Bureaucracy and Political Development

STUDIES IN
POLITICAL DEVELOPMENT

1. *Communications and Political Development*
Edited by Lucian W. Pye

2. *Bureaucracy and Political Development*
Edited by Joseph LaPalombara

3. *Political Modernization in Japan and Turkey*
Edited by Robert E. Ward and Dankwart A. Rustow

4. *Education and Political Development*
Edited by James S. Coleman

5. *Political Culture and Political Development*
Edited by Lucian W. Pye and Sidney Verba

6. *Political Parties and Political Development*
Edited by Joseph LaPalombara and Myron Weiner

7. *Crises and Sequences in Political Development*
Edited by Leonard Binder, James S. Coleman, Joseph LaPalombara, Lucian W. Pye, Myron Weiner, and Sidney Verba

Three additional volumes are planned for this series.

Sponsored by the Committee on Comparative Politics of the Social Science Research Council

Lucian W. Pye, *Chairman*
Gabriel A. Almond
Leonard Binder
R. Taylor Cole
James S. Coleman
Herbert Hyman
Joseph LaPalombara
Sidney Verba
Robert E. Ward
Myron Weiner

Bryce Wood, *staff*

Bureaucracy and Political Development

Edited by Joseph LaPalombara

CONTRIBUTORS

CARL BECK
RALPH BRAIBANTI
JOHN T. DORSEY
S. N. EISENSTADT
MERLE FAINSOD
BERT F. HOSELITZ
J. DONALD KINGSLEY
JOSEPH LAPALOMBARA
FRITZ MORSTEIN MARX
FRED W. RIGGS
WALTER R. SHARP
JOSEPH J. SPENGLER

PRINCETON, NEW JERSEY
PRINCETON UNIVERSITY PRESS
1967

L.C. Card: 63-11059
SBN 691-07502-6

Second Edition, 1967
Second Printing, 1970

This 1967 edition includes a selected bibliography in the study of administration and political development.

Printed in the United States of America
by Princeton University Press, Princeton, New Jersey

TO THE MEMORY OF

Sigmund Neumann

WHOSE INTEREST AND FRIENDSHIP

GUIDED THIS ENTERPRISE

FOREWORD

THIS volume is the second in a series of Studies in Political Development sponsored by the Committee on Comparative Politics of the Social Science Research Council under a grant from the Ford Foundation for the period 1960-1963. The Committee has been strongly impelled to explore those aspects of rapidly changing societies that are of particular interest to the political scientist. As we are able to gather more information concerning the political forms, processes, and policies with which the newer nations experiment, it is hoped that our theoretical understanding of the dynamics of political change will be enriched and that, as a result, additional contributions can be made to the evolution of a genuine comparative political science.

In furthering these aims, the Committee has sponsored a series of conferences and research institutes in which the insights of American and foreign social scientists, educators, journalists, political leaders, and government officials have been brought to bear on the problems of modernization and democratization in the developing areas. The first volume to emerge from this activity is *Communications and Political Development*, edited by Lucian W. Pye. Other volumes scheduled for early publication include *Political Development in Turkey and Japan*, edited by Robert E. Ward and Dankwart A. Rustow; *Education and Political Development*, edited by James S. Coleman; and *Political Parties and Political Development*, edited by Joseph LaPalombara and Myron Weiner. In addition, volumes based on the Committee's two summer institutes, and individual scholarly efforts, will deal more directly with the theory of political culture and political change—with political typologies conceived in developmental terms, and with factors that affect the pattern, direction, and tempo of political change.

The papers which appear in this volume were prepared for the Conference on Bureaucracy and Political Development which was held from January 29 to February 1, 1962, at the Center for Advanced Study in the Behavioral Sciences, Stanford, California, under the direction of Taylor Cole and Joseph LaPalombara. In several cases, the papers were substantially revised in the light of the conference discussion, as well as on the basis of written critiques submitted by conference participants. In his introductory chapter, the editor attempts to pull together the threads of theory and direct attention to common theoretical and empirical problems that are scattered throughout the volume.

Members of the Committee on Comparative Politics and all but one of the authors of the papers were able to attend the conference. Others who participated, and whose many contributions and suggestions found their way into the revised papers, include: George I. Blanksten, Northwestern University; James W. Fesler, Yale University; Bertram M. Gross, Syracuse University; H. Field Haviland, The Brookings Institution; Ferrel Heady, University of Michigan; James Heaphey, University of Pittsburgh; Takeshi Ishida, Tokyo, Japan; Victor Jones, University of California (Berkeley); Guy Pauker, University of California (Berkeley) and the Rand Corporation; Robert Tilman, Tulane University; Edward W. Weidner, East-West Center of the University of Hawaii; and Bryce Wood of the Social Science Research Council.

GABRIEL A. ALMOND

PREFACE AND ACKNOWLEDGMENTS

THIS volume is part of a larger effort, fostered by the Committee on Comparative Politics of the Social Science Research Council, to explore various salient aspects of the process of political development and modernization. Events of recent years have forced social scientists and policy makers to come to grips with the momentous and often unsettling changes that are taking place in the so-called less developed portions of the globe. These changes are not restricted to any single sector of society; they affect every facet. In the economic sphere, the mechanization of agriculture, the development of crops and other goods for the world market, and the encouragement of capital accumulation and industrialization appear as universal goals. In education, the need for raising levels of literacy is everywhere articulated and in many places now involves massive inputs of human and material resources. In the social sphere, economic change and the removal of literacy are directly responsible for fundamental changes in social stratification and in human interrelationships. All of these mutations are, in turn, both encouraged and made public through the dynamics of traditional and modern networks of communication.

In this dynamic process, political institutions and behavior are also undergoing change. Moreover, we now understand that the changes themselves, whether they be economic, social, educational, or political, emerge in large measure as the result of direct governmental intervention. Whereas much of the Western world developed with relatively little direct intervention by the "public sector," this history clearly will not repeat itself. For reasons that range from economic necessity to ideological rigidity, the developing nations insist that government—particularly the bureaucracy—should play a major, even exclusive, role in effecting the changes that are sought. Thus, whether it is the building of roads, the creation of new industries, or the radical transformation of traditional villages, one can usually expect to find the bureaucracy intimately involved. Even in those places where some concessions are made to the participation of the "private sector," such activity will be and probably must be carefully integrated with what government itself does.

Given these conditions, there are a number of reasons why the social scientist, particularly the political scientist, must be concerned with the topic which this volume encompasses. We need to know more, for example, about the various ways in which public bureaucracies can be more or less effective as instruments of change. Additionally—and this is frankly a central concern of those involved in this venture—we wish to have more reliable knowledge about the consequences of certain patterns of change for the probable evolution of democratic polities. Thus, we are asking not merely where the developing new states may be going politically but how development might be pushed in the direction of freedom rather than tyranny.

The Committee on Comparative Politics has thus felt the need to encourage careful exploration into this as well as other aspects of political development. The first volume in this series, *Communications and Political Development*, edited by Lucian Pye, appeared in April 1963. The present volume is the product of the Committee's effort to encourage a number of outstanding scholars to provide both theoretical and empirical information on the role of public bureaucracy in bringing about change. Papers were prepared, discussed at a conference held at the Center for Advanced Study in the Behavioral Sciences, Palo Alto, California, revised, and finally edited for this volume. Several of the contributors are greatly indebted to participants at the conference whose remarks and observations helped to sharpen the focus of attention of specific contributions.

A venture of this nature will lack the tight integration of a work which is by a single author. In addition, the relative newness of the central topic treated causes, and perhaps requires, that this initial effort make some sacrifices in the interest of broad and tentative exploration. It is out of such a broad approach that we can hope for eventual insights that will serve to buttress both the field of comparative politics and the development of free societies.

In a very profound sense this volume is the product of many collaborators. Gabriel A. Almond, Chairman of the Social Science Research Council Committee on Comparative Politics, has provided continuous and dynamic leadership. The Committee members themselves, and particularly Taylor Cole in this case, have helped to see the conference and the volume through various stages of planning and execution. Pendleton Herring and Bryce Wood have managed to give all sorts of intellectual, organizational, and administrative aid that I will not try to enumerate here. Suffice it to say that it is difficult to conceive that this, as well as other volumes, would emerge without their valued counsel.

My own contribution to this volume was immensely facilitated by the availability of an extraordinary fellowship year at the Center for Advanced Study in the Behavioral Sciences. Although it is not possible to recognize individually all those at the Center who made my own task easier, I do wish to acknowledge the creative and devoted work of Anne Bernstein, who helped to organize the conference, who typed the original manuscript, and who saw to various other important stages of its evolution. Ann McNaughton should be recognized for her meticulous editorial assistance. The index is largely the work of Mrs. Janet Brooks. Finally, I wish to express appreciation to Michigan State University, which has in many ways encouraged and made possible my involvement in this particular academic enterprise.

JOSEPH LAPALOMBARA

CONTENTS

Foreword vii

Preface and Acknowledgments ix

1. An Overview of Bureaucracy and Political Development 3
by Joseph LaPalombara

2. Bureaucracy and Political Development: Notes, Queries, and Dilemmas 34
by Joseph LaPalombara

3. The Higher Civil Service as an Action Group in Western Political Development 62
by Fritz Morstein Marx

4. Bureaucracy and Political Development 96
by S. N. Eisenstadt

5. Bureaucrats and Political Development: A Paradoxical View 120
by Fred W. Riggs

6. Levels of Economic Performance and Bureaucratic Structures 168
by Bert F. Hoselitz

7. Bureaucracy and Economic Development 199
by Joseph J. Spengler

8. Bureaucracy and Modernization: The Russian and Soviet Case 233
by Merle Fainsod

9. Bureaucracy and Political Development in Eastern Europe 268
by Carl Beck

10. Bureaucracy and Political Development, with Particular Reference to Nigeria 301
by J. Donald Kingsley

11. The Bureaucracy and Political Development in Viet Nam 318
by John T. Dorsey, Jr.

12. Public Bureaucracy and Judiciary in Pakistan 360
by Ralph Braibanti

13. International Bureaucracies and Political Development 441
by Walter R. Sharp

Contributors 475

Bibliography 479

Index 505

Bureaucracy

and Political Development

CHAPTER 1

An Overview of Bureaucracy and Political Development

JOSEPH LA PALOMBARA

Introduction

It is now a commonplace to depict the contemporary world as one of rapid, increasing, and frequently cataclysmic change. Such forces as disappearing colonialism, revolution in communications and technology, international technical assistance, and spreading ideology cancel out centuries of relative stability, replacing it with conditions of economic upheaval, social disorientation, and political instability. While the so-called developed nations prepare to harness at least a portion of space, most of the rest of the world—spurred along by the West and by the revolution of rising expectations—struggles to cross the threshold of social and economic modernity.

Indications of this mutation could be endlessly multiplied: political maps of the world become obsolete almost as soon as they are published; school children must add continually to the number of nation-state names they commit to memory; debater and voter in the United Nations dramatically announce the presence of new sovereignties and the shifting balance of power they portend; newspapers flash the names of exotic countries that may or may not have existed a few years ago, where conditions of economic distress, physical violence, or political maneuvering somehow seem to have a direct bearing on the peace and tranquility of the entire globe. The utterances of new leaders of small African states are as carefully pondered by the statesmen of the West as the pronouncements of a major power. Coalition government in Laos, agricultural reform in China, India's Five-Year Plan, jungle warfare in Viet Nam, industrial development in Ghana, village change in Pakistan, a campaign to wipe out illiteracy in Nigeria, military coups in Turkey or Korea, civil war in Indonesia, spectacular economic changes in Brazil—all of these are symptoms of a tempo of development and change that the Western world simply cannot ignore.

Perhaps because the changes now experienced are unprecedented in both tempo and scale, they have attracted the attention of a great many scholars, as well as those whose immediate concern is international politics and diplomacy. Some of these scholars are strongly motivated by an urge to provide useful counsel concerning governmental policy; others see in rapid processes of transformation an unparalleled opportunity both to apply and to test theories and methods of the social sciences, thus adding to our storehouse of theoretical and empirical knowledge. Whatever the motivation, the urge to sharpen our understanding of the propellants, processes, and consequences of change is clearly overwhelming, as the outpouring of professional literature in recent years attests.

For many reasons that do not require elaboration here, the professional literature concentrates largely on social and economic change. We now have a fairly vast bibliography of studies dealing with both of these phenomena, particularly with the conditions—social and economic variables—that accompany and to some extent govern the evolution and the probable direction or modification in the social system and in the production and allocation of economic goods and services. By way of sharp contrast, relatively little systematic attention has been accorded the phenomenon of *political* development, i.e., the transformation of a political system from one type into another. Even more curious is the lack of attention accorded the public sector—particularly the bureaucracy—as an important independent variable that greatly influences any kind of transformation in the developing countries, be it social, economic, or political.

It scarcely requires exhaustive documentation to demonstrate that major changes in both the developed and the developing nations are inconceivable today without the massive intervention of government. The time is evidently past when public officials are expected to sit on the developmental sidelines, limiting their roles to the fixing of general rules and to providing certain basic services and incentives for those private entrepreneurs who are the major players in the complicated and exciting game of fashioning profound changes in economic and social systems. Whether it is the encouragement of electronic industries in the industrialized West, or the improvement of rice production in Pakistan or Viet Nam, or an increase in medical care in the United States, or the exploitation of petroleum resources in Latin America or the Middle East, the direct participation of government is immediate and intimate, if not to say exclusive. When our focus shifts from the economic to other areas of activity, the presence of government is revealed in even sharper relief. Systematic campaigns to eradicate illiteracy, create or revitalize village-level government, remove ancient social barriers, or to replace atomistic parochialism with a sense of nationhood are unthinkable without the participation of government. The same may be said for any effort to forge major transformations in the political institutions that characterize any particular society.

The reasons for heavy public or governmental involvement in the phenomena of economic, social, and political change are as myriad as the kinds of development actually underway. In many places, government is the only significant social sector willing to assume the responsibility for transformation. In others, the bureaucracy husbands the vast majority of whatever necessary professional, technical, and entrepreneurial resources may be available to a society committed to change. In still other areas, the primary—even monopolistic—involvement of the public sector in programs of social and economic development may be a manifestation of fierce ideological commitment. Moreover, in every type of situation, both historic and contemporary, the creation of social overhead capital is a matter that requires the application of the full resources of political and bureaucratic capacity. Without such public participation, very few other plans for basic changes in the economic or social structure are meaningful or feasible. The chapter by Fritz Morstein Marx in this volume clearly demonstrates how unreal it would be to think of any type of national development in which the bureaucracy, even if its role is limited to the provision of data, advice, and management expertise, is excluded.

This book (as well as the conference out of which it emanates) is an effort to direct attention to the vital role that bureaucracies can and do play in the various kinds of transformations that the developing nations are experiencing. While some attention is accorded certain problems and phenomena of social and economic change, the major focus is on political development. It goes without saying that we need to know more than we do about the forces that mold one configuration of political institutions rather than another. If, as we assume, the bureaucratic sector in most of the developing nations is to be heavily involved in the general processes of transformation, we must be able to suggest with greater confidence than is presently possible what alternative roles are open to the bureaucracy—and with what probable consequences for the emerging political systems. If, as many of us hope, political development is to move in a generally democratic rather than anti-democratic direction, it is essential that we know in greater precision what patterns of bureaucratic organization and behavior aid or handicap the achievement of this goal. If, finally, we ever expect to be able to deal comparatively and scientifically with the process of political development as a generalized phenomenon, we simply must accord greater attention than in the past to the bureaucracy as a critical variable that both affects and is conditioned by the process itself.

The chapters that follow range from theoretical speculation to empirical case studies of the role of bureaucracy in political and economic development. They raise questions of conceptualization, suggest basic hypotheses or generalizations, and alert us to certain problems that must yet be confronted before the field of "comparative development administration" can move from its present state of infancy to the first glimmerings of maturity. In this introductory chapter I shall touch on only some of these questions, generalizations, and problems that strike me as particularly salient. In assuming this responsibility, I am mindful that not all of the authors may share my sense of the important or my interpretation of the inferences to be drawn from the data presented. Moreover, as the reader will surely discern for himself, an endeavor of this kind can do little more than suggest the richness of thought and information that the varied papers of the authors represent.

Definitions and Models

At first blush, bureaucracy does not appear to offer any difficulties of definition. On closer inspection, however, it is apparent that the meaning of this concept is far from self-evident. Does it refer to all persons, at whatever level, who are on the public payroll? Does it make much sense to cluster under the same generic category a postal clerk and a national planner, a local policeman and an undersecretary in a Home Office or Ministry of the Interior? When we speculate about the consequences of bureaucratic organization and behavior for political development, are we interested in the relationship of the "administrative class" to the legislature, as well as that of a field representative of a Ministry of Health or Agriculture to the rural village?

There is no single or simple answer to these queries. For some purposes, as for instance when one is concerned with the kinds of public attitudes toward government that bureaucrats help to inculcate or fortify, it is reasonable to think of bureaucracy as encompassing all public servants. When such public attitudes are the paramount concern, the village aid worker may be a much more significant bureaucrat than the remote top-level officials of the ministry he represents. For the great mass of people in most countries, government is scarcely much more than the specific public officials with whom they come in direct contact. The upper reaches of a public administrative hierarchy may constitute a paragon of skill, rationality, and humaneness, but all of this will go relatively unnoticed if those who deal directly with the public are arrogant, aloof, arbitrary, and corrupt in their behavior. Those at the center of administration may spin out beautiful and extremely insightful national plans, but these will appear as not very meaningful—or even bizarre—to the population if field administrators do not have the talent for translating what exists on paper to meet the requirements of human situations.

On the other hand, where one is concerned with the relative roles of bureaucrats and legislators in the formulation of public policy, a more restricted conceptualization of the bureaucracy is required. The same is true when the problem at hand is that of discovering what major internal characteristics evolve for any bureaucratic apparatus. In short, there are some occasions on which only those public servants at a relatively high level in the hierarchy constitute the relevant bureaucracy.

The issues treated in this volume to some extent require an accordian-like conceptualization of the bureaucracy. Problems regarding the development of effective field administration in Viet Nam bring us to a relatively low level in the public administrative hierarchy, as do observations regarding the use of the extraordinary writs to protect both citizens and public servants against arbitrary and excessive bureaucratic behavior in Pakistan. When comments are made regarding venality and corruption in the public service, every level of the bureaucracy is involved. By and large, however, the bureaucrats of major interest to us are generally those who occupy managerial roles, who are in some directive capacity either in central agencies or in the field, who are generally described in the language of public administration as "middle" or "top" management. The reason for this more restrictive use is self-evident: the managerial group in the bureaucracy is more likely to have a direct bearing on political and other kinds of national development. It is those public servants at the upper administrative levels who will be called upon to provide policy counsel, to assist in the formulation of programs, and to engage in the management and direction of the people in the interest of translating policy hopes into realities.

Given this somewhat restricted view of the bureaucracy, is there any particular framework within which bureaucracies may be viewed? The several models of bureaucratic systems provided by the authors suggest that no obvious single approach is available. If, as John Dorsey suggests, change is essentially the outcome of modifications in the amount of information available to a society and the way that information is converted into energy, we may want to look at bureaucracies as they relate to that important process. It is obvious, for example, that the Vietnamese bureaucracy enjoys a near monopoly of certain crucial categories of information available to that country and that, for this and other reasons, it exercises a quantum of power that has had to be harnessed politically. It is equally obvious that, if power centers other than the bureaucracy are to be created in the developing nations, information that is essential to development will have to be more widely shared. Methods whereby such a situation might be brought into existence must certainly be suggested before we can solve the problem of creating the democratic pluralism which underlies many of the contributions to this volume.

Bert F. Hoselitz offers a structural-functional model of bureaucracy, and would presumably classify public administrative systems according to how they relate to the critical sectors of cultural maintenance and transmission, national integration, systemic goal gratification, and environmental transformation. Where a reasonable amount of national integration has occurred and the basic concern of a system is economic development, the role of the bureaucracy in the goal gratification and allocative sectors is of critical interest and importance. All of these sectors are closely related and, although the bureaucracy will always be concerned with all of them to some degree, major involvement in the integrative sector will clearly limit the amount of involvement in sectors that are more intimately related to economic development.

A somewhat similar structural-functional model is suggested by S. N. Eisenstadt, wherein the major perspective in viewing a bureaucracy is the manner in which it handles the flow of demands and organizations that interact with the political system. What the bureaucracy does in this sense will have an immediate and direct bearing on the kind of development that occurs and on how rapidly change will proceed. Merle Fainsod develops a typology based on the relationship of bureaucracies to the flow of political power and suggests that others might be constructed that reflect the bureaucracy's range of functions, its internal characteristics, or its role as a carrier or inhibitor of modernizing values. Other treatments of bureaucracy reflect exactly some of these latter orientations.

It would certainly be premature at this time to attempt to make a final choice among various conceivable models or taxonomies. Each of them offers a particular window, perhaps a magnifying glass, through which to view an important aspect of the political process. What one glass may obscure, another may illuminate. Until we have seen more varied detail than we have thus far, no single vantage point is likely to serve our needs adequately. Moreover, it is apparent from what is said about bureaucracies, and the concerns that are expressed with regard to them, that the central focus of all of the suggested models is far less diverse than might appear at first glance.

The Problem of "Modernity"

Somewhat more perplexing are problems of conceptualization and theory that confront us when we approach the subject of "modernization." This concept is often used in a shifting and imprecise way. When it is equated with "development," it can mean everything from increases in the amount of information and energy that societies use, to increased ability to absorb new demands and organization, to structural differentiation for the performance of systemic functions. For some, a modern system is essentially a society that has become urban and industrial. For others, a system cannot be modern which has not achieved a high degree of political pluralism. Some would stress gross or net national product as an index of modernization; others would look for the degree of popular participation in politics and government as the most meaningful measure. Often several meanings can be detected in the same piece of writing.

The confusion induced by the shifting content of concepts like modernization and development is compounded by what appears to be an underlying culture-bound and deterministic unilinear theory of change. If modernization or development simply means industrialization and the mechanization of agriculture, the concept is reasonably neutral and does not necessarily imply a unilinear theory of evolution or a particular institutional framework within which this kind of economic change must take place. But as soon as either of these concepts takes on social and political content, it is apparent that what many scholars have in mind when they speak of a modern or developed system is one that approximates the institutional and structural configuration that we associate with the Anglo-American (in any event, the Western) democratic systems. When, in addition to such culture-bound conceptualization, it is implied that the evolution of political and social systems is moving in this direction and that any other line of development is an aberration, all sorts of difficulties arise concerning the matter of dealing empirically with existing social and political systems.

It is apparent, for example, that rapid economic change leading to industrialization can be effected without conformance to the social and institutional patterns that we might ascribe to the Anglo-American model. Indeed, it may very well be that rapid change in the economic sector is much more meaningfully related to what we might call an undemocratic pattern of social and political organization. This is certainly one of the principal—even if depressing—hypotheses that emerges from the contributions of Merle Fainsod and Carl Beck. In any event, if any kind of clarity is to emerge from our use of such concepts as modernization and development, it will be vitally necessary to specify what we mean by the concepts and to indicate explicitly when a shift in meaning occurs. Failure to do this is certain to encumber our discussions of political change with confusion and with culturally limited and deterministic baggage.

The limitation of our conceptualization is equally apparent when we shift our attention to public administration. Regardless of what Max Weber himself may have intended, it is apparent that his classical formulation of bureaucracy has come to be inextricably associated by some with the highly industrialized and democratically pluralistic society. Thus, the role of bureaucracy in effecting socio-economic-political change is said to require, as central tendencies, such Weberian attributes in public administration as hierarchy, responsibility, rationality, achievement orientation, specialization and differentiation, discipline, professionalization. Insofar as public administrative systems fall short of this Weberian legal-rational model, they are said not to be modern. Moreover, it is often either claimed or implied that a public administrative sector that does not manifest these attributes cannot be an effective instrument for bringing about the kind of economic, social, and political change that one associates with modernity.

Our ability to understand the process of change, and the role of the public sector in bringing it about, is considerably damaged by any neat association of the classical conceptualization of bureaucracy with a particular configuration of institutional or structural arrangements in economic, social, or political sectors. To assume, as have some of the public administration technical assistance advisors who have ventured abroad, that such an association is necessary is to neglect the nature of change in the West and in other countries. We know, for example, that at the time that Britain and the United States experienced their most rapid economic change, the respective bureaucracies, to considerable degrees involved in the facilitation of change, were conforming much less to the Weberian model than they are today. A striking degree of particularism and corruption in public administration can be associated with economic development in both of these countries.

Recognizing this, several of our authors come close to stating that corruption or its functional equivalent may be critically important to the developing nations. Fred Riggs, for example, suggests that a developing political party system may require spoils and that a bureaucratic system based on "merit" may aggrandize bureaucratic power at the expense of political institutional development in the early stages of growth of a party system. Hoselitz, who argues that economic development requires a shift from corruption to rationality in the bureaucracy, concedes that venality in the bureaucracy is acceptable when the primary need of a society is integration rather than goal attainment. Morstein Marx argues cogently that a merit bureaucracy makes constitutionalism more viable and helps to legitimize government, but his hypothesis need not be viewed as being at odds with the others mentioned if it is conceded that the particular *stage* of political development may call for different kinds of bureaucratic structure. The point seems to be that classical bureaucracy is not necessarily a precondition of development.

This last observation is made even more starkly apparent when we analyze the Fainsod discussion of the Soviet Union and the Beck examination of development in Eastern Europe. The former makes the central point that economic modernization and democracy do not necessarily travel hand in hand. Moreover, it is apparent that the economic development that preceded the advent of the Bolsheviks evolved largely at state behest and under the guidance of a venal, corrupt, autocratic, inefficient, and particularistic bureaucracy that the efforts of neither Peter nor Alexander succeeded in reforming. One of Fainsod's important conclusions, which deserves more treatment as an interesting hypothesis, is that a bureaucracy can instill and implement economic modernity without itself absorbing any of the changes it seeks to disseminate.

That industrialization does not necessarily carry the seeds of democracy nor require the development of a Weberian bureaucracy is also suggested by Carl Beck. He shows that the countries of Eastern Europe have been able to absorb changes in their economies, administrative systems, and elites without creating classical administrative systems. While some flexibility in the Communist doctrine of development is evident, it cannot be traced to bureaucratization. Indeed, recent patterns of administrative devolution make the achievement of classical bureaucracy even more unlikely, but it may nevertheless play an important role in the future development of these societies. As Beck puts it, the classical theory seriously underestimates the role of political power and ideology in national development. His chapter, as well as that of Fainsod, should be sobering for those who associate a particular configuration of public administration with economic and social development.

To attempt to remake the bureaucracies of the developing states to conform to any abstraction derived from a Weberian model involves more than an effort of herculean proportions. The effort itself, insofar as it may succeed, is of dubious value in that a bureaucracy heavily encumbered by Weberian-derived norms may for that reason be a less efficacious instrument of economic change. To put the matter succinctly: one might simply observe that, in a place like India, public administrators steeped in the tradition of the Indian Civil Service may be less useful as developmental entrepreneurs than those who are not so rigidly tied to notions of bureaucratic status, hierarchy, and impartiality. The economic development of a society, particularly if it is to be implemented by massive intervention of the public sector, requires a breed of bureaucrats different (e.g., more free-wheeling, less adhering to administrative forms, less attached to the importance of hierarchy and seniority) from the type of man who is useful when the primary concern of the bureaucracy is the maintenance of law and order. On the other hand, as Ralph Braibanti notes for Pakistan, bureaucrats deeply rooted in the traditions of the Indian Civil Service, which are essentially British, may be much more effective as guardians of law and justice than the more impatient types for whom the single and essentially exclusive goal is economic development.

Hoselitz states that, as a practical matter, all of the bureaucracies of the developing areas are likely to be dual in character, reflecting the transitional nature and the conflicting needs of the societies themselves. In such a setting, the "primitive" will be juxtaposed with the "modern," the traditional with the legal-rational. If, as Hoselitz hypothesizes, economic development requires a streamlined and highly rationalized bureaucracy, many of the structures of a dual society will tend to undercut this goal. Whether, in order to push ahead economically, the political elite should seek to eradicate the traditional structure or seek somehow to harness it to developmental plans is not as easy a problem to resolve as we might assume. Westernized elites in the developing areas, imbued with notions of Western technology and organization, are prone to ride roughshod over the traditional elements in their society. Yet, as Morroe Berger discovered for the Egyptian bureaucracy,[1] traditional ways have amazing survival power; they are capable of adapting to even the most radical changes in formal organizational structure. And, as national bureaucratic planners in India are learning, the implementation of developmental schemes will have to occur as modified by traditional and parochial influences or it may not take place at all.

We need to know more than we do about how and why traditional patterns survive formal modifications in administrative structure, how and with what consequences they manage to exist side by side with so-called modern bureaucratic patterns, and what implications such patterns have for national plans to effect social, political, and economic change. For this reason we must take as merely tentative or limited the suggestion of Eisenstadt that a developed political system requires the centralization of the polity. This need may be greatest when the primary goal is integrative, that is, when the central effort is that of creating a sense of nationhood or national identification. Certainly the histories of Japan after the Meiji Restoration, of Prussia in the eighteenth century, and of Germany and Italy in the nineteenth century clearly demonstrate that a centralized bureaucracy can be a vital factor in the molding of a national entity out of disparate ethnic, regional, feudal, or otherwise atomistic groupings. Indeed, whether we are thinking of nation-states or empires, both their historical evolution and their maintenance reveal a central, perhaps critical, role played by the public administrative apparatus.

It is not obvious, however, that a centralized bureaucracy is required

[1] *Bureaucracy and Society in Modern Egypt: a Study of the Higher Civil Service*, Princeton, Princeton University Press, 1957.

when the basic concern shifts from the integrative to the goal gratification sector, or when the end in view is the development of a pluralistic society. Such goals may very well require considerable administrative decentralization as well as efforts to encourage at the local level the kinds of political institutions that can serve both as supports for and as watchdogs over administrative officials. The revival of the panchayats in India is having exactly this kind of impact. Fred Riggs argues with great cogency that, from the standpoint of political development, it may be essential to create a fairly high degree of local political and administrative autonomy. To do so would presumably limit the centralized bureaucracy's tendency to displace its service orientation with that of aggrandizing its own power—a danger which Eisenstadt recognizes as clear and present in most of the new states.

We must, then, look with greater care to traditional structures before concluding that they are incompatible with social, political, or economic change. The vital question to pose is what the national goals of a society are, what role in accomplishing them the public sector is expected to play, and, given these aspirations, what patterns of public administration seem to be the most efficaciously related to goal achievement.

The Neutrality of the Bureaucracy

What we have said thus far has certain implications for the role of the bureaucracy in encouraging the evolution of democratic, constitutional systems. If, as seems essential, we must concede that the Weberian conception of the bureaucracy is nothing more than an ideal formulation not subject to empirical verification, and that the classical democratic formulation of a strictly neutral and instrumental bureaucracy is an equally idealized and probably unattainable standard, it is necessary to modify somewhat the general frame of reference within which the role and function of the bureaucracy is evaluated.

We may begin by noting—as several of our authors do—that the bureaucracy, particularly in its upper reaches, will always be deeply involved in the political process. Indeed, it is impossible even in the most structurally differentiated political systems to conceive of the complete separation of function that would be required were there to be an attempt to restrict the bureaucracy strictly to an instrumental role. Those who have looked closely at the public administrative systems of the Western world have long since abandoned the misleading fiction that assumed a neat, dichotomous separation between policy and administration. Among other things, we know that some policy implications are implicit in all significant administrative behavior and that the power and influencing-seeking groups of a society, sensing this, will cluster about administration decision points, hoping in this way to exert some leverage over the quite clearly political decisions that emanate from the bureaucracy. What is true of the more advanced countries is probably accentuated in developing nations, where the bureaucracy may be the most coherent power center and where, in addition, the major decisions regarding national development are likely to involve authoritative rule making and rule application by governmental structures.

In order to sharpen our understanding of the political role of the bureaucracy, it is also necessary to note that the bureaucratic arena will almost invariably reproduce in microcosm many of the basic political conflicts that characterize the developing system itself. If the "traditional" and the "modern" are in conflict, this tension will surely be reflected among bureaucrats. The bureaucrats in the field may ally themselves with local elites and politicians and to some extent oppose well-made developmental schemes that emanate from national planners at the center. If, as is invariably the case, capital and other developmental resources are in short supply, those who populate the bureaucracy's infrastructure will to some extent be at war with each other over the definition of goals and the allocation of resources. Whether a developing society is characterized by several competing political parties or is dominated by a single party, we can assume, first, that views concerning the setting of developmental goals will differ and, second, that the competing members of the political elite will search for and find allies in the bureaucracy. Not only will shifts in political power be reflected in the balance of power within the bureaucracy; the bureaucrats themselves, through the myriad policy-related functions they perform, will have much to do with the major shifts—even the slight nuances of change—that occur from time to time.

Tension between the political leaders and the bureaucrats of the developing nations grows in large measure out of the recognition that bureaucrats are never passive instruments to be manipulated at will, like inert pawns. Where the indigenous bureaucracy is deeply steeped in colonial traditions of law and order, or in the use of the bureaucratic apparatus for control rather than development, politicians bent on change, as well as intellectuals impatient with the rate of progress, will find themselves at odds with the more conservative bureaucrats. When, in the interest of staffing administrative positions vacated by colonial administrators, or of filling new positions directly relating to economic change, a new group of ambitious and often badly trained bureaucrats is added to what had existed previously, a considerable amount of turmoil, with definite consequences for the political system, is predictable. Aspects of this problem are explored in Braibanti's chapter on Pakistan and Dorsey's contribution regarding Viet Nam. In these chapters, as well as others, the conclusion is inescapable that keeping the bureaucracy out of politics is a vain hope. Riggs, who pointedly observes that in transitional societies inter-bureaucratic conflict may become the main form of politics, cautions that such a situation has ominous implications for democracy, and he explores what might be done to reduce this phenomenon to less disturbing proportions. Eisenstadt, too, is aware of this danger and notes that its alleviation lies in the development of structures that would make a political process outside the bureaucratic setting a viable possibility.

Of particular interest to us in this regard is Morstein Marx's chapter. Recognizing that the higher bureaucracy will be deeply involved in the politics of development because of the crucial place it occupies in the power structure, he wonders what might be done to guarantee not inert but responsible neutrality in the bureaucracy. Responsible neutrality would not in any way deny the society the benefits of the considerable talent that the bureaucratic apparatus may husband. Indeed, responsible neutrality would require that bureaucrats play a major role, not merely in the implementation of programs, but in their definition and development into policies as well. One of Morstein Marx's salient conclusions is that responsible neutrality is inextricably tied to the status position of the higher civil service. If the bureaucracy is to act in the public interest, it must be permeated by a consciousness of both its legal and its social status in the system. For Morstein Marx, this kind of essential status is unattainable if bureaucracy based on kinship is not replaced by one based on hierarchy, if bureaucratic office is not protected by certain guarantees that safeguard tenure and imply a recognition of the expert advisor's role that a bureaucrat can perform. He sees responsible neutrality emanating from a status officialdom protected by a highly rational merit bureaucracy. Riggs views the premature creation of such a structure as possibly minatory to the goal of democratic political development. Each of these propositions is examined in some detail by the authors. Neither of them supports the unacceptable notion that a neutral bureaucracy implies an ostrich-like withdrawal and isolation from the nerve centers of the political process.

Scarcity of Bureaucratic Talent

It is also apparent that few if any of the developing nations possess the resevoir of bureaucratic skills that their often grandiose developmental schemes would require. Some new nations, such as India, are reasonably well endowed with first-class administrative talent, particularly at the highest levels. In Africa, where the Congo would be an extreme but not untypical example, the situation is much more desperate. Colonial administration, which emphasized the services of police and law and which did not recruit large numbers of Africans to positions of policy responsibility, has been replaced by public administration that is closely tied to goals of national development. African administrators whose responsibilities until recently were characterized by routine are catapaulted to the top of the hierarchy, where they are expected to advise ministers and politicians regarding major programs of economic and social development. As J. Donald Kingsley aptly observes, the inexperience and other limitations of unseasoned public administrators necessarily set limits to the dreams of politicians. How much the state can accomplish in a setting that manages to steer clear of administrative chaos, to say nothing of just plain inefficiency, is clearly circumscribed by the nature of the bureaucratic talent available.

This is not to say that a few high-level administrators are of little use to a new nation. Kingsley shows us that in Nigeria top-level officers with a common education and tradition constitute a vital factor in the national integration of that country. Equally impressive are the related data that Braibanti adduces for Pakistan, which was compelled to create a state *de novo* with extremely limited administrative talent at its disposal and against great odds. A handful of men, some indigenous, some foreign, utilized extraordinary skills and creative leadership to hold the national house together during critical formative years. One is tempted to say that a central operating proposition can be extrapolated from the experiences of Nigeria and Pakistan, but doing so raises the frustrating question of how other new nations can get their hands on a reasonable quotient of bureaucratic leaders who display the Anglo-Saxon traits of respect for law and order, intellectuality, pragmatism, objectivity, and rationality in the organization and management of public administrative machinery. These traditions somehow enable the bureaucrats to survive the tensions that grow up between themselves and the politicians, as well as the tendency of the politicians, abetted by intellectuals and the citizenry, to lay the failures of development at the doorstep of the bureaucracy.

Even in places like Pakistan and Nigeria, it is abundantly apparent that much must be done to train the desperately needed administrative cadres at all levels. To some extent, revolutionary changes in secondary education will eventually fill the needs of the public sector. Yet changes in the opportunity for advanced education do not automatically take care of the matter of providing specific training for those who will enter the public service. What kind of training should lower-level administrators receive to assure, not merely that they can handle the technicalities of a particular position, but also that they will manifest the kind of behavior toward superiors and toward the public that is consistent with the particular kind of *political* system that may be the end in view? If field administrators in colonial areas have been aloof from and disdainful toward the public, how can such an orientation be changed. If higher-level bureaucrats have been primarily concerned with the maintenance of law and order and the rigid application of colonial regulations (often designed to inhibit economic development), what must be done to make them better attuned to the problems of development and change in the future?

One of the generalizations that emerges from Merle Fainsod's analysis of the Soviet Union is that there is probably no obvious substitute for a massive program of education maintained for at least a full generation. Those who are sanguine about the benefits to be derived from the use of international technical assistants in the field of administration should read with care what Fainsod reports of efforts to reform the Russian bureaucracy under Peter the Great. Hoping to borrow liberally from the Swedes, Peter the Great put into motion a striking program to bring about bureaucratic change. Fainsod concludes that, for all of his efforts, he left Russia pretty much as he found it. It required the single-minded campaign inaugurated by the Bolsheviks, and knowingly calculated to have its impact in the long run, to effect the profound modifications in the Soviet bureaucracy that have evolved over the last four decades. I might add that the same thing is true of Japan. Statements regarding bureaucratic change there after the Meiji Restoration often obscure the fact that many of the modifications we associate with the period since 1868 were evidently already very much in motion for at least a century during the Tokugawa Shogunate. It seems reasonable to suppose, then, that even those new nations which begin the process of nation building and political development with few deeply rooted structures at the national level will have to develop a more reasonable expectation concerning the tempo with which political and administrative institutions can be built.

Regardless of the rate at which the training of new public administrators may proceed, the question must be posed concerning what kinds of top-level personnel are desirable. Braibanti, in his discussion of Pakistan, points out something that is typical of indigenous bureaucrats in countries where the British and French enjoyed relatively long periods of colonial control, namely, that the upper-level administrators are generally hostile to the scientific, mechanistic, egalitarian, and anti-intellectual bias of American public administration. It should be pointed out that efforts of Americans to export scientific public administration have met with negative responses not only in such widely dispersed places as Pakistan, Viet Nam, Turkey, and Brazil, but in West European countries like Italy as well. American public administration, like the Taylorism which influenced the shaping of its traditional principles, is not very palatable in societies where science is less than a god, where traditional forces are still at work, even among the Westernized elites, and where the administrative legacy the new nations possess comes from older European countries that continue to have greater prestige among the political and administrative elite than does the United States. That the ability of these countries to resist American efforts to "modernize" public administration is formidable is clearly discernible in the reports of federal administrators and academicians—many of them experts in "O and M," personnel, classification systems, budgeting, and planning, etc.—who ventured abroad with great expectations, only to have their hopes shattered by the discovery that, even where institutional transfer is achieved, the consequences are often unanticipated. Thus, even where some evidence of the American institutional impact can be detected, it is hazardous to conclude that the heavy investments of money and men pay the anticipated dividends.

Moreover, the authors of this volume suggest that it is far from obvious that the bureaucracies of the new states should uncritically adopt American principles of scientific management. Braibanti concludes that the British influence on Pakistan's bureaucracy has been anything but detrimental to the nation. He suggests that a bureaucracy less tied to the British tradition—i.e., less generalist in its orientation—would not have been as stable in an unstable situation. One of his generalizations that deserves further investigation is that the introduction of an egalitarian system of recruitment in a highly status-conscious society would serve to reduce the status of public servants. If this is true, the role of the bureaucracy as a politically stabilizing influence would be seriously undermined. He also hypothesizes that, in a setting where voluntary associations are unavailable to the political system, almost every act of government involves bureaucratic behavior. In this type of setting, he remarks that the isolation and aloofness of the bureaucrat from the public may be his only protection against an avalanche of demands for particularistic considerations. In other words, if Braibanti is correct, as he certainly seems to me to be, in asserting that the bureaucracy is necessarily a reflection of the larger social environment of which it is a part, it would appear somewhat irrational to superimpose on any of the developing nations the principles and organizational characteristics of public administration that have evolved in the United States. Indeed, the irony in much of this is that the principles we try to export do not even operate in the United States. Many scholars and professional administrators who went abroad on technical assistance missions in recent years are the first to attest to this axiom.

In thinking about what kinds of training programs should be instituted for top public administrative management, we must come to grips with what Morstein Marx has to say about the administrative specialist—the functional expert whose superiority over the British generalist is so often lauded in the textbooks. His central proposition is that the growth of functional expertise in the bureaucracy seriously weakens the integrative function of status officialdom. The specialist is insular, narrow in his vision as well as his desires; he tends to turn the bureaucracy into a house divided against itself. This insularity and concern with limited interests blurs the bureaucrat's vision of the broader national problems and reduces his capacity to fulfill his vital role as a policy advisor. In Morstein Marx's terms, metaphysics yields to technology. In Braibanti's formulation, the loss of a strong intellectual orientation in the leading bureaucrats makes it less likely that they will play a creative and stabilizing role in the economic and political development of society. In short, the implied proposition here is that, particularly in the new states where the need for national integration is paramount, the proliferation of functional specialists in administration will add to the many centrifugal forces that already exist. When a society is rent by all sorts of social and political forces pulling in conflicting, disintegrative directions, the administrative generalist may be a vital cement, holding the system together. It may well be that programs of economic development require a certain amount of functional expertise in administration; indeed it is difficult to imagine how the many technical activities implied by economic modernization could evolve without them. But there must be accorded equal attention to the critical political role that the administrative generalist can perform, as well as to the need for preventing these generalists from impeding the development of countervailing centers of political power.

I might add here that the literature of political science in the West raises a number of problems regarding the functional specialist that are also worthy of consideration. The most critical of these involves the general problems treated below regarding the exercise of effective political control over the bureaucracy. If it is true that legislative rule-makers find it increasingly arduous if not impossible to maintain meaningful control over the bureaucratic experts, proliferating these bureaucrats early in the histories of the developing new states may very well serve to tip the political balance permanently in favor of a bureaucratic elite. It is fairly obvious, for example, that the specialists in destruction, the military, often enjoy a position of superior power precisely because they are technologically the most "modern" element in the developing areas. To be sure, their power is often also owing to their control of troops and weapons, but they remain, nevertheless, among those groups more readily willing to accept change. In any event, if the new states are going to emphasize functional expertise in public administration, they should be clear regarding the possible political price that such a program may imply.

Finally, on the subject of finding adequate personnel for the developing nations, Walter R. Sharp's chapter is very suggestive. He notes, for example, the value that may be derived from integrating technical assistants directly into the bureaucratic systems of the new states. Presumably, persons so placed will have a greater impact than those who function as advisors to host country counterparts. In addition, Sharp offers a number of generalizations of considerable importance. For example, he notes that most efforts to reform public services have tended toward too much centralization of administrative agencies. His axiom would be that where there is little decentralization there is very little creativity and innovation forthcoming from the bureaucracy. Riggs, who spends much time discussing the need for local politics, would certainly concur. So would John Dorsey, who recognizes that the need for greater administrative decentralization in Viet Nam is seriously impeded by the security situation in that unfortunate country. Presumably, Eisenstadt may be of the same view, if his comments regarding the need for administrative centralization are applied to the early activities of the bureaucracy in the integrative sector.

Another of Sharp's propositions is that the impact of United Nations (and presumably other) technical assistance programs depends on people and not on money. Plans for bureaucratic reform or economic and social change will be seriously inhibited if they run counter to powerful interest groups, if aid is sought to mask human failures in politics and administration, and if changes in political leadership cause, as they usually do, upheavals in public administrative leadership. For these as well as other reasons that we have already discussed, it is critical to understand—and for the developing nations to accept—that the short-run impact of strategies of bureaucratic reform, capital investment, social change, and the like will be very slight indeed. As Sharp notes, how the impact can be increased is a matter concerning which our information will remain limited until further research is undertaken.

Bureaucracy and Other Political Institutions

As several of our authors indicate, the bureaucracy is often called on to play a critical role when the major need of a society is that of creating a sense of nationhood. Bureaucratic behavior that relates to this function takes place in what Hoselitz calls the integrative sector. When, in addition to national integration, economic development also becomes an overriding goal, the bureaucracy, or "public sector," may also be asked to participate in the goal gratification and allocative sectors. When this happens, the probability of the bureaucracy's becoming deeply enmeshed in the function of rule making (as well as rule application) is enormously increased. Such an increase in bureaucratic power in the developing areas may clearly inhibit, perhaps preclude, the development of a democratic polity.

As Riggs notes, the presence of a strong bureaucracy in many of the new states tends to inhibit the growth of strong executives, political parties, legislatures, voluntary associations, and other political institutions essential to viable democratic government. Indeed, a significant problem in many of the ex-colonial areas is not that bureaucracy is too weak but that, as a result of the colonial experience itself, the bureaucracy in the post-independence period is the only sector of the political system that is reasonably cohesive and coherent—and able to exercise leadership and power. Where this is true, political parties tend to be ineffective, and voluntary associations, rather than serving as checks on the bureaucracy, tend to become passive instrumentalities of the public administrators.

The problem of how much control should be exercised over the bureaucracy is very perplexing. As John Dorsey illustrates for Viet Nam, President Diem's strategy has involved a combination of bureaucratic centralization, a network of tight political controls, the inculcation of attitudes of political reliability, and the use of a combination of kinship and personal charisma to assure the preponderance of the executive over the bureaucracy. Diem seems very much to have satisfied the Riggs stricture that in order to keep the bureaucracy in check, the executive needs a power base outside the bureaucracy itself. However, the general price of this control in Viet Nam has meant a political regime that is anything but democratic in its total configuration. In Pakistan, the civil bureaucracy has to some extent been checked by the military and martial law, but the situation there appears somewhat healthier from a democratic standpoint in the sense that the judiciary is functioning to check the excesses of both the military and the civil bureaucracy. It is apparent that finding the kind of balance that increases the chances of democratic development is extremely arduous and that it must be a task adapted to the particular set of circumstances that each developing area manifests.

Where economic development as a national goal is paramount, and its attainment is expected to take place largely at public hands, public administrators are in the political limelight because they tend to be injected into policy-making activities. Some feel that there is little alternative available to this pattern in the developing new states and that the question of how to relate bureaucrats to other political authorities is appropriately raised at a later stage. It is also asserted that what is political or non-political, partisan or non-partisan, varies from culture to culture and that in transitional societies the distinction is never neat. Yet, both the long-range development of a democratic system and the short-range goal of achieving a sense of the economy of the polity as a whole requires that some distinction between political and administrative roles be made, understood, and adhered to. To cite one of the least negative consequences of a failure in this area, one risks the consequence that few if any standards of professional competence will ever permeate the bureaucracy. This type of politicization can in turn weaken the capacity of the bureaucracy to perform its long-range developmental tasks.

I am arguing here that democratic development requires some separation of political and administrative roles. Joseph J. Spengler adds that economic development in turn cannot proceed with maximum efficiency unless it is managed by a combination of both the private and the public sector. Spengler suggests that the public sector is less rational in the recruitment of the manpower needed for economic development and less efficient in the management of the important economic input transformation function. He would, therefore, limit the economically relevant role of bureaucracy to the selection of the ends or objectives of development, the provision of objective conditions that aid the growth of an entrepreneurial middle class, and the addition of certain input transformation activities where the private sector is inadequate.

Spengler's is strictly an economic argument for limiting the role of the bureaucracy in economic development. He, like others, warns against having the public sector become an omniverous and unproductive consumer of a nation's limited resources. Yet his position clearly has important political implications. Riggs, for example, sees the development of a middle class as a vital means of limiting bureaucratic power in favor of democratic development. The data, however, are discouraging. Kingsley tells us that in Africa the economic involvement of the bureaucracy is essential if the "leap to modernization" is to take place where a private entrepreneurial class is simply nonexistent. Dorsey stresses that the public sector is often emphasized precisely because little or no economic development would otherwise occur. The problem for the developing countries seems to be that of finding entrepreneurial skills and motivation wherever they may exist. That the bureaucracy usually harbors the vast concentration of this talent is the consequence of a particular pattern of historical and colonial evolution.

However, it is also apparent that, for ideological or other reasons, the bureaucracies of the developing areas will often hamper the growth of a private entrepreneurial class. Merchants and others who might work to transform the economy are incessantly harassed; what appear on the surface to be rational tax systems amount, in fact, to tribute. The price of commercial survival becomes a systematic campaign to corrupt the bureaucracy itself. Often whatever indigenous entrepreneurial talent there may be is concentrated in pariah classes, of foreign origin, and therefore not politically available to the society at large. Thus, forces that might be harnessed to the tasks of nation building are dissipated in the most unproductive kind of petty political maneuvering which enshrines corruption as the means of commercial and fiscal survival. Neither meaningful economic development nor political democracy are likely to emerge unless, as Spengler suggests, the bureaucracies of the new states make quite deliberate efforts to encourage the flourishing of the private sector. Spengler's general warning has a ring of authenticity: when the bureaucracy is once mobilized for the achievement of systemic goals, it is not likely to withdraw willingly when the pressure of systemic goals diminishes.

From a democratic standpoint, the general picture is not completely discouraging. Even where the bureaucracy is deeply involved in goal setting, the extent of its power may be checked by such factors as increased literacy, strong traditional institutions, and strong social elites of which the bureaucracy is not a part or into which it has not yet been absorbed. We know, for example, that even after a century of Prussian bureaucratic centralization, encompassing developments from the Great Elector to Frederick William I, the bureaucracy was limited in its powers by the necessity of having to effect all sorts of compromises with the Junkers. In Meiji Japan, at least until the upper-level bureaucrats began to be absorbed into the nobility, the dominant social class served as a check on bureaucratic excesses. In contemporary India, the Congress Party, the traditions of the Indian Civil Service, and the growth of strong and articulate local centers of political power appear as partial checks on the central bureaucracy. In many of the developing areas—as witness abortive efforts to ride roughshod over village-level forces—a kind of *de facto* federal structure tends to circumscribe the amount of power the bureaucracy can exercise.

By and large, however, we are witnessing in many places the emergence of overpowering bureaucracies. Some feel that there is little alternative to a cautious acceptance of this development. It is pointed out that rapid economic change is the overriding need and that little can be done to moderate the revolution of rising expectations. In these circumstances one must accept an increasingly powerful bureaucracy and hope that, in the long run, other political institutions will catch up. Moreover, it is not always certain that attempts to limit bureaucratic power will have the desired results. For example, the encouragement of stronger political institutions, say, a two- or multi-party system, might be counter-productive as far as economic development is concerned. On this reasoning, one should prefer a one-party-dominant system and hope that the party itself might serve as a check on the bureaucracy, as it does in the Soviet Union or as it may do in Ghana. As another example, it is far from clear that encouraging the growth of local governmental institutions will give anticipated results. Where this was attempted by Alexander II in Russia, those who went into the zemstvos were, indeed, at war with the central bureaucracy, but so much so that many of them became Cadets and made their appearance in the 1905 Revolution. It is also noteworthy that in many places in Africa strong bureaucracies are needed in order to hold together new countries that would otherwise fall apart under the impact of the many centrifugal forces that beset them. In places such as these, a powerful bureaucracy is said to be essential if one is to override the disintegrating influences of artificial political boundaries, the competitive force of familial and tribal structures, the difficulty of organizing and financing political parties, the low energy output of the population, and the tendency of the population to want to expend funds on consumer gadgets rather than on a capital formation. In sum, there are those who hold that, in the developing states, powerful bureaucracies are simply necessary evils that one must learn to tolerate, hoping for the best from a democratic standpoint.

For those such as Fred Riggs who are not sanguine about the probable political outcome of trends now in motion, it is necessary to take certain positive steps. Riggs' chapter contains a number of concrete suggestions. He would encourage the long ballot at the local level, as well as greater local autonomy of taxing power. He rightly notes, as do others, that central planning aggrandizes bureaucratic power and that local participation in developmental plans is not meaningful unless local citizens are asked and empowered to pay for economic change through taxation, if they want to and can. It may sound like a tired cliché, but there is apparently more than blind faith in the generalization that political democracy begins at the grass roots. The need for national integration, which calls for centralized administration, must give way to greater decentralization if the need for democratic development is to be met.

To summarize, there appears to be some incompatibility between rapid economic development, on the one hand, and democratic political development, on the other. Riggs flatly states that the price of democratic development may have to be slower development in the economic sphere. Certainly it is anything but apparent that a planned increase in the material well-being of a society will automatically bring about democratic institutions. Planned economic development, in which the public sector is dominant, tends to imply centralized control, the curtailment of public wants to increase surplus value for investment, the weakening of traditional institutions of a society, particularly when they manifest values antagonistic to economic development, and an intolerance of institutional arrangements, such as many political parties or strong interest groups, that might divert the society from its central purpose.

Bringing about democratic political development must be a consciously sought goal. If it cannot be encouraged through a de-emphasis of economic goals, it might be possible to experiment with such mechanisms as local governmental autonomy, the integration of traditional structures into developmental plans, the use of democratic ideological indoctrination as a means of controlling bureaucracies. Equally vital to democracy, it would seem, is the development of the private economic sector. The bureaucracy might limit its role to that of setting systemic goals and of providing the objective conditions without which economic development is seriously hamstrung. Beyond this, the bureaucracy might exercise self-restraint, relying as much as possible on the private sector for the performance of the function of input transformation. To be sure, in most of the developing societies input transformation would require the dual participation of both the bureaucracy and whatever business community exists. But only if the latter is encouraged substantively to participate can one expect to witness the growth of the kind of social and economic milieu in which eventual democratic development amounts to more than a pious hope.

Demands and the Bureaucracy

Eisenstadt tells us that all political systems are subjected to a pattern of demands and that all of them have some capacity to deal with increases in demands and organization that may develop. In reaction to demands, alternatives are available to the authoritative structures in the sense that the development of demands may be minimized, controlled or manipulated, or absorbed by responding to them with governmental policies. The particular combination of these three patterns of response will divulge the degree to which a political system approximates democracy or totalitarianism. A modern democratic system would be one in which there exists both a high degree of structural differentiation for dealing with demands as well as a reasonable correspondence between the level of demands and their substantive satisfaction. In the satisfaction of demands, in any system, the bureaucracy inevitably plays a very vital role. The point to note is that there are functional requisities for any given political system and that, if a democratic industrial society is desired, requisites such as the above, in which the bureaucracy is intimately involved, must be met.

In the developing areas, the bureaucracies are normally confronted with a level of demand that the system is simply not able to satisfy. Kingsley points out that colonialism itself leaves a legacy of greatly increased demands for the symbols of a well-endowed materialistic society. Dorsey phrases this problem as resulting from the permeation of low-information-energy societies with the information and values of high-energy societies. Morstein Marx, looking to the consequences of this, notes that the bureaucrats in developing societies are often squeezed by the excessive demands of politicians who tend to reflect and to generate what the masses seek from the political system. Whatever the formulation, it is obvious that bureaucrats often find themselves confronted by requests that they cannot meet. The situation is particularly difficult in those political systems where there are no well-developed political parties and voluntary associations that might serve to temper and aggregate demands and to provide an orderly means of communicating demands to the bureaucracy.

One bureaucratic response to this situation is what Riggs calls "formalism," involving the creation of the formal structures of high-energy societies but not their content. Another related response involves the encouragement, even the creation by the bureaucracy, of seemingly voluntary associations that are nothing more than the bureaucracy's instrumentalities. Such associations afford some structural means whereby demands can be transmitted in a reasonably orderly way. They help the bureaucracy, to some degree, to control the flow of demands and to implement policies that emanate from the bureaucracy itself. Needless to add, such a pattern of response is not consistent with the development of a pluralistic democracy.

Nevertheless, in any political system, something has to be done about the growth of political demands that occur as a social system moves from a traditional into a transitional situation. In the development of Western systems the situation was different in an important respect. There, the capacity of political systems for enforcement of decisions and the allocation of values increased along with the capacity of the society to generate demands. Where, as in the new nations, demands clearly outstrip any capacity of the system to meet them institutionally, one witnesses the evolution of symbolic and demagogic politics—an inflation of the language of politics as an effort to soak up those demands which cannot be met by concrete output. This is merely another mode of responding to the general problem—a mode in which the bureaucracy itself may play a central role. The fact is that, when confronted with this set of circumstances, the bureaucracy, by various devices, is forced to (1) limit the creation of demand, as in Salazar's Portugal, (2) control those demands not emanating from the government itself, as in the Soviet Union, and (3) absorb as many of the demands as possible through the utilization of existing institutions and the creation of new ones. While all political systems will exhibit some combination of these three responses to demand, the developing nations tend to focus primarily on the first two. This tends to institutionalize an unstable situation and to bring into operation patterns of political and bureaucratic behavior that are incompatible with democracy.

The management of demands is a deeply perplexing problem and in the developing nations the bureaucracy is certain to be heavily involved in the process. Unfortunately, the widest possible range of demands is directed against the government. The demands for independence against colonial powers accustomed the masses to convert most of their grievances into demands against the government of the central state. Additionally, in the post-independence situations, the existence of a bi-polar world helps to generate additional demands which are still directed against the central government. In any case, the capacity of the government to meet demands will be limited by the capacity of the economic system. Here lies the pressure for rapid economic change which leads the bureaucracy to push hard in this direction. That demands are not always spontaneous, that they may be manipulated and generated by elements of the articulate, educated elite, is not immediately relevant. The fact is that the demands are there and the bureaucracy is compelled to respond to them in some meaningful way. For, unless some way of institutionalizing and otherwise coping with demands is devised, the system itself is certain to disintegrate into violence and chaos. Certainly the nature, flow, and magnitude of demands will make any kind of development, political or economic, easier or more difficult. Difficulties are certain to increase in the degree to which the bureaucracy fails to manage demands in some systematic way.

This leads me to speculate whether it would not be possible to manipulate demands so that goals of democratic political development enjoy a status equal to that of economic change. Less emphasis might be given to grand schemes of economic development, more to local-level development that might bring forces of local political participation into play. This might also be a means of encouraging the evolution of the kind of private economic sector that would constitute an embryonic middle class and an eventual counterpoise to the power of the centralized bureaucracy. I might say that I strongly believe that it is more than historical coincidence that economic liberalism preceded the emergence of political liberalism in the West. A similar, even if not exactly duplicate, type of evolution might be encouraged in the developing nations. Some political benefits would surely derive from encouraging the kind of economic enterprise that is individually rather than collectively oriented, that exalts the place of the private entrepreneur rather than that of an all-embracing collectivity symbolized by large-scale, unwieldly, and unbending public bureaucracies. While I do not expect the intellectuals, bureaucrats, and politicians to accept a Spencerian definition of the role of the public sector, it does seem possible that greater acceptance might be accorded the model assigning a more significant role to the private sector of the economy.

I am aware that it will be difficult to implement what is suggested here. Progressive limitations on the powers of bureaucracy are not easy to come by; de-emphasizing economic development goals will meet with a great deal of opposition everywhere in the new states. Yet, without some conscious effort in this direction, the pattern of political development in the new states will probably follow the Soviet—or Chinese—rather than the Anglo-American model. It is this possibility that compels us to give even greater attention to the role of the bureaucracy in political development.

Some Unanswered Questions

The chapters in this volume, while providing a number of generalizations such as those I have reviewed, raise more questions than they answer. Much more needs to be done in the field of comparative research—both historical and contemporary—before we can speak with confidence about the variables that push a nation in one political direction rather than another. How, for example, does a society go about inculcating the set of attitudes toward government and voluntary associations that are compatible with a pluralist democracy? What role can the bureaucracy play in this important function? What instruments of political socialization are most efficaciously related to this process? What kinds of training and statuses does the bureaucracy require if it is to exercise the quantum of self-restraint that will make of it a bulwark of democratic rather than totalitarian development? If economic and political development are to move ahead simultaneously, what kind of balance of objectives and tempo of movement is to be prescribed for each sector? If, in the developing areas, the public sector is to achieve a position of great prominence from the very beginning of nation-statehood, what can be done to guarantee that healthy centers of countervailing power will come into existence? Questions such as these will surely suggest themselves to the reader. They deserve continuous attention from the practitioners of social science.

It will doubtless be noted that one important topic not treated in this volume is the role of the military in economic and political development. This subject was discussed at some length by those who attended the conference out of which this volume emerges. There was unanimous agreement that the increasing interest in the military is amply justified by events that have occurred in varied developing areas around the globe. It is apparent, for example, that in many of the new states, what development does occur will be managed by the military bureaucracy, either working largely alone, as the military has tried to do in places like Burma and Thailand, or in some kind of collaboration with the civil bureaucracy, as has been true of countries like Egypt, Turkey, and Pakistan.

From the standpoint of nation building and economic development, the military can often work as a very effective instrument. The role of the centralized military in breaking the power of feudal nobles, warlords, and caudillos is well known. The military was effectively used in this sense in Prussia after the Great Elector and in Japan following the Meiji Restoration, to cite only two of the obvious examples. The military can very quickly acquire a sense of the nation and develop hostilities toward vested interests and parochial enclaves. The military organization itself, by recruiting from disparate groups throughout the society, can be an important socializing instrument, inculcating values that are nation-oriented.

By its very nature, the military will also tend to be the most modern group (in the technological sense) that one encounters in a transitional society. Defense needs move military leaders to accept new technologies and to train recruits in skills that one associates with an industrial society. These skills can be put to use when recruits are released from military service. Moreover, in situations where the military becomes directly involved in the creation of social overhead capital, it can be quite effective in the construction of roads, bridges, dams, and other projects essential to rapid economic change.

The list of positive characteristics does not terminate here. Armies can be important transitional experiences for those who leave the villages and wind up in urban centers. As officers are recruited from other than the dominant aristocratic strata of societies, armies can become a means of strengthening the middle class. The military, through its formal and practical educational opportunities, can be a most significant means of providing a reservoir of future administrative and technological leadership. In short, the military can be a very important impetus for change.

Yet, where the military has assumed control, it is often apparent that democratic development is impeded. The case of Japan following the American military occupation seems to be an exception, and, until recently, so was Turkey. Pakistan may offer another interesting exception, but it is yet too early to draw firm conclusions there. By and large, when the military assumes control it does not tend to encourage democratic institutions and practices; it is suspicious and disdainful of politicians; it is apt to short-circuit and to delay constitutionalism; and it is inclined either toward becoming a part of the existing aristocratic strata or toward developing a vested-interest status of its own. The history of Latin America clearly illustrates one pattern of political development that can emerge when the military bureaucracy gets into the driver's seat.

Nor should one exaggerate the utility of the military bureaucracy in economic development. For one thing, military leaders infrequently understand the myriad and subtle problems involved in the business of giving rational and coherent fiscal and financial leadership to the community. As national political policy makers, they tend to be less able than their civil bureaucratic counterparts. For another thing, military regimes invariably divert to the military area limited resources that might be better used for economic development. Perhaps the point to make here is that, whereas the military can be very useful as a limited instrument of economic development, its utility and effectiveness greatly diminishes as it moves toward complete control of the social system. In any event, it is reasonably clear that, where the goal-setting and goal-implementing bureaucracy is military rather than civil, the prospects for democratic political development are even more dismal than I have suggested above.

Other topics that directly relate to the central focus of this book might be cited. We have embarked on only the beginning of an intellectual journey that is fraught with all sorts of conceptual and theoretical difficulties. Some of these are empirically visible only above the surface, and we shall have to probe to greater depths before moving ahead with confidence. Unhappily, time does not stand still for the new states, and forces already in motion will probably lead to destinations that were set long before these pages were written.

CHAPTER 2

Bureaucracy and Political Development: Notes, Queries, and Dilemmas[1]

JOSEPH LA PALOMBARA

Introduction

Every political system must include some patterned means whereby wishes or statements of public policy are transformed into action affecting those within the system over whom political power is exercised. In earlier, less complex systems, the activity of transformation could be carried on more or less effectively by the prince and members of his household. In many contemporary tribal and peasant systems, the activity or function of administration is still performed by a chief and his family or personal entourage, by leaders who frequently combine political with religious or other roles, by kinship groups, clans or castes that enjoy a privileged place in the making and administration of public policy. But as the volume and tempo of public business increase, for whatever reasons, there tend to follow both a growth in the number of administrators and a division of labor among those entrusted with public policy administration. Not only does there occur a specialization of activity among administrators; the function of administration itself is increasingly differentiated from that of policy formulation.

Public administrative systems extant in the contemporary world run the gamut from the most "primitive" functionally diffuse variety, where it is difficult to isolate the specific function of policy administration from other activities, to the most "modern," in which a relatively very high degree of specialization and differentiation of both function and structure has occurred. Whether a particular structural and behavioral configuration in the public administrative sector is required in order to achieve change or development in the social, economic, and political sectors is one of the problems that will be examined below.

[1] For several of the ideas and problems treated in this paper, I am indebted to my colleagues on the Committee on Comparative Politics of the Social Science Research Council, as well as to my colleagues at the Center for Advanced Study in the Behavioral Sciences, Bernard Cohen and Warren Miller. Fred W. Riggs also took the time to make many pointed observations of great usefulness.

Our more basic concern is to speculate regarding what might be the alternative roles of public administration in bringing about particular kinds of change, especially in those newer nation-states that are now undergoing rapid transformation.

In order to do this meaningfully, we must first confront a number of perplexing problems, the most important of which, in my view, involves the use of the concept "modern" or "modernity" when we refer to political systems or sub-systems within them. Failure to confront at least the major contours of this conceptual problem at the outset is certain to lead to considerable misunderstanding.

In this chapter I wish to raise several questions that seem particularly relevant to the problem of probing the relationship of public administration to political change. The first of these is whether it makes any sense—whether it is useful—to think about development or change in terms of some conception of the politically "modern," whatever may be the attributes that one ascribes to "modernity." I will suggest that the concept is essentially a serious pitfall and that, for the time being at least, we should suspend its use. I shall then provide several dimensions along which we might fruitfully analyze change in political systems. I shall also ask whether political change of a particular kind requires any specific set of characteristics in public administration, especially that set of characteristics which we associate with the Weberian concept of bureaucracy. I shall also consider what may be the relationship between particular characteristics of the public administrative system and the development of the kinds of political institutions and behavior that we associate with democratic systems.

While exhaustive answers to the queries posed cannot be provided here, it is possible to offer some hopefully suggestive notes and to point our attention to some topics that are worthy of further discussion. Finally, I believe it may be useful to highlight some apparent dilemmas that seem to emerge for those in the West whose great concern and aspiration are that the developing nations move in directions that will make their political, social, and economic systems reasonable approximations of what we may call the Anglo-American model.

On the Concept of "Modern" or "Modernity"

My first concern with the use of the concept of "modern" or "modernity" as applied to political systems is that there exists considerable confusion and disagreement regarding its meaning. One important source of confusion is the implicit or explicit free substitution of society, economic system, or social system for political system. With distressing regularity, one is led to infer that a "modern" political system is one which operates in a society that is relatively highly urbanized, that manifests a relatively high degree of literacy and social mobility, that contains a relatively high degree of specialization of occupational roles, that has gone considerably beyond the "take-off" stage in economic development, that has achieved a high degree of sophistication and efficiency in the conversion of information and resources into energy, and that is secular or rational in the performance of societal functions.

The problem of clarity is exacerbated by the tendency among economists to define "modernity" in terms of quantitative increments in the per capita output of goods and services produced by societies. When "modernity" really refers to economic modernity, it is difficult to avoid the snare that a "modern" political system is simply one that exists in a society that is highly industrialized. This confusion has been greatly abetted by the developmental goals of the new nations which are primarily and dramatically economic, secondarily social, and only casually political in character. After the achievement of the overriding political goal of national independence, little if any attention is paid to the problem of political development; almost no systematic articulation takes place regarding the possible characteristics of political "modernity," whether such characteristics are desirable as developmental goals, and, if so, what policies and action would be essential to their achievement. At best a certain amount of lip service is paid the matter of political development; at worst, the whole area is demagogically treated or submerged to the prior needs or goals of effecting economic development. To be sure, many of the economic or social development programs have latent consequences in the political sphere. My point is that these consequences are not generally overtly explored or consciously and systematically posited as ends to be achieved.

A second objection to the use of "modern" or "modernity" when referring to political systems is that the concept is often implicitly and perhaps unintentionally normative. For example, definitions of "modernity" that rest primarily on economic criteria often result in one's having to place in the same taxonomic category totalitarian systems such as the U.S.S.R. and democratic systems such as the United States. This grates on the sensitivities of those who consider the former an aberrant political system and leads to attempts to append to the definition of "modernity" characteristics that are parochially and normatively derived. What begins explicitly as an effort to define "modernity" in terms of easily measurable economic criteria ends as a suggestion that those political systems are "modern" which possess the structural and behavioral attributes that can be associated with Anglo-American democracy.

Such normative definitions naturally grow out of the fact that, over many decades, the most "advanced" countries of the world were generally identified as those of North America and Western Europe. Viewed by the Anglo-American standard, a "modern" political system would necessarily have to possess more than those empirically determined characteristics that countries like the United States and the Soviet Union have more or less in common. A "modern" system would be one in which achievement rather than ascriptive criteria in political recruitment and role differentiation are maximized, in which group interests are articulated by a plurality of competing voluntary associations, and the interests in turn aggregated by more than a single political party and by governmental institutions over the membership of which the adult citizens exercise some measure of ultimate control. Nor is that all. To qualify as "modern" such a system would have to be responsive to the needs and articulated demands of the people or the electorate; it would necessarily involve universal suffrage and a high degree of popular participation in the political process. Elements of particularism in the exercise of every aspect of the political function would be considerably moderated by a pragmatism and secular rationality that would characterize most of the secondary system-wide structures.

Obviously, a definition that proceeds along such lines has serious limitations from the standpoint of a comparative political science. However, without becoming involved in the problems of what is or is not "modern," one could certainly use the Anglo-American political systems as a working example of the kind of arrangement of institutions and behaviors that is desired and then proceed to raise and answer questions concerning the conditions under which political development might or might not move in the desired direction. Anglo-American democracy then becomes the dependent variable in the analysis, and attention can be focused on those variables which seem to be independently related to the development and maintenance of such a system. We will suggest below several variables by which one may judge, not merely the potentiality of the emergence of democracy, but also the possible emergence of political systems that are non-democratic.

A third objection to the use of "modern" or "modernity" when dealing with problems of political systems is that the terms tend to suggest a single, final state of affairs—a deterministic, unilinear theory of political evolution. It seems to me that this is well illustrated by the extent in recent years to which both scholars and technical assistance personnel who have confronted problems of development have had the Anglo-American model in view as not only desirable but as a "naturally" ultimate stage of development as well. This bias is often not apparent because of the confusion that prevails between the application of economic and other criteria of "modernity." As long as it could be persuasively argued that totalitarian and undemocratic systems were not as economically efficient as systems found in democratic societies, no particular problems were forced to the surface. However, the contradictions and dilemmas involved in working with a hodge-podge conception of "modernity" which is part economic and part Anglo-American political are made apparent when the evidence demonstrates that the total Anglo-American set of political institutions and behaviors is not a necessary condition of "modernity" in the economic sense and that, indeed, it may actually constitute a hindrance to rapid economic growth. Were one at this point to pursue the conceptual and definitional problem with vigor, the need to separate what is meant by a "modern" economic system from what is meant by a "modern" political system would be obvious. It is precisely at this point that it becomes apparent that comparative analysis is not facilitated by a definition of political "modernity" that is culture-bound and narrowly restrictive through its assumption of the evolutionary inevitability of the Anglo-American model. Only a rigid Wilsonian faith in the inevitability of democracy would justify a retention of a parochial and deterministic definition in the face of the historical and contemporary evidence that surrounds us.

The danger of determinism and of unilinear evolution remains even if one is prepared to specify the general attributes of "modernity" that are not normatively derived. The very words "modern" or "modernity" imply a social Darwinian model of political development. They suggest that change is inevitable, that it proceeds in clearly identifiable stages, that subsequent evolutionary stages are necessarily more complex than those which preceded them, and that later stages are better than their antecedents. What we need at this time are genuinely open models of political change that will permit us to identify the various ways in which the many variables that bear on change are interrelated. At least until our knowledge is greatly increased, change in political systems should be viewed as neither evolutionary nor inevitable. Such systems may remain in a given stage for exceedingly long periods, and when change does occur it may not necessarily represent a step forward. What we should accept is that there may be a number of paths in political change, that widely varying structural arrangements may emerge from differing total conditions of development, and that, if this is so, it makes little sense to confuse the issue by trying to attach the label "modern" only to a particular and possibly unique structural configuration. Such an approach may not appear as elegant as one that proceeds from a definition of the "modern" and the "primitive," but it will surely save us the energy that will be expended, with dubious pay-off, in our search after the will-o'-the-wisp of the "modern" and "modernity" in political systems. Concern with the nature of change rather than with definition is likely to permit the development of a science of comparative politics.

Some Characteristics of Political Change

It may be that the definitional problem will one day be resolved and that we will be provided with a definition of political change that both liberates us from cultural bias and provides the basis for some hypotheses concerning the process of development. Here we will turn our attention instead to the matter of exploring several dimensions along which basic changes in political systems—in any political system—might usefully be measured. In listing these dimensions, I do not mean to be exhaustive; however, I believe that they represent significant variables that bear on the political institutional changes that occur in political systems from time to time.

I wish to explore four dimensions, or variables, and to suggest how they relate to one particular kind of political system or another. The first of these is the *degree of structural differentiation*[2] that exists for those institutions involved in the performance of political functions. It is possible for us to detect the type of societal development that results

[2] I am using "structural differentiation" here to mean essentially what Fred W. Riggs intends by "refraction." See his "Prismatic Society and Financial Administration," *Administrative Science Quarterly*, Vol. 5, June 1960, pp. 1-46.

in a distinct separation of the performance of political functions (here understood as David Easton's authoritative allocation of values) from the performance of other functions such as the economic or the religious. Separation, or differentiation, involves the creation of new structures and roles for the performance of political functions; it implies an increased specialization or division of labor among those who are responsible for the performance of political functions.

One way of handling the specific political function of rule application, for example, may be that of entrusting it to a group of administrative officials who handle many varied kinds of activities, both political and non-political. When the role of government is limited, when rule application or administration is largely a matter to be handled by the prince's household, only a minimum amount of division of labor occurs; each of a few administrators covers a broad general area of governmental activity. That this was the earliest kind of public administration is reflected in what we know about ancient political systems, as well as in the training programs or educational preparation for public administrators that have come down to the present day. However, another way of approaching the rule-applying function is to place it in the hands of very highly trained and specialized functional specialists whose work is considerably more subdivided and differentiated. Not only do these men not perform non-political roles in the system; the roles that they do perform are highly differentiated and generally require the full-time attention of the persons involved. We have experienced the growth of this type of administrator, and of educational and training programs that produce him, in several of the societies of the present-day world.

The combination of these two general types of political (in this case administrative) roles which are required for a political system will depend in part on the kinds of goals that are set for the system. If, say, rapid industrialization at the hands of public authorities is an important end in view, the pressures for functional specialists who can accomplish this end will be great. This can be generalized to read that the pressure to proliferate the functional specialists in administration will bear a direct relationship to the degree in which government becomes involved in technical activities ranging all the way from public health to the development and preservation and use of natural resources. The growth of general technology, itself, will have a bearing on such a development in that increased technology creates both opportunities and problems of governance that did not previously exist.

The particular combination of specialists and generalists that is most desirable may be strongly affected if a central value of the society is the maintenance of democracy in the political system. The literature of political science and public administration in the United States and Great Britain clearly points up the danger for democratic values that may grow out of a strong emphasis on the growth of administrative specialists. It is apparent that the central idea in democratic theory of an instrumental bureaucracy is seriously challenged in its efficacy as we learn of the increasing complexity, even the impossibility, of keeping the specialists in government meaningfully responsible to those in the political system who are theoretically responsible for setting the ends of government. We shall return to this dilemma later in this chapter. The point here is that a public administrative system that maximizes the degree of differentiation and specialization of administrative roles is not necessarily more "modern"; it is merely different, in its relevance for one set of national goals (e.g., democratization, industrialization, social pluralism) from another system that, for whatever reasons, does not go as far along in this direction. To put this differently, the national goal of industrialization may require a very high degree of differentiation of administrative roles. On the other hand, great differentiation does not seem to be a requisite of political democracy. One of the great dilemmas of many of the developing countries is that they seem to want economic development more than freedom.

As a general rule, specialization and differentiation of political roles and structures will be accompanied by similar differentiation and specialization in other sectors of society as well. This would be true of commerce, agriculture, industry, services, and communications, to name only some of the more obvious sectors. However, such development does not and need not occur in a setting of balance or equilibrium, nor is it apparent that development in one sector must necessarily precede or follow similar developments in another sector. For example, there might occur considerable differentiation of political roles in a society in which a concomitant division of roles had not occurred in the economic or commerical sectors. Or, within the same society, we might find isolated portions of each sector that manifest great differentiation of structure and other portions that do not. Or, we may discover that, notwithstanding the formal differentiation of political structures, the political function itself is largely handled by structural arrangements that carry over from the past. All of this could be well illustrated by the histories and contemporary situations of many West European countries. There are parts of Italy, for example, in which structural differentiation in the political sphere is substantively meaningful in the sense that the new structures actually work—that is, they perform the formally prescribed functions. This would be true, say, of administrative field offices, prefectures, provincial councils, and municipal assemblies in cities like Turin, Milan, Bologna, Venice, and other places in the north. In the south, however, notwithstanding the existence of similar formal political institutions, the effective authoritative allocation of values continues to take place through the intervention of the local priest or bishop, the great family, and so on.

This situation suggests that, in addition to verifying the existence of high structural differentiation in a given political system, we must examine these structures closely in order to determine exactly what political function they do perform. Certainly, for any political system, and particularly for those of the developing nation-states, one of the important questions begging attention is how and why political structures that have been formally replaced by newer ones continue to persist as viable elements of the political system. We know of this survival power not only with regard to "dual" or "transitional" systems, but also with regard to those which have presumably come some distance away from that status.[3] I believe that our ability to understand and to deal with this phenomenon has been considerably hampered by the primitive-transitional-modern model which somehow presupposes that change moves in a determined direction.[4] It is the particular configuration of structures that is of interest to us. We need to know the circumstances under which such configurations occur, without regard to whether there is implied a ubiquitous, deterministic evolution.

A second dimension along which change in political systems might be viewed and plotted is *magnitude*. By magnitude I mean essentially the ratio of political activity, however institutionalized, to all of the other activity that takes place in society. We know, for example, that

[3] Fred Riggs notes that the failure of actual behavior to conform to what the formal structure suggests or anticipates is "formalism" and should be subjected to analytical treatment as a separate variable.

[4] A less deterministic, more promising model is the "fused-prismatic-refracted" conceptualization of F. W. Riggs. See his forthcoming *Comparative Bureaucracy*.

significant growth in population will require more than a mere arithmetic increase in the activities of government. We understand that highly populated nation-states must confront problems of public policy and governance that do not exist in smaller historical and contemporary communities. The same specific and limited activities of government take on different dimensions, and require an increase in magnitude, as we move from Joliet, Illinois, to New York City.

The kind of structural differentiation and specialization to which I refer above may or may not carry with it a change in the magnitude of government. Highly undifferentiated political systems might manifest great or little magnitude; the same is true of systems that achieve a high degree of differentiation. However, one can probably assert that, as a general rule, magnitude and differentiation will vary with each other, with the scope of governmentally made decisions increasing as the political system develops greater structural differentiation. In other words, while the same political functions are performed everywhere, the magnitude of governmental decisions will increase as greater structural specialization evolves.

In two highly differentiated systems, magnitude will naturally be greater in a totalitarian than in a liberal democratic society, or greater in a society that emphasizes the public over the private sector. Our concern with this variable, then, is to discover how extensive a role a particular social system ascribes to specific political institutions. Some of these will be very severe in limiting government, perhaps insisting that its appropriate concern is merely the maintenance of internal order and protection against external aggression. Others societies will turn over to those who occupy political roles great responsibilities concerning almost every facet of human existence.

Thus, it is both fruitless and misleading to confuse an increase in magnitude with "modernity," although it is obvious that some observers equate the more "modern" with the more positive state. Whenever this relationship is expressed or implied, it must mean that a society in which economic planning and development take place largely through the energies of the public sector is more "modern" than one in which such decisions are left to the market mechanism, voluntary associations, and other non-governmental structures. When laid perfectly bare, this approach would necessarily force the ludicrous conclusion that not only the Soviet Union but countries like India and Pakistan are more modern than the United States. It is critical, therefore, if it is to serve us in understanding political change, that the concept of magnitude as I have defined it be left unencumbered by notions of what is or is not "modern." Our concern, as with the case of structural differentiation, is to specify and verify the circumstances in which there is likely to occur an increase or decrease in magnitude. This, too, is an item to which we shall briefly return in the portion of this chapter that examines the problem of bringing a democratic structural configuration into existence in the developing new states.

A third way of looking at political systems is to ask what *degree of achievement orientation* applies to political recruitment and role differentiation. The question of central tendency is crucial here; we are certainly not interested in establishing that a particular type of political system requires the exclusive application of achievement or ascriptive criteria in the selection and placement of those who are asked to perform political roles. As a matter of empirical reality, all systems will manifest a particular combination of ascription and achievement. The matter of interest then becomes that of trying to relate a given combination of these criteria to the maintenance or transformation of a specified social, political, or economic configuration.

We might say, for example, that the democratic ethic requires that achievement be the dominant method in political recruitment, placement, transfer, and promotion. Or, we might assert that certain kinds and levels of economic development demand a combination of achievement and ascription within certain limits, and that if ascription exceeds a given limit the goal of economic development itself will be adversely affected. Only if particular patterns are related to other structural elements of the system are discussions centering on "how much achievement or particularism" likely to make very much sense. Moreover, in making comparisons between or among political systems it is important not to draw facile assumptions, say, about the United States and then leap to the conclusion that, in order to attain democratic development (or some other form of development), the developing nations should be endowed, just as quickly as possible, with the attributes we associate with Anglo-American democracy.[5]

We clearly need to know more about the relationship of achievement orientation to development and change. For example, while I concede that the goal of industrialization requires more of this than one usually finds in primitive or transitional societies, I would suggest that

[5] The same general point can be made for the use of other pattern variables such as "particularism-universalism," "intimacy-avoidance," etc. which are not treated here as separate dimensions.

the same is not true of the goal of political democratization. Depending on the specific nature of developmental goals, it may be that one would want a dominant political party that recruits public administrators primarily from among its own membership.

What is of vital concern is the job to be performed, and it is entirely possible that non-achievement criteria can be applied in part without destroying a reasonable relationship between the method of recruitment and what has to be accomplished. The fact that Soviet administrators may be recruited largely from the Communist party, or that Italian administrators tend to come primarily from the southern provinces, or that in the United States women are clearly discriminated against in public administrative occupations may very well violate democratic values, but it does not tell us that, for this reason, the functions of government will be inadequately performed. The notion that one gets the best performance only if all members of the society have an equal opportunity of contributing their talents to political functions may look neat and persuasive on paper, but is not clearly supported by the empirical evidence we have about recruitment and role differentiation in many political systems.

The crucial question to pose is what is the consequence of particular patterns of political recruitment for the ends that society sets for the political system. If, for example, it is expected that government will play a direct role in industrial management, and a system of recruitment exists that excludes those who are best fitted to perform these roles, we can conclude that there is present an irrationality of means that will adversely affect goal achievement. But we must bear in mind the lesson of the Soviet experience which teaches that political functions in the hands of those narrowly recruited from the dominant political party can be efficiently and effectively performed. The same thing may today be true of some of the one-party dominant newer states where political talent may be even more heavily concentrated among party members than was the case with the Bolsheviks forty-five years ago. Spoils may not be an efficacious way of creating neat democratic institutions and practices in the short run; but they may represent the most rational way of moving the newer states along in certain developmental directions that they greatly desire. That there may be a dilemma of both ends and means implied here for those of us who wish to see democracy emerge in the newer states is a matter which we can try somewhat to clarify later. The point is that maximum achievement orientation in political recruitment may be critical for a society that deeply and directly involves the government in economic development while only optimum achievement orientation may be necessary for democratization.

The last dimension along which we might view political systems in the *degree of secularization* that persists in performing all of the political functions. Maximum secularization would require that the political process proceed primarily on the basis of a rationality of the ends of government and of the means utilized to achieve these ends. Although we would not expect to find any system free from irrational behavior in this regard, we would be interested in identifying central tendencies and in analyzing the consequences for the system of a particular pattern or another. Obviously, many of the complex functions that we associate with contemporary government require systematic and reliable means of gathering information, of processing and evaluating such information, and of using it to govern the kinds of goals that are set and the kinds of means adopted for goal implementation. For many of the developing countries, we understand that goals are unrealistic in part because the approach to information is chaotic and because the environment is not confronted in an essentially rational and empirical manner. Given certain national aspirations, we can say that a given degree of secularization is necessary to make politics truly the "art of the possible." We might be able to contend that before certain goals are either set or achieved, the determination of ends and means must be based on information as opposed to, say, religious revelation; on pragmatic considerations rather than arbitrary, a priori prescriptions; on systematic manipulation of the human environment rather than magic; and so on.

Having said this, I should add that the idea of rationality cannot be too parochial—too narrowly associated with patterns of organization and behavior that evolved in Western Europe in the eighteenth and nineteenth centuries. Nor is it of any apparent use to argue a concept of rationality that involves accepting both the premises and the logic of those who hold a democratic view of the nature of man and who insist that those political structures and processes are best (i.e., most rational) which reflect this nature and permit its fullest development. Some of us may not like the political systems that are emerging in the newer states, but this abhorrence does not alone establish that the reason for these "aberrations" lies in the limited degree of secularization that one can associate with such systems. It seems to me that while democracy may require maximum secularization, secular attitudes as a central tendency in the political process can be manifested by political systems that range all the way from the Anglo-American democratic to the most pervasive totalitarian types. The most we can say at the moment is that, if the newer states wish to move in given economic, social, or political directions, they will have to develop a degree of secularization that is consistent with such movement. Whether, in so moving, they take on the trappings of democracy or totalitarianism seems to me to depend on some other considerations that are outlined below.

We now have a four-dimensional way of looking at political systems. It should be reasonably clear that development along these dimensions can occur irrespective of whether the population participates in the political process, whether one or more political parties exists, whether civil liberties are institutionalized, whether public policy is responsive to the wishes or demands of the people, whether a high degree of political pluralism is present, and so on. From the standpoint of possible change, there is nothing magical about the relationship of any of these dimensions and the particular institutional and behaviorial characteristics we have come to associate with the United States or Great Britain. A particular combination of attributes along these dimensions might still evolve in either a democratic or a non-democratic framework. In other words, if *democratic* political development is the end in view, it must be analyzed in terms of variables that are additional to those we have been discussing.

If these dimensions, or others that might be added, embrace the aspects of change that must be dealt with, it may be important to re-emphasize that our interest should now be in analyzing the consequences for society or any of its institutions of increases or decreases in any of these dimensions. We should recognize that movement in either direction is possible. For example, the degree of achievement orientation in political recruitment might diminish (and carry certain consequences) as ascriptive considerations take on more importance. To some extent, these may have happened in the Soviet Union in all sectors of society in the later Stalinist years. Generational data may show that the same long-range trends are now at work in the United States. Or one might detect periods in any political system during which there occurs a diminution of the degree of secularization that characterizes the political process. The history of the United States clearly demonstrates that the quantum of human reason applied to the problems of public policy varies considerably, particularly during times of stress. We may discover that, for the developing newer states, one important way of maximizing the chances for democratic political development is to de-emphasize the rationality implied by secularization and to emphasize instead arguments that do not necessarily appeal to man's reason. My view is that this kind of approach is essential if we are to prevent patterns of development that resemble not so much democracy as the polar political systems to which democracy is compared.

Finally, to close this portion of the discussion, it should be noted that in the process of change a political system might simultaneously move toward or away from the specific structural arrangements of democracy and totalitarianism. Ascription or achievement might characterize political recruitment in both a one-party and two- or multiparty system; terror and coercion as instruments of control might accompany a great proliferation of voluntary associations; a high degree of popular participation in the selection of policy makers might take place in a system that is minimally responsible to the wishes of the public. It therefore appears probable that as the newer states continue to develop along social, political, and economic lines, they will evolve novel combinations of institutions and behavior—combinations that may have only the vaguest resemblance to the nation-state types from which some models are now derived. It is for this reason that, as one approaches the problems of political development and change, not rigid and closed but broadly open models of probable combinations and outcomes must be what guide research and theorizing.

Public Administration and Political Change

Because public administration is a vital part of any political system, what we have said about dimensions of change for political systems as a whole has implications for this sector as well. It is obvious, for example, that depending on what one expects of government, certain combinations of differentiation, magnitude, achievement orientation, and secularization must be applied. If increased productivity is the end desired in government, then administrative output, like economic output, must be increased. This requires certain levels of differentiation, achievement, and secularization. If development is to take place at public hands (and this implies the risk of despotism), then the magnitude of government must also be increased. To put this differently, one might say that there must be some reasonable relationship between the articulated ends of government and the capacity for transforming public policy into meaningful implementative action. But, just as ideas of political development have been somewhat clouded by reliance on an Anglo-American political model, notions of the relationship of administration to change have been hampered by talk of a "modern" public administration in which "modern" is usually equated with Max Weber's concept of the bureaucracy. It is true that for Weber development (or "modernization") requires a certain amount of differentiation. This is illustrated by what he has to say about bureaucracy, as a public administrative method, the development of which, as an integral part of a rational-legal authority system, requires the evolution of functionally distinct and specialized roles. Weber's model would move systems from the functionally diffuse patterns of administration in traditional systems, to administration by personal charismatic leadership in transitional systems, to administration by bureaucracy in the "modern" rational-legal system.

In a traditional system public administration would be intermingled with the performance of religious and economic functions, recruitment to salient roles would proceed on the basis of particularistic considerations, qualifications and job performance would be evaluated in terms of ascriptive rather than achievement criteria. In the transitional situation, dominated by personal charisma, public administration would be in the hands of a great leader—of a Diem or Nkrumah—and of those who are chosen members of his entourage. Administrators would be evaluated on the basis of the extent of their fierce personal loyalty to the great leader, and rewards would also be closely tied to loyalty and the leader's favor. In the transitional or "dual" situation, one would expect to find a tension-creating juxtaposition of traditional and rational-legal structures.

In Weber's rational-legal phase, we get public administration by bureaucracy. The crucial characteristics of bureaucracy, in the classical sense, are: (1) specialized, highly differentiated administrative roles, (2) recruitment on the basis of achievement (measured by examination) rather than ascription, (3) placement, transfer, and promotion on the basis of universalistic rather than particularistic criteria, (4) administrators who are salaried professionals who view their work as a career, and (5) administrative decision making within a rational and readily understood context of hierarchy, responsibility, and discipline. Ideally, neither traditional (family, fuedal) nor transitional (charismatic leadership) considerations affect the operation of the bureaucracy; rational and enlightened man in the public administrative sector proceeds by essentially the same "scientific" laws that operate in the economic sector. These Weberian ideas concerning bureaucracy are generally included in most definitions of a "modern" system of public administration.

From the standpoint of analyzing and predicting particular patterns of change, the Weberian ideal type may be useful, but it can also be misleading as a model of development. As Weber himself would be the first to concede, in a highly differentiated and specialized political system, public administration can be managed—even managed well in terms of measurable outputs—without the existence of every ideal element of a classical bureaucracy. Research on organizations has shown that particularism, charisma, irrationality—even ascription—have striking power to persist. This suggests that, to some extent, such patterns are integral characteristics of all systems or organizations, no matter how "primitive" or "modern." We need not wonder whether Weber's observations on the German bureaucracy were accurate in order to question whether the empirical existence of one of the ideal types is essential to a public administration attuned to new demands and new roles of government.

The point is that large-scale governmental enterprise can evidently be managed through structures that do not rigidly adhere to the requisites of classical bureaucracy. Patterns of administration that have evolved behind the Iron Curtain attest to this. What we know about the administration of government and publicly controlled industry there challenges the notion that complex systems require particular structures in order to work well. What appears to the Westerner as rampant particularism and irrationality need not inhibit the accomplishment of designated tasks of development and governance. Indeed, the Soviet situation illustrates that public administration can be managed through the omnipresent domination of a political party that is formally outside the governmental system. To call the party an effective part of the Soviet bureaucracy may help to explain what happens, but it also clearly damages the elegance of the Weberian model.[6]

[6] It also confuses the picture in the sense that it obscures the fact that the party also stands outside the bureaucracy and certainly manages to bring it under political control.

One might also cite developments in the U.S.S.R. and Eastern Europe aimed at placing some portions of public administration in the hands of the citizenry. This now involves lower courts, some simple police functions, as well as some significant local roles in economic administration. These developments suggest that there may be ways of handling administration in a highly differentiated system that are far removed from Weber's idealized bureaucracy as well as from the norms of those of us who share an Anglo-American view of the appropriate functions and procedures of the public bureaucracy.

It may be worth recalling the Anglo-American norms that incorporate and extend the idealized concept of bureaucracy. They apply not merely to the internal characteristics of bureaucracy but also to the way in which bureaucracy is related to its setting. If what one means by "modern" bureaucracy is essentially what exists, more or less perfectly, in the West, there are certainly behavioral and attitudinal norms that can be added to what has already been said about Weberian bureaucracy.

First, the democratic Westerner expects that bureaucracy will be instrumental for the various political institutions of the society—the chief executives, legislatures, councils, cabinets, and assemblies. Although it is conceded that policy and administration can never be fully separated, bureaucracy is expected to be less directly involved, as a *de facto* matter, in policy making than is true of less developed systems. Policy-making institutions are presumed to be strong enough to limit the bureaucracy to its instrumental role. Administrators—from the military to the local tax collector and public health officer—are expected to see their own roles in instrumental ways. They are not supposed to "usurp" the rule-making function.

To a considerable extent, in the West, bureaucrats share this norm and go to some pains to convince themselves and others that their essential role is primarily instrumental. These men eschew politics even when it is strikingly apparent that they are deeply involved in the rule-making process. The extent of their involvement, of the "perversion" of the role of the administrator, is attested by the considerable literature that deals with the problem of generalist control over the functional specialists in public administration. It is, perhaps, correctly felt that such a situation endangers the vitality of democratic government. However, it is not at all evident that public bureaucrats as active and vital policy formulators will impede the attainment of basic changes in the economic and social spheres. As far as the newer states are concerned, it is apparent that the top-level bureaucrats provide one of the few sources—perhaps the sole source—from which one can expect a rational confrontation and management of the problems of public policy. In short, it may be that the goals of these systems require roles for bureaucrats that do not conform to the Weberian ideal of the public administrator.

Second, democratic Westerners expect that public administrators will interact on a free and open basis with a plurality of voluntary associations that exist in society. Emphasis is on "free," "open," and "voluntary." Voluntary associations are viewed as an important means of popular control of government and participation in the political process. From a democratic standpoint it is considered dangerous—perhaps abnormal—for public administrative agencies to create their own clientele associations, make them economically or otherwise dependent on government, and use them instrumentally to aggrandize the interests (e.g., policies, power, organization) of the bureaucracy itself. By the standards implied here, many of the associated groups of totalitarian societies, or of many of the newer states, are considered bogus, not capable of fulfilling their normatively prescribed function. Once again, the inconsistency of such patterns with a democratic ethic is apparent. Furthermore, if economic development is a high-priority goal of a society, this kind of organized manipulation of populations and groups may be more positively related to goal achievement than would be the ideally democratic pattern itself.

Of equal importance to the democratic Westerner is the avoidance of patterns whereby a limited number of groups acquire either privileged access to administrative decision making or a high degree of dominance over the administrative or rule-application process. It is assumed that administrators share this attitude, that they wish freely to interact with their clienteles, that they welcome the services that associations can perform but wish to keep the bureaucracy free of any limited group domination. Thus, while the bureaucrat's ideal self-image requires, on the one hand, that he see his role as instrumental vis-à-vis formal policy-making institutions, it also demands, on the other hand, that he see his role as that of mediator, or interest aggregator, vis-à-vis the organized voluntary associations of society. For some, all of this is condensed into the stricture that it is the business of the public administrator to know, implement, and guard the "public interest."

Fourth, it is expected that administrators will consider the electorate sovereign and that those who are elected to policy- or rule-making roles are legitimately endowed, for the duration of their office, with the power and the right to specify what is or is not in the public interest. This means not merely that the administrator sees himself as instrumental for political institutions but that he will not, alone or in concert, seek to undo or pervert what the electorate may have decided. Among other things, this would demand that the administrator not become involved in factional fights, either among political parties or within the dominant party. It means a conscious, continuous effort to steer clear of "politics," however manifested. That this ideal is imperfectly realized, even in Western democracies, does not diminish the vigor with which the norm is held. That it fails to be perfectly realized even in systems where the economy is largely in the hands of the private sector suggests how much more unattainable the ideal is for systems in which the public sector is intimately and massively involved in programs of social and economic development.

Fifth, public administrators, by Western democratic standards, are expected to be honest and free from corruption in the performance of their functions. Just as they are presumably recruited, assigned, transferred, and promoted on the basis of universalistic and achievement criteria, they are expected to behave on the basis of similar considerations toward their authority. Another way of putting this is to say that administrators must evince a high degree of professionalism with regard to every aspect of the official roles they occupy.

Finally, administrators are required to accept and to be loyal to the administrative and political system of which they constitute an integral part. This means accepting as reasonable and desirable the normative aspects we have mentioned, particularly those characteristics of universalism, rationality, hierarchy, discipline, and responsibility which form a part of a democratic bureaucracy, at least as one would wish to see it operate.

All of these norms are commendable, and I, for one, share them for my own society. However, I suspect that, while they may be more closely related to economic than to political development, they are not absolutely essential for either. We know that, if industrialization is society's goal, it can be achieved with striking rapidity through the use of public administrative patterns that defy most of the norms we have enumerated. To be sure, one cannot reasonably hope to achieve systematic, rapid development in the economic or related sphere if the public administrative sector contains scarce differentiation and specialization of roles. It seems clear that one serious impediment to economic development in the newer states is the domination of public administration by the administrative generalist. Insofar as developmental goals imply highly specialized administrative roles—in either the public or the private sector—the persistence of administrative generalists will constitute an impediment to economic change.[7] What Ralph Braibanti has to say about the public administration of Pakistan[8] is a clear and dramatic illustration of this. The same can be said for developing countries ranging from Viet Nam to Nigeria, from Colombia to the Congo.

Yet it may be an error on a grand scale for those engaged in technical assistance to assume that the quickest and only road to national development is the prior "Westernization" of public administration. I fail to understand why it is assumed that neat organization, encompassing all of the organization and management principles of American public administration, is a requisite of effective bureaucratic intervention in the developmental process. Once a reasonable differentiation of administrative roles has occurred, once these roles are filled with minimum attention to achievement criteria, once the bureaucrats themselves are persuaded to approach the tasks in hand on the basis of secular attitudes, the minimum conditions of a developmental bureaucracy are met and it can proceed with its responsibilities. That the bureaucrats may usurp the policy-making role is no reason for great concern. That the bureaucracy is rampant with particularistic behavior is not evidence in itself that it cannot function with reasonable effectiveness as a developmental instrument. That hierarchy is fragmentary, discipline sloppy, reporting and accounting unsystematic may be causes of great distress and exasperation for the technical assistance specialist; but we have evidence from the Soviet Union that national development can proceed apace despite the existence, by Anglo-American standards, of a chaotic and archaic public administration.

Obviously, the relationship of developments within the bureaucracy

[7] On the other hand, the administrative "generalist" may be a bulwark of democracy or democratic practice, less likely to be a ruthless driver for single and narrow-minded goals than a technocratic specialist.

[8] See his contribution to the present volume as well as his excellent "The Civil Service of Pakistan: A Theoretical Analysis," *South Atlantic Quarterly*, Vol. 58, 1959, pp. 258-304.

to political development in general is vital. This means that any conscious program of national development must pay great attention to administrative change. It does not mean, however, that before the bureaucracy itself can serve as an effective instrument of economic change it must acquire the complex set of characteristics that stem from a literal empirical application of Weberian ideal types and of Western democratic norms concerning public administration. In this regard, it might be worth recalling that an enormous amount of national development took place in the United States and Western Europe long before the public bureaucracies achieved even the approximate degree of rational organization and behavior that characterizes them today. To cite the current example I know best, it is significant that in Italy the most dramatic national development occurred, until his untimely death, at the hands of Enrico Mattei, the economic czar and manager of a public corporation that defies many of the organizational and behavioral norms that Western democrats hold so dear. If the strictures of Weber and of democratic ideology were applied to Mattei's ENI (Ente Nazionale Idrocarburi), it would wither on the vine, never bringing forth the important fruit in national development that it now promises. The particularism of ENI's operation, its unbelievable freedom from any kind of close public scrutiny, the reckless way in which it intervenes in elections, subsidizes newspapers, and buys support are exactly the ingredients which make the operation successful. It may not be democratic, but it works. There may be a lesson here for developing newer states that find their bureaucracies excessively encumbered by formal administrative patterns imposed by or imported from the West. If economic change is the desired goal, it may be desirable to provide much more achievement orientation and secularization than is required by democracy. Additionally, such a system may also have to achieve greater magnitude than is consistent with democracy. Perhaps we can explore what this means.

Relationships of Bureaucracy to Other Political Institutions

I have suggested that, given certain national developmental goals, a bureaucracy that does not fully conform to democratic norms may be more effective in bringing about certain kinds of change than one that does manifest such conformity. I believe that many of the leaders of newer states, for whom economic development is an overriding value, understand this, and that they are led to accept "tutelary bureaucracy" even while paying lip-service homage to democratic values. It will take considerable empirical evidence, set off against the Soviet and similar experiences, to persuade these leaders that national development can be just as expeditiously managed in a setting of democratic institutions and behavior. So far, there is scant indication that such evidence will be forthcoming. Even India, the real hope of the democratically inclined developers, is not very promising in this regard. The domination of the country by a single party, the massive role of the bureaucracy in both policy planning and implementation, and the unspectacular results of efforts to revitalize local-level forms of political participation and involvement are significant support for this generalization. Much more striking is the military's control of development in Pakistan, where efforts at strengthening the "basic democracies" are feeble and half-hearted, or the "guided democracy" of Indonesia. Illustrations of national development in contexts of non-democratic political institutions might be produced in considerable profusion from other newer states.

But what if some segment of the change-oriented elite of a developing country were consciously to set as developmental goals the specific structures that we associate with Western democracy? How might such goals be achieved? Without attempting to specify the minute particulars of building a healthy party system, strong and responsive legislatures, vigorous voluntary associations, responsible bureaucracies, and strong restraints on government, we can enumerate some broad outlines of policy and strategy that might be followed.

The first suggestion is that there emerge a strong de-emphasis on goals of economic development. One way to approach this problem is that of articulating less about collective economic goals and focusing more attention on individual and local-level economic change that might evolve on a more sporadic, piecemeal, basis. The articulation of grand schemes of economic growth immediately orients the political system to the ways and means of overcoming the various obstacles that stand in the way of goal achievement. It is a natural step to conclude that a certain amount of coercion is necessary, that power to control people and resources must be tightly centralized, that the luxury of organized opposition to national policies cannot be permitted, and so forth. In the name of the economic developmental interests of the whole community, a whole congeries of non-democratic behavior can be rationalized in Turkey or Ghana, Pakistan or Viet Nam.

The point is that if economic development is the all-embracing goal, the logic of experience dictates that not too much attention can be paid to the trappings of democracy. When confronted by the real dilemma of choosing between political and economic goals that are probably incompatible, the decision to move in the economic direction is necessarily taken at the expense of the political. To be sure, one might single out places and examples where the sacrifice of political institutions seems excessive. I personally wonder, for example, whether the crisis situation in Viet Nam justifies the essentially police state that has evolved there. I wonder, too, whether some goals of economic development might not have been facilitated if the dominant elite had been less hysterical and paranoid toward oppositional groups. But, for all such countries, there looms not in the shadows but in the bright sunlight the prototype example of Soviet Russia. That close examination would show that the Russian situation of 1917 is not comparable to the contemporary situations confronting most of the newer states is not immediately relevant; it is the belief in the relative efficacy of a given set of means that is overpowering. It is not merely coincidence that, in several newer states where a military establishment exists, the military bureaucracy has moved in to assume responsibility for national development. The military tend to be more empirical, more technologically oriented, more responsive to crises and emergency than the civil bureaucracy. Moreover, military leaders the world over are masterful articulators of the axiom that one does not quibble about the means when a job affecting the national interest and security is the most important end in view.

At whatever cost in delayed material gain may be implied, the elite of the developing newer states might be persuaded to downgrade national plans for economic development and to make democracy a goal in itself, worth sacrificing speed in economic development in order to obtain. Moreover, it is probable that these same persons should be encouraged to limit the role in economic development of the public sector and to encourage the development of the private economic sector. I strongly believe that it is more than historical coincidence that economic liberalism is associated with the emergence of political liberalism in the West. The set of attitudes that we identify with Western democracy were also strongly inculcated in the economic sphere and with reference to concrete economic interests rather than the vaguer, more abstract interests that might be called political. It may be that one critical way of developing important attitudes concerning the freedom and the dignity of the individual in the developing countries is to encourage the kind of economic enterprise that is individually rather than collectively oriented, that exalts the place of the private entrepreneur rather than that of an all-embracing collectivity symbolized by gigantic, unwieldy, and unbending government. To do this in the newer states—to develop a national bourgeoisie—would require the genuine integration and assimilation into the social system of the now harassed, bedeviled, and persecuted pariah entrepreneurial groups. If the relationship between economic and political liberalism is not inextricable, it appears to be nevertheless intimate. It may be short-sighted to assume that one form can be achieved completely in the absence of the other.

This is not to suggest a Spencerian notion regarding the appropriate role of the public sector. Obviously, the politicians and intellectuals of the developing countries who are so hostile to private enterprise would never accept such a state of affairs. But they might accept a greater effort to create genuinely dual economies than is presently the case. One potential ground for appealing to some of the political and intellectual elite is that of pointing out that a reasonably vigorous private economic sector would provide an important source of countervailing power against the bureaucracy, or the dominant party.

Another means of encouraging the development of democratic-type institutions would be to control the demands made on the political system. It is now abundantly apparent that the level of such demands far exceeds the capacities of most of the newer nation-states. Unsatisfied demands are a continual source of instability. Furthermore, they induce political leaders frequently to take arbitrary, non-democratic steps to keep demands in check.

By control I do not mean limitation. I mean instead that it might be possible to shift these demands from the economic to the social and political realm. The same energies that are used to keep dissident groups in check might be utilized to generate great national commitment to and demand for democratic development. For many of the newer states, grandiose schemes of economic development and future material well being are clearly myths. Why should it not be possible to raise a belief in and desire for democracy to the same level? One irony in the activities of indigenous leaders of developing countries, and of the many technical assistants who advise them, is that they proceed on the clearly implied assumption of an *homo economicus*, for whom all other values and motivations are presumed to be secondary. It is easy to assert that strong psychological motivations lean strongly in this direction; but national developmental plans that proceed on this assumption are certain to make the development of democratic structures improbable.

Even if these changes in emphasis could be achieved, they represent nothing more than temporary measures alongside the prime need for a massive program of education. Only by raising the level of literacy, by inculcating a national sense of secularization, and by considerably reducing the great hiatus between elite and masses can one hope to see political change move in a democratic direction. More is implied here than the need for training people, say, in the technical skills necessary to the management of complex industrial or governmental enterprise. Again, the experience of the Soviet Union indicates that literacy alone will not necessarily bring about greater democratization. The educational apparatus itself would have to be geared to the business of socializing people to democratic values and democratic roles. It is unlikely that such an orientation of education will take place if the nationally articulated goals of the dominant elite concentrate on the economic. While man is probably not by nature economic or anything else, the basic socializing institutions of a society can prepare him for a variety of political roles—from passive and unquestioning obedience under authoritarianism to vibrant participation in a democracy.

Much of what has been said here is intended to limit the power of bureaucracies in many of the newer states. From a democratic standpoint, this need is particularly great in those ex-colonial areas where indigenous bureaucrats were accustomed to unrestrained governmental behavior, where they developed toward the masses a sense of guardianship, at best, and disdainful superiority, at worst. Following independence, the only political structure with any strength and organized sense of purpose is the bureaucracy. To endow this structure with the major responsibility to set society's goals and to implement them is certain to impede the development of other strong political institutions or other important power centers in the society. This is not to say that the bureaucracy would have no important role to play in political as well as economic development. In the economic sphere, it could do much, as Joseph Spengler points out,[9] to facilitate the growth of the private economic sector. The bureaucracy could help to create an

[9] See Chapter 7 for a detailed and provocative analysis of the role of the bureaucracy in encouraging the private sector in the function of economic input transformation.

"objective setting," characterized by law, order, and security; it could facilitate credit, allocate scarce resources, and provide numerous fiscal and related inducements to economic growth. In order to maximize its own participation in a dual economic system, it could carry the major responsibility for limited national economic planning.

In the political realm, the bureaucracy could set an example by spearheading democratization in its own sphere. It could also encourage the healthy growth of legislative and executive power, as well as voluntary associations, by exercising a judicious self-restraint in the use of its own powers and capacities. Since it is unreasonable to expect that such a pattern of action would materialize spontaneously, it would be essential for members of the political elite of the newer states to push in this direction. Clearly, one important goal in the campaign to create a democratic political system would be that of forcing the bureaucracy to adhere to the organizational patterns and norms expounded previously in this chapter.

Insofar as the United States is involved in programs of assistance to the newer states, it could share in the responsibility of encouraging democratic development. To do so effectively would require a radical transformation of assumptions and strategies that have thus far prevailed. It now seems obvious that there is no one-to-one relationship between economic and democratic development; that industrializing a country, supplying it with food or guns, or training its military or technicians will not automatically bring democratic political development. It appears equally clear that emphasis on economic growth may actually run directly counter to such a goal. Under these circumstances there must be less emphasis on techniques and technology, more on democratic values and ideology. Rather than send Pakistan, Turkey, or Viet Nam public administrative experts in the refinements of organization and management, we might concentrate on those able to explain the vital role and function of public administration in a free society. Hopefully, we might send both types, but, in a setting of scarce resources, I would send the latter. Examples could be repeated ad nauseum. The point is that there should be more open and conscious effort to export not merely American technical know-how, but our political ideology and reasonable facsimiles of our political institutions and practices as well.

I am aware that the above suggestion is fraught with great difficulties, that our representatives are already suspect abroad, that leaders of the newer states are jealous, suspicious, and hostile toward any effort to tamper with the obviously political. Yet I am also reasonably confident that, without such an effort, the probability of attaining democratic configuration in most of the newer states is very low indeed. This, too, represents a dilemma that must be confronted.

CHAPTER 3

The Higher Civil Service as an Action Group in Western Political Development

FRITZ MORSTEIN MARX

I. Introduction

QUEST OF ADMINISTRATIVE STRENGTH

In the newly rising nations of the world, much is expected of the early attainment of an adequate administrative technology. Governmental machinery to carry out continuing public functions with at least minimal efficiency is a basic requirement of national advance, even of political survival. Indeed, a reasonably resourceful officialdom may prove to be a significant asset if only as a reservoir of competence for the building of a governing class, in Gaetano Mosca's meaning.[1] The need is initially for elementary experience, for general ability to sustain the essential presence of government, as much as for technical proficiency.

The expectations associated in the new nations with the formation of an effective administrative system have their foundation in the historical evidence furnished by the older countries. The present volume is not intended to dwell upon the evolution of the contemporary merit bureaucracy. But some benefit will be gained for purposes of comparison by providing at this point a quick summary of the pertinent parts of the record. What needs to be brought in focus are the varieties of influence that have come to the fore in the role played by the higher civil service as one of the contributing elements in Western political development, especially in the European context.

To be sure, the lessons, such as they are, cannot claim universality. They do not admit of ready transfer to environments that reflect varying stages of growth as well as cultural, climatic, and other differences. Yet certain characteristics of the career man's response to

[1] The English edition of Mosca's *Elements of Political Science* (trans., Livingston, New York, McGraw-Hill, 1939) tends to blur his meaning. He was not concerned with describing the tasks of a "ruling class" as a self-constituted and self-perpetuating elite with its own power base.

the course steered by government stand out and manifest themselves with great persistence. These contradict the widespread assumption that the modern bureaucracy fits only one mold of behavior.

A bureaucracy, it is true, is an aggregation of many factors rather than a monolith. It contains both high and low, though the rank and file is bound to form the main body. Its weight cannot be ignored. It may wield considerable autonomy in determining the rules of acceptable official conduct, including how much work is to be done during the allotted hours and how much deference is to be accorded nominal authority.

Despite such gravitational pulls, the institutional orientation of Western bureaucracies, by and large, has proceeded from the top to the bottom. The public service had a public mind as well as a public voice. The directing cadre, usually drawn from among the academic output of the educational system, generally succeeded in maintaining a commanding position. It had the triple advantage of greater intellectual resources, elevated social status, and close identification with government. This is not to gloss over occasional stretches of serious friction within the hierarchical structure or to minimize the material pursuits of civil service unionism. In the main, however, the bureaucracy tended to generate its sense of purpose and its institutional drive in the higher ranges of formal authority. Thus, if one views the bureaucracy as an acting force, it makes sense to think primarily of the groupings of advanced rank, normally combined into a recognized career category.

On the other hand, when we speak here of the higher civil service, it is not necessary to attempt a legally precise definition. We do not need to scrutinize in detail a mass of statutory and interpretative pronouncements to establish which positions are and which are not included. What is meant is simply the relatively "permanent" top group composed of those who share, in different degrees, in the task of directing the various administrative agencies.

In other words, the emphasis is not, in British nomenclature, on the "administrative class" alone, to the exclusion of the top ranks in the "professional" or the "industrial" categories. Nor do we mean to exclude, in American usage, either the "staff" personnel or the "field service." Planning, quite naturally, is considered an integral part of direction, as are other specialized functions that underpin the administrative process. Higher civil service in the present sense is hence intended to denote both a functional proximity to the channels of decision making and a relative homogeneity as a result of common professional standards.

BUREAUCRACY AND CONSTITUTIONALISM

What, then, has been the performance of the higher civil service in terms of its effects upon the political development of the modern nation-state? No single answer will suffice. If a brief answer is attempted as a point of departure, much of its significance will emerge from the qualifications that must serve as the indispensable accompaniment. Although we shall begin with a brief answer, most of the pages that immediately follow will have to deal with the necessary qualifications, clarifying the dimensions of our topic and indicating important variables.

In broadest language, the chief effect of the emerging merit bureaucracy may be said to have been in the direction of vastly increasing the viability of constitutional government. Popular rule, easily distorted by volatile partisanship, cries out for the counterweight of considered assessment of issues. Representation was strengthened rather than weakened by being linked with the sober insights that originate in the perspective of public management. The political spokesman and the practitioner of administration, though often at odds with each other, learned to appreciate their separate yet mutually dependent contributions.

Although at the outset the civil servant was pledged to bear personal loyalty to the dynasty, his occupational bond to the activities of government as a going concern introduced, with time, an impersonal disposition. Service as well as *the* service invited the career man's commitment. The bureaucracy, looking toward its enduring tasks and gradually gaining an intimate familiarity with the realities surrounding them, became an objectifying influence in public affairs. It grew into a storehouse of information. It projected policy in terms of demonstrable cause-and-effect relationships, thus erecting barriers to both despotic fiat and mere off-the-cuff judgment.

In these several aspects, the bureaucracy operated as both a source and a manifestation of rationality, to use Max Weber's phrase, even though remaining subject to challenge in the competition of values, attitudes, and inferences. To that extent, the workings of the administrative system helped to legitimize governmental authority. Public policy acquired an aura of fundamental propriety. Objectives of administrative action had to undergo the test of accepted purpose. Responsibility was made to submit to an accounting for motives as well as for choices.

Moreover, capacity for public management greatly enlarged the range of effective political action. The new administrative profession served as a multiplier in the expeditious discharge of responsibilities assumed by government. It turned into a principal instrumentality for the accommodation of demands made upon the body politic. It even participated significantly in the formation of an order of priorities to be superimposed upon these demands. In exerting itself as a force that worked toward stability and continuity, the bureaucracy spoke as a recognized voice of self-evidence. In these respects, the administrator fostered the consolidation of a common public outlook with direct practical consequences.[2]

So much for a first general answer. In tracing it out into the particulars, we might do well to examine next one important change in the institutional orientation of the merit bureaucracy: the change from the earlier self-identification with the business of government as a whole to the rise of a new divisionist functionalism. Thereafter the main action patterns available to the bureaucracy need to be set forth. Additional sections of this chapter will deal with the higher civil service in its prevailing attitudes, either as defender of the status quo or as supporter of reform. The concluding pages will outline certain ingrained occupational habits, including the defensive employment of the concept of administrative neutrality.

II. Sense of Engagement

RESPONSIBILITY AND SELF-INTEREST

Thus far we have looked primarily to the effects of the merit bureaucracy as a governmental instrumentality upon the practical operation of popular rule. This, however, is but one side of the picture. How about the career man's self-interest, especially any unacknowledged, implicit partisanship he may be expected to harbor? How does the bureaucracy act when it acts competitively in the political arena, as a group projecting itself into the struggle between power centers and organized interests?

[2] Commenting on his visits to "many lands" in an address delivered at the United States Civil Service Commission's 1962 honor awards ceremony, Vice President Lyndon B. Johnson spoke of ". . . the inescapable fact that in the modern world, no nation—new or old—can have unity and prosperity without a trained civil service." *The Federal Employee*, Vol. 47, No. 3, March 1962, p. 10.

In the Western world, the rise of popular rule has given an ostensible sanctity to the maxim that day-by-day administration—the business of civil servants—is to be carried on solely as the arm of public policy. Granting the fact that the comfort as well as the capacity of the arm cannot be disregarded, the maxim insists that ultimately the responsible determination of public policy is the business of political leaders. Although in need of refinement to serve as an adequate statement of the "facts of life," the maxim expresses in prescriptive language a vitally important and widely accepted guideline. It aims to hold administration to an instrumental role and to keep it politically responsible. How, then, can the higher civil service be an action group going its own way in political development?

There is more than one simple answer to this question. In the first place, when the top element of the bureaucracy displays durable cohesiveness, in conduct as well as in point of view, it is bound to make its influence felt upon the choices that mark the progress of political development. It is thus functioning as an action group. To be sure, no group is capable of poising itself for action unless the unifying factors at work within it, such as a sense of common purpose, are stronger than the dividing factors, such as differences of opinion on fundamental matters. The higher civil service normally shares a prescribed educational and training experience. The limitations of access to it and the "sense of belonging" encourage and reinforce broadly identical social attitudes and political dispositions. As a rule, these disintegrate only under unusual stress.

Secondly, although occupational doctrine and instinctive caution tend to keep the ranking groups in the civil service from reaching for command over the ship of state, an action group can be effective even when it submerges itself in alliances with other more conspicuous action groups. Indeed, in the day-by-day conduct of public management the general outlook of the directing cadre in administrative offices may have far-reaching consequences for the government of the day. For one thing, it makes a great difference whether the higher civil service happens to identify itself emotionally with a particular political leadership, whether it firmly sits on its hands when displeased, or whether it can be trusted to perform its tasks loyally and without reservations in support of lawful government independent of party label. In this regard, it can be said with considerable justification that the bureaucracy is an action group for the simple reason that it exists. It inevitably casts a shadow because it occupies a crucial spot in the power structure and provides indispensable support in the operation of the modern state.

Thirdly, it is not unrealistic to refer to the higher civil service as an action group even though, as a matter of fact, action in almost all instances neither follows an obvious line of group strategy nor reflects a position adopted by the ranking elements as a body. Instead, action is likely to take one of two main forms. The first is that of official proposals, openly advanced as recommendations for consideration and acceptance by those bearing political responsibility. Such recommendations may be vehicles for the conscious or unconscious expression of group preferences. The other main form is that of acts of highly placed individual members of the bureaucracy or of closely knit elements within it. These may become molders of administrative career opinion; in turn, such opinion may not divorce itself intelligibly from the position signaled by those who remain unchallenged as spokesmen. By comparison, organized action on the part of the top bureaucracy as a unified force, apart from observable tendencies in the exercise of its official responsibilities, has been very rare.

STATUS OFFICIALDOM

Even more relevant has been another distinction. The sense of engagement in a bureaucracy may embrace government as such, in all of its functions. The opposite is full absorption into one or another function, with a corresponding disengagement from other functional concerns. We shall speak of the first as status officialdom, the second as functional expertise. The historical shift from the one to the other has profoundly influenced the record of the higher civil service as an action group in political development. A brief review of the principal effects should be useful.

Status officialdom is a term that is employed here as a product of utility. In the light of the ascendancy of functional expertise, it refers, in point of time, to the formative period in the consolidation of the merit bureaucracy.[3] In point of structural design, it refers to an organizational pattern of the higher civil service that promotes dedication to a public interest truly general in character, in contrast to an allegiance that is centered on one or another functional segment of government.

[3] Status officialdom and functional expertise, in our present sense, hence represent distinguishable emphases within the framework of the merit bureaucracy, which I have contrasted elsewhere with the patronage bureaucracy, the caste bureaucracy, and the guardian bureaucracy. See F. Morstein Marx, *The Administrative State: An Introduction to Bureaucracy*, Chicago, University of Chicago Press, 1957.

To be guided by a truly general concept of the public interest, the higher civil service must be permeated by a consciousness of its status as a necessary element of the body politic. Such status calls for more than recognition under civil service law, in the legal dimension. It must have reality in the eyes of the public, in the social dimension.

In certain respects, these two dimensions of status have a common origin. The legal status guaranties traditionally enjoyed by the German career service, for example, were the echo of history. They were largely the result of a prestige position acquired during the battles over royal power in the emerging national state of Brandenburg-Prussia. The king's men, though indifferent to the common man's affection, helped to break ground for a common order. In its erection they won an invisible stripe of distinction. The bureaucracy maintained a key position as absolutism in the raw yielded to enlightened monarchy. Rulers began to proclaim their new mission as "first servants of the state." In due course of time, law conquered most of the authority once claimed by despotic command, however responsive to recognized need. The higher civil service thus came to see itself as a steward of authority under law.

Legal status means vastly less in the rank order of social standing when it represents but a degree of occupational security for unimportant clerks. The same is true of tenure privileges possessed by a patronage bureaucracy stuffed at the top with a coterie of expendable partisans, who are unable to assume an institutional role as both the brain and the control center of the administrative system. The situation is not much different, though in a sense reversed, when organizational arrangements and training requirements for the higher civil service tend to deny its identity, as was long the case in the United States. Again, status will have relatively little weight in political decision making when public agencies can remain altogether insulated from the struggles of competing forces for a share in the exercise of power. Such a condition of weakness is also likely to prevail as long as government generally does not play a noticeable role in the life of the people.

By contrast, certain circumstances magnify the effect of legal status guaranties of the bureaucracy. Formal safeguards of permanence may be greatly amplified by the prestige enjoyed by top civil servants in the centers of power. Such prestige usually flows from the general characteristics of the directing cadre. For instance, the higher civil service may be recognized in the performance of its functions as a dependable umpire in the contest between interest groups. It may be held together by a strong ideology of service. It may consist of a body of university-educated, professionally oriented practitioners of public management making their work a life career. Or, at an earlier stage of development, it may enjoy a recognized standing simply because its members are drawn from social groupings that successfully claim an elite position for themselves.

The practical significance of status in the official conduct of the higher civil service lies mainly in the assurance of a certain degree of administrative independence. Expression of responsible judgment is thus encouraged instead of being hampered or suppressed. Ideally, such judgment must acknowledge the political frame of reference. This frame of reference may be supplied in basic commitments laid down in public law. Alternatively, it may take the form of Aristotle's constitutional rule, in the sense of understandings embedded in the conscience as well as in the habits of the community.

Actually, however, a bureaucracy does not of necessity lose its footing by setting itself off to a certain degree from what is verbally honored as common dogma. Administrative agencies may be somewhat casual toward implications that are assumed to be settled in the constitutional frame of reference, as long as the managerial bias is recognized and can thus be discounted or combatted. In a political order torn by dissension, elements of the higher civil service may even emerge openly among the partisan forces. But when such intense discord gives way, the career man can withhold himself only at grave risk from the general course steered by the government.

Under reasonably stable conditions and in a relatively mature state of political, economic, and social development, the higher civil service is unlikely to acknowledge and pursue aims of its own as an aggressive force. Its role in the affairs of state is limited as well as strengthened by its status. As a source of strength, status serves as the cement by which the bureaucracy is held together. The resulting degree of unity allows the administrative system to operate both as an institution endowed with considerable coherence for action and as a serviceable instrument available to the government for the accomplishment of its program. A hierarchical order unified by status is more durable and more readily subjected to accountability than a free association based on a feeling of kinship. It is a superior device for fashioning a self-perpetuating body suitable to function in the forms of large-scale organization. To this extent, status is an essential foundation for the creation of a productive administrative system.

At the same time, status holds the bureaucracy to its basic assignment, to doing what it is told to do by those legitimately in political control. In turn, to provide a system of public responsibility, such control must not run free of rules. There must be a corresponding self-restraint imposed on political power. The implications of administrative status need to be accepted in the exercise of ultimate authority on behalf of the electorate. Otherwise, political leaders would be able to change the machinery of government radically in accord with their temporary preferences or the expedient of the hour, thus destroying the basis of effective rule by any group lawfully carried into control.

To sum up, status gives the bureaucracy a much needed adviser's voice in the determination of public policy as well as a defined sphere of public management. But status cannot simply be ordained. It becomes a tangible thing principally by behavior—the behavior of the public as well as the rules observed by politicians and bureaucrats. For reinforcement or clarification, not to mention the comfort of whistling in the dark, such rules are often written out in the prescriptive language of law.

FUNCTIONAL EXPERTISE

Status officialdom, in the meaning attached to it here, shows several main tendencies. It demonstrates a consciousness of basic purpose in support of operative government as such. In this perspective Mosca long ago saw the outline of responsible government. He visualized the structure of representation side by side with the structure of administration, each complementing the other, each making a contribution of its own. To be sure, both were not to be truly coequal. The power base required for final policy choices could be gained only in the political sphere, outside the range of administration. By contrast, public management would be the primary means of accomplishing the ends adopted by those placed by the electorate on the level of highest responsibility. Another tendency displayed by status officialdom is its attention to the long-run performance of government as a going concern, if only from the angle of its institutional stake in it. Finally, status officialdom is prone to show a moralizing disposition both toward its own conduct, as a professional group, and toward the abiding goals to which political leadership ought to devote itself.

As mentioned earlier, historically the modern bureaucracy came into its own when it had matured in the pattern of status officialdom. The ever-increasing specialization that gained full momentum in the twentieth century in all branches of public administration brought about a significant shift. In the old view, administration was to serve an essentially indivisible basic purpose as the acting arm of government. This view was challenged by the continuing proliferation of specific functions typical of the contemporary "service state." More often than not, a new function created its own world, self-contained and self-sufficient.

Compared with the relative unity of the directing estate under auspices of status officialdom, public administration came to look like a house divided against itself. The old and the new often remained far apart. Small wonder that a practical mind like Lenin's knew how to feel for breaches. Looking at Imperial Russia before the uprising of 1905 from the vantage post of his exile in Switzerland, he proposed a fresh approach toward the tsarist bureaucracy by intellectual infiltration of its most recent addition, the reform-minded factory inspection service.

Functional expertise, rushing into the public service from all sides, was bound to weaken the bureaucracy as the embodiment of an integrated administrative branch. The specialist was insular in his outlook. He mastered the know-how, the techniques of his own methodology. Government dissolved into a maze of tunnels, each inhabited by a separate class of technicians. The counter-drive for a restoration of the sphere of the "generalist" and for deliberately prepared coordinators is unlikely to reverse the situation.

In these circumstances, the mission of administration as such appears quite blurred even to the higher civil service. Fewer and fewer eyes proved searching enough to bring in focus the structure of government as a whole, the general output of public management in its social effects, the longer-range implications of what the epoch demanded. The ethics of administrative behavior went out of fashion. "Idle metaphysics" had to yield while the technology of "getting things done" conquered the official's realm.

Paul Appleby once pointed out, on the strength of his experience in the United States, that the commodity in shortest supply in any governmental agency, as in any large-scale undertaking, is reasonably close knowledge of the whole organization. The same fact has been documented many times in the professional literature of public administration in other lands. A point of view that seeks to grasp the entire field of governmental operations is becoming rare. The occupational interest of the bureaucracy is being deflected toward individual strips of highly specialized activity. Each branch of the public service invents its own jargon, its own mental shorthand, its own compass. The common bond survives mainly as an appealing figure of speech.

The effects are far-reaching. Formerly, an unflinching exercise of power was commonplace in the administrator's life because power was a steady companion in his identification with government as such. Today such self-exposure, too often, is something to be avoided. Responsibility, even when its weight is slight, is best hedged about with all the safeguards of interest consultation as well as objective marshaling of data, in fastidious reliance on the scientific approach.

As a result, the political mind and the administrative mind frequently lose sight of each other. Those who say that they have to do no more than to carry out the law seek refuge behind a defensive phrase, if a noble one. They withdraw into a growing neutralization toward the serious political business of building a general power base without which policy making for specialized objectives would falter for want of support. Stress is being placed on the functional focus as well as the dependent character of administrative authority. The theory is propagated that administrative responsibility compartmentally begins where political responsibility ends. This theory is easing the new career man into a functional niche, into a safely circumscribed condition, despite his often dramatic pleading for his special area of concern.

Undoubtedly the outcome is not all on the negative side. In part, it spells a gain, besides being an inevitable product of the undirected interaction of the social and economic forces at work. Functional expertise has reduced the quest for solution of many problems encountered in the formulation of public policy to an analytical exercise. There is an assessment of facts, a listing of findings, a presentation of conclusions. That is an approach more readily susceptible of critical review, within the administrative branch as well as in the legislative forum and in the arena of public opinion. Experts have become modern medicine men. Yet their ministrations are open to challenge by other experts, not to mention the legion of those who are ready for a horselaugh when confronted with the expert's dictum couched in language that leaves them floundering in a swamp of new-fangled terminology. Functional expertise has further reduced caprice in free discretion and substituted an answerable rationality for the fervor of ideological faith.

All of this has injected into the operation of administrative responsibility an additional degree of concreteness it did not possess before.

On the other hand, the orientation of the career man's responsibility has lost depth. It has gravitated toward the technical adequacy of particular categories of decisions, with stress on the procedural requirements of specialized patterns of decision making. Responsibility has been enslaved to a considerable extent to individual functional interests. By being pressed into the grooves of specific processes, responsibility has suffered a measurable loss of acuteness, of perspective, of comprehensive involvement. It no longer molds and redeems concern with the special.

Under the aegis of status officialdom, the directing cadre sees in the deficiencies of the administrative system a personal challenge that cannot be overlooked. From the angle of functional expertise, the specialist is more likely to hide in his little pile of sand, asking evasively, "Who, me?" The time-honored self-designation of the public officer as servant of the state survives largely as a bit of institutional poetry.

Above all, and of immediate significance for the bureaucracy's ability to reflect a view of its own, functional expertise is a destroyer of esprit de corps, as a set of attitudes observable throughout the directing cadre. As administrative responsibility undergoes fragmentation, so the intellectual and emotional cohesiveness of the higher civil service is greatly curtailed. Fundamental agreements within the top group about power and purpose, however vague or inarticulate, come to revolve less about primary preferences in relation to the general course of public policy. They center more upon matters affecting the institutional prerogatives and the economic condition of the bureaucracy or the political support for particular functions.

A continued broadening of the recruitment base for the higher administrative career has been noticeable in many countries during the past generation. In consequence, traditional class leanings and corresponding political inclinations have gradually eroded on the top levels of the public service. But democratization at the turnstiles, leading to the ranking positions, has resulted in diversity of outlook rather than a new homogeneity. It has not produced a relatively consistent democratic bent of mind.

We may therefore advance the general proposition that present-day Western bureaucracies have grown more multi-minded than they were before. In turn, they are less capable of staging their own campaigns over general issues of public policy. Activation of administrative specialists is toward the special. Activation is likely to be broader only when policy ends impinge on the immediate occupational interests of the career service as a whole.

UMBRELLA OF DUTY

Perhaps it is well to summarize the conclusions suggested by the preceding discussion. We began with the obvious though usually neglected point that the history of modern government and the evolution of the merit bureaucracy are inextricably intertwined. Each is part of the other. Indeed, a mature political system needs to be partly nonpolitical so as to possess adequate managerial capacity. By helping to provide such capacity, the bureaucracy has had a hand in the making of the contemporary state. If this be "action," the bureaucracy has mostly acted by seeming not to act, by being neither heard nor seen.

But "action" in this meaning is rather in the nature of doing an assigned job. Is there still other action? Who is the agent of such action? Who acts when it is said that the bureaucracy acts? After all, even the higher civil service is far from being a completely cohesive element. Capacity for action is not "natural" for human beings sharing a particular occupational experience. Nor is a potential for action clearly inherent in the bureaucracy. It needs to be built up by an organizing or integrating pressure, from within or from without. It needs the formative influence of incentive and stimulus, to overcome the pluralism of personal inclination and conviction.

In the interplay of these factors, status officialdom provides a more hospitable climate for a relatively independent role of the bureaucracy than prevails in the setting of functional expertise. Experts carry the field when they succeed in escaping challenge. That is why the contemporary state requires organs of general government, administrative as well as political, to cope with the centrifugal tendencies of specialized bureaucracies. One aspect of such redress is to strengthen the integrating faculties of *the* bureaucracy.

Expressed differently, specialist groups are not "the bureaucracy," though nominally part of it. They talk function, not general public policy. Moreover, the primary mode of action available to functional expertise is persuasion, practiced openly in the market of opinion. Such action relates to the exercise of normal duties, to the higher civil servant's sphere of official responsibility. It has thus become exceedingly rare for other actions by the directing cadre to encompass the extremes of conspiratorial intransigence. If there is hidden play, it usually shows the custodian of a specialized function reaching out for allies in unadvertised corners.

In most instances, therefore, the higher civil service acts under the convenient umbrella of official responsibility. Other forms of action by the bureaucracy are mostly action ascribed to it, though almost never taken collectively. These may originate with particular clusters within the career service, held together by special links. More frequently, action may come from self-assured and self-appointed spokesmen or from intrepid rebels in administrative posts. Perhaps we may dismiss the often powerful bread-and-butter manifestations of rank-and-file civil service unionism as marginal to our survey.

III. Action Patterns

FORMAL LEGITIMACY

We have seen that the higher civil service, viewed as an action group exerting influence upon a country's political development, usually leaves quite indistinct tracks. Its role is neither easily assessed nor predictable. Aside from institutional variables, we must allow for differences not only between countries but also between stages in each country's evolution. With these considerations in mind, we need next to take a closer look at the forms of action usually relied upon by the bureaucracy.

Common forms of action may be contrasted with exceptional ones. Generally speaking, the rise of functional expertise has tended to split the merit bureaucracy into specialized groups which found it safest as well as most productive to appeal to both political decision makers and the public from their official pedestal, observing by and large the accepted proprieties of administrative consultation and of legislative-executive relationships. To that extent, the higher civil service has gained increasing comfort from deference to a formal legitimacy, however high at times the passions underneath.

Conversely, exceptional modes of action, unless supported by a feeling of great urgency shared widely in the career service, are rarely resorted to today by Western bureaucracies. Exceptional action too often flounders for the simple reason that it compels the participants to violate generally accepted canons of official behavior or even explicit obligations anchored in law. It has not proved easy to push aside the traditional idea of the administrative officer's personal self-limitation as a vital safeguard of responsible and responsive administration. To be sure, from almost imperceptible slowdown to outright sabotage, disruptions of normal work processes occur repeatedly as isolated phenomena, and for various reasons. But there are no conclusive illustrations in the Western world of successful action taken by the higher career group either to mount a roadblock or to attain policy objectives thumbed down by the political leadership.

The facts are instructive. In England, for instance, Harold J. Laski's gloomy forecasts promised the rebellion of the "administrative class" against a Labor cabinet ready to govern. Plausible as it might have seemed to some, it did not come off. Indeed, it was never actually attempted. Although in France the authoritarian shadow of the *ancien régime* followed the higher civil service through most of the lifetime of the Third Republic, the main result was administrative self-isolation rather than a whittling down of the government's freedom of political choice. Again, after the collapse of the German empire in 1918, the new republic and the old bureaucracy were far from thinking alike. But the initial antagonism did not set off destructive explosions. With time the uneasy relationship improved as a new generation made its way into the public service.

Similarly, the deep cleavage between Slavophiles and Westerners that divided Russia during much of the nineteenth century failed to tear asunder the tsarist bureaucracy. Though felt acutely, the tensions did not cause a stalemate in the traditional structure of control. The upsurge of a heterogeneous progressive sentiment changed neither official habits nor administrative morality—such as it was. Perhaps part of the explanation lay in the fact that in its intellectual sensitivities the directing element was accustomed to the coming and passing of ephemeral ideas. Moreover, civil servants could not be expected to possess sufficient abandon for a counterpart to the Decembrist palace coup of 1825, managed mostly by young officers, with but slim support from like-minded men in the ministries.

On the other hand, a different situation presents itself when both the political system and the bureaucracy experience the impact of sweeping change that is likely to last. There were times in modern Western history when the higher civil service consciously abetted reaction. There were other times when it assumed the character of an unorganized reform party. Equally, in newly consolidated nations, the bureaucracy may turn into a nucleus of partisans in the face of dynamic pressure for political, economic, and social innovation. As there is hands-off administration, so there is messianic administration.

But one fundamental fact remains. Bureaucracies are caught in their experience as engineers of the administrative process. Theirs is the task of operating governmental machinery in the day-to-day accomplishment of public purposes. Not surprisingly, the directing cadre cannot readily slip out of character. It is rarely seen on the barricades or in revolutionary conclaves.

POLICY COUNSEL

An adviser who thoroughly knows the field about which he is to give advice is not easily ignored. That is true especially of one who, in addition, knows about practical ways of applying such knowledge to given circumstances. This kind of counsel rendered to chosen leaders who bear political responsibility, together with skill and experience in carrying out their decisions, is at the heart of the bureaucracy's contribution to the effective conduct of modern government.

If there were no other avenue for action available to it, the higher civil service would have ample opportunity for an active part as a direct consequence of the key position it occupies. It functions as a control tower for the flow of information arising from countless routine operations. It is a prime source of proposals moving up to the points of political determination. It oversees the deployment of competence in the execution of public policy. In modern government, the administrative system is called upon to perform a unique combination of tasks. These interrelated tasks, as Max Weber recognized with great astuteness, cannot be transferred without serious loss to any other organ of the body politic. Nor can they be handed over to an improvised body of fluid manpower.

The natural base for the bureaucracy's role as policy counselor is found in its exceptional resources. It is a gatherer of facts that constantly accumulate as a byproduct of administrative activities. It is a surveyor of public needs as well as of governmental performance in meeting such needs. It is a recorder of interest pressures and public sentiments affecting the political course. It is an inaugurator of organizational devices and technical procedures suitable for attaining the government's ends. It is a fountain of ideas about what ought to be done to redress conditions that cry for remedy. Finally, it is a knowledgeable and skillful draftsman in converting broad understandings about desirable goals into the detailed language of regulatory measures.[4]

Some of these functions admit of being shifted to other places. One may think of a professional staff attached to legislative committees, of advisory bodies, of study groups established outside the official machinery of government. Moreover, the administrative system does not possess a monopoly in the discharge of its main tasks. On the contrary, it must be prepared to compete with many rivals, including the formidable army of lobbyists and other special pleaders. But as an integrated and mutually reinforcing complex, the formal responsibilities and informal involvements of the bureaucracy make for a large package for which there is simply no other taker.

At the same time, if policy counsel is viewed as an avenue of action available to the higher civil service, we must single out the factors that make action likely. Is there something of a common platform in the mentality or orientation of the ranking groups of the bureaucracy? Is there a point of view that is likely to show up in the formulation of decisions?

One answer is suggested by the degree to which the career man accepts and is guided by a basic rationality. Such a rationality may come to the fore as a moral standard to insure objectivity. It may also express itself as a commitment to apply the insights of a learnable administrative technology, without brooking interference. As indicated earlier, the rationality of the bureaucracy cannot ordinarily survive when it divorces itself too far from the ideological tenets professed by the political community at large. At the same time, it may sustain a distinctive intellectual disposition such as "administrative reasoning," as a counterpart to "political reasoning."

In this respect, it obviously makes a difference whether the higher civil service, in background and outlook, is generally homogeneous or

[4] In these respects, an alert bureaucracy acts frequently "on its own steam," in an anticipatory fashion. For example, almost as soon as President Truman had announced (on March 29, 1952) that he would not be a candidate for another term, staff planning for the orderly transfer of power to the next man in command got underway almost automatically. To quote an authoritative account, "In the White House and several other strategic points in the government, both political and career officials began to consider the specific problems of turnover. . . . One locus of such thinking was the Budget Bureau, . . . now staffed by experienced professionals who regarded themselves as reliable custodians of the President's—any President's—interests. Within a few days after Truman's announcement, staff papers on transition . . . were circulating in the bureau." Laurin L. Henry, *Presidential Transitions*, Brookings Institution, Washington, 1960, p. 471.

heterogeneous, whether it is a small corps or a spreading multitude, and whether it is pre-sorted by identical educational and training requirements or freely accessible from any occupational escalator. Again, it is of great importance whether the bureaucracy is traditionally nonpartisan or whether it is molded periodically to represent the changing specter of political control. Nor can we ignore the large distinction between a higher civil service that sees itself as an organ of the "living constitution" and one satisfied with the image of a mechanism used pragmatically because of its proficiency.

Illustrations of such differences are not difficult to find. Even though the "university man" in public administration has come close to representing a unified type, it shows many variations. In Britain, for instance, one variation could be found in the product of the old universities before World War I. Another leaf of history presented the new subsidized scholar, whether from Oxford or from Manchester. Each, in turn, was set apart in more than one way from the old-time German *Akademiker* in office garb. Still another race rushed forth with the late Professor William E. Mosher's practical missionaries from Syracuse a generation ago.

Again, in France the aroma of political reaction which aspirants for the higher administrative career acquired during their preparation for entrance as late as in the 1930's has gone out of style. The turning point had been reached with the creation in 1945 of the now widely acclaimed National School of Administration. Many of its graduates take pride in a zest for the general interest under auspices of "positive government," in seeking to oppose government by or for the special interests through the tactics of a "counter-lobby." Another illustration is furnished in the effects of professionally oriented institutes of public administration founded in recent years in various newly important parts of the world. In good measure, these institutes have helped to crystallize attitudes of service as well as to promote knowledge of the art of management, thus laying a basis for a vitalized bureaucracy.

Moreover, once sturdy institutional molds are provided, they become host to living substance. If that living substance is kept in touch with national thought through the higher learning, it cannot be expected to insulate itself against the changing spirit of the era. This explains, for example, why Bismarck, while steering Prussia through the constitutional conflict between king and parliament, came to bemoan the attitude of the ministerial bureaucracy. To him, the career man of the early 1860's was too often a partisan of the nineteenth-century liberal upsurge, a traitor to the cabinet. Similar situations arise in contemporary Africa and Asia. Under strong-man regimes, the modern-minded administrative officer is often torn in two directions. He may be both a hopeful loyalist in the cause of reform and development and a frustrated opponent because of his aspirations for lawful government.

PROGRAM FORMULATION

Policy counsel and program formulation are often spoken of as if they were about the same thing. If one were to think of "program" in the most comprehensive sense, it would delineate, by withdrawal or assertion, the sphere within which policy choices are to be made. Program would then be the framework of policy, or the anterior condition.

Actually, however, this is a relationship rarely encountered even in approximate form. Moreover, where it is customary to accept the primacy of a political program, such a program is normally a party platform. In the making of such a program the bureaucracy is usually at best an indirect participant. Even where it is commonly accepted that the majority will seriously pursue its party program while holding the reins of government, a degree of discretionary freedom does remain. Opportunity must be preserved for last-minute decisions about what matters, on fresh appraisal, should be tackled first, and when.

In the era of the special, American bureaucratic lingo has further devaluated the concept of program by applying it with sinister passion to everything from replacement of desks to handing out service pins. More appropriately, program refers to a blueprint covering a major functional segment in the range of governmental activities. Inevitably, its formulation has to assume the priority of basic policy positions, as a way of gaining steppingstones. Formulation of a program, in this derivative sense, is mainly an analytical rather than a freely creative enterprise. It converts ideas into relationships, ends into means, objectives into organizational and procedural patterns. Here understanding of these inferential connections is at a premium, second only to experience, to a grasp of how so many parts can best be fitted together to accomplish "operations."

Program formulation supplies the higher civil service with an action pattern somewhat less consequential than policy counsel. But it allows for proportionately greater freedom of initial decision.[5] Advice received will be pondered, especially on principal issues. It may be good advice, as far as it goes, and yet it may have to yield to technically irrelevant impositions of political tactics or of the ultimate decision maker's personal comfort in the face of risk. Indeed, the administrative adviser himself is often not present at the point of final determination to block the adulteration of his proposal. If it stands up in the face of counter-pressures, it will survive because it may be so perceptive or cogent as to argue strongly against being watered down.

By contrast, program formulation means coming up with a completed edifice, whatever the scope or size. Each brick has to support another, kept in place essentially by the professional skill of a craftsman who asks to be judged by the total outcome rather than by any part or the detailed sequence of his work. For him, identification and solution of the policy problems involved are really not his business. These matters must necessarily precede program design and construction. But thereafter, in piecing together the program, the bureaucracy has a relatively free hand, although it is not the last hand. The final test comes with close assessment of the results by those who have to launch the program in the political market.

Nor can one say that in the task of program formulation the higher civil servant is the only one to stir the broth. He normally is given sharply limiting directions for the recipe from other quarters. Such directions reach him through legislative surveillance or party intercession as well as in the channels of executive authority. If these limiting directions prove flexible in realistic bickering, it is due in most instances to the independent pressures coming from the organized special interests. Indeed, here we encounter a broad proposition which deserves great emphasis. It may be stated in different ways. One way would be to say that the effectiveness of the top bureaucracy as an action group in political development, in present-day Western experience, is in almost exact proportion to the ingenuity it shows in enticing interest organizations into the harness of program commitment.

Political leadership is properly concerned with the general plan.

[5] A recent German newspaper cartoon, entitled "Glad Tidings from the Federal Ministry of the Interior," shows two overjoyed bureaucrats reaching into a desk drawer filled with neat folders and the following text: "The construction market begins to quiet down? Well, then we must introduce right away our Bill on Compulsory Erection of Bomb Shelters!" *Die Zeit* (Hamburg), January 5, 1962. In terms of the rationality of program making, this manner of describing a frequently essential phase is not necessarily a joke.

But in coming to terms on critical details, the specialized resources inherent in the bureaucratic structure must be brought to bear on the specialized pleadings of organized interests. By and large, however, interest politics and functional expertise pull in the same main directions. This explains why the modern state is habitually short on program, long on programs. One discerns a built-in bias in support of case-by-case "positive government"—expansion of individual public tasks, consolidation of the resulting organizational patterns, and methodical exploration of what is still beyond the horizon.[6]

In short, program formulation on a functional basis is an important means by which the higher civil service can attain self-expression in the sphere of politics. The potential is heightened with the increasingly technical character of the program in question. It is lowered to the extent that each program is forced before generally oriented review agencies.

Examples of general review agencies are the British Treasury and the Bureau of the Budget in the United States. The effect is lost when the review agency is itself freely challenged in the legislative forum. It is easy to perceive the precarious foundation on which such review agencies rest, short of a high degree of public sophistication needed in their support. Hence the popular observation that they have "nothing to sell." We must also recall that legislatures do not necessarily enforce unity, even for themselves. It may be a hard thing for the legislative majority to hold the standing committees in line. It may be a harder thing for each committee to forego the splendor of its *de facto* autonomy.

The trend toward the special is a chief feature of the modern Western world. As a unifying influence on program formulation as well as on public policy, the bureaucracy no doubt has lost ground during the past hundred years. The perspectives documented in the earlier administrative writings of Continental Europe, especially in the aftermath of the revolutionary storm of 1789, illustrate a different point of view. The government officer's concern was with the state as guardian of society, as an agency exerting itself toward the general welfare. This comprehensive engagement gave great strength to the administrative system. It made it possible for the bureaucracy to produce such leaders of political reform as Baron vom Stein, one of the main

[6] For a fresh probing of the operation of this built-in bias, see Carl Hermann Ule, ed., *Die Entwicklung des Öffentlichen Dienstes: Berichte, Vorträge, Diskussionsbeiträge,* Heymanns, Cologne-Berlin, 1961.

architects in the rebuilding of Prussia after her defeat at the hands of Napoleon.

PUBLIC MANAGEMENT

Administration is often called the fourth branch of government. There is something awkward about such numerical labeling, and the metaphor has little chance of proving acceptable to an arboriculturist, who is more interested in trees than in branches. But if the metaphor is objectionable, it does suggest certain salient features of the administrative state.

For one thing, the day-by-day administration of public functions is, by quantitative measurement, one of the biggest parts of contemporary government. This is a task that cannot be entrusted safely to the first available supply of willing hands. It requires the continuing effort of a carefully recruited body of trained manpower. In addition, successful operation depends to a very large extent on allowing administrators appropriate freedom in the utilization of their managerial resources.

To be sure, precisely because administration has come to be so important, it must bow to the logic of Lloyd George's World War I dictum about the folly of having wars run by generals alone. Who would doubt that it is politically impossible to leave public management completely in the hands of administrators? Nowhere, however, is the higher civil service generally as much in command as in the daily business of administration. That is the sphere in which the detailed fashioning of the administrative process occurs. It is here that we observe the intricate operations by which the modern state carries out its day-in-day-out functions.

The character of these functions inevitably mirrors the structure of the national economy as well as that of society. Normally, they show great diversity when seen as one package and demonstrate highest vitality individually. Whether regulatory, promotional, equalizing, or reinforcing, the continuing functions of government interlace the private sector of the economy at countless places with the public sector. All of this serves to emphasize that another significant springboard for action is available to the bureaucracy in its superintendence over the administrative process.

To an increasing degree, Western man is being accompanied by a condition still relatively new to him—the condition of being administered. The results, although defying exact assessment, are varied and often striking. They include the maintenance of mountains of public records, the sprouting of prohibitions, and the rise of minimum standards of individual well-being.

In the United States, for instance, administered man benefits from public provision for his likely needs almost from the cradle to the grave, though mainly without having such care forced upon him when there is no necessity. In a potentially sharpest disruption of his life, he can entrust himself to a selective service administration that is much superior to earlier methods of calling men to military duty. He appreciates the great gains in public health; beholds the halting advances in low-rent housing; is comforted by a respectable showing in sustaining industrial peace; and enjoys reasonable assurance that the food and drugs he buys are what they say they are and, by and large, do not expose him to unusual hazards concealed by irresponsible manufacturers. The more assiduously the individual is being looked over and looked after as the object of public administration, the more knowledgeable and experienced has the bureaucracy become. It has no serious rival in finding suitable organizational and procedural forms for dealing with new tasks and for adapting old ones to the inroads of change.

It should be noted, however, that the everyday administration of public functions is not to be compared in impact with the breakthrough of a fresh program or with the establishment of novel policy positions. To put it differently, although the higher civil service enjoys the greatest measure of leeway within its four walls in attending to the administrative process, the effects of its own discretionary choices are far less than momentous. They do not normally affect the course of political development, except in providing indirectly a continuum of governmental capacity which in itself is likely to influence policy.

The outstanding restraint in this sphere is an institutional factor, compounded of law, doctrine, and habit. Authority is under "government of laws." Perhaps no less important, the contemporary merit bureaucracy is too busy doing its job to stray from it. Moreover, for all of his skill in large-scale administration, the career man is held in place by the service doctrine he has created for himself. The "spirit of the constitution" no less than the legal order denies the administrative officer any right to negotiate on his own terms with political superiors about the measure of loyalty and cooperation to be pledged by him. He cannot bargain about how far—and at what price—the bureaucracy's capacity for administration is to be made available to a new government.

At the same time, government itself tends to be identified in the eye of the citizen by the welcome he is given when appearing as applicant in public offices. Hegel, with his realistic grasp of the shape of things to come, assigned to the bureaucracy the role of the state's receptionist. He was much concerned with turning each contact between agents of public authority and private individuals into a mutually elevating experience. He saw each contact as an opportunity for reinforcing the very idea of the state, as an expression of its vitality. He feared that thrones could be lost through the arrogance of thoughtless underlings.

But the public Hegel had in mind was not the common multitude. It was, in the main, one favored stratum—the rising urban middle class, sufficiently self-reliant and public-spirited to have found shelter even under the roof of Jefferson's agrarian commonwealth. Citizens in this simplified image knew what they needed, and field officials could be expected to be close to these needs. To talk about such matters with the proper official was—or could readily be made to be—a social affair. It was unencumbered by long forms to be filled out in triplicate or by similar ritualistic exchanges in the contrived language of the bureaucratic world.

This kind of field officialdom, best exemplified perhaps by the French prefect during the nineteenth century, was bound to cultivate its own shadow. Its clientele was relatively stable and represented a rather thin social layer. Dispensers and recipients of advantages came broadly from the same class. Understandably, discretionary freedom of official action was neither unduly hedged about nor frequently begrudged.

The delicate balances that could be worked out in human terms under such circumstances are unattainable under present-day mass procedure. Administration in the interest of a select minority invited political responsiveness as well as political accounting—on either end of the relationship. But when "caseloads" press upon administrative offices like a black flood, the overwhelming need is for keeping the lines moving. Emphasis is on substituting a limited number of objective, and therefore quickly reviewable, criteria for an elaborate scale of discretionary factors. The need is for minimizing the free play of judgment and for maximizing general dispatch. The heavier the pressure of numbers on mass procedure, the fewer opportunities survive for the bureaucracy to throw its weight around in an attempt at guiding political development according to its own preferences.

On the other hand, when the higher civil service is recruited mainly from a particular economic stratum, it can be expected to drag its feet in carrying out governmental tasks detrimental to that stratum. The administration of land reform measures has been a stumbling block in countries where the top groups of the bureaucracy were linked with the large landholders. Similarly, regulatory programs aimed at urban commercial enterprise have usually not fared well in the hands of an officialdom that was town-based and profit-minded.

Growing democratization in the methods of staffing for higher administrative responsibility, besides insuring other advantages, interferes with the formation of such special links or dependencies. Equally important are the subtler variables grouped between mere gestures of cooperation with the demands of policy, on the one pole, and demonstration of high spirit in the performance of duty, on the other. In the early years of the Weimar republic, for instance, top civil servants in Germany, still rooted in the monarchy, often held themselves coldly aloof from the new democratic leadership. At the opposite side, Bismarck's revolutionary venture into social insurance, initiated in 1883 during a period of political unrest, did not stall for want of administrative support. A comparable example was supplied when England, a generation later under Lloyd George's Liberal cabinet, adapted the same concept to the achievement of employment security. Neither development would have been conceivable without the bureaucracy's acceptance of a reorientation toward the public interest.

IV. Defense of the Status Quo

ADMINISTRATION AND STABILITY

The preceding section has sketched the principal action patterns at the disposal of the higher civil service in influencing political development. Now we should turn to a review of some of the main ways in which the bureaucracy tends to deploy itself in the contest for change. The directing cadre may line up as participant on one side or the other. It may also play the part of an inactive "third force," to be reckoned with by both sides. Each way of deployment is affected by circumstances inherent in the nature of the administrative process as well as by factors external to it.

To begin with the obvious, public management is a stationary, not an ambulant, business. It is tied to a fixed locus. There must be offices, manned during set hours, if not all the time. There must be workers who can find papers and refer matters to superiors when the exigencies of a case so demand. There must be space for clients or idlers to stand or sit. More important, each office must provide for a physical order of placement for the men of importance, a reasonably clear chain of decision making, and a scheme of channeling administrative output without confusion or loss of time.

Again, fixed locus carries with it the need for a certain cohesiveness. It is necessary to have cooperative understandings among the office staff, procedures to assure a sound division of functions, and organizational design to make it easy to assert control and assume responsibility. The stress placed in all of this on acquired knowledge and experience discloses how much administration, as a mastered craft, has reason to treasure the learned, the familiar, the recurrent. Indeed, one hallmark of good administration is the degree to which it "rolls by itself." The waste of never-ending improvisation has to be replaced by quasi-automatic routines—closely interlocked, relatively free of discretion, and functioning with a minimum of high-level supervision.

These occupational phenomena breed an institutional disposition. True enough, administration, especially in the mass state, lives inevitably close to the common stream of life, and hence near the signal masts of change. But, as a going concern, it bears a distinctly conservative streak. It responds to the present in the light of the past, confining the future to the immediately foreseeable. It has an operational interest in stability, in an undisturbed working rhythm, in today's repetition of yesterday. Not unnaturally, the higher civil service usually favors a firm structure of political power as something to lean against. Expressed differently, administrative systems normally have a professional predilection for the status quo. Higher civil servants often emerge as emotional defenders of the given order of things.

ENTRENCHMENT OF TRADITION

A stable power structure is not simply a political rampart. It is also a generator. It contributes greatly toward the sort of coalescence of symbolisms, ideological commitments, value systems, and official mores from which come forth durable goal-oriented concepts such as the general interest. A settled order encourages the formation of shorthand catechisms to guide civic as well as administrative behavior. When a higher civil service is immersed in its sense of institutional identity, when it sees itself as possessed of a mission, it will automatically police official conduct. It will evolve its own *Staatsgesinnung* as well as its own code of honor. It will devote itself to the building, refining, and enshrining of its traditions. It will raise the stature of the state or the nation to gain height for itself.

Tradition seeks kinship. Worship of tradition makes the civil servant a ready ally of the military,[7] of the clergy,[8] of the nobility,[9] of the economic upper dog. A community of interests is formed, providing each partner with an enlarging stake. In turn, it may entice each partner to turn militant in preserving the "good society." When such allegiances have become a mark of public propriety, it makes little difference whether the good society is in fact but a decrepit order parading as the permanent answer to the future. Illustrations of this kind of alignment are supplied not only in European history but also in the evolution of the new nations of Asia and Africa.

DIVISIONIST TENDENCIES

The result is in most instances a bureaucracy displaying caste features and class preferences. The higher civil service will give itself an elitarian air. It will entrench itself behind formal educational qualifications, such as completed academic study. Entrance requirements of this sort are used to erect insurmountable barriers so as to prevent the influx of members of the middle career groups, who are not university men. The middle groups, in turn, while prone to imitate the manners of their superiors, may think of them as a demonstrative lot, each a Colonel Blimp, each as good as his astute assistants succeed in making him appear to be. When the drawing of lines assumes such proportions, it is not surprising that the rank and file surrenders to a violent trade unionism.

In its effect upon public policy, a stand-pat top cadre in administrative offices will show inflexibility. Prompted by its dedication to the status quo, it will sport a corresponding social gospel. It will act upon

[7] It is useful to recall, however, that elements of the military may rally to the phalanx of reform. Army concern with the physical condition of recruits, for instance, has converted itself into pressure for general public health programs. The military also may assume a task of political rejuvenation. Thus, in Egypt, Nasser and his aides have sought to identify themselves with the aspirations of the people, especially the rising educated class of business and professional men, but also the underprivileged peasants. See P. J. Vatikiotis, *The Egyptian Army in Politics: Pattern for New Nations?* Bloomington, Indiana University Press, 1961.

[8] Churches, too, may gravitate in different directions. The social teachings of the Catholic Church, for example, have had a significant impact on ameliorative public policies.

[9] Again, where the nobility is conscious of a cultural role, it is bound to bring forth from within itself reformist drives intensified by the educational resources it can muster.

the self-evident truth accepted by those who pronounce themselves as "sound." A bureaucracy that feels pledged to uphold the status quo will see nothing wrong with repressive tendencies. The more conspicuous the higher civil service becomes as the caretaker of the given order, the less can it expect to be judged truly non-partisan.

One must add, however, that bureaucracies enmeshed in the defense of the status quo usually trigger off rebellion in their own midst. What are the reasons? We need not search too far for them.

In the first place, administration is compelled to look forward, despite its fondness for precedent and routine. This determination to look ahead may be displayed also by kings and statesmen under constitutional government or by rulers under authoritarian regimes in young nations still in search of popular rule. Next to these, however, the modern bureaucracy is almost the single remaining force to concern itself with government as a going enterprise, in its long-run prospects. The higher civil service is therefore impelled to think ahead of the national development, to keep its eyes on the general administrative evolution, in contrast with cabinets carried along with the tides of public sentiment. However deep the roots the directing cadre may have in the status quo, its nervous preoccupation is with the shape of tomorrow. It cannot banish from its mind the nagging thought that today's rationale may prove a cul-de-sac. Affirmation and doubt are peculiarly linked in the bureaucratic mentality. Administrators wear worry like a coat.

This leads to a second point. Bureaucrats are doers, but they are also planners. To proceed by plan—or at least by planning—is a necessity when the administrative resources required to support governmental programs are usually so large. Whether expressed in money or manpower, they are frequently tremendous, viewed in relation to the decision maker's personal responsibility. As a planning agency, the higher civil service is an instrumentality for social calculus, for policy thinking. To this extent, it is an intellectual agency, even when keeping a jaundiced eye on eggheads, as befits the "practical man." Unquestionably, the administrative system is an important center for the drafting of alternative blueprints for national action.

In this internal process that presumably is not to be embarrassed by the ears of curious outsiders, idea battles idea without imposition of control. The value of agreement among the participants is reduced to minimal operational necessity, to the need for hammering out proposed solutions. To differ is a common propensity in staff units, even though etiquette may demand keeping differences within the four walls of the bureaucratic setting. If nominal unanimities are insisted upon too pedantically, all that may happen is that the differences will be driven underground.

V. Support of Reform

SOURCE OF IDEAS

As we saw, the milieu of administration engenders an inclination toward holding on to familiar ways. The prevailing habit of thought in the bureaucratic setting attributes great value to stability of political power and gives the status quo the aura of a superior order. But counterforces have never been completely absent.

Administrative discontent with antiquated and cumbersome procedures has often been acute enough to push civil servants into a search for new and better methods. Nor must we overlook the intrusion of more profound anxieties. Despair over the impotence of a wilting political regime makes administrators as well as citizens scan the scene for alternatives. Similarly, when the inherited social order shows itself beyond repair, the allegiance of the higher civil service may come to an end. Such conditions are likely to bring into play the adaptive faculties inherent in a bureaucracy that benefits from the steady influx of young men and women from the universities. This is the main reason why during the last two hundred years the directing cadre in the administrative system has repeatedly functioned as a party of reform.

To such a role the higher civil service brings considerable qualifications. It substitutes for vague humanitarian aspirations the realistic language of concrete information and statistical data. It thus functions as an intelligence center supplying observation, evaluation, and inference. It provides society with a magnifying glass. It is a general staff available to those assuming political responsibility for carrying forward the reform movement.

Top civil servants sit in a grandstand when it comes to gauging the effect of administrative action upon current economic and social conditions. As a result, the directing cadre gains a close view of the strong and the weak points of governmental programs. That is why alert bureaucracies, aware of shortcomings and inadequacies, are quick to come forth with considered proposals for change.

A reform movement in pursuit of a program is likely to find a suitable display in the desks of the higher civil servants. One agent of "millennial" change—Hitler—drew from these desks a mountain of policy recommendations that differed sharply in sober content from his own bizarre brand of political reform. He simply capitalized on the log-jam of draft measures kept out of circulation by the prolonged stalemate that accompanied the slow disintegration of the republic.

PARTICIPATION IN STRATEGY COUNCILS

But the higher civil servant is more than a channel of hard-to-get intelligence, more than a fountain of program ideas. His presence in the improvised strategy councils of reform has an important additional reason. He has the technical knowledge required for putting ideas to work.

His practical experience makes him an authoritative judge in determining which particular way of accomplishing objectives agreed upon is to be preferred over other seemingly equally feasible ways. He is not fazed by the difficult task of designing administrative machinery to achieve the policy goals of the sponsors of reform. The question of what things are desirable is often answered by strength of political influence. What is administratively attainable, especially when time is of the essence, is a far more specific and narrowly technical question. To venture answers on such questions is peculiarly within the competence of the bureaucracy.

More, however, is involved in the presence of administrators in the strategy councils of reform. Even in nationally integrated bureaucracies such as prevail in the contemporary Western world, there remains a counter-pull of loyalty and interest toward locality, district, and region. In addition to dircct forms of representation through party, faction, or junta, civil servants who for particular areas "know all about how people think" cannot be overlooked. They are usually at a premium in attempts at plotting the course of a reform movement. Ranking field officers often combine skill in handling the apparatus of administration with a sure sense of how local and regional sentiment can be enlisted in a "fair deal." Such field officers play an important role in the applied geography of politics.

This aspect is proportionately magnified where the configuration of political power is strongly influenced by local or tribal allegiances. Today that is particularly true of many of the new nations of Asia and Africa. Frequently, what is most significant about an administrative official is where he comes from and what his standing is with the group to which he belongs. Compared with his status as, say, the son-in-law of the leader of the dominant element in the northern region, how much weight he has on the scales of public management may be quite immaterial. If he is credited with having experience, it may be only in inflicting authority crudely upon a resentful population.

LANGUAGE OF ACHIEVEMENT

Generally, however, one observes in the rising nations the growth of a nucleus of trained or training-minded administrators. These contribute a professional outlook to the everyday conduct of governmental activities. They are usually relatively young, responsive to modern ways, and simultaneously aroused partisans of the new order. To be sure, being heavily dependent on support from the political leaders in control, they are not seldom despondent over the incidence of free-wheeling opportunism displayed in factional tactics. But one cannot ignore the fact that the new practitioners of an administrative technology are leaving a visible imprint.

They have begun to occupy a key position in maintaining the pace of development—political, economic, and social. Indeed, some of the novel jargon of administration is being accepted as the language of achievement in lands where time used to walk slowly. "Planning" is an illustration. So is "management." So is "projection." So is, finally, "development" itself.

But the fresh wave of governmental involvement must run with the tides of political power. This is the reason why professionally oriented administrators have not yet had much of a chance to neutralize their task in the political game of musical chairs. They are squeezed between the massive remnants of the old order and the personal regimes that spring up when feuding politicians drift toward bankruptcy. Strong-man government settles some irritating questions for frustrated officials eager to carry forward their programs. But it simultaneously introduces additional irrationalities in allowing the whims of the "redeemer" and the interests of his cohorts to control many administrative decisions.

Political factors penetrate into public management also as a result of other circumstances. For want of effective democratic instrumentalities, the government may be compelled to maneuver between full-speed progress everywhere and responsible adaptation of programs to available financial resources. Typically, this dilemma pits the budget agency, encouraged to pursue a realistic course, against enthusiastic program departments. The most important of these may be a ministry for development, which usually combines considerable audacity in taking economic risks with an unlimited supply of popular pressure in favor of racing into utopia. The resulting tensions become especially serious when one of the departments engaged in the argument is still directed on a contract basis by experts from another—perhaps even the old colonial—country.

VI. Prudential Neutrality

THE VIRTUE OF NON-COMMITMENT

The constitutional law of administrative behavior properly stresses the instrumental character of the career establishment. The arm of the state cannot be permitted to defy the political brain, nor is it free to separate itself from the body politic. The restraining implications of these broad maxims are the test of a bureaucracy's maturity, sophistication, and rectitude.

On the other hand, administrative neutrality does not mean an ostrich-like withdrawal of the directing cadre from the arena of governmental choice. Policy, program, and management pose countless issues on which the higher civil servant is obligated to come forth with his best judgment. He fails to do his duty if he tries to wash his hands of these questions. He has no warrant for simply passing them to the politicians, without first contributing his special competence for professional analysis. Here, one large question is how to keep the spokesman of functional expertise from pre-empting the decision, instead of providing a factual foundation for it.

What administrative neutrality does mean is something else. It means acceptance of the discipline of working without reservation—indeed, with devotion—for the success of every government lawfully in power. Conversely, it carries with it a prohibition. Permanent officers cannot allow themselves so intimate an identification with a particular policy or program as to create for them an emotional disability when it comes to turning in the opposite direction under a different government.

Between the two poles of single-track partisanship and conscientious neutrality there are numerous notches on the scale of behavior. Official verbalization may be mere window-dressing. Often the character of a particular stage of development, leavened by cultural factors, supplies a temporary logic for the general acceptance of certain rules of official conduct.

Different times and different conditions hold out their own answers to delicate questions of institutional ethics and pragmatic feasibility. Bureaucracies are molded to a significant extent by what is demanded of them. But they also mold by their own momentum the essence of government as a force in the lives of men.

MOTIVATIONAL FACTORS

Ultimately, the effects of the higher civil service as an action group in political development flow from the bureaucracy's skill and resources for bolstering the long-run performance of government. The career man's concern with governmental machinery, irrespective of who happens to be at the helm, refers his attention primarily to the administrative process as such. This is in contrast with the military, for instance. Control over sufficient means for planned violence to force shifts in power does not spell capacity for sustaining durable political change.

Civil servants do not drift naturally into the camp of change. For a permanent establishment there is obvious advantage in avoiding exposure to serious public controversy. From these cautions simultaneously develops the bureaucratic habit to seek full political cover, to fall back on two-faced answers in order to get by, and to hide behind the smoke-screen of busy business.

Clearly, there is advantage for the administrator in passing the buck to the place where it must go on grounds of political logic. He is bound to show adroitness in substituting prudence for courage. Such tendencies do not detract from the fact that the higher civil service functions near the heart of government. This fact alone makes the bureaucracy a prompter in the determination of the national agenda.

The prompting role of the bureaucracy relies on the exercise of the administrator's normal responsibilities in aiding political decision makers. It does not require resort to scheming, to the formation of camarillas or janizariats. In the day of functional expertise, however, the bureaucracy speaks too often through the voices of groups of single-minded specialists rather than with the single voice of generally oriented responsibility. This is a source of disorganization. It weakens political leadership and is fatal to its sense of direction. But here a larger failing becomes manifest—the failure of the institutions of modern government to integrate the special in the discipline of the general.

As in all occupational groups, certain patterns of leadership or spokesmanship evolve in the higher civil service through voluntary bodies or informal relationships. It is toward these spokesmen that outsiders as well as group members turn for cues to indicate common attitudes, inclinations, and intentions. But spokesmen, too, act in a given context. Part of it is the strength of service doctrine. Here we find one of the lifelines of motivation in the behavior of the directing cadre as an action group in political development.

CHAPTER 4

Bureaucracy and Political Development[1]

S. N. EISENSTADT

I

The term "political development" has recently evoked much discussion and is often used in conjunction with the term "economic development." To some extent, the latter's criteria are "objectively" or quantitatively determined, but the meaning of political development has not yet been precisely or clearly established. In this chapter political development will be used in a specific way. It will be used, if with less precision, as the economist uses "self-sustained" growth to mean a continuous process of growth which is produced by forces within the system and which is absorbed by the system.

Within the political sphere, the equivalent of such self-sustained growth is the ability to absorb varieties and changing types of political demands and organization. It also includes the skill to deal with new and changing types of problems which the system produces or which it must absorb from outside sources. The concept complies with two views. It is closely related to a view of a political system which emphasizes authoritative decisions by rulers over subjects who pressure for such decisions, as well as to an approach which stresses the articulation of many interests, as it is to one which is concerned with the aggregation of political functions in the ruling institutions.[2]

Neither the different analytical implications of such approaches nor the actual differences between them will be discussed. Suffice it to indicate that according to this view every political system, by its nature, deals with demands and issues of political struggle. The demands and struggles are a very part of the definition of any such system. They may be classified according to the extent to which they seek either to

[1] This chapter is based on a series of comparative studies of political systems and bureaucracy by the author. Some of these studies which contain full bibliographical references on source material are quoted in the footnotes.

[2] D. Easton, *The Political System, An Inquiry into the State of Political Science*, New York, Knopf, 1953. G. Almond, "A Functional Approach to Comparative Politics," G. Almond and J. Coleman, eds., *The Politics of the Developing Areas*, Princeton, Princeton University Press, 1960, pp. 3–65.

determine broad policy or simply to accrue particular benefits to individuals and groups. Those which seek to influence or determine policy are usually articulated as specific political issues, while those which seek to accrue personal benefit are usually much less articulated in political terms.

Political organizations may also be classified according to whether they are concerned with political activities alone or whether they also deal with other social activities and kinds of groupings. Accordingly we may distinguish between different types of political organization and activities. There is the simple petitioning which may range from that of an individual to that of a group. There may be attempts to obtain group representation or to usurp power positions. There is also the structural accumulation of different kinds of cliques and the formation of political groups and parties which participate in and attempt to influence central political decisions.[3]

II

Different types of political systems are able to deal with specific types of political demands and organization which have different levels of articulation. The capacity to deal with these is actually built into the structure of a political system. The more a political system is differentiated or organized into specific roles and structures, the more it can develop autonomous orientations and goals. It enlarges the scope of policies as well as the administrative services which are provided to the various groups in the society. The variety of political demands and organization which the system can absorb increases, especially those demands and organizations which are specifically political.

It seems that the more the political system is differentiated, the more sensitivity it has also to "objective" problems like international relations, population movements, or economic fluctuations. External events may obviously impinge upon any given polity. But the more differentiated the system, the greater is its ability to cope or to attempt to cope with such problems as well as to manipulate and influence such external conditions. If we make a general comparison of historically different political systems, such as primitive with feudal, or feudal

[3] In concrete cases an overlapping of these criteria always exists, but they have been found useful for analytical distinction in comparative studies. For a fuller exposition of these criteria see S. N. Eisenstadt, "The Comparative Analysis of Historical Political Systems," a mimeographed paper prepared for the Committee on Comparative Politics, Social Science Research Council, 1958. Also S. N. Eisenstadt, *The Political Systems of Empires*, Glencoe, Ill., The Free Press, 1963.

with centralized empires, differences in the elements already discussed will be readily apparent.[4]

Related to, though not identical with, the ability of a political system to absorb varied types of demands is a political system's capacity to deal with orientations which were not anticipated in its basic framework or ideology, even if they were actually generated by the system's own internal forces.

Various political systems may exhibit different degrees of flexibility when it comes to their ability to absorb such "unexpected" changes. Despite the variety which different historical political systems exhibit when compared with one another, most of them evince relatively little of such capacity. Some partial institutionalization of the capacity did, however, develop in some of them—especially in those of the centralized empires. This ability is probably connected both with the extent to which the political system is differentiated and with the major goals upheld by the rulers and the major value orientations prevalent among different strata in the society.[5]

III

Generally, this potential capacity to sustain continuously changing, new types of political demands and organizations develops only within those processes which can be denoted as political modernization or initial "pre-modernization." Historically, political modernization can be equated with those types of political systems which developed in Western Europe from the seventeenth century and which spread to other parts of Europe, to the American continent, and, in the nineteenth and twentieth century, to Asian and African countries.

Typologically, political modernization is characterized by the development of a series of basic features. Some of these features also existed in the pre-modern systems and often served as precursors and prerequisites of modernization.

[4] S. N. Eisenstadt, "Primitive Political Systems: A Preliminary Comparative Analysis," *American Anthropologist*, Vol. 61, No. 2, April 1959, pp. 200-220. S. N. Eisenstadt, "The Political Struggle in Bureaucratic Societies," *World Politics*, IX, 1, October 1957, pp. 15-36. S. N. Eisenstadt, "Internal Contradictions in Bureaucratic Polities," *Comparative Studies in Society and History*, VI, October 1958, pp. 58–75. S. N. Eisenstadt, "Les Causes de la Désintegration et de la Chute des Empires, Analyses Sociologiques et Analyses Historiques," *Diogene*, Vol. 34, Avril-Juin 1961, pp. 87-112.

[5] These problems as related to the political systems of the centralized empires are dealt with in S. N. Eisenstadt, "Internal Contradictions . . . ," *op.cit.* S. N. Eisenstadt, "Les Causes . . . ," *op.cit.* S. N. Eisenstadt, *The Political Systems . . .* , *op.cit.*

The first characteristic of political modernization is a high degree of differentiation in political roles and institutions and the development of a centralized and unified polity with specific goals and orientations. The second characteristic is the extension of the activities of the "central" administrative and political organizations and their gradual permeation into all spheres and regions of the society. The third is the tendency of potential power to spread to wider and wider groups in the society—ultimately to all adult citizens. Fourth, it is further characterized by the weakening of traditional elites and traditional legitimation of rulers and by the increase in ideological and institutional accountability of the rulers to the ruled who hold potential power.

These transformations are all connected with the continuous development of great fluidity in political support while political allegiance based on ascriptive commitment to a given ruler or groups of rulers diminishes. This diminution of ascriptive commitment forces rulers continuously to seek the political support of the ruled in order to maintain themselves in effective power. This support is also needed for specific goals and policies which rulers propagate and want to implement. The culmination of the process, as it has gradually developed in the outright modern systems, is the citizen's participation in the selection of rulers and in setting up major political goals. To a smaller extent they further take part in the formulation of policies. In most modern political systems elections have evolved in different ways to allow for the formal expression of this participation. Even the rulers of the totalitarian regimes, unlike the rulers of traditional regimes, cannot take political passivity and traditional identification for granted. They are even afraid of such passivity, for it has the potential of becoming a focus around which the citizens' political power may crystallize. The difference between modern democratic, semi-democratic, and totalitarian political systems does not lie in the spread of power, for this is common to all of them. The difference lies in the ways in which the rulers react to this power. The spread of potential political power is a characteristic of all modern political systems, including the totalitarian as distinct from pre-modern or traditional.

Though the citizens of totalitarian regimes are not allowed to exercise their potential power, it is formally recognized in their right to "vote." Most of the very restrictive measures of the rulers of these regimes, unlike those of the rulers of traditional ones, are based on the recognition of this potential power. The rulers also fear the potential dangers to themselves of its spontaneous organization—hence their attempts to organize, to manipulate, and to direct its expression.

Charismatic and traditional (feudal) relations between rulers and ruled still prevail in modern political systems. This is particularly the case with charismatic relations. Legitimation or "accountancy" of the rulers to the ruled may be based upon charisma, rational legality, or the "social" when the latter term is used to mean devotion to secular social values (this category may be akin to Weber's "Wertrational," though he did not use it in his classification of types of legitimation). But in no modern political system can traditional legitimation or criteria of accountancy of the rulers to the ruled be the predominant ones.

The analysis of political modernization presented here does not postulate any overall evolutionary trend. The dominance of the traditional ceded to some non-traditional elements though the strong possibility of reversal remains. But this is not related to whether the orientation will be charisamtic, legal-rational, or "value" based.

IV

It is necessary to distinguish between the scope of the demands which a given political system can absorb in general and the general propensity of a political system to change and the ability to absorb such changes continuously within its institutions. These continually changing demands and issues are specific to modern political systems, where they derive from the broader conditions of modernization which will be analyzed shortly.

Political leaders and institutions, in the modern systems as in all others, have to deal with both "objective" problems like international relations, economic conditions, economic resources, and the mobilization of political support. The connection between these two in modern political systems is much closer than in other types of political systems. The growing participation of wider strata of the population in the political struggle increases sensitivity to and interest in, if not always understanding of, the objective problems.

Similarly, the ways in which political demands and activities are articulated in modern political systems is closely related to the provision of resources for the political elite. Continuous use of these resources by the polity requires that the ruled be effectively organized politically. This prerequisite, which enables the political elite to mobilize support and to articulate political demands, is of crucial importance to the working of modern systems. Different patterns of articulation of political demands and of mobilization of political support developed at various stages of the modernization process. But it is possible to discern some general institutional devices in almost all modern political systems.

Interest groups, social movements, public opinion, and political parties are the specific types or organizations through which political demands are articulated. The first three may to some extent be seen as components of the last—the parties—which are the most articulate forms of modern political organization. They also, however, have autonomous existence and orientations of their own.

The interest or pressure group is usually directed to gaining concrete and specific ends—whether economic, religious, cultural, or political. It is concerned primarily to promote this interest or at least to assure its optimal promotion in a given situation. Interest groups are, of course, diverse. They may be economic, professional, religious, ethnic, or tribal, and their specific interests may vary greatly from situation to situation.

Social movements are a second type of organization through which political adaptations and demands are articulated. Social movements usually aim at the development of some new total society or polity. They attempt to interject certain values or goals into a given institutional structure or to transform such a structure according to these aims and values. These aims are usually inclusive and diffuse. A social movement usually has a strong future orientation. It tends to depict the future as greatly different from the present and to fight for the realization of this change. It very often contains some apocalyptical semi-messianic elements, and it usually makes demands of total obedience or loyalty on its members while making extreme distinctions between friends and foes.

The third element through which either the membership or leadership articulate political demands in a modern political system can be called "general, diffuse, and intelligent interest in public issues." This refers to people or groups who have a more flexible attitude to both specific issues and to "total" ideas and claims. They are not firmly attached to any given interest group, movement, or organization but are mainly interested in the "sober" evaluation of a political program, in values, and in concrete possibilities.

Each of these ways of articulating interests also existed in premodern political systems—but with differences. One of the differences was the lack of firm legitimate recognition within the central political institutions of processes for representation. Petitions or entreaties by interest groups or cliques were a partial exception. But social or social-religious movements were either entirely a-political or non-legitimate in the view of the existing institutions. A second difference was that these groups were mostly concerned with petitioning the rulers for various concrete benefits, and not with the determination of major political goals or the selection of rulers. A third factor is that only in modern political systems do these different interest groups and movements tend to become integrated into the framework of a common continuous political activity and organization. A continuous orientation develops to the central political institutions, namely in political parties.

Political parties tend to integrate the different types of political organizations. They attain this integration within their own organization through the development of specific party organs, leadership, and programs. The integration is effected through the subsumption of various concrete interests under some more general rules or aims which have some appeal to a wider public. It also occurs through the translation of the inclusive, diffuse aims of the social movements into more realistic terms of concrete goals, issues, and dilemmas.

Different parties may evince different degrees of predominance of each of these elements. But whatever such relative predominance, the integration of each of these elements into the parties is never complete. Interest groups, social movements, and public opinion may retain autonomous orientations and activities which often tend to burst the frameworks imposed on them by the parties. Their autonomy is maintained by presenting demands directly to the central political institutions of the executive, the legislature, or the bureaucracy without the mediation of any given party. They attempt to mobilize support and resources for themselves directly and not through a party.

V

The tendency was for these various characteristics of modern political systems to develop gradually. Not all of them developed in any given regime, and the tempo or temporal sequence differed in different countries. But their development and crystallization may be seen as the focus of the process of political modernization. They developed within the wider framework of social, economic, and cultural modernization. The combined impact of these conditions gave rise to the continuous production of new types of political demands and organization which the central political institutions had to absorb. Within any modern political system there is a continuous interplay between changing political demands and forms of political organization. There is also an interplay between attempts by the political elites to direct and channelize these demands and the possibilities of absorption and of non-absorption.

Hence the central problem of modernization in any modern political system is the ability to deal with such changing demands. They must be absorbed in policy making while assuring continuity to the system. Sustained political growth thus becomes a central problem of political systems.

At different stages of modern development different problems and different types of political organization appeared. Suffrage and the definition of the new political community were of the greatest central importance at one stage. At other stages problems of religious toleration and secularization of culture predominated. Economic and social problems, and problems of organization, have been dominant at various times. The appearance of each of these problems was connected with the entrance of different groups and strata into the political arena, and has sharply posed the question of the ability of the political institutions to cope with them.

VI

In principle any modern political system could deal with this problem in several distinct ways. One is to attempt to minimize the development of any changes which would generate new political demands and patterns of development. The second is to control and manipulate such changes and their political expressions. The third is to absorb, within certain limits, such new demands and organization.

Obviously, in any concrete regime there exists some mixture of these three orientations. It is the nature of the mixture which varies among different regimes, and the relative predominance of any of them which also differs. But not even those regimes which prefer to minimize changes can entirely neglect the problem of absorption of change which is inherent in any modern system.

Although the propensity to generate changes and to deal with them is built into the institutional structure of modern political systems, the capacity to deal with them effectively varies greatly.

The history of modern political systems is full of cases of unsuccessful adaptation or lack of adaptation of existing political structures to new types of demands and organization. Or, in terms of this discussion, the capacity for continuous growth and continuous sustenance of such growth can be blocked or impaired. This impairment is manifested in the inability of various groups to articulate demands clearly, or in not providing resources for political elites and institutions, or by presenting demands more intensively or extensively than existing institutions can absorb them.

Political eruptions, or more or less violent outbreaks of political activities with symbols which are directed against the existing system and its symbols, are external manifestations of blocking. Such eruptions are usually very closely related to and manifested in the lack of integration of interest groups into any wider common framework. They result when social movements are not institutionalized within the framework of parties and policy making.

The more "primitive" eruptions or mob activities are evident in the simple lack of ability of elites to organize and articulate the potential political demands of various groups. When the eruptions are articulated they are manifested as organized political activities with discordant premises from those of prevailing parties and political institutions. It signifies a failure on the part of the erupting leaders to integrate their demands within the existing framework. If such eruptions are not merely transitory, they may cause either the destruction of a given political system or the successful suppression of the new demands by the rulers to a level at which they and the institutions are capable of dealing with them.

VII

Modern political systems, like other political systems, are, then, faced with the problem not only of balancing demands and policies but of balancing through absorption. Sustained political growth is thus the central problem of modernization, and ability to deal with continuous change is the crucial test of this growth.

A modern system may itself retard further political modernization, but this does not make it non-modern. There is a basic difference between Nepal prior to the 1950's, Franco's Spain, or even Salazar's Portugal. The difference lies in the suppression and manipulation by Spain and Portugal of demands which are partially rooted in the system but which are denied free political expression. There is no provision for making demands on the central political authorities in either formulations or decision making. In a traditional system, on the other hand, this problem does not exist because various groups and strata do not evince such needs.

The only way in which a modern system can entirely obliterate, rather than simply limit or retard, modernization is if it can succeed in changing the basic social conditions which cause such demands to develop. Obliteration may temporarily succeed in systems which are just on the threshold of modernization, but it does not succeed in the more autocratic modern systems.

VIII

The ability of modern political systems to absorb changing political demands is closely related to the development of several basic institutional frameworks. First in importance are the various executive and legislative bodies. Political parties through which the political demands of different interest groups and social movements are articulated are second, and, third, there are the centralized bureaucratic administrations. Though the tempo of development differs from place to place, all three are to some extent basic corollaries of any process of modernization. Their role in the institutionalization of the capability to absorb changing political demands and organization is crucial.

It is with the place of the bureaucracies in this process that this chapter is concerned. An attempt will be made to analyze the bureaucratic administration's role in both early and late modernization. Early and late modernization constitute the two main types of political systems which can be classified as precursors, or as initial stages, of modern political systems as they developed in centralized empires—especially in the centralized European states during the Age of Absolutism and in the nineteenth century post-colonial regimes in Asia and Africa.

In both of these cases bureaucracies were of crucial importance in shaping the framework of differentiated systems as well as in serving as important instruments of political unification and modernization. They also proved capable, however, of becoming important impediments to further modernization. A brief comparative analysis of the bureaucracies in historically early and late cases of initial modernization may provide some important clues for the conditions under which these bureaucracies may facilitate or impede the establishment of unified centralized polities. It may also indicate how systematic capacity for change and the absorption of change develop.

The creation of a "historical centralized" polity was very often aimed against various groups—aristocratic groups and strata, traditional urban groups, and religious elites. It was either through the invention of a bureaucratic administration or the reorganization of an existing administration on a centralized pattern that the strength of these traditional strata was undermined. Their privileges and monopolies in political and administrative positions were also withdrawn.

Whether the rulers succeeded in establishing these polities usually depended upon either the existence or the creation of specific conditions within those societies. The most important of these conditions were a relatively differentiated social structure, elements of a market economy, some degree of flexibility in the status system, and the growth of some universalistic cultural orientations. All of these were connected with the development of free-floating resources and with the emerging predominance of non-ascriptive rural and urban groups.

The expansion of bureaucratic organizations and their activities in turn contributed to the establishment and continuation of conditions and premises upon which the polity was based. The relatively differentiated and non-traditional strata were the backbone of these polities. They provided the free resources needed by the rulers and maintained dependable relations for them.[6]

IX

Bureaucratic administrations played a similarly crucial part in cases of late initial modernization in the post-colonial empires.[7] Most of these countries usually had two or three bureaucracies or layers of bureaucratic organization and structure. What remained in the post-colonial new states was the personnel, organizational structure, and tradition of the old colonial civil service. After the attainment of independence, it provided the basic framework for further extension and development of bureaucratic administration.

Within these societies, this initial extension of administration was

[6] For a fuller exposition see S. N. Eisenstadt, *The Political Systems . . . , op.cit.*

[7] A more complete discussion can be found in S. N. Eisenstadt, "Problems of Emerging Bureaucracies in Developing Areas and New States," a mimeographed article prepared for the North American Conference on the Social Implications of Industrialization and Technological Change, Chicago, 1960. R. Braibanti, "The Relevance of Political Science to the Study of Underdeveloped Areas," R. Braibanti and J. J. Spengler, eds., *Traditions, Values and Socio-Economic Development*, Durham, University of North Carolina Press, 1961, pp. 139-181. R. Braibanti, "The Civil Service of Pakistan: A Theoretical Analysis," *South Atlantic Quarterly*, Vol. 58, Spring 1959, pp. 258-304. W. J. Siffin, ed., *Toward the Comparative Study of Public Administration*, Bloomington, University of Indiana Press, 1957.

rooted in the need of the colonial powers for resources and for the maintenance of law and order. It was based on political control by the metropolitan powers who participated only minimally in the indigenous life of the community. This way of functioning greatly affected the scope of the colonial powers' activities. They were necessarily limited to basic administrative services. It also determined the administrations' structural characteristics and resulted in a high degree of centralization, of adherence to legal precepts and rules, and a small amount of internal differentiation.

Thus, on the one hand, these colonial bureaucracies helped to establish the framework of modern legal and administrative practices. On the other hand, they were highly a-political since they did not meddle in politics, maintained the ideal of a politically neutral civil service, and refrained from participating in the political life of the country in which they served. Their very limited goals were set by the colonial powers who were neither responsible to the political groups nor to the opinions of the country in which they ruled. They performed only secondary functions in the regulation of internal political interests and activities among the colonial population. Whatever internal political activities were undertaken by them were perceived mostly in terms of administrative injunctions and enforcement of law.

The second layer of the bureaucracies in the new states consists of those departments and echelons which were developed after attainment of independence. Here a new civil service was developed. It was new in personnel, goals, and even departments and activities. This new bureaucracy had to be staffed with new recruits, often inadequately trained, whose main qualification for office was former participation in the nationalistic political movements. These new bureaucracies were the bearers of new types of goals such as economic advancement, social betterment, educational advancement, or other types of community development.

Most of these new recruits usually had a much clearer, more articulate political orientation and a sense of political responsibility than did the former colonial civil service. They very often saw themselves as representatives of their respective movements, parties, or sectors. They saw their function as mainly political, and sought to fulfill it by either implementing political goals or representing, articulating, and regulating the political interests and activities of different groups and social strata.

The relations between the older bureaucracy and the newer echelons were not always easy, especially in the first period after independence when an attitude of distrust on the part of the nationalist leaders toward the remnants of the older colonial services usually prevailed. In some cases this may have led to an almost complete destruction of the older structure. In most cases some sort of *modus vivendi* developed between the older and newer echelons in which one or the other tended to predominate. The implementation of new social, political, and economic goals were strongly emphasized and envolvement in the political process was much greater than before.

X

The bureaucracies in developing countries which have not been under colonial rule exhibit a somewhat different although not entirely dissimilar pattern. Within them there first existed a traditional bureaucracy whether "royal," as in the Middle Eastern countries, or "oligarchical-republican" as in most Latin American countries. These bureaucracies usually dominated the political scene until the end of the Second World War. Some traditional elements were mixed with more modern ones which were very often copied from some European country. The strong influence of the French pattern in most Latin American countries is an example.

These administrations tended usually to uphold the interests of the ruling oligarchies and to implement rather limited social and economic objectives. Whatever tendency to modernization they may have exhibited, as in the fields of military affairs or education, their major political aim was to limit those minimal spheres which were necessary to maintain the viability of the then existing system.

With growing modernization came an increased impact of internal democratization and the development of new social, political, and economic goals which caused the bureaucracies to extend the scope of their activities and to recruit new personnel. The older pattern continued to leave its imprint on the new echelons and departments through administrative training and organizational methods. Social and political orientations also reinforced these to some extent. Only in a few of these countries like Mexico did widespread, well-organized, semi-revolutionary parties succeed in upsetting the oligarchy and in establishing a stable and viable modern political framework. A somewhat new pattern of bureaucratic organization was established which was not dissimilar from those of new states, although much more efficient and stable.[8]

XI

In all these societies, whether historical or new states, the bureaucracies were posed between the rulers and some of the major groups and strata. There was a conflict between the rulers' desire to use the bureaucracies for their own needs and purposes, and the rulers' and administrators' need to mobilize economic resources and political support. A further factor was the development of expectations of service and some standard rules from the bureaucracies by the non-ruling power groups.

In conjunction with these varied pressures, the bureaucratic administration, and especially their higher echelons, tended to develop some specific organizational characteristics and political orientations of their own. The most important of these was the tendency to emphasize internal organization and professional autonomy.

This tendency was manifest in two major aspects of their activities. Some autonomy developed toward both the rulers and the various strata as a result of attempting to meet the demands and interests of both. Certain general usages, or rules and standards of service, developed. General interests of the population were considered, and ability grew to resist the pressures of those seeking continuous and intermittent change for their own benefit. Secondly, most of these administrations tended to develop some conception of themselves as servants of the state or the community. They conceived of themselves as having a responsibility to the polity and developed criteria of service and professional performance.

These tendencies could combine with different types of organizational structure. Needless to say, many of these administrations did not necessarily develop all the characteristics of pure Weberian bureaucracies. The extent to which such characteristics were developed differed greatly from case to case and should constitute a subject of separate study. But even the preceding analysis tends to show that these organizational characteristics of the administration did not appear in a void but were to a large extent a product of the broader social conditions. Because of this, whatever their exact organizational char-

[8] See, for instance, R. E. Scott, *Mexican Government in Transition*, Urbana, University of Illinois Press, 1959.

acteristics, the bureaucracies performed broader social and political functions and participated in the political process from their beginning.

XII

It was these characteristics that facilitated the bureaucratic administrations' performance of several important functions in the polity. They helped to maintain the framework of a unified polity as well as the capacity to absorb varied demands and to regulate them effectively. Not only were they important instruments for unification and centralization, but they enabled the rulers to implement continuous policy. In addition, they also served as important instruments for mobilization of resources—taxes, manpower, and political support.

Beyond these, the bureaucracies performed crucial functions of the bureaucratic administrations in regulating the political struggle. When continuous administrative organizations were staffed by professional personnel whose activities were regulated by mechanisms independent of other groups, technical services and facilities became assured for the wide strata of the population. These administrations also facilitated the regulation of several aspects of the interrelations and potential conflicts between the main groups of the society, assured them of continuous service and upheld their rights, irrespective of momentary changes in their power relations.

In a similar way, the bureaucratic administrations also helped to regulate the relations between the political sphere, the rulers, and other groups in the society. To some extent they regulated the demands of the rulers for various resources from the main social groups, assured some regularity and continuity in the mobilization of these resources, and provided the major social groups with some continuous services on behalf of the rulers. In this way they could segregate the provision of services from the daily political struggle. The latter centered in other institutional frameworks such as court-cliques, royal councils, parliaments, and parties. By providing different services, they gave the rulers a framework through which the satisfaction of some of the interests and demands of various groups could be assured.

Once these bureaucracies were established and used, they could perform very important duties in political socialization. They could function in accommodating various groups to the framework of the centralized polity and to its basic institutions and norms. They could also facilitate identification with the goals of the rulers of these polities. In this way they could not only enhance the ability of these political systems to absorb different types of political demands; they could also enhance their own ability to deal with the varying types of demands.

XIII

The very performance of these functions has necessarily involved the bureuacratic administrations in the political process within these societies. But the ways in which they become involved in this process of modernization differed in historical empires, in colonial and in post-colonial countries. The main difference lay in the extent to which wider groups in the society participated actively in politics and in the nature of the basic legitimation of the rulers.

In historical empires the bureaucratic administrations provided the rulers with the basic resources which they needed and participated in the formulation as well as the implementation of policies. To some extent, they also participated with other active groups, such as the aristocracy and the religious elites, in the more central political struggle. This struggle was not yet fully articulated and what interests it did articulate were relatively simple. There were large parts of the population which did not participate and many interests were neither articulated nor organized into specific political forms. By providing services and through its general framework, the bureaucracy was able to keep these demands at a relatively low level. The functions it performed in political socialization were to accustom the various groups to the framework of a centralized polity, to uphold the traditional legitimation of the rulers, and to maintain the basic social framework for these groups.

In post-colonial societies which are cases of initial late modernization, the bureaucracies became much more involved in the political process. They became geared to having wider groups participate in the central political process at a higher level of activity. They also helped to confer legitimation on rulers who did not enjoy any traditional base.[9] This greater extent of the bureaucracy's involvement in the political process can be seen in several ways.

In many of these countries it constitutes itself as an effective executive or part of it, in addition to being the administrative arm of the

[9] For a wider discussion of the problems of new states see G. Almond and J. Coleman, eds., *The Politics . . .* , *op.cit.* E. A. Shils, "Political Development in the New States," *Comparative Studies in Society and History*, II, 3, April 1960, pp. 266–292, 379-410. S. N. Eisenstadt, *Essays on Sociological Aspects of Political and Economic Development*, The Hague, Mouton, 1961. J. J. Spengler, "Economic Development: Political Preconditions and Political Consequences," *The Journal of Politics*, Vol. 22, August 1960, pp. 387-416.

empowered executive. It plays a part in setting up, determining, and implementing political goals as well as in establishing major policy directives. Apart from the head of the executive, it is the only body, in many countries, which is capable of formulating clear objectives which may be either political or administrative.

The second major aspect of the bureaucracy's involvement in the political process in these countries is its tendency to develop as one of the main instruments of political regulation. It is one of the main channels of political struggle in which and through which different interests are regulated and aggregated. Its role in this aspect of the political process may be not only important but predominant. In some cases the bureaucracy may become a very important pressure and interest group in its own right with strong alliances with other oligarchical groups, as in some Latin American countries.

Thus in all these countries the bureaucracy may tend to fulfill different types of political functions and, like parties, legislatures, and executives, become a center of different types of political activity. Through these activities it may establish some of the basic frameworks of modern politics, but it may also minimize the extent of differentiation of various types of political roles and activities. It thus impedes the development of autonomous and differentiated political activities, organizations, and orientations.

The emerging bureaucracies are also the major instruments of social change and of political socialization in their respective countries. They are initially, at least, based on universalistic and functionally specific definitions of the role of the official and the role of the client. But the majorities of the populations of these countries have a different orientation. In their social life their traditional orientations and structures, such as the extended family, are predominant. The major part of a person's role-relations in these societies are set within traditional groups. Rights and duties are defined in terms of personal relationships. Previous experience with bureaucratic organization is restricted and rarely of great importance.

Thus the contacts of the public with governmental organizations may provide a framework for a wider and more intensive process of political socialization. The public's accommodation to the new political structure becomes dependent, to a considerable extent, upon its successful learning in these situations of contact. This has very often forced the bureaucracies to go beyond their specialized roles and to assume various roles of social and political leadership and tutelage.

This is what enabled them to effect changes in the behavior of the population at large. It was this need to foster change which often extended the scope of the activities of bureaucrats beyond those of specific goals and made them reach out into the realm of family, kinship, and community life of wide strata of the population.

XIV

Whatever the differences between these cases of initial early and late modernization, the bureaucracy performed some crucial functions of political socialization and regulation in both. But the continuous performance of these functions by the bureaucracies was neither given nor assured by the continuity of their existence. In many cases they could develop into stumbling-blocks on the road to political unification, to continuous modernization and development. These possibilities were rooted in the inherent tendency to bureaucratization which is the extension of a bureaucracy's sphere of power and influence beyond what is deemed to be its legitimate concern.[10]

In the cases just discussed this tendency toward bureaucratization could occur because the bureaucracies became involved in the political processes in these societies. In conjunction with this involvement they tended to develop several distinct types of political orientations, and some of these were closely related to the potential tendency to bureaucratization which could undermine the very premises of the unified polities within which they developed. They could also act to minimize the bureaucracy's ability to deal with changing problems.

Despite many differences in detail, some crucial similarities can be found in the political orientations of the bureaucracies in cases of both early and late modernization.

There were three important political orientations developed by the bureaucracies in the historical empires. They could maintain service orientations to both the rulers and the major strata with greater emphasis on the services to the rulers in the societies in early stages of modernization. It was possible for them to develop into a merely passive tool of the ruler with but little internal autonomy or performance of services to the different strata of the population. They might displace service goals to the various strata and to the polity in favor of goals of self-aggrandizement, usurpation of power exclusively in

[10] On this tendency of bureaucracies see S. N. Eisenstadt, "Bureaucracy and Bureaucratization: A Trend Report," *Current Sociology*, VII (1959). S. N. Eisenstadt, "Bureaucracy, Bureaucratization and Debureaucratization," *Administrative Science Quarterly*, Vol. 4, December 1959, pp. 302-321.

their own favor, and the favoring of a group with which they became closely identified.

In the last case, the bureaucracy tended usually to weaken and to de-emphasize the distinctiveness of its occupational and career patterns as well as of its professional ideology and self-image as servants of the country. It tried to lend to its positions the basic attributes of aristocratic status and to make the offices into some sort of private hereditary possessions or fiefs. It sought also to limit recruitment into the bureaucracy to members of the bureaucratic families and to minimize its accountability to various strata and, in extreme cases, even to the rulers.

Needless to say, all the bureaucratic administrations in the historical bureaucratic polities usually evinced some mixture or overlapping of these tendencies or orientations. However, a particular tendency usually could become predominant in any of them.

Similar but not identical social and political orientations of the bureaucracy can be discerned in the later stages of modernization in post-colonial regimes. In these cases some of the orientations become somewhat more crystallized and sharpened.

The first such orientation is similar to the first, and to a smaller extent to the second, political orientation of bureaucracies in the centralized empires. It is manifest in the development of a relatively efficient framework of modern administration. Legal norms and rules are upheld and basic services maintained even if this is effected through the monopolization by the bureaucracy of many political functions. Thus it extends the scope of its activities and its officials assume many social and political leadership roles. In such cases the bureaucracy may generate, through the establishment of new political frameworks and through the development of such activities, many new social organizations and activities on both the central and local level. It may also contribute to the establishment of viable political frameworks and conditions conducive to economic and political development.

The second major type of possible orientation of the bureaucracies in the new states is characterized by its development in a direction similar to that of the last two, and especially of the third, orientation in the centralized empires. In such cases the bureaucracy tends not only to monopolize some central political functions but also to become a major interest group. As such it is usually closely allied with some institutional groups and with various oligarchical strata. Because of this alliance the bureaucracy tends to become a center of attraction for various white-collar aspirants and over-staffed. It may also easily become a narrow interest group which tends to stifle any development of independent political action.

XV

These different types of political orientations were similar in the initial phases of both early and late modernization, and may similarly influence the ability of these systems to maintain their basic frameworks as well as to foster and absorb further modernization.

In the historical empires when the bureaucracy maintained its basic service orientations to both the rulers and the major strata it was able to contribute to the continuity and stability of the regime. It was able to maintain the basic conditions of the centralized bureaucratic regimes even when it more strongly favored the rulers. In those societies, in periods in which the bureaucracy maintained service orientations, their help enabled rulers to maintain both their own and supporting strata's positions. This was partially achieved by keeping in check those strata which were opposed to the prerequisite of the centralized political systems as to the development of the more flexible political orientations. This was the way in which the bureaucracy could contribute to the maintenance of the unified, relatively differentiated political systems, and to their ability to absorb relatively articulated political demands and organizations.

The total subservience of the bureaucracy to the ruler as found in the cases of Prussia and the Ottoman Empire was usually connected with a very high degree of the use of force. The rulers implemented their goals by force against a very strong opposition. They received relatively little direct support from groups such as urban classes or free peasantry which could provide the requisite types of resources which the rulers needed to implement their goals and to develop centralized bureaucratic polities. When the bureaucracy had this kind of orientation, usually rigid political systems were involved which did not suffer any high degree of articulated political demands and organizations. Such orientations contributed to the weakening or alienation of the more flexible groups and strata, and to the freezing or undermining of the centralized political systems.

When service goals were displaced by the bureaucracy with illegitimate, usurpatory goals of self-aggrandizement, the flexible non-traditional strata tended to be gravely weakened. Self-aggrandizement was usually connected with at least the partial aristocratization of the bureaucracy. Economic resources and political support were withheld by the non-traditional strata from the aristocratized bureaucracy, thus leaving it without the support it required to continue functioning. This process became a contributory cause to the gradual disintegration of these policies into a more differentiated type of political structure.

Similar potential effects of the different orientations of the bureaucracy on the stability of political systems may be discerned in the new states. When these bureaucracies maintain some basic loyalty to the overall goals of the polity, in combination with a service orientation to the ruling elites and the major social groups, they are able to contribute to the establishment of the frameworks of unified centralized polities. They can also further the development of the capacity to absorb changing new political demands and to solve changing political problems.

The structure and patterns of activities of the bureaucracies which develop under these conditions may differ greatly from those of classical bureaucratic organizations. The relatively wide scope of their activities, especially when combined with a firm political orientation and a high measure of political consensus, may facilitate the maintenance of relative stability and continuity. It may induce and generate various new types of economic entrepreneurship, professional activities, and political leadership on the local and even on the central level. The bureaucracy may further give rise to a gradual diversification of functionally specific groups as well as to independent public opinion and leadership. It is interesting to note that in these cases there usually also exist rather strong party-bureaucracies. Conflicts may develop initially between them and the civil service. But the existence of some initial diversification of functions within a relatively unified political framework may help to produce change and economic development.

The second major type of political orientation of bureaucracies in the new states may easily contribute to what Riggs has called "negative development."[11] As it becomes a relatively narrow and yet very strong pressure group, it may easily obstruct schemes of economic development which threaten its own level of income, power, and influence. Such a bureaucracy may often attempt, through suppressive policies, to lower the level of political demands and organization. It may undermine the framework of a unified polity and facilitate the outbreak of various types of eruptions.

[11] F. W. Riggs, "Economic Development and Local Administration: A Study in Circular Causation," *Philippine Journal of Public Administration*, Vol. 3, January 1959, pp. 56-147.

XVI

Thus we see that in the initial stage of either early or late modernization a bureaucracy's similar political orientations may produce similar results. These orientations influence the extent of institutionalization of a centralized polity and facilitate or block further political development and modernization. These varied types of political orientations of the bureaucracy tend to persist, if somewhat transformed, in later stages of modernization. They are rooted in the internal structure of the bureaucracy and in the wider framework of the political process in these societies. Truly enough, in these later stages of modernization the bureaucratic administrations tend to become somewhat more specialized, professionalized, and fully organized bodies. Even here, however, it is only in the fully constitutional-democratic regimes that the ideal of the politically neutral civil service develops, though it may never become a full-fledged reality.

Even this type of neutral civil service constitutes only a specific subtype of what has been called service bureaucracy in this chapter. It necessarily denotes a certain type of engagement in the political process. As with all other types of political orientations which the bureaucracy may hold, this one too develops under certain specific structural conditions. It is important for this discussion to analyze what these varied conditions are.

The extent to which the bureaucracy maintains some basic service orientations while restraining both its inherent tendency to displace goals and its tendency to obtain autonomous power depends upon the interplay between several basic components of the political process in the pre-modern and modern societies.[12]

The first such condition is the existence of strong political elites. They must be able to articulate political goals. They must also establish and maintain frameworks of both political and legal institutions as well as direct communication with the major social and political groups. The second is the continuous development and vitality of groups and strata which are politically and socially articulate. They must be able to implement various social and political goals through their own activity. And they must concurrently provide the bureaucracy with a broader social setting from which to recruit its manpower.

Thus the existence of strong elites in the initial stages of political unification and modernization is to some extent more important than

[12] S. N. Eisenstadt, "Bureaucracy . . . ," *op.cit.* S. N. Eisenstadt, "Primitive Political . . . ," *op.cit.* S. N. Eisenstadt, "The Political Struggle . . . ," *op.cit.*

the existence of political groups which are strongly articulate. Such groups which tend to develop very intensive political demands and pressures may undermine the stability and viability of the political framework, and may also inhibit the rulers' ability to implement realistic policies. They are highly necessary, however, to provide resources to rulers and to restrain their autocratic tendencies.

The weakness of rulers and of such various strata may facilitate, in the initial stages of modernization, the development of the bureaucracies into an omniverous consumer of resources. It may give them a monopoly on the articulation of political demands which acts to undermine the incapacity to provide services and the rulers' capacity to absorb demands coming from wider strata.

As has been indicated above, the concrete manifestations of these tendencies varied in different historical settings. In the centralized empires the bureaucracy's maintenance of a service orientation to the rulers and the major strata was very closely related to its partial incorporation in various flexible and "free" strata. When it was not incorporated, it was at least not alienated from such strata. At the same time it accepted and expanded the duty of service to the rulers, and of power as an autonomous criterion of social status.

On the other hand, the development of tendencies in the upper echelons of the bureaucracies to displace service-goals was closely connected with the development of the bureaucracy into some sort of ascriptive stratum. It either grew into an independent, semi-aristocratic, or gentry stratum, or it became part of the already existing aristocratic stratum. This alienated it from the rulers, to some extent at least. When there was a similar tendency on the part of the rulers to ally themselves with aristocratic elements the structural positions and the frameworks of the centralized polities were weakened.[13]

In the new states one of the main problems facing the elites and the bureaucracy is the extent to which they may be able to overcome the pressure for a higher level of consumption. They must foster wider educational schemes which can provide adequate training for personnel in technical fields while regulating the pressures on the white-collar jobs.

Here the maintenance by the bureaucracy of a basic service orientation and of activities which can facilitate the solution of these problems depends upon the existence of some basic unitary political framework. There must also be a relatively unified political elite and some degree

[13] This is more fully analyzed in S. N. Eisenstadt, *The Political . . .* , *op.cit.*

of political consensus. Institutional interest groups such as the army or the churches which can easily monopolize power and economic positions must be relatively weak. Their position must be subordinate to the ecological strata and the more modern functional groups which are able to provide resources to the ruling elites while also tending to identify with the new centralized framework.

These bureaucracies may develop a negative orientation when a unified political framework and consensus does not exist. This is likely to occur when there is either a rift between the traditional and modern elites, or when a lack of consensus within the modern elite is very great. It also occurs when institutional interest groups like the church, the army, and other narrow oligarchical groups predominate in the social and economic structure.[14]

In later stages of modernization, when more specialized types of bureaucracy develop, the stage shifts to the stability of the general framework of political struggle. Emphasis is also upon the continuity of political symbols, the extent of political articulation, and the cohesion within and between major social groups. At this stage the very availability of ruling elites with their political and organizational ability depends on the stability of such framework as well as on the availability of cohesive articulated strata. The interaction between these frameworks and the different strata influences the development of the bureaucracy's different political orientations. But the analysis of these historical manifestations is already beyond the scope of this chapter.

[14] S. N. Eisenstadt, "The Problems . . . ," *op.cit.* S. N. Eisenstadt, *Essays on Sociological . . .* , *op.cit.*

CHAPTER 5

BUREAUCRATS AND POLITICAL DEVELOPMENT: A PARADOXICAL VIEW[1]

FRED W. RIGGS

Introduction

A PHENOMENON of the utmost significance in transitional societies is the lack of balance between political policy-making institutions and bureaucratic policy-implementing structures. The relative weakness of political organs means that the political function tends to be appropriated, in considerable measure, by bureaucrats. Intra-bureaucratic struggles become a primary form of politics. But when the political arena is shifted to bureaucracies—a shift marked by the growing power of military officers in conflict with civilian officials—the consequences are usually ominous for political stability, economic growth, administrative effectiveness, and democratic values. It seems important, therefore, to give serious attention to the relation between political and administrative development, to the question of how balanced growth takes place.

In this chapter, accordingly, I deal with the way in which bureaucratic interests affect political development; not how the declared political aims of officials impinge on politics, but how the existence and self-interest of bureaucratic institutions affect, directly or indirectly, the growth of political institutions. My theme will be the conditions under which non-bureaucratic power centers capable of subjecting bureaucrats to political control flourish or decline. I recognize that there are other important respects in which political development can and does occur, but this paper will be limited to this particular aspect of the subject.

In Western countries it has become a habit to think of the bureaucracy as an instrumental apparatus for the execution of policies established through "political," non-bureaucratic institutions. There have, of course, been serious scholars, as well as emotional writers, who have

[1] The author is grateful for many useful suggestions made by participants of the Social Science Research Council Conference on Bureaucracy and Political Development, and particularly for the help provided by Professors John T. Dorsey and Edward W. Weidner.

stressed the difficulty of keeping bureaucrats under control or, as the administrative cliché has it, "on tap but not on top."[2]

One consequence of this conventional attitude is that relatively few scholars have devoted themselves to an analysis of the political role of bureaucrats, the part they play in politics or in political development. However, in my opinion bureaucrats probably always have some influence in politics—although the extent of such influence varies from precious little to a great deal. In the developing countries the extent of bureaucratic involvement in politics is exceptionally high. If this opinion is correct, then it is even more important in the study of the developing countries to consider the role of bureaucrats in politics than to examine this topic in the study of more advanced political systems.

In his major work on government,[3] Carl J. Friedrich suggests that constitutionalism can emerge only after a substantial development of the bureaucracy, for without a governmental apparatus to bring under control, the challenge would not be present to bring into being a system designed to impose limitations and rules upon those who exercise administrative authority. I believe the experience of the developing countries is consistent with Friedrich's observation, but it suggests a corollary, namely that the imposition of constitutional control over a bureaucracy is a difficult task, and the more powerful, relatively, the bureaucracy becomes, the more arduous the achievement.

If we make a quick survey of the transitional societies today, we will be impressed by the weakness of their extra-bureaucratic political institutions in contrast with the burgeoning growth of their bureaucracies. In every country a great expansion of governmental agencies and a proliferation of functions has taken place, especially in the new nations that were recently under colonial rule. By contrast, parliamentary bodies have, in the main, proved ineffectual and, even in the countries like India and the Philippines where they have been most vigorous, their role in basic decision making has been questioned.[4]

[2] As one example of a serious analysis of the problem of maintaining bureaucratic accountability see Charles S. Hyneman, *Bureaucracy in a Democracy*, New York, Harper, 1950.

[3] *Constitutional Government and Democracy, rev. ed.*, Boston, Ginn, 1950, pp. 25-27, 57.

[4] For example, Norman Palmer, a careful observer of Indian politics, has written in connection with the operation of the constitutional and parliamentary system, "the main decisions are made to a large degree outside normal channels. This fact calls attention to the great influence of 'nonpolitical' forces in India, to the role of personalities and charismatic leadership. Most of the major policies are in fact determined within the Congress Party and not by the agencies of government; and within the Congress Party they are made by Jawaharlal Nehru and a handful of associates.

Elections have often been conducted in such a way as to give but a poor reflection of the popular will; the courts have not generally shown themselves to be bulwarks of the rule of law; and chief executives have more often than not shown themselves to be arbitrary and authoritarian, relying on their charismatic leadership qualities or a party machine rather than on formal political institutions as the basis of power. Under these conditions it is not surprising that bureaucrats themselves have often had to play a crucial part in determining what would, or perhaps *would not*, be done.

In speaking of non-bureaucratic power I have in mind, of course, primarily those institutions through which, in democratic countries, public interests are articulated, aggregated, and communicated to policy makers, there to be translated into decisions which can and are to a large extent subsequently implemented.

However, I do not rule out of the concept those systems in which the representation of popular interests is highly defective, but in which, nevertheless, a non-bureaucratic political system exists which is able to impose its control upon the governmental apparatus. I have in mind those states—whether of the Fascist or Communist type—in which a political party under highly centralized guidance seizes power and uses its party machinery to impose discipline upon the governmental bureaucrats. Because of the close affinity of the party bureaucracy to the formal bureaucracy in such states, some students lump the two groups together as a single bureaucracy. In my opinion this obscures a fundamental political issue, and hence I shall use the term "bureaucracy" to refer only to the formal hierarchy of government officials, speaking of all other bureaucracies, whether of corporations, trade unions, churches, or political parties, as "non-bureaucratic" or as "non-governmental bureaucracies."

Development as Differentiation

The phenomenon of development involves a gradual separation of institutionally distinct spheres, the differentiation of separate structures for the wide variety of functions that must be performed in any society.

It is clear that in very traditional or simple societies such differenti-

. . . there is a kind of unreality about the operation of the governmental agencies in India, and any examination of their functioning soon leads to other sources of influence and power." "The Political Heritage of Modern India," in George McT. Kahin, *Major Governments of Asia,* Ithaca, Cornell University Press, 1958, pp. 294-295. This seems like an overstatement—but perhaps it is sufficiently true to support the position taken in this paper.

ation has taken place to an extremely limited extent. A single set of officials or authorities, as in feudalism, may exercise undifferentiated military, political, administrative, religious, and economic functions.

By contrast, a highly developed political system contains a large number of explicitly administrative structures, each specialized for specific purposes: agricultural, transport, regulatory, defense, budgetary, personnel, public relations, planning, etc. Moreover, a set of political structures—parties, elections, parliaments, chief executives, and cabinets—are designed to formulate the rules and pose the targets which the administrative structures then implement.

Undoubtedly the principle of the separation of politics and administration is as much a target for aspiration as a statement of actual conditions in a real government, like that of the United States; but the extent of realization of this separation is marked indeed if one compares it with what prevailed in any traditional or primitive folk society. Moreover, the separation of politics and administration is only one facet of a differentiated society, since both the political and administrative institutions are themselves differentiated from economic, religious, educational, and social structures of a distinct and separate character in the advanced Western societies.

The process of modernization in the developing countries is marked by the progressive creation of formally distinct social structures, adapted from Western models, to which differentiated political and administrative tasks are assigned. But in this process the older institutional base of a traditional society lingers on. Although eroded and embattled, it struggles to remain alive, to retain positions of influence.

We find, then, in the transitional society, a dualistic situation. Formally superimposed institutions patterned after Western models coexist with earlier, indigenous institutions of a traditional type in a complex pattern of heterogeneous overlapping. The new patterns thrive best at the center and in the higher levels of society; the older patterns persist most vigorously at the periphery, in the rural hinterlands and the lower levels of society; but the mixture is everywhere present and produces new forms characteristic of neither the Western nor the traditional institutional systems.[5]

The relative speed of change in the functional sectors of a transitional society also varies. Those sectors in which technology, the purely

[5] Even the most developed societies retain admixtures of traditional elements and are therefore also to some extent "transitional." The differences are not absolute, but in degree and proportions.

instrumental means, predominate are able to change more rapidly than those in which social and personal values are implicated. For this reason it was often in such spheres as military technology, agricultural crops, formal schooling in science, language, and Western learning that innovations were first made in non-Western countries.[6]

In the governmental sphere, this principle means that development in public administration, bureaucratic change, takes place more readily than counterpart changes in politics: technics change more easily than techniques. The reasons are apparent. The initial demand for Western institutions in many non-Western countries was in the military sphere, for defense against an intrusive imperial power. To develop the means of defense, rulers employed foreign military advisers and sent students to European military academies. The costs of modern arms were high, and so in national finance, in taxation, especially in customs, and state monopolies like salt, in budgeting and accounting, transformations were carried out. Defense needs also created a demand for effective control over outlying areas of a traditional realm, and so led to a reorganization of territorial administration, the creation of a Ministry of Interior, recruitment of a career service of district officers, prefects, governors, and a central secretariat to control their operations.[7]

While this proliferation and expansion of bureaucratic machinery was taking place in most of the non-Western countries, no corresponding development of the non-bureaucratic political system occurred. In the independent countries, political leadership was still provided by traditional rulers—as in Siam, Iran, Ethiopia, Japan—although in the

[6] This proposition has been elaborately demonstrated with historical examples by Arnold J. Toynbee. By way of summary he writes, in *The World and the West*, New York, Oxford, 1953, p. 68: "When a travelling culture-ray is diffracted into its component strands—technology, religion, politics, art, and so on—by the resistance of a foreign body social upon which it has impinged, its technological strand is apt to penetrate faster and farther than its religious strand . . . the penetrative power of a strand of cultural radiation is usually in inverse ratio to this strand's cultural value."

Harold Lasswell and Abraham Kaplan distinguish "techniques" from "technics." The former consist of those parts of a technology which belong to the social order, hedged about by sanctions, mores, values; the latter those which are free of such involvements. "Technicalization" refers to a transformation from technique to technic. (*Power and Society*, New Haven, Yale University Press, 1950, p. 51.) In this terminology, the process of modernization has involved technicalization, and change has been more rapid in technics than in techniques.

[7] The general pattern of such transformations is discussed in my article, "Prismatic Society and Financial Administration," *Administrative Science Quarterly*, v, June 1960, espec. pp. 9-16. For a detailed case study of one such transformation, see Walter Vella, *The Impact of the West on Government in Thailand*, Berkeley, University of California Press, 1955. See also E. Herbert Norman, *Japan's Emergence as a Modern State*, New York, Institute of Pacific Relations, 1940. The sequence in areas under colonial rule has been different in important respects, but fundamentally similar.

Japanese case perhaps the greatest success was achieved in establishing new political institutions, a central legislature, political parties, and a cabinet system. This success is, of course, directly relevant to the phenomenal Japanese achievement of industrialization and the greater effectiveness of its governmental institutions as compared to those of other non-Western countries. Even here, however, bureaucratic elements, especially from the armed forces, tended to exercise disproportionate influence in the political structures, notably in the period leading to the Second World War.[8]

In the countries under colonial rule the proposition is even more patently true—at least until recently. Here the colonial administration itself created a bureaucratic apparatus not subject to political control within the dependent territory, so that administrative institutions proliferated while political structures remained embryonic and largely extra-legal, hence unable to relate themselves effectively to control over the bureaucracy. A striking exception was the Philippines under American administration where nationalist opposition groups were quickly given opportunities to share in the conduct of the government. In India, especially after the First World War and the Montagu-Chelmsford reforms, Indian participation in formal politics, notably in provincial government, laid a substantial foundation for the post-independence development of vigorous political institutions. Subsequently in other British dependencies legislative bodies and political parties were permitted, and they began to share in the formation of policy and control over administration. In a somewhat different way, the same has been true, perhaps, in some of the French-controlled territories. Ultimately this legislative experience, plus the ordeal of revolutionary opposition, provided the ex-colonial countries with a stronger political foundation than the countries which never felt an imperial yoke.

In the contemporary era of large-scale technical assistance under international and bi-national programs, we see a continued infusion of external pressure and assistance in the expansion and proliferation of bureaucratic organs, with relatively little attention to the growth of strictly political institutions. The reasons are quite evident. Administration is regarded as a technical matter (technics) subject to foreign, "expert" advice, whereas politics is so closely linked with fundamental

[8] The extent to which postwar, extra-bureaucratic political development in Japan was influenced, directly or indirectly, by the Occupation, will long remain an interesting subject of study.

values and social mores (techniques) that aid would be construed as "intervention."[9]

Moreover, the demand for economic development and modernization impinges directly on agricultural, industrial, public health, and educational spheres in which external assistance is fed directly to segments of the bureaucracy, and only weakly mediated through central political institutions. The foreign experts and advisers, for their part, while competent to deal with technical matters in a variety of program fields, and even the related administrative questions, would scarcely claim any competence to assist in the establishment of new political institutions.

The question naturally arises: what is the relationship between this burgeoning of bureaucratic institutions and the course of political development? The relationship may be examined from two sides: the effect of political weakness on administrative effectiveness,[10] and the consequences of bureaucratic expansion for the political system. In this chapter I shall limit myself to an examination of the latter set of relationships.

My general thesis is that premature or too rapid expansion of the bureaucracy when the political system lags behind tends to inhibit the development of effective politics.[11] A corollary thesis holds that separate political institutions have a better chance to grow if bureaucratic institutions are relatively weak.

[9] Until the last few years it perhaps did not even occur to U.S. policy makers that political development should or could be a goal in overseas programs.

[10] In another paper, "Bureaucracy in Transitional Societies" (mimeo. 1959), I have argued that political weakness has led to administrative ineffectiveness in many of these countries.

[11] A perceptive public administration advisor shrewdly pointed to this problem in the following words: "Efficient administrative machines can be used to prevent as well as to promote development, and much of the effort that it takes to produce the appearance, if not the reality, of improvement in public administration can become, as it has in the Philippines, a means of concealing inability or unwillingness to undertake needed action on other fronts." Malcolm B. Parsons, "Performance Budgeting in the Philippines," *Public Administration Review*, Vol. 17, No. 3, Summer 1957, pp. 173-179.

The view taken here is not, of course, that bureaucrats or bureaucracy are essentially evil monsters, and certainly the need for administrative services which can be performed only by public officials argues for an expansion and improvement, not curtailment, of bureaucracy. The argument is presented, however, that effective administration by bureaucrats is contingent upon the simultaneous growth of extra-bureaucratic institutions capable of maintaining effective control over officials, of keeping them responsible to the formal political authorities, and responsive to the public and clientele interests directly affected by their work. Ideally, such responsibility is to the whole population through democratic processes, but even under totalitarian conditions there must be responsiveness to a party control machine with an extra-bureaucratic power base.

Some historical evidence for this proposition is suggested by a comparison of the history of feudal societies with those in which traditional government had a more bureaucratic basis. An outstanding example of a traditional bureaucratic system was imperial China.[12] Here the elaborate complexity and pervasiveness of an ubiquitous bureaucracy may be related to a notable weakness of autonomous political structures. In modern times it was only on the wreck of the bureaucracy, in a period of war-lordism and administrative anarchy, that political parties were finally able to emerge and lay the basis for a powerful one-party structure capable of re-organizing and controlling the bureaucracy. In a sense, the war-lord period represented a feudalization of Chinese society.

Russian history is parallel to Chinese in this respect. The Czarist bureaucracy left little scope for autonomous politics and revolutionary movements could survive only abroad. The war-caused bureaucratic collapse cleared the ground for a short-lived florescence of free politics, followed by the triumph of a monocratic party.

In the West, autonomous political institutions developed best in countries with a feudal background, where bureaucratic power was weak and fragmented. This was notably true in England. For different reasons—its frontier character, for example—American bureaucracy was also relatively weak and fragmented. In France, despite a long feudal background, the absolute monarchy consolidated national power through a growing bureaucratic apparatus, and this course of development may be related to the continuingly precarious basis of French political life.

But such historical examples are merely suggestive. Rather than explore them in more detail, it may be more fruitful to investigate the inner workings of the political and bureaucratic systems in contemporary transitional societies to see whether or not we can discover some more specific reasons for the suggested relationships. I will examine, in turn, the relation of bureaucracy to party systems, the electorate, legislatures, courts, and executive leadership.

Bureaucracy and the Party System

Let us consider, first, the basis of recruitment to a bureaucracy and its relation to political development. It has become axiomatic in mod-

[12] Karl A. Wittfogel, *Oriental Despotism* New Haven, Yale University Press, 1957, is a comprehensive examination of the history and dynamics of bureaucratic systems.

ern public administration that bureaucrats *ought* to be selected on the basis of universalistic, achievement criteria, best expressed in an examination system; and that employment should be for a career. The pressure of international advisers and the demand for technically qualified personel to staff the program-oriented services of modern government has meant the proliferation in all the developing countries of civil service and personnel systems rooted in the merit and career concepts. Indeed, so deeply engrained are these ideas that even to question their utility is to risk castigation as a heretic and subversive.

Yet the merit system cuts at the root of one of the strongest props of a nascent political party system, namely spoils. Once political parties are strongly established, once the public is widely mobilized for political action, prepared to give volunteer support, and to contribute financially from a broad base of party membership, it is possible to reduce or perhaps even eliminate spoils as an element of support for party activity.

Certainly, if American history can be taken as suggestive, the spoils system played an important part in galvanizing the parties into action. Even today, although national politics and the federal administration has been substantially purged of spoils, a strong residue of spoils appointments still remains. If local politics, on which our party machines rest, were to be deprived of spoils, they might well lose much of their vigor. Without for a moment denying the evils associated with the spoils system, one cannot escape noting the intimate relation between spoils and the growth of political parties.

It is, of course, no easy matter to organize spoils in such a way as to strengthen political parties. A natural tendency exists to use opportunities for patronage appointments and graft through public contracts to favor relatives and friends of individual politicians rather than to reward those who work for a party as an organization. But without official sanction for at least some degree of spoils in the bureaucracy, it is difficult to institutionalize procedures and rules for the use of spoils to reward bona fide party workers.[13]

A second relation of spoils to political growth ought to be considered. No doubt a career bureaucracy of specialists is administratively more capable than a transitory bureaucracy of spoilsmen. But, by the same token, the career bureaucracy can project greater political power

[13] Even the hope of contracts might open sources of finance to opposition parties which would otherwise be doomed to poverty and ineffectiveness.

on its own, resist more successfully the politician's attempts to assert effective control. What is lost in administrative efficiency through spoils may be gained in political development, especially if party patronage can also be used as a lever to gain control over administration.

The existence of a career bureaucracy without coresponding strength in the political institutions does not necessarily lead to administrative effectiveness—as I have argued elsewhere.[14] Without firm political guidance, bureaucrats have weak incentives to provide good service, whatever their formal, pre-entry training and professional qualifications. They tend to use their effective control to safeguard their expedient bureaucratic interests—tenure, seniority rights, fringe benefits, toleration of poor performance, the right to violate official norms—rather than to advance the achievement of program goals. Hence the career, merit bureaucracy in a developing country not only fails to accomplish the administrative goals set for it but also stands in the way of political growth.

Not, of course, that one would want to see a wholesale transformation in developing countries of their present career bureaucracies into spoils. However, it might be that, by judicious selection, a range of positions, a "schedule C," could be declared open for political appointment with a counterpart provision that they should be filled only by persons who meet requirements for service to a winning party.[15]

It is characteristic of a one-party state for the dominant group to eliminate all rivals. The loss for freedom is a gain for political and administrative development in the perverse sense that policy direction is sharpened and bureaucratic performance held to a higher level.

But in a polity shaped by bureaucratic dominance, opposition groups tend to be tolerated, and a ruling party takes shape as a coalition of diverse elements. The ruling coalition lacks coherence or unity—although it may well be the inheritor of a revolutionary tradition from an earlier period of common struggle against foreign rule. It would perhaps be too strong to say that the coalition is formed of elements congenial to the bureaucrats, but at least they are typically ambitious men attracted by the crumbs to be gathered off the tables of the elite, rather than by any hope of creating a better political or social order. In

[14] "Bureaucracy in Transitional Societies," *op.cit.*

[15] Moreover, the needs for technical competence in the twentieth century are undoubtedly greater than they were in the nineteenth. Hence any move to open the door for spoils appointments certainly ought to set minimum standards, and reserve key technical positions for non-partisan recruitment.

a sense they form a sodality of the gentry.[16] Because the distribution of crumbs—"pork," to use the American equivalent—can reach far corners, the coalition, with bureaucratic backing, can usually count on electoral success.

Without the hope of spoils, and with minimal opportunities for penetrating the career services, the opposition parties can attract only the confirmed idealist, the bitterly disappointed, the fanatic, and the maladjusted: all predominantly drawn from the intelligentsia. Moreover, without real hope of an electorial victory and spoils, there is no strong incentive for these hostile fractions to coalesce, to form a unified opposition, nor is there much reason for them to be loyal to a system of government which offers them no hope of rewards. The hostile political fractions then become cults, sectarian, a total way of life, an absorbing preoccupation for the small minorities attracted to them. Addicted to violence and extremism, to poly-functionalism[17]—since they cater to the religious, social, and economic as well as the political interests of their members—they form cancerous growths in the body politic. They serve, also, as the breeding grounds of a one-party dictatorship since, with an appropriate spin of the wheel of fortune, one of them may someday find itself catapulted into power.[18]

In a working democracy the opposition parties help to keep the party in power politically alert and responsible to public demands. The hostile fractions in a bureaucratic polity, although labeled opposition parties, cannot really have this effect. Instead, they undermine the system, weaken the coherence of the ruling party, and strengthen the

[16] The word "gentry" is here used in a technical sense to refer to a "ruling class" whose members base their power primarily on access to bureaucrats or bureaucratic status. Both an aristocracy and a gentry possess wealth (chiefly in land) and power, but an aristocracy's wealth is the source of its power, whereas a gentry's wealth is the fruit of its power. For a perceptive analysis of the most classical instance of a gentry see Chung-li Chang, *The Chinese Gentry*, Seattle, University of Washington Press, 1955.

[17] "Poly-functionalism" may be defined as a condition intermediate between being functionally "diffuse" and functionally "specific." In other words, it serves fewer ends than a traditional family, but many more than a Western-style "association." Elsewhere I have called such poly-functional groups "clects."

[18] Examples of such tightly knit minority "parties" or fractions are described in many works, but their characteristics are often attributed to racial, ethnic, religious, or other local and cultural features rather than to general functional relationships common to most of the "transitional" societies. See, for a good example, Myron Weiner, *Political Parties in India*, Princeton, Princeton University Press, 1957, especially pp. 223-264. Although Indian political development has been outstanding in comparison with most of the other new states, the inability of sectarian opposition parties to form a stable coalition or unified opposition is a major obstacle to further strengthening of democratic politics in India.

relative power of the bureaucracy which may be called on—through police or army—to suppress one or more of the fractions as they resort, in turn, to violence. (In pointing to the role that spoils played in the growth of the party system in the West, I do not mean to suggest that the same course should or will be followed elsewhere—but some functional equivalent must be found if effective party systems are to grow.)

Bureaucracy and the Electorate

It was one of the favorite theses of the colonial regime that political participation ought to begin at the local level. The administration of central government, it was said, ought to be left to the colonial bureaucracy; the development of village, communal, and municipal councils would provide ample opportunity for the political education of the indigenous population. After having mastered the techniques of democratic politics at this level, the population would be prepared to take over a major share in government at the provincial level, ultimately at the national. This theory was also propagated by Sun Yat Sen and the Kuomintang for Nationalist China, and has been tested in recent years in Taiwan.

Strangely enough, nationalist revolutionaries and the intelligentsia of the dependent countries never looked with favor on this thesis. They called it a delaying tactic of imperial rule, and sought to plunge immediately into national politics, by-passing the local level. The same tendency has persisted since independence in the new nations. The dominant elite, having gained control in the center, manipulate the bureaucracy as an instrument of control over local government, giving little more than lip-service to the philosophy of decentralization and local autonomy. One suspects there must be some deep-seated dynamism that moves the ruling groups in a developing country—whether under colonial or native control—to strengthen central bureaucratic administration at the expense of local self-government.

Let us seek clues to this paradox by considering the changes taking place in these countries.

In the former, traditional situation, local affairs were, in fact, largely controlled by local leaders—gentry, notables, petty chiefs, or headmen —and even within the community, the affairs of sub-groupings came under caste, clan, family, and temple control.[19]

[19] For an explicit account of this system in village India, see Bernard S. Cohn, "Some Notes on Law and Change in North India," *Economic Development and Cultural Change,* VIII, October 1959, pp. 79-93. An earlier characterization of the same situation in India is provided by Henry Maine in *Lectures on the Early History of*

The new regimes in developing countries, whether ruled by foreign imperialists or a native intelligentsia, have sought major socio-economic transformations in their societies. In this effort, they uniformly met resistance from traditional leaders and groups at the local levels. Insofar as their modernizing goals were limited, they permitted local affairs to be run in the age-old fashion, but to the extent that they wished to extend the domain and speed of development, they had to seize administrative control and impose change. For a modernizing elite—whether native or foreign—the value of development always outweighs local autonomy.[20]

As, gradually, local populations became enmeshed in the transformation, some among them began to desire the products of the new order, and so the modernizing central leadership discovered new allies in the small community. It then seemed practical to urge local self-government, with the expectation that rural elites, when exercising local autonomy, would continue and finance the very policies desired by the central authorities—the extension of roads and bridges, building of schools, improved sanitation and health measures, more rational agricultural practices, further expansion of the market system. Interestingly, spokesmen of local interests came, in large measure, to accept these targets, but not their costs. Who would pay for change?

Although central governments always imposed some taxes on the rural population, most of the revenue of the new nations comes from the more productive sectors, located in the major urban areas, and from customs revenues imposed on international trade. Hence the cost of local improvements has been largely financed from the center. Indeed, only this ability to pay for modernization enabled national governments to extend the range of their control as far as they have. If the center had merely demanded change, requiring localties to finance their own development, it is doubtful if the modernization of rural hinterlands would have gone as far as it has—limited as that is.

Proposals for more local self-government, however, have met an

Institutions, London, J. Murray, 1893, p. 380. For an account of Chinese local control in the traditional system see Martin Yang, "Former Rural Control in China" (Unpublished manuscript, no date). Even Karl A. Wittfogel, who argues most strongly for the totally despotic character of the traditional bureaucratic system in China, refers to this characteristic local sphere of autonomy as a "beggars' democracy," *op.cit.* pp. 108-125. In feudalistic societies the extent of autonomy for local ruling groups was, of course, even more marked.

[20] The developmental patterns desired by the elite, of course, are typically one-sided—they serve their own economic, political, or national interests more than the interests of the local populations concerned.

impasse, for, while local leaders have been all too willing to manage local improvements, they have been unwilling to finance them. They want the central government to pay for development programs, but not to staff and control them. Naturally, no central regime is willing to turn over its funds for unsupervised use by local authorities. Every bureaucracy insists on maintaining some control over the use of its own money.

By contrast, in the "developed" countries, local self-government, to the extent that it is effective, rests on the ability and willingness of local communities to tax themselves for a substantial part of the services they want. When central funds *are* allocated for use by local authorities, they often involve matching of contributions and, necessarily, some central supervision. Even in developed countries, any programs which are fully financed from the center arc typically run by field offices of central government rather than by autonomous local authorities, even where co-opted grass roots organizations participate in making and implementing policies. The measure of local autonomy in a country is certainly related to the ratio of locally financed and controlled programs to local programs which are centrally financed and controlled. In developed countries this ratio is large; in the developing ones, very low.

The weakness of local self-government in transitional societies means, of course, that the bulk of the citizenry are denied meaningful participation in modern-style politics. Of course, traditional forms of self-rule may persist. Even where local elections are held, they tend to be of limited significance. They may, of course, become the focus of great local excitement, and certainly they can have an impact on the local scene.[21] The question is: to what extent do such elections give the population a significant political experience, i.e., one in which meaningful choices are made. Insofar as effective control of developmental programs are retained—because financed—by field agents of the central bureaucracy, elected local officials lack significant powers of decision making. Their function becomes primarily ceremonial. Electoral contests then determine relative prestige ratings, not program or policy issues. Insofar as any appointments are made by the locally elected officials, purely personal patronage rather than party or program needs are considered. Electoral victory may depend on

[21] See Morris Opler, "Factors of Tradition and Change in a Local Election in Rural India," in Richard L. Park and Irene Tinker, eds., *Leadership and Political Institutions in India*, Princeton, Princeton University Press, 1959, pp. 137-150, for a dramatic case study of the impact of elections on a village community.

who can marshal more of the electorate by mobilizing his kinship alliances, rather than on party commitments to specific policy issues. No doubt in all patronage, personal motives are mixed with policy and program goals—but in significant politics there would have to be at least a minimal concern for issues in the contest and resulting patronage.

For local self-government to be significant as a training ground for national politics, I think it must involve electoral choices between alternative programs for which the voters themselves must pay, at least in part. If one party offers an expanded road and school program at the cost of heavier taxation, and the rival party offers a reduced benefit program with lighter taxation, then the community can make a significant choice. Or, the rival parties may offer different packages of public benefits, undertaking to collect the cost by contrasting tax schedules, in which the burden would fall more heavily upon one group or another in the community. Only in this way can both politician and voter learn the meaning of political choice instead of agitation and demagoguery.

These statements should not leave the impression that in the more developed countries local politics always measure up to this idealized account of effective self-government. However, it is argued here that, relatively speaking, local politics and significant choices by local electorates tend to be more meaningful in the industrialized than in developing countries.[22]

The weakness of local government—at its best—in the more developed countries shows how much room for growth still remains in these societies. It should also be noted that in traditional societies, prior to the impact of industrialization, there often existed a substantial measure of local autonomy, though without the formal machinery and ideology of modern self-government.

The most typical situation in the transitional societies, as I see it, weakens political institutions and strengthens bureaucratic. The more local communities have their appetites whetted by the "demonstration effect" for improvements which can be paid for only by the central government, the more unrealistic local politics becomes, and the more extended the central bureaucratic apparatus.

Even the goals of economic development are not necessarily advanced under these conditions. If local schools are built, for example,

[22] See, in this connection, A. B. Lewis, "Local Self-Government: a Key to National Economic Advancement and Political Stability," *Philippine Journal of Public Administration*, Vol. 2, No. 1, January 1958, pp. 54-57.

the most energetic and intelligent young people to graduate leave for higher schools in market centers and universities in the urban areas, where they seek posts in the expanding bureaucracy. The frailty of local politics and development means there is little to hold the most able. Instead of contributing to the vigorous growth of a locality, centrally based development deprives it of its best potential leadership, leaving a residue of partially educated men and women whose level of aspirations has risen more rapidly than their capabilities. Hence the bitterness and frustration of local politics increases without compensating successes in self-realization and achievement.

No doubt similar phenomena can be found in the more developed countries, but there are significant differences of degree. Since the over-all level of education is higher in the developed countries, those who remain in rural areas, while less schooled than the urbanites, nevertheless reach a higher level of training than the village folk of transitional societies. Rural families in developed countries, moreover, are typically closer in terms of communication and transportation to secondary urban centers than are the villagers of non-industrialized countries.

The speed of social transformation also means that the gulf between traditional- and modern-minded people—the unschooled and the schooled—is greater in transitional than in industrial societies. This not only reinforces the motivation for those with schooling to leave their uncongenial, rural homes; it also tends to block the application, by those who remain, of skills and values they acquired in school. The level of effective modern education of rural youth does not equal the level of formal schooling they may have enjoyed, and this differential is probably much greater in the newly developing than in the more developed countries.

It may be that political development, at least toward a democratic type of political action, can be attained only at the cost of slower economic and social development. It is often said that authoritarianism can force economic development at a more rapid rate than democracy. Less familiar is the corollary that efforts to speed the rate of economic development may lead toward bureaucratic authoritarianism.

Is there any way to invigorate local self-government, both as a way of providing significant political experience to large sectors of the population, and also as a way to limit the expansion of central bureaucracies through proliferating field offices, and so to make it easier for national political institutions to gain control over the governmental apparatus?

A look at our own political history may provide a clue of value. A great battle in modern American reform has been the struggle to replace the long ballot with a short ballot. Yet even today our communities must elect a surprisingly long list of candidates. Just as spoils in American politics has fulfilled a key political function, so the retention of the long ballot has, perhaps, a functional significance, and need not be explained only by social inertia.

The arguments for the short ballot resemble those for the merit system: they both enhance administrative efficiency. When a congeries of independently elected officials begin to get in each others' way, administrative confusion results. Moreover, with the expansion in size of jurisdictions and the increasingly technical character of administrative work, even in local government, citizens find themselves choosing among strangers, with little knowledge of their abilities or character. They begin to cast a party-line ballot. Significant choice passes to the machine leaders.

But do these arguments apply to the new nations, especially in rural communities? Here, just as in matters of recruitment, the impulse of foreign experts is to recommend what we have found useful in America rather than to inquire whether our doctrine offers a solution to another's problems. Thus, the tendency has uniformly been to simplify the new voter's problems by asking him to choose only one name—i.e., the short ballot. As in national administration, the proposal is made to put all positions—at least formally—on a merit basis.

It is assumed that the political inexperience of new voters in a peasant population makes it impossible for them to choose candidates for several offices, but easy to choose for one. Are these assumptions valid? Have they ever been tested? I do know that where a single executive is elected in local government, say as a mayor or headman, and is authorized to appoint other local officials—policemen, clerks, peons—he typically makes the appointments on a narrow, nepotistic basis, antithetic both to good administration and political development.

Consider, as an alternative, a proposal to fill several local offices by election. Each would be carefully chosen to concern matters in which the community takes a real interest. Indeed, a study of rural communities in transitional societies will show, I believe, that several positions of local importance are now, and have traditionally been, filled by community choice. These may involve supervision of local religious activities and fiestas, maintenance of market places, conduct of traditional schools, etc. An American equivalent might be the volunteer fire department, or the proverbial dog catcher. Although age, generation, and family play an important part in such choices, I doubt if local headmen in traditional societies, for example, are recruited by hereditary right as much as we often assume. The position has often involved as many onerous duties as special privileges, and so may not be universally desired. Indeed, it may sometimes be necessary to press a man to induce him to accept the post.[23]

As to the ability of voters in a rural community to choose, I suggest that in the rural setting every potential candidate is already well known to his neighbors. He would scarcely need publicity. Moreover, if the office to which a man were seeking election carried simple and concrete duties, our village voters could readily judge which of the candidates would be most likely to do a good job. The compensation would necessarily be minimal and the duties heavy enough so that the honor and income of office would be barely enough to attract candidates without tempting profiteers or opportunists. The community, knowing the duties of each office, could easily judge how well they had been performed. Terms would be short, and rotation in office frequent. The compensation would be raised by local levies, probably in a form directly related to the benefits provided.

Obviously the limited scope of activities that could be carried out under such a scheme would impose a brake on development. An outside administrator, with more formal training and experience, could no doubt spur economic development more rapidly, but not political development. The community might choose to use its resources for purposes scarcely judged important by the central authorities. In an example from Furnivall, they might buy electric power to illuminate a pagoda rather than to provide household lighting.

Another component of the short ballot complex is the secret ballot. In an advanced society, where public office carries high prestige and power, the secret ballot is indispensable to honest elections. But in a peasant, largely illiterate community, the secret ballot is pretty meaningless. Moreover, it limits the possible complexity of voting, since pictorial symbols or equivalent devices must be used to represent the

[23] For further light on this question in the Chinese case see Hsiao-tung Fei, *Peasant Life in China*, New York, Dutton, 1939. The more autonomous the local structure, as in a tribal or feudalistic system, the greater the benefits of "chieftainship," and correspondingly the greater the likelihood of recruitment by strict hereditary right. However, we are then dealing less with "local government" than with small-scale, independent government. See also Robert E. Ward, "The Socio-Political Role of the Buraku (hamlet) in Japan," *American Political Science Review*, XLV, December 1951, pp. 1,025-1,040.

candidates or their parties. Hence the short ballot is linked with illiteracy and secrecy. Even under these conditions, secrecy can scarcely be maintained, and one often finds unanimous balloting, at least among sub-groups of the community.[24]

If votes are being cast for a plurality of positions, and if the competition for any one of them is not keen, it is doubtful that secrecy would add much to the value of the election. The desirability of the chief local position itself declines if other positions are filled by election instead of appointment. If the requirement of secrecy is lifted, the technical problems of recording votes are, of course, greatly simplified.

As communities gained experience in political participation and office holding, they might advance to a more sophisticated pattern of political action—including shorter and secret ballots. It would not be difficult to design a sequence of charters or options for local self-government, each more advanced and privileged status—linked with more central help—being accompanied by higher requirements for local self-financing. Determination of the pattern for local government in each community would then be made by referendum, rather than by fiat at the center. Urban centers could start with the more advanced patterns. Thus incentives for political growth would be linked with opportunities for increased participation. If the goal of policy is political experience and development rather than a sudden leap to the most sophisticated but perhaps unattainable political techniques, then one might think experimentation along such lines as I have suggested should be encouraged. However, the price might be slower economic development and less bureaucratic expansion. In effect, the number of local appointments to field offices of central agencies would be reduced, the work being transferred to locally elected and financed officials. This would be resisted by the bureaucracy and central administration, but it would be a gain for local self-government, and hence for political development.

This is not an argument for the immediate grant of local self-government to rural communities. Quite the contrary, I think such a policy would lead to stagnation in rural areas.[25] The first stages of economic development in a traditional society probably require the infusion of an external stimulus, if not from abroad, then from a central or regional

[24] See, for example, R. Ward, *op.cit.*, pp. 1,028-1,036.

[25] An argument to support this view is presented in my essay, "Economic Development and Local Administration: a Study in Circular Causation," *Philippine Journal of Public Administration*, Vol. 3, No. 1, January 1959, pp. 86-146.

government. Once well started, however, it appears that further growth in a locality may be accelerated by the reduction or withdrawal of central controls, especially if this devolutionary transfer of authority can be carried out in such a way as to stimulate local initiative and responsibility. Ultimately balanced political development requires not only the emergence of institutions strong enough to control bureaucracy, but probably also a territorial reallocation of power from central to regional and local levels.

Bureaucracy and Interest Groups

One of the pillars of political action in advanced countries is the "association," through which functionally specific interests are articulated and communicated to decision-making centers. Although interaction between associations and government takes place through bureaucracy as well as through political institutions, the dominant mode tends to be with political party and legislative organs. The importance of interest groups in politics has only recently been recognized, but research on the subject has by now produced a substantial literature.

These same associations also play a key role in policy implementation or rule application. The literature of public administration has made this process a subject of study to some extent. Thereby an unfortunate dichotomy has arisen: interest groups as originators of policy proposals, in the "input" process, are regarded as playing a political role, whereas when these same groups participate in policy execution they are regarded as playing an "output" or administrative role. The activities of the groups are thus viewed from two perspectives, but not as a whole. However arbitrary the dichotomy in the context of advanced societies, in the study of developing countries it has a particularly confusing effect.

If by political development we refer primarily to the process of democratization, the growth of popular control over government, then perhaps this distinction is useful. But in another sense political development refers to the process of politicization: increasing participation or involvement of the citizen in state activities, in power calculations, and consequences. In this sense the regimentation of citizens by the rulers is as much politicization as the initiation by citizens of demands upon the rulers. From this point of view, a modern totalitarian regime, with its total political regimentation, is as much politicized as a fully democratic regime. Both differ from the traditional polity in which, to a great extent, the mass of the subject population is little involved in political decisions, largely ignored by the rulers, and hence predominantly indifferent to their actions.

In the process of development the citizenry becomes progressively involved in matters of state, i.e., politicized. The primary vehicle or "transmission belt"—to use Joseph Stalin's colorful phrase—for such politicization is the interest group. However, in view of its dual role as instrument for popular regimentation as well as for public control, both should be considered in a full analysis of this process. The politicization of a population by its progressive involvement in groups organized by the state as transmission belts for policy implementation is a political matter, even if we label it an administrative development. But the fact that we do label such developments administrative blinds us to their political significance.

In contemporary developing countries, bureaucratic agencies are set up to implement new programs oriented to the concept of the welfare state, intimately affecting much of the population. Ranging from public health, educational, and agricultural services to community development, these programs necessitate a massive coordination of the population. To carry them out, officials must mobilize those affected in many special-interest groups. Educational programs, for example, may require something like the parent-teachers' association to promote family cooperation for the school attendance of children, and to prepare even more ambitious programs of community or fundamental education. Agricultural programs require the creation of farmers' associations to transmit new techniques, improved seeds, fertilizers, and farm equipment. Women's groups and "4-H clubs" carry innovations into the home. Cooperatives handle credit and marketing problems. Community health units facilitate the dissemination of new drugs, police water supplies, enforce immunization drives, and sponsor clean-up campaigns or the installation of privies. Capping all the special interest groups are community development programs which call for the creation of all-purpose councils to plan and implement, under government supervision, a wide range of activities.

Without questioning the utility of these programs, I wish merely to note their political implications. In almost every case, the creation of these interest groups follows a bureaucratic initiative. They are not a spontaneous product of citizen demand in response to felt needs. The groups extend the reach of the bureaucracy, providing it with transmission belts through which total mobilization can, protentially, be achieved. Hence the growth of state-sponsored interest groups augments bureaucratic control, without necessarily strengthening any centers of autonomous political power capable of bringing bureaucratic machines under popular control. In other words, this process leads to political development in the sense of politicization, but not democratization. Quite the reverse, for here we see how accelerated economic and social development contributes to bureaucratic power, and lays the foundation for totalitarianism, weakening the prospects for democratic control over government.

There are many reasons for the weakness of autonomous interest group formation in the developing countries. One is simply the propensity for bureaucrats to be suspicious of autonomous groups outside their control. It is easier to deal with an orderly, unified system, especially if it has been set up to meet their specifications. Hence groups that start to organize on their own, or with external support—from a foreign government, foundation, or religious body—are viewed with hostility and, if not actually suppressed, are at least given little cooperation as compared with officially sponsored groups.

A second reason is financial. In poor countries the cost of voluntary organization can scarcely be obtained from members who barely get enough to meet their own minimum living needs. After collecting dues and contributions, voluntary groups find their resources still hopelessly inadequate. They must succumb to necessity, and either content themselves with a largely ineffective marginal existence or go, hat in hand, to government, begging financial help. The same dynamism that cripples local government weakens voluntary associations that rely on governmental subventions for existence. Inevitably the government takes control as a condition of granting assistance, and so the would-be private group becomes another transmission belt.

Thirdly, the leadership for modernization comes predominantly from the intelligentsia, an intellectual class schooled in the concepts and aspirations of the "modern" world. This leadership, as I have indicated above, tends to be funneled into the central cities, leaving the hinterland starved of modern leadership. Into this partial vacuum the bureaucracy steps, the local representatives of central government being, by and large, the most modern and best educated persons in their districts. The result, quite naturally, is that in rural areas the bureaucratic leaders of interest groups usually dominate by relative superiority of talent and training the private citizens with whom they deal.[26]

No doubt governmentally sponsored associations sometimes become

[26] For a case study illustrating these and other factors responsible for the weakness of interest groups see my "Interest and Clientele Groups," in Joseph L. Sutton, ed., *Problems of Politics and Administration in Thailand,* Bloomington, Ind., Institute of Training for Public Service, Indiana University, 1962, pp. 153-192.

strong enough to declare their independence of the officials who brought them into being. This might happen in some developing countries. There seems no reason to assume that it would necessarily happen, and under totalitarian conditions mass organizations have remained passive tools of autocracy for a considerable time. Perhaps steps could be taken, as a matter of policy, to offer incentives for the achievement of autonomy by such associations. In any event, the degree of independence of private associations may be determined only by empirical investigation in each case. It is not something which can be assumed a priori.

Urban Interests and Pariah Entrepreneurship

It may be suggested that the situation differs in the urban areas where modern commerce and industry and the non-bureaucratic intelligentsia are concentrated. Here also the example and influence of other countries is strongest. Yet even here powerful factors operate to inhibit the effective political influence of interest groups. Moreover, a new set of factors show up which give a perverse twist to the relation between interest groups, bureaucrats, and politics.

It is at the urban core of government that the processes of development—especially commercial and industrial development—come to focus in the new states. These activities depend for their success upon the enterprise and skill of entrepreneurs who combine the various factors of production and control the process of distribution.

Here is a class which surely has the need, knowledge, and financial capacity to support interest groups—chambers of commerce, trade associations—through which to exercise pressure for the control of government. At least, this has been the history of the democratic developed countries, and an analogy is suggested for the developing areas. However, close inspection suggests risks in this analogy.

All too frequently, the private entrepreneurial class in the new nations suffers from lack of formal access to the political process. Its members are often drawn from a marginal group—racially, ethnically, or religiously—or of alien origin. Discriminatory laws and regulations are imposed against them. In applying these rules, members of the bureaucracy often exploit their power to penalize the entrepreneur unless he rewards them for overlooking infractions of the law.

Hence there develops a symbiotic relationship of "antagonistic cooperation" between government official and private entrepreneur. The official supplements his inadequate official income. In exchange, the businessman is permitted to violate regulations.

Why does such a situation continue? Characteristically in the new nations those who can acquire status, prestige, and power through land or official positions do so in preference to a business career—both because of the low status and the risks involved. Hence only those who cannot follow the preferred occupations choose entrepreneurship. Thus a self-selecting mechanism restricts the entrepreneurial role to members of marginal or alien communities.

How can the obvious evils of this situation be overcome? Apparently only by imposing the rule of law upon bureaucrats, requiring them to enforce the law impartially. At the same time, a legal structure is needed which favors the development of commerce and industry by protecting property and contract rights, imposing non-confiscatory tax rates, opening economic opportunities to all candidates without regard to particularistic criteria, etc. But how can such a regime be established? Clearly a prerequisite is the achievement of sufficient political power by the business community to impose responsibility and favorable laws upon the bureaucrats.

One cannot realistically expect uncontrolled bureaucrats to impose this kind of regime upon themselves when it is clearly against their immediate interests. Moreover, it is in the bureaucratic interest to prevent the creation of any groups in the business community that have a chance of gaining enough power to impose the rule of law upon government. Because entrepreneurs have the greatest potential for group formation, the bureaucrats use their sharpest weapons against them.

A classic bureaucratic weapon designed to meet the threat of entrepreneurial organization is to set up a counter-organization based on would-be entrepreneurs drawn from the dominant community. This counter-organization then seeks policies that discriminate in favor of their members against those of the established entrepreneurial community. Thus political support is mobilized for a continuation of basically anti-entrepreneurial policies, without risking the formation of a strong new entrepreneurial class, since the members of the favored group find it easier to convert their special privileges into cash on the black market than to learn a difficult business and do the hard work required.

Another bureaucratic tactic to counter the threat of growing power in an entrepreneurial community is to establish a public sector, to organize a mixed economy and use public enterprise to set the pace, regulate, or fill the gaps of the private sector. In practice, of course, these governmental undertakings are often run at a loss, requiring subvention from public funds. This enables them to compete with the private entrepreneur, and limit his growth or even force him into bankruptcy. Enterprises which can be readily controlled, especially where the state is the main customer or supplier, are turned into government monopolies, and the private sector eliminated. If a state enterprise is profitable, there may be an irresistible temptation to use official pressure—taxes, regulations, licenses, exchange control—to hamper, perhaps destroy, the competing private enterprises. As a result of these maneuvers, the private entrepreneur is forced to the wall, losing his capacity to organize effective political power. So long as he continues to buy protection from the bureaucracy, he is permitted to survive as a marginal or pariah entrepreneur, but not as a politically influential class.

As to the public sector, it is scarcely possible to expect efficient and honest management of enterprises run by a bureaucracy that is not under political control. Who will prevent officials vested with authority to run public enterprises from dipping into the till, from squeezing the state just as they squeeze the private businessman? If conspicuous peculation is eliminated, more inconspicuous forms abound. Where effective political control over a bureaucracy is lacking, there is no institutional means for preventing bureaucrats from exploiting their power position at the expense of both private entrepreneurs and public enterprise. (Under such conditions, of course, to expect a public sector to remedy the developmental weakness of the private sector is delusory.)

The condition described is scarcely one of equilibrium. Only a relatively passive bureaucracy, drugged by its own self-indulgence, can perpetuate its own regime indefinitely. With the growing pressure of international opinion and example, and the impact of bi-lateral and multi-lateral aid programs, systems of bureaucratic power are energized and thrown on the defensive. They must create more and more mass organizations as instruments for program administration. But the dissemination of organizational skills is the sowing of dragon's teeth. If the entrepreneurial community could organize power effectively, it might impose a middle class revolution on the government, establish the rule of law, create a favorable environment for economic development and administrative efficiency by means of a democratically controlled bureaucracy. This has been the history of the Western democracies, and to a considerable extent also of Japan. The pre-condition, however, was a relatively weak bureaucracy and a socially entrenched burgher class.

The alternative course of events is, unfortunately, more likely. In the inter-organizational struggle reaped from the Cadmean harvest, victory is more likely to go to a mass-movement led by a political fraction under the leadership of an embittered intelligentsia group of the type described above under political parties. Such a group will build a new Thebes. It may embrace the doctrines of international Communism or, perhaps more likely, it will espouse a national-chauvinistic ideology, fascistic and zenophobic. Among the chief targets of its hatred will be the pariah entrepreneurial community, and so its program will almost surely involve destruction of this group and expansion of state power through nationalization and government monopoly of industrial development.[27] It will, of course, bring the bureaucracy under control. But the price of this kind of political development is social disaster—the loss of individual freedom and the risk of international war.

Bureaucracy and the Legislature

With but few exceptions the history of parliamentarism in the new nations is without lustre. In many, as in Egypt, military regimes have suspended representative institutions altogether, after a period of noisy but ineffective experimentation with legislative bodies and ephemeral constitutions. "Guided democracy" is Sukarno's alternative to parliamentary politics after a period of unsuccessful trial and error. Turkey, Pakistan, Burma, the Sudan, many Latin American states fit this pattern. Since the revolution of 1932, Thailand has tried a variety of parliamentary systems and constitutions, but they have uniformly been pliant tools for the group in power. Since the first republic in 1912 the Chinese have followed parliamentarism as a will-o'-the-wisp.

Notable exceptions have been India and the Philippines. In both instances several decades of vigorous parliamentary experience under colonial rule preceded independence,[28] and the political habits established during dependency have stood these nations in good stead since obtaining their freedom. But even in these exceptional cases, closer scrutiny reveals serious weaknesses in parliamentary power.

The case of Japan is instructive for, with all its weaknesses, the Diet

[27] For an extremely suggestive discussion of the emergence of mass-movement, single party regimes, see Robert C. Tucker, "Towards a Comparative Politics of Movement-Regimes," *American Political Science Review*, LV, June 1961, pp. 281-289. Anti-semitism and the myth of racial superiority were the typical signs of such a path in European political development.

[28] Plus, in the Philippine case, the energetic parliamentarism of the Malolos Constitution during the transition period to American rule.

has shown itself, despite black periods and long-term deficiencies, a notably effective legislative body. Perhaps the astonishing success of Japan's industrialization drive and the relative efficiency of its bureaucracy is not unrelated to this fact.

If we ask for an explanation of the miserable record of parliamentary institutions in the new nations, we may look for an answer to the range of parliamentary sub-structures already examined in this chapter. A parliament or congress is not just an assembly to pass resolutions. As a supreme decision-making body for a polity, it must effectively represent its constituencies and have weapons with which to command the obedience of the governmental apparatus, the bureaucracy.

Among the supports of the legislative body are the electoral system, political parties, and interest groups. Unless the assemblymen have been chosen through an electoral process in which significant choices are registered, they cannot have a meaningful popular mandate. Each or all of the candidates for election may be equally unrepresentative and unresponsive to political demands. If picked by a ruling clique under plebiscitary conditions, or chosen in a popularity contest or bandwagon-hopping situation where electoral divisions reflect no significant political differences, what and whom do they represent?

As I have suggested above, electoral ineffectiveness largely prevails in the new nations—with some notable exceptions—and the extension of bureaucratic control into local government is one of the reasons for this ineffectiveness. Hence the parliamentary system is undermined at its foundations in most of the new nations, and bureaucratic patterns can be identified as a key element in this weakness.

Unless the political party system is vigorous, assemblies lack an indispensable means of organizing their activities. It is true, I believe, that a strong one-party system can achieve effective control over a bureaucracy. In such a case, however, formally elected parliaments become puppets of the party. If a collegial process does take place in top-level decision making, it is likely to be in a central or political committee of the party rather than in the formal legislature.

One requisite of effective parliamentary life seems to be a vigorous and loyal opposition. But as we have seen, the lack of an effectively organized spoils system in the bureaucracy is one of the reasons why opposition parties are unlikely to be either loyal or unified. Dissident elements take on a sectarian character, and only those driven by fanatical devotion to an alternative political formula are willing, as we have seen, to devote the time and energy needed for the creation of opposition parties or fractions. Such parties undermine the legislative process. They use their positions to disrupt legislation rather than to modify it. Their fanaticism prevents unity as well as loyalty in their opposition. Here again, a fundamental basis of parliamentary vigor is lacking, and one of the contributory factors is the merit and personal patronage system in a bureaucracy oriented to careerism and seniority.

The third pillar of parliamentary vigor is a proliferation of associational interest groups, prepared to speak on behalf of the myriad functional interests of a complex society. Here again, as we have already seen, the weakness of such associations in the new nations, and especially the tendency for bureaucrats to control what associations do exist, deprives legislatures of a major source of independent ideas for policy and for critique of the bureaucracy's performance. In a functioning democracy it is in the bureaucrat's interest to encourage access of interest groups to the legislator—assuming that the bureaucrat's program is already a response, in some degree, to the demands made by the interest groups. In the new nations, by contrast, it is often against the bureaucrat's interest for such a liaison to occur unless the groups are securely under bureaucratic control. Independent interest groups might criticize administrative performance, providing legislators with ammunition for use in establishing legislative supremacy.

But all of these factors are indirect. They involve legislative weaknesses based on non-bureaucratic factors in which bureaucratic factors play an indirect part. In addition, there are reasons for legislative weakness which can be directly attributed to the interaction of bureaucrats with parliamentary bodies. These include matters of *finance* and *policy*.

Finance

The traditional basis of parliamentary power in the Western democracies was control over the purse. The need of rulers to seek authorization for new taxes from the representatives of the burghers forced them to limit administrative arbitrariness as a quid pro quo.

In the new nations, under the doctrine that democracy is enhanced by universal suffrage, the vote has been given to a mass public, composed largely of poor peasants and workers who lack any resources for tax purposes. Conversely, those elements of the population which have the most wealth, and hence provide the most promising base for public revenues, are legislatively impotent or disfranchised. The business community in the new states is often composed largely of aliens who, as a matter of constitutional law, are deprived of the vote. Others are drawn from marginal or pariah communities within the state, as we have seen, and lack political power. Even if they can vote, they are swamped in electoral districts where the majority community naturally wins.

Decisions about taxation, therefore, largely involve schedules under which those formally represented in parliament impose taxes upon elements in the population which are not represented.

When those who might pay but are not effectively represented in parliament are called upon to supply the lion's share of the public revenues, it is not surprising that they resist payment—on a principle familiar to all Americans: "no taxation without representation." When revenue officers approach them suggesting that they pay their taxes, they not unexpectedly employ their sharp wits to find ways to evade. One of the most effective ways is to share part of their wealth with the tax collector in order to avoid sharing more of their wealth with the state. Since the bureaucrats are notably underpaid everywhere, and especially in poor countries whose public services expand more rapidly than their national income, they have powerful economic motives for collusion.

To the extent that this situation prevails, bureaucrats even have expedient reasons for encouraging legislatures to impose penalizing taxes and regulations upon the business community. Such measures do not strike at the apparent interests of the majority of the constituents, and they provide a basis for bureaucratic self-enrichment.

A second financial factor has become increasingly important in recent years, namely the extent to which the revenues of many new nations come from external sources. To cite an extreme case, Viet Nam, "more than half of the governmental revenues are directly contributed by American aid, and most of the rest comes from taxes levied on the U.S.-supported commercial import program."[29] While extreme, this situation is typical of many countries, ranging from Korea and Formosa around the Asian rimland to some of the new African countries at the opposite end. The oil-rich lands of the Middle East similarly depend on their royalties.

Insofar as foreign financing prevails, it is apparent that legislatures must again act without effective power. They may adopt budgets ex-

[29] John D. Montgomery, "Political Dimensions of Foreign Aid," in Ralph Braibanti and J. J. Spengler, eds., *Tradition, Values and Socio-Economic Development*, Durham, N.C., Duke University Press, 1961, p. 266. Montgomery goes on to note that only 15,000 of the total population of 12.3 million paid income taxes, of whom 12,500 were military and civil bureaucrats paying only a nominal amount.

pressing a hope for foreign aid, but are scarcely in a position to make the decisive judgment. Even a country like India, which is more nearly self-supporting than most, has adopted development programs which call for substantial foreign subventions. Success in obtaining these funds depends, in large measure, upon bureaucratic rather than political performance. It is the national planners and the diplomatic representatives of the new nations, the bureau chiefs and counterparts who negotiate with their opposite numbers in the USOM's, international banks, and specialized agency headquarters, who influence the extent and type of foreign aid received. Thus external financing serves, effectively, to reinforce bureaucratic control at the expense of legislative authority.

A third major source of revenue in many developing countries consists of income from state monopolies, lotteries, and other income-producing ventures. Here again, elected representatives have only marginal influence. It is perhaps true that these programs rest upon prior legislative authorization—although even this is not always the case—but, once established, such programs become relatively autonomous bureaucratic empires. The scale of revenue depends upon the economics of the operation, and the skill with which they are managed. Even those which lose money have revenues of their own which can be manipulated to political effect.

If the legislatures are deeply handicapped in their efforts to control public revenues as contrasted with bureaucratic influence in these processes, the same is true of budgetary and expenditures controls. Although data are weak, I do not fear refutation of the statement that in very few of the new nations do the budgetary systems actually used offer legislatures an effective instrument for control over the bureaucracy. Generally old-fashioned types of line-item budget, without much distinction between capital and current expense items, are furnished by the administration. Such budgets may enable the legislators to play bureaucratic politics, supporting their friends in the bureaucracy and punishing their enemies, but they give them no effective weapon for influencing the content and conduct of governmental work. Even where a performance budget has been established, as in the Philippines, it remains largely unimplemented while the legislators cling to the particularistic advantages that the old, line-item budget gives them. The bureaucrats are probably also reluctant to implement the performance budget because in the process they would be compelled to reveal crucial defects in their own performance.

An extreme case, but perhaps illustrative, is that of Bolivia, whose budget office and procedures were created in 1928 in accordance with recommendations of the American Kemmerer mission. A more recent American expert writes of the current state of the Bolivian budget, which includes national and local government expenditures, that it:

". . . is prepared by an office that has twelve employees, half of whom have only stenographic and clerical duties. No distinction between capital and current expenses is indicated. Functionally, expenses are broken down by agency into 'Salaries' and 'Other Expenses.' Thus six 'professionals' prepare a budget of better than thirty million dollars . . .

". . . only once in the last thirty-one years has the Congress approved the budget prior to the beginning of the fiscal year. Phrased differently, in thirty of the last thirty-one years, the fiscal year has been at least two-thirds over before the Congress has approved the budget."[30]

In the matter of expenditures control, legislatures in developed systems rely upon some form of auditing which enables them to judge the extent to which funds have been spent in accord with the law. Here again, although the documentation is inadequate, I suggest that in most of the new nations legislatures lack effective machinery for auditing administrative spending. Even where, under technical assistance, new tools of accounting and auditing have been provided, they have been largely conceived for management purposes, and hence have perhaps strengthened the internal control system of the bureaucracy, the office of president or prime minister, but not the legislature as a political control center.

No doubt these financial powers of legislative bodies are not highly effective in many of the industrially developed countries themselves. It may also be that such procedures as the line-item budget served a useful purpose in helping legislators achieve effective control over bureaucrats, just as the spoils system did. However, these techniques can also be used for personal patronage and favoritism as well as to strengthen party organization. Thus the crucial test is not so much the particular techniques of financial control used—important as they may be—as the way or the purposes for which they are employed.

The position taken here is that, whatever the weaknesses of parliamentary financial controls in developed countries, they have been strong enough to give legislatures substantial leverage in their struggle to impose the rule of law and political policy upon officials. The same

[30] Allan R. Richards, *Administration—Bolivia and the United States*, Albuquerque, University of New Mexico, 1961, pp. 11-12.

cannot be said of most legislative assemblies in the developing countries. But without such controls, how can these bodies hope to formulate enforceable laws?

Policy

Needless to say, financial control is only one of the supports of legislative effectiveness. Even a good budgetary system—such as may exist in the Philippines, Viet Nam, or India—does not by itself assure parliamentary control over the bureaucracy. If the political party, electoral and associational base is weak, parliaments will still be weak. An effective legislature must also be able to formulate clear and mutually compatible laws. The strange fruit of legislative necrosis is to be found in the realm of policy making.

According to our conventional model, adoption by congress or parliament of a law gives it legitimacy in the popular mind, enforceability through the courts, and a binding authority upon the bureaucracy charged with its implementation. The source of this legitimacy is a political formula, or constitution, on which substantial consensus prevails throughout the population.

Where bureaucrats exercise considerable power, as in most of the new nations, they may themselves take the initiative in seeking legislative authorization for what they wish to do. When such legislation is adopted it does not represent political control over the bureaucracy so much as bureaucratic manipulation of the symbols of legitimacy.

A major source and symptom of weakness for legislatures is even more potent, namely the phenomenon of formalism. Laws on the statute books of the new nations are often not well enforced by the public bureaucracy. The prevalence of corruption in a country is an index of the extent to which bureaucrats are able and willing to violate laws or permit their violation. Bribes may be given to induce officials to perform their duties—as when granting licenses and permits—as well as to overlook non-performance.

Funds and personnel for the enforcement of a law may not be available, so that laws remain dead letters for lack of resources to implement them.

The lack of adequate information—related to the weakness of interest groups—means that legislation is often inherently unenforceable because of technical defects in draftsmanship and unfounded assumptions as well as mutually contradictory norms.

To the extent that formalism prevails in legislation, laws enacted by legislatures cannot be regarded as real decisions. Rather, we have a process of pseudo rule making. It may, of course, be difficult for legislators to tell whether a particular bill or amendment would or would not be enforceable. Moreover, it must be acutely frustrating for a conscientious legislator to learn that hours of work invested in the preparation of a law were of no avail because of non- or mal-administration. Such frustration leads to a variety of responses, including an apathetic disillusionment with the legislative process and hence diversion of interest to other more rewarding types of activity, including direct intervention in administrative processes, appointments, contracts, etc. Another response might be to superimpose new, more drastic laws upon the old, unenforced ones, as though a more severe piece of formalistic legislation could correct failures in a milder rule on the same subject. Other legislators, in disgust, become apathetic and turn to private pleasures. The cynicism and hostility of the political fractions toward the whole legislative process is increased.

Here it ought to be acknowledged that one of the forces which aggravates legislative formalism is foreign pressure, precisely because international agencies and aid programs tend to be preoccupied with technical matters of economic development and administration rather than the crucial problem of political development. For example, pressure is applied to the new nations to live up to international standards in a wide variety of fields—health, labor, statistics, legal standards, civil rights, etc. Indeed, model codes are often drafted and adopted by international bodies to provide a guide for developing countries. The governments concerned find that their international status can be improved at relatively little cost merely by putting such laws on their statute books. The prevalence of legal formalism makes it easy to do this since, if laws are widely disregarded, one can virtually adopt any law that will satisfy the foreign critics without having to worry about enforcement. Thus international standards may weaken legislative vigor without securing the hoped-for substantive effects. Such model legislation, indeed, may contribute to administrative corruption and popular disgust with governmental processes. Examples could be cited from laws setting minimum wage standards and regulating labor relations, providing for the control of drugs and food, for sanitary inspection and quarantine of pests.

At a different level, under the impact of technical assistance programs, reorganization plans may be submitted to institutionalize a distinction between line and staff, to decentralize a government agency, establish a position classification scheme, or organize an "O & M" program. Legislation and even formal bureaucratic reorganization to meet these recommendations—including, especially, expansion of the number of governmental units and positions—often follows. But the advisers responsible are subsequently discouraged to find that the anticipated benefits do not result. Indeed, the costs of government may be increased, but not the output of services. The changes have merely rearranged the formalistic surface structures, but not seriously affected the underlying social and power structure which actually determines bureaucratic action.

It is often thought that a constitution provides the major foundation for effective parliamentary rule. However, we might gain a different perspective on this relationship if we tried reversing it, i.e., suggesting that effective legislative performance validates a constitution. When a legislature is unable to make enforceable decisions, public disillusionment and apathy turns against the constitution as well as the assembly. When the constitution itself rests upon a precarious base of support, reflecting the wishes of a small intelligentsia or aristocratic group, it has to legitimate itself by growing success. Without such success, the system is discredited and easily overthrown. Consensus fails to develop.

It would seem that in the transitional societies, with but few exceptions—the Philippines, India, Meiji Japan—parliamentary structures have proved expensive but largely fruitless. They can be given life only by a middle-class revolution capable of imposing the rule of law on the bureaucracy. If a mass-movement regime is installed, they will be totally crushed as a useless decoration. So long as bureaucratic rule predominates, the assembly may be tolerated as an additional crutch to give some color of legitimacy to the administration, but it will not be permitted to exercise the substance of political power.

Parliamentary and constitutional theory in the advanced countries assumes that legislative action provides an effective lever for the control of bureaucratic behavior. My analysis leads me to conclude that this theory works only under special conditions, and that the formal creation of an elected and voting assembly by no means assures its success.

Bureaucracy and the Courts

In the politically advanced countries the courts play a key role in helping to keep bureaucrats under control. The process of rule adjudication, considered as one of the output functions of the governmental system, is designed not only to test specific applications of public policy but to restrain bureaucrats from arbitrary exercise of their power.

In the Common Law countries a single autonomous judicial system carries out this administrative law function in addition to its general jurisdiction over civil and criminal cases. Because of this institutional separation, the tendency in American thought has been to classify administrative law with other legal processes and to segregate its study in the law schools. As a consequence, the relevance of judicial institutions to politics is often overlooked. Yet a more comprehensive view of government cannot ignore the fact that, by helping to keep bureaucrats responsible, courts can play a decisive political role. In so doing, the judiciary assists the legislature by holding the administrative arm to a full and fair implementation of politically determined policies.

In the Civil Law countries, by contrast, a system of administrative courts within the bureaucracy is vested with special responsibility for enforcing bureaucratic accountability to the law as declared by the legislature. The result, however, has been that, in these countries, administrative law is identified with public administration, and its political significance is again neglected.

It is when we turn to a study of the new nations that we suddenly become aware of the crucial role of the courts in maintaining the viability of a politically developed system. Yet even here it is possible to miss the significance of the relationship because, of all the governmental institutions imported from the West, the judicial ones appear, on the surface, to have been most successful. Everywhere modern codes have been formally adopted, new style courts established, and an incredible outpouring of lawyers generated.

Yet the consequences of this new institutionalization have been perversely different from those originally intended. By and large, judicial structures have protected the interests of Westerners. Under colonial rule, the connection between imperialism and legal safeguards was apparent. But even those countries which never experienced direct foreign rule were induced to adopt Western legal codes in order to abolish the hated system of extraterritoriality. What mattered for the powers, of course, was not so much the formal adoption of the codes as their application to the interests of Western residents and business. For the rest, it was easier to permit customary or "adat" law to persist. Neither the customary law nor the new codes provided effective restraints upon arbitrary bureaucratic conduct, except in matters affecting the privileged interests of Westerners and, increasingly, a gentry class of indigenous power-holders.

In traditional societies the formal machinery for imposing limits on bureaucratic excesses was feeble. Even so, it did provide some safeguards, as in the famous Chinese censorate. But the main restrictions were furnished by the technological limits of administrative machinery. A law of diminishing returns served to keep bureaucratic rapacity within bounds since, beyond a somewhat flexible line, the cost of further exactions exceeded the returns. Traditional officials also recognized the futility of "killing the goose that laid the golden eggs."

But in transitional societies these factors no longer operate in the same way. The new administrative technology, based on functional specialization (differentiation, refraction) gives the official keener weapons with which to subject the population to control. Among these weapons one of the most useful is precisely the judicial system. Instead of serving as an instrument to safeguard the public interest by holding bureaucrats to their official responsibility, it reinforces administrative abuse.

One of the most famous examples of a highly developed judicial system introduced under Western auspices is that of British India. Here, to cite but one example, a class of officials known as *tahsīldārs* was authorized by the British to act as their agents in local revenue and land administration. According to a student of the subject in the Benares region,

"Since the *tahsīldār* controlled the land records and the revenue records and knew well which estates were profitable to their owners because they were underassessed, and since they knew all the *legal maneuvers* and also had great illegal powers, they were able to acquire large estates in a very short time. . . .

"The Indian officials were in the best position to understand and manipulate the new situation. They knew *how the courts worked*, because they worked in them. They knew which estates were valuable, because they kept the records and collected the taxes. Many of them acquired capital quickly through bribery and corruption. It became a simple matter for them *legally* or fraudulently to bring to auction those estates which were valuable because underassessed, and to acquire them for themselves."[31] (Italics added.)

[31] Bernard S. Cohn, "The Initial British Impact on India; A Case Study of the Benares Region," *Journal of Asian Studies*, XIX, August 1960, pp. 426, 429.

Elsewhere we read:

"A wealthy Thakur who went to court looked forward to not just one quick case, but to a series of cases, appeals, adjournments, and counter appeals, through which a poorer competitor could be ruined. Since British procedure and justice appeared capricious to the Indians, someone with a bad case was as prone to go to court as someone with a good case. The standard was not the justice of his case, but his ability to outlast his opponents. It became a mark of pride among the Thakurs to outwit an opponent through the use of the courts and law, and the prestige of a family, was tied to its success as a litigant and its ability to ruin its competitors in court."[32]

Elsewhere courts were usually less effective than in India, and correspondingly they proved less efficacious for bureaucrats in quest of wealth and power. Unfortunately we lack systematic data on the social and political consequences of the judicial establishment in the new nations. To a considerable extent the literature that is available is concerned with the technical success of the courts in following procedures and enforcing laws which bear primarily upon the administered population, not on the administrators themselves.

To the extent that European observers have been interested in the consequences of judicial action, they have naturally been most sensitive to the consequences for their own interests as businessmen, missionaries, and foreign service officers. Insofar as this foreign sector has been the beneficiary of special privilege—the more so when we consider that Europeans also understood best how to manipulate legal procedures first designed in the West—the courts in the new nations have been given high marks for excellence. This helps to account for the singular reputation for effective adaptation to local conditions that the judicial systems of the new states enjoy. Evaluated in the abstract—judicial procedure for the sake of judicial procedure—it may be true, as suggested above, that the new law codes and courts have been uniquely successful. But judged by their political consequences, the courts would appear to have heightened bureaucratic irresponsibility rather than reduced it.

If we search for reasons to explain the limitations of judicial action in the new nations, we might start by reflecting on the history of legal institutions in the West. On the continent, for example, the *parlement* was once a predominently judicial body with substantial power. The

[32] Bernard S. Cohn, "Some Notes on Law and Change in North India," *op.cit.*, p. 93.

present *Conseil d'état* rests on a long tradition of autonomous collegial judicial bodies. Even here, however, the imposition of bureaucratic responsibility could be attained only by the ascent to power of the *Conseil* as the key managerial body of the whole French bureaucracy.[33] Similarly in England, the courts, especially the King's Justice, grew out of a long tradition of autonomous legal institutions based on customary law.

But courts would scarcely be effective without strong social backing. In its modern development judicial power has had the powerful support of a middle class which used the courts to safeguard its property and contract rights against official intervention and arbitrary penalization. The lawyers have also formed a powerful autonomous guild in Western society. By their solidarity and ubiquitous penetration of government, especially as politicians in the legislatures, they have helped to write enforceable laws and sustain their implementation. Even the lawyers in bureaucratic administration have worked as much to secure the enforcement of the laws as to find loopholes for their evasion.

By contrast, the courts in the new nations have lacked this kind of non-bureaucratic support. By default, they have been exploited by bureaucrats to give a factitious legitimacy to their abuse of power. In so doing, the popular view of judicial institutions has turned from an initial apprehension of the courts as an alien institution to fear and hostility generated by experience of their actual operations. The entrepreneurs, normally the bulwark of judicial power in the developed areas, have become the worst enemies of the courts in countries where their very survival as a class depends upon their ability to violate formal governmental regulations. For them, resort to law courts can bring only disaster. The lawyers, too, have scarcely developed as an autonomous group. Rather, they have sold themselves as panders to the gentry and bureaucracy.

Because of the paucity of the literature exploring these relationships —and the preoccupation of comparative law with the formal aspects of judicial and legal development whenever it ventures outside familiar Western grounds—I cannot go farther than to propose the foregoing observations as a set of hypotheses. Whether field research will sustain or demolish them, I submit that here is another subject worthy of study. If my surmise turns out to be correct, we will discover that

[33] See a discussion of this phenomenon in Alfred Diamant, "The French Administrative System," in William Siffin, ed., *Toward the Comparative Study of Public Administration,* Bloomington, Indiana University Press, 1957, pp. 199-203.

the courts and codes of the new states, instead of helping to vitalize a developing political structure, have undermined its foundations and sapped its vitality by catering to, rather than containing, arbitrary exercise of bureaucratic power.

Bureaucracy and the Chief Executive

The central controlling structure of bureaucratic authority is the chief executive. He is, in one sense, the highest bureaucrat, if we conceive of the bureaucracy as a hierarchy of graded authority. But in order for him to control the bureaucratic system, the executive needs a power base outside the bureaucracy itself. Otherwise he becomes a prisoner of his own bureaucracy. Consequently we find that chief executives either have, or strive for, extra-bureaucratic sources of power which enable them to consolidate their role as manager of the bureaucracy.

In the developed political systems of the Western democracies this non-bureaucratic power base is provided through the electoral and party system. He is either directly elected, as in presidential systems, or indirectly chosen, as in parliamentary regimes. The political party, of course, provides an apparatus for relating the executive to his constituency, both mobilizing support and helping to guide him. Thus the bureaucrats know that, in accepting the direction of the executive, they are not merely obeying a man but, through him, implementing their responsibility to the public and the state.

In totalitarian systems the electoral principle is vitiated, but the party system becomes enlarged as a compensation. Through the ruling party, as a control system, not only is the power base of the executive established, but he is provided with a complex and ubiquitous apparatus through which to bring the bureaucracy under his direction.

By contrast, traditional systems of bureaucratic government involve a sacred sanction whereby the ruler, a king or emperor, is crowned with a divine mandate. Hence his exercise of control over the bureaucracy is backed by religious authority, since anyone who questions his edicts does so at the risk of supernatural punishment—outcasting or excommunication.

Normally the power of traditional rulers is also backed by kin-based control institutions. In Asian empires and kingdoms this often took the form of an enlarged royal family, including marriage alliances with influential families. Such families generated many princes to whom controlling positions could be assigned. Since the maintenance of their special privileges depended on their ascribed status as members of the royal family, they could be counted on to cooperate in supporting the ruler as against commoner bureaucrats, recruited on a more achieved basis. Finally, the princesses of the royal family could be given in marriage to key families, and thereby further kin-based loyalties brought to the support of dynastic control over the bureaucracy.

I cannot enumerate all the institutional bases of royal or imperial control over traditional bureaucracies, nor classify the many variations in historical systems, but perhaps enough has been said to show that traditional rulers were able to invoke extra-bureaucratic sources of power to maintain their supremacy over the administrative apparatus.[34]

In contemporary transitional societies—at various stages of development—the sacred and kin-based sanctions of traditional monarchic rule have been undermined, and new sources of executive power based on party and electoral systems are but weakly instituted. Hence the rulers find themselves in a precarious power position, the more so because simultaneously the processes of modernization have led to a proliferation of specialized bureaucratic structures and to great increases in the size and scope of public bureaucracies.

We may classify the transitional societies with respect to the base of executive authority into three categories or, perhaps better, three sets ranged on a scale from the most traditional to the most modern.

At one end of the scale we might place countries in which traditional rulerships have survived with greatest strength to the present day. At the other extreme are governments in which new political institutions of a Western type have been most securely established. Midway on this scale are a group of countries in which traditional rulers have been overthrown or gravely compromised, and new institutions but weakly established. The chief executives rely heavily on charismatic leadership, violence, and whatever color of legitimacy they can squeeze from the fragments of any old and new political institutions allowed to exist.

In the first category we would include the more remote and inaccessible countries which, for one reason or another, escaped colonial rule, including Ethiopia, Afghanistan, Saudi Arabia, Yemen, Iran, and Thailand. To these countries should be added a number of protector-

[34] For further discussion of traditional bureaucratic polities and the relations between the bureaucracy and "head of state," see S. N. Eisenstadt, "Political Struggle in Bureaucratic Societies," *World Politics*, IX, October 1956, pp. 15-36; and *idem*, "Internal Contradictions in Bureaucratic Polities." *Comparative Studies in Society and History*, I, October 1948, pp. 58-75.

ates or regimes under indirect rule, where monarchies have survived the transition to independence. Examples are Malaya, Laos, Cambodia, Jordan, Morocco, Kuwait, Libya. African chieftains, especially in more remote areas, also retain their sacred aura, though under growing attack.

The residual basis in custom and religion, however, has been enough to give these monarchs—or the men acting in their name, whether called viziers or prime ministers—a significant power base for the control of the bureaucracy.

An outstanding example of such traditional power was King Chulalongkorn of late-nineteenth-century Siam who brought about an astonishing transformation of the bureaucratic system. But even here the very process of transformation cut the roots of the monarch's sacred authority, and by 1932 the absolute monarchy in Siam fell a victim to resurgent bureaucratic power. The princes were ousted from key positions in the government service by a revolution conducted by military and civil bureaucrats, and a constitutional monarchy was promulgated.

The regime of Mussaddig in Iran revealed the serious weakness of the Shah's position, but his successful comeback shows the continuing strength of the Iranian monarchy, or perhaps of its present incumbent.

An exceptional case is that of the Japanese Emperor, who became the focal authority for the modernization of Japan in the Meiji Restoration. But the essence of the Restoration was the overthrow of the Shogunate, which had usurped the imperial authority, and so the new regime became strongly identified with the process of modernization. Moreover, because the Emperor exercised primarily legitimizing authority rather than active control, his position remained strong, even growing in prestige until defeat in the Second World War. Now, even in Japan, constitutionalism prevails, and the Emperor has been humbled from a divine to a symbolic status. The Japanese example—and, indeed, the British case, itself—suggests the possibility of evolving a modern democratic polity within the chrysalis of a fossilized monarchy.

The countries at the other end of the scale are fewer in number, and include those territories formerly under direct colonial administration —especially by the industrially advanced powers—where the traditional basis of royal power was largely destroyed and Western political institutions were most strongly established. The disastrous attempt of the French to base a regime in Viet Nam on the discredited authority of the Emperor Bao Dai—despite the continuing vitality of lower-level, traditional institutions in Northern and Central Viet Nam—and the comparable Japanese experiment in Manchukuo with the last scion of the Manchu dynasty, Henry Pu-yi, illustrate the collapse of the traditional rulership. Another example is the paralysis of the princes in the Indian Native States immediately after independence.

Perhaps the best examples of vigorous Western-style constitutional politics can be found in India and the Philippines, where, as we have seen, party, electoral system, and legislatures have combined to give the executive substantial non-bureaucratic support. Here the supportive role of a declining monarchy was provided by a foreign imperium—perhaps a functional equivalent—during the birth of the democratic polity.

The third group, the intermediate situations, includes many of the semi-colonial states, those in which full control by a modernizing industrial empire was not established, but yet the impact of industrial imperialism was sharply felt. The degree of independence and the degree of colonial rule, of course, varied.

China is probably the most outstanding instance. But Turkey, Egypt, and the larger Arab states are also illustrative. Here the traditional monarchy collapsed, although at different times, ranging from the downfall of the Manchus in 1911 to the elimination of the Egyptian and Iraqi kings in 1952 and 1958, respectively. On the ashes of the monarchies, or during the decades of their decline, constitutional parliamentary and electoral systems with political parties came into existence. But by and large they proved completely ineffective and became as widely discredited as the monarchies themselves. Hence a power vacuum arose into which the warlord and dictator emerged as a personal or charismatic leader.

For charisma is a third possible legitimating principle, but the weakest of all because attached to a mortal man. Upon his death there is no way of automatically perpetuating the rule. Traditionally, pure sacred charisma could be institutionalized, in Max Weber's terms, by the establishment of a hereditary dynasty. But today personal charisma has to be institutionalized in modern ways, namely through party and electoral systems. Of these two, it is easier to establish a mass-movement party as the focus of control than to create a viable electoral system.

We can, therefore, vaguely discern two likely patterns of development in this intermediate category—the semi-colonial states with charismatic leadership—those in which charisma is poorly or not at all institutionalized; and those in which a mass-movement, single party system arises. Here the prospects for evolution of a democratic polity are faint.

Under charismatic rule the leader seeks to gain control over the bureaucracy through projecting an image of himself as the savior or hero who leads his people through a time of troubles to independence, progress, and power. The new media of communication made available by modern technology help him to project his image at mass meetings, over the radio and through motion pictures. His picture is everywhere apparent, larger than life. His name is invoked in cheers and rituals. By one means or another the public and the bureaucracy are conditioned to accept his will as their own. Thus the leader seeks—with varying degrees of success—to bring the governmental apparatus under his control.

Often he also tries to put on whatever shreds of legitimacy can be pulled out of both traditional monarchic and new parliamentary-electoral-party structures. A puppet king is called upon to confer a sacred mandate on the leader by royal proclamation, and a puppet parliament is enjoined to name him prime minister. Recent Thai history affords several examples. Where one or both of these formal institutions has been too much discredited, they may be discarded, as happened in Nasser's Egypt. Alternatively, one or the other may be used by itself, as "President" Sukarno has done in Indonesia.

Unfortunately, personality changes and age weakens. The charismatic leader begins to lose his charm. His authority is undermined. Syngman Rhee, at first unquestioned national hero for the Koreans, became, at the end, a villain. Chiang Kai-shek, who never quite attained true charismatic stature, lost disastrously until the Taiwan refuge made it possible for him to rescue a few remnants of his former aura.

Even more disastrous to the charismatic regime is the sequel to the leader's death. Who will take his place? How can a new leader be found, or how can an institutional basis for choosing the executive be created? If not, a successor may grasp the penumbra of power, holding in weak hands the charismatic umbrella of his predecessor. Gradually the bureaucrats become more and more unruly, impatient, or apathetic. Governmental administration declines, and inter-bureaucratic rivalries sharpen. The leader is reduced to playing one bureaucratic agency or clique off against another just to keep his precarious title.

A characteristic sequel, under these conditions, is the seizure of power by the military bureaucracy, or rather by a clique of military officers who appoint themselves to positions of authority over the civilian bureaucracy and name one of their members as permanent or temporary leader. Many Latin American, Middle Eastern, and Southeast Asian countries have witnessed this sequence. An early modern example was Yuan Shih Kai, commander of the new army created to defend the declining Manchu power. He became the first president of the Chinese Republic, and shortly thereafter named himself first emperor of a new but illusory dynasty.

In this sequence of military coup after coup we see the nadir of executive authority and the supremacy of bureaucratic power—military or civil. After each coup, the military leaders appointed to run civilian departments gradually become captives of their own subordinates, and converted from officers to officials. Hence the triumph of the military group is by sudden violence; of the civil group by slow penetration. But the essence of politics becomes intra-bureaucratic struggle, a pathetic denouement for the charade of charismatic politics.

Perhaps aware of this fact, some military juntas have tried to create a mass base for their power, and so have turned to the creation of a party or movement from the top. The Egyptian National Union seems to be one of the most successful efforts of this kind.

But perhaps more often the mass movement arises outside the government and the bureaucracy, in one of the opposition political fractions created by an embittered intelligentsia, men caught in the cross-fire of native tradition and foreign learning, who seek a new ideological as well as power base for restructuring a fractured social and political order. Once they have found a way to capture mass support, and when the existing regime totters, about to collapse, they strike, bringing the shaky superstructure down in ruins.

The bureaucracy may then be drastically reshaped, members of the new regime put in key positions, placed as political commissars to control the older bureaucrats, or as spies in strategic positions for reporting on the performance and loyalty of hold-over officials. The leader of the mass movement becomes a new charismatic leader, but he now has the basic advantage of a large party or movement base for his control over the bureaucracy: mortal man reborn as immortal party. The Chinese and Vietnamese Communists illustrate this sequence in the East, perhaps Castro's Cuba in the West.

The rise of the mass-movement regime appears to provide one road for an escape from the political weakness of unsubstantial charisma to the disastrous power of totalitarianism. The alternative pattern, of course, requires an invigorated parliamentary and open party system, resting on free elections and autonomous interest groups to provide the basis for executive power legitimated by effective constitutionalism. So far, it is hard to find any examples where such a development is likely to occur in the semi-colonial group of countries, at least if no basic changes in international pressures can be anticipated.

Conclusion

The Western countries evolved their political institutions, in a sense, independently. There were, of course, cross-influences within Western society, and it would be wrong to suggest that the development of American, or British, or French politics was fully autonomous. But at least the growth patterns for Western politics, as a whole, were autonomous as compared with the dynamics of change in the new nations. We have seen, before our eyes and in the space of scarcely more than a hundred years, a series of fundamental transformations in the non-Western countries. In many instances the transformation was rudely launched under direct colonial administration by a Western power; in other instances as a response to the challenge of Western power but, even then, with the help of Western advisers and Western-trained native leaders.

More pervasive, perhaps, than the impact of Western politics has been the thrust of the industrial revolution and the new science-based technology which has transformed the economic basis of traditional societies, substituting the market and a cash nexus for a framework of custom, seriously undermining religious and social systems, attacking the basis of individual security and identity.

A typical byproduct of this transformation has been the expansion and proliferation of bureaucrcay. This expansion has been both a conscious result of efforts to reform administration, and an indirect consequence of program-oriented efforts to modernize education, agriculture, transportation and communications, national defense and diplomacy: to consolidate territorial administration. The recent popularity of economic development has simply intensified these trends.

Characteristically, however, neither Western advisers nor the leaders of the new nations were equally concerned with the bases of political power or the requisites for political development. They assumed that bureaucrats would passively serve, or could be induced to serve, the political authorities, and that no particular difficulty would arise in establishing political control. At most, they expected that the mere creation by fiat of a democratic constitution, the establishment of electoral procedures, the seating of a parliament, and the organization of one or more political parties would do the trick. Only recently have we begun to see more clearly how shallow was this reasoning, and how much more there is to the operation of an effective political system than its mere political forms.

However, despite this growing intellectual recognition, we have not translated these insights into practical policy. By and large American foreign policy goals—and the goals of international agencies—are expressed in technical, programmatic, and economic terms. Even the writing on non-economic factors in development largely reflects a preoccupation with the impact of these factors on the course of *economic* development. The result is that the actual character of conscious international programs—public and private—and the economic and religious activities which have indirect consequences for the new nations, all tend to reinforce historic trends which contribute to bureaucratic proliferation but weaken the bases for democratic control over politics. At most they contribute, indirectly, to the rise of political fractions and mass-movement parties—authoritarian types of political development.

Not only is there limited recognition of the problem of political development in Western lands, but even in the countries concerned the whole subject is swathed in confusion. Explanations for the difficulties encountered are sought, I believe, in every direction but the most relevant ones. It is perhaps assumed that, if the level of literacy and mass education were to rise, then political institutions would be invigorated. Alternatively, if economic development takes place, these problems will be solved. Perhaps the difficulties arise from foreign intervention and imperialism, and so independence is looked upon as a panacea.

The result of such shallow analysis is that programs are undertaken which aggravate the very ills most feared. Public health and famine control measures—designed from the most admirable motives—have produced a population explosion which threatens to cancel out whatever gains in living standards might have been achieved by urgent and painful efforts to spur economic development. At the same time, new medical and health agencies are added to the proliferating growth of bureaucracy. With rare exceptions, the problems of reducing birth rates and strengthening political institutions—the urgently necessary countervailing measures for the reduction in mortality—receive no attention.

Another example: few will question the desirability of education, and so mass literacy and free compulsory schooling are pushed with massive vigor in the new nations. Combined with other developments in the new technologies of transport and communications, the result is explosive social mobilization, the sudden entry of new populations into political participation. Unfortunately, assimilation cannot proceed as rapidly, and little enough attention is given to the need for bringing the newly mobilized into community with the elite. Yet this is precisely one of the most acute problems of political development. Failure means the rise of separatist movements, demands for local autonomy, and partition. The catastrophic collapse of colonialism in Africa, following by only a decade its collapse in Asia, is only one sign of the effect of social differentiation among the mobilizing populations. The next stage is partitionist movements within the new states, following the India-Pakistan pattern. The strength of linguistic sub-nationalisms in India already augurs darkly for the future. The Congolese chaos suggests the strength of fissiparous forces about which we shall hear much in the years ahead. Yet the internationally encouraged mania for educational development and the spread of the mass media is scarcely counter-balanced by pressures for political assimilation. We blithely support self-determination and independence, reckless of the Pandora's box that is being opened. Nor is there recognition of how the growing educational, transportation, and communications bureaucracies add to the difficulty of creating viable political institutions.

If soundly conceived programs for political development are to be launched, I believe they must be based on much deeper insight into the interrelationships between factors operative in the transitional societies. In this chapter I have tried to cast a shadow of doubt on some of the clichés used to rationalize our present international policies and programs.

It may appear to some that in discussing such practices as spoils and the long ballot I have, in effect, been arguing that transitional societies must go through the same stages of growth as those experienced by the West. This was not my intention, for the new technology and the international system, with its resources of international trade, foreign assistance and stimulus, basically changes the circumstances under which development takes place today.

My chief concern is that the developmental problems of the new states should be examined in their own terms, and not as possible arenas for the importation of methods and solutions which have proved useful to other countries facing a different set of problems. It is just as fallacious to think that transitional countries can or should take over intact the latest political and administrative techniques of the most developed countries, as to think that they should go through the same stages of change as were experienced in the eighteenth or nineteenth century by the Western nations.

However, just because developmental sequences elsewhere may be different from those of the West is no reason for assuming that these polities can escape the necessity for building viable political institutions—whether democratic or despotic—to control their burgeoning bureaucracies, nor that such institutions can be built without using some functional equivalents for the means by which the growth of effective political institutions in the West took place.

It is certainly too early to say—before much more substantive research has been done—that any of the suggestions offered here ought to be made the basis for action. However, I do think enough is clear to indicate that political development is itself a fundamental requisite for a better life, for the world and the people of the new nations, and that progress in public administration and economic growth will not automatically promote political development. Moreover, although many factors are surely involved in the phenomena of political development, among them one of the most crucial, and, therefore, one which we ought to study with increasing intensity, is the role of bureaucracy.

CHAPTER 6

Levels of Economic Performance and Bureaucratic Structures[1]

BERT F. HOSELITZ

THE purpose of this chapter is to examine in what way some current views on political modernization, e.g., those proposed by Gabriel A. Almond in the introductory chapter to *The Politics of Developing Areas*, can be meaningfully applied to a concrete problem, in particular the analysis of the interrelations between levels of economic performance of different societies and the bureaucratic structures which they create for themselves. Among various possible ways of carrying out an exercise of this kind, I propose to start with a brief examination of the model of a social system from which Almond's concepts and the relations posited by him are derived and to develop more explicitly the generalized interrelations between levels of output and bureaucratic structure, attempting at the same time to present whatever empirical validation for these relationships can be found.

It will be recalled that it is Almond's purpose to describe a political system in its most general structural and functional aspects and to identify those forms of social action which, regardless of what level of economic performance and social complexity has been reached, are characteristic manifestations of the political needs of any society.[2] The model which Almond develops is derived from a more general model of social action systems originally presented by Talcott Parsons and his associates.[3] It may be useful to present here once more those features of this model which are of special relevance for our discussion.

[1] This paper was written while I was holding a John Simon Guggenheim Memorial Fellowship. I wish to express my gratitude to the officers of the Foundation for having afforded me the time for research and reflection which made possible the writing of this paper. I also wish to express my indebtedness to S. N. Eisenstadt and to Neil Smelser, who have made valuable comments on an earlier draft of this paper. I have greatly profited from their suggestions, but I am alone responsible for any blemishes which remain.

[2] Gabriel A. Almond, "A Functional Approach to Comparative Politics," in Gabriel A. Almond and James S. Coleman, eds., *The Politics of Developing Areas*, Princeton, Princeton University Press, 1960, pp. 3-64.

[3] The model was first developed in Talcott Parsons, Robert F. Bales, and Edward A. Shils, *Working Papers in the Theory of Action*, Glencoe, Ill., The Free Press, 1953, pp. 163ff. It was elaborated in later writings of Parsons, e.g., the book jointly

I

The model is based ultimately on the observation and ordering of a set of empirical data among which we may identify as the most elementary units a series of socially relevant actions. These actions may be ordered into a series of sub-systems of social action, each of which is normally bounded and tends to maintain the boundaries within which action relevant to the system occurs. As we shall see later, this postulate focuses attention upon certain social institutions which are the central points around which each of the boundary-maintaining action systems cluster. In more general terms, we may classify socially relevant actions into four groups which are customarily designated as the latency sector, the integrative sector, the goal-gratification sector, and the adaptive sector.

Actions in the first of these sectors have as their main objective the maintenance of cultural patterns and their transmission from generation to generation, as well as their internalization in the individuals born into a culture. The major institutions around which pattern-maintaining actions cluster are the family and other more extended kinship groups, the school and other groups of persons of similar age who stand normally in close face-to-face relation to one another. Among institutions in this sector which accommodate and through which are transmitted the more highly formalized expression of social values and basic beliefs are religious communities and other groups concerned with the high esthetic, literary, and philosophical tradition of a society.

In what follows we will be relatively little concerned with the institutions primarily located within the pattern maintenance set of action since we will focus our primary attention upon social relations which occur in relatively large and complex societies in which secondary and tertiary social relationships, rather than primary ones, prevail. However, to the extent to which such processes as socialization are of interest, the function of institutions in the latency sector are obvious. These points will be brought out in the later course of this chapter. On the whole, however, we will assume that the problem of pattern-maintenance is "solved" in the societies with which we deal and that

written with Neil J. Smelser, *Economy and Society*, Glencoe, Ill., The Free Press, 1956, and other works. The statement of the problem in the *Working Papers* is the freshest and most adequate for our purposes and we will build on the model presented there. This will also make superfluous repeated citations, since the materials on which the argument in this section is based may be found in the work mentioned.

none is in a crisis situation in which its cultural cohesion and the continuity of its basic values are in question. In accordance with this view we stipulate the latency of this process of pattern maintenance, i.e., though it goes on as a continuing process it poses no major problems for the societies under examination. It is routinized and, from the point of view of the society as a whole, is of subordinate significance, though it may be of fundamental importance within the social system of a given family or other small group.

The next set of social actions for which we find a common group of institutions is that which deals with the integrative needs of a society. Since—as already stated—we are concerned in this chapter chiefly with entire large societies, e.g., nations or similar entities, the major set of integrative actions are those which are associated with determining membership within the society as a whole and the relations between the members and groups of members among one another. This problem is crucial on a level of nationhood, especially in periods when new nations are formed, when a previously colonial country gains independence, or when—as a result of war and other upheavals—a new political entity develops. Integrative needs were paramount, for example, in the immediate post-independence period of most ex-colonial countries or—to choose an example which lies farther back in history—during the formative stage of Western nations, at a time when the territorial organizations of European populations were created after the cessation of barbarian invasions in the tenth and eleventh centuries. We shall see later that these periods in which integrative needs predominate call for particular administrative adjustments and are characterized by peculiar motivations on the part of individuals forming the cadres of the bureaucratic apparatus.

Though integrative needs are most powerful during periods when a nation is formed, they do not subside completely at other times. For even if membership criteria in a national society have once been established, there still remain problems of the rights and obligations of the various members towards one another. An example of a problem of national integration, for example, is the linguistic controversy in India; another even more telling example is the prevalence of various centrifugal tendencies in the outer provinces of Indonesia. Any reshuffling of the relative power positions of different groups may provoke new integrative problems, and the potentially very far-reaching changes in social prestige provoked by economic growth and political modernization produce new problems in the system of social action in the integrative sector. Since political modernization almost by definition is associated with profound changes in the prestige and power position of different social groups, the integrative needs created by this process will have their reflection in the functioning of the bureaucracy.

The third major sector of social action is that directed towards the meeting of systemic goals. All social action is goal-oriented, i.e., it is designed to meet some proximate or more distant objective. But much of social action and many institutions around which action sets cluster are concerned only with goals of limited scope, i.e., goals of a person or a more or less small group of persons. The institutions located within the goal-gratification sector of social action are concerned with the meeting of the goals of the system as a whole, i.e., of all members of the system. In short, the major institutions through which goal-gratification activity is mediated are political institutions, and the bureaucracy is of course located within this sector. In other words, the bureaucratic apparatus is one of the institutions through which goal-gratification activity is performed; it is a central focus around which clusters a whole series of social actions designed to meet systemic goals.

We shall see later that certain actions of bureaucracies in economically little developed countries are often directed, not towards the fulfillment of systemic goals, but rather of private or sectional goals. Moreover, not all social action performed with the objective of systemic goal gratification actually meets this objective. In other words, certain actors attempting to perform acts which are destined to meet the goals of the community as a whole will often antagonize certain members of the community and engage in acts which are opposed by some. In still more concrete terms, the head of a state, acting for his nation, may engage in action which is considered by a portion of his constituents as being opposed to the best interests of the nation. But we are not concerned here with whether or not any actions taken within the goal-gratification sub-sector of a social action system meet with opposition. Even if they meet with opposition they are usually binding on those who oppose them. For example, a treaty concluded by the proper authorities of a nation also binds those who may have opposed the treaty and those who may continue to regard it as pernicious and contrary to the best interests, i.e., the systemic goals, of their country.

The importance of the goal-gratification sector for our analysis should be obvious, since we are concerned with political modernization and, in particular, with an institution functioning primarily within this sector. One of the principal problems around which much of the subsequent discussion will turn is the interaction between an institution located primarily within the goal-gratification sector and developments partly within the same sector, but outside the institution (political modernization) and associated developments in another, the adaptive sector (economic growth).

This observation has brought us to the fourth sub-sector of social action, the adaptive sector. By adaptive social action we understand that kind of behavior which is designed to manipulate or transform the non-human environment in such a way as to make it more appropriate for the ends of the members of the society. In particular, adaptive behavior is concerned with production of goods and services and related activities subsidiary to production. The typical institution in the adaptive sector is the firm, the business enterprise, or whatever other productive agency there exists in a given society. It is quite clear that in modern societies, and especially in societies in which the achievement of higher levels of economic performance has been made a systemic goal, there exists strong interaction between the adaptive and the goal-gratification sectors. This interaction may be observed in two ways, depending upon whether we have in mind an ideally "autonomous" or an ideally "induced" system of economic growth.[4] In the first case there is a series of inputs passing from the adaptive to the goal-gratification sector, designed to bring about legislation and administrative prescriptions which will become the outputs of this sector, but which will aid in the better performance of adaptive social action. In the case of induced growth, outputs will emerge from the goal-gratification sector—in the form of economic programs, plans, etc.—and be transmitted to the institutions located within the adaptive sector, the outputs of which, in turn, will, in part, become inputs of the goal-gratification sector in the form of raw materials, finished goods, and services destined to meet the systemic goals of the national society. These interrelations between different institutions located in different action sub-systems need not be reciprocal, i.e., the input-output mechanism is not one which corresponds to a market exchange. Also, the output of the goal-gratification sector may issue from one institution within it and a related input may be destined for another. For ex-

[4] For the distinction between autonomous and induced patterns of economic growth, see Bert F. Hoselitz, *Sociological Aspects of Economic Growth,* Glencoe, Ill., The Free Press, 1960, pp. 97ff.

ample, the economic plan may emanate from a part of the civil bureaucracy, but the corresponding inputs to the goal-gratification sector may be destined for use by the military.

We will be primarily concerned in what follows with the integrative, goal-gratification, and adaptive sub-systems. But each sub-system may itself be treated as a four-sector system, and each institution located within the action-sphere of any sub-system may also be so regarded. This may easily be explained as follows: we have seen earlier that social institutions may be considered as sub-systems of social action whose predominant function falls within one of the four sectors depicted in our diagram. For example, the legislative institutions of a national society or the administrative institutions of that society may be interpreted as forming a cluster of social actions in which goal gratification as an objective predominates. But this does not mean that all social actions performed by a bureaucratic or legislative body fall into the sphere of systemic goal gratification. A bureaucratic entity has its integrative and its adaptive and also its latent pattern maintenance functions, though these are subordinate to the predominant systemic goal-gratification problems of that entity. Hence we find in each of the various sub-systems numerous institutions which, in turn, may be regarded as constituting in itself a social system with its various needs and functions, and these needs and functions may be interpreted in the same fashion and by using analogous reasoning to that employed earlier, when we were examining the entire nation-state as a social system.

II

We will now turn briefly to an examination of the bureaucracy as a social system and apply to it the type of analysis we employed before with reference to the nation. First let us look at the function of pattern maintenance. Each bureaucracy, whether private or public, whether large or small, whether efficient or inefficient, has its system of values. In fact, attempts have been made to distinguish different bureaucracies in terms of different value systems: for example, those acknowledging the supremacy of purposive rationality, as against those acknowledging the even higher principle of welfare maximization of the community.[5] One could cite a whole series of other values, some of an intermediate or lower level of significance which prevail within bureaucracies of

[5] See, for example, Robert V. Presthus, "Weberian v. Welfare Bureaucracy in Traditional Society," *Administrative Science Quarterly*, VI, 1, June 1961, esp. pp. 2-4.

various sorts: there is the concept of service, the concept of justice, and the concept of efficiency which have at various times and in various contexts formed the values to which bureaucracies—at least modern bureaucracies—were expected to assent. For example, Frederick the Great was speaking as the head of the Prussian administrative service when he is reputed to have said: "I am the first servant of my state." These words are an explicit acknowledgment of public service as a major value in the bureaucratic institutions of eighteenth-century Prussia.

Bureaucratic institutions also have integrative needs. In fact the very rationalization of bureaucratic organization, the hierarchical relations with clearcut distinctions between the various layers of the hierarchy, the rights and duties of the persons and groups of persons on each layer, and the standard forms of interaction between persons on different levels of this hierarchy show the importance of integrative needs. But, as we shall see, the integrative sector of action also comes into play when we examine in more detail the process of political socialization and recruitment, especially the latter. Some phases of the process of socialization which tend to lead to the formation of political attitudes and understandings clearly belong to the latency sector of social action. They consist primarily of forms of behavior designed to produce certain attitudes and to lead to the internalization of norms designed to affirm a person's loyalty and his sense of belonging to a national society as a whole. It is indifferent for this phase of the socialization process what particular institutional attachments a person has with certain organizations in the goal-gratification sector. With specific reference to the bureaucracy this means that the political socialization process of an individual is independent of his eventual association with the bureaucracy, though children destined for government service may receive a different education and may be brought up in a different home environment from children destined for other careers. This special socialization process is possible, of course, only in societies in which a bureaucratic career appears as something desirable. Instances which may be cited are traditional China and almost all the developing nations of the present day, in which government service is considered one of the most highly prized occupations among almost all social classes.[6] But perhaps even more important than the socialization process

[6] See, for example, Edward A. Tiryakian, "Occupational Satisfaction and Aspiration in an Underdeveloped Country: The Philippines," *Economic Development and Cultural Change*, VII, 4, July 1959, pp. 437ff.

in families in which it is hoped that children will embrace a career as public servant is the pattern of socialization in the families of public servants themselves who wish to pass on to their children the status of the father. Hence, even in the early stages of socialization certain differences in the socialization process may be discernible depending upon the occupational role of the head of the household, and this may in a certain manner influence the future career of persons educated and socialized in this way.

In studying socialization patterns among different social classes, we come close to the consideration of how certain integrative patterns impinge upon action in the latency sub-sector, i.e., we are confronted with a problem of reciprocal inputs and outputs between the latency and integrative sectors. We could extend this discussion by distinguishing the various phases of the process of political socialization. As long as it centers around the acquisition of the most basic political attitudes, it has a different function from when it enters a stage in which more specialized skills in the realm of political action, or loyalties not to the nation as a whole but to particular groups with political objectives, are transmitted and instilled. In this second phase the socialization process moves progressively away from the latency sector into the integrative and even goal-attainment sectors. Hence the analysis of the process of political socialization shows that the structure of a social system must be described and evaluated in strict concordance with the diverse functional requisites and objectives of social action.

A more crucial problem from the standpoint of this chapter is the question of political recruitment. Here also the general norms prevailing in a society will be applicable. For example, in societies with strongly held ascriptive norms in the distribution of occupational roles, i.e., in societies in which status considerations predominate in determining who gets what jobs, procedures of recruitment into the bureaucracy will also exhibit a strong admixture of ascription. This is reflected in the integrative patterns prevailing in such a society, both on the level of the integrative sector of social action of the society as a whole, and also on the level of any one institution within the society. Hence, it should not surprise us if we find that such behavior as the appointment of relatives to official posts, succession to a bureaucratic office by a family member of the holder, and similar aspects of recruitment along ascriptive lines which are often encountered in societies at the threshold of political modernization, are merely a transference of generally valid norms regulating social action designed to meet the integrative needs of the society as a whole to a peculiar institution in this society. In other words, practices which are designated by some observers as corruption are really nothing but the generalization of commonly accepted principles of recruitment and selection for occupational roles to a special institution—the administrative services—which in its Western variant is highly rationalized and to which recruitment therefore is based on strict achievement rather than on ascriptive criteria.

It is easy to see that such a situation of double standards creates conflict. It creates conflict in the bureaucracy, especially in countries whose bureaucracies were once manned entirely or predominantly by Westerners, since there is ambiguity with reference to the proper method of recruitment. It creates conflict between the bureaucracy and other institutions, since there is a danger that alternative standards of recruitment—i.e., integrative patterns—may be applied. Finally, it creates conflict within the individuals who man the administrative apparatus, since the latent values governing action in the society as a whole may not apply to certain institutions in it, and antagonism may develop between the basic values of social life as a whole and those applying to a particular institution in the society. We shall see later how these factors may lead to a fractionalization of the bureaucracy, i.e., the dual economy which is so often stipulated by some observers as necessary in modernizing countries may have its counterpart in a dual bureaucracy.

It is not necessary to discuss in great detail the goal-gratification functions of a bureaucracy. Since the overwhelming part of its activity is devoted to devise or implement acts which have the attainment of systemic goals as their objective, this aspect of a bureaucracy's activity is too obvious to require extensive comment. It may be useful, however, to mention in this place one interesting point which also will concern us later. One of the points stressed by Almond is the multifunctionality of political structure. In particular, he says that the "rejection of the 'state and non-state' classification . . . is not merely a verbal quibble. It is a matter of theoretical and operational importance. Such a dichotomous classification could come only from an approach to politics which identifies the political with the existence of a specialized, visible structure, and which tends to restrict the political process to those functions performed by the specialized structure. . . . It is this emphasis on the specialized structures of politics which has led to the stereotyped conception of traditional and primitive systems as static systems. . . . The mechanics of political choice are there as well, but in the form of *intermittent* political structures. . . . If the functions are there, then the structures must be, even though we may find them tucked away, so to speak, in nooks and crannies of other social systems."[7]

In the light of the preceding discussion we must explain this statement and translate it into the terms used in this chapter. Almond begins with political structures, i.e., entities which are very similar to what is called here "institutions," whereas we started with sets of socially relevant action. Hence if we cannot find in a society institutions which have primarily goal-gratification functions—in our terms, institutions located in the goal-gratification sector because they represent a clustering of social action designed to meet the goal-gratification needs of the society—this does not mean that other institutions located in other sub-sectors do not perform some of the functions which in other societies are allocated to specialized institutions located in the goal-attainment sector. With special reference to the bureaucracy and the performance of administrative acts, this means that in some simple societies specialized institutions charged with the exclusive or predominant performance of administrative functions may not exist, but institutions do exist which may be located elsewhere in the social system, and which do perform these administrative functions. Just as we have shown that the bureaucracy may be considered as a social subsystem of its own, exhibiting latent, integrative, goal gratification, and adaptive needs of the sub-system, so we will find institutions in the adaptive or integrative sub-sectors which perform, among other things, goal-gratification functions of the kind characteristic of the actions of a bureaucracy. For example, it can easily be shown that productive enterprises which, as we have maintained, are institutions of the adaptive sub-system perform many acts which overlap or substitute for bureaucratic activities of the central administrative services of a nation.

This brings us, however, to a very important point. For in some relatively simple societies there do not exist specific institutions charged with the performance of administrative tasks. In fact the clearcut distinction between administration and other political tasks is relatively new in political thought. But unless the executive power of government is clearly seen, many institutions charged with administrative duties may, at the same time, have judicial and legislative tasks, so that their specific bureaucratic peculiarity is not too pronounced. In

[7] Almond, *op.cit.*, p. 12 (italics in original).

other words, instead of being clearly bureaucratic institutions, they are institutions of general government. Many of the higher authorities of the medieval church, for example, were institutions of general government within their area of competence, and so were several of the temporal authorities of feudal Europe.[8] Now these general governmental institutions performed acts designed to meet the systemic goals of the society of various sorts, many of which would have fallen into the specific resort of a bureaucracy if it had existed.

But once we admit that specific administrative acts may be performed by a general governmental institution, we have no reason to deny that they may also be performed by institutions whose primary function is even further removed from specific goal-gratification activities, i.e., by institutions whose major purpose is to provide a focus for a cluster of social action designed primarily to meet the integrative, adaptive, or pattern-maintenance needs of the society. In fact, the very example I have given, the performance of administrative acts by feudal authorities, leads us very close to this interpretation. For it may be argued with a good deal of force that the typical feudal institutions had primarily integrative rather than goal-gratification functions. In more primitive societies than that of medieval Europe, the central focus of the institution which performs certain administrative acts may be even further removed from goal gratification, and in still less complex societies the institutional structure may be so bare and simple, and any one of the existing structures may have such multiplex functions, as to make it extremely difficult, if not impossible, to assign specific administrative functions to any regularized institutional entity. This is precisely the case in which Almond would expect to find bureaucratic structures tucked away in the nooks and crannies of other social systems.

The important conclusion which we can draw from this analysis is not that bureaucratic "structures" may be encountered in other than the goal-gratification sub-system of social action, but rather that the development of a reasonably rationalized administrative service requires the conscious establishment of a set of permanent administrative institutions in the goal-attainment sector. In other words, it means a conscious organizational change in the society, the creation of something new—new not only in the sense that such an entity has not existed before in the society, but new in the sense that the society may not have

[8] See Marc Bloch, *Feudal Society*, Trans. L. A. Manyon, Chicago, University of Chicago Press, 1961, pp. 408ff.

known any entity before which was so uniquely concentrated upon the performance of functions and the meeting of needs in the goal-attainment sub-sector. Hence we may say that there is more than a quantitative difference between the structures (using Almond's term) in simple non-complex societies which perform political functions, and allegedly analogous structures in more modern "rationalized" societies. The difference is one of kind. The *action systems* may have analogies, but the *institutions* differ profoundly. In terms of the concepts used in this chapter the meaning of the word "structure" by Almond then becomes crucial. If he means by it merely a set of actions, we can agree with him, but if he means by this term what is called an institution in this chapter, we differ. I believe that the preceding discussion has shown, however, that it is useful to make the distinction between action systems (or sub-systems of social action), on the one hand, and institutions, on the other, simply because this distinction permits a more extensive characterization and analysis of the various functional dimensions of each structural complex.

We now turn, finally, to a brief examination of the adaptive functions of a bureaucracy, and here we find again that they are manifold and relatively easy to describe. We are not concerned here with the outputs of bureaucratic institutions which become inputs in the adaptive sub-sector. For example, we are not considering directives given by executive organs which are addressed to various productive organizations in a society and which induce these productive organizations to perform various acts related to the production of goods and services. We are concerned, on the contrary, with the productive activity of the bureaucracies themselves, and, in particular, with products other than red tape.

This problem may in my opinion be considered on two levels: on the level of relatively simple non-complex bureaucratic organizations, and on that of rationalized modern bureaucracies. As concerns the latter, we merely state that certain productive tasks in a modern society are directly performed by a bureaucracy. For example, the bureaucracy produces research reports, handbooks, and various other objects which may be regarded not as containing directives for other agencies, but rather which are final products. That is, the product of the activity of the bureaucracy is an object which may be used by anyone for whatever purpose he sees fit. Just as a business firm may produce some object which the purchaser may use for any legal function, the product of the bureaucratic apparatus may be used in a similar manner. For example, a research report produced by a government bureau may be used by an educator for purposes of teaching, by a businessman for purposes of changing certain practices in his firm, and by a political party as a basis for a change in its appeal to the public. This aspect of the adaptive function of a bureaucracy is trivial from an analytical point of view, but it must be noted that with the great rise of scientifically trained personnel and the large numerical growth of experts in modern bureaucracies, this kind of adaptive function tends to be quantitatively on the increase.

More interesting is the adaptive function of bureaucracies in simpler societies, because there the adaptive functions are a consequence of the multi-dimensionality of most social institutions rather than of the conscious specialization of tasks within the bureaucratic apparatus. In his discussion of bureaucracy, Max Weber maintains that the development of a money economy is a presupposition of bureaucracy, since a rational system of bureaucracy requires a pecuniary compensation of officials. But he goes on to cite cases in which rather efficient and quantitatively large bureaucracies were developed in societies in which pecuniary compensation of officials was not the rule, but which presented strong "patrimonial and prebendal elements." In these societies the remuneration of officials was primarily in kind. But it is here that the adaptive needs of a bureaucratic organization of a pre-modern type become clearly visible. It may be most appropriate to cite Weber's own discussion of this point: "According to historical experience, without a money economy the bureaucratic structure can hardly avoid undergoing substantial internal changes, or indeed, turning into another type of structure. The allocation of fixed income in kind, from the magazines of the lord or from his current intake, to the officials easily means a first step toward appropriation of the sources of taxation and their exploitation as private property. . . . Whenever the lord's prerogatives have relaxed, the taxes in kind as a rule have been irregular. In this case, the official has direct recourse to the tributaries of his bailiwick, whether or not he is authorized. . . . Another process involves fixing the official's salary—the official hands over a stipulated amount and retains the surplus. In such cases the official is economically in a position rather similar to that of the entrepreneurial tax-farmer."[9]

This description of the arrangements of the role of officials in so-

[9] See H. H. Gerth and C. W. Mills, *From Max Weber: Essays in Sociology*, New York, Oxford University Press, 1946, p. 205.

cieties in which a money economy is not generalized shows clearly the intimate association of the performance of goal-gratification functions with adaptive functions within the same institution—or, if we wish to choose Almond's term, the same structure. This is apparently characteristic also of bureaucratic structures in countries at the threshold of modernization. Some administrative tasks in these societies are still performed by persons and institutions who live in a non-pecuniary environment and whose remuneration consists either in kind or in the accrual of prestige and power which, in turn, may, under certain circumstances, be converted into income of some sort. Modernization of these bureaucracies then consists, among other things, also in a conversion of the principles of remuneration and the strict separation of the goal-gratification functions of the officials from their function in meeting the adaptive needs of the system.

In these instances we may encounter what has been termed earlier "dual bureaucracies." The administrative apparatus in these societies is not uniform, even though they have a structure which externally appears as a unitary hierarchy. In other words, although there may exist in theory (and perhaps even in practice) a single line of command reaching from the central top positions in the administrative structure down to the most widely dispersed local bottom positions, the values and norms according to which different layers of the bureaucracy operate do differ. There is a break somewhere in the structure which clearly distinguishes the two parts of the bureaucracy certainly in terms of the underlying principles of action and often also in terms of routine practices.

In colonial times and in colonial countries, this break was often coterminous with the break in the administrative structure along ethnic lines. In a sense, the entire principle of indirect rule is based upon the assumption of such a break as this in the administrative structure of a colonial area. The native pattern of government—including, of course, local, municipal, and district administration—was supposed to remain as intact as possible, but was related through one or several intermediary officials (often the District Officers), with the central administration on top. The central administration was run along rationalized lines of modern European bureaucracies, the native government continued to conform to traditional values and norms. In fact, it was considered the very virtue of the principle of indirect rule that the indigenous system of government was disturbed as little as possible, provided it could be adapted in some crucial features—usually those relating to the raising of revenue and the maintenance of law and order—to the requisites of the metropolitan power.

The principle of indirect rule, therefore, clearly implies the existence of a dual bureaucracy; in fact, it may be said to be designed to bring about this form of administrative structure. But many features of a dual bureaucracy were also present in the administrative structures of colonial countries which were not governed on the basis of the principle of indirect rule. Dual bureaucracies, or certain aspects of them, continue to be discernible in the administrative structures of the newly independent nations. In these cases it is not the intentional differentiation between governmental values on the central and local level which account for this, but rather the insufficient penetration of all levels of the administrative structure with the values and behavioral norms of a modern bureaucracy. It has been maintained that the concept of dual economy was applicable only to countries in which a native traditionally oriented society became subdued by a conquering colonial power, and in which the traditional economic values proved themselves resistant against penetration by the capitalist ethic of the metropolitan power.[10] It follows from this that with the emancipation of the colonial country and its adoption of a uniform economic policy the feature of the dual economy tended gradually to disappear.

Perhaps the fate of dual bureaucracies is similar. But, for the time being, there continue to exist very strong features of dualistic bureaucratic structures in developing countries. In a certain sense they have even become strengthened. It is strange that these developments occur not in the countries in which direct rule was widely applied, but rather in those in which it had never been used. In countries with an ancient high culture, such as India or Ceylon or Pakistan, the attainment of independence also has led to a revival of many values really or allegedly derived from a past golden age of the culture. These values have been most easily applied in the realms of religion and government, and with the revival of traditionalistic norms—born out of the newly fostered nationalism—they have been applied with increasing frequency in the general political and more narrowly administrative realms of action. Hence the nationalist revival in newly independent

[10] See, for example, the paper by Yoichi Itagaki, "Some Notes on the Controversy Concerning Boeke's 'Dualistic Theory': Implications for the Theory of Economic Development in Underdeveloped Countries," *Hitotsubashi Journal of Economics*, 1, 1, October 1960, pp. 13-28. In this article all the relevant literature dealing with the problem of the dual economy is critically surveyed.

countries, by introducing more numerous appeals to traditionalistic political ideals and forms of behavior, tends to strengthen the dualistic bureaucratic structure in these countries. For, on the one hand, the time-honored old-fashioned ways of government and administration are extolled, and at the same time the pressure for economic advancement places stress on the development of a streamlined, highly rationalized modern bureaucracy. But the implementation of the policy of administrative modernization is often confined only to the capital and a few other large urban centers, whereas the rest of the country continues to be administered by officials who conform only externally to the principles of a rationalized achievement-oriented bureaucracy and who, in substance, adhere to a set of behavioral norms which are of a very different order and either stress what Weber would call patrimonial and prebendary objectives, or are reasserting ascriptive norms in the distribution of administrative services and returns from such services.

III

The discussion of dualistic bureaucratic structures has deflected us from our main problem: the tracing through of the interrelations between economic development and the change of administrative services. For although the dualism which we discussed is one aspect of political modernization, its incidence appears to be confined to the special cases of countries experiencing either indirect rule or the emancipation from colonial rule and the revival, for nationalist reasons, of a great old cultural tradition. The principal line of the argument, developed in this chapter so far, has focused on the following conceptions: I attempted to delineate the generalized social action system in terms of which Almond's model of political structures must be interpreted, and I tried to show also that this procedure may be applied to the study of an entire national society as well as a given institution in that society, in our particular case, the bureaucracy. So far the treatment has not gone beyond that of a static system, though in some instances comparisons were made which show that the social system as a whole, or the particular institution under examination, may perform on various levels of complexity and efficiency. It may be assumed that in the course of its development and social change any society or institution passes through these various levels.

It now becomes our task to dynamize our model more explicitly. In other words, we must try to throw more light on two problems: (1)

What changes does an administrative apparatus undergo in the process of modernization, and (2) how are these changes related to the improvement in economic performance of the society?

If we are to identify a single overriding factor which provides the impetus for internal autonomous changes in the social s, stem and the various structures into which it may be disaggregated, we find it in the process of social differentiation and subsequent reintegration. On the lowest, most elementary levels social differentiation may be a consequence of population growth, a change in the environment, such as the gradual alteration of climatic conditions, or such externally induced factors as war or conquest. As one looks, for example, at the history of tropical Africa, say in the region along the great Rift valley, one finds that social differentiation has taken place there gradually, and that it has occurred mainly as a consequence of many piecemeal, small-scale changes: population displacements, alterations in the ecology due to different effects of the cattle complex, accommodating and antagonistic consequences of lineage loyalty, interest in social stability and personal security in each village, and others.[11] As population grows, the customarily used land is insufficient for the normal needs for food of a given society. Some members either migrate, set out to conquer new lands, or alter the manner of exploitation of the resources they command. All these adjustments to an environmental situation produce certain forms of social differentiation; and although we know as yet very little about what factors are responsible for what specific patterns of differentiation, it is easy to see the intimate causal nexus between environmental changes, needs for adjustment within a society, and social differentiation.

In the context of the problems of primary interest in this paper, we need not worry too much about the causes which initiate an autonomous process of differentiation, simply because we are concerned with instances of consciously induced modernization, primarily modernization of the economy. The societies we concentrate on are not the simple African peoples of the last four or five centuries, but modern nations whose leaders have become persuaded of the need for economic growth, and who are trying to implement, as rapidly as possible, policies which will bring about a rise in output per capita, diversification of productive patterns, a reallocation of human and non-human natural resources,

[11] Though he does not deal with the problem of social differentiation explicitly the views expressed in the text owe a great deal to a perusal of the work of Max Gluckman, especially his *Custom and Conflict in Africa*, Glencoe, Ill., The Free Press, 1955.

and a large-scale change in the ecology, the pattern of population distribution, and the occupational structure in the society. In other words, the introduction of a new technology, the transition from handicrafts to machine-driven industry, from subsistence farming to cash crop farming, and the ubiquitous rural-urban migration, have the effect of producing a higher degree of structural differentiation, i.e., of the evolution of more specialized and autonomous social units and of the development of new institutions with highly specific functions.

In the introduction to their collection of essays on the political systems of indigenous Africa, M. Fortes and E. E. Evans-Pritchard present a series of comparisons which they derived from the empirical, inductive studies reported in the case study chapters of the book. This introduction is a masterpiece of anthropological method. In the section headed "Kinship in Political Organization," Fortes and Evans-Pritchard write: "It seems probable to us that three types of political system can be distinguished. Firstly, there are those very small societies . . . in which even the largest political unit embraces a group of people all of whom are united to one another by ties of kinship, so that political relations are coterminous with kinship relations and the political structure and kinship organization are completely fused. Secondly, there are societies in which a lineage structure is the framework of the political system, there being a precise co-ordination between the two, so that they are consistent with each other, though each remains distinct and autonomous in its own sphere. Thirdly, there are societies in which an administrative organization is the framework of political structure.[12]

Let us note that the two writers also report that the societies of the third type are substantially larger, i.e., more populous, than those of the second type, and that the larger societies also exhibit a much higher degree of hierarchical social stratification than the smaller societies of type 2. Fortes and Evans-Pritchard use these three types of societies to show significant comparisons in political organization among different African peoples. We do not know whether societies of type 3 were once similar to those of type 2, i.e., whether there is an evolutionary pattern leading from type 1 to type 2 and ultimately to type 3 societies. What the two writers assert is merely that societies exhibiting these different forms of kinship and political organization may be found contemporaneously in Africa.

[12] M. Fortes and E. E. Evans-Pritchard, eds., *African Political Systems,* London, Oxford University Press, 1940, pp. 6-7.

Now if we translate the categories mentioned by Fortes and Evans-Pritchard into the language we have used earlier in this chapter, we note two things. First, as we move from societies of type 1 to those of type 2 and finally those of type 3, we find a growing degree of structural differentiation, due perhaps to larger size and greater structural heterogeneity of the society. But we also find that at the basis of the classification proposed by Fortes and Evans-Pritchard is the fact that societies of type 3 have specialized political—among them also administrative—institutions, whereas societies of types 1 and 2 do not have such specialized institutions. In the societies of type 1, institutions primarily located in the latency or the integrative sector also perform certain political functions. In societies of type 2, there is still overlap between the integrative and the goal-gratification sectors of action; but the institutions to which political functions are assigned are more specialized, their connection with specific political purposes more clearly recognized. This does not mean that they are recognized as political institutions; rather, the lineages are entities to whom loyalty is owed and which, especially in situations of stress, act as unitary groups with common purposes. As Günter Wagner has said very appropriately of such a tribal group in his discussion of the Bantu of Kavirondo in Kenya:

"The political unit must thus be defined in terms of *consciousness of unity and interdependence* rather than in terms of submission to a central authority. . . . This tribal political unit does not necessarily act as a body in all its foreign relations, but it is merely the largest unit of people which feels as a unit and which—on certain occasions—acts as one. . . . An *institution thus has political significance if it fulfills a political function, regardless of what other functions it may perform besides*. The political structure, in this sense, is the sum total of all forms of sanctioned behavior which serve, directly or indirectly, intendedly or not, to integrate the political unit."[13]

Finally, the societies of type 3 are structurally most highly diversified and differentiated. They have not only specific political, but in most cases also specific administrative, institutions. In other words, these societies harbor bureaucracies in the proper sense of the word, though the values and norms of these bureaucracies may differ profoundly from their Western counterparts and from the ideal-typical bureaucracy stipulated by Max Weber. When I discussed systems of dual bu-

[13] Günter Wagner, "The Political Organization of the Bantu of Kavirondo," in M. Fortes and E. E. Evans-Pritchard, eds., *op.cit.*, p. 201. (Italics added.)

reaucracy earlier, I had in mind certain societies of type 3, since in societies of types 1 and 2—which do not have proper administrative institutions—the term "dual bureaucracy" would be strictly speaking inapplicable.

On the basis of the case studies presented in a work like *African Political Systems* alone, we are not able to postulate the existence of a genuine dynamism, since the empirical evidence that we derive from these essays does not show that societies of type 1 develop into those of type 2, and further into societies of type 3. But there exists a great body of literature which shows that the differentiation exhibited in these comparative cases is paralleled in the dynamic development of societies as they undergo the process of modernization and economic development.[14] Just as these societies exhibit in their economies various phases of transition from traditional to more modern modes of production, so they present various stages of development in their political institutions, and, in particular, in their administrative structures. The three types of societies postulated by Fortes and Evans-Pritchard may then be assumed to be ideal types (or structures close to ideal types) which represent various phases in the dynamic process of political modernization. The concrete forms of political, social, and economic structures may vary greatly in different societies and the phases which we here describe (and which must not be confounded with stages of growth) may succeed one another at intervals of widely varying duration. The factors which will affect the concrete manifestations of the concrete structures are manifold and range from such strictly structural factors as the specialized forms of kinship organization in different societies to such environmental factors as climate and the nature of the crops that can be grown, as well as the technical conditions under which food and other objects of common usefulness are produced.

IV

It would be inadvisable to discuss the various forms of interrelations which may exist between economic, integrative, and bureaucratic institutions and to show how each of these patterns of interaction (or

[14] An extensive discussion with abundant citations from the pertinent literature is presented in a concise and insightful paper of Neil Smelser, "Mechanisms of Change and Adjustment of Change," presented at the North American Conference on the Social Implications of Industrialization and Technological Change, held at Chicago, Ill., September 15-22, 1960. A final version of this paper is scheduled to appear early in 1962 in Bert F. Hoselitz and Wilbert F. Moore, eds., *The Impact of Industry*, the Hague, Mouton & Co.

boundary exchanges, if the more rigorous terminology of Parsons is to be applied), are related to certain levels of economic performance and/or modernity of political organization.[15] What I should like to do instead is to discuss two more specific cases of dynamic change. One centers around patterns of interaction between bureaucratic structures in developing societies and certain integrative structures, the other with interaction between the bureaucracy and certain significant economic variables. Let us consider first the interrelationship between integrative and goal-gratification needs, and apply this specifically to the study of bureaucracy. This interrelationship is closely related to our previous discussion of political systems in primitive societies, such as those of tropical Africa.

In a paper published almost three years ago, I suggested hypothetically that the overall historical course of a society could be interpreted as passing through several phases of secular evolution; that it is first confronted as a major functional requisite with problems of solidarity or integration, then with those of systemic goal attainment, and finally with those of adaptation.[16] In more concrete terms, in its initial period a society is concerned primarily with problems of determining who are its members and how they are related to one another. We note these integrative concerns in the formation of simple societies, but also in newly constituted nation-states, e.g., the countries which emerged after the First World War out of the shambles of the Austro-Hungarian Empire, or more recently the newly independent nations which had shaken off the colonial yoke. In the course of time integrative concerns tend to become less pressing; methods of solving the needs of the solidarity sector tend to become routinized; and systemic goal gratification comes to occupy the first place among the needs of the society. Only at a late stage of development do adaptive needs

[15] It goes without saying that a very useful task may be performed if different patterns or constellations of modernizing polito-economic systems are devised. One example of a very fruitful attempt along this line is the classification presented by David E. Apter and Carl Rosberg, "Some Models of Political Change in Contemporary Africa," in D. P. Ray, ed., *The Political Economy of Contemporary Africa*, Washington, D.C., National Institute of Social and Behavioral Sciences, 1960. It would have been instructive to apply the categories developed in this chapter to the problems of bureaucratic structures in the three types of modernizing political-economic systems postulated there, but my information on recent developments in African countries is too scanty to permit me to attempt such an exercise. I hope that someone more familiar with the recent history of Africa may be encouraged to undertake this task.

[16] See Bert F. Hoselitz, "Economic Policy and Economic Development," in Hugh G. J. Aitken, *The State and Economic Growth*, New York, Social Science Research Council, 1959, pp. 333ff.

come to occupy a principal place, but their supremacy, except in relatively crisis-free situations, is constantly threatened by the pressure of meeting the collective goals of the system. It is, of course, not maintained that this schema presents a full description of the evolution of social systems through time. In particular, it is not maintained that any of the needs, integrative, goal attainment, or adaptive are ever absent, but merely that during different phases of the development of a society different sets of needs tend to predominate. This phasing, on the whole, follows a course of evolution in which primary concern with solidarity is replaced by goal attainment, and this latter by adaptation as the major problems faced by a society.

If we apply this schema to the study of bureaucracies, we find that in societies in which integrative needs predominate, administrative behavior is strongly influenced by these integrative needs. In fact, in little differentiated societies administrative functions are often performed by institutions located primarily in a sub-sector of social action in which the maintenance of solidarity is paramount. Hence, it is not surprising at all that Fortes and Evans-Pritchard point to segmental lineages as the carriers of administrative functions in certain African societies. And we find that even on a much higher level of differentiation administrative functions are performed by structures which have strong integrative admixtures, or are institutionalized primarily with reference to the integrative, rather than to the goal-attainment needs of the society. For example, in the patrimonial bureaucracies of the early Middle Ages, described by Weber, the performance of public office was basically subject to the integrative action system. Thus under European feudalism, at a time when integrative needs appeared predominant, the holding of public office was a function of the solidarity structure. I refer to the period during the ninth and tenth centuries when the various political entities in Europe began to be formed, many of them arising, in part, out of the consolidation of territories reconquered by a local magnate and his followers from the retreating barbarians. It was the time when counties and, in some instances, dukedoms or even petty kingdoms began to emerge. A public office was held in those days, at least ideally, as a fief. It was exercised in the particularist interest of its holder, and through this interest his integration into the solidarity structure was assured. The very definition of an administrative position as a fief shows the close connection of the public office with the solidarity structure, since the fief itself was the object merely of establishing a relationship between lord and vassal.

The major nexus of classical European feudalism was the tie establishing a solidarity structure throughout society.[17] This interpersonal relationship often established the social status of the vassal. Hence the exercise of an office was tied to the ascriptive position of this individual in the social structure. In other words, the granting of a fief to which was tied a public office not only established the right and the charge to execute the administrative task, but also defined the social rights and obligations of the holder of the office vis-à-vis his lord, as well as vis-à-vis the public at large. What mattered most in the context of building an administrative structure by this means was not so much the constitution of a bureaucracy, but rather the fulfillment of the integrative needs of a society in process of formation.

Feudalism changed greatly in the course of its later evolution. Much of what had been real in its early phases became a pure formality later. But even in its earlier stage, it was a relatively highly formalized system, with elaborate ceremonial and extensive and explicit legal sanctions. But similar structural relations, also with primarily solidarity-forming or solidarity-enhancing functions, based on some form of ascriptive norms may be found in many fairly differentiated, non-industrial societies. Superficial observers who have studied the social and economic relations of many traditional societies, have found extensive feudal elements in them. Though they have, on the whole, employed a vague and ill-defined concept of feudalism, they have sensed correctly that all social institutions in these societies were still strongly influenced by the persistent integrative needs of the society and that ascriptive, rather than rationalized, achievement-oriented, norms determined the behavior of persons entrusted with administrative functions. Much of the alleged corruption that Western technical advisers on administrative services of Asian and African states encounter, and against which they inveigh in their technical reports with so little genuine success, is nothing but the prevalence of these non-rational norms on the basis of which these administrations operate. Moreover, as we have seen earlier, when we discussed the case of dual bureaucracies, the very existence of these structures, based on ascription and survivals of the phase of integrative predominance, constitutes a contrast and results in a clash with the rationalized achievement-

[17] On the nature of European feudalism, see Marc Bloch, *op.cit.*, esp. Part IV, pp. 145ff. On the connection between public office and the grant of a fief, see the extensive literature on *Ministeriales* and *Dienstlehen*; an abbreviated statement may be found in F. L. Ganshof, *Qu'est-ce que la Féodalité?* Bruxelles, Office de Publicité, S.C., 1947, pp. 137ff.

oriented bureaucracies of the central government—or at least some of its branches.

The process of bureaucratic modernization in developing countries seems, therefore, to be tied up closely with the struggle for greater national unity, and, above all, the decrease, destruction, or fundamental modification of particularist tendencies still prevailing in these countries. Political modernization in the new nations of Asia and Africa implies, among many other things, a transfer of a person's loyalty from a small, particularistic group to a large entity, ideally the entire nation. In some societies this process takes place stepwise as, for example in India, where linguistic groups and linguistically defined states intervene between the small particularist group (caste, tribe, or village community) and the nation as a whole. There exist similar interstitial structures in other countries, e.g., Nigeria or Indonesia, which plainly acknowledge this federated character, but we find them even in countries which do not officially acknowledge them. In these latter the struggle against the nuclei around which particularist sentiments can crystallize is much sharper.

The demands of economic development in all these countries require the elimination or effective reduction of particularist loyalties and action based upon them. For if the human and non-human resources of a country are to be allocated optimally, strict principles of efficiency, rather than familiarity or other forms of personal and local preference, must rule in the assignment of economic and occupational roles and similar contractual relations pertaining to allocation of resources. But local, tribal, and linguistic particularisms stand in the way of this process of generalization of interpersonal economic relations in a developing country and hence the pressures for economic development tend to support the struggle against them. But, as we have seen earlier, particularistic loyalties are also at the bottom of these political sentiments which prevent the development of an achievement-oriented rationalized bureaucracy. As Dr. Wagner pointed out, in the passage cited earlier, a political unit in segmented (i.e., strongly particularistic) societies may be defined in "terms of consciousness of unity and interdependence," i.e., in terms of loyalty towards and identification with a more or less narrow group of individuals. It is this segmented structure of political organization with strong admixtures of kinship, i.e., ascription-oriented features, which militates against the establishment of specialized political (and among them also specialized bureaucratic) institutions.

Hence the requisites imposed on a society by the pressures for economic development are parallel to those made by the demands of political and especially administrative modernization. The protective shelter of predominantly integrative functions in the existing institutions must be modified or abolished, and institutions with differentiated functions in the adaptive and goal attainment sub-systems of the society must take their place. This is the basic meaning of social-structural differentiation in modernizing societies.

There is still a final point that needs to be discussed, since it is tied up with those mentioned so far, and that is the relationship between the bureaucracy and the development of a money economy. As we have already seen, Max Weber regarded the presence of a money economy as a prerequisite for a rational system of bureaucracy, and again in the discussion of the feudal, patrimonial bureaucracies of early medieval Europe, we found that by granting a public office in the form of a fief, the office tended to become exercised in the particularist economic interest of the holder. In more concrete terms, a person who received, say, a tax collection job as a fief, was supposed to gain his income from part of his receipts, and other more strictly administrative posts were granted often with a piece of land attached from which the public official was expected to provide for his livelihood. As Weber argued, this system tends to produce pressures fostering the breakup of the bureaucratic structure, but also to force upon the official the role of entrepreneurial tax farmer. Hence, in systems such as these there is a strong conflict between the bureaucracy becoming institutionalized in the adaptive as against the goal-attainment sector.

We know that medieval feudalism, in the course of its development, made the fief inheritable. This established progressively a proprietary interest of its holder in the landed property attached to it, but often also in the office itself. In some cases the office provided an income in and of itself, in others it determined the social status of the holder, and in still others it gradually became, as we shall see, an object of trade and exchange. For once a proprietary interest in an office had been established, it was only natural that whoever controlled it should regard it as a good which could be bought and sold. Even if the holder of the office wished to pass it on to his son, it had to be evaluated so as to compensate other children accordingly. But since, in the last resort, an office was held not in the holder's own right, but from his superior lord, the lord—in most instances the king—wished to share in the transaction, regardless of whether the office was to be passed on by sale, inheritance, or dot. The venality of office thus arose in a context in which in the realm of public administration, goal-attainment, and adaptive system problems occupied a somewhat ambiguous position but in which gradually the natural economy had given way to a money economy, and in which it became customary to transfer property—including property in certain privileges and rights—by sale or inheritance.[18]

With the expansion of a moneyed class of traders and the simultaneous growth of a territory controlled by a monarch, conditions are established in which possibilities for demand and supply of new offices are created. For the buyer of an office it holds out not only a continuing source of income, but in a society in which the holding and exercise of an office are as yet regarded as a privilege of the nobility, the acquisition of an office also means an advancement in social status. For the crown the sale of offices provided a new, previously untapped source of revenue, especially in times of fiscal emergencies. It was this coincidence of interests on the part of important social groups, the rising entrepreneurs and the court, which caused the saleability of offices to become a widely practiced procedure. And although it was perhaps most highly developed in France, it was also common in the sixteenth, seventeenth, and eighteenth centuries in all other European countries and their colonies, as well as in the Ottoman Empire and China.[19]

The institution of sale of public office fitted very well into a social system in which goal-attainment needs tended to predominate, but in which on the institutional level clearcut structures concerned solely with meeting these needs did not yet exist. At the same time, as yet no sharp distinction was made between the attainment of systemic goals and the private goals of members of the social and political elite. It is, therefore, no wonder that in the early stages of the formation of centralized national states the practice of the sale of offices became widespread and that, with few exceptions, all administrative and municipal offices, and often also military and naval commissions, could be obtained only by those who were willing and able to pay for them or who inherited them.

[18] See G. Pagès, "La venalité des offices dans l'ancienne France," *Revue historique*, CLXIX 1932, pp. 477-482.

[19] See K. W. Swart, *Sale of Offices in the Seventeenth Century*, The Hague, Nijhoff, 1949; also Martin Göhring, *Die Aemterkäuflichkeit im Ancien Régime*, Berlin, Verlag Dr. Emil Ebering, 1938; and J. H. Parry, *The Sale of Public Office in the Spanish Indies under the Hapsburgs*, Berkeley, University of California Press, 1953.

But the sale of public offices ceases to be a useful instrument of recruiting and remunerating a civil service if the systemic goal-attainment problems tend to diverge from the private goal-gratification needs of the social elite. Though a system of sale of offices is intrinsically subject to corruption, it is doubtful whether, under the conditions existing in sixteenth and seventeenth century Europe, the saleability of offices had any significant impact upon the degree of corruption in government. The alternative method of selecting bureaucrats which was then common—the granting of offices to favorites—was no less conducive to the exercise of corrupt practices and was no more capable of attracting genuinely qualified persons to public service. This point was stressed sharply by Montesquieu, who favored the sale of public office over other methods of appointing civil servants, because, as he said, "chance will furnish better subjects than the prince's choice." But he preferred this method of recruiting a civil service also, because he regarded it as an orderly means of advancement in the social scale, assuring thereby a rendering of "the several orders of the kingdom more permanent."[20]

I have presented in some detail the case of venality of public offices, as it was practiced in European countries, particularly in France, during a period in their social development when the elaboration of fully institutionalized structures in the goal-gratification sector was as yet incomplete and when, especially in structures performing administrative tasks, integrative and adaptive needs played an important and occasionally even overpowering role. But although the concrete facts in the distribution of administrative positions and the recruitment to bureaucratic service vary in non-European societies, they all pass through related or analogous phases in their process of political modernization. In China, for example, the sale of offices became quite common under the Ch'ing dynasty and reached its widest extension during the nineteenth century.[21] In other countries it was never much in vogue, but the method disavowed by Montesquieu of selection by a superior, often on the basis of ascription, was not infrequent. In still other places, there existed numerous other traditional forms of recruitment of public servants, which all exhibit, however, the common feature of being associated with ambiguous and highly undifferentiated

[20] Charles Secondat de Montesquieu, *The Spirit of Laws*, translated by Thomas Nugent, Book v, Chapter 19, Quest. 4, New York, Hafner Library of Classics, 1949, p. 69.

[21] See P. C. Hsieh, *The Government of China, 1644-1911*, Baltimore, Johns Hopkins University Press, 1925, pp. 106ff.

institutions in which integrative and adaptive needs play as prominent a role as those of the systemic goal-gratification sector.

All these systems of bureaucratic structure, recruitment, and remuneration then appear to be suited to societies in the process of transformation from a phase in which integrative problems predominate to one in which systemic goal-attainment problems become most urgent. But with the accomplishment of this transformation the sale of offices, or any analogous form of constituting the civil service, ceases to be a suitable method, not so much because of the possibility of corruption which these systems entail, but because of their inefficiency in procuring bureaucrats who owe primary loyalty to the optimum attainment of systemic goals. Moreover, the control by the centralized authority over the composition of the administrative structures is rigorously limited in a system in which office holders have either proprietary or ascriptively sanctioned claims on their jobs. Thus in the various countries of Europe in which economic development actually took hold, various institutional patterns were designed to eliminate the sale of offices and to replace this form of social action by one better suited to the needs of optimum goal attainment.

Let us once more take France as an example. There the crown was confronted with the dilemma between a serious loss of revenue if it abolished venality of public office, and inefficiency in administration if it retained it. A way out was found by robbing the offices which remained for sale of their administrative significance and introducing a series of new offices whose incumbents were selected on the basis of their fitness for the job rather than their ability to pay for it. In other words, the way out of the dilemma was found by rejecting both principles of selection examined by Montesquieu and by replacing them by a third, the recruitment of a centralized bureaucracy on the basis of achievement norms. In this way the *intendants* and their assistants gradually replaced the *parlements* in the administration of France. The final step in this drama was taken when, in the memorable session of August 4th, 1789, all the three estates, moved by a spirit of generosity and national unity, sacrificed some of their privileges on behalf of the national welfare. The third estate, i.e., the representatives of the wealthier classes of the bourgeoisie, offered as their contribution the abolition of the venality of office.[22] Though this step was regarded as a sacrifice of a privilege at the time it was taken, it logically fitted into the overall historical development of the interests of the third

[22] Cf. Swart, *op.cit.*, p. 17.

estate. For it subjected the governmental bureaucracy to the same principles of rationality and achievement orientation which came to prevail during the nineteenth century and after in the institutions of the adaptive sector. And the bourgeoisie, more than any other social group, occupied the most responsible positions of leadership and decision making in this sector of social action.

V

I have dwelt so long on the historical development of the public service of France because it shows in a clearcut logical fashion the parallelism between the intensification of adaptive needs, the successful improvement of economic performance, and the change in basic values and underlying principles of the bureaucracy. The French Revolution, which put an end to so many social traits and social institutions whose ultimate roots go back to the hoary antiquity of the early feudal period, also drew a stark line under any and all forms of patrimonial and prebendary bureaucracies which still had survived for several centuries, after they had lost their functional utility. If in the *ancien régime*, parts of the bureaucracy, even in France, were still operating in realms of action far removed from the bureaucracy's full institutionalization in the goal-attainment sector, and were still exhibiting traces—and often more than traces—of meeting integrative needs, in the new post-revolutionary age this intimate nexus between administration and social solidarity was broken. A new nexus of a different kind with the adaptive sub-sector of social action was established. But now, with clearcut institutions within the goal attainment and the adaptive sub-sectors, the question of the nature of boundary exchanges, of the interdependence of inputs and outputs, for the first time took on real meaning. Now the boundary relations can be empirically studied. The inputs from the adaptive to the goal-gratification sector and vice versa can be clearly identified, even if it may still be difficult to measure their magnitude or intensity without ambiguity. The whole schema presented by Almond in the discussion to which I have already referred several times makes full sense within this modern political-economic system, because clearcut and easily identifiable institutions, the administrative apparatus, the business firm, and others, are available whose operations, interchanges, and social behavior with relation to one another can be subjected to precise empirical research. One example of how well this can be done is provided by the initial chapters of a work by Dahl and Lindblom, in which varying patterns of interaction between the bureaucracy and productive enterprises are discussed.[23]

We are now on familiar ground and may summarize briefly the main points made in the last few sections of this chapter. It will be recalled that we tried to examine the general outline of the dynamics of the process of change which economic and administrative structures undergo in their transition from a high degree of tradition-orientation to modernity. We found that in the course of this evolution both economic institutions and governmental administrations tended to become subject to the process of structural differentiation, that this process had its beginning in almost imperceptible, small changes within a relatively primitive system of social relations, but that it received a significant impetus through the conscious policy of economic advancement and political modernization which had become the rule in the new states of Asia and Africa. With special reference to the administrative services, this process of structural differentiation has taken the following general course:

On a more primitive level, the specific institutions which perform bureaucratic service are little differentiated, and specific administrative institutions squarely within the goal-gratification sub-sector are absent. Institutions with primarily integrative functions also have the subsidiary purpose of performing administrative acts, and the values and norms appropriate to a solidarity-maintenance system determine the performance of administrative actions rather than the rational, achievement-oriented norms of a modern goal-gratification system. In the course of the process of structural differentiation of bureaucratic institutions, the old restrictive garments of the integrative sub-system are sloughed off as time proceeds and specific institutions with differentiated political functions are created.

As long as integrative institutions predominate, not only the administrative but also the adaptive needs of the society are subordinated to the functional requisites of the solidarity system. Significantly, it is not the growing importance of the adaptive, but of the goal-gratification sector, which tends to destroy the primacy of the integrative subsystem of action, and to lead to a greater degree of structural differentiation. But in going through this process, the rational achievement-oriented principles of the adaptive system are applied also to the institutions which gradually emerge within the goal-attainment sector of

[23] See Robert A. Dahl and Charles E. Lindblom, *Politics, Economics, and Welfare*, New York, Harper, 1953, chapters 1-4.

social action. The closer any of the institutions in this sector resembles certain adaptive entities, the more profoundly does it adopt the principles elaborated by them. The bureaucratic apparatus in its modern "Weberian" form, among all political institutions, resembles most a productive enterprise. It is hierarchically organized, its members are engaged almost constantly in a process of choice and allocation, and its performance is judged essentially by the same standards of efficiency (cost versus benefits) as a business firm. In fact structurally a bureaucracy and a large firm are so similar that the new science of management does not distinguish in its basic principles between public and private bureaucracies. What distinguishes the two is, therefore, not the principle of performance, and perhaps not even the underlying values on the basis of which they function, but the objectives of their action. A civil service is engaged in meeting the systemic goals of the society as a whole, the business firm is attempting to meet the private goals of those who own and/or direct it.

Thus, if on a certain level administrative actions are performed by institutions with strong integrative functions, on another level they are performed by institutions whose behavior distinguishes them little from entities in the adaptive sector. This change clearly also alters the nature and frequency of boundary exchanges between the goal-attainment sector, on the one hand, and the integrative or the adaptive sectors, on the other. And, finally, by emphasizing more clearly the place of the various institutions, and allocating them squarely to the different sub-sectors of social action, it allows a neat description and evaluation of the system of interaction (or of inputs and outputs) between the different sectors of the social system and especially their various institutionalized entities. It is in this context alone that a proper evaluation of a bureaucratic structure becomes fully adequate.

CHAPTER 7

Bureaucracy and Economic Development[1]

JOSEPH J. SPENGLER

"Whoever wills the end must make his peace with the means"—T. Veblen, *Imperial Germany and the Industrial Revolution*, p. 240.

This chapter studies the role of the public bureaucracy in economic development, to ascertain what may be done to increase the effectiveness of this role. It relates only to the role of bureaucracy in a mixed economy, that is, one in which the public sector is of significant size and yet not almost coterminous with the economy, as in the Soviet Union. For this role can only be negligible if the state does little more than function as a night-watchman and order-keeper; and it cannot be dealt with effectively in terms of public-private intersectoral relations if the private sector is very small. Even so, this role may vary appreciably from one mixed economy to another for diverse reasons, among them the fact that the developing countries embrace economies ranging from the small and primitive to the large and promising.

I. Economic Development Defined

Economic development entails both accretion and differentiation. At any given point in time there may be said to exist a population inclusive of a labor force, together with a stock of man-made equipment, a natural environment that has been more or less modified by man's past activities, a set of ideas and concepts and aspirations that bear positively or negatively upon economic development, and a variety of institutions that condition what use is made of this complex of equipment, natural environment, and development-affecting ideas. At a subsequent, proximate point in time the population inclusive of the labor force may be unchanged in size, or it may be somewhat larger or smaller; its natural environment may remain substantially as it was while its stock of man-made equipment may be somewhat larger or somewhat smaller; and its ideas, concepts, aspirations, and institutions may remain much as they were, or they may have undergone some

[1] I am very much indebted to Mr. Walter L. Johnson for suggestions and assistance in the preparation of this chapter. I am also indebted to the Ford Foundation for financial assistance. I completed this study while on a Guggenheim fellowship.

change, in which event it is probable that the qualitative composition of the population and its man-made equipment will have been modified somewhat. What has been said boils down to this: the state of development of a changing economy (or system) at time period t is a function of its state of development in the preceding time period t-1, together with whatever development-affecting activity was undertaken in this time period. Accordingly, even though such a given state of development is related as described to the states preceding and, therefore, partially reflects the sequence of states immediately preceding, the amount of reflection will be relatively small if the amount of development-affecting activity undertaken is large and increasing.[2]

I have not yet attempted to define at all specifically that system or sub-system in which growth and development are taking place, nor have I indicated with precision the components of this change-undergoing object. In fact, a definition that is both inclusive and easy to follow is not to be had; for that in which development is (or may be) taking place is a matrix of somewhat interrelated objects, any or all of which may be changing even as the total number of objects included in the matrix may be increasing or decreasing. Accordingly, because it is difficult to communicate in terms of such a matrix, howsoever amenable it may be to conceptualization, one is inclined, when discussing economic development, to employ some single-indicator end-result and to suppose that changes in this indicator reflect changes in the seemingly more important of the elements included in the matrix. As useful an indicator as may be had of this end result is Gross National Product (GNP), or, if allowance is made for capital consumption, Net National Product (NNP) compiled and computed in accordance with current or some other commonly accepted conventions; one or the other of these indicators will be employed in much of the discussion that follows.

It will be taken for granted, at least for purposes of exposition, that

[2] Let S represent an economy's state of development; D, developmental activities undertaken; and t, the time period to which S and D refer. Then

$$S_t = f(S_{t-1}, D_{t-1});$$

and, since S_{t-1} is a parameter, $\Delta S/\Delta t$(i.e., $S_t - S_{t-1}$) $= f(D_{t-1})$. Furthermore, if the amount of change in state S per unit of time (i.e., $\Delta S/\Delta_t$) is an increasing function of the amount of developmental activity D carried on within such unitary time span, then we may say:

$$\frac{\Delta \frac{\Delta S}{\Delta t}}{\Delta D} = +;\ \text{or}\ \frac{\Delta^2 S}{\Delta t^2} = f(\Delta D)$$

growth has taken place if GNP, or NNP (which usually moves in close sympathy with GNP), has increased. This does not mean, of course, that well-being at the individual level has moved correspondingly; for population may have increased at the same rate as GNP or NNP. Accordingly, if the subject of inquiry be well-being at the individual level, it is essential to employ as an indicator, per capita GNP or NNP, for it is at the individual level that one encounters sensibility of income received and of change therein, and it is of his own share, or at most of the share of his primary group, together with changes therein, that the individual is highly sensible.[3] It does not follow, however, that the movement of GNP, or of NNP, per capita is a virtually perfect indicator of the movement of individual well-being, even when that individual is free to dispose as he chooses of the share that passes into his hands. For both GNP and NNP are imperfect measures which have not been entirely divested of costs or adjusted to the task of measuring social income; their increase may have been accompanied by increase in the inequality with which product is distributed; and there may have been a decrease in the degree to which the composition of output has been accommodated to the composition of tastes, or of demand. It is much more likely, nonetheless, that, within a given country or cultural sphere, an upward movement of GNP or NNP per capita makes for an increase than that it makes for a decrease in well-being per capita.[4]

[3] I have neglected the so-called external economies and diseconomies of consumption, the satisfaction and the dissatisfaction that others than the consumer proper experience in consequence of his consumption. These economies and diseconomies seem to be of very minor significance for the purposes of this essay, and they are not easily woven into the discussion.

[4] This statement may need qualification in that, as familial income rises, a family may find itself shunted from its old milieu of tastes and aspirations into a new and more demanding and expensive milieu, with the result that its level of satisfaction is diminished. Within most low-income countries, however, this outcome is unlikely. More pertinent presumably is that which the author of the *Panchatantra* tales wrote many centuries ago:

> Until a mortal's belly-pot
> Is full, he does not care a jot
> For love or music, wit or shame,
> For body's care or scholar's name,
> For virtue or for social charm,
> For lightness or release from harm,
> For godlike wisdom, youthful beauty,
> For purity or anxious duty.

On the communally disorganizing effect of extreme poverty see Edward Banfield, *The Moral Basis of a Backward Society*, Glencoe, Ill., The Free Press, 1958. See also Oscar Lewis, *The Children of Sanchez: Autobiography of a Mexican Family*, New York, Random House, 1961.

II. Developmental Processes

The processes underlying economic development are ultimately reducible to two: the selection of ends or objectives which entail or are associated with development, and the transformation of inputs into outputs in such ways as to materialize these objectives.

The value system dominant in a society, particularly among its elites, is of primary importance. For it can generate a system of virtually unchanging routines which allow for little or no increase of NNP per head, as has happened in traditional and tribal societies. Or it can generate a system of routines which embodies change-producing forces (e.g., capital formation, technical education) that gradually modify some of the routines, usually in a manner to intensify rather than to diminish the change-producing forces at work; illustrative is the experience of England between, say, 1600 and 1800. Or, finally, it can generate a system of changing routines which gives rise to arrangements that institutionalize the science and the art of technical invention and innovation, together with capital formation and technical education, and (in some degree at least) the production of relevant scientific information. Illustrative is the experience of advanced societies in the past fifty to a hundred years.

Unless many among the elite of a society are animated by values favorable to these change-producing forces and seek objectives realizable only through the operation of these forces, a society is not likely to undergo much economic development. If these values are present, and particularly if they are also being diffused more widely, the objectives in question will be sought. They may be sought in a hit-or-miss fashion, as would initially be characteristic of a purely laissez-faire economy, or they may be sought through varying degrees of organized planning in the public or the private sector. As a rule, such development as has taken place has been a sequel to both kinds of planning or fixing of objectives, with planning in one sector tending to make for complementary activity in the other, and with both modes of planning tending to give rise to change-producing routines of the sort mentioned above.

If only a small fraction of the members of the elite in a society are animated by values making for the choice of objectives whose realization entails the enlistment of change-producing forces, getting economic development underway is beset with many difficulties and may even prove impossible. Such is the situation faced in many developing countries, particularly in those shot through with traditionalism or tribalism. Under these circumstances one of the tasks of a development-seeking minority element among the elite is the communication of aspirations after development to members of both the elite and the underlying population, and another is to obtain sufficient control over what may be called a society's input-transforming agencies to get some economic development under way.

The second process, that involving input transformation, had best be described before the interrelations of the two processes are touched upon. Put very simply, there are available at any point in time quantities of disposable inputs (labor, capital equipment, land, etc.) which may be transformed into products for use today or tomorrow, or which may simply be allowed to remain idle. What these inputs will be transformed into depends upon the objectives sought in the society by those with the requisite purchasing power or in possession of alternative means of control over the uses to which inputs are devoted. Inevitably some of these inputs will remain idle, and most of those that are used (perhaps 80-99 per cent) will be transformed into consumer goods and services, that is, into goods and services which, even though essential to existence, contribute little or not at all to the subsequent flow of inputs and the possibility of augmenting NNP per capita; the balance (say 1-20 per cent of the inputs used) will be transformed into income-producing or future-oriented goods and services, that is, into goods and services that make for increase in NNP per capita. In the situation here assumed, therefore, whether or not there will be economic growth and development turns on whether some of the available inputs are transformed into income-producing goods and services. Whether or not inputs are so used depends in turn upon the objectives sought by those able to decide what input-transforming agencies must do, and these objectives reflect the values regnant in a society, particularly those regnant among the elite.

I have sought to show that the two processes underlying economic development—the fixing of appropriate objectives and the transforming of inputs into goods and services realizing these objectives—are separate and distinct. It is possible for individuals to fix objectives and cause them to be materialized so long as they exercise control over some of a society's inputs, or over the decisions of some of those who manage input-transforming agencies. These objective-fixing individuals do not also have to administer or supervise the input-transforming agencies. Similarly, it is immaterial to those administering input-transforming agencies what kinds of transformation they undertake, so long as the transformation in question is as profitable as any alternative kind of transformation.

I have also sought to show that these two processes are distinct and separable because only if this distinction is recognized can the possible roles of a public bureaucracy be discussed fruitfully. For if the processes are distinct, either one or both may be carried out by the public bureaucracy, or one or both may be carried out under private auspices. I shall argue later on that in a mixed economy comprising a public and a private sector the major concern of the public bureaucracy will be, and on grounds of efficiency should be, the specification of ends and objectives, more or less pursuant to the indications provided by the legislative branch of the government or (when the executive is so empowered) by the executive branch of the government.[5] The actual business of transforming inputs will normally be only a minor concern of the bureaucracy. The concern of input-transforming agencies will be the transforming of inputs into outputs, in keeping primarily with demands originating in the private sector and secondarily with demands originating with agencies of the government or in the public sector. In reality, of course, because there is always present a tendency for decisions respecting both processes to become lodged in a single decision-making organization, there often come into being various sorts of arrangements which are designed to establish more than a fortuitous connection between those carrying out one or the other of the two processes (e.g., the public corporation); some of these will be touched upon later.

III. Determinants of Economic Development

The factors making for economic development in the sense of increasing GNP or NNP have been variously classified. For purposes of the present discussion, however, we shall classify them as follows: (1) the elements requisite in a political milieu if it is to be conducive to

[5] Here the executive branch is understood to embrace only the top executive, together with his immediate cabinet and his and their important aides, though not also the underlying bureaucracy, which is responsible for carrying out but not for initiating decisions. In practice, of course, this distinction is blurred, since the underlying bureaucracy (components of which often are in competition and even in conflict respecting either objectives or the the means best suited to realize such objectives) frequently plays a major role in the generation of objectives subsequently endorsed by the legislative or the executive branches of the government.

economic development; (2) the objective and the subjective factors making for economic growth through time; and (3) the effectiveness of the allocative system.

(1) In order that economic growth may take place, the state must meet two responsibilities, above all in the developing countries. It must provide a minimum of public services and legal conditions; and it may also have to support a number of growth-stimulating policies. Under the head of minimal public services and legal conditions, at least the following may be indicated:

(a) Law, order, and security must be maintained, and their maintenance must be accompanied by a minimal degree of public probity, since otherwise improbity, together with its uneven incidence, will too markedly reduce the effectiveness of the arrangements designed for the maintenance of law, order, and security.[6]

(b) There must exist a legal and administrative structure which guards and guarantees the prerequisites of both private and public property, which permits the various required types of business organization (e.g., partnership, limited liability companies, syndicates, etc.) to function, and which allows quite full scope to economic competition, in part by preventing the persistence of unregulated monopoly in any important sector of the economy.

(c) There must be a suitable monetary and banking structure; an adequately controlled supply of paper money and bank credit; and a system of banks designed to assemble savings, to supply credit for short and intermediate periods of time, and to afford access to domestic and foreign long-term capital.

(d) There must be increasing provision per capita for the support of education, public health, and various overhead capital outlays, the returns from which cannot be wholly recaptured by sale of their services because these flow also to beneficiaries from whom the collection of payment is impractical. The amount of provision annually made must more than cover depreciation on past outlays and allowance for

[6] Undoubtedly an illuminating essay might be written on the role of increasing probity in the facilitation of growth; for in the absence of a minimal degree of probity it is difficult to achieve growth. Presumably traders and manufacturers could guard themselves against the improbity of their fellows, even though consumers might not be able to do so unless competition reigned and agencies of the state did not undergird the aspirations after monopoly so common among manufacturers and tradesmen. Against improbity in government, however, it was difficult for enterprise to guard itself, even as it is difficult to do so today, with the result that various activities are handicapped or not undertaken at all.

population growth; it must permit increase in the stock of overhead capital available per capita.

(e) Inasmuch as most countries, and especially those which are still developing, stand to benefit greatly from the inflow of foreign personnel and capital, it is essential that provisions be made for their satisfactory juridical and economic treatment.

The minimal conditions I have outlined are those one expected in a pre-1914 "liberal" state. Furthermore, of the conditions listed, only the last two tend to be continuously contributive to economic development. The others simply provide a framework within which economic development is possible, given the presence of active agents. Under these circumstances, therefore, the role that the bureaucracy as such could or would play in economic development would be quite small.

There are many countries in which provision of these minimal conditions, while necessary if growth is to take place, is insufficient to set continuing growth processes in motion, for other of the pre-conditions to self-sustaining growth are not present, or at least are not present in sufficient degree. When this is so, corrective action on the part of the state is necessary. It may be necessary only to introduce from abroad agencies which can generate this growth. It is more likely, however, that the state will have to undertake appropriate input-transformation, or induce input-transforming agencies to transform inputs into growth-producing objectives. Whether or not this is done, or whether it can be done in sufficient degree, depends upon the strength of the growth-favoring values present in a society, upon how effectively they are expressed by the bureaucracy, and upon the capacities of its input-transforming agencies or of those to which access is possible. Attention will be given later on to specific tasks which may confront the bureaucracy in a developing country at various levels of its progress. At present it is essential to touch upon objective and subjective factors making for the growth of NNP per capita as well as upon the price system; for how effectively a public bureaucracy can promote economic development turns ultimately upon how effectively it can cope with the specific determinants of economic development and with the transformation of inputs into outputs.

(2) Under the head of objective determinants of the growth of NNP per capita we may include those whose influence is immediate (i.e., capital, technological progress, enterprise) and those whose influence is less immediate (i.e., technical education of the labor force, accumulation of scientific knowledge). If we are interested also in the

growth of total NNP or GNP we must include growth of the labor force, or more specifically, growth of the aggregate input of manhours, which depends also upon the proportion of the population of working age who are employed and upon the average number of hours worked per year per employee.[7] Of the immediately influential objective determinants, technological progress and enterprise seem to be the more important, though their effectiveness is limited by the amount of capital available.

The precise importance of capital is not easy to assess. Under static conditions, if capital employed per worker increases by one per cent, output per worker under otherwise *ceteris paribus* conditions will normally increase by between about 0.2 and 0.4 per cent, with the higher rate to be found in capital-short countries in which the new nations abound. When, however, the role of capital under dynamic conditions is examined, it is found that over sustained periods (say forty to fifty years) only a small fraction of the increase in output per manhour is attributable to capital. This fraction may be somewhat more or somewhat less than 20 per cent of the total increase in output per manhour; the balance seemingly is attributable largely to technical progress, with economies of scale and agglomeration perhaps making some contribution. The significance of capital investment is probably greater, however, than these figures suggest. Capital is essential, of course, to give expression to new inventions; for even though an invention is capital-saving, its introduction is likely to entail an initial increase in capital outlay. More to the point, however, invention and innovation and the science and engineering technology underlying them are the product of past investment in various kinds of scientific skill and equipment; and the general improvement in the quality of the manhours supplied by the labor force is the product of past investment in the education of the labor force.

A complete discussion of the role of capital, which is here understood to embrace only reproducible equipment and information, involves discussion also of land and other natural resources. For, while the development of natural resources absorbs capital, such resources amount to substitutes for or complements to capital. A developing country well-endowed with good land and natural resources will be

[7] I am largely neglecting the impact of population growth, even though this growth may variously influence the course of output per worker by affecting the rate of capital formation per head, the proportion of the population of working age, the behavior of tendencies to increasing or decreasing returns, the flexibility of the economy, etc.

able both to attract foreign capital and to derive a relatively large income from a given amount of reproducible equipment. A country not so well-endowed will find it more difficult if not impossible to achieve a given high level of development as evidenced by level of income.

The precise contribution of technology, usually arrived at by allowing for the supposed contribution of other factors and attributing the residuum to technical progress, is not easy to determine, given the margin of error surrounding estimates of the contribution of these factors. The gross contribution of technology is very great, however, as is suggested by estimates which attribute as much as four-fifths or more of the increase in output per manhour to the cluster of elements grouped under technological progress. It follows, therefore, that economic development is assured so long as heavy enough investment is made in technical progress and the factors closely associated with it. Unlike a developed country which usually must contribute to the pool of basic knowledge that underlies technical progress, a developing country can rely largely upon the world pool of relevant knowledge and confine its efforts to introducing this knowledge and utilizing it to improve domestic methods of production.

The role played by enterprise is subject to controversy, even when enterprise is defined to include such functions as organization of the activities of a firm, the bearing of risk, the innovation of invention, the continual discovery of business opportunities and the direction of inputs to the realization of these opportunities, and so on. Some economists associate economic development primarily with the activities of the entrepreneur, suggesting that his activities generate a good deal of the capital available in an economy and that, even though industry supplies only a small fraction of the basic research undertaken, it is largely through his leadership that the findings of basic science are made subservient to man's welfare. In the opinion of these economists the entrepreneur is the prime mover in an economy, while the economy itself cannot function very dynamically unless there is a sufficiency of entrepreneurs. Other economists admit the importance of the various functions associated with enterprise, but suppose that these functions will be performed well in any society in which there is a sufficiency of technically trained people who are not unduly constrained. These economists thus make the supply of enterprise dependent, even as is the supply of engineers, upon efforts to train individuals appropriately; they thus place less emphasis upon the uniqueness and the art-like quality of the entrepreneur's contribution. Despite the way in which these two interpretations differ respecting the role of the entrepreneur and of the augmentation of the supply of persons to perform this role, they do agree on the importance of the role; and this has a strong bearing upon the place to be assigned the public sector in a developing mixed economy.

Of the less immediate objective determinants of growth, the education of the labor force and accumulation of scientific knowledge appear to be the most important. Not much need be said of these determinants. Regarding the first, inasmuch as the opportunity cost of investment is very high in a capital-short country (say somewhere between 10 and 20 per cent), expenditure upon education needs to be concentrated upon kinds of education which are essential to production rather than upon kinds which are decorative or of little productive worth (e.g., ecclesiastical, much that is legal or traditional). It is essential that primary education be continued until functional literacy is achieved, since otherwise the primary training will prove worthless; and it is important that heavy emphasis be placed upon secondary education and upon technological education at this level since most jobs can be filled with persons of such education. More advanced education can be afforded only in a limited degree, so long as a country is short of educational facilities, with the result that major emphasis must be put upon scientific training that can facilitate economic growth. Regarding the accumulation of scientific knowledge, it is to be noted that, as the initially small and now growing contribution of Japan suggests, a developing country can contribute little thereto until it has progressed sufficiently; during this incubation period, therefore, a developing country can proceed most economically by drawing upon the world pool of scientific information and adapting this information to its requirements. Both because of the difficulties and the financial uncertainty that beset the introduction of new methods at the pilot stage in a developing country and because of the external economies that may be associated therewith, some subsidization of this process may be indicated. The circumstances surrounding an enterpriser introducing new methods from abroad are somewhat similar to those surrounding an enterpriser who undertakes basic research in a developed country; for since this research can pay satisfactory returns only under certain conditions, it is essential either that such research be subsidized or that it be carried on in universities and other institutions where immediate profitableness is or may be of little or no concern.

Under the head of subjective factors affecting economic development may be included the systems of values which orient the conduct of the elite and the underlying population considered above and the apparatuses of thought (or sets of concepts) wherewith scientists, artisans, administrators, etc., approach problems in the realms of politics, economics, the life sciences, the inorganic sciences, medicine, and so on. These two subjective categories may be distinguished analytically, since the uses to which apparatuses of thought are directed is largely under the governance of the regnant systems of values. In reality, however, these two kinds of furniture (or contents) of the mind are not wholly independent and may even be mutually re-enforcing; for given values may be favorable to some apparatuses of thought and unfavorable to others, whereas what is revealed by a given apparatus of thought may result in a modification of some values.

The subjective factors are very important in that one generally finds economic development associated with some and not with others. They are not susceptible of rapid modification, however. The most that can be done in a developing country encumbered with unfavorable subjective factors is to shunt power into the hands of the minority equipped with favorable factors in the hope that appropriate input transformation will be encouraged and that the views of this minority will be diffused to other elements in the population. This observation implies that economic progress will be facilitated through the replacement, in important positions in the bureaucratic structure, of bureaucrats with a traditional subjective equipment by bureaucrats with both a modern, more scientific point of view and a greater disposition to bring about development-favoring changes. If, in addition, control can be established over the educational system and over what is taught, a very great change in the conspectus of subjective factors may be produced in ten to twenty-five years.

(3) The allocative system operative in a society, together with its instrumental effectiveness, may be dealt with either in terms sufficiently broad to cover various reward systems and to take account of the respective contributions of ascription and competitive assignment, or in terms confined to economic or market competition.[8] Here, however, notice will be taken only of the price system. In order for an economy to function effectively and for consumers, suppliers of personal service or skill, and input-transforming enterprisers to choose rationally among the alternative courses of action open to them, a fairly well-developed

[8] E.g., see T. Parsons, *The Social System*, Glencoe, Ill., The Free Press, 1951, pp. 114-132, 175-176, 243-248, 414-427.

and flexible price system must exist and be at their disposal.[9] Such a system not only facilitates the making of rational economic decisions by assembling and diffusing information rapidly; it also functions as a servo-mechanism in that it enables decision makers to modify their courses of action whenever prices relevant for them undergo sufficient change. In consequence, the behavior of participants in the economic system is easily kept adjusted to changes in the underlying structure of income distribution, taxes, scarcities, tastes, etc. A price system of this sort is found in advanced countries where, even though it is subject to somewhat misleading rigidities imposed by the state or by monopolistic elements, it makes for quite rational decision making within both the public and the private sectors. In a developing country, however, the price system is likely to be imperfect and in need of supplementary estimation (based perhaps on external experience) if it is to supply adequate information for the forming of various future-oriented decisions, among them important ones relating to economic development.[10] Imperfections of this sort handicap both bureaucratic and private decision makers and may have a bearing upon attempts to determine what functions should be assigned to the public sector in given situations.

Even when those in control of an economy have sought to institutionalize a "basic obsession for economic growth," as has the Communist party in the Soviet Union, selection of inappropriate indicators of success, together with their misuse, will reduce the return from growth-oriented investment below the realizable level. Misuse of inputs results; motivation on the part of management to innovate and to improve methods of production is weakened; and the composition of the output of consumer goods is maladjusted to the composition of demand.[11] These tendencies, always present in some degree, are ac-

[9] One might fall back upon an analogue of the price system, but only in an advanced country equipped with the requisite instruments.

[10] For a discussion of shortcomings in the price systems of developing countries, see T. Balogh, "Economic Policy and the Price System," *Economic Bulletin for Latin America*, VI, 1, March 1961, pp. 41-53. He includes among the shortcomings of such price systems not only their imperfections respecting the assembly and the diffusion of necessary information, but also the insensitivity of various price-makers and price-takers to the system of prices as such. These insensitivities, granted that they exist, are of a different order than imperfections in a system's capacity to assemble and diffuse information.

[11] E.g., see A. Pepeliasis, L. Mears, and I. Adelman, *Economic Development*, New York, Harper, 1961, pp. 144-149; F. D. Holzman, ed., *Readings on the Soviet Economy*, Chicago, Rand McNally, 1961, Parts II, V-VI; also Harry Schwartz's account of current non-synchronization of fixed and other forms of capital investment in the Soviet Union, *New York Times*, October 29, 1961, Sec. 1, p. 7.

centuated when the execution of plans is rendered inflexible by excessive routinization and when ideological hostility to the use of servomechanistic systems (e.g., the price system) is on the rise.

IV. Inter-Sectoral Relations

Inasmuch as the public sector of an economy is under the control of the bureaucracy, whereas the balance of such economy is under the control of private enterprise, we may, for purposes of discussion, look upon an economy as bi-sectoral in composition. When this is done, it becomes evident (among other things) that each sector is drawing upon the stock of inputs available to the economy, with the result that, so long as all these inputs are employed, expansion of one sector will be at the expense of the other. The relation between the two sectors is substitutive in character, in part because similar activities are pursued in both sectors and in part because similar inputs enter into dissimilar outputs, some of which originate only in the public sector and others only in the private sector. Of course, if the available stock (or flow) of inputs increases, a portion of the increment will tend to flow to the one sector and the balance to the other; for, when an economy expands, a complementary inter-sectoral relationship is likely to emerge.[12]

It is because the public and the private sectors are variously interrelated that assessment of the effects of a policy initiated in one sector is seldom adequate unless account is taken of the effects produced by such policy in both sectors. Illustrative are the possible repercussions of efforts on the part of a developing country's bureaucracy to increase the stock (or flow) of available inputs through measures designed to increase the rate of saving or capital formation in the public sector.[13]

[12] The precise nature of inter-sectoral connections and behavior depends, in any given situation, upon the concrete circumstances present, among them the actual composition of each of the sectors involved. E.g., see Leif Johansen, *A Multi-Sectoral Study of Economic Growth*, Amsterdam, North-Holland Publishing Co., 1960; J. S. Chipman, *The Theory of Inter-Sectoral Money Flows and Income Formation*, Baltimore, Johns Hopkins University Press, 1960.

[13] Such measures are widely favored and quite appropriate when properly formulated and executed. For, "by and large, countries with relatively high rates of investment have achieved relatively high rates of growth." See United Nations, *World Economic Survey, 1960*, New York, 1961, p. 15. This relationship is somewhat more pronounced in advanced countries (*ibid.*, p. 16) than in developing countries, where other obstacles to economic growth are distributed in such wise as partially to reduce the correlation between rate of capital formation and rate of growth (*ibid.*, pp. 57-58). When these obstacles have been removed, the correlation increases. For a detailed empirical account of the role of investment in economic development, see United Nations, *World Economic Survey, 1959*, New York, 1960, Part 1.

Such increase might be accomplished through taxation and other measures that divert resources from consumption to capital formation, at least within the limits that seem to be set by constraints to which capital formation is subject.[14] If, however, such increase is attempted through measures that divert to the public sector resources that would otherwise have been employed in capital formation in the private sector, the resulting increase in public capital may be accompanied by little if any increase in the aggregate (i.e., public plus private) stock (or flow) of capital.[15] Similarly, an increase in the amount of manpower employed in the public sector may be at the expense of the private sector. It is essential, therefore, when increase in the employment of inputs in one sector is at the expense of their employment in the other, to determine in which sector marginal inputs are more productive, given the objectives (shorter- and longer-run) sought by a society.

The relative importance of the public sector and hence of the bureaucracy required to carry on the functions assigned to this sector may vary, and does vary considerably, even in societies with mixed economies. Various circumstances affect its importance: (a) The prevailing ideology exercises some influence, though how much it is difficult to estimate; for when this ideology is unfavorable, as was the case in England or in the United States in the mid-nineteenth century, governmental functions are held at a minimum, whereas when it is favorable, functions may be turned over to the state which could be

[14] Even in Communist countries capital formation has not been raised much above 15 per cent on a net basis, or above 25 per cent on a gross basis, though conceivably a high-income authoritarian regime might raise capital formation above 15-20 per cent of NNP. See S. Kuznets' discussion of the limits on saving in "Quantitative Aspects of the Economic Growth of Nations," Part v, *Economic Development and Cultural Change*, Vol. VIII, No. 4, Part II, July 1960, pp. 22-32. Concerning what taxes are least incident upon savings see R. A. Musgrave, *The Theory of Public Finance*, New York, McGraw-Hill, 1959, chaps. 15-16; also P. T. Bauer, *Indian Economic Policy and Development*, New York, Frederick J. Praeger, Inc., 1961, pp. 89ff., 124ff.

[15] Indian economic policy is a case in point, Bauer states (*op.cit.*, pp. 124ff.). It is not easy to estimate with precision offsets in the private sector to savings in the public sector, or to infer much from inter-country comparisons, given the fact that high levels of government savings often are found in countries with high levels of total saving, and that the private sector has been the main source of domestic saving in industrial and in some though not all developing countries. In industrial countries the private sector has been the source of roughly 65-80 per cent of total fixed investment (United Nations, *World Economic Survey 1959*, pp. 39-44); in developing countries the corresponding percentage has ranged roughly between 40 and 80 per cent (*ibid.*, pp. 83-84). See also United Nations, *World Economic Survey 1960*, pp. 19-31, 67-73. Fixed investment, of which about three-fifths consists in construction, forms about 90-95 per cent of all investment. See Kuznets, *op.cit.*, pp. 33-34, also pp. 85-87 on public and private fixed capital formation.

performed at least as well in the private sector.[16] (b) A limit to the size of the public sector may be imposed by the scarcity of personnel (see below) capable of filling bureaucratic positions, together with such technological constraints as hold down the amount of work a bureaucrat can do; this limit is encountered in all developing countries and probably accounts in part for the comparative smallness of the ratio of governmental expenditures to GNP encountered in many such countries.[17]

(c) Growth of the public sector may be fostered by the presence of potential external economies, particularly if it is believed that expansion releasing such economies will not or cannot be undertaken by private enterprise; and it is likely to be fostered by the belief that, as incomes rise, demand increases even more rapidly for supposedly "collective" and "indivisible" goods which the state is best able to supply.[18] Such growth has been fostered also by recurring crises which make necessary increases in the relative amount of revenue raised by the state and thereby gradually adjust upward a people's ideas respecting the tolerability of tax burdens; and this decline in public resistance to increase in tax burdens may be facilitated by shifts in the responsibility for governmental functions and costs from local authorities to the central authority.[19]

[16] Concerning the changing role of the public sector see United Nations, *Economic Survey of Asia and the Far East, 1960*, Bangkok, 1961, Part II, and *Economic Survey of Latin America, 1955*, New York, 1956, Part II; also *Economic Survey of Europe in 1959*, Geneva, 1960, chaps. 5-6. In the United Kingdom government expenditure amounted to 9-12 per cent of GNP during the last two-thirds of the nineteenth century; it rose from about 13 per cent around 1910 to about 26 in 1920-1933 and to about 40 in 1950-1955. See A. T. Peacock and Jack Wiseman, *The Growth of Public Expenditure in the United Kingdom*, Princeton, Princeton University Press, 1961, pp. 37, 42-43.

[17] Government consumption (including defense) has been ranging from about 10 to 18 per cent of GNP in industrial countries and from 6 to 19 per cent in developing countries. See United Nations, *World Economic Survey, 1960*, pp. 22-23, 68-69. Government expenditure and consumption appear to be increasing somewhat in relative importance in the new nations, especially in Asia and Africa. See United Nations, *Economic Survey of Asia and the Far East, 1960*, pp. 55-64, and *Economic Bulletin for Africa*, I, 2, June 1961, pp. 1-28. Somewhat parallel data are presented by Simon Kuznets in *op.cit.*, pp. 84-87, and in "Quantitative Aspects of the Economic Growth of Nations," Part II, *Economic Development and Cultural Change*, Supplement to V, 4, July 1957, pp. 62-65, 68-73, 75-81.

[18] Views of this sort were expressed in the late nineteenth century, particularly in Germany. See R. A. Musgrave and A. T. Peacock, eds., *Classics in the Theory of Public Finance*, London, Macmillan, 1958, pp. xvii, 8, 29, 233ff. See also Peacock and Wiseman, *op.cit.*, pp. 16-21, 23-26, 39-40. Many of the goods represented as being collective and indivisible are not so; for the services flowing from such goods are usually quite divisible and hence saleable in large or small quantities to given purchasers.

[19] See *ibid.*, pp. xxiii-xxvii, 24-30, and passim; also p. 149, where it is concluded

(d) A somewhat similar set of circumstances, responsible for changes in the relative importance of the public sector and hence of the bureaucracy, has been identified by T. Parsons and N. Smelser and elaborated by B. F. Hoselitz. According to this view, varying demand is made upon the economic sub-system of a society by its polity, a subsystem having to do with the attainment of collective goals and the mobilization of resource for this purpose. As a result, when collective or system goals increase in importance, the public sector expands, but when, the important goals having been realized, emphasis upon such goals diminishes, the public sector contracts, at least relatively. On this theory, relative size of the public sector, together with the bureaucracy required to man it, tends to fluctuate, sometimes rising and sometimes falling.[20] This theory is compatible with the great importance attached to the state's assuming responsibility for investment in socio-economic overhead capital and various developmental expenditures which (at least in poor countries) cannot be borne by domestic private enterprise; but it fails to account for the fact (given that estimates of prospective public expenditure are tenable) that there is little likelihood that the ratio of public expenditure to GNP will decline sharply after having risen.[21]

V. Inter-Sectoral Factor Movement

GNP will be at a maximum, other conditions given, when inputs are optimally distributed between the public and the private sector; and the rate of growth of GNP will be at a maximum when inputs are distributed between the two sectors in such wise as to give the same

"that the rate of growth of public expenditures is likely to be such as at least to maintain the share of government in GNP broadly at present levels." Compare Otto Eckstein's estimate that federal expenditures may increase less rapidly than GNP, in *Trends in Public Expenditure in the Next Decade*, New York, Committee for Economic Development, 1959. See also B. U. Ratchford, *Public Expenditures in Australia*, Durham, N.C., Duke University Press, 1959.

[20] See Hoselitz, "Economic Policy and Economic Development," in H. G. J. Aitken, ed., *The State and Economic Growth*, New York, Social Science Research Council, 1959, pp. 330-333.

[21] This ratio has declined in the past after having been greatly elevated by war. In Asian countries the share of investment in governmental expenditure, usually 20-40 per cent, has risen somewhat as has the share of the public sector in national expenditure. See United Nations, *Economic Survey of Asia and the Far East, 1960*, pp. 56-59, 67-74, also 75-83 on allocation of governmental expenditure. A similar trend is reported for Africa but not for Latin America. See United Nations, *World Economic Survey 1959*, pp. 83-87, and *Economic Bulletin for Africa*, 1, 2, June 1961, pp. 1-28. Even in the United Kingdom the enlargement of the role of the public corporation has appreciably increased the role of the public sector in capital formation. See Peacock and Wiseman, *op.cit.*, pp. 127-131.

marginal impetus to economic growth in each sector. Of most concern, in this connection and for the purposes of the present chapter, is the fact that the public sector may differ from the private sector in two respects: (1) its personnel is recruited differently; (2) the business of fulfilling functions in the public sector is subject to a somewhat different set of sanctions and a somewhat different set of corrective or homeostatic pressures.

(1) We find that admission to the bureaucracy and perhaps also advancement within it depends upon the possession of certain attributes disclosed by examination, education, personal history, etc. Admission into corresponding segments of the private sector, on the contrary, depends largely upon the manifestation by individuals of a capacity to perform particular functions effectively; unless certain professional qualifications have been imposed by the state (e.g., qualifications deemed requisite at a minimum for the performance of the duties normally associated with such a profession as medicine, accounting, etc.) selection of individuals will be made in the light of such manifestation.

The mode of selecting personnel within the public sector is thus likely to exclude from it various individuals who are quite capable of performing the functions of the offices for which selection is being made. Let us suppose that effective performance of a set of functions F associated with a given office is contingent upon an individual's possessing attributes *abcd*. Within the private sector, an individual with attributes *abcd* would probably be selected to perform the functions F, for if the specified attributes are relevant (as is here assumed), the individual possessing them would probably have manifested ability to perform F. In the public sector, however, it is quite likely that when individuals are being selected for the performance of functions F, they will be required to possess more than the requisite attributes *abcd*. They will also be required to possess attributes *ef* which are not requisite for the effective performance of functions F and which may even be irrelevant or disadvantageous—or six attributes in all, *abcdef*. The effect of this over-requirement of attributes is discriminatory and restrictive in character; it limits the number of persons available, at least in the public sector,[22] for the performance of F. For if S designates all

[22] Over-requirement of attributes is encountered not only in the public sector but also in monopolized occupational areas (e.g., those in which outmoded apprentice systems operate) and in every area in which capacity for achievement is partially subordinated to compatibility with ascriptive allocation. While the addition of attributes may be employed to restrict admission to occupational areas to those who are

persons with attributes *abcd* and *S′* denotes all persons with attributes *abcdef*, and, as is very likely, *S′* is significantly smaller than *S*, the imposition of qualifications *ef* will have artificially and substantially limited the supply of persons qualified to carry out *F*. Of course, if *S′* sufficiently exceeds the number of persons needed in positions involving the performance of functions *F*, the imposition of qualifications *ef* will not reduce the number available below the number required. If, however, the number required for these positions is in excess of *S′*, the imposition of irrelevant qualifications *ef* will retard those forms of economic development in which *F* is required; shortage of persons permitted to perform *F* will have become a limitational factor.

The type of argument just advanced, while also of general application, is of particular application with respect to the performance of the functions normally grouped under "enterprise."[23] The combination of traits that makes for success in enterprise not only varies considerably but is sufficiently unique to make it very difficult (if not impossible) to identify in a useful way what specifiable attributes are essential. This observation holds even though it is true that, within limits, possession of technical information tends to enlarge the realm within which an enterpriser may undertake to function.[24]

What has been said may be formulated in quasi-monopolistic terms. We are dealing with two sectors between which the movement of fac-

competent to perform the tasks encountered therein, it is often used to discriminate on irrelevant grounds in favor of some and against others. Over-requirement of attributes tends to arise in the public sector because it is much easier to group heterogeneous posts and to prescribe requirements for them as if they were homogeneous than it is to recognize heterogeneity of posts and allow men to undergo sorting until (as in the private sector) they finally come to occupy posts roughly in keeping with their abilities. In essence, bureaucratization of selective procedures tends to reduce the number of classes into which men or commodities are assembled below the number that is optimal or that emerges under free-market conditions; for bureaucratic control abhors fine distinctions, much as Aristotle's "nature" abhorred a vacuum. In practice the misuse of attributes, whether in the form of over-requirements or in the form of discriminatory rationing or selective systems, depresses the output or welfare maxima realized below what might have been realized. Such misuse tends to characterize apprenticeship systems, civil-service recruitment arrangements, etc. E.g., see unsigned, "The Most Acute Case," *The Economist*, CCI, November 25, 1961, p. 733; M. A. Chaudhuri, "The Organization and Composition of the Central Civil Service in Pakistan," *International Review of Administrative Sciences*, XXVI, 3, pp. 279-292; Jean Chatelain, "Le recrutement et la formation des cadres superieurs de l'administration générale en France," *ibid.*, pp. 249-255. The conduct of civil-service recruitment in some of the new African states is also illustrative.

[23] E.g., see my "Public Bureaucracy, Resource Structure, and Economic Development: A Note," *Kyklos*, XI, Fasc. 4, 1958, pp. 460-486.

[24] Relevant here might be consideration of the circumstances under which an entrepreneur at (say) the peddler level, common in developing countries, is likely to rise to a level involving heavy investment in fixed capital. See notes 32 and 39 below.

tors should be unimpeded. Yet, the addition of attributes *ef* to the relevant ones, *abcd*, limits the movement of the factor enterprise from the private into the public sector. Even then, no untoward effect would result if all other factors were also free to move in either direction, for then the final factor combinations would be about the same in each sector. If, however, other factors do not flow freely from one sector to the other, there tends to result a situation in which too little enterprise is combined with other factors in the public sector and too much is combined with them in the private sector. If, at the same time, the public sector is made responsible for a considerable share of the input transformation intended to foster economic development, and as a result of public expenditure other factors than enterprise are drawn into the public sector in greater measure than is enterprise, then the ratio of enterprise to other factors will be too low in the public sector and the productivity of other factors, irrespective of what they are paid, will be lower in the public sector than they are in the private sector.

(2) In the discussion so far it has been assumed that the public sector is just as congenial to input transformation as is the private sector. If this does not happen to be the case, or if the two sectors are equivalent only in respect to some kinds of transformation, but not in respect to all, then overall output will be reduced if transformation is carried on in the sector less favorable, rather than in the one more favorable, to efficiency in transformation (i.e., to the minimization of composite input per unit of output). This would be true even if no barriers were placed in the way of the movement of the enterprise factor. This unfavorable outcome would be accentuated if, supposing the public sector to be less favorable to efficiency in some respects, factors other than enterprise were drawn into it while the inflow of enterprise was restricted and thereby diverted into the private sector. This outcome would also be accentuated if, even though the public sector were potentially as well adapted to input transformation as the private sector, the relevant institutional structure of the public sector were imperfectly organized.

VI. Concrete Situations

The actual significance of what has been said in Sections IV-V turns, in any country, upon the concrete circumstances obtaining therein. Among these circumstances are the availability of capital, the availability of suitably educated or experienced personnel, the attitudes of educated personnel toward economic development, and the institutional complex within which private and public activity are currently pursued.

Capital is never available in relatively large amounts and at low supply prices in typical developing countries even though the capacity of such countries to absorb or make use of specific types of equipment (usually of foreign origin) is limited.[25] This comparative non-availability of capital has its origin in part in the lowness of per capita incomes and savings rates and in part in the fact that so large a fraction of the capital currently available must be diverted to equipping increments to the population instead of to the augmentation of the amount of capital available per head.[26] This non-availability may be partially relieved by a net inflow of funds from abroad, though subject to the limitation that countries possessing mineral resources and/or basic facilities (e.g., transport) tend to attract the major share of foreign funds.[27] In general, however, shortage of capital, together with foreign exchange, is a major deterrent to economic development; and this shortage is reflected in the fact that the rate of return on capital, correctly computed, probably exceeds 10-12 per cent in capital-short countries. Capital should, therefore, be distributed between the public and the private sectors and among industrial sectors compatibly with the relevant high rates of return. Whether the bureaucracy having to do with the allocation of scarce public capital is as likely as private investors to insist on so investing it is questionable, however.[28]

"Shortage of capital is not the only, and indeed not the principal, obstacle to more rapid economic progress in the less developed coun-

[25] Limitations of this sort flow from shortages of inputs complementary to the equipment in question and essential to its use.

[26] Pertinent data are to be found in United Nations, *World Economic Survey 1960*, chap. 2, and *World Economic Survey 1959*, chap. 2. On the impact of high rates of population growth upon the formation of capital per capita see United Nations (ECAFE), *Economic Bulletin for Asia and the Far East*, X, 1, June 1959, pp. 33-45; XII, 2, September 1961, pp. 1-28.

[27] United Nations, *World Economic Survey 1960*, pp. 60-66. See also P. N. Rosenstein-Rodan, "International Aid for Underdeveloped Countries," *Review of Economics and Statistics*, XLIII, May 1961, pp. 107-138; also on the comparative importance of the contributions made by different sorts of foreign investment, A. Y. C. Koo, "A Short-Run Measure of the Relative Economic Contribution of Direct Foreign Investment," *ibid.*, August 1961, pp. 269-276.

[28] A detailed examination of public investment policies in various developing countries is needed to establish this point. In the United States the public authority tends to underestimate the cost and overestimate the benefit deriving from investment in water resources. See C. L. Barber's review of recent literature, "Water Resource Development," *Canadian Journal of Economics and Political Science*, XXVII, November 1961, pp. 533-540.

tries. Inexperience and lack of trained manpower at every level are even more serious handicaps." So remarked Mr. Eugene R. Black, President of the World Bank, recently.[29] These lackings are reflected in educational data. For example, although the ratio of college students to the population is only 35-70 per cent as high in Asia and Latin America as in Northwest Europe, the highly significant ratio of secondary students to the population is even lower, being only 20-40 per cent as high.[30] Moreover, in some though not all developing countries, only a relatively small number of the college students are enrolled in engineering or in the natural sciences;[31] and in most of the underdeveloped countries the annual number of graduates with scientific degrees remains very small in comparison with the population.[32] The current shortage of appropriately educated manpower is even

[29] Press release N. 718, November 1, 1961. Shortage of skilled and experienced manpower is stressed in many of the country studies done by missions of the World Bank (International Bank for Reconstruction and Development). Edward Shils, having noted the dearth of indigenous industrial entrepreneurs in the new states, the hostility of new-state intellectuals and intellectual-politicians to private enterprise, and their disposition to seek economic development under the auspices of a greatly enlarged civil service, points out that "almost every new state, except India, Ghana, Nigeria, Tunisia and the Sudan, is defective in its civil service. All except India, and possibly Nigeria lack an ample corps of politicians with devotion to parliamentary institutions and skill in working them. . . . Only India has succeeded in inculcating the army with civil loyalty." See his "Political Development in the New States," reprinted from *Comparative Studies in Society and History*, II, 1960, pp. 279, 409. On the dearth of managerial personnel in the new nations and on difficulties attending the use of foreign personnel, see Mary E. Murphy, "Management Science in the Less Developed Countries," in Donald P. Ray, ed., *Series Studies in Social and Economic Sciences* (National Institute of Social and Behavioral Science), No. 7, Washington, June 1961, pp. 13-21. See also United Nations (ECAFE) *Economic Bulletin for Asia and the Far East*, VII, November 1956, pp. 37-38.

[30] Based on UNESCO, *Basic Facts and Figures 1960*, Paris, 1961, p. 20. In Middle and South Africa the ratio of college students to the population is 1/13 of that found in Northwest Europe; the corresponding fraction for secondary students is 1/10. The data given above do not reflect disparities in the quality of the education available at various levels. On illiteracy and primary-school data see *ibid.* and UNESCO, *World Illiteracy at Mid-Century*, Paris, 1957. For a detailed account of the educational and personnel situation in one country, Nigeria, see the report prepared by the commission headed by Sir Eric Ashby, *Investment in Education*, Lagos, 1960.

[31] Data presented in UNESCO, *Basic Facts and Figures 1960*, Paris, 1961, pp. 56ff., indicate that in Brazil and the Philippines nearly 1/6 of all college students are enrolled in natural science or engineering; in Egypt, Mexico, and Argentina, about 1/8; in Ghana and Syria, about 1/12; in Thailand, only 1/16. In India and Pakistan as in Canada, by contrast, the corresponding fraction is about 3/10. While the comparable fraction for Japan is 1/6, its smallness is offset by the higher rate of overall college enrollment found in Japan. Business education is lumped with social science and history in the UNESCO report; hence the attention given it, though increasing, cannot be compared on a country basis.

[32] Some data are presented in *ibid.*, pp. 65-66. See also United Nations, *Economic Bulletin for Asia and the Far East*, XII, 2, September 1961, p. 25.

more pronounced than these college enrollment data suggest, since the relative number attending college has risen, but too recently to reduce greatly the shortages which obtained ten to fifteen years ago.

These shortages of appropriately educated personnel, together with the shortage of personnel possessing experience in the organization and management of manufacturing and mining and public utility establishments,[33] underlie the almost universal complaint in developing countries of a dearth of manpower with managerial and related skills.[34] These shortages are accentuated, of course, by the fact that the attitude of many intellectuals renders them unfit for effective service within the bureaucracy,[35] and that the behavioral tendencies of many in the bureaucracy are unfavorable to the effective conduct of affairs within the private sector.[36] It is these accentuated shortages that

[33] It is entrepreneurial or managerial skill adapted to the conduct of manufacturing, mining, and public utility enterprises that is particularly scarce and not skill adapted to trading, finance, and speculation, practitioners of which are unlikely, in developing countries, to launch successful manufacturing, mining, or public utility enterprise. See B. E. Supple, "Economic History and Economic Underdevelopment," *Canadian Journal of Economics and Politics*, XXVII, November 1961, pp. 473-475; B. F. Hoselitz, *Sociological Aspects of Economic Growth*, Glencoe, Ill., The Free Press, 1960, pp. 149-154, also pp. 143-149, 154, on the distinction between the managerial and the entrepreneurial role and personality and on the greater compatibility of the former than of the latter with the conduct of enterprise under bureaucratic state auspices.

[34] E.g., see United Nations, *Public Industrial Management in Asia and the Far East*, New York, 1960, pp. 11, 26-27, 41-43, 47-48, 57, 114, 120, 125, and *Management of Industrial Enterprises in Under-Developed Countries*, New York, 1958, pp. 8-11.

[35] What Shils says about India probably is pertinent to other developing societies with a long religio-intellectual tradition: "But the great majority of intellectuals in India are alienated from the centers of public life. They are disillusioned and unhappy about the course of events. They feel great ideals have been deserted for the sake of trivial advances. Their disillusionment is a response to the real difficulties of independent national existence, and also the product of the confrontation of the vague and heroic idealism of opposition by the obduracy of reality. Whatever its causes, Indian democracy, with all its difficulties and inadequacies, the best of the democracies of Asia and Africa, will not long persist under the conditions of this civil abdication of the Indian intellectual class. India might make economic progress, it might be efficiently governed, but it will not continue to be a democracy without a reinforcement of the civil will of the intellectuals." See Edward Shils, *The Intellectual Between Tradition and Modernity: The Indians Situation*, Supplement I to *Comparative Studies in Society and History*, The Hague, Mouton, 1961, p. 116. On Ceylon see Bryce Ryan, "Status, Achievement, and Education in Ceylon," *Journal of Asian Studies*, XX, August 1961, pp. 463-476. What Shils says is much less applicable to African societies, inasmuch as African intellectuals do not number among their mental encumbrances a written history and tradition; it is much less applicable to India than it was a decade ago.

[36] Shils remarks that the great increase "in the size of the Civil Service," prompted by the belief that economic development is "a major task of government," makes contact with the bureaucracy "more frustrating for members of the public which must deal with it. Delays are increased, rebuffs more frequent and the populace forms a distrustful image of government. Murmuring and complaint become widespread, tales

make the economic use of skilled manpower so significant for economic development in countries in which (e.g., India) the absolute (if not the relative) number of skilled personnel is large as well as in those in which both the absolute and the relative numbers of skilled personnel are very small.

As has already been suggested, the complex of institutions within which public and private activities are carried on may further accentuate the shortages described by making for ineffective use of skilled manpower and other resources. For bureaucrats frequently are unsuited, because of their training and experience and outlook, to create an administrative and procedural milieu congenial to private enterprise or to carry on enterprise effectively in the public sector.[37] Accordingly, if reliance must be placed in public enterprise, it is desirable that there be developed managers free of the shortcomings of both civil servants and private entrepreneurs and that these managers remain free of ordinary civil service rules.

Before we turn to means of dealing with the domestic scarcity of high-level personnel, it should be noted that this scarcity has been greatly accentuated in many countries which have recently achieved political independence. On the one hand, many of the expatriate civil servants have been replaced by native personnel, often of inferior training and relatively inexperienced, on the ground, among others, that such action is essential to an emerging state's dignity. On the other hand, independence, together with the importance attached to the public sector, has greatly increased the need for skilled personnel in the public sector.[38] The impact of this scarcity has been accentuated

of irresponsibility, inefficiency and corruption increase." See "Political Development in the New States," *op.cit.*, p. 279. Bauer states: "In India, where even minor civil servants have great powers over those subject to their authority, these controls are often very irksome and their results costly to individuals and to the economy. Resources are also wasted in the absorption of time and effort of civil servants in the production and enforcement of regulations, and of others in trying to evade or change them." See *op.cit.*, p. 89. These remarks probably are applicable also to Pakistan and other countries.

[37] United Nations, *Management of Industrial Enterprises*, p. 8, and *Public Industrial Management*, pp. 125, 130-131.

[38] E.g., see Murphy, *op.cit.*, pp. 15ff.; E. P. Laberge, "The Development of Public Administration in Central America Since the Second World War," *International Review of Administrative Sciences*, XXVI, 2, 1960, pp. 166-180; A. L. Adu, "Problems of Government in Emergent African States," *ibid.*, No. 1, pp. 61-69; R. Taylor Cole, "Bureaucracy in Transition: Independent Nigeria," *Public Administration*, XXXVIII, 1960, pp. 321ff.; A. A. Williams, "Administrative Adjustment of a Colonial Government to Meet Constitutional Change," *ibid.*, XXXV, 1957, pp. 267-288; W. F. Fixnan and A. L. Dean, "Procedures for the Preparation and Implementation of Administra-

also by the difficulties which have attended efforts to introduce Western selective criteria and administrative practices into developing countries and by the disposition of newly emerging national bureaucracies to view private and foreign entrepreneurs and enterprise more or less unfavorably.[39]

VII. Bureaucracy's Role in Economic Development

There are usually though not always three groups to be found in a developing society whence may flow a will and a capacity to plan for the future of a society and so to organize and administer that society's manpower, resources, and external relations as to set (or continue) growth processes in motion. These are the civilian bureaucracy, the military, and the growth-oriented members of the so-called middle class. The first two have more or less at their command the apparatus of state, whereas the power of the last depends largely on the nature and strength of market and market-related contractual ties. While all three are committed to shaping the future through deliberate, future-facing action in the present, the bureaucracy and the military tend to stress action at the national instead of at the local level. It is among these three groups that nearly all personnel with managerial, entrepreneurial, analytical, and planning skills are distributed. How great will be the relative importance of the role played by any one of these three groups depends in considerable part upon the size of its share of a society's growth-oriented personnel and upon the extent to which each group complements or re-enforces the growth-oriented activities of the other two. Thus, if the middle class is of negligible importance (e.g., in Ethiopia),[40] the role of the bureaucracy will be great and that

tive Reforms," *International Review of Administrative Sciences,* XXIII, 1957, pp. 437-452.

[39] E.g., see Murphy, *op.cit.,* pp. 18ff.; M. R. Goodall, "Issues in the Transference of Western Administrative Practices to Contemporary India," *World Affairs Quarterly,* XXX, 1959, pp. 154-160; A. H. Hanson, "Public Enterprise in Nigeria I. Federal Public Utilities," *Public Administration,* XXXV, 1958, pp. 366-384; W. J. Siffin, "The Civil Service of the Kingdom of Thailand," *International Review of Administrative Sciences,* XXVI, 1960, pp. 256-269; unsigned "Administration Under Strain," *Eastern Economist,* XXXIII, 1959, pp. 798-799, and "Private Foreign Investments: An Open Door," *ibid.,* Vol. XXXVI, 1961, p. 768; Committee for Economic Development, *Economic Development Abroad and the Role of American Foreign Investment,* New York, February 1956, pp. 16, 23. The need to reorient the recruitment, training, and use of civil service personnel, together with changes in the relation of the bureaucracy to other elements in the population, is outlined and emphasized by Lim Tay Boh in his admirable address, "The Role of the Civil Service in the Economy of Independent Malaya," *Malayan Economic Review,* IV, April 1959, pp. 1-9.

[40] It is here implicitly assumed that the attitudes and interests of large land-owners are not such as to permit their inclusion among the growth-oriented component of the

of the army may be important, particularly in times of peace when it can supply administrative skills, access to foreign technology, and opportunity for able men of humble origin to rise, and when it can function as a modernizing agency.[41] The role of the bureaucracy may be great even when the middle class is quite powerful; for it is primarily the duty of the bureaucracy to insure that a society diverts enough of its resources into growth-producing activities by devising, on its own motion or in compliance with legislative and/or executive instruction, measures which effectively and economically accomplish such diversion.[42] It is the continuing duty of the bureaucracy of a growth-seeking society to insure that due weight is given to long-run economic considerations, since these are likely to be played down by the small-scale entrepreneurs of short time-horizon who predominate

"middle class." E.g., see Z. Y. Hershlag, *Turkey, An Economy in Transition*, The Hague, Van Kulen, 1958, pp. 34-35, 243; Pedro Tei-chert, *Economic Policy and Industrialization in Latin America*, Oxford, University of Mississippi Press, 1959, chap. 6; United Nations, *Progress in Land Reform*, New York, 1954, *passim;* Robert Solo, "The Accumulation of Wealth in the Form of Land-Ownership in Underdeveloped Areas," *Land Economics*, XXXI, May 1955, pp. 156-159. This assumption is frequently, though not always, valid. Even when it is invalid or only partially valid, however, the contribution of the land-owning element is likely to be restricted by the difficulties that often stand in the way of the rapid modernization of agriculture. The contribution of the land-owning element is much more likely to be capital and foreign exchange (especially in mineral-poor countries) than managerial or entrepreneurial leadership for the non-agricultural sector. Compare B. F. Johnston and J. W. Mellor, "The Role of Agriculture in Economic Development," *American Economic Review*, LI, September 1961, pp. 566-593. An analogous problem is posed by traders, speculators, and money lenders when these show little disposition to invest in fixed capital and other relatively illiquid prerequisites to self-sustaining economic growth. Presumably, if these individuals are not so disposed, their growth-fomenting role will be small unless their activities serve to complement and supplement the activities of growth-oriented undertakers.

[41] E.g., see Lucian W. Pye, "Armies in the Process of Political Modernization," *Archives of European Sociology*, II, 1961, pp. 82-92, to be included in John J. Johnson, ed., *The Role of the Military in Underdevelped Counries*, Princeton University Press, 1962. But compare E. Lieuwin, "The Military: A Revolutionary Force," *Annals of the American Academy of Political and Social Science*, CCCXXXIV, March 1961, pp. 30-40; B. R. Chatterjee, "The Role of the Armed Forces in Politics in Southeast Asia," *International Studies*, II, 3, 1961, pp. 221ff.

[42] When a country's economic policies are strongly influenced (as were pre-independence India's) by external agencies, economic development may be retarded. E.g., see Helen B. Lamb, "The 'State' and Economic Development in India," in S. Kuznets, W. E. Moore, and J. J. Spengler, eds., *Economic Growth: Brazil, India, Japan*, Durham, Duke University Press, 1955, pp. 464-495. This may be true even of sovereign states, when, as in Libya, foreigners dominate industrial enterprise and purveyors of foreign aid misapply such aid or utilize it to serve the interests of nationals of the aid-supplying state. E.g., see International Bank for Reconstruction and Development, *The Economic Development of Libya*, Baltimore, Johns Hopkins University Press, 1960.

in the private sectors of developing economies, or to be subordinated to considerations of external and internal security even when, as is usually the case, military personnel are modern in view and alert to the dependence of military upon economic strength.

The propensity of an economy to grow and develop will be much greater when the activities of the bureaucracy, the military, and the middle class complement one another than when they are at variance. In reality, of course, these activities are bound to be somewhat competitive at best, both because there is competition for inputs and because the bureaucracy, if it gives due emphasis to long-run economic considerations, frequently has to give a longer-run tilt to the objectives sought in the private and in the military sectors. Even under optimum conditions, therefore, conflict in purpose is likely to be present and in need of composition. What must always be sought, therefore, is a rational delimitation of the area within which a stable compromise is to be found; and what must be avoided is the intrusion of ideological or attitudinal considerations which make difficult the delimitation of such area.[43]

The contributions that the bureaucracy can make to economic development are of three fairly distinct sorts. First, it can help to establish and strengthen what we have called (see Section III above) the minimum legal and public-service preconditions to economic development, namely, law and order and security in general, infra-structural elements, money and banking institutions, and a legal and administrative structure favorable to the conduct of economic activities by both domestic and foreign enterprise. What the bureaucracy can do in any specific situation, independently or in conjunction with the military, turns largely on how much has been accomplished already. In the past it has often been a rudimentary bureaucracy of foreign origin that has helped to bring into being and spread various of these preconditions, finally to be assisted by a growing domestic bureaucracy. The bureaucracy is thus both an element in and a fomentor of ele-

[43] Illustrative of these considerations is the ideological hostility that the bureaucracy or the military often manifest toward middle-class elements. Thus when *étatism* was introduced into Turkey in the 1930's, the regime "relied mainly on the Military and the Civil Service, which were apprehensive lest the power of the middle class increase." See Hershlag, *Turkey, An Economy in Transition*, *op.cit.*, p. 88. This attitude flowed at least in part from the failure of private initiative to launch economic development. *Ibid.*, pp. 171-172, 243, also p. 244 on the improvement of mutual relations as the economy progressed. See also United Nations, *Economic Survey of Africa since 1950*, New York, 1960, pp. 188-189.

mentary pre-conditions as well as a force serving to direct some of the existing achievement motivation into channels favorable to economic growth.

Second, the bureaucracy can, by fixing on certain general or specific output objectives, play an important if not a major role in so modifying the resource-structure of a country, together with its exploitation, as to make it more favorable to economic growth. For, while a country will always enjoy a potential comparative advantage in certain respects, its development-potential cannot be realized until both strategically and tactically important agencies are introduced. These agencies will normally consist of individuals with requisite technical skills, of others with managerial (or entrepreneurial) and suitable organizational ability, and of equipment embodying needed modern technology. These agencies will assume the form of firms, of firms that are wholly new and foreign, of firms that represent varying combinations of foreign and domestic capital and enterprise, or of firms that, while domestic and public in character, rely almost entirely upon foreign personnel and skill. In time, of course, these firms will bring into being a body of domestic personnel possessing all or most of the skills and traits requisite for the exploitation of a country's labor force and resources. Under this second approach the bureaucracy plays little or no part in the actual business of transforming inputs into desired output, behaving much as does a government when it utilizes tax or other revenue to buy output from private input-transforming firms.

Third, if private enterprise shows insufficient initiative in exploiting a country's labor force and resource-equipment in ways deemed essential to its economic development, the bureaucracy may establish public corporations, or mixed public-private corporations, or alternative organizational forms to supply the necessary initiative. When this is done, a government agency takes on responsibility for transforming inputs into the kinds of output the bureaucracy believes essential to economic development. Employment of this third approach therefore entails problems and responsibilities of a different order than does the second, with its delegation of responsibility for input transformation to agencies in which the government's direct role is negligible or small. In both approaches, however, it is the bureaucracy that fixes the major objectives or product-mix that is to be supplied, and it is the bureaucracy that determines, or may determine, within limits, how much capital is formed and how much attention is given to training and modernizing the domestic labor force.

If this paper had to do also with the growth-fomenting role of the bureaucracy in economically advanced countries, a fourth approach would be indicated. This approach would include the tax, fiscal, and investment policies fashioned by the bureaucracy for advanced states—at least insofar as these policies are intended to maintain employment, sustain savings and capital formation, and provide for investment in educational, scientific, and technological progress.[44]

What has just been said may be put somewhat differently. If a country is still developing, though possessed of a considerable economic potential, exploitation of this potential can be accelerated through the introduction from abroad of entrepreneurial or managerial talent capable of developing portions of this potential, together with technical and skilled personnel and requisite forms of capital equipment. A country's bureaucracy may initiate such introduction, or facilitate it after it has been initiated, but (presumably) subject to the condition that firms from abroad develop a domestic staff of workers and technical people as rapidly as feasible and reinvest in the country (as taxes or ploughed-back profits) as much of pre-tax profits as is compatible with retaining old and attracting new foreign investment.[45] By so doing, the bureaucracy may foster the growth both of technically competent and experienced personnel and of the pool whence civil servants may be drawn.[46]

The conditions under which domestically scarce factors can be drawn

[44] Some but not all aspects of this fourth approach are touched upon by A. T. Peacock, "The Public Sector and The Theory of Economic Growth," *Scottish Journal of Political Economy*, VI, February 1959, pp. 1-12. I distinguish this fourth approach because there is more scope for growth-oriented fiscal policy in advanced than in developing countries.

[45] Whether what is collected as taxes contributes to economic development turns on the uses to which this purchasing power is put. If it is devoted largely to current consumption or to the construction of relatively unproductive buildings, etc., little long-run benefit will be realized. If it is invested in divers forms of productive enterprise, in suitable education, and in essential types of overhead capital, long-run benefits will result. The bureaucrarcy may be able to divert the expenditure of tax revenue into benefit-yielding channels. Of pertinence in this connection is the tendency in newly emerging states, inherited from pre-independence days (when civil-service rates of remuneration were adjusted to the needs of nationals from the controlling or mother country), to provide civil servants and governmental officers with very high rates of pay even though considerable prestige supposedly attaches to service with the state. The effect of this policy at the input-use level is to draw too many people into government service. Its effect at the capital-formation level depends upon whether the bulk of this excessive payroll is invested in the country's development by its recipients or merely consumed.

[46] E.g., see Roy Lebkicher, *Aramco and World Oil*, New York, R. Moore, 1952, *passim;* Murphy, *op.cit.*, pp. 16ff.; also the National Planning Association Series of reports on United States Business Performance Abroad, Washington, 1953-1957.

from abroad and utilized to develop a country's economic potential vary. Individual firms acting on their own will be attracted, as a rule, only if the prospective rate of return remains sufficiently high, after allowance has been made for juridical and other uncertainties and risks.[47] Such firms are likely to be attracted to a newly developing country, therefore, only if it possesses exploitable natural resources (e.g., gold, copper, petroleum, land suitable for cultivating such marketable specialties as bananas); not until after development and the construction of an infrastructure have proceeded far enough to provide an internal market or ready access to an external market will processing and other manufacturing firms, public utilities, and trading firms find investment opportunities sufficiently attractive. The coming of foreign manufacturing and trading firms may be accelerated not only by the construction of an infra-structure but also by other arrangements. For example, the government of the developing country, or domestic firms situated therein, may enter into a joint arrangement with a foreign firm and supply some of the required capital and (above all) juridical security and freedom for maneuver in that country and (possibly) access to markets in neighboring lands.[48] The bureaucracy may contribute to the coming of such firms by removing the many man-made obstacles and sources of delay frequently encountered by foreign firms as well as by small and even large domestic firms interested in investing in developing countries, by providing certainty about administrative and legal conditions, by supplying relevant information, and by facilitating necessary or advantageous contacts. It may contribute also by requiring competition in every branch of industry as early as feasible, by fostering the development of new and small firms (and hence of a growing body of entrepreneurial and managerial skill), especially in areas ancillary to large-scale or foreign firms,[49] and by facilitating the corporate organizational device as well as investment therein. The bureaucracy can, however, do what is required and provide an environment generally favorable to foreign and domestic enterprise only if its values and attitudes are appropriate. It must ap-

[47] Investment in relatively less attractive regions may at times be prompted by the fact that such action is believed essential to protecting a firm's position in that region and its overall earning capacity.

[48] While capital is always a consideration in such an arrangement, the main considerations are the know-how and organizational skill supplied by the foreign firm and freedom from administrative and other man-made encumbrances supplied by the domestic partner.

[49] On the recruitment and training of small-industry managers, see J. E. Stepanek, *Managers for Small Industry*, Glencoe, Ill., The Free Press, 1960.

preciate the great and strategic importance of the private sector (in any but a completely state-centered economy); it must look upon the entrepreneurial elite as an ally instead of as a competing and less prestigious elite; and it must contribute to the dissipation instead of to the re-enforcement of values which derogate entrepreneurship and cause able young people to avoid instead of engaging in private (and perhaps also public) entrepreneurial activity.

If there is a dearth of capital available to particular firms in the private sector and this dearth cannot be corrected through governmental and/or foreign credits, or if for various other reasons private initiative is lacking or indisposed to undertake activities essential to a country's economic development, the bureaucracy may fall back upon one or more of several organizational arrangements, any one of which can draw on skilled foreign personnel and firms. A governmental department or bureau may carry on the activities in question, or a public corporation may be set up, or the state may establish a company under company law and supply all or most of the company capital, or the government may enter into a contract with a domestic or a foreign company which engages to do what is required for a negotiated fee.[50] Of these organizational forms, the state company or the public corporation is generally deemed preferable except in situations when, because quick action is wanted, the operating contract may offer the best solution. Hanson probably expresses accepted opinion when he states that "there is precious little evidence that the company is either conspicuously better or conspicuously worse than the public corporation. Both have certain theoretical advantages, which may or may not be realized in practice; and both suffer from certain diseases, which in underdeveloped countries often assume pathological proportions."[51] In India, however, preference is now being shown for the company in which the state owns half or more of the stock.

What is required of the public corporation or alternative organizational form is the transformation of inputs into specified output as

[50] E.g., see A. H. Hanson, *Public Enterprise and Economic Development*, London, Routledge and K. Paul, 1959, chap. 11; also V. V. Ramanadhan, *Problems of Public Enterprise*, Chicago, Quadrangle Books, 1959; United Nations (ECAFE), *Economic Bulletin for Asia and the Far East*, VII, November 1956, pp. 33-39; Parmanand Prasad, *Some Economic Problems of Public Enterprise in India*, Leiden, N. E. Stenfert Kroese, 1957.

[51] *Public Enterprise*, *op.cit.*, p. 356. In 1956 a tabulation of public enterprises other than utilities in ECAFE countries indicated 92 to be department organizations, 80 to be public corporations, and 49 to be companies in most of which the state had a controlling ownership. See United Nations, *Economic Bulletin for Asia and the Far East*, VII, November 1956, pp. 34, 35-36.

economically as possible. This means that inputs, and particularly labor, should be hired as economically as possible; that transformation processes should minimize economic input per unit of economic output (compatibly with what is the appropriate aggregate output); that output should be sold and used at prices appropriately reflecting costs and demands for this output; and that, through time, improvements in transformation methods and quality of product should be introduced as rapidly as economically desirable. The corporation or organization should be held accountable to parliament or its agents only on these grounds; it should be judged in the light of its accomplishments along these lines; and its management should be allowed to operate in such wise as to carry out these assigned objectives effectively. Under these circumstances the public corporation or alternative organization will function much as a well-run private corporation, but accountable to parliament or its agent instead of to stockholders.

If a public corporation or other organization proceeds in this manner, it can largely avert the two shortcomings to which attention has been directed, requiring more attributes on the part of personnel than are essential to the accomplishment of allotted tasks, and conducting a firm's transformation assignment in ways that utilize more inputs than necessary. The first shortcoming can be avoided so long as a firm's employment policy remains free of rules so rigid as those usually applicable under civil service regulations and it may employ, utilize, discharge, promote, and remunerate personnel much as a private corporation does. It is difficult in practice, however, to achieve these objectives, and it remains a challenge to bureaucratic formulators of arrangements to approximate them.[52] If the first shortcoming is not avoided, a country's labor force and resources will be used less effectively than they might.

The second shortcoming is likely to be more serious than the first even though a public corporation or other governmental organization is engaged in transforming inputs into fairly simple product-mixes (say steel or rail transport) for which an adequate and growing demand exists. If what is done can be evaluated in terms of the price system and the combination of inputs within the firm can be made to

[52] E.g., see Hanson, *Public Enterprise, op.cit.*, chap. 15, and "Public Enterprise in Nigeria . . . ," *op.cit.*, pp. 366-384; United Nations, *Public Industrial Management*, pp. 41-42, 47-48, 57, 63-64, 67-68, 91-92, 120, 125-126, 131. Remuneration may be too low for some and too high for others, given a country's wage and salary structure; and it may be pressed up out of keeping with productivity indicators when trade unions are strong, as in England.

reflect external prices, a fairly accurate measure of comparative performance can be gotten, particularly if allowance is made for the cost of training new personnel for this and other firms.[53] This is not always done, however, in part because those responsible for the management of public enterprise are less disposed to discover and rectify mistakes, and in part because insufficiently exacting criteria of judgment may be employed.[54] When new undertakings are contemplated, costs may be underestimated and gross returns overestimated; thus in India in 1959 five-sixths of the public enterprises earned no profit and all of them together earned one-fifth of one per cent or less on the capital invested.[55]

In practice, public corporations are seldom permitted to exercise the autonomy they supposedly were allowed when created,[56] and the risks to which management is exposed on this score probably affect their hiring and pricing policies adversely and may re-enforce what March and Simon call " 'Gresham's Law' of planning: Daily routine drives out planning"; they strengthen the disposition to continue in old and seemingly tested grooves.[57] In short, because of the rules under which public corporations must carry on, and/or because of the various restraints imposed by the government and by pressure groups, it is much harder in the public than in the private sector to carry on transformation processes efficiently and to price inputs and output economically. Of course, if bureaucratic attitudes and rules and governmental practices were sufficiently modified, much of this disparity between the public and the private sector would be removed. In any event, if a superior alternative is not available and private initiative cannot be mobilized to undertake activities essential to economic development,

[53] For accounts of criteria see *ibid.*, pp. 30-36, 66-75, 126-129; H. K. Paranjape, "Measurement of Management in the Public Sector," *Indian Journal of Public Administration*, VI, 1960, pp. 158-176; Claudio Alhaique, "La productivité dans l'administration publique en Îtalie," *International Review of Administrative Science*, XXIII, 1957, pp. 497-502.

[54] For example, the management may be satisfied with a rate of return (corrected for external short-run economies and for longer-run prospects) below that which correctly reflects the scarcity of capital; or allowance may not be made for inputs supplied at less than market prices; and so on.

[55] See unsigned, "Public Sector Returns on Capital Employed," *Eastern Economist*, XXXVI, 11, March 17, 1960, pp. 786-787; also United Nations *Public Industrial Management*, pp. 70-75.

[56] E.g., see *ibid.*, pp. 11-14, 49-50, 67-68, 93, 94, 130-132; Hanson, *Public Enterprise*, *op.cit.*, chap. 12.

[57] J. G. March and H. A. Simon, *Organizations*, New York, Wiley, 1958, p. 185. In his autobiography, *Memoirs of a Public Servant*, London, Faber, 1961, Lord Salter implies that the civil service can provide scope for initiative and enterprise.

recourse must be had to a public corporation or a state company *faute de mieux.*

VIII. Conclusion

In this chapter I have been concerned less to arrive at specific conclusions respecting the developmental role of the bureaucracy than to indicate the main considerations that need to be taken into account when determining what this role might be in concrete situations. The most important responsibility of the bureaucracy in a developing country—in addition to that of strengthening the pre-conditions of development—is that of supplying a long-run and broad time horizon and an expanding set of developmental objectives to be realized through input transformation in both the private and the public sectors. It is evident that the relative importance of the role of a bureaucracy will be greater in developing than in developed economies, even though bureaucracies are much weaker in developing than in developed societies. This disparity between required role and bureaucratic capacity can be effectively reduced principally through modernization of the outlook and technical skills of the bureaucracies emerging in developing societies and through directing achievement motivation into economic developmental channels.

CHAPTER 8

Bureaucracy and Modernization: The Russian and Soviet Case

MERLE FAINSOD

THE role of bureaucracies as determinants of social, political, and economic change has been subjected to relatively little systematic analysis. Broadly speaking, the tendency has been to view bureaucracies as dependent rather than independent variables, to see their activities as the product of larger social, political, and economic forces which condition the content, scope, and incidence of bureaucratic authority. Where bureaucracies are weak, possess limited powers, and lack the technical means to make their will effective, their role is necessarily a subordinate one and there is relatively little opportunity for the exercise of bureaucratic initiative. As the functions of government multiply and its activities affect society in a direct and immediate sense, bureaucratic power begins to magnify, and bureaucracies move into a much more central role. Perhaps the extreme case is the totalitarian party-state bureaucracy as it has developed in the Soviet Union and in Communist China, where the objective is nothing less than the use of political and administrative means to reshape man and society in the collectivized industrial image which lies at the heart of the Communist ideal. With totalitarianism we approach the apotheosis of politico-administrative social engineering as a means of achieving fundamental change.

The concern of this chapter is with the potentialities and limits of bureaucracies as modernizing instruments. Primary attention will be devoted to Russian and Soviet experience insofar as it purports to serve as a model for the less-developed nations. But before we embark on an analysis of the specific case, it may be desirable to try to define terms and to set the problems of the relationships between bureaucracy and modernization in a larger context.

First, what do we mean by modernization? An easy answer, but I fear an increasingly parochial one, is to point to the development of the United States and Western Europe and to cite their combination of high industrialization, social mobility, legal norms, and democratic practices as defining the end results of an inevitable onward and upward progress which all "backward" nations are duty-bound to recapitulate. If Soviet experience has proved nothing else, it has demonstrated that rapid industrialization can be achieved by dictatorial methods, and that democratizing and industrializing tendencies do not necessarily go hand in hand. In other words, the process of modernization need not be a seamless web in the Anglo-American, West European sense. It may be highly selective and differentiated. Industrialization carries a train of social consequences in its wake, but, as Max Weber was perceptive enough to recognize more than a half century ago, the discipline which it imposes has very little "real affinity for democracy."[1] The Communist response to industrialization has been to recognize its rational imperatives where productivity considerations are involved, but to permeate and control the new social groupings which it creates in order to preserve the party's monopoly of power. Political modernization, as the Communists conceive it, has nothing to do with competitive party politics and a system of regularized institutional restraints on the exercise of political power. It involves using all of the powerful instruments which modern science and technology make available to enforce political unanimity and to mobilize the energies of the nation to carry out the leadership's plans. Communists and Western democrats share a vision of modern industrial society, but their views of the requirements of political modernization are at opposite poles.

The competing models which Communists and Western democrats offer the developing nations do not exhaust the alternatives from which they may choose. There are, needless to say, other patterns, and the roles which bureaucracies play vary with the systems of which they are a part. Bureaucracies may be classified in a variety of ways, and the scheme of classification one adopts will depend on what aspects of bureaucratic behavior one wishes to highlight and contrast. Some of the possible permutations and combinations are suggested by the very different classificatory schemes which emerge when one emphasizes such diverse characteristics as the relationship of bureaucracies to the flow of political authority, the functions they perform, their internal arrangements, or their modernizing role.

If the criterion of classification is the relationship of bureaucracies

[1] "Zur Lage der bürgerlichen Demokratie in Russland," *Archiv für Sozialwissenschaft und Sozialpolitik*, XXII, 1906, pp. 347-349.

to the flow of political authority, at least five different forms can be distinguished: (1) representative bureaucracies, (2) party-state bureaucracies, (3) military-dominated bureaucracies, (4) ruler-dominated bureaucracies, and (5) ruling bureaucracies.

Political democracies characteristically produce representative bureaucracies which are responsible to, and in greater or lesser degree responsive to, the political forces which command the support of the electorate and dominate the political organs of government at a given time. Bureaucratic representativeness is defined, not so much by the extent to which its members constitute a social cross-section of the population which they serve, but rather by the fact that their powers and activities ultimately derive from a process of competitive party politics, and that the policies which they espouse are shaped by and adapted to the popular support which they can muster. The initiative which representative bureaucracies exercise must be adjusted to an underlying political consensus; the dynamics of change are regulated by the competitive political process. Competition for electoral support usually involves the need to woo significant voting blocs by promising them immediate benefits. Sacrifices and deprivations are not easily imposed, nor is long-term planning based on austerity ordinarily feasible.

Party-state bureaucracies are the byproducts of totalitarian regimes and other one-party dominated political systems. In these systems it is the party, and more particularly its leadership, which plays the transcendent role. The state bureaucracy, where it exists as a distinctive structure, is penetrated, controlled, and dominated by the party bureaucracy; the present arrangements in Khrushchevian Russia illustrate this relationship in extreme form. Modifications of the pattern permit varying degrees of autonomy to the state bureaucracy, and indeed in some cases, perhaps most forcefully illustrated in the Stalinist system of rule, both party and state bureaucracies become equally subordinate instruments of a supreme leader whose will is the final law. Party-state bureaucracies in their various forms are usually associated with strong charismatic leadership claiming a monopoly of wisdom, intolerant of opposition, and impatient to move ahead with the tasks of nation building, social reconstruction, industrialization, or other forms of modernization which they have set themselves. Totalitarian party-state bureaucracies seek to encompass the whole of society in their embrace; some of the one-party movement regimes in the new nations of Asia and Africa have similar ambitions, but so far at least, have lacked the will or the means to make their pretensions equally effective.

Military-dominated bureaucracies usually arise in societies in which the armed forces occupy a strategic power position. Not infrequently they take shape as a result of a *coup d'état* or seizure of power by officers of the armed forces who install their representatives in key civilian posts and endeavor to give direction to the state bureaucracy. Their purposes may be conservative or modernizing, but in either event they tend to give priority to strengthening the military establishment and building the supporting institutions which will sustain it. The tendency of military-dominated regimes is to stress the military virtues of hierarchy and discipline, and to give short shrift to the processes of explanation, persuasion, and discussion. Typically, officers of the armed forces are most at home in areas of decision making which are closest to their professional concerns; the complexities of economic development tend to elude them. As their field of responsibility widens, they are not infrequently driven to lean more heavily on expert civilian administrators for advice. As the recent experience of Pakistan illustrates, the transfer of power from a politician-dominated regime to a military regime may have the paradoxical result of reinforcing the influence and the authority of civilian administrators, even though they remain subject to military direction in an ultimate sense.

The category of ruler-dominated bureaucracies embraces those cases in which bureaucracies are the highly personal instruments of an autocratic ruler or dictator who exercises an approximation of absolute power and who uses his bureaucratic establishment to project his control and impose his purposes on the people whom he rules. In such systems, individual members of the bureaucracy may exercise considerable influence because of their personal qualities and the confidence which the ruler reposes in them; indeed, the existence of court favorites only underlines the subservient character of the bureaucracy's institutional role. Whatever elements of dynamism the system possesses derive from the ruler and his surrounding court. A ruler intent on change will seek out bureaucratic instruments suited to his purposes, but the nature of the underlying relationship is such that bureaucratic innovation is unlikely to develop as a spontaneous process.

There remains a final category in which the bureaucracy itself is in effect the ruling element in the political system. Examples can be found in certain phases of colonial rule, where the administrators on the scene function with minimum direction from the metropolitan center and with more or less absolute authority over the local inhabitants. In another variant, the formal structure of authority may appear to deposit ultimate power in a monarch or some other political organ, while in fact it will be the bureaucracy which makes the determining political as well as administrative decisions. In such systems the bureaucratic establishment is likely to think of itself as playing the role of Plato's Guardians, but such devotion to duty as it displays is usually also combined with a lively sense of bureaucratic self-interest. It is unlikely to welcome any derogation of its powers, and it is apt to reserve a major role for itself in any development program which it sponsors.

Bureaucracies may also be classified in terms of the range of functions which they perform. Here the continuum runs from the limited law and order and revenue collection functions performed by colonial bureaucracies at a certain stage of their development to the comprehensive planning and management of a whole society associated with the totalitarian party-state bureaucracies of the Soviet type. In between, there are a host of variant combinations involving different degrees of emphasis on national defense, welfare functions, regulation of the private economic sector, enlargements or limitations of the public economic sector, and planning of economic and other aspects of the nation's life. Looked at broadly in contemporary terms, the trend among the Western political democracies has been toward one or another form of mixed economy in which defense expenditures bulk large, the private sector remains vigorous, and bureaucracies play an important promotional, regulatory, and welfare role, administer a number of nationalized enterprises, but stop short of comprehensive social or economic planning. Among the new nations of Asia and Africa the dominant tendency has been to regard private enterprise with suspicion and to reach out for a socialist-welfare pattern of economic organization, a development which has been congenial to the expansion of bureaucratic authority. In some instances—and here the example of Pakistan can again be cited—the expansion of the public sector and emphasis on defense have been combined with efforts to invigorate and develop the private economic sector.

Still another possible scheme for classifying bureaucracies looks to their internal arrangements and the degree of rationality which these arrangements embody. Here the relevant questions and distinctions may include the degree of professional training required in order to qualify for entrance into the public service, whether appointments and promotions are made on the basis of merit, favoritism, venality, or some combination of the three, whether the system of allocating and distributing authority bears some rational relation to the functions which the bureaucracy is expected to perform, and whether the processes of decision making are regulated by general rules applicable to like instances or determined by arbitrary considerations unique to the individual case. These criteria may be used to try to define the place of each bureaucratic system on a rational-irrational curve. There is danger, however, of falling into the all-too-easy trap of assuming that the bureaucratic system which most closely approximates the model of Weberian rationality will necessarily function most effectively as an instrument of modernization and change. No bureaucratic establishment can be divorced from the political or social system of which it is a part. When the Weberian model is superimposed on a social or political system which is not prepared to assimilate it, the result can only be stalemate or frustration. A system less "rational" in its pattern of organization but capable of sustaining a living connection with the modernizing forces in its society may be much more effectively adapted to initiate change.

Bureaucracies may also be classified in terms of the degree to which they embody or serve as carriers of modernizing values. Here too it is possible to envisage a continuum in which bureaucracies at one end of the scale seek to safeguard the traditional structure of society in all its aspects, while bureaucracies at the other end operate as spearheads of fundamental social, economic, and political transformation. In between one can identify many variants. There are conservative bureaucracies which try to protect the political and social status quo, while undertaking to modernize their armed forces and the parts of the economy which support them in order to ward off external military threats. There are modernizing bureaucracies which are hospitable to Western administrative and political practices, but resist innovation in the economic and social realm. There are still others which turn their backs on the Western political heritage and confine their borrowings to the area of technology and advanced industrial practice. Even among bureaucracies which accept the goals of modernization, however interpreted, there may be sharp differences in the extent to which they are able to translate aspirations into action. The capacity of any modernizing elite to fulfill its ambitions depends not only on its own commitment but perhaps even more on its ability to communicate its vision to the rest of society, or, alternatively, on its readiness to employ the most ruthless measures to liquidate stubborn opponents who stand in the way.

Classifications of the kind outlined here have their obvious inadequacies as well as their suggestive applications. Every array of data may be viewed from a variety of perspectives, and each perspective may be legitimate to the extent that it illuminates characteristics and relationships which go unidentified when one views them from other perspectives. But however useful taxonomy may be, it has an inevitable static quality. It tells us little or nothing about the motive forces of change, their direction, or trend of development. If one is interested in the dynamics of change and the relation of bureaucracy to development, the problem can perhaps be most fruitfully attacked within a historical context. Judgments will, of course, vary on the weights to be assigned to one or another factor in unraveling the historical skein, and problems of ultimate causation may well be beyond scholarly reach. At the same time, unless one is prepared to try to come to grips with historical experience in all its complexity and time dimensions, one runs the very real danger that any comparative treatment of the modernizing role of bureaucracies will be shallow, narrowly time-bound, and reflective of little more than contemporary melioristic concerns. Comparisons can be significant, not merely cross-culturally, but as they embrace the sweep of history within a single culture, and, indeed, it is when they combine both that they yield their richest fruits.

All of this can be and should be read as an apologia for prefacing a treatment of the Soviet pattern of modernization with an analysis of earlier Russian efforts to use the bureaucracy to foster development and change. Russia, both in its tsarist and Soviet guise, has been characterized by a system of autocratic rule which has been little touched by the constitutional restraints and democratizing tendencies that flowered in the West. The concentration of power in the hands of the tsars and their successors, the Communist party leaders, provides an element of continuity in Russian history which transcends the drastic social upheavals of the last decades. Whatever the explanations for the remarkable persistence of monocratic rule, its consequence has been to reserve major powers of initiative to the tsar or party leader, the ruling elite which has surrounded them, and the bureaucracy which has served them. At most stages of Russian history the bureaucracy has taken its lead from the autocratic personality and his group of favorite advisers; when the interests of the bureaucracy have sharply diverged from the innovating purposes of a particular monarch, the typical response has been to resort to passive inertia and delaying tactics rather than to indulge in outright defiance. For the most part, however, Russia has had a serving bureaucracy, privileged but duty-bound.

The Russian bureaucratic establishment began, as in so many other rising monarchies, as an extension of the prince's household. In the early Muscovite conception, the state was regarded as the patrimony of the tsar, his own private domain which it was his privilege to exploit and manage as he wished. As the princes of Moscow expanded their domain at the expense of neighboring princelings, as they found themselves compelled to raise armies, to support them, and to govern the new territories which they conquered, the outlines of a primitive administrative system began to emerge. But it was primitive indeed. To begin with, the tsar simply entrusted any executive function which needed to be performed to one or another of his *boyars,* members of the land-holding aristocracy who, as their tasks became more complex and required record-keeping, gathered small staffs of secretaries (*diaki*) and clerks (*podiachi*) around them.[2] With time the *prikazy,* or commands, as they were known, hardened into regularly established official positions. All *boyar* families and their members had an assigned place in a rank order of social and political precedence; all official positions, similarly, were classified in a rank order of precedence. Tradition dictated that the two be matched. As the power of the *boyars* declined and the authority of the tsar was exalted, the latter exercised increasing freedom in recruiting his officialdom according to his own preferences; the bureaucracy was increasingly transformed into the tsar's personal instrument. In warding off the ambitions of the *boyar* aristocracy to share his authority, the tsar relied on the support, as well as the submission, of the lesser landed nobility. The rewards which went to them, in the form of offices, land, and serfs, helped to consolidate the position of serfdom and landed property in Russia and to weaken and delay the emergence of a Russian equivalent of the bourgeoisie, which played such a powerful role in the modernization and industrialization of the West. An autocracy rooted in peasant bondage and dependent for its ongoing momentum on social formations which profited by it could hardly be a congenial vehicle of social change. At the same time the commitment of the tsars to expand their domains or to defend their patrimony brought them into collision

[2] See Jesse D. Clarkson, *A History of Russia,* New York, Random House, 1961, pp. 92-94.

with more advanced nations where the imperatives of survival dictated an effort to overcome backwardness by adaptive modernization and selective borrowing of more advanced Western techniques.

The case of Peter the Great (1682-1725) may serve to illustrate the problem. Peter did not begin his career as a great reformer. As the great Russian historian Klyuchevsky justly noted, he "became a reformer by accident, as it were, and even unwillingly. . . . Reforms were stimulated by the requirements of war, which indeed dictated the nature of the reforms that were undertaken. . . . War was the most important circumstance of his reign. . . . Of the thirty-five years of his reign, beginning with autumn 1689 when the regency of Sophia came to an end, only one year, 1724, was completely peaceful; in all the rest it is possible to find only thirteen months of peace."[3] It was Peter's early defeats at the hands of the Swedes that furnished much of the impetus for his modernizing efforts.

This is not the place for a detailed analysis of Peter's reforms. It is perhaps enough to note their major direction. His determination to overcome Russia's military backwardness provided the key to his policies. Not only did he himself travel abroad to study Western techniques; he also sent scores of young Russians abroad to do likewise, and he imported great numbers of foreign specialists. As Klyuchevsky writes, "The young Russian was sent to study mathematics, the natural sciences, naval architecture, and navigation; the foreigners who came to Russia were officers, naval architects, sailors, artisans, mining engineers, and later on jurists and specialists in administration and finance. With their help Peter introduced into Russia useful technical knowledge and skills lacked by the Russians. Russia had no regular army; he created one. It had no fleet; he built one. It had no convenient maritime commercial outlet; with his army and navy he took the eastern littoral of the Baltic. Mining was barely developed, and manufacturing hardly existed, yet by Peter's death there were more than two hundred factories and workshops in the country. The establishment of industry depended on technical knowledge, so Peter founded a naval academy, and many schools of navigation, medicine, artillery, and engineering, including some where Latin and mathematics were taught, as well as nearly fifty elementary schools in provincial and subprovincial main towns. He even provided nearly fifty garrison schools for soldiers' children. There was insufficient revenue, so Peter

[3] Vasily Klyuchevsky, *Peter the Great* (Archibald translation), London, Macmillan, 1958, pp. 57-58, 255.

more than trebled it. There was no nationally organized administration capable of managing this new and complicated business, so foreign experts were called on to help to create a new central administration."[4]

The American public administration expert who has met frustration in trying to superimpose the *Report of the President's Committee on Administrative Management* on the administrative institutions of one or another developing nation might profitably review Peter the Great's experience in borrowing "advanced" Swedish administrative practices toward the end of his reign.[5] The bureaucratic legacy which Peter inherited was chaotic, disorganized, and shot through with bribery and corruption. Peter was determined to rationalize it, and, having heard that the Swedish colleges or ministries had the highest reputation for administrative efficiency in all Europe, he decided to use them as models for reforming his own central institutions. He called in foreign experts familiar with Swedish collegial institutions; they drew up the appropriate blueprints and in due course *ukazes* were issued putting the new scheme into effect. On paper the reorganization had much to commend it. It greatly simplified the central administration by reducing the number of units and bringing related functions together. Each college had its president, vice-president, four councillors, four assessors, and one foreign councillor or assessor, and two secretaries, one of whom was foreign. Business was to be conducted on a consultative basis in accordance with prescribed procedures. There was provision for a systematic division of duties both in the central and provincial administrations. Yet somehow the miracle on which Peter counted failed to happen, and the quality of administration did not noticeably improve. The ignorant and venal officials who carried over from the old to the new system remained the same men they had been before. His foreign advisers suggested that Russians be replaced by foreigners, but this Peter was loath to do. Then they suggested that suitable training schools be established, and this Peter approved. He did what he could to widen the field of recruitment for the public service and flouted the social conventions of the day by disregarding rank and giving offices to literate serfs as well as to members of the petty nobility. But, despite all his efforts, the new institutions failed to take root, and bribery and large-scale embezzlement persisted very much as before. In a towering rage Peter ordered the immediate publication of an *ukaze* "that whoever robbed the state of so much as the value

[4] *Ibid.*, pp. 263-264.

[5] For details, see *ibid.*, pp. 209-213.

of a piece of rope would hang for it." According to Klyuchevsky, "the Procurator-General, Yagushinsky, the sovereign's eye in the senate, exclaimed: 'Would your Majesty like to be a ruler without any subjects? We all steal, only some do it on a bigger scale, and in a more conspicuous way, than others.' Peter laughed, and did not publish the *ukaze*."[6]

Reacting to such experiences, Peter once observed, "You know yourselves that anything that is new, even though it is good and needful, will not be done by our folk without compulsion."[7] Nor did Peter hesitate to employ compulsion. He was prepared when the occasion demanded to resort to the most ruthless methods to destroy those who stood in his way. But impressive as his innovations were, he left the social configuration of Russia much as he found it—a pyramid of castes, with serfdom at its base, the landed nobility dominating the countryside, and the autocrat presiding over all. Because his reforms never reached deep into society, he found himself thwarted and frustrated by inertia and passivity at every turn.

In one important respect, however, he did leave his mark. More than any other tsar before him, he was the builder of the modern Russian state. Before his reign, Russia was still conceived of as a private domain of the tsar. Peter recognized that the state was a political entity separate from the person of the ruler, and he provided that his subjects take two oaths, one to the state and the other to the ruler. He insisted that the interests of the state were supreme, and, however absolute his power, he still thought of himself as the state's first servant. He saddled the administration with new tasks and problems, and in the process he built up a tradition of state power in which the bureaucracy was assigned and assumed the major responsibility for organizing the state's military strength, accumulating the resources to sustain it, and building the economic structure to support it. The administrative machinery which he established was not equal to the burdens which he imposed on it. He modernized its structure, but in the last analysis he failed to modernize its spirit. Like many administrative reformers before and after him, he discovered that it was far easier to draft blueprints than to find the men capable of translating them into reality.

A backward society is a poor nursery for a modernized bureaucracy,

[6] *Ibid.*, p. 244.

[7] Quoted in B. H. Sumner, *Peter the Great and the Emergence of Russia,* New York, Macmillan, 1951, p. 162.

and when efforts are made to combine them one or the other must yield. In Western Europe the modernization of the bureaucracy developed hand in hand with the modernization of society. Men of experience and learning, recruited first from the church and the nobility, and later from the rising bourgeoisie, were available to staff the bureaucratic structure, and when they were not readily available, they could be trained. In post-Petrine Russia a stagnant society produced its counterpart in an equally stagnant bureaucracy. Until past the middle of the nineteenth century, despite the valiant efforts of Speranskii and other administrative reformers, officialdom remained largely untouched by the winds of change. In the words of Professor Marc Raeff:

"The incredibly large amount of routine paper work in [the provincial and district government bureaus] was performed by lowly clerks, the sons of completely impoverished local gentry, merchants, or village priests. There was no regular procedure for recruiting these clerks that would insure some degree of uniformity in the staffing of local offices. Nobody expected them to have a standardized or uniform level of education. Whatever knowledge was needed they received on the job, an apprenticeship which did not make for a widening of their intellectual horizons. They were an underpaid, demoralized lot, open to corruption and the worst kind of graft. Possessing neither education nor ambition, they were utterly incapable of giving useful advice to their superiors. At best, they could apply blindly the prescriptions handed down from St. Petersburg. . . .

"At the top, in St. Petersburg offices, the run-of-the-mill scribes, the minor officials, were every bit like their confrères in the provinces. Like their colleagues, the vast majority of clerks in the capital had but the bare minimum of education and received no special training; they too learned their limited duties by experience alone. As the majority remained in the same department or bureau throughout their careers, they mechanically learned only a few routine operations. And so it was that the lowly clerks in the capital had as much difficulty in accepting and adjusting to innovations as their counterparts in the provincial offices."[8]

The task of directing this army of clerks fell to a relatively small group of high-ranking officials of whom the most influential were likely to be the personal favorites of the autocrat. Like the clerks whom they supervised, they usually lacked professional training for their

[8] Marc Raeff, "The Russian Autocracy and Its Officials," *Russian Thought and Politics, Harvard Slavic Studies*, IV, 1957, p. 81.

jobs. Recruited initially from the nobility, they tended almost unthinkingly to reflect the interests of the class from which they derived, and they were ill-fitted to discharge the increasingly complex and specialized functions which the burdens of managing an expanding empire thrust upon them. Under Alexander I and Nicholas I there was an increasing disposition to turn to the military to perform functions of civil administration. As the need grew for specialists to perform technical functions and for educated men to fill responsible intermediate positions, the social basis for bureaucratic recruitment was reluctantly broadened. During the nineteenth century ambitious sons of the clergy and the merchant classes who had succeeded in obtaining a formal education were increasingly successful, not only in penetrating the bureaucracy but in rising to high positions where, by virtue of their ascent on the bureaucratic ladder, they automatically attained noble status. Such careers, however, were fairly exceptional. By and large, the upper ranges of the bureaucracy remained a noblemen's preserve.

It was not a setting calculated to spawn innovation and experiment. Most tsars saw their duty as dictating the preservation of the established order, and this meant keeping people of lowly social origins in their appropriate place. In the words of the notorious Ministry of Education instruction of 1887:

"Gymnasiums and progymnasiums are freed from receiving the children of coachmen, servants, cooks, laundresses, small tradesmen, and the like, whose children, with exceptions, perhaps of those who are gifted with extraordinary capacities, ought by no means to be transferred from the sphere to which they belong and thus brought, as many years' experience has shown, to slight their parents, to feel dissatisfied with their lot, and to conceive an aversion to the existing inequality of fortune which is in the nature of things unavoidable."[9]

Yet, committed as the autocracy was to safeguard the traditional social structure, it found itself forced on the path of modernization despite itself. As in Peter the Great's time, military setbacks served as the great awakening. The shock of defeat in the Crimean War, the realization that Russia was falling behind the rapidly industrializing countries of the West, the increasing awareness that its administrative and economic institutions were obsolete and inefficient compared to their counterparts in the West opened the way for a wave of reforms

[9] Quoted by Alf Edeen, "The Civil Service: Its Composition and Status," in C. E. Black, ed., *The Transformation of Russian Society*, Cambridge, Harvard University Press, 1960, p. 281.

under Alexander II which began with the Serf Emancipation Edict of 1861 and extended to the *zemstvo*, or local government reforms of 1864, the judicial reforms of the same year, the municipal reforms of 1870, and, perhaps as significant as any of these, the series of steps which were taken during the 1860's and 1870's to reorganize the armed forces and to make literacy one of the objectives of military training.

Following the Petrine tradition, it was the "state" which took the lead in promoting Russia's economic development. State investments played a major formative role, and state policy in the form of concessions, subsidies, and guarantees gave every encouragement to both domestic and foreign investment capital. Reutern, who served as Minister of Finance from 1862 to 1878, dedicated his energies to fostering industrial development, and it was largely under his ministrations that the great burst of railroad construction in the 1865-1875 decade occurred. During the 1890's, Russia entered on a decade of intensive industrialization; its growth rate during that decade compared favorably with that of any country in the world. Again, it was the "state" that took the lead, and the guiding genius was Count Witte, Minister of Finance from 1892 to 1903.

The auspices under which the belated Russian industrialization drive was conducted were not such as to create a favorable milieu for the liberalization or modernization of its political institutions. Russia's economic development was intimately intertwined with the state and heavily dependent on bureaucratic guidance and tutelage. Industrial growth was based on sustained intervention by the government. By 1913 two-thirds of the total railroad mileage was owned and operated by the government; the private lines that remained were subject to strict state supervision. Government enterprise was extensive. The state owned valuable mines and processed their ores in state plants. It operated a liquor monopoly. It controlled vast tracts of lands and sixty per cent of the country's forests. Through the state bank and other credit institutions, it financed private enterprises. It extended protection through the tariff. It granted concessions and subsidies. Government orders and contracts largely sustained heavy industry and were important in other areas as well. Private industry operated within the framework of governmental direction and supervision. The bourgeois stratum of society was still weakly developed and was hampered in its aspirations for independence by its excessive dependence on the state. In the years before World War I, native business leadership in Russia showed many signs of restlessness and some signs of self-assertiveness, but the economic and bureaucratic fetters which bound it operated as a serious barrier to full emancipation.

The heavy responsibilities which were thrust on the tsarist bureaucracy represented a greater burden than it could effectively discharge. Paradoxically, the modernizing impulses which it transmitted to industry did not permeate the bureaucracy itself. Although there were the usual striking exceptions on whom the system depended for such initiative and momentum as it achieved, the bureaucratic mass continued to pursue its traditional bureaucratic ways. The sharp upsurge in the favors which the bureaucracy had to dispense was matched by an increase in corruption, as the more venal bureaucrats traded privileges for bribes. Jealous of its position, the bureaucracy resisted any diminution of its authority, and because its authority derived from the undiluted power of the autocrat, its influence was predominantly exerted to buttress the autocracy rather than to impose restraints on its rule. The *zemstvo* reforms, which provided for a degree of local self-government and introduced doctors, veterinarians, agricultural specialists, engineers, teachers, and other professionally trained functionaries into the local government service, were regarded with the deepest suspicion in high bureaucratic circles, and the restrictions which were imposed on *zemstvo* initiative owe much to bureaucratic fears. The coalescence of the reactionary impulses of Alexander III and Nicholas II with the views of their highest bureaucratic advisers served to erect a barrier to all efforts to widen popular participation in government. Symptomatic of the attitude of the bureaucracy was the gloom with which it greeted the creation of the Duma after the 1905 revolution and the undisguised joy with which it welcomed the whittling away of the Duma's authority in succeeding years. An article which appeared in the leading Russian encyclopedic dictionary in 1895 neatly summed up the tsarist bureaucracy when it defined the term bureaucracy as "denoting a method of administration peculiar to political communities in which 'the central government authorities have concentrated all power in their hands' and in which there exists 'a privileged segment' of officials who display 'caste exclusiveness' and 'are poor members of communities' because of their full identification not with the society which they serve but with the authorities who employ them."[10]

It may seem a harsh indictment to assert that the alliance of the

[10] A. Iu., in "Biurokratiia," *Entsiklopedicheskii Slovar*, Vol. v, St. Petersburg, F. A. Brokgauz and I. A. Ebron, 1895, p. 293, quoted by A. Vucinach, "The State and the Local Community," in C. E. Black (ed.), *The Transformation of Russian Society*, Cambridge, Harvard University Press, 1960, p. 204.

bureaucracy and the autocracy bears a large share of responsibility for the series of revolutionary upheavals which ultimately led to the Bolshevik triumph in November 1917. At a sheer technical level, the inefficiency and venality of the bureaucracy helped to contribute to the disastrous military defeats and the economic breakdown of the home front which prepared the way for revolution. In a more profound sense, the reluctance of the autocracy and the bureaucracy to share their authority with the rest of society transformed would-be moderate liberal-minded reformers into revolutionaries and imposed a maximalist and authoritarian temper on Russian political life. The bureaucracy and the autocracy, to be sure, had achievements to their credit. The belated industrialization drive which they sponsored left its modernizing mark on a sector of the economy, though Russia on the eve of World War I was still far behind the more advanced industrial countries of the West. The agricultural reforms associated with the name of Stolypin, who sought to break up the *mir* and to build up a class of sturdy peasant proprietors, represented a bold and intelligent effort to provide a bulwark against revolution, but the slowness with which the reforms were executed and their virtual suspension during World War I largely robbed them of their intended effect. In the years before World War I there were undoubted signs of social progress in such varied fields as education, trade union rights, welfare provisions, and medical care, but the difficulty with these reforms was that they were too little and too late. A policy of grudging concessions was increasingly outmoded by rapidly growing demands.

As one reviews the modernizing role of the bureaucracy in Tsarist Russia, one cannot escape the conclusion that it was much more successful in the economic than in the political sphere. Even in the economic area, there were long periods of stagnation; the driving energy of a Peter the Great or a Count Witte or the shock of military defeat was required to stir the bureaucracy into action and to make it function with any effectiveness at all. Its torpidity and passivity reflected the backwardness of society. An institution which itself resisted modernization could hardly serve as an efficient instrument to transmit modernizing values to a society which was dominated by elements who were themselves fearful of change. Perhaps the greatest failure of the bureaucracy was in the political sphere. Identifying its own authority with that of the tsar, it found itself increasingly isolated from the new social forces which were pressing for recognition in twentieth-century Russia. Instead of seeking terms of accommodation with them, or assimilating and incorporating them in its formula of rule, it regarded their pretensions with suspicion and helped to force them on a revolutionary path. It thought that it was building a dam against revolution; it ended by opening the dikes.

When revolutions erupt in a society in which the bureaucracy has been among the staunchest defenders of the status quo, one would expect that its position would be in serious danger. Actually, during the first phase of the Revolution, changes were slow in coming. Although there were replacements in the upper levels of the bureaucracy under the Provisional Government from March to November 1917, the middle and lower ranks were left largely untouched. Amid the exigencies of war and revolution, the bureaucracy continued to perform routine functions, but its actual authority was thoroughly undermined. Formal responsibility was assumed by the Provisional Government, but beneath it there developed a vacuum of power, which was in part occupied by the Soviets, in part by other locally chosen or self-constituted bodies, and in part not occupied at all. What the Provisional Government would have done to reorganize the bureaucracy had it been permitted to continue must remain an open question; in any case the Bolshevik seizure of power on November 7, 1917, rendered the question moot.

The Bolsheviks came to power promising a thoroughgoing purge of the bureaucracy. Indeed, Lenin, in one of his more utopian moments, declared that the whole inherited administrative apparatus would have to be destroyed and replaced by "a new one, consisting of the armed workers."[11] But this phase did not last long. The chastening responsibilities of power introduced a new perspective. On April 28, 1918, Lenin addressed himself to the theme of "The Immediate Tasks of the Soviet Government." It was far easier, Lenin admitted, to expropriate and nationalize industry than to manage it. "Our work of organizing proletarian accounting and control has obviously . . . *lagged behind* the work of directly 'expropriating the expropriators.'" "The art of administration," he proclaimed, "is not an art that one is born to, it is acquired by experience. . . . Without the guidance of specialists in the various fields of knowledge, technology and experience, the transition to socialism will be impossible."[12]

From the beginning the new Bolshevik regime set itself the double

[11] In "The State and Revolution." See Lenin, *Selected Works*, Vol. II, Moscow, Foreign Language Publishing House, 1947, p. 220.

[12] *Sochineniya* (Collected Works), third edition, XXII, Moscow, Partizdat Tsk VKP (b), 1935, pp. 439-468.

task of building an administrative apparatus that would be loyal to the Revolution and efficient in executing its mandate. The difficulties were enormous. What remained of the pre-Revolutionary bureaucracy was a repository of traditional governmental routines and procedures, but its skills were not readily adaptable to the new order, and, in any event, many of its members regarded their new overlords with enmity. The pool of bourgeois managerial, technical, and scientific talent which Russia had accumulated under the tsars was depleted by flights into White territory or escape abroad. The party itself had few members with any experience in civilian or military administration, and the qualities which made for success in revolutionary agitation and propaganda were not easily transferable to industrial management or other administrative responsibilities. What the party leadership did possess was a disciplined party organization and a determination to hold on to power. To insure that it would do so, it assigned key positions in the administrative structure to its most trusted cadres. Yet even so, in the first post-Revolutionary years, its control remained precarious. Five years after the Revolution, Lenin commented:

"We now have a vast army of governmental employees, but we lack sufficiently educated forces to exercise real control over them. Actually, it often happens that at the top, where we exercise political power, the machine functions somehow; but down below, where the state officials are in control, they often function in such a way as to counteract our measures. At the top, we have I don't know how many, but in any event, I think several thousand, at the outside several tens of thousands, of our own people. Down below, however, there are hundreds of thousands of old officials who came over to us from the Tsar and from bourgeois society and who, sometimes consciously and sometimes unconsciously, work against us. Nothing can be done here in a short space of time, that is clear. Many years of hard work will be required to improve the machine, to reform it and to enlist new forces."[13]

The party leadership resorted to a variety of expedients in order to cope with the problem of its inadequate administrative resources. Since it could not dispense with the old regime specialists, bureaucrats, and army officers, it enlisted them in its service and surrounded them with party and police controls in order to ensure their loyalty. As Lenin put it, "We have had to resort to the old bourgeois method and to agree to pay a very high price for the 'services' of the biggest

[13] *Ibid.*, XXVII, 353.

bourgeois specialists. Clearly such a measure is a compromise . . . a *step backward* on the part of our Socialist Soviet state power, which from the very outset proclaimed and pursued the policy of reducing high salaries to the level of the wages of the average worker."[14] But Lenin justified the measure as a necessary "tribute" which the Soviet state was compelled to pay to compensate for the backwardness of the masses. The "tribute," he predicted, would cease when the Soviet state had trained its own specialists. Meanwhile, every effort was exerted to identify party members who displayed a talent for management, to give them intensive training and to assign them to responsible posts.

If the first priority of the Bolsheviks was to consolidate their power, there remained the question of what they would do with power once they were in a position to exert it. In orthodox Marxian terms, Russia was a backward country which had still to complete its bourgeois, capitalist phase of development and which was not yet ripe for a proletarian socialist revolution. Even in Bolshevik ranks, this consciousness of Russian backwardness was so strong that in the early years after the Revolution there was general agreement among the party leaders that they would encounter the greatest difficulty in moving forward to socialism, or even holding on to power, unless there was also a successful proletarian revolution in Germany, or in other advanced industrial nations of the West. When the revolutionary aid from the West on which they counted failed to develop, the Bolsheviks were thrown back on their own resources, still hoping against hope that the Western proletariat would ultimately come to the rescue. As Lenin put it in 1921, "While the revolution in Germany is slow in 'breaking out,' our task is to *study* the state capitalism of the Germans, to spare *no effort* to copy it and not shrink from adopting dictatorial methods to hasten the copying of Western culture by barbarian Russia and not hesitate to use barbarous methods in combatting barbarism."[15] Restated in non-Leninist language, the historic burden which the Bolsheviks assumed was that of modernizing a developing country by dictatorial and totalitarian means.

Consciously or unconsciously, willingly or unwillingly, the Bolshevik leadership found itself thrust into the role of an industrializing elite. From the beginning Lenin provided the lead. As early as April 1918

[14] *Ibid.*, XXII, 447.

[15] In "The Tax in Kind," see Lenin, *Selected Works*, Vol. II, Moscow, Foreign Language Publishing House, 1947, p. 705.

we find him urging the adoption of the Taylor system in Soviet industry and proclaiming, "The Soviet Republic must at all costs adopt all that is valuable in the achievements of science and technology in this field. The possibility of building Socialism will be determined precisely by our success in combining the Soviet government and the Soviet organization of administration with the modern achievements of capitalism."[16] In the midst of civil war he commissioned some two hundred of the best scientists, engineers, and agronomists to prepare a plan for the electrification of the Russian Soviet Republic, and though Lenin did not live to witness its execution, he had the vision to see its importance in laying a base for the later industrial drive.

After the exhaustion of the civil war and the famine which accompanied and succeeded it, the Bolsheviks were compelled to beat a retreat, to make concessions to the peasantry, and to permit a revival of private trade. During the years of the NEP, pre-war industry was rebuilt, but the state encountered the greatest difficulty in accumulating the investment funds to finance a further expansion of the industrial sector. Agricultural production increased, but so did peasant consumption, and efforts to increase the tax burden on the peasantry met formidable resistance. The stalemate which this produced was eventually resolved by forcing the peasants into collective farms, which operated as a device to extract agricultural output from them without equivalent compensation and thus transferred a large part of the burden of accumulating an industrialization fund to the countryside.

The industrialization controversy which agitated top party circles in the middle and late 1920's has been treated extensively elsewhere.[17] Here perhaps it is enough to note that none of those who participated in it questioned the goal of industrialization. The disagreements which developed centered on pace and methods, how its burdens were to be distributed, the relative weight to be given light and heavy industry, the size of the commitment, and the swiftness and ruthlessness with which it was to be pursued. The goals which were ultimately incorporated in the revised First Five Year Plan involved a victory for the super-industrializers (a cause, incidentally, with which Stalin belatedly identified himself). Although not openly recognized or acknowledged at the time, the victory carried with it a train of consequences; emphasis on heavy industry at the expense of light; the suppression of the claims

[16] "Immediate Tasks of the Soviet Government," *Ibid.*, p. 327.

[17] See Alexander Erlich, *The Soviet Industrialization Debate 1924-1928*, Cambridge, Harvard University Press, 1960.

of consumption; the "revolution from above," as Stalin termed it, by which the peasantry was brought to heel and collectivized; and the strengthening of the coercive and totalitarian features of the regime to deal with the opposition which the new program generated.

Implicit in the victory of the super-industrializers was also a tangled skein of ideological considerations. In Marxist terms the firmest support of a socialist revolution was a strong proletariat. In Russia, where the industrial working class was weak and small in numbers, the party in effect functioned as a surrogate of the interests of the proletariat. But doctrine also dictated that the party do all in its power to strengthen its working-class base, and this meant rapid industrialization. The party, moreover, by seizing power before the historic mission of capitalism had been discharged, had the added obligation of telescoping a phase of capitalist development within the framework of a socialist society. In this sense too the claims of industrialization could not be denied. Finally, there was an increasingly powerful nationalist or patriotic ingredient in the industrialization drive. As the prospects of world revolution dwindled, Russia, the home base of the revolution, became the central preoccupation of the party leadership, and the need to strengthen its defenses and build up its power loomed as a more and more important task. In the process the legacy of Russian national interests became inextricably intertwined with broader Soviet goals and objectives. Industrial backwardness operated as a barrier both to the assertion of Russian national claims and to the realization of Communist revolutionary hopes. Nowhere did this newly emergent Soviet patriotism receive clearer expression than in a speech by Stalin in 1931 when he rejected the views of those who urged a slowing down in the pace of industrialization. These were Stalin's words:

"To slacken the tempo would mean falling behind. And those who fall behind get beaten. . . . The history of old Russia is the history of defeats due to backwardness. She was beaten by the Mongol Khans. She was beaten by the Turkish beys. She was beaten by the Swedish feudal lords. She was beaten by the Polish and Lithuanian gentry. She was beaten by the British and French capitalists. She was beaten by the Japanese barons. All beat her—for her backwardness: for military backwardness, for cultural backwardness, for political backwardness, for agricultural backwardness. . . . Do you want our Socialist fatherland to be beaten and to lose its independence? If you do not want this you must put an end to its backwardness in the shortest possible time. . . . There is no other way. That is why Lenin said during the October Revolution: 'Either perish or overtake and outstrip the advanced capitalist countries.' We are fifty or a hundred years behind the advanced countries. We must make good the distance in ten years. Either we do it, or they crush us."[18]

The Soviet Union launched its series of Five Year Plans in the late 1920's and 1930's under the aegis of a ruling elite that was by that time thoroughly committed to the goal of rapid industrialization. It was also an elite that was prepared to resort to the most drastic and ruthless expedients in eliminating opposition and in enforcing the sacrifices necessary to accumulate an industrialization fund. It commanded a monopoly of political, military, and police power, dominated the instruments of mass communication, and presided over a centrally directed economy through which its industrial priorities could be imposed on the land. At the same time its zeal and its loyalty were far more impressive than its knowledge or technical competence.

Perhaps the greatest single problem which the Soviet Union faced in the first stages of the industrialization drive was the lack of experienced and trained cadres capable of performing the technical and administrative tasks which industrialization required. Perforce, the party leadership found itself compelled to improvise and to draw on every resource which could be tapped. Much as it distrusted the old-regime specialists who remained, it used them where it could; when difficulties developed, it also found it convenient to make them scapegoats for popular wrath. It loaded such few party specialists as it had in industrial management with huge responsibilities, and it sent others who had shown some aptitude for administration to special "industrial academies," where they were given intensive training and then quickly assigned to responsible managerial posts. It made effective use of the Great Depression to recruit thousands of foreign engineers, technicians, and other specialists who were eager for employment at the attractive rates which the Soviet government then offered. Its orders abroad for plants and machinery were frequently accompanied by technical assistance contracts, under which foreign firms agreed to train Soviet personnel either in their own plants abroad or at the sites in Russia where the plants and machinery were being installed. In order to meet the need for trained native personnel quickly, courses focussed on a relatively narrow specialization were established, and young Soviet students were rushed through these courses in considerable numbers

[18] J. Stalin, *Problems of Leninism*, Moscow, Foreign Languages Publishing House, 1940, pp. 365-366.

so that they could fill their designated posts on the industrial front. The training of those who were assigned to positions of technical or administrative responsibility in the initial spurt of industrialization frequently left much to be desired, but all of these measures represented hasty improvisations to meet emergency demands, and the regime had no other choice.

At the same time, the Soviet leadership launched a major long-term effort to educate the oncoming generations in the technical and scientific subject-matter which an industrializing society requires. Beginning in the early 1930's, the schools were reorganized to stress solid training in mathematics and the natural sciences. Habits of order, precision, and discipline were instilled. So-called *tekhnikums* were greatly expanded in numbers to train skilled workers and technicians, and over the next years a host of higher technical institutes were created in a variety of specialized fields to supplement the more academic training provided by the universities, which were also multiplying in number and size. The new Soviet technical intelligentsia, which presently plays such a major role in the management of the Soviet economy, is essentially a product of this massive educational reform.

An industrializing society needs industrial culture heroes, and this too the Soviet leadership supplied. The incentive system was reorganized to provide the highest awards to talented managers, engineers, and scientists, and at lower levels compensation was carefully graded to reward productivity and to penalize sloth. All the resources of agitation and propaganda were mobilized to instill a production ethic; the new heroes of fiction and drama, of poetry and song, were the Stakhanovite workers who performed prodigious production feats, the engineers who built the dams, the managers who exceeded their output quotas, and the scientists in their laboratories exploring new trails. These were the models held out to the children of the oncoming generations, and the careers to which they aspired reflected the values they were taught.

Without this positive and continuing emphasis on education, incentives, and indoctrination, it is doubtful that the Soviet leadership would have been successful in realizing its industrial goals. For it was not enough that the top echelons of the Soviet ruling elite were committed to industrialization. Peter the Great in his day also dedicated his enormous energies to modernization, but a backward bureaucracy and a backward society largely frustrated his designs. The Soviet industrializing elite crossed its Rubicon when it managed to create a technical intelligentsia capable of staffing a modernizing bureaucracy and when it began to succeed in communicating the values, the habits, and the requirements of industrialization to the backward society which it sought to transform.

It would be hard to exaggerate the difficulties of the task. The obdurate resistance of the peasantry to collectivization was overcome only by the massive application of force. The disciplining of industrial labor was enforced by repression and terror. The whole society operated under intensive pressure to produce results.

Every totalitarian system has a style which reflects the tasks it undertakes and the color and dynamism of the ruling personality who directs its course. Under Stalin the dominating priority was forced-draft industrialization. In more specific terms, this meant concentrating on building the elements of military strength and constructing a heavy-industry base which would accelerate the rate of industrial growth and provide modernized armaments, machinery, and factory plants. This ruling priority affected every aspect of Soviet life. It meant that consumer goods, housing, and agriculture were neglected and ignored. It made the fulfillment of planned industrial targets the central preoccupation of every sector of the party, police, and administrative apparatus. It also meant a strengthening of the repressive organs of the state to deal with the discontent generated by the sacrifices which a high rate of capital expansion imposed.

The system of administration which developed under Stalin was shaped to a very considerable extent by his own personality—his paranoiac suspicion, his fear of rivals, his distrust of those around him, and his desire to hold all the strings of power in his own hands. In his drive for total power, he evolved a system of competing and overlapping bureaucratic hierarchies in which he depended on the party apparatus and the police to penetrate and watch each other and made use of both to control the administration as well as all other branches of Soviet life. The administrative pattern on which he relied was one of extreme centralization, a pattern which he not only found personally congenial, but which had more generalized advantages as long as trained and experienced administrators were scarce and the economy was not too complex. As the Soviet Union entered a more mature phase of industrialization, the centralized control which he exercised became increasingly anachronistic. It induced congestion at the center and a paralysis of initiative below. The super-centralization on which Stalin insisted hampered the operations of an economy which was becoming increasingly complex.

Indeed, super-centralization and the superhuman demands which Stalin made on his administrators and his people produced by way of reaction a pattern of informal evasive arrangements which offered a striking contrast to the totalitarian model of absolute control. Thus, collective farmers who could not subsist on their earnings from the collective farm spent a minimal time on their collective farm duties and reserved their major energies for their private plots, where the potential returns were substantially greater. Depressed living standards and scarcity of goods stimulated thievery, black market operations, corruption, and bribery on a not inconsiderable scale. Factory managers and collective farm chairmen who could not meet their planned targets resorted to all kinds of ingenious subterfuges to conceal their deficiencies from the center, and not infrequently found at least temporary protection in a network of "family" relations with local party and administrative officials with whom they were deeply involved. Under Stalin, the most drastic sanctions were invoked to prevent such phenomena from getting out of hand; their persistence throughout the Stalinist period is a testimonial to the limits of totalitarian power even in its most extreme form.

The death of Stalin marked the end of an era and opened the way to a readjustment of political and administrative arrangements to the more mature stage of industrialization which Stalin himself had done so much to create. Once the succession crisis had been resolved by Khrushchev's purge of his competitors, the outlines of a new model of Khrushchevian totalitarianism began to crystallize. It can best be described as a form of "enlightened" or rationalized totalitarianism which seeks to eliminate or mollify the worst grievances of the Stalinist epoch and rationalize the system of administrative and economic controls while preserving the substance of totalitarian power itself. His formula of governance relegates terror to a much less central role than it occupied under Stalin, and the welfare concessions and improvements in the incentive structure which he has sponsored are designed to broaden the popular support which the regime enjoys. But Khrushchev's vision of society remains total, and he sees nothing within it that can be permitted to remain free of the party's paternal guidance and care.

Like Stalin before him, Khrushchev is committed to a continuation of the industrialization drive, but his political style is uniquely his own. He has made the most assiduous efforts to create an image of himself as a leader who is close to the people. In striking contrast to Stalin, who rarely ventured forth from the Kremlin and whose charisma of godlike infallibility was magnified by the aura of mystery, aloofness, and remoteness which surrounded him, Khrushchev has been the agitator par excellence, in constant motion, addressing meetings from one end of the country to the other, visiting collective farms and factories, speaking the language of the people, and reaching out for popular support. The common touch which he radiates and the sharp criticism which he has directed at Stalin's pretensions to omniscience have not prevented him from launching his own "cult of personality," albeit cloaked in a more earthy guise. The new populism which Khrushchev has articulated seeks to mobilize the energies of the masses by providing for their more active participation in the tasks of Communist construction, but subject, of course, to party guidance and control. He has sought to recapture some of the egalitarian appeal of the earliest years of the Revolution by correcting the grosser inequalities of the Stalinist era, though he has also insisted that differential rewards tailored to productivity are essential if the dynamic momentum of industrialization is to be maintained. The educational reforms which he has sponsored are intended to bring the schools and production closer together; by insisting that most candidates for higher education serve an apprenticeship in industry or agriculture, he hopes that the educated elite of the future will preserve a link with the masses and be prevented from developing into an isolated ruling caste. In struggling with the problem of reconciling the elitist and populist strains in Communist ideology, Khrushchev seeks, in essence, to give elitism a wider base of popular support.

Again, in contrast to Stalin, Khrushchev has used the party as his primary instrument of rule. Under Stalin, the party declined in vitality, and its apparatus became simply one of several channels through which he communicated his commands. Khrushchev has poured new life into the party and lifted its apparatus to a central position in his structure of direction and control. Within the party itself he has sought to revive what he describes as Leninist norms—more active participation in the party rank-and-file in party discussions, encouragement of greater criticism from below, more frequent assemblages of party congresses, conferences, committees, and other important party organs, and greater emphasis on the recruitment of leading workers and collective farmers in order to strengthen the party's popular roots. But the revival of the forms of intra-party democracy should not be confused with its essence. Khrushchev, like Stalin before him, tolerates no derogation of his authority, permits no opposition to raise its head within the party, and insists that the party function as a monolith in executing his will. The party functionaries, nevertheless, have flourished under Khrushchev. He has depended heavily on them to strengthen his control of the armed forces and the police, to achieve centralized direction of industry and agriculture, and to provide the coordinating framework which holds Soviet society together and forces it to march in step.

Khrushchev's use of the party apparatus as an integrating force has been combined with a pragmatic willingness to adopt forms of decentralized administration where they promised more effective operational results. His recognition that the super-centralization of the Stalinist era was ill-suited to the rational management of an increasingly complex economy has led him to experiment with delegations of authority which Stalin would probably have sternly disapproved. He has enlarged the decision-making prerogatives of factory managers and collective farm chairmen, transferred important administrative functions from the center to the republics, dissolved a large number of central economic ministries, and replaced them with a network of regional economic councils which have shifted the weight of supervisory authority much closer to the grass roots. His restless search for more rational forms of administration has resulted in a series of major reorganizations in agriculture as well as in industry, but behind them all is a drive to push the experts and the specialists into the production process and to bring his administrators nearer to factory and farms. The responsibilities which he has delegated run the danger of pluralizing his authority, but he has sought to guard against it, not always altogether successfully, by invoking the unifying discipline of the party to hold fissiparous tendencies in check.

Like Stalin before him, Khrushchev has discovered that the party-state bureaucracy on which he has to depend to carry out his directives will do what it can to protect its own interests when they diverge from his own overriding concerns. In the aftermath of the industrial reorganization of 1957, a number of regional economic councils were found guilty of the crime of "localism," which, as the term implies, involved putting local interests above the broader interests of the state.[19] Resources allocated for centrally approved projects were diverted to provide local amenities not provided for in the plan. Priority was given to supplying local industries, and interregional delivery commitments were simply not met when to do so would have imperiled the fulfillment of the local plan. Some recent even more dramatic examples of administrative evasion and sabotage are provided by the series of agricultural procurement "scandals" ventilated at the January 1961 plenum of the Central Committee and in the press afterwards.[20] After the bumper crop of 1958, extremely ambitious agricultural goals were incorporated in the Seven Year Plan, and Soviet administrators undertook pledges to fulfill and even exceed them. The excellent harvest of 1958 was followed by two mediocre harvests in 1959 and 1960, and in the event many of the pledges turned out to be unrealistic. But rather than plead excuses or confess failure, many party officials and local agricultural administrators resorted to various ingenious and not so ingenious forms of fraud and statistical manipulation to simulate plan fulfillment and even over-fulfillment. With the connivance of party and governmental officials, procurement organizations issued fictitious receipts to *kolkhozes* and *sovkhozes* in order to allow them to report exaggerated output and delivery figures. *Sovkhoz* and *kolkhoz* managers were permitted and even encouraged by higher officials to purchase such products as meat, milk, eggs, and butter at state stores or *kolkhoz* markets and then to credit them to the output plan of the *kolkhoz* or *sovkhoz*. Still another common practice was the delivery of feed and seed stocks in order to fulfill the grain procurement plan. False data were fabricated on a widespread scale, and even agencies such as the Central Statistical Directorate connived in the padding of accounts.

To read the proceedings of the January 1961 plenum of the Central Committee is to gain a new appreciation of the dilemma of the Soviet bureaucrat who is caught between the demands of his superiors for higher and higher production and his own inability to meet these expectations. The answer which Khrushchev gave at the plenum was clear: "If a leader sees that he cannot cope with the job, he should come and say: 'Comrades, I have failed in the work. I cannot lead the province, I have discredited myself— Let me resign.' "[21] But this course

[19] See Howard Swearer, "Khrushchev's Revolution in Industrial Management," *World Politics*, XII, 1, October 1959, pp. 45-61.

[20] See Arcadius Kahan, "Troubles in Soviet Agriculture," *Problems of Communism*, X, 2, March-April 1961, pp. 62-66.

[21] *Pravda*, January 22, 1961.

of action obviously held out less attraction to those to whom he was commending it than it did to Khrushchev himself. The alternative course was to seek to conceal one's deficiencies, to hope to get away with it, and to run the attendant risks. Many Soviet party and governmental officials opted for the latter course and paid the penalty when they were caught.

What is perhaps more significant than the specific details of particular administrative scandals is the fact that they are endemic in the system and that the pressures under which Soviet administrators operate impel them to shield themselves against the drastic consequences of failure. In one important respect, the Soviet administrator is not unlike his colleagues elsewhere in the world. He is not anxious to assume obligations which he knows he cannot perform, and he does what he can to secure plan targets which are feasible and within his capacity. But unlike his colleagues in many other parts of the world, the Soviet administrator, since the inception of the industrialization drive, has had to make his way in an atmosphere of storm and fury, constantly prodded and goaded to increase his exertions and courting disaster if he fails. Under Khrushchev he has been given more elbow room to exercise initiative; his conditions of work have become more normalized; and he need no longer live in perpetual fear that a mistake may result in a sentence to a forced labor camp. But the race is still to the tough and able, who can hammer their way through to new production records. The price of failure remains a quick end to a career and a swift descent in the Soviet social ladder.

As one looks back on the Soviet period of Russian history, perhaps the most important single development is the continuing transformation of the Soviet Union from a predominantly agrarian into a highly industrialized society under totalitarian auspices. Industrialization has set new forces into motion. In bureaucratic terms, it has meant a vast expansion of managerial, engineering, technical, and scientific personnel and a recognition that they constitute the spearhead of an "industrializing elite" who must be appropriately rewarded for their crucial contribution to the industrialization process. In party terms, it has brought a different type of party apparatchik to the fore in those areas of party activity concerned with the management of the economy. For these party functionaries mastery of the classics of Marxism-Leninism is no longer enough; technical knowledge is required if they are adequately to perform their role of economic controllers. The armed forces too have undergone a radical transformation as the result of advancing technology. Ballistic missiles and H bombs introduce new scientific and technical dimensions into warfare, demand a fundamentally different order of skills, and pose problems of control which are as perplexingly intricate for the Soviet leadership as they are for us. The dominating role of science and technology in the economic life of the nation and the habits of thought which they breed make many of the dogmatic constraints of Marxism-Leninism appear obsolete and implicitly challenge the party to accommodate its ideological heritage to a new set of expectations rooted in methods of scientific inquiry. With advancing industrialization come the first tastes of leisure and affluence, with all their distracting temptations and new delights. The austere production ethic of the early phases of the industrialization process is increasingly challenged by a consumption ethic to which concessions have to be made. The spread of elementary and higher education stirs rising aspirations and presents the regime with new problems in adapting its system of controls and indoctrination to these expectations and demands.

There are some who argue that totalitarian dictatorship and a highly industrialized society are fundamentally incompatible, that the necessary result of industrialization is to pluralize authority among the functional groups created by it, that the diverse interests of these groups are likely in the first instance to reflect themselves in the emergence of factions within the ruling party, that these factions are likely to overflow the bounds of the party and find roots in Soviet society, and that the end result of this process will be the emergence of some form of constitutional order which will make room for the legal interplay of parties or factions within the framework of a socialized economic order.[22] While such a consummation would be warmly welcomed by all those who believe in the superior virtues of constitutional systems, the likelihood that it will soon take place does not appear great.

Both the doctrines and practice of Bolshevism militate against such a development. The expectation that a party leadership which bases its authority on the suppression of factions would accede to a course of development which produced splits in its ranks and loss of its monopoly of power is a Utopian fantasy that no one who has mastered the ABC's of Communist organizational theory is likely to entertain. Nor should one be unduly beguiled by that special variety of technological deter-

[22] See Isaac Deutscher, *Russia, What Next?* New York, Oxford University Press, 1953, and *Russia in Transition,* New York, Coward-McCann, 1957.

minism which assumes that those who possess improtant technical skills in a society inevitably transmute these skills into political power. There is no iron law which prevents dictators from presiding over the destinies of highly industrialized societies.

This does not mean that the Communist party leadership may not find it desirable to make continuous readjustments in its method of rule to take account of the increasing complexities of managing an industrializing society. It already insists that the party cadres to whom it entrusts economic control functions possess a degree of technological and managerial sophistication adequate to cope with the coordinating and supervisory responsibilities which they must discharge. Experimentation is likely to continue in the search for a proper balance between the centralization of policy-making and control functions and delegations of operational authority calculated to increase efficiency. The party leadership will undoubtedly persist in putting a special premium on the complex of skills essential to industrialization. But while it counts heavily on the contributions of its industrializing elite, and rewards its members accordingly, it is highly unlikely to permit them to emerge as autonomous power centers, and even tentative moves in this direction are likely to be nipped in the bud. The first law of the party leadership is its own self-preservation; it can be expected to take the sternest prophylactic measures to prevent any encroachment on its supreme authority.

Nor need the education of the masses or the spread of higher education necessarily operate as a grave threat to party rule. Universal literacy in some circumstances may open the door to political freedom; in the Soviet setting it is deliberately used as a powerful weapon of indoctrination, and its political purpose is to inculcate faith and belief in the regime rather than to generate doubts about its premises. The Soviet educational system is designed to produce scientists, engineers, and technicians who will bear comparison with the best that the West has to offer, but it also makes strenuous efforts to ensure that they will loyally serve the Communist cause. A goodly portion are enrolled in party ranks, and those who are not are not immune from party pressure. Even where indoctrination is weak or ineffective, the regime disposes of a powerful array of instruments calculated to enforce compliance with the system and to discourage deviant behavior of any sort. Careers and assignments are at the mercy of the party, and the incentive system can be manipulated to reward the faithful and penalize the untrustworthy. In extreme cases, police sanctions may be imposed. Even when the effect of exposure to the educational process has been to plant doubt and stimulate independent thought, most Soviet citizens are deterred from active opposition because the system of controls which encloses them makes the consequences of dissidence very painful indeed.

This does not mean that there are not, and may not in the future be, more Soviet citizens prepared to risk these consequences. Much will depend on the course which the party leadership steers. If its record is one of continuing success in domestic and foreign affairs, its position will not easily be challenged. If its performance over the years is dotted with broken promises and failures, a rising tide of disappointment and disillusionment may prepare the way for an eventual erosion of its power.

Currently there is little to indicate that the process of disintegration has begun. Soviet power still appears to be on an ascending trajectory. Its industrial growth rate is markedly higher than that of the United States; its educational system is geared to continued rapid scientific and technical progress; and its military strength needs no underlining in an age of rockets, missiles, and H bombs.

The attraction which the Soviet model of industrial development has for many non-Communist as well as Communist intellectuals in the developing countries is by now a familiar tale that requires little elaboration. For minds and imaginations possessed by the mystique of industrialization, with its promise of growing power and a swift solution to pressing economic problems, the Soviet experience provides a living demonstration that a backward country can industrialize rapidly and in the space of decades take its place as a leading industrial and military power. Admiration for Soviet achievements is transposed easily into admiration for the political and economic system which has presumably made these achievements possible. Glib slogans borrowed from the Russians, such as planned economy and the priority of heavy industry, take on an almost magical hortatory force. Emulation of the Soviet example is seen as a shortcut to Utopia.

There are, of course, many members of the industrializing elites in the developing countries, particularly those in responsible positions, who do not view their problems so simply and who have a much more sophisticated and critical view of Soviet accomplishments. But it remains true that there is much misunderstanding of the implications of the Soviet experience for the developing countries and an all-too-frequent tendency to take at face value Soviet claims of having created an earthly paradise.

Some of the misunderstandings perhaps bear elaboration. It is too easily forgotten that Russia was launched on the path of industrialization long before the Bolsheviks took power, and that the economy which the Bolsheviks inherited, while backward when compared with the industrial West, was relatively advanced when compared with most present-day developing nations. Without in any way detracting from the remarkable advances which were subsequently made under Soviet auspices, it remains true that its leaders built on a base which few developing countries today possess. The natural resources on which the Soviet state could draw were also incomparably richer than those of most developing countries, and the capacity to exploit them was also at a much higher level.

Even with these substantial advantages, the story of Soviet industrialization remains a gruesome tale, and its human impact in terms of suffering, deprivation, and denial of human rights finds all too little resonance in discussions of the significance of the Soviet experience among the intellectuals of the developing nations. For one thing, it was enforced by the most stringent totalitarian controls, which left no place for the liberal and humanitarian values which many members of the new industrializing elites in the developing nations still cherish. For another, it involved decades of grim sacrifice, during which there was a decline rather than an improvement in the material condition of the mass of the population. Until Stalin's death it left little or no room for the realization of the welfare objectives on which many of the new nations put such a high priority. The Soviet Union built a powerful heavy industry base and a formidable military establishment, but the cost must also be measured in the millions who were consigned to forced labor camps, in the suppression and purge of all oppositionists, and in the shortages of food, consumer goods, and housing which accompanied industrialization. It may well be that many members of the industrializing elites in the developing nations who advocate emulating the Soviet example would be prepared to pay this price if it would guarantee rapid industrialization, but as yet there appears to be little realization that there is a price to be paid.

If these more negative and sobering aspects of the Soviet experience have yet to sink deep into the consciousness of the industrializing elites of the developing nations, it is perhaps also worth noting that the more positive features of the Soviet achievement are also not always fully understood or appreciated by them. In a positive sense, the success of the Soviet industrialization drive was insured by its massive investment in the expansion of elementary and higher education, in the emphasis which educational institutions laid on the training of engineers, technicians, and scientists to serve expanding industry, in the reorganization of the incentive system to attract and reward the crucial skills necessary for the effective operation of industry, and in the prestigious place accorded to the new industrializing elite in Soviet society. These measures transformed the Soviet bureaucracy into an effective instrument for technical modernization, and they made the Soviet populace receptive to the values of industrialization. There is much which the developing nations can learn from this experience, and it holds out a special lesson for countries which pay lip service to the goal of industrialization but fail to adjust their educational and motivational infrastructures to its demands. In this area at least, Soviet experience has a generalized application which transcends the question of whether the new nations model their political or economic systems on the Soviet pattern. Regardless of whether they find themselves attracted or repelled by Soviet totalitarian social engineering, they can rediscover in Russian and Soviet history that industrialization is crucially dependent on an educational base and that an industrializing elite is condemned to frustration unless it shapes its policies with this in mind.

In a recent article in *Encounter* (October 1961), Professor Edward Shils has eloquently observed, "Modernity is not just an advanced technology with a complex division of labor, nor is it merely a relatively higher standard of living; it is not just a bureaucracy recruited and organized on relatively rational principles. Modernity is an opening up of the creative powers of ordinary people; it involves an appreciation of their rights and potentialities as individuals, of their capacities for expression, for happiness, for knowledge."[23] In Professor Shils's terms, the "modernity" of Russia "is a tyrannically deformed manifestation of potentialities which are inherent in the process of modernization," since it bases its control on "a coerced conformity" and "mobilization of the masses" rather than on personal liberties and freely given consent. For those (and I include myself) who are committed to Western liberal values and would like to see them universalized, Professor Shils strikes a welcome note. But the question which neither Professor Shils nor any one else can answer is whether the newly emergent nations will view their priorities of development in these same terms. In

[23] P. 45.

making their choices, it is of utmost importance that they possess a sober and realistic understanding of the meaning of the Soviet experience. Such knowledge may help to insure that decisions to borrow from Soviet practice will be made with some appreciation of the losses that may ensue as well as of what may be relevantly learned and gained.[24]

[24] The author wishes to thank the Harvard University Press for permission to utilize in this chapter extracts from the 1963 revised edition of his *How Russia Is Ruled.*

CHAPTER 9

Bureaucracy and Political Development in Eastern Europe[1]

CARL BECK

THE central purpose of this chapter is to explore the relationship between bureaucracy and political development in Eastern Europe and to evaluate the utility of bureaucratic theory as a means of explaining the short-run development of these Communist states.

The departure point for the analysis will be the set of hypotheses that are suggested when classic bureaucratic theory is used as an analytical framework for explaining the impact of modernization upon the political system.

The core of the chapter consists of a description and analysis of the impact of the social process of bureaucratization upon the political systems of Eastern Europe. In this endeavor, primary emphasis will be placed on political doctrine, the system of administration, and the character of the political elite. These subjects have been selected for emphasis because they are critical indicators of the impact that the creation of a modernized society has upon political totalitarianism. Primary attention will be given to the social process of bureaucratization rather than to the role of the formal state bureaucracy.

Conclusions will be drawn about the utility of classic bureaucratic theory as a means of explaining political change. Because of the nature of the systems of Eastern Europe, and because of the partial nature of bureaucratic theory, it will be argued that bureaucratic theory is of limited utility. It will also be argued that to view these systems as frozen—one popular view of Communist states—is likewise not a fruitful approach.

[1] I would like to thank the Social Science Research Council for a grant received in 1958-1959 for research on the administrative system of Czechoslovakia; my colleagues in the Administrative Science Center, particularly Dr. James D. Thompson and Dr. Robert W. Avery; and my colleagues in the Department of Political Science at the University of Pittsburgh, particularly Dr. Holbert N. Carroll, for their advice and criticisms.

Legal-Rationalism and Bureaucracy

Discussion of a process of political development has been heavily influenced by extracts from the writings of Max Weber.[2] His typology of authority structure, in particular, has been used to explain the process of "modernization."[3] The belief that the course of political development is reflected in a change from traditional to charismatic to legal-rational authority structures has had a great deal of appeal. It also has pitfalls.

Certainly the traditional authority structure of a society is disturbed as that society undergoes the pangs of modernization. The primary organization of a traditional society (family and family-type groups), the primary form of inter-personal relationships (face-to-face contact), the primary form of economic organization (agriculture), are all shattered as a new type of society is being built. Traditionalism is no longer the point of reference which sets for the citizenry their perception of accepted patterns of behavior, their aspirations, and their goals.[4]

The first stage of modernization is often one which results in the fragmentation of the pre-existing social order. The acute problem facing society at this point is that of reintegration. According to the Weberian derived theory, society is amenable to the emergence of a charismatic type of authority structure. Here one individual, endowed with exceptional sanctity, establishes the normative patterns for all.[5]

Reliance on a charismatic type of leader and a charismatic authority structure is by nature transitory because of the relationship between modernization and industrialization. One of the drives of a society attempting to become modern is towards the construction of an industrial society. Industrialization has both a prestigeful and a meaningful economic appeal to societies undergoing transition. Industrialization requires an ethic stating that the environment can be controlled and not left in the hands of fate. It also requires technical knowledge

[2] See Max Weber, *The Theory of Social and Economic Organization*, transl. Talcott Parsons and A. M. Henderson, Glencoe, Ill., The Free Press, 1947, p. 328.

[3] See Roy C. Macridis and Bernard E. Brown, *Comparative Politics: Notes and Readings*, Homewood, The Dorsey Press, 1961, pp. 437-439.

[4] *United States Foreign Policy: Economic, Social and Political Change in the Underdeveloped Countries and Its Implication for United States Policy*. A report submitted to the United States Senate Committee on Foreign Relations (Study Number 12) by the Center for International Studies, Massachusetts Institute of Technology, Washington, D.C., 1960.

[5] H. H. Gerth and C. Wright Mills, *From Max Weber: Essays in Sociology*, New York, Oxford University Press, 1946, pp. 245-252.

for the reshaping of the physical environment.[6] Industrialization places a premium on technology and science, not on charisma. Industrialization requires routinized economic and political processes, not inspiration. In short, industrialization demands the establishment of a legal-rational authority structure.

This belief in a movement toward the construction of a legal-rational authority system draws support from the classic theory of bureaucracy. Concomitant with the development of a legal-rational system, a rationalized administrative structure is constructed. The impact of modernization upon the role and character of bureaucracies is summed up in a recent study in this manner:

"It is one of the characteristics of industrialized societies, irrespective of their form of government, to develop a civil service recruited on the basis of specific technical requirements. 'Bureaucratic administration means fundamentally the exercise of control on the basis of knowledge,' observed Max Weber. It is above all a rational organization characterized by: a) a clearly defined sphere of competence subject to impersonal rules; b) a hierarchy which determines in an orderly fashion relations of superiors and subordinates; c) a regular system of appointments and promotions on the basis of free contract; d) recruitment on the basis of skills, knowledge, or technical training; and e) fixed salaries."[7]

The model of political development that is founded on theories of change in the authority structure and the classic theory of bureaucracy takes this form. The establishment of a legal-rational system is the end product of the process of modernization. As society becomes rationalized, a specialization of roles takes place. Specialization of roles requires the development of formal rules and a hierarchical structure for the enforcement of these rules and the settlement of conflicts. These pressures cluster together to dictate a bureaucratization of society with an increased power position for members of the formal bureaucracy. As this occurs, the non-rational (ideological) components of the political milieu tend to be dissipated. The political style tends to become pragmatic. The political culture tends to become rational and secular. In this transformation the formal state bureaucracy plays a major role, so the arguement continues, as it has in many polities undergoing change.

[6] Talcott Parsons, "Some Principal Characteristics of Industrial Societies," reprinted in Cyril E. Black, editor, *The Transformation of Russian Society*, Cambridge, Harvard University Press, 1960, pp. 13-42.

[7] Macridis and Brown *Comparative Politics*, *op.cit.*, p. 305.

In some polities the relationship of the governmental bureaucracy to political development is a key relationship. In some polities the bureaucracy has become the "core of modern government."[8] In these polities the bureaucracy assumes both an instrumental and a policy-making role, and the action of the bureaucracy regarding political change is crucial.

There are a series of factors which influence the course of interaction between bureaucracy and political change. In those cases where there is a homogeneous civil service with its own political and social profile which is in conflict with the proposed change, subversion of change can be expected.[9] In those cases where the bureaucracy has only an instrumental image of itself, an instrumental role towards change can be expected.

It is recognized that it is not enough to know the character of the bureaucracy. Some analysts relate the form of interaction between a bureaucracy and political change to the political culture in which the bureaucracy operates: "The ideal of a neutral, instrumental bureaucracy, responsible to the political arm, comes closest to being realized in political systems where the political culture tends to be secular and rational, and where the functions of political choice—that is, the articulation and aggregation of interests and the making of public policy—are performed by specialized agencies."[10]

It cannot be postulated that all bureaucracies are carriers of an antiquated political philosophy and therefore will impede change, or that all bureaucracies press toward a further rationalization of society. But the important variables that determine, or at least satisfactorily explain, a particular case can be isolated. Because of the Western experience the conclusion is often reached that a bureaucracy will be a

[8] Carl J. Friedrich, *Constitutional Government and Democracy*, rev. ed., Boston, Ginn and Co., 1950.

[9] Excellent studies of bureaucratic conservatism can be found in studies of the Social Democratic party of Germany, which held political power from 1918-1920; the Labour Government of 1929-1931 in Great Britain; and the Cooperative Commonwealth Federation Government of Saskatchewan. Seymour Martin Lipset, "Bureaucracy and Social Change," in Robert K. Merton, ed., *Reader in Bureaucracy*, Glencoe, Ill., The Free Press, 1952, pp. 221-232. This and other studies seem to substantiate the conclusion reached by Max Weber that control of the existing bureaucratic machinery is the crucial qusetion and this control resides in the long run with the trained permanent official, not with the cabinet minister. Weber, *The Theory of Social and Economic Organization*, *op.cit.*, p. 128. See also, S. Soemardjan, "Bureaucratic Organization in a Time of Revolution," *Administrative Science Quarterly*, Vol. 2, Sept. 1957, pp. 182-199.

[10] Gabriel A. Almond, "Research Note: A Comparative Study of Interest Groups and the Political Process," *American Political Science Review*, Vol. 52, March 1958, pp. 279-280.

harbinger of legal-rationalism. This conclusion tends to reinforce a concept of political development that has as its ultimate stage the establishment of a legal-rational authority system.

If these sets of statements about bureaucracy and political development were entirely applicable to the Communist states, the course of their development would be predictable. The political structure, as a reflection of the social structure, would become increasingly rationalized; rules, both formal and informal, would become increasingly codified; career channels would become increasingly routinized, with a major emphasis placed upon expertise; and decision strategies would be based more upon computation and bargaining than on inspiration.[11] These changes would not necessarily be incremental in nature, but the political systems of totalitarianism would move in this direction. Such a movement would mean the eventual erosion of the ideology and revolutionary character of Communist regimes. It is this forecast that forms the frame for this chapter. It will be explored by reference to the doctrine, the administrative system, and the political leadership of the Communist states of Eastern Europe.

Political Doctrine

Three phases can be isolated in the fluctuating political development of the Communist states of Eastern Europe.[12] The first, the early period of People's Democracies, was marked by political action based more upon power considerations than upon doctrine.[13] It was a

[11] James D. Thompson and Arthur Tuden, "Strategies, Structures and Processes of Organizational Decision," in James D. Thompson, Peter B. Hammond, Robert W. Hawkes, Buford H. Junker, and Arthur Tuden, *Comparative Studies in Administration*, Pittsburgh, University of Pittsburgh Press, 1959, pp. 195-216. Computational decision strategies take place in situations where there is agreement on preferences about possible outcomes and agreement on beliefs about causation. Bargaining decision strategies take place in situations where there is non-agreement on preferences about possible outcomes but agreement on beliefs about causation. The first is reflective of a bureaucratic structure; the second is reflective of a representative structure.

[12] For an excellent study of the phases of political development in Eastern Europe, see Zbigniew K. Brzezinski, *The Soviet Bloc: Unity and Conflict*, Cambridge, Harvard University Press, 1960.

[13] Because the governments established after World War II could not qualify as dictatorships of the proletariat and because they had to cooperate in coalition governments with hostile political forces, a more elastic concept than that of the Soviet model was required. A new concept had to be created requiring a " 'creative' application of Marxism-Leninism to the new and complex environment." Brzezinski, *The Soviet Bloc, op.cit.*, p. 25. According to I. P. Trainin three types of democracy existed following World War II: bourgeois democracy, democracy of the transitional form existing in the People's Democracies, and the purer democracy of the Soviet Union. The People's Democracies were recognized as temporary deviations from the Soviet pattern. I. P. Trainin, "The People's Democracies," *Sovetskoe Gosudarstvo i*

period in which Communist leaders in each country stressed the national and democratic character of their movements and the uniqueness of their own road to socialism.[14] The second, the period of the consolidation of People's Democracies, was marked by political action in the mold of Stalinism. Each Communist leader acknowledged the hegemony of the Soviet Union and the relevance of the Soviet model for the construction of socialism.[15] The third, the period of "thaw"

Pravo, Nos. 1 and 3, 1947. See also Y. M. Shavrov, "The Constitution of the Czechoslovak Republic," *ibid.,* No. 8, 1956. The Communist leaders of Eastern Europe did not have a clear idea as to the character of People's Democracies. See Jozsef Revai, "The Character of a 'People's Democracy'," *Foreign Affairs,* Vol. 28, October 1949, pp. 143-152.

[14] It is difficult to determine whether political leaders in Eastern Europe who espoused unique and national roads to socialism were sincere in this conviction or whether they were making an appeal to a larger population than that of the Communist parties in their respective countries. However, all of them went on record as supporting unique roads to socialism. "During the last 25 years the Communist Parties of the world learned that there are several roads which lead to socialism and accordingly we cannot build socialism if we did not build our own road taking into account the special conditions prevailing in the country. . . . This will be socialism born on Hungarian soil and adapted to Hungarian conditions." Speech by Rakosi before the Second Congress of the Hungarian Communist party. Prior to the *coup d'état* of February, 1948, Czech Communist leaders supported this position. On September 25, 1946, Klement Gottwald, Communist Premier of Czechoslovakia, announced to the Central Committee of the Communist party that "experience in the principles of Marxism-Leninism tells us that the dictatorship of the proletariat and of the Soviets is not the only road to socialism." Reported in Winifred N. Hadsel, "Czechoslovakia's Road to Socialism," *Foreign Policy Reports,* Vol. 22, February 15, 1947, p. 270. A few weeks later he stated that it was the historical and cultural background of the country rather than an abstract ideological pattern that determined the methods to be adopted in establishing a socialist state. Klement Gottwald, *O Ceskoslovenske Zahranicni Politice,* Prague, Svoboda 1946. The Yugoslavs asserted on the other hand that their People's Democracy was the Soviet model. "And we, who contended that we had won our socialist revolution, that our People's Democracy was of the Soviet type, we were told that we were narrow-minded sectarians and entirely incapable of inventing something new, despite the fact that practically everything is really new in the present People's Democracy. In the present, People's Democracy has been created in our country." E. B. Kardelj, "On People's Democracy in Yugoslavia," *Komunist,* Belgrade, July 1949, pp. 3-4.

[15] By 1948 Soviet and Eastern European leaders had proclaimed the applicability of the Soviet model to their own experiences and denied there were as many roads to socialism as there were countries. This recognition was made explicit when the All Union Institute of Juridical Sciences published *Gosudarstvennoye Pravo Stran Narodnoi Demokratii,* Moscow, 1949, by N. P. Farberov, a leading Soviet theoretician. Farberov argued that the People's Democracies met the doctrinal criteria established by the Soviet Union. They acknowledged the dictatorship of the proletariat and the vanguard of the party; they acknowledged that the revolutions were anti-fascist, anti-capitalist, people's democratic revolutions aimed at smashing the bourgeois state; they accepted the concept of the working class state in which the dictatorship of the proletariat performed the same cohesive and educational functions as in the Soviet Union and they accepted the fundamental law of the transition of socialism. Farberov concluded, "all the basic principles and institutions of the constitutions of the People's Democratic states bear on them the stamp of the magnificent influence of the Stalin

and "deluge,"[16] was marked by a reaction, sometimes violent, to the totalism of Stalinism. Today the bloc is beset with the legacy of all of these pressures as it confronts the problem of harmonizing diversity and polycentrism with unity in Communism.

When the Communist parties of Eastern Europe seized control over their respective countries, each leader of each party proclaimed the construction of a socialist state as his aim.[17] Soon after, the era of Stalinism in Eastern Europe was well underway. Diversity in theory and pluralism in politics were no longer acceptable. The Soviet model of building socialism was the only model.[18]

The construction of socialism in Eastern Europe has not been a simple process. Each country has been pressured into serious deviations from the Soviet model. These deviations have resulted, not in a rejection of party doctrine, but in changes in the tempo and the violence which were a part of the Stalinist system. The broad political, economic, and social policies which are intrinsic to the Soviet model of Marxism-Leninism have remained, with minor exceptions, the political, economic, and social policies of the Eastern European states.

In the political sphere the doctrine demanded the establishment and implementation of the Communist party as the vanguard of the dictatorship of the proletariat, and the intensification of the class struggle against both traditional class enemies and the more devious

constitution." See also article by I. Yutin, *Pravda*, April 27, 1949. Gustav Bares, one of the leading intellectual spokesmen of the Czechoslovak Communist party, summed up the Eastern European response to this new theory of People's Democracies. The conception of a distinctive Czechoslovak path to socialism, different from the path taken by the Soviet Union after the October revolution, was replaced by the conception of a common Leninist path different only in secondary features. H. Gordon Skilling, "People's Democracy, The Proletarian Dictatorship in the Czechoslovak Path to Socialism," *The American Slovak and East European Review*, Vol. 10, April 1951, p. 103. Bedrich Rattinger, "Stalinska Ustava a Ustavni Vyvoj Lidove Demokratickeho Ceskoslovenska," *Za Socialisticky Stat*, No. 6, 1951, pp. 592-598.

[16] Brzezinski, *The Soviet Bloc*, *op.cit.*, p. 23.

[17] Constitutions recognizing the establishment of People's Democracies were established in Bulgaria on November 4, 1947; Rumania, April 13, 1948; Czechoslovakia, May 9, 1949; Hungary, August 20, 1949; and Poland, July 22, 1952. For a discussion of these see P. B. Steanu, "Constitutionalism in the Satellite States," *Journal of Central European Affairs*, Vol. 12, April 1952, pp. 56-69, and Pavel Peska, *Ustavy Lidove Demokratickych Zemi*, Prague, Orbis, 1954.

[18] The Soviet position on building socialism was made clear as early as November 1947. N. P. Farberov, writing in *Bolshevik*, stated "the general laws of transition from capitalism to socialism, discovered by Marx and Engels, tested, put to concrete use, and developed by Lenin and Stalin on the basis of the experience of the Bolshevik party in the Soviet state, are binding upon all countries." This position was made clear to the Eastern Europeans when it was reprinted in *For a Lasting Peace, for a People's Democracy*, No. 1, November 10, 1947, pp. 1-2.

class enemies such as opportunists, internationalists, and others who had infiltrated the party. In the economic sphere the doctrine demanded the construction of a socialist economy defined as industrial and collectivist. In the social sphere the doctrine called for the creation of socialist man. Each of these principles was pursued by all of the states of Eastern Europe, with varying intensity, since 1948.

Disagreement and even conflict took place on how these doctrines are best achieved and at what speed. When the party first came to power, its methods were similar to those used at the height of Stalinism in the Soviet Union. Terror, purge, forced collectivization, unmanageable commitments to heavy industry, and control over all social and educational organizations were the hallmarks of this period.[19]

The unrealistic demands of the period of Stalinism and the brutal methods employed developed counter-pressures in the countries of Eastern Europe. These pressures ruptured when the Stalinist monopoly of power and ideology was faced with the problem of succession. The death of Stalin did not result in the disintegration of either the Communist doctrine or the Communist structure of Eastern Europe, but it did result in the seeking of a variety of solutions to the problems raised by that doctrine and structure.

The Malenkov New Course in the Soviet Union had a great deal of appeal to some leaders of the People's Democracies. Professor Brzezinski has analyzed that appeal in the following terms: "Without yielding the most important Stalinist positions, it seemed to permit them [the leaders of the People's Democracies] to reduce somewhat the accumulated economic tensions."[20] In each country the period of the New Course took a separate form determined by the peculiar facts of that country. In Bulgaria, Czechoslovakia, and Rumania there was no major retreat from Stalin's policies or from Stalin's doctrines, and no major changes in the power structure.[21] For the most part limited

[19] It should be pointed out that these are generalizations about the entire area. Actually there were many variances in each country. Poland and Rumania were relatively moderate. The Czechs and Bulgarians engaged in the most radical and violent policies.

[20] Brzezinski, *The Soviet Bloc*, *op.cit.*, p. 157.

[21] E. O. Stillman and R. H. Bass, "Bulgaria: A Study in Satellite Nonconformity," *Problems of Communism*, Vol. 4, November-December 1955, pp. 26-33. Ivo Duchacek, "Czechoslovakia: New Course or No Course?" *ibid.*, Vol. 8, January-February 1959, pp. 12-19. Hugh Seton-Watson, "Eastern Europe since Stalin," *ibid.*, Vol. 3, March-April 1954, pp. 10-17. See speech by Chervenkov on September 8, 1953, *Rabotnichesko Delo*, September 9, 1953; and the report of the Fourth National Congress of the TAZS, February 15-17, 1955, in *Zemedelsko Zname*, February 17, 1955. For Rumania, see speech by Gheorghiu-Dej, August 25, 1953. In Czechoslovakia the New Course was referred to as a program "to raise the working peo-

economic concessions were made to the peasants, industrial targets were scaled down, increases in consumer goods were planned, protection against arbitrary state acts was promised by rigid adherence to socialist legality, and there were promises of increased cultural freedom. In Hungary, where the impact of Stalinism was as violent as anywhere, where the party was split into various groups, and where the Soviet Union entered in directly, the New Course had important political implications. But, prior to the revolution, emphasis was placed upon economic concessions, greater independence for the peasant, and protection from arbitrary power.[22] Poland was the last to adopt a New Course. Here again the emphasis was upon economic concessions.[23]

In general, the New Course affected the doctrine by legitimizing collective leadership in the party, de-emphasizing class warfare, scaling down commitments to heavy industry, and in some cases allowing withdrawal from the collective farms.[24] But these infringements upon the doctrine were recognized as expedients because of "objective" circumstances, not changes in the steps necessary to advance toward socialism.

A political movement that directly challenged the doctrine and therefore would have had profound consequences upon the political development of Eastern Europe was revisionism. Revisionism was the result of protest by Communist intellectuals against the doctrinaire character of totalitarianism. At first the revisionists' protest was against the curbs imposed by the party upon intellectual activity. This protest soon spilled over into politics, including criticism of the hallowed party doctrine. Revisionists did not accept Khrushchev's explanation that Stalin's crimes were merely a function of his egomania; they saw them as manifestations of the system. As a result, revisionists soon ques-

ple's economic and cultural standards." *Rude Pravo*, October 4, 1954. This period was inaugurated in a speech by William Siroky on September 15, 1953 before the National Assembly in Prague, *ibid.*, September 16, 1953.

[22] Speech by Imre Nagy before Parliament on July 4, 1953. His program called for price reductions, wage increases, cancellation of agricultural deliveries, reduction of taxes on peasants, some withdrawal from collective farms, greater religious tolerance, abolition of internment camps, and partial amnesty. *News from Behind the Iron Curtain*, August 1953, p. 47.

[23] Speech by Beirut before the Ninth Plenum of the Central Committee of the United Polish Workers' Party, October 29, 1953. See also Jean Malara, "Poland since the Death of Stalin," *Problems of Communism*, Vol. 4, March-April 1955, pp. 12-19. It was not until the period surrounding the Polish October that the New Course in Poland moved outside the realm of economics.

[24] Nagy talked about sanctioned withdrawal from collective farms; Siroky promised limited permission to withdraw from collective farms. Beirut called for a continuing struggle against the Kulaks.

tioned the basic features of Leninism, including proletarian internationalism, the dictatorship of the proletariat, and the forced character of a socialist economy. Revisionism, however, never became an organized political movement. The inherent Communism of Gomulka, the sweeping aside of revisionism by the aroused nationalism of the Hungarian Revolution, the failure of revisionists to get support from the peasantry, the branding of revisionism as the major threat to the communist camp by the Moscow twelve-party declaration of November 1957, and the conviction of many revisionists that attempts to reform Marxism-Leninism were bound to fail—all contributed to its atrophy.[25]

The Polish road to socialism has often been presented as unique and revisionist, but the deviations from the doctrine are more than matched by the adherences to it.[26] The Polish road includes an expressed belief in the political doctrine, including a leading role for the party[27] and the building of a monolithic labor class.[28] Its most serious deviation is in regard to collectivization of agriculture. Within a short time following Gomulka's rise to power, only 1,700 of the 10,600 farms were in existence as collective farms.[29] Most of the other changes were in regard to social and intellectual freedoms. The Polish road to socialism has been a combination of pragmatism and national interest within Communism, in the direction, as the position of Gomulka became consolidated, of orthodoxy. The impact of Gomulkaism on political doctrine is centered upon intra-bloc relations, not

[25] William E. Griffith, "What Happened to Revisionism?" *Problems of Communism*, Vol. 9, March-April 1960, pp. 1-15; Heinz Kersten, *Aufstand der Intellektuellen, Wandlungen in der kommunistischen Welt; ein dokumentarischer Bericht*, Stuttgart, H. Seewald, 1957. For an optimistic appraisal of the future of revisionism, see Jean-Paul Sarte, *Les Temps Modernes*, November, December 1956, January 1957, pp. 1-29, 1-30, 1-31.

[26] For an excellent discussion of the Polish road to socialism, see Brzezinski, *The Soviet Bloc, op.cit.*, pp. 331-357. See also Jan Przblya, "Gomulka and the Peasants," *Problems of Communism*, Vol. 7, May-June 1958, pp. 23-30; Leon Lewins, "The Polish Economy, The Problems and Prospects," *Problems of Communism*, Vol. 7, May-June 1958, pp. 14-23; K. A. Jelenski, "Revisionism—Pragmatism—Gomulkaism," *Problems of Communism*, Vol. 7, May-June 1958, pp. 5-13.

[27] Gomulka's speech before the Tenth Plenum, *Trybuna Ludu*, October 26, 1957. In fact, following the Tenth Plenum, a purge took place in the party which resulted in the dropping of 200,161 members. *Sztandar Mlodych*, May 15, 1958.

[28] Wladyslaw Gomulka, *Przemowienia*, Warsaw, Ksiazka i Wiedza, 1957.

[29] Brzezinski, *The Soviet Bloc, op.cit.*, p. 344. In addition to these changes, the right to buy and sell private land was restored to the peasant, compulsory milk deliveries were abolished, other delivery quotas were reduced, prices paid by the state for agricultural products were doubled, restrictions on sale of products outside the network of state-purchasing stations were eliminated, tax rates were lowered, and larger credits were made available.

upon the doctrine of socialism. In the field of foreign affairs Gomulkaism advocates "close alliance with the U.S.S.R. but not domestic subordination to it, domestic autonomy without external ideological ambitions."[30]

It would be a mistake to view the doctrine of Communism as formulating a rigid pattern of development which must be adhered to at all times. But the syndrome of the Communist state has been defined. This definition has been accepted by the political leadership of Eastern Europe with deviations viewed as only temporary due to "objective" circumstances. Public policy is designed to limit the number and range of "objective" circumstances. In this respect, the Communist political movement and its leaders have been generally successful. The doctrine has been followed more than it has been violated. The violations that have occurred are not directly traceable to conflict between totalitarianism and bureaucratization.[31]

The System of Administration

The administrative structure of Eastern Europe is highly complex, determined to a large extent by the nature of the doctrine, particularly those parts of the doctrine which demand that the leading role be played by the party and at the same time that administration be a mass affair.[32] Generally speaking, it is possible, as some Communist theorists have done, to divide the system of administration into three hierarchies: (1) the National Front, consisting of all political parties and mass organizations which together represent "under the leadership of the Communist Party, the supreme power of the people";[33] (2) the organs of state power which include those bodies established to add legitimacy to decisions such as the National Assembly, the President in Czechoslovakia, the Council of State in Poland and Rumania, the National Council in Hungary, and the Presidium of the National

[30] *Ibid.*, p. 356.

[31] Despite all the conflicts that have occurred in Eastern Europe, there is little evidence of conflict between individuals who drew their source of support from the party against those who drew their support from the state apparatus.

[32] V. I. Lenin, "Speech to the VII CPSU Congress, 1918," *Selected Works*, Vol. 8, New York, International Publishers, 1943, p. 318. For more recent assessments of the role to be played by the masses, see C. A. Jampolskaja, "The Part Taken by the Masses in the Administration of the State," *Sovetskoe Gosudarstvo i Pravo*, No. 12, December 5, 1956; Ladislaw Hrzal, "The Party and the Masses," *Nova Mysl*, June 6, 1958.

[33] Juraj Hromada, *Prehl'ad Ceskoslovenskych Statnych Organov*, Bratislava, Slovenske Vydavatel'stvo Politickej Literatury, 1955.

Assembly in Bulgaria;[34] and (3) the organs of state administration. The major organs of state administration are the councils of ministers in each country and the people's committee systems.

The powers of the Council of Ministers under the 1952 constitution of Poland are typical. The Council coordinates activities of ministries and gives direction to their work; it adopts and presents the proposed state budget; adopts and presents the long-term national economic plans; ensures the proper execution of the laws; issues executive orders; and exercises general direction over national defense and foreign affairs. Theoretically the Council of Ministers is the supreme agency of governmental and executive power.[35] The Council, composed of administrative, political, economic, social, and cultural ministries and the prime minister and deputy prime ministers, is generally regarded as the apex of the state structure in the countries of Eastern Europe. Agencies of state administration directly subordinate to a particular ministry exist at all levels. Although in time this state apparatus is supposed to wither away, leaders in Eastern Europe are quick to point out that the state apparatus is important in the present phase of socialist development. If anything, it needs to be strengthened.[36]

The state agencies of administration on a regional and local level are the people's committee systems. These committees are "the bearers and executors of the state power and the local authorities of the state power in a People's Democratic Republic."[37] The main tasks of each component in this system is to "direct and plan the complex development in all sectors of the economy within its territory and, on the

[34] Only in Poland does the National Assembly play a significant role in political life. This was particularly true in the Eighth Parliamentary Session, April 23-28, 1956, when many critical speeches were made in regard to both policies and the role of the Sejm itself. Some deputies argued that the Sejm should control the Council of Ministers and the Council of State. There have been actual cases of negative votes being recorded. For a discussion of the way in which these organs bring legitimacy to the system, see Bedrich Rattinger, *Nejvyssi Statni Organy Lidove Demokratickeho Ceskoslovenska: Narodni Shromazdeni a President Republiky*, Prague, Statni Nakladatelstvi Politicke Literatury, 1958.

[35] *Sbirka Zakonu a Narizeni Republiky Ceskoslovenske*, 1948, No. 150, Article VII.

[36] Speeches by Maurer and Ceausescu before the National Assembly of Rumania; speeches by Stoice and Draghici before the Third Congress of Rumania. See also Herbert Ritvo, "Totalitarianism without Coercion?" *Problems of Communism*, Vol. 9, November-December 1960, pp. 19-29; K. Frolov, "The Class Struggle in the Period of Socialism," *Partiinaia Zhizn*, No. 20, 1956. Khrushchev explained in a speech at the 21st CPSU Congress: "There will be no weakening of the role of the state in the building of Communism," *Pravda*, January 29, 1959.

[37] *Rude Pravo*, March 28, 1952.

other hand, to allot in accordance with the targets of the state plan the basic economic tasks . . . and to control the fulfillment of these tasks."[38] In all of the countries the powers and functions of the people's committee systems have been continually strengthened. Recently the people's committee system of Czechoslovakia was made responsible for the development of agricultural production, local industry, warehouses and shops, construction enterprises, kindergartens, schools of general education, professional schools, hospitals, etc. In exercising these and other responsibilities the people's committee system will control 30.6 per cent of the total state expenditures.[39]

In addition to these two hierarchies a multitude of other organizations exist to administer the state. In Czechoslovakia, for example, commissions of the people's committees have been established as "effective instruments for organizing the working people, for solving and fulfilling the tasks of economic and cultural construction, for working and securing of the plan and budget, for managing enterprises and cultural and social establishments."[40] In December 1960, 310,000 persons were members of these commissions. Citizens' committees have also been established to overview the functioning of the people's committees. In September 1960 Czechoslovakia had 10,200 citizens' committees with 105,000 members.[41]

The people's committee system is assisted by a whole series of mass organizations who also are concerned with the effectiveness and direction of administration in the socialist states. In Hungary, a special people's control committee was established in 1957 directly responsible to the Council of Ministers. This control commission with its network of metropolitan, urban, county, and district committees is to keep a constant check on the economy.[42] By January 15, 1960, 32,000 "people's controllers" had been employed.[43] Other assisting and cajoling organizations are trade unions, youth organizations, socialist brigades,

[38] "Organisace Spravy Planovacich Komisi," *Hospodarske Noviny*, February 19, 1960.

[39] *Politkia Ekonomie*, No. 6, June 1960.

[40] *Pravda*, Bratislava, December 26, 1960.

[41] *Rude Pravo*, September 22, 1960.

[42] *Nepszabadsag*, January 15, 1960. Geza Szenasi, Public Prosecutor, has stated: "People's Control is in many respects similar to the work of the police and public prosecutor's office, and this control has many points of contact with the particular fields for which the police and prosecutors are responsible. It is very important that the two should exchange their experiences. The People's Controllers must cooperate with the police, the prosecutor's office and above all work with the party cells." *A Torvenyesseg Orhelyen*, Budapest, Kossuth, 1958, p. 136.

[43] *Nepszabadsag*, January 15, 1960.

associations for relations with Soviet Russia, peace committees, societies for the dissemination of science and culture, and national councils of women.

The cement that is used by the leaders to hold this diffuse structure together is the party. The leading role of the party is not merely a shibboleth expressed by Communist leaders and theorists. It is a fact of administrative existence in each of the Eastern European states. This "law" gives the party the authority to operate at all levels upon all other hierarchies within the system. The facts of existence, including the necessity of the system being productive, limit interference, but few deny the right of the party to exercise control when and where the totalitarian leaders determine that it shall.

Among the formal and informal methods of control exercised by the party over other administrative agencies is that of dual office holding. Almost all members of the administrative hierarchies are members of the Communist party and therefore subject to its hierarchy and its discipline. Often the leading administrative boards are staffed with the same persons as the leading party boards. At lower levels, party committees are created in conjunction with the network of people's committees, factory committees, collective farm committees, and even block committees. By creating this system the party can be assured that it has a great deal to say in the decisions and staffing of non-party agencies.

This complex system seems effective from the party point of view because it allows the expert to participate in decisions without inordinately increasing his power and because it allows the party to shift the blame for mistakes and failures. Conversely it is a danger to the party. The party is placed in the position where it must rely to a large extent upon the good faith of members of many other organizations.

Because of the pervasive role played by the party apparatus, totalitarian political systems have often been described as monolithic and bureaucratic. Unfortunately, this description implies that the administrative structure is one that functions and behaves in the classic bureaucratic manner. The administrative structure of totalitarian political systems, as evidenced in Eastern Europe, is not that simple. These are structures that are marked by a series of hierarchies, a series of conflicting controls, a series of conflicting demands, and a series of interests. In short, the administrative structure of totalitarian political systems is highly complex.

It is impossible, for example, to pinpoint a formal state bureaucracy in Eastern Europe in the sense that one can do so in describing politics in Great Britain or France. The course of administration is not determined by a bureaucracy in the sense of a formal state administrative system that is independent and instrumental; it is determined, instead, by the interplay between the leaders, the movement, and a series of administrative organizations. The latter, because of the power of the party to intrude at any time and at any level, displays few of the functional and behavioral characteristics that are ascribed to a classical bureaucracy.[44] Indeed, a totalitarian political movement would find an administrative structure that developed in the classical manner to be a threat to both its power position and its ideological posture.

Similarly, the dynamics of administration in Eastern Europe is not a simple process. Tensions and conflict are inherent in each of the political systems under discussion. Some of the tensions stem from the doctrine itself. The requirement to preserve a leading role for the party and to continue the class struggle complicates profoundly the achievement of a rational industrial society. Industrialization tends to breed an interest in economic optimization. Such an interest places its emphasis upon technical competence and economic rationality, not upon political loyalty and ideological pronouncements. Industrialization tends to demand autonomy for the technical decision maker and the decision-making aparatus, which the party must control. Collectivization adds to the price that agruculture must already pay for industrialization, and this further complicates the establishment of an optimizing economy.[45]

All of these tensions and pressures disrupt any clear trend in the political development of Eastern Europe. The multi-directional posture of politics in Eastern Europe can be demonstrated by reference to two important characteristics of bureaucratization: (1) the development of autonomy in the decision-making apparatus, and (2) the selection of decision makers.

The Development of Autonomy

The right of the Communist party to exert pressure and to control performance at all levels and in all dimensions of society is one of the mainstays of the Communist system of government. An important

[44] For a discussion of this conclusion as drawn from a study of administration in Czechosolvakia see, my "Party Control and Bureaucratization in Czechoslovakia," *Journal of Politics,* Vol. 23, May 1961, pp. 279-294.

[45] Fritz Schenk, *Magie der Planwirtschaft,* Cologne, Kiepenheuer und Witsch, 1960.

area for exploration, then, to understand the impact of industrialization and the possibilities of a trend toward bureaucratization and the construction of a legal-rational system is the extent of autonomy developing within the system. To explore this area of inquiry, reference will be made to the character of administrative reorganization, industrial decentralization, and devolution in Eastern Europe. In conclusion, signs of a developing autonomy and the relevance of autonomy to bureaucratic theory will be discussed.

A. ADMINISTRATIVE REORGANIZATION

Reorganization of regional administrative units took place in Bulgaria, Czechoslovakia, Rumania, and Poland. Reorganization is also being discussed in Hungary and will probably take place in the near future.[46] In each of these countries larger regions have been created "in maximum accordance with the economic areas that are already virtually existing."[47] In some cases ministries have been abolished and their functions turned over to the people's committees of the new regions.

Economic considerations have influenced this change in structure. The new regions are supposed to reflect an economic unit characterized by some degree of specialization. This form of organization will simplify planning and management in the Eastern Europe states. In addition, the establishment of amalgamated regions leads the way to the future amalgamation of *kolkhozes* and villages.[48]

The reorganizations were not motivated by economic reasons alone. Nor will future decision making in these newly established regions be dictated solely by economic motives.

From the beginning, stress was placed upon the political goals of reorganization. All of the Eastern European leaders were quick to point out that reorganization will bring the administrative structure closer to the "revolutionary organizations of working masses" which are the "political basis of a socialist state."[49] Reorganization has, therefore, been defined as an extension of democratic centralism, not as a substitute: "The sense of the new measures is not some 'shifting of chairs' as such, but in the first place the effort to create the conditions

[46] *Nemzepor*, February, 1961.

[47] Speech by Antonin Novotny and declaration of the Czechoslovak Central Committee, *Rude Pravo*, January 17, 1960. In Czechoslovakia 10 regions and 108 districts replaced 19 regions and 270 districts.

[48] *Ibid.*, February 13, 1961.

[49] Frantisek Koranda, Radio Prague, May 14, 1960.

for a further development of a higher degree of participation of the people in the direction of economy and culture, which would be linked with a further deepening of the Leninist principles of a central direction of both these sectors. The deepening of initiative and of centralism —two mutually joined aspects of democratic centralism—is a law of the development of socialism."[50] Others have suggested that the extension of democratic centralism has little to do with reorganization,[51] but none has suggested that democratic centralism is being abandoned.

In all cases territorial reorganizations have meant an increase in the concerns of the regional people's committees. At the same time, the leading role of the party within the people's committee systems has been stressed in all countries following reorganization. *Rude Pravo*, the newspaper of the Communist party in Czechoslovakia, has stated: "We shall fully apply the leading role of the party in the people's committees.[52] . . . The activities of the people's committees are being guided by the decisions of the party."[53] It has warned that "any lowering or denying of the leading role of the party in the administrative reorganizations equals a complete disarmament of the proletariat to the benefit of the bourgeoisie."[54] In Czechoslovakia trained members of the party apparatus were sent to key posts in local and district people's committees to insure that reorganization proceeds smoothly. They have remained as officials of the reorganized people's committees.

Administrative reorganization may help to put the regional administrative organs of Eastern Europe on a more rational basis and simplify the tasks of centralized planning.[55] It may help to differentiate the resources available in each region. It may help to prune the administrative apparatus. It could even lead to a greater degree of autonomy, but the party is taking many measures to assure that this result is kept to a minimum.

[50] Jaromir Sedlak, "Territorial Reorganization," *Rude Pravo*, March, 19, 1960.

[51] "If in their previous forms they [the replaced regions] rested on principles of democratic centralism, why do we undertake a new reorganization of our state apparatus and management of our national economy. The reason for the reform is that the old forms were in contra-distinction with the economic, cultural and other changes which have taken place," Professor Hapasov, *Rabotnichesko Delo*, March 23, 1959.

[52] *Rude Pravo*, July 22, 1960.

[53] *Ibid.*, October 27, 1960.

[54] *Ibid.*, June 21, 1960.

[55] Boris Burov, "The Reorganization and the Administration of the Bulgarian National Economy," *Pravna Misal*, Vol. 4, July-August, 1960, pp. 3-13.

B. INDUSTRIAL DECENTRALIZATION

The management of the industrial empire that has been created in each of the Eastern European countries has raised a myriad of problems. In addition to the normal (although not necessarily solvable) problems associated with industrialization, the Communist legacy of Stalinism, the Communist doctrine of administration, and the character of the revolutionary political movement itself have further complicated an already involved subject. However, some general statements about methods of management can be made.

Although Soviet economic models have shifted rapidly and often,[56] the general theme in the Soviet Union which has been reflected in Eastern Europe has been to toughen industrial targets, to increase the exercise of sanctions and controls, and to proliferate the number of targets in order to make up for loopholes in the centralized command system.[57] These tactics often led to the issuance of incompatible orders, thereby giving sanction to illegal behavior by managers, absence of coordination in planning, and a series of conflicting interests between planners and managers.[58] The Soviet response to this dilemma has been the establishment of territorial economic councils responsible for the enterprises within their regions, and the abolition of some twenty-five central ministries.[59] These structural changes have been called decentralization.

[56] For an excellent discussion of Soviet economic models see P. J. D. Wiles, "Rationality, the Market, Decentralization, and the Territorial Principle," in Gregory Grossman, ed., *Value and Plan*, Berkeley, University of California Press, 1960, pp. 184-203. For recognition that a variety of economic models is possible in a socialist economy, see Czeslaw Bobrowski, "Economy on a Panoramic Scene," *Przeglad Kulturalny*, November 29, 1959.

[57] Francis Seton, "Soviet Economy in Transition," *Problems of Communism*, Vol. 10, January-February 1961, pp. 34-41.

[58] See, for example, Joseph S. Berliner, *Factory and Manager in the USSR*, Cambridge, Harvard University Press, 1957; Gerhard W. Ditz, "Industrial Administration in Communist East Europe," *Administrative Science Quarterly*, Vol. 4, June 1959, pp. 82-96; and the mimeographed studies done by the research section of Radio Free Europe: Ladislav Stepan, "The Coal Industry in Czechoslovak," 1954; Vratislav Busek, "Studies in Vulnerabilities of Management (Czechoslovak Engineering Industry)," 1957; and Gerhard W. Ditz, "Studies in Vulnerabilities of Management (Czechoslovak Coal Industry)," 1957. For an assessment by a Hungarian, see Janos Kornai, *Overcentralization in Economic Administration: A Critical Analysis Based on Experience in Hungarian Light Industry*, translated by John Knapp, London, Oxford University Press, 1959.

[59] Michael Kasar, "The Reorganization of Soviet Industry and its Effect on Decision Making," Grossman, *Value and Plan*, *op.cit.*, pp. 213-234. See also A. Jurczenko, "Administrative Reorganization and the Building of Communism," *Bulletin of the Institute for the Study of the USSR*, Vol. 7, January 1960, pp. 14-23.

Eastern Europe has undertaken a similar decentralization program in conjunction with the territorial reorganizations discussed above. The important question to be asked about decentralization for our purposes is whether this program has served to reinforce the managerial elements in society whose major professional interest is with optimization, predictability, and routinization. If managerial autonomy was a result of the decentralization program, this would have an important impact upon politics in the Eastern European countries. In this section emphasis will be placed on a discussion of the formal placement of power and authority under the decentralized system. Unfortunately, we know little about the day-to-day operations of the various councils involved, and the way in which they relate to each other. Therefore we cannot note with any degree of satisfaction whether decision strategies and influence patterns have changed as a result of decentralization.

Territorial reorganization and industrial decentralization went together in Eastern Europe. In addition to other newly assigned tasks the regional people's committees have been given a greater degree of supervision over the operation of local industry. In some countries these regional people's committees were assisted by technical commissions. In Rumania, for example, regional economic councils similar to the Soviet *sovnarkhozes* were established. These councils are composed of technical experts brought together to coordinate the plans of local industry, check fulfillment of plans, and submit proposals to the people's committees.[60] In other cases the regional people's committees were authorized to construct their own apparatus. In Czechoslovakia, for example, the authority of the leading secretary of the regional people's committee was enhanced and special sub-divisions for agriculture, industry, and ideology established under his supervision. There has been discussion of establishing technical councils, but so far there is no indication that they are operating.

The response to the decentralization program has varied from country to country. This variance is indicative of the disparity in the freedom of action that local agencies enjoy. In Poland, on the one hand, frequent criticism of decentralization appears with the general tone being that meaningful decentralization has not occurred: "Budgets are corrected and approved in all details by the ministries and this

[60] Speech by Dej at the submission of the new economic plan, *Scanteia*, December 6, 1959.

does not in the least give the impression that the associations [combinations of local industries] are their own economic accountants. Inspectors from the Supreme Chamber of Control often do not accept the explanations of the director concerning post-inspection observations on the activity of subordinate enterprises. There are signs of technical interference of ministries in the activity of enterprises. . . . Associations do not have much authority in the work. . . . Does all this not mean that the superior authorities do not have confidence in the associations!"[61]

In Bulgaria, on the other hand, warnings have been issued that excessive decentralization would lead to excessive bureaucracy, more costly production, and lack of initiative. Decentralization in Bulgaria, at least, is to be guided by the principle of democratic centralism, and democratic centralism "does not lend itself to decentralization."[62] Bulgarian theorists accept the form of industrial decentralization because this form of "decentralization in the administration of the national economy is a new form of central administration."[63]

As far as can be ascertained, on very scanty evidence and little empirical research, the decentralization program has not meant a diminution in the power and role of the party apparatus. The factory councils, the people's committees, the technical commissions, and all of the other paraphernalia have been warned that the party committees still have the power to co-administer.[64] Soviet theorists have concluded that the reorganization of industrial enterprises has "considerably increased the role of Party organizations in economic construction."[65]

Most Western analysts seem to agree that the decentralization program has not meant greater autonomy for the individual decision maker in industry, except perhaps in Poland, nor the creation of a state bureaucracy with a more independent position. One concludes that the "scope for choice at the operational level of the economy . . .

[61] Jerzy L. Toeplitz, "The Counsel and the Complaints," *Zycie Gospodarcze*, November 10, 1960.

[62] Boris Burov, "The Reorganization and the Administration of the Bulgarian National Economy," *Pravna Misal*, Vol. 4, July-August 1960, pp. 3-13.

[63] *Ibid.*, p. 12.

[64] "The Role of the Party in Places of Work," *Nowe Drogi*, February 1959; Istavan Oroszi, "The Workers' Part in Factory Management," *Nepszabadsag*, February 11, 1959; D. Miladinov and P. Manolov, "The Role of the Manager," *Rabotnichesko Delo*, May 7, 1960; W. Migon, "Decentralization Means Not Only Prerogatives," *Trybuna Ludu*, July 7, 1961.

[65] "Several Organizational-Legal Problems of the Administration of Industry," *Sovetskoe Gosudarstvo i Pravo*, No. 3, August 1960.

seems to have been little affected by the reorganization."[66] A relatively enduring judgment as to whether this assessment is accurate will have to wait until systematic investigation of decision making at various levels in the industrial system has been undertaken.

C. PROFESSIONAL AUTONOMY

The evidence is sparse and the trends unclear as to other signs of a developing autonomy. Professor Ulam has noted that one of the three social pressures developing in the Soviet Union that are intrinsic to any modernized society is a pressure toward professional autonomy.[67] Professional groups, he argues, have natural demands for autonomy—intellectuals for freedom to discuss and debate, workers for real autonomy in the trade unions (including the right to bargain), lawyers for a routinization and regularization of legal administration. In Eastern Europe there has been some evidence of professional groups making demands for less control by political agencies. For the most part these have been confined to intellectual groups. Some Polish and Hungarian sociologists have argued that Western-type sociology is a discipline that can be treated scientifically.[68] Some Hungarian writers have demanded that Western writings of all sorts be available for appraisal.[69] Polish economists have held discussions on price systems unfettered by Marxist-Leninist orthodoxy, including discussion of such economic mechanisms as interest charges on fixed capital, differential rent, and

[66] Kasar, "The Reorganization of Soviet Industry and its Effect on Decision Making," *op.cit.*, p. 230. Jerry F. Hough sums up the situation by stating that instead of the emancipation of the technical intelligentsia from political control the recent period has witnessed the expansion of the party's role of authority not only in industry but in almost every other sector of Soviet life. "The Technical Elite vs. the Party: A First-hand Report," *Problems of Communism*, Vol. 8, September-October 1959, pp. 56-59.

[67] The other two social pressures are for a higher standard of living and protection against arbitrary acts by the state. Adam B. Ulam, "The New Face of Soviet Totalitarianism," *World Politics*, Vol. 12, April 1960, pp. 391-412.

[68] Statement by Julian Hochfeld, a leading Polish sociologist, quoted in *East Europe*, Vol. 10, April 1961, p. 2. Sandor Szalai, professor of sociology in Hungary, acknowledged that "this new type of sociological research (empirical-scientific), very practical in its nature and developing strongly specialized data collecting and processing and other surveying techniques on the factory, the family and other areas, has produced in the course of its large-scale and concrete examinations, besides assumptions for various propagandistic and ideological purposes, also realistic results and methodological solutions which are applied in the most highly developed capitalist countries very successfully." He then criticizes Hungarian sociologists for not doing the same. "Marxism and Sociology," *Elet es Irodalom*, April 14, 21, and 28, 1961.

[69] Aron Tamasi, "The Works Decide," *ibid.*, November 28, 1959.

obsolescence.[70] Polish lawyers have argued that a routinization of legal processes should take place.[71] All of these are indicative of a greater range of intellectual freedom than was allowed in the earlier period. As yet these scattered events do not seem to constitute a significant threat to the basic organization of the Soviet states in Eastern Europe.

D. DEVOLUTION

One of the doctrinal prescriptions that has plagued Communist leaders is that sometime in the future the state must wither away.[72] This tenet becomes more ominous as the socialist states prepare to become Communist. Khrushchev has recently stated that in the immediate future the state must be strengthened; East European leaders have concurred. Khrushchev has suggested that a way to resolve this incompatibility is by a reaffirmation of the leading role of the party to the point of stating that in the period of Communism the party will completely supplant the state. At that time persuasion alone rather than persuasion plus force will be the means for the propagation of the great ideas of Marxism-Leninism.[73] Khrushchev has further suggested that one way to spur the twin goals of lessening the role of the state and establishing persuasion as the "sole regulator of relations among people" is by expanding the role of public organizations.[74]

Concurrent with the reorganization and decentralization programs, some state functions were passed on to public organizations in Eastern Europe. The two major groups that have been affected are the police and the judiciary. Para-police organizations have long been a part of the Eastern European scene. In Bulgaria, Czechoslovakia, Hungary, and Rumania citizens can expect to be scrutinized and propagandized by block janitors, tenant committees, residential groups, local people's

[70] During the lifetime of Stalin, defense of economic rationalism was a precarious undertaking. In 1950, N. A. Vornesensky, former planning chief and member of the Politburo, was shot for overemphasizing the law of value and suggesting that economic laws can be manipulated by willful action.

[71] *Zycie Warszawy*, December 30, 1960; *Trybuna Ludu*, February 23, 1961.

[72] V. I. Lenin, *State and Revolution*, New York, International Publishers, 1932; J. Stalin, *Mastering Bolshevism*, New York, International Publishers, 1937. For an early assessment of this phenomena, see Calvin B. Hoover, "The Soviet State Fails to Wither," *Foreign Affairs*, Vol. 31, October 1952, pp. 114-127. Khrushchev resolved all doubts and confusions when he stated that "the state proceeds towards its withering away via its maximum strengthening." Speech to the 21st Party Congress, *Pravda*, January 28, 1959.

[73] Herbert Ritvo, "Totalitarianism Without Coercion?" *Problems of Communism*, Vol. 9, November-December 1960, pp. 19-29.

[74] Speech to the 13th Komsomol Congress, *Pravda*, April 2, 1958.

committees, and agitators of all sorts, in addition to the public prosecutor's office. The effectiveness of such groups can be judged by a report of the tenant committees in Hungary. In Budapest, in 1960, tenant committees initiated 40,000 prosecutions for "asocialist" behavior.[75]

Comradely courts, the major para-judicial bodies, were established in Poland in 1955, in Hungary and Czechoslovakia in 1956, in Rumania in 1958, and in Bulgaria in 1960. They did not become active until recently. Comradely courts usually consist of five members, elected by the enterprise in which they are established. In Czechoslovakia, for example, such courts are to be established in every enterprise that has a permanent staff of fifty persons.[76] They are empowered to consider offenses against socialist and private property; against social living, including family relations; and against work discipline. They are not bound by legal rules. They hold their sessions in public. They can punish by public admonishment and fine.

The establishment of comradely courts has caused a great deal of confusion. It has been suggested by some that their areas of concern be increased.[77] They have been criticized by others for "considering everything, even matters which could be settled far more effectively by simple talk."[78] They have been chastised in Czechoslovakia for attempting to establish routinized court procedure.[79] In Poland the lawyers' association has criticized them for failure to develop standard procedures.[80] Despite this confusion as to their proper functions and methods they seem to have been firmly established as a part of socialist legality.

In addition to para-police and para-judicial bodies other citizens' committees were recently established. Among these are cooperative control committees to supervise accounting.[81] Coordination committees have been created in many factories to "control the administration of the enterprise, manage and appraise socialist competition, supervise collective agreements, establish technical conferences, and assure the participation of the masses in management."[82] In Bulgaria, the suggestion has been made that public organizations assume responsibility

[75] Radio Budapest, February 8, 1961.

[76] *Rude Pravo*, April 10, 1960.

[77] Veronika Bajaki, "Proposal for an Extension of Courts," *Jogtudomanyi Koslony*, July-August 1960.

[78] *Rude Pravo*, April 5, 1960.

[79] *Ibid.*

[80] *Pravo i Zycie*, December 11, 1960.

[81] *Szabad Fold*, August 14, 1960.

[82] *Pravda* Bratislava, March 5, 1959.

for physical culture, sports, tourism, social security, health administration, and the maintenance of public order.[83] The party will, of course, remain the leading force with respect to all of these public organizations.[84]

So far only minor functions of state administration have been transferred to social organizations, and evidently with a limited degree of success. What is significant is that this emphasis upon devolution occurred at a time when other changes in the structure of administration in Eastern Europe are being undertaken which could be considered as leading to an increased routinization of the state apparatus.

We are suggesting that an autonomous structure in which organizational roles are performed in accordance with expertise, rather than in accordance with a grand ideological scheme, is important for the establishment of an independent bureaucracy. The establishment of this type of autonomy can be seen as a function of industrialization. Recent developments in Eastern Europe show that there has been some movement in this direction. At the same time, though, emphasis has been placed even more firmly on the leading role of the party and the necessity for expanding mass participation in administration. Until we know more about the decision-making processes and the patterns of influence of the various components making up this system we cannot single out a trend in any one direction. Devolution, however, cannot help but further atomize the administrative structure, thereby complicating the creation of rountinized political processes and a bureaucratized system of administration. It is probably not by chance that such a program was undertaken at a time when pressures toward autonomy were beginning to rupture.

The New Class

Communist states are run by an elitist political movement. Therefore, any change in the character of the political elite can have dramatic consequences for the political style of Communist states. Some observers have argued that new classes have been created in the Communist states and that these new classes will play an instrumental role in political development.

Discussion of new classes takes two forms: (1) that Communist

[83] Yanko Yanov, "A Transfer of the Functions of State Organs to Public Organizations," *Pravna Misal*, Vol. 4, August 15, 1960.

[84] "The chief guarantee of a successful advance of all mass organizations as well as of the socialist state, is the leading role of the Communist Party." Ivan Bystrina, "The Growing Importance of Mass Organizations," *Rude Pravo*, October 15, 1959.

elites have become a ruling class; and, (2) that a new managerial class is now developing within the political systems of Eastern Europe. The first conclusion was stimulated by the publication of Milovan Djilas, *The New Class*.[85] Djilas argued that the ruling elite of Communist states was made up of individuals whose status was determined, not by training and professional qualifications, but by the fact of membership in the victorious revolutionary movement. Members of this New Class were crude political types whose sense of power and intrigue pushed them into the circle of power holders. The closer they came to the inner circle, the more power they wielded.

Recently, others have argued that the New Class that Djilas found is already being replaced by a second New Class. They argue that under the impact of industrialization a new managerial class has been created that is relatively unconcerned with maintaining revolutionary fervor and with ideology, but highly concerned with personal security, protection from arbitrary state acts, material welfare, and the development of predictable political and economic processes.[86] It is with the development of this second New Class in Eastern Europe that this section is primarily concerned.

Discussion will center on two aspects of the second New Class theory. What form has change in the aggregate composition of power holders in Eastern Europe actually taken? What is the impact of these changes upon the political style of Eastern Europe? Once again, we are forced to draw conclusions from a modicum of information. There has been no systematic study of the aggregate composition of political elites over time in Eastern Europe. Communist statistics on the social composition of the party are unreliable,[87] not comparable,[88] and unavailable for certain periods of time. Without systematic analysis and statistical evidence it is hard to assess the size and the behavior of any second New Class. But there are indications that a different type of person has entered the elite group.

In recent years the Communist states of Eastern Europe, like the Soviet Union, have been emphasizing technological progress. Special state committees concerned with technological improvement, technical

[85] London, 1957.

[86] See for example Ernst Halperin, "The Metamorphosis of the New Class," *Problems of Communism*, Vol. 8, July-August 1959, pp. 17-22; Hugh Seton-Watson, "Eastern Europe since Stalin," *ibid.*, Vol. 3, March-April 1954, pp. 10-17; Richard Lowenthal, "The Logic of One Party Rule," *ibid.*, Vol. 7, March-April 1958, pp. 21-30.

[87] An individual who comes from a working class background, for example, often appears in the statistics as a worker even if he has become something else.

[88] The categories used are rarely constant, and not very meaningful.

commissions to work in conjunction with the people's committees, factory level technical groups, and others have been established to improve the efficiency of the system. Employees are encouraged to further their technical knowledge.[89] And it is pointed out repeatedly that

TOTAL BULGARIAN SPECIALISTS WITH ADVANCED AND SECONDARY EDUCATION

31 Dec. 51	*1 Dec. 53*	*1 Dec. 54*	*1 July 56*	*1 July 57*	*1 July 58*
99,517	119,880	143,353	159,943	186,383	205,144

Source: Statistika, Vol. 7, March-April 1960, pp. 75-79.

EDUCATION OF PARTY MEMBERS IN POLAND

Year	*Primary Incomplete*	*Primary Complete*	*Secondary*	*Higher*
1953	40.9	42.2	14.6	2.3
1958	31.5	44.9	19.0	4.6
1959	27.6	48.2	19.3	4.9
1960	26.1	49.1	19.5	5.3

According to survey data from Poland, 63,570 members and candidates are completing their education. Of those, 58.4% are completing secondary education and 14.8% higher education. *Nowe Drogi,* May 1961.

the accepted criteria for advancement is no longer class background and political loyalty alone: "Each time we have mentioned that class loyalty and puritan aims alone do not suffice to achieve good state and economic management, that expert knowledge is indispensable, we are accused of knowing everything better. . . . It is very sad that some comrades living on their past express the desire that it should be clarified whether class loyalty or knowledge is of prime importance. They wait in vain for the reply that expert knowledge is of second rate importance because unwavering loyalty to the people is not worth anything without thorough knowledge."[90]

The composition of the party reflects an increasing interest in technological advancement. It is impossible to deal satisfactorily with statistics from Eastern Europe on social composition, but all of the parties indicate that the number of intellectuals in the party has increased.[91] Table 1 an page 294 seems rather typical.

The Eastern European states have developed their own industrial

[89] *Scanteia,* August 11, 1960; *Praca,* June 17, 1959; *Rude Pravo,* July 21, 1960. Janos Csergo, "More Concern for the Young Technical Intelligentsia," *Magyar Ifjusag,* February 7, 1961. There has been a general increase in the number of persons with advanced training. The following statistics from Bulgaria and Poland seem to be typical.

[90] *Del-Magyarorszag,* May 11, 1961.

[91] For an excellent discussion of the intelligentsia as a recognized class in the Soviet Union, see Alex Inkeles, "Social Stratification and Mobility in the Soviet Union: 1940-1950," *American Sociological Review,* Vol. 15, August 1950, pp. 465-479.

TABLE 1: COMPOSITION OF PARTY MEMBERSHIP IN HUNGARY [a]

Class	*1951*	*1954*	*1957*	*1959*	*1961* [b]
Workers	56.9	60.5	57.9	60.9	58.8
Peasants	15.4	14.45	16.7	12.8	15.0
Intelligentsia	4.0	4.99	6.9	7.6	9.1
White collar workers and others	23.7	20.6	18.5	18.7	17.1

[a] Peter A. Toma, "Revival of a Communist Party in Hungary," *Western Political Quarterly,* Vol. 14, March 1961, pp. 87-104.

[b] Jonsef Sandor, "A Few Points on the Organizational Development of our Party," *Tarsadalmi Szemle,* June 1961.

and technical intelligentsia. There is every indication that a high degree of social stratification has taken place and that the industrial and technical intelligentsia rank directly below the ruling elite.[92]

An important question is how influential the technical intelligentsia has become in the major governing councils. A study of the Czechoslovak Council of Ministers gives some indications of the answer to this question. By constructing a political-technical scale based upon the careers of everyone who was a member of the Council of Ministers, it was possible to group them into three relatively pure categories and two mixed categories. The pure categories are Communist party *apparatchiki,* puppet parties' *apparatchiki,* and technical experts. The mixed categories are combinations of these. Certain trends emerge when the aggregate composition of the Council of Ministers is plotted over a period of years.

The most obvious trend is the increasing reliance on technical skills in the aggregate composition of the Czechoslovak Council of Ministers and a decreasing reliance on members of puppet parties. In absolute numbers technical experts increased from 2 to 7. Communist party *apparatchiki* with technical experience increased from 3 to 10. Communist party *apparatchiki* increased from 6 to 8. Puppet parties *apparatchiki* decreased from 7 to 6. Puppet parties' *apparatchiki* with technical experience decreased from 4 to 0.[93] Although there was gen-

[92] Inkeles, "Social Stratification and Mobility in the Soviet Union, 1940-1950," *op.cit.,* pp. 465-479.

[93] Using Friedman's two-way analysis of variance,

$$Xr^2 = \frac{12}{Nk(k+1)} \sum_{j=1}^{K} (Rj)^2 = 3N(k+1)$$

it was possible to test the null hypothesis that all the samples came from the same population. The results show that the change was significant at the .001 level, thereby indicating that the changing aggregate composition of the Council of Ministers was not the result of chance.

CHART I

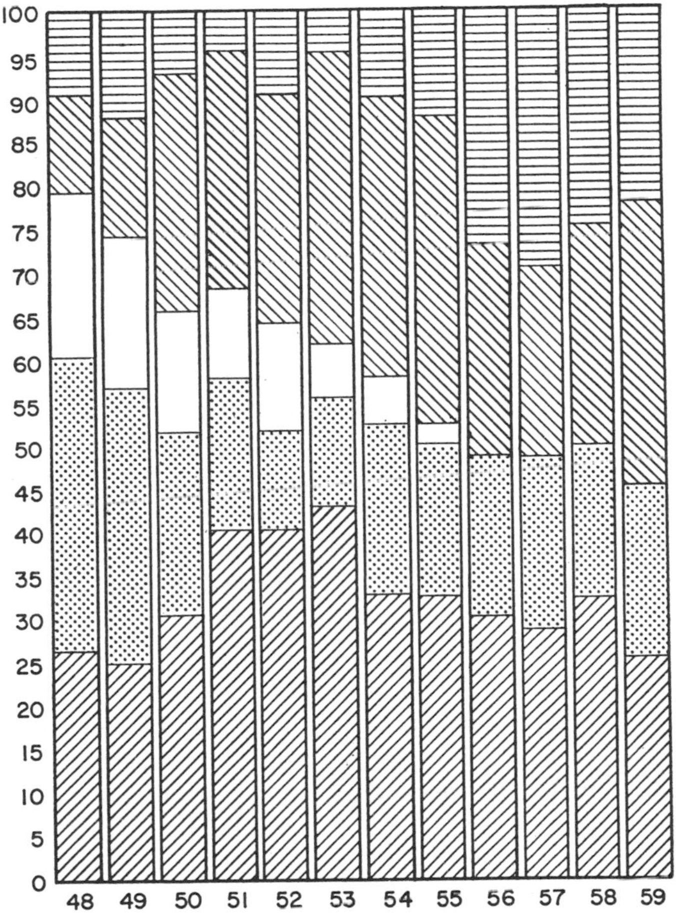

COMPOSITION OF THE CZECHOSLOVAK COUNCIL OF MINISTERS
1948-1959
(Per cent)

Communist party appartchik

Puppet party appartchik

Puppet party appartchik and technical expert

Communist party appartchik and technical expert

Technical expert

erally an increasing concern with technical considerations and a decreasing concern with the legitimacy and representativeness that puppet parties' *apparatchiki* bring with them, it is important to note that in periods of organizational and political crisis, 1953, for example, there was a marked tendency to revert to the selection of political types. In all periods, organization men—Communist party *apparatchiki* with and without technical experience—have dominated the Council.

The political elite groups have been also influenced by the need to recruit technically competent individuals but not as much as the administrative organs. In the Politburo of Czechoslovakia, for example, three groups are discernible: the old professional revolutionaries, the party *apparatchiki*, and the technical and administrative experts. The most numerous group is that of men like President Novotny who have made their careers within the existing party bureaucracy, but who have little formal training and little managerial experience. Others have been accepted.

There are signs that a new managerial class is being created in the Eastern European countries and that this new managerial class is beginning to be represented in the leading administrative and political councils. To some this portends the beginning of a new revolution in Eastern Europe, a revolution in which the logic of political Communism will become dissipated under the impetus of the rational interests of this new group.[94] This argument assumes that industrial man will come even further into the forefront in the future. It also assumes that this new group per se holds different political perspectives from those now in control and that these perspectives are in opposition to the less rational characteristics of the system. It can be demonstrated that industrial man has become more important in Eastern Europe. It cannot be demonstrated that industrial man has achieved, or will automatically achieve in the future, a dominant position. Further, there is little support for the view that industrial man must be a different type of political man than those now in power.[95]

It is true that one of the basic questions concerning the style of politics in any political system undergoing industrialization is the terms on which the newly recruited industrial man will be incorporated

[94] Alex Inkeles and Raymond H. Bauer, *The Soviet Citizen: Daily Life in a Totalitarian Society*, Cambridge, Harvard University Press, 1959; Adam B. Ulam, *The Unfinished Revolution*, New York, Random House, 1960.

[95] The German bureaucracy of the 1930's is an excellent case study of a conservative managerial class operating within a highly routinized bureaucracy which did little to mitigate the irrationality (much less the brutality) of the Nazi regime.

in the political community.[96] But the political perspectives of industrial man will depend upon the way in which he is socialized[97] and upon how successful the systems have been in achieving material and prestigeful goals. His position will depend upon the kind of informal agreement established between him and the political leadership, and this agreement will be determined by a myriad of factors both external and internal.

The New Class may move in many directions, and the direction in which it moves will be determined by more than the fact that the people populating this New Class grew up in a society undergoing industrialization. If all the forces and pressures external to the New Class were to remain equal, the proclivity of this class to push in the direction of a legal-rational system might be enhanced. But in any political system forces and pressures external to a new generation affect that generation's political profile. This is particularly true of a political system ruled by the elite of a political movement which has as one of its major aims the institutionalization of revolutionary zeal and one of its major supports striking successes in technology and science.

Conclusion: Evaluating Change

The preceding analysis and description have focused upon the impact of the creation of a modernized society upon the political structure and political style of Eastern Europe. Indicators of this impact have included changes in political doctrine, in the system of administration, and in the elite group. In this final section, emphasis will be placed on the validity of methods used to evaluate these changes, particularly the adequacy of classic bureaucratic theory.

Evaluation of the significance of the changes in the doctrine, the administrative system, and the elite depends upon the baselines that the analyst uses for comparison. If these changes are assessed from the viewpoint of an idealized concept of a frozen, monolithic, totalitarian society, departures from this concept cannot be satisfactorily

[96] For a perceptive analysis of this subject in which the "Ideologies of Management" in Tzarist Russia and Soviet Russia are compared, see Reinhard Bendix, "Industrialization, Ideologies and Social Structure," *American Sociological Review,* Vol. 24, October 1959, pp. 613-623.

[97] As Professor Pye has pointed out, the pattern of political socialization is crucial in determining the elements of stability and the dynamics of change in political systems. Lucian W. Pye, "Political Modernization and Research on the Process of Political Socialization," *Social Science Research Council Items,* Vol. 13, September 1959, pp. 25-28. Unfortunately this is a subject on which little systematic research in the Eastern European political systems has been accomplished.

explained. If what has occurred is compared with forecasts stemming from bureaucratic theory, a major conclusion of this chapter cannot be explained: that the political systems of Eastern Europe have been generally successful in absorbing these changes without creating a bureaucratized administrative system.

Students of bureaucracy recognize that bureaucratic behavior and function are affected by extrinsic factors. Deviations from the behavioral characteristics of the classic model can be attributed to the social values of a particular society.[98] Deviations from the functional characteristics of the classic model can be attributed to the configuration of the polity in which the system of administration is embedded.[99] Basically, however, the classic theory of bureaucracy points toward the hypothesis that over time a particular type of organization and administrative system will develop as a country becomes modernized. This type of organization, called a bureaucracy, is marked by a hierarchical structure in which there is a specialization of function. It is staffed by individuals chosen because of their expertise. These individuals are then placed in tenure positions. The theory holds that this type of system will generate decision-making behavior that is stable, predictable, continuous, precise, and rational. This is the type of decision-making behavior, it is argued, which all industrial societies require. To those who have surveyed the impact of industrialization upon Western political systems this theory seems highly relevant for the prediction of the development of those countries now becoming industrialized.

Why is bureaucratic analysis not adequate when used as a framework for the analysis of political development in Eastern Europe? The answer lies partly in the nature of bureaucratic theory itself and partly in the characteristics of the political systems under discussion.

Classic bureaucratic theory, concerned with isolating certain factors, is only a partial theory. If this partial character is not stressed sufficiently, bureaucratic theory seems to be deterministic. It seems to state that, under the impetus of a drive toward rationality, organizations and systems of administration will evolve into rational-legal structures in which decision-making processes become bureaucratic. In constructing this model, bureaucratic theory underplays, if it does not ignore com-

[98] Robert V. Presthus, "Weberian v. Welfare Bureaucracy in Traditional Society," *Administrative Science Quarterly*, Vol. 6, June 1961, pp. 1-24.

[99] Beck, "Party Control and Bureaucratization in Czechoslovakia," *op.cit.*

pletely, the relevance of politics. Political power and political ideology are assumed to be of no consequence. When the political environment of the system of administration is brought into the analysis, as it must be in order to explain political change, bureaucratic theory is found wanting.

The environment that we have been discussing in this paper is shaped by the existence of a revolutionary political movement, led by an elite which exercises political power virtually without institutionalized restraint for the purpose of maintaining power and furthering the revolutionary movement. In this setting the creation of an independent bureaucracy, even of an instrumental type, would become a threat to the power position of the elite and the goal of maintaining revolutionary political zeal.

Implicit in much of the writing in which bureaucratic theory is utilized to forecast political change is the belief that only when a legal-rational authority structure is created is the problem of legitimacy solved.[100] We can accept as given that all political systems seek legitimacy.[101] There is little reason to believe that only a particular type of authority structure is legitimate. Legitimacy can be built in many ways. It is not built for all times. Legitimacy can rest upon a crude nationalistic appeal: many Germans believed that Hitlerism was in fact a legitimate form of government if not *the* only legitimate form of government. At least one analyst of the American scene attributes legitimacy to a sense of "historical givenness."[102] Soviet successes in space, industry, and science have probably endowed the government and regime of the Soviet Union with a great deal of legitimacy. In Eastern Europe the problem of legitimacy is more complex than in

[100] Macridis and Brown, *Comparative Politics: Notes and Readings*, *op.cit.*, p. 429.

[101] Legitimacy is used in the sense that Seymour Martin Lipset uses it as involving "the capacity of a political system to engender and maintain the belief that existing political institutions are the most appropriate or proper ones for the society." "Some Social Requisites of Democracy: Economic Development and Political Legitimacy." *American Political Science Review*, Vol. 53, March 1959, p. 86.

[102] Daniel J. Boorstin, *The Genius of American Politics*, Chicago, University of Chicago Press, 1953; see also Charles Dickens, *Our Mutual Friend:* " 'We Englishmen are Very Proud of our Constitution, Sir. It Was Bestowed Upon Us By Providence. No Other Country is so Favoured as This Country. . . .' 'And other countries,' said the foreign gentleman. 'They do how?' 'They do, Sir,' returned Mr. Podsnap, gravely shaking his head; 'they do—I am sorry to be obliged to say it—as they do.' 'It was a little particular of Providence,' said the foreign gentleman. . . . 'Undoubtedly,' assented Mr. Podsnap; 'But so it is. It was the Charter of the Land. This Island was Blest, Sir, to the Direct Exclusion of such Other Countries as—as there may happen to be.' "

the Soviet Union. In an Eastern Europe setting nationalist appeals are anti-Soviet in nature; the Eastern European countries are not full partners in the exploits of Soviet science and technology.

In order to evaluate and to explain the uneven course of political development in Eastern Europe it must be recognized that totalitarian political systems, like other polities, are *systems*.[103] Because they are systems, factors over which the political movement itself has little control create situations to which the system and the movement must respond adaptively. Some of these pressures stem from phenomena which are intrinsic to any system such as feedback and adjustment. Others stem from the unanticipated consequences of action. Pressures that exist in the environment, stimulated by such drives as nationalism and the peculiar religious, economic, and social facts of each country, complicate any pattern of integration. Forces external to the system, such as the character of bloc relations and the status of the cold war, add further difficulties. Such a "model" suggests that the countries of Eastern Europe will develop on a pattern that over time demonstrates surges in one direction and then in another, with those areas which are neglected becoming the source of future problems. Such a theory accounts for what bureaucratic theory cannot: the unanticipated character of changes in doctrine, structure, and the system of administration that have marked the political development of the Communist states of Eastern Europe.

[103] For an excellent discussion of the fallacy that it is possible to construct an unchanging social order, see Raymond A. Bauer, "N + 1 Ways Not to Run a Railroad," *The American Psychologist*, Vol. 15, October 1961, pp. 650-655.

CHAPTER 10

Bureaucracy and Political Development, with Particular Reference to Nigeria

J. DONALD KINGSLEY

I

THE most significant legacy of colonialism is the existence of institutions in the newly emerged states which reflect levels of political development not yet reached by those states. Of these, the most important are political or administrative in character, including a sophisticated bureaucratic organization and—in some instances—a relatively seasoned if numerically inadequate cadre of officials.

These institutions were devised in the first instance for the purposes of the controlling metropolitan power and reflected the general level of political and institutional development of that power. They were staffed and manipulated by it for its own particular ends. But all, in the course of time, developed to a greater or lesser degree indigenous elements and even grew indigenous roots. In the process, their character was necessarily modified and they sometimes even became instruments in the hands of nationalists for weakening or destroying colonial control. Their role in this respect requires far more careful study and analysis than has yet been undertaken, especially in respect to the psychological reorientation of the bureaucracy in the critical years just before independence.

For the purposes of this paper, it is enough to note, first, the existence at independence of such "advanced" institutional structures in all of the former colonial areas; second, that the existence of such institutions is crucial in terms of the deeply desired "leap to modernization"; third, that their alien origin and association with colonialism make them convenient targets for nationalist attack even when their importance to the early attainment of nationalist objectives is recognized. The result is the oft-noted tendency toward political schizophrenia which goes so far to explain many political developments in the new African states and which is particularly in evidence with respect to the civil services. The political dialectic resulting from this ambivalence leads to modifications in both the inherited institutions and the surrounding political environment.

In this situation, there is not much in the classical theories concerning relations of bureaucratic evolution to political development that seems directly useful in predicting or even in interpreting the course of events in the new African states. This is true in large part because both their political and their institutional development under colonialism were highly selective and correspondingly uneven. Sophisticated institutions were created and imposed as required by the metropolitan power, but without any systematic attempt to relate them broadly to problems of indigenous growth and development or even to other existing social structures and institutions.

To this, one exception needs to be made. Since the over-riding objective of colonial institution building was political control, there was always either a positive or a negative relationship to traditional power structures. In the former British areas, where indirect rule was the guiding principle of control, the imported institutions were closely geared to and served to strengthen the traditional patterns of power. As a consequence, they acted for many years as a brake on modernization. Modernized institutions were themselves employed to sustain archaic political structures.

It is, then, characteristic of the new states, born in the twilight sleep of an expiring colonialism, that they come into the world equipped with a baffling and contradictory assemblage of modern and traditional institutional limbs. They embark upon independence with an administrative structure already in being (often a highly sophisticated one in terms of its limited functional objectives) and with a functioning bureaucracy, however evident its inadequacies to new tasks. The bureaucracy, also, is composed of a relatively sophisticated elite, but one which may or may not reflect in its indigenous elements the power and authority structures that emerge after the withdrawal of the colonial power. But an inherited administrative structure and a bureaucracy in the full sense of the term already exist at independence. They have to be reshaped and rebuilt; they do not have to be created.

This is true, of course, even of the Congo, where a violent birth followed the too-abrupt withdrawal of the Belgian midwife. But, even there, the administrative framework remained as did a bureaucratic ethic and a skeleton bureaucracy.

Since the institutions of administration have been imported, since they are not African but European in origin, their ethos, structure, and functional character all reflect European more than African conditions. Indeed, the organization of offices, the demeanor of the civil servants, even the general appearance of a *bureau*, strikingly mirror the national characteristics of the bureaucracies of the former colonial powers. The *fonctionnaire* slouched at his desk in Lomé or Cotonou, cigarette pasted to his underlip, has his counterpart in every provincial town in France; and the demeanor of an administrative officer in Accra or Lagos untying the red tape from his files would be recognizable to anyone familiar with Whitehall or, more specifically, with the Colonial Office.

These are not superficial but profound evidences of successful institution building. But their existence illustrates a whole series of difficult problems for the future. Africanization is, in the first instance, a matter of replacing white colonial officers with indigenous blacks. This is difficult enough within a brief space of time. But it is a minor problem compared to those of redefining the functions and objectives of an independent civil service, of restructuring it in the light of the redefinition, of adjusting conditions of service to African realities rather than to recruitment requirements in Paris or London, and of developing incentives which will have effect in a culture where the extended family is a deeply rooted social organism and where the prestige value of the bureaucracy will inevitably change as it becomes recognized as an instrument of government policy rather than the fountainhead of power.

II

So much by way of introduction. In the body of this chapter, I shall confine my observations largely to the four governments of the Federation of Nigeria, with only occasional glances elsewhere in sub-Saharan Africa. Nigeria is a large and complex country, and the problems of bureaucracy and political development it presents are representative in degree of all the former British areas in Africa, east or west. To a considerable extent, also, they typify problems in the former French areas, but variations in detail and in political and social environment are such that far more space than can be occupied by this chapter would be required to deal with them.

Nigeria presents fascinating opportunities to the student of politics because of its size, its diversity, its federal structure, and its varying rates of development. A vast land larger than California, Texas, New York, and New England combined, its thirty-eight or forty million citizens comprise by far the largest political unit in Africa. The three hundred or so tribal groups among them reflect almost every conceivable stage of social and political development, from that of the naked pagan tribes of the Jos Plateau to the great medieval Emirates of the Haussa-Fulani in the north, the highly developed chieftaincies of the Western Yoruba, or the village democracies of the Ibo in the east. In economic terms the contrast is equally great, ranging from the most primitive agriculture (little more than collecting the fruits of the forest as they mature) to the growing industrial complexes around Port Harcourt or in Western Nigeria.

Politically, the many tribal groups have coalesced around three major tribes, each of which dominates one of the three major political parties and in turn controls one of the three regional governments: the Haussa-Fulani in the north, the Ibo in the east, and the Yoruba in the west. Of the three regions, the north is the largest both in terms of area and of population and the Northern People's Congress (the party dominated by the Haussa-Fulani) has the largest representation in the Federal House of Representatives. But it does not control a safe majority of seats and the federal government is a coalition of the NPC and the National Council of Nigeria and the Cameroons (the Ibo-dominated party of the east).

There are those who have argued that a more logical coalition (as though politics were governed by logic) would have been between the east (the NCNC) and the west (the Action Group). Together, the two regions comprise the south as opposed to the north and they have generally reached a "higher" level of development in such measurable terms as education or degree of industrialization. The application of indirect rule in the north served to strengthen and maintain the Muslim Emirates there, and Lugard committed the British to assist the Emirs in keeping out the Christian missionaries who were already well-represented in the coastal areas of the south. As a consequence, the north lagged behind the rest of the country in the development of schools; and the shortage of educated northerners has directly affected the pace of political development and the Africanization of the bureaucracies of both Northern Nigeria and the federal government.

The northern region did not, for example, request internal self-government until two years after it had been granted the western and eastern regions, and the pace of "Nigerianization" of the federal bureaucracy before and after independence has been slowed by the understandable desire to hold a proportion of posts open until northerners are available to fill them.[1] While it is difficult to establish in any particular instance, there is no doubt that British colonial or contract officers have been retained in both the northern and the federal services whose posts could have been Nigerianized by the recruitment of southerners. In the north, indeed, "northernization" is the objective, rather than "Nigerianization," and—since independence—there has been a significant number of dismissals of southern Nigerians, particularly of Ibos, from the northern service.

The reasons for this are both political and cultural. The identification of political parties with particular regions and particular tribes, the religious difference between the largely Muslim north and the predominantly Christian or pagan south, the striking contrasts in social organization and way of life between north and south—all have an impact on both political development and bureaucratic evolution.

To a somewhat lesser degree, similar factors have affected the Nigerianization of the public services in Western and Eastern Nigeria, though the absence of northerners from significant posts in those services may be rationalized in terms of the general shortage of qualified northerners everywhere. This is not, however, the entire story. In looking through the civil list of the government of Western Nigeria, I do not identify a single Ibo in a controlling post, although there may be one or two whose names I did not properly classify. There are representatives of some of the smaller tribes associated with the action group, but the bulk of senior officials would appear to be Yoruba. A comparable situation exists in the civil service of Eastern Nigeria, where the top Nigerian officials are all easterners.

This was not always the case. In colonial days there was a considerable movement of officials from one region to another, including the handful of senior Nigerian officials in the service. I have, indeed, been told by Nigerians that it was once the policy to move Nigerian officers out of the region of origin; and that this policy served colonial objectives. Whether or not the policy did serve "colonial objectives" in the African sense, it was a rational one in terms of assuring more objective administrative and judicial action. It is less difficult to act ob-

[1] There is no quota system as such and proposals to establish one and to earmark certain posts formally for northerners were rejected by the northern government. However, extraordinary efforts are made by the federal government to recruit northerners, including the establishment in the north of a branch of the Federal Civil Service Training School and—most recently—preferential treatment in the important matter of housing in Lagos.

jectively among strangers than when surrounded by one's family and friends.

The present situation does not primarily reflect extensive politicalizing of the Nigerian bureaucracies in the traditional American sense of party spoils. There is certainly an element of this, but the basic reasons are more deeply rooted and more complex. They spring from a culture in which the word "brother" may be used to describe a spectrum of relationships from those of blood, to village, to tribe; and in which the antonym is the word "stranger." A brother is a member of the in-group; a stranger is not. In the not very distant past, he was probably a mortal enemy. A stranger is not to be trusted—is, perhaps, even to be feared.

It is possible to make too much of the deep feeling represented by the opposed words "brother" and "stranger" when dealing with sophisticated groups like the higher civil service. Nevertheless, it represents a political fact of pervasive influence, serving to retard the growth of truly national political parties—and unquestionably affecting the character of the bureaucracy.

The impact of the extended family is also of importance, and nepotism is a larger problem than political patronage. This is especially true in Eastern Nigeria, where population pressure is heavy, but it is a factor everywhere. Politicians and civil servants alike are under extreme and constant pressures to support or give assistance to a circle of relatives which seems to expand geometrically as one's status and income go up.

Standing over and against these pressures are the institutional devices and the service ethic inherited from the Colonial Service. They are powerful: the Public Service Commission, with its control of selection, promotion, and discipline resting on a body of long-established rules and regulations and of quasi-judicial precedent; the schedules of service with their hierarchies of posts linked to requirements of training and experience; the body of procedures in which bureaucratic relationships are embedded and which circumscribe not only the relations among officials but between officials and ministers as well.

These are, of course, all subject to change in the course of time. All public service commissions in Nigeria were "Nigerianized" within a year of independence, and their actions now unquestionably reflect more closely government policy, particularly political and cultural considerations, than was formerly the case. There have been some departures, as is noted later, from established entrance requirements and established schedules of service; and the transition from government by Whitehall to a responsible parliamentary system has necessitated modifications in bureaucratic relationships and procedures. But in the first years after independence, such changes are amazingly few. The bureaucracy is remarkably resistant to significant change.

This is, in part—and perhaps largely—due to the strong corporate spirit of the service: a sense of identity and purpose inherited from the Colonial Service. That service governed as none can in a democratic state and had the prestige associated with the direct exercise of power. The District Officer (or District Commissioner), the Resident, and the Governor, each in his geographical area, *was* the government so far as the governed population was concerned. And—more often than not—in the more remote areas, a strong administrative officer was the government in fact. Communications were poor (and could readily be made to appear poorer than they were at a particular time), Whitehall was far away and had other problems on its collective mind, and the District Officer or Resident could interpret the law in his own way and act on his own initiative. It is not hard to understand the nostalgia of many Colonial Service officers for the good old days. Such exercise of power coupled with breadth of discretion lent great prestige to the Colonial Service even when its acts were resented.

That prestige has been strengthened by the competence and character of the small number of Nigerians who were taken into the Colonial Service in the transitional years just before and after the war and who are now among the service leaders. These had to be men of exceptional merit to make it and they were often also well-connected in Nigerian society. They constituted, in the strictest sense of the term, an elite, and they have tended to stamp the service with their image. They are jealous of its competence and status and constitute a bulwark against the deterioration of standards or ill-considered change. With few exceptions, they have remained aloof from party politics except for the considerable roles they have played behind the scenes in the formulation of party and government programs. But they wield great power and influence on the civil service. A man like Chief Simeon Adebo, formerly the head of the Western Nigerian civil service, was only a good administrator but a leader whose spirit pervaded the service.

What we have been discussing may be described either in terms of institutional inertia or of institutional momentum. I prefer the latter term because this ethic constitutes in and of itself a political force. The direction of bureaucratic evolution is determined by the dynamic interplay of this force with other political forces. In most of Africa it is too early to predict that evolution in detail. But it is not too early to identify some of the problems involved in transforming a colonial service and a colonial administrative structure into an indigenous administrative arm.

III

At independence, or in the months immediately preceding it, the replacement of expatriate officials with indigenous personnel (a process variously termed "Africanization," "Localization," "Nigerianization," "Northernization," etc.) always proceeds at a faster pace than anyone imagines it will or can and—perhaps—at a pace faster than might be dictated by prudence. To judge by experience in English-speaking West Africa, it may be taken as a rule that the administration (the administrative and controlling posts, though not the professional and technical ones) will be "localized" within a very few years of independence: perhaps three to five years at the outside. In the instance of Western Nigeria, the transformation was effected within the first year, although it was more than three years after the region had become internally self-governing.

The pace of localization is determined as much by voluntary resignations of expatriate officers, particularly younger ones with good career alternatives, as by the effective application of political pressures for Africanization, though the two are obviously closely related. Those who have or believe they have alternative opportunities anticipate the pressures and depart before they fully develop. It has been the general experience in former British West Africa that about a third of expatriate officers leave just before or immediately after independence and another third leaves within the first eighteen months, despite the incentives devised by the Colonial Office to encourage a more leisurely and orderly withdrawal.[2] In the second third are large numbers who leave because their posts either have been "Africanized" or have been designated for early Africanization by the Africanization officer or bureau usually established for this purpose. They include large numbers of senior officials.

[2] The incentives were ingenious and generous, though probably offered too late to West Africa. It will be interesting to observe their effect in Tanganyika, by contrast, where there has been more time. They are fully described in Kenneth Younger's *The Public Service in New States,* London, Oxford University Press, 1960. See particularly Part I and Annexes I and II.

After these initial surges, a sort of plateau is reached, and there may even be an increase in the total number of expatriate officers in the service, as was notably the case in Ghana and as may well occur in the Federation of Nigeria.[3] But these are officers on term contract and they tend largely to be in technical and professional, rather than administrative (and thus directing) posts. Thus, the technical competence of the new services tends to be maintained even as dilution and inexperience reduce the levels of their organizational and managerial capacities.

It is entirely understandable that an independent state should wish to staff, manage, and control its own civil service. In anticipation of this, a special committee of the Nigerian House of Representatives stated a year before independence that "all policy making posts must be Nigerianized now, or latest on the attainment of independence . . .";[4] and went on to quote (what has become a classic in newly emerged countries) the statement of the government of Malaya that "one of the fundamental rights and privileges of a self-governing country is that it must have control of its public service." The government did not accept the recommendations of the special committee, and a substantial number of "policy making posts" is still filled by expatriates as of this writing. But the committee report was a part of the political pressure brought to bear on expatriate officers, and I know from personal contact that it was not without effect. Similarily, the "Stallard must go" campaign, directed against the Chief Secretary to the Prime Minister (Peter, now Sir Peter, Stallard), undoubtedly led to his departure, although the Prime Minister presumably wished him to stay on. In the face of such political pressures, the orderly transformation of the administration is difficult.

There are, of course, many reasons for the rapid localization of the administration in addition to the natural desire of an independent country to control its civil service. As we have seen, the District Officer (an administrative officer) under colonialism *was* the government, insofar as the people in the bush were concerned. He has to be changed, if for no other reason than to dramatize independence for the masses of the people. Thus, the first African administrative officers put into training by Tanganyika in anticipation of independence were not central

[3] The fact of the increase in Ghana was obscured by various devices such as the use of blanket "votes" or appropriations and the exclusion of many posts from the "establishment."

[4] *Final Report on the Nigerianization of the Public Service,* Sessional Paper No. 6 of 1959, para. 200.

government administrators, but district commissioners. Similarly, in the various regions of Nigeria, the District Officer positions have been the first to be Nigerianized.

But localization of the controlling posts in the central government staffs cannot lag far behind. Ministers—many of them new to public life, unused to dealing with the old Colonial Service and insecure and unsure of themselves in a new administrative setting—may be exceptionally touchy and sensitive in the matter of advice from an expatriate. In extreme cases—and I have known some—they may fail at all to consult their officials in such circumstances, or may develop informal channels of consultation which disregard the hierarchy. In either event, the responsible official soon resigns and the Minister—even though then served with far less competence—breathes easier.

Finally, to complete this far from exhaustive list of contributing factors, mention should be made of the generalist background of the British administrative officer. In the Colonial Service, as in the Home Civil Service, his educational background was usually a good university degree in no matter what field. These posts thus appear to be much easier to fill than those requiring professional education. It is hard to establish to a nationalist politician that experience as a Colonial Service officer does not have negative as well as positive aspects and that a post requiring only general education cannot easily be filled by an African graduate. This is one of the penalties for having failed to recognize that administration is a science as well as an art.

I do not wish to burden this chapter either with statistics illustrating the rapidity of the Nigerianization process or with a description of matters already fully covered elsewhere, such as in the lectures of Kenneth Younger[5] or in the excellent paper by Professor Taylor Cole on aspects of the Nigerian bureaucracy.[6] But events do move with astonishing rapidity in Black Africa and I should like to illustrate this fact by citing a few changes in the situation since it was described by these authors.

Mr. Younger dealt with all the governments of Nigeria, while Professor Cole concentrated primarily on the federal government. When Mr. Younger delivered his lectures just a few years ago, only one of the eleven permanent secretaries to ministries in Western Nigeria was a Nigerian. Today, all permanent secretaries and virtually all ad-

[5] *The Public Service in New States*, *op.cit.*

[6] "Bureaucracy in Transition; Independent Nigeria," *Public Administration*, Winter 1960. Professor Cole's paper has an excellent description of the Nigerian Federal Service.

ministrative officers are Nigerian. I surveyed the staffing and training problems at the request of the Western Nigeria government in the summer of 1958 and then believed they could not hope to Nigerianize these controlling posts much before 1963. They have done so already, and the western civil service is a well-functioning organism.

In Eastern Nigeria, at the time Mr. Younger wrote, there were three Nigerian permanent secretaries out of a total of thirteen. Today, a majority of such posts are held by Nigerians and the transformation just below the top has been even more striking. In 1961, of 558 serving officers on the two top salary scales (superscale and scale A), only 92 were expatriates on pensionable terms. Three years earlier, more than half had been.[7]

As suggested earlier, the pace of Africanization has been slower in the north and in the Federation. In January 1961, there was only one Nigerian permanent secretary in the northern government,[8] although there are now four, including "acting" appointments. In the federal government, nearly two-thirds of the permanent secretary posts are currently filled by Nigerians, whereas there was only one Nigerian in such a post in 1959. Substantial numbers of expatriate officers are still employed by the federal government, however.

IV

The first result, then, of independence is to replace relatively experienced administrative officers with young men fresh from the universities or with limited experience in other fields like teaching. The dilution of the pool of service experience is sudden and severe. In the civil service of Eastern Nigeria, to take a single example, the median age of administrative officers in 1961 (including the surviving expatriates) was thirty-three and the average officer had had only three and a half years of any kind of government experience. Only thirteen officers (most of them expatriates) in the entire administration had been in government service as long as ten years.

Service in a particular post, or even in a particular ministry, had, of course, been much shorter than this. It is characteristic of such situations that the game of official musical chairs is played with abandon as crises shift from ministry to ministry. Under such circumstances, the

[7] J. Donald Kingsley, *Staff Development in the Public Service of Eastern Nigeria*, Government of Eastern Nigeria, Official Document No. 7 of 1961 (Enugu).

[8] J. Donald Kingsley, and Sir Arthur Rucker, *Staffing and Development of the Public Service of Northern Nigeria*. Report of a Commission organized at the request of the government, Kaduna, 1961.

traditional method of training administrators by a kind of process of osmosis from superior to understudy breaks down completely.

The young and inexperienced service is immediately confronted with a complex of major problems, most of which I can do no more than list: rationalization and reorganization of the administration in terms of responsible parliamentary government; integration of departments (formerly with head offices in Whitehall) into ministries; creation and organization of planning and programming units to perform functions formerly centered in London or in inter-territorial bodies; and the development and execution of the new programs a newly independent government understandably wishes to have in evidence before the next election. All of these demands and many more descend en masse on the shoulders of an untried and largely untrained service. That it survives the impact is remarkable and in good measure a testimony to that institutional momentum mentioned earlier.

Let me refer only to the impact of the introduction of responsible parliamentary government on the organization, functioning, and status of the bureaucracy as a single illustration.[9] The Colonial Service was a highly unified and centralized instrument. Headed by the Governor (or, during the period when Nigeria had a unitary constitution, by the Governor-General), the "administration" was composed of a central secretariat under a Chief Secretary and field officers (Residents, District Officers, etc.) also under his control and direction. The function of this highly centralized body was essentially the political control of the country through the maintenance of "law and order." The central secretariat was organized into functional departments (like Education and Health) directed in professional matters by London, but serving in a staff capacity to the Governor, who reported to the Secretary of State for the Colonies.

Under the system, administrative officers in the field, charged with limited and well-understood functions and subject only to administrative and not to political pressures, had considerable discretion and autonomy. In pursuance of their "law and order" mission, they served as policeman, prosecutor, and judge and their role was substantially more significant than that of the official in the central secretariat.

With independence and the establishment of responsible ministerial government, all of this changes.[10] The principal functions of the civil

[9] Professor Cole has treated another major problem, that of the integration of departments into ministries, *op.cit.*, pp. 329-330.

[10] It had, of course, begun to change even earlier. There was a considerable erosion of the magisterial powers of the district officer even before self-government.

servant are to advise ministers on the formation of policy and to be responsible to them for the execution of any policy formulated. The magisterial functions of the civil servant are increasingly transferred to the judiciary and the police functions to the police. Insofar as "residents" and "district officers" are continued, their functions change radically. In Eastern Nigeria, for example, the former Resident has been transformed into a political commissioner with the status of a junior minister. In the Sudan, the district officers have become local government officers responsible to the Ministry of Local Government.

No general pattern of transformation has yet emerged, and my only purpose here is to indicate a basic problem and the extent to which the inherited bureaucracy must ultimately be altered in the light of the changed political conditions.

Even with stability in such institutional relationships as these, there obviously are limits to the load that a young and inexperienced civil service can bear; and those limits have profound political significance. It is, for example, at least possible to argue that the quasi-military governments in such countries as Pakistan or even the Sudan were the product as much of administrative weaknesses as of political (parliamentary) defects. In many newly emerged states the army has the most experienced bureaucracy and the officer cadre is the most numerous and highly trained group of administrators. In times of peace, this cadre also has less to do.

In a broader sense, the limitations of a youthful and unseasoned bureaucracy undoubtedly set limits to the sometimes extravagant dreams of politicians and circumscribe the possible areas of state action. There seems little doubt, for example, that inadequacies in the civil service and attendant administrative weakness were largely responsible for the recent relaxation of commercial controls in Guinea with the abolition of the *Comptoirs Guinéens de Commerce*. Indeed, Guinea's ambassador to Paris and London (M. Tibour Tounkara) was recently quoted as saying: "The abolition of the Comptoirs occurred because although the objective of a planned economy was sound, the means were not the right ones: people were not up to it."[11] The Ambassador may have had in mind the consumers rather than the bureaucrats when he observed that "people were not up to it," but the bureaucracy certainly was not, in any event.

Similarly, I am of the opinion—despite the relative competence of the public service in Ghana—that the current tendency to extend gov-

[11] *West Africa*, December 16, 1961, p. 1,381.

ernmental activity into complex economic areas (like the recent imposition of detailed import and export controls) is likely to be checked by administrative realities and inadequacies.

We have here, indeed, another example of that ambivalence which affects all new states, at least in the sub-Sahara. On the one hand, their rapid development requires that government undertake many activities and many direct operations that might be left to private individuals or institutions in countries with more mature economies and thus with a wider range of established economic institutions. On the other hand, the shortage of managerial skills and competence in the new bureaucracies makes it difficult or impossible to carry out too many or too elaborate governmental programs. The new states are, to a considerable degree and each in its own way, socialistic. But the difficulties even the Russians continue to encounter in the control of agriculture—after more than a generation in which to develop an adequate administrative machine—suggest the existence of practical limits to the extension of state activity. While the existence of functioning bureaucracies is a condition to any development, their capacities also determine the scope and direction of effective development efforts.

V

The first phase in the adjustment of the inherited bureaucracy to the political environment of independence (localization) is soon over, except for professional services requiring long training leads. At its conclusion, there remains a reasonable facsimile of the Colonial Service now staffed by young Africans: the same structure, the same posts, the same emoluments and other conditions of service. To be sure, the pressures to replace expatriates in a hurry have often led to some temporary waiving of rigid educational and other entrance requirements, but this has been regarded as an expedient in an emergency situation and not as involving a question which ought to be examined as a matter of principle. The Colonial Service entrance requirements remain on the books and are considered operative, even though they are obviously related to labor market conditions in England, Scotland, and Wales rather than to those prevailing in Africa. There is to be no "lowering of standards" in the new African civil service, even though certain standards have no demonstrable relation to anything but the strength and restrictive practices of British trade unions. The point is a psychological and emotional one with strong political overtones (as well as a reflection of bureaucratic conservatism).

So it goes, as well, with salary, retirement, and leave policies. In the Colonial Service, all of these were more or less logically related to problems of recruiting and maintaining a staff of overseas officers whose families were often home in England and whose children were certainly in school there, who lived in government houses with government furnishings and rode in government cars. The Colonial Officer never—well, hardly ever—walked.[12] But as Africans came into the service, it was obviously undesirable as well as politically impossible to treat them differently from their British colleagues in comparable positions. They thus fell heir to a scale of emoluments totally unrelated to indigenous living standards or to the economic development of the country—a situation which could easily spell political difficulties in the future.

In Nigeria, the difficult process of trying to relate conditions of service a bit more closely to local conditions is now underway. The practice of Nigerian officers taking home leave in England has gone. Car allowances have been reduced and there is talk of charging economic rents for government houses. But, thus far, only the surface of the problem has been scratched. In economic terms, the civil service is a highly privileged group. In political terms it is a highly influential group and it is probably unlikely to reform itself in any very drastic way.

There are other difficulties for the future which may prove troublesome. The youthful character of the service from top to bottom will distort the promotional picture for many years to come and—unless there is substantial expansion in the public services—a real career ladder will not exist for most. This is especially serious since many of those recruited under the pressures for rapid Nigerianization were less well prepared and perhaps less able than those who are now, or in the future will be, coming into the entrance grades as the educational base expands. If able young people find their careers blocked by less able young people only a few years their seniors, political difficulties are likely to result.

While no one can now foresee the outcome in respect to any of these related problems, it seems probable that the civil service together with the politicians will continue to make up a power elite in the new states and will therefore continue as an economically privileged class. There

[12] A Colonial Service friend of mine who arrived as a young district officer in the bush just after restrictions had been placed on the indiscriminate use of litters and before the day of the motor car cried out in pain at this. However, it has been true in recent years.

is no substantial middle class in existence and few independent centers of economic power. These facts, combined with the drive for development, clearly push towards socialism, or, at the most, a mixed economy in which the role of the government will be as large as it practically can be. So, therefore, will be that of the bureaucracy.

VI

In this final section I should like to refer briefly to the potential importance of the bureaucracy as a factor in the political unification of Nigeria. Like the other new African states, Nigeria is an historical accident insofar as her boundaries and the peoples within them are concerned. Her boundaries originally represented no more than the limits of British power at the time of the partitioning of Africa.

Moreover, the existence of Nigeria as a constitutional entity dates only from 1914, when the Protectorates of Southern and Northern Nigeria and the Colony and Protectorate of Lagos were unified. At that time, the British established a unitary political system and administration for the country as a whole. By the 1930's, administrative convenience led to the grouping of provinces into three main regions (north, east, and west) and the existence of the regions as political entities was recognized in the 1946 Constitution. From that time through the grants of self-government to the east and west in 1957 and to the north in 1959, the political forces of separatism were strong.[13] Until the Constitution of 1951, the Governor-General continued to serve as the head of a unified public service, with a chief secretary and a secretariat located in Lagos and with chief commissioners in charge in the regions. Thereafter, the service was broken into four parts, although all were still parts of the Colonial Service and there was a good deal of fluidity of movement from one to another service. This came very nearly to a halt with the grants of self-government to the east and west in 1957 and while the federal service has drawn heavily from the regional services, there is today very little movement between or among the regional governments. The inter-regional character of the federal civil service is, however, a potent instrument of unification.

Moreover, high-ranking officers from the regions and the federal government meet regularly in various official federal bodies like the

[13] For an excellent brief account of constitutional and political developments see R. Taylor Cole, "The Independence Constitution of Federal Nigeria," *The South Atlantic Quarterly*, LX, 1.

Joint (Economic) Planning Committee (the JPC), share a common tradition and common aspirations, and are beginning to develop a common professionalism. It is still not easy to organize a meeting of top officials from the various governments to discuss a problem having even potential political implications. On this point, many political leaders are extremely touchy. But to a constantly increasing degree, officials are meeting on technical and administrative problems and developing national rather than provincial outlooks.

It will, I think, be a long time before anyone might realistically suggest a unified civil service for the country, even though such an instrument might substantially contribute to the "leap to modernization." Tribal and local feelings still run too deeply for that. But the existence of even four separate bureaucracies which share a common history and tradition, with common attitudes and ideas, and with essentially common conditions of service, will undoubtedly have a significant unifying effect.[14]

[14] This chapter reflects developments in Nigeria up to January 1962.

CHAPTER 11

The Bureaucracy and Political Development in Viet Nam

JOHN T. DORSEY, JR.

1. Introduction: Development in Terms of Information and Energy

OF THE currently fashionable areas encompassed by the fluid and porous boundaries of political science, that suggested by the term "political development" is perhaps the most underdeveloped. One might even consider this appropriate as an aesthetic parallel, since concern with problems of political development tends to center around geographic areas of the world which are also dubbed "underdeveloped" in various ways. As a practical matter, both for the state of political science and of those areas of the world, this is unfortunate. Unless we are able to bring to bear a greater measure of systematic understanding on the political problems of the "underdeveloped" areas, the conflicts they generate may mushroom—literally as well as figuratively—beyond all human proportion.

What is "political development"? Obviously the term implies change, but with equal obviousness it implies more. It suggests change in some direction: from something toward something. For lack of better theoretical formulations we often use terms like "transition" from "traditional" to "modern" conditions, structures, values, or practices. Or, with an implicit but possibly uneasy bow to economic theory, we use the ambiguous adjective "developing" to denote the kinds of societies and political systems we want to talk about.[1] Undoubtedly these terms all communicate with a reasonable degree of efficiency, and we have gotten substantial mileage out of them. But they are all imprecise, highly relative, and even temporally parochial. The phenomena and problems of political development have been with us a long time (how long has it taken the British political system to develop to its present state?) and will undoubtedly be with us for years

[1] Dissatisfaction with such terms as these has led Professor Fred W. Riggs of Indiana University to propose an entirely new vocabulary based on optics. See, for example, his "Prismatic Society and Financial Administration," *Administrative Science Quarterly*, Vol. 5, June 1960, pp. 1-46.

to come. How will our concepts of "traditionality" and "modernity" look to the political scientists of the twenty-first century?

If the preceding observations have any validity, they impose the obligation of suggesting alternative concepts which might be more useful in elucidating the notion of political development while avoiding the more serious shortcomings of current concepts. Since this chapter is to be concerned primarily with the problems of a specific political system, that of the Republic of Viet Nam, the presentation of such alternative concepts must be compressed into a few preliminary pages. But it can be hoped that some of the values sacrificed to brevity can be regenerated through the critical appraisal and discussion that the concepts may provoke in their bare and unadorned form.

One of the most striking and consistent differences between the "highly developed" and the "underdeveloped" societies is the amount of energy which they extract or capture from their environments and utilize (consume, expend) or convert from one form to another. The amounts of energy consumption from inanimate sources in 1952, for example, ranged from 2 megawatt-hours per capita or less (Ethiopia, Afghanistan, Haiti, Somalia, and several others) up to 75.9, with six countries consuming over 30 megawatt-hours per capita (Belgium, Luxembourg, United Kingdom, Canada, the U.S.A., and Bahrein).[2] These contrasts are not surprising, given the evident correlation between industrialization and energy consumption. But several other relationships are relevant: (1) high average standards of living as measured, for example, in per capita income, are not found in societies of low energy conversion—i.e., while high levels of per capita energy consumption can, as in Bahrein, exist without corresponding high levels of per capita income, the reverse does not hold; (2) low levels of per capita income (e.g., $200 or less in U.S. dollars) are found almost invariably in societies with low per capita levels of energy consumption (e.g., 7.7 megawatt-hours or less, with all but a few in this category falling below 4 megawatt-hours per capita).[3] But of greater significance for present purposes is the fact that societies of high per capita energy conversion require technologies (including social and economic struc-

[2] Norton Ginsburg, *Atlas of Economic Development*, Chicago, University of Chicago Press, 1961, p. 80. See also United Nations, *World Energy Supplies, 1955-1958*, Statistical Papers Series J, No. 3, New York, United Nations, 1960. Ginsburg remarks that "many experts believe that energy is a more precise and useful indicator of the general development of an economy than any other single factor," *op.cit.*, p. 78. The anomalous presence of Bahrein in the latter list of examples results from its very unusual combination of high petroleum production with a very small population.

[3] Ginsburg, *op.cit.*, pp. 18 and 80.

tures and processes) that differ radically from those required by societies of low per capita energy conversion. Is it not to be expected that they would require different *political* structures and processes as well?

The central idea of a developmental theory based on changes in energy conversion levels can be formulated as follows: as levels of energy conversion in a society rise, political, social, and economic structures and processes undergo transformations. Such structures and processes are the means of maintaining sufficient degrees of internal integration and control and external adaptation to keep the social system as a whole viable. The structural patterns and the processes sufficient for "low energy" societies must be replaced by or transformed into different patterns of structure and process in societies of rising and high energy levels.

Clarification of these transformations, however, will require brief mention of the varieties of energy conversion in social systems and consideration of certain other factors closely involved in energy conversion. First, if the concept of energy is to be useful as a basic element of a theoretical approach to political development, we will have to recognize that the total energy converted by a given social system includes not only the fuels, water power, etc., used to run machines of varying degrees of efficiency, but also energy expended in the physical work and other activities of people as well as the work of domesticated animals employed for human purposes. Thus manpower and employment figures and work animal statistics, converted into the same standard equivalent measures as those used for fuels and electricity, would modify the figures referred to above—although not their relative magnitudes.

Even more important for theoretical purposes, the humanly controlled conversion of energy presupposes the acquisition of information organized as knowledge. The technology of energy conversion, from the simplest tool (e.g., the hand-ax) or technique (e.g., the use of fire for warmth or cooking) to the most sophisticated and complex machinery (e.g., atomic reactors) requires as a pre-condition the systematic abstraction, organization, accumulation, and transmission of increasing amounts of information about empirical reality.[4] And the coordinated expenditure of large quantities of human energy (which

[4] John T. Dorsey, Jr., "The Information-Energy Model," in Ferrel Heady and Sybils Stokes (eds.), *Papers in Comparative Public Administration*, Ann Arbor, Institute of Public Administration, University of Michigan, 1962, pp. 37-57.

through large-scale ogranization is in turn necessary for the conversion of the even larger quantities of non-human energy, as for example in industrial or military enterprises) depends upon the degree to which individual actions are "informed" by knowledge and skills, and upon the patterns of communication between individuals employing such skills and knowledge in organizations.[5] The kinds, amounts, and patterns of distribution and circulation of information, then, determine the amounts of energy in a social system that are converted from one form to another (released, expended, consumed, etc.) and the processes and applications of such energy conversion. The crucial significance to development of the kinds and amounts of information, and the organized patterns in which it is stored, circulated, and exchanged, becomes apparent when it is recognized that per capita human energy conversion can vary only within relatively narrow limits. Factors such as knowledge, skills, and organization account for the difference in energy conversion levels when societies are compared.

I am proposing, therefore, that for purposes of theory construction it may be fruitful to view the over-all level of development of a social system as an expression of its energy conversion levels,[6] but that the latter depend upon the information (using the term in its broadest sense) available to, stored in, and circulating within the system. According to the purpose of analysis, either total or per capita energy conversion figures would be useful to indicate the level of development. The possibility of analyzing rates, processes of change, and trends in energy levels and information circulation makes the concepts suitable for dynamic as well as for static models.

It should not be inferred that what is being proposed here is essentially an economic foundation for social and political theory. Energy conversion and its prerequisite and concomitant information processing are broad cultural phenomena, with separately significant social, economic, and political sources, ramifications, and aspects. For example, analysis from a sociological perspective would involve the patterns of communication manifested in social organization and control through which the behavioral energy of individuals and groups is mobilized, directed, or limited in a social system. Economic analysis would deal with the technologies and exchange relationships by means of which

[5] John T. Dorsey, Jr., "A Communication Model for Administration," *Administrative Science Quarterly*, Vol. 2, December 1957, pp. 307-324.

[6] Fred Cottrell, *Energy and Society*, New York, McGraw-Hill, 1955, and Leslie A. White, *The Science of Culture*, New York, Farrar, Straus and Co., 1949, pp. 363-393 ("Energy and the Evolution of Culture").

both human and non-human energy forms are utilized in the production, distribution, and consumption of other energy forms. Political analysis would focus on certain of the structures and processes which, through communication, function to integrate and adapt the system as a whole, directly or indirectly through the use of political power. The latter would be conceptualized as the control of energy conversion (especially in human behavior) throughout the system by the communication of symbols referring directly or indirectly to the use of more or less legitimate compulsion.[7] "Political development," consequently, would refer to the changes in power structures and processes that occur concomitantly with changes in energy conversion levels in the social system, whether such conversion levels change primarily in their political, social, or economic manifestations or in various combinations of the three. Although there is no inherent reason for doing so, it may be convenient for present purposes to limit the use of the term "development" to *increases* in energy levels of societies, since increases rather than decreases have been the underlying dynamic factors in the changes of recent centuries.

The role of bureaucracies[8] in political development is manifold and awkwardly little understood. As structures they marshal and pattern the energy expenditure of their members. Since they both manipulate and are justified by the symbols of legitimacy, they function as complicated concentrations of political power in their social systems. To the extent that they are controlled, they are potent instruments in the hands of those who control them, but to regard them only as instruments is to vastly oversimplify their roles. They cannot be manipulated as mere neutral and passive machines, for to varying extents they generate their own interests and values, and their actions are compounds of the partly conflicting and partly harmonious goals, desires, calculations, errors, and successes that characterize human behavior in general. Nevertheless, it may be that with the aid of the ideas sketched above we can single out a few variables that would help significantly to understand how bureaucracies can stimulate, increase, and maintain, or prevent and even lower, the over-all levels of energy conversion in the social system. These would include the sources and kinds of information and energy "inputs" to the bureaucracy (identification of which would clarify the means and degree of control from

[7] Gabriel A. Almond and James S. Coleman, eds., *The Politics of the Developing Areas*, Princeton, Princeton University Press, 1960, p. 7.

[8] The term "bureaucracy" will be used in this chapter to refer to the "public" or civil governmental administrative components of political systems.

extra-bureaucratic power centers, as well as the power bases and objectives of those who control them), the bureaucracy's share of the total information and energy available to the entire social system, the values and practices which pattern their information handling and energy conversion (particularly as manifested in the behavior of bureaucrats), and the modes and extent of their articulation with other components of the social system (with reference both to the bureaucracy's "intake" and to its "outputs"). In postulating the significance of these "input," "conversion," and "output" processes, it is possible to accommodate the view that neither the bureaucracy nor its environment changes simply as a function of the other, but that each may incorporate dynamic factors which influence the other. Thus in political development, the bureaucracy may respond to changes in energy conversion levels and processes in other components of the social system—but also, changes in the bureaucracy may bring about changes in energy conversion in such other components.

An important reason for the tensions, turmoil, and not infrequent convulsions that societies undergo in the process of developing from low to higher levels of energy conversion is to be found in the uneven and uncoordinated emergence of higher levels of energy conversion in different parts of the social system, and in the uneven adaptation of structures and processes throughout the system to such changes. Contributing to and underlying both of these are changes in the concentration and distribution patterns of various kinds of information. For example, changes in information concentrations (manifested in such things as the appearance of new skill groups or new ideological orientations of various groups), or changes in energy conversion rates (represented by such things as dietary changes, the application of a new technology, or the evolution of new organizational forms—e.g., the corporation), may change the power bases and objectives of those controlling or seeking to control the bureaucracy. This in turn results in new patterns of inputs into the bureaucracy in the form of demands that clash with previously established patterns of values and practices in the bureaucracy. Or bureaucratic outputs stemming from changes in the values and practices governing bureaucratic information processing or energy conversion may come into conflict with traditional values and practices in the bureaucracy's environment—just as a changed environment may not be receptive or responsive to unchanged or traditional types of outputs. In developments such as these, the articulation of the bureaucracy with its environment is lessened, making it either more difficult to control from outside or less effective in its output relations with the environment, or both. The consequences are aggravated tensions and lesser integration of the social system as a whole.

A sequence which has occurred fairly frequntly in low energy level societies and which illustrates articulation problems in particular can be outlined in the following terms:

Contact between high and low energy level social systems (often through colonialism) resulted in a proportion of the population of the low energy level society learning the language of the high energy level society, thereby increasing the "complementarity"[9] of the two. This led to an increased flow of information from the high to the low energy level society. As it became diffused in the low energy level society, this information modified values and produced demands for some of the perceived benefits of high energy technology—political and social benefits as well as economic. It also weakened or disrupted previous structures and processes in the low energy level society. But since demands can evidently develop and spread more rapidly than information of the sort required for the development of knowledge, skills, and organizational structures and processes needed for high levels of energy conversion, imbalances between such demands and the capacities of various components—particularly the political—of low energy level societies are produced. Often the political systems of such societies have responded to such demands by adopting formal structures associated with high energy level societies. But the formal structures alone are unable to produce the transition to high levels of energy conversion, so marked discrepancies develop between the formal and the effective.[10] At the same time, to prevent disintegration under the pressure of new demands, the political system (whether controlled by colonial authorities or indigenous groups) often finds it necessary to impose broader and tighter controls throughout the social system. Or, the same result can follow from the political elite's developmental efforts—all the more so if strong efforts are being made to accelerate development. The spread of demands is in most instances an irreversible process, so increased political controls lead to increased frustration and tensions, which foster extremist views and violence. In situa-

[9] Karl W. Deutsch, *Nationalism and Social Communication,* New York, John Wiley and Sons, 1953, pp. 68-74.

[10] The tendency toward wider gaps between the formal and the effective in "transitional" societies as compared with both "traditional" and "modern" ones has been pointed out frequently as a significant phenomenon by Fred W. Riggs.

tions where a revolutionary counter-elite has been able to establish, openly or underground, a network of communication within politically significant segments of the society, such tensions can be systematically exploited to the serious detriment of stability, order, and development. Eventual disruption and even disintegration may result, unless the new demands can be diverted from vulnerable points in the political system while the latter's effective capacity (as well as that of the economic system) is being increased to a degree commensurate with the demands, through the development of appropriate structures and processes.

As a means of tracing the relevance and implications of these ideas, let us now attempt to examine political development and the bureaucracy in Viet Nam.

2. *Changing Energy Levels and Communication Patterns in Viet Nam*

When measured by any of the currently available indices, Viet Nam is one of those nations which manages to derive relatively little energy from its environment. For example, gross energy consumption in Viet Nam was only 2 megawatt hours per capita in 1952 when the world mean was 10 and the figure for the U.S.A. was 62.1.[11] At about the same time, commercial energy consumption in Viet Nam (excluding fuelwood and other vegetable fuels) was 0.3, while the world mean was 10.2 and in the U.S.A. it was 66.[12] Although these figures do not include the human energy expended through work and other activities (expressible in principle as manpower) and are based on years when Viet Nam was suffering the destruction of the Indochinese war, it is safe to assume that current figures, if they were available, would not significantly alter Viet Nam's relative position.

As would be expected from the relationships postulated in the first section of this paper, information and its circulation are also relatively limited. Adult literacy, estimated about 1950, was 15-20 per cent, compared to a world mean of 56 per cent and a U.S.A. figure of 96-97 per cent. The ratio of daily newspaper circulation to population was estimated as 1.7 for (South) Viet Nam, when the world mean was 106.7 and the ratio for the U.S.A. was 325. The primary school enrollment ratio (the proportion of children 5-14 enrolled in primary school) was 7 in Viet Nam, 42 for the world mean, and 86 for the

[11] Ginsburg, *op.cit.*, p. 80.

[12] *Ibid.*, p. 82. The higher figure of 66 for the U.S.A. results from commercial energy figures based on 1955 rather than 1952.

U.S.A. The percentage of total population enrolled in secondary and higher education was .40 (South Viet Nam only), 2.29 for the world as a whole, and 6.02 in the U.S.A. Again, while improvement in these indices has undoubtedly occurred since the end of large-scale fighting in Viet Nam, the figures substantiate the assertion that Viet Nam is well down on any scale of modern technological information available in and circulating in its social system. As might be expected, gross national product per capita was low, coming to the equivalent of only 133 U.S. dollars.[13]

These indices reflect a socio-economic reality in Viet Nam which, with the exception of conditions related directly to the war being fought or just concluded when the estimates were made, is common in the literature of economic underdevelopment. Viet Nam was and is overwhelmingly rural and agricultural, with most of the population living in traditional-type villages. The urban minority, dominated by a Westernized elite, is largely concentrated in a single urban metropolis. There is relatively little industry. The usual pattern of "gaps"—urban-rural, elite-mass, wealthy-poor, Westernized-traditional, with large but by no means complete congruencies among the first halves of these dichotomies on the one hand and the second halves on the other—characterize the social structure. These "gaps" inhibit communication by limiting the distribution of many types of information, and consequently lower the degree of integration of the whole.

Prior to its period of intensive contact with the West, the Vietnamese social system as a whole was more homogeneous and its political components were more highly integrated than they have been since.[14] All but a tiny minority of the population lived within the confines of thousands of tightly knit agricultural villages, or "communes," where family relationships were interwoven with most other local institutions, including the "councils of notables" that governed them. With its roots in these villages and in part sustained by recruitment from them was a centralized mandarinal bureaucracy, Confucian in inspiration and training. Over this traditional agrarian society reigned the *Hoang De* and his court, a monarchy patterned closely on the classical Chinese model.

[13] All figures are from *ibid.*, pp. 18, 38, 40, 42, and 44, and refer to years in the first half of the 1950's.

[14] For two centuries (the seventeenth and eighteenth) Viet Nam was divided and governed by two rival political systems, one in the north and another in the south. During this period the homogeneity and integration of each, separately, were comparable to the homogeneity and integration of the whole in previous and subsequent periods.

Although largely independent of Chinese rule since the tenth century A.D., the Vietnamese had found the political institutions inherited from the preceding millennium of Chinese domination to be viable enough to withstand Mongol and Chinese assaults from the north and conflicts with its southern and western neighbors, Champa (eventually engulfed) and the Khmer empire. Moreover, while its unity and cohesion were not complete and should not be overstressed, this political system had facilitated the southward expansion of the Vietnamese down the east coast of the Indochinese peninsula as the population grew; a moving frontier of new villages based on fishing and/or the culture of rice had reached the Gulf of Siam and threatened to spread through Khmer territories in present-day Cambodia when France intervened.

During the several centuries preceding the arrival in force of the French, per capita levels of energy conversion for the society as a whole had probably remained relatively stable. The Confucian-style bureaucracy and the army based on village conscription had adequately mobilized and directed sufficient manpower to maintain internal order most of the time and resist external threats, some of which, such as that of the Mongols in the thirteenth century, were of spectacular proportions. Communal village organization and the technologies of rice culture and coastal fishing were sufficient to extract nutritious energy from the physical environment which not only sustained the villagers but also provided a surplus that could support the bureaucracy, the army, and the court. There was relatively little commerce, internal or external. Communication linking provinces to the capital and binding all into a single political system (except for the abovementioned period of partition) was largely maintained by the mandarins and their official couriers. The kinds and amounts of technological information, however, were not such as to permit per capita rates of energy conversion to increase beyond a fixed and rather low ceiling. Information relevant to inter-personal relations, social and political organization, and the supernatural was patterned by the partly blended and otherwise interwoven values and insights of primitive ancestor worship, animism, Confucianism, Taoism, and Buddhism. The result was a strongly conservative social system whose resistance to change could be overcome only by the force of a higher energy physical and social technology—such as that of France.[15]

[15] I am indebted to Professor Roy Jumper for reminding me that much fundamental research remains to be done in Vietnamese history, and that subsequent findings might require qualification of some of the generalized remarks in the two preceding

Without attempting to summarize the historical events and developments through which it occurred, we need at least to sketch some of the major consequences of the French domination of Viet Nam. By the time of World War II, Viet Nam had been largely or wholly under French domination for about three-quarters of a century. This domination produced disruptions in a number of dimensions of the traditional social system. Politically, boundaries were relatively stabilized (thus ending further Vietnamese expansion) and the institution of the monarchy was retained under rather close French "protection." The legitimacy of the monarchy in the eyes of its subjects was thereby seriously weakened. In the south ("Cochinchina"), which was under direct colonial administration, the mandarinate was replaced by the colonial counterpart of *Monsieur le Bureau* from France, while in the central and northern regions (separate countries according to French colonial policy), French *Résidents* ruled through the indigenous bureaucracy at both central and provincial levels, into which they introduced various changes. The integrity of what remained of the traditional mandarinate was consequently undermined; mandarins who had formerly enjoyed respect as members of the intellectual elite and who had partaken of the Emperor's "Mandate of Heaven" came to be viewed as collaborators by many of their compatriots. At the village level, French penetration was less, although efforts to modify the powers and composition of the village councils and, in the north, to change the manner of their selection, brought the forces of change to that level also.

The economic impact of French rule did not affect a large proportion of the Vietnamese directly, but its indirect effects and ramifications were widespread. In the north, mines and a limited industrial development introduced high energy technology; in the south, rice and rubber plantations were established to produce exports. Hanoi, Haiphong, and Saigon became commercial centers and entrepôts for exports to and imports from France. Banking and commerce, with the legal institutions to support them, grew in the cities. In the colonial pattern, Viet Nam was viewed by the French as a source of raw materials and as a market for French goods. The result was the appearance of a dual economy: a French-dominated sector geared to trade with France, and a Vietnamese sector producing for the subsistence needs of the vil-

paragraphs. The most useful general histories currently available are Le Thanh Khoi, *Le Viet Nam*, Paris, Les Editions de Minuit, 1955, and Joseph Buttinger, *The Smaller Dragon*, New York, Frederick J. Praeger, 1958.

lagers. A growing community of "overseas Chinese" participated in each sector and in some ways linked them. But the two sectors were not integrated with each other; one of the consequences was that, while the mean level of energy consumption was undoubtedly raised for Viet Nam as a whole, the distribution of consumption was highly skewed in favor of the French-dominated capitalist sectors of the economy. However, the repercussions of the new economic system reached the countryside in the form of increased tenancy, sharecropping, absentee ownership, and rural indebtedness. At the same time, French public health programs and measures to prevent revolts and famines lowered the death rate, and the population grew at a rapid rate. Population density in the Red River delta in the north and in the narrow central coastal plain increased, and rural poverty fed discontent. But demands for relief were not adequately satisfied by the colonial administrative system. Meanwhile, French schools in the cities had opened up channels for the introduction of French culture and had begun the process of partial Westernization of a portion of the urban population. Knowledge and values based on ideas of materialism, secularism, rationalism, democracy, and revolution, as well as Catholic religious ideas, flowed in to compete with weakened traditional concepts. Under these conditions the traditional bases of consensus began to erode, the vitality of traditional structures of organization and control was sapped, and resistance movements fed by nationalist demands grew in strength.

The fall of France in World War II and the Vichy government's alliance with the Axis powers brought Japanese troops to Viet Nam as the occupying power. Although the Japanese left the French colonial authorities in place during most of the war, they deposed them in 1945 and allowed the installation of an independent Vietnamese regime under the auspices of the Communist-dominated Viet Minh, which had won the leadership of the nationalist movement in Viet Nam. After the Japanese surrender, the French attempted to re-establish their former position, and the attempt led to the long (1946-1954) and bitter Indochinese war.[16]

The colonial period had brought processes of energy conversion and patterns of information and communication which, as we have seen, began to disrupt the traditional Vietnamese social system in basic ways.

[16] The best sources on the war period are Ellen J. Hammer, *The Struggle for Indochina*, Stanford, Stanford University Press, 1954, and Philippe Devillers, *Histoire du Vietnam de 1940 à 1952*, third edition, Paris, Editions du Seuil, 1952.

The war accelerated and spread disruption and disintegration. Large quantities of energy, human and chemical, were concentrated and expended destructively in military manpower, explosives, and fuels. Within the villages established patterns of communication were shattered or restructured: in Viet Minh-controlled areas by reorganization of the villages along Soviet or committee lines, and in French-controlled areas by military efforts to establish control and weed out Viet Minh sympathizers. Networks of civil communication and transportation throughout Indochina were broken or destroyed, to be replaced in part by military communication networks. Some sectors of the economy were interrupted by destruction or abandonment; rice and rubber production fell sharply. At the same time, some of the commercial and service sectors were stimulated into rapid expansion by the presence of large numbers of French troops. Urban populations were swelled by refugees from the fighting or from devastated areas.

In the course of the war, the French trained and armed anti-Communist Vietnamese troops and threw them, under French officers, into the struggle against the Viet Minh. These troops were to become the foundation of the Republican army after the war. The French also armed certain politico-religious sects, notably the Cao Dai and the Hoa Hao, who, while they fought the Viet Minh much of the time, sometimes also fought the French. The municipal police force of Saigon-Cholon fell under the control of the Binh Xuyen, an organization of former river pirates who also controlled organized vice in the city. In the hope of winning popular support against the Viet Minh, the French reinstated the former emperor Bao Dai, and his government was given increased, although still circumscribed, autonomy. The bureaucracy remained under French control, but in the early 1950's the French began systematically to turn over positions and responsibilities to Vietnamese officials.

The French defeat at Dien Bien Phu in 1954 during the international conference at Geneva led to an armistice based on the partition of Viet Nam at the 17th parallel. The Bao Dai regime, still under French sponsorship, was to govern the southern half of the country, and the emperor appointed Ngo Dinh Diem as President of the Council of Ministers. The new President arrived in Saigon from France in July 1954 and began to form his government.

The formation of a new political system south of the 17th parallel occasioned further dislocations. Previously the southern and northern ends of the country had complemented each other economically, with the southern rice surplus being exchanged for coal and some of the industrial products of the north. This ended with the drawing of the new boundary between the two, as did all other economic transactions. However, by this time economic activity had slowed significantly in the south anyway. Motivated both by the pessimistic prospects of the new southern regime and the nationalistic impression given by Ngo Dinh Diem, French businessmen began to transfer their capital back to France. Large numbers of French enterpreneurs, technicians, professionals, business and plantation managers, and troops began to withdraw.

South Viet Nam at this point faced a disintegrative crisis of monumental proportions. Political consensus had largely dissolved from the effects of colonialism and the war, and conflicts between the demands of various groups appeared irreconcilable. The effective structures of power, the bureaucracy, the armed forces, and the police, were either weakened or under the control of groups hostile to or unwilling to commit themselves to full support of the Ngo Dinh Diem. The legitimacy of the latter was questionable among important segments of the population. The economy was faltering, if not tottering, and hundreds of thousands of refugees from the north began to flood into the south.[17] If a chart could be drawn of overall energy conversion levels, including military, they would undoubtedly show a significant drop-off in the years 1954 and 1955.[18] The departure of large numbers of French civilians and troops from Viet Nam likewise represented a net loss of information in the form of knowledge and skills. The destruction of war had patently reduced energy extraction and conversion capacities, and had severely disrupted transportation and communication networks and facilities.

3. *Reintegration and Control of the Bureaucracy*

Developments in the bureaucracy of South Viet Nam after partition can best be understood in terms of the regime's strategy for dealing with the two major tasks imposed by the disintegrative situation. The major tasks were, first, to establish and consolidate control of the main

[17] Discussions of refugee, economic, and other problems are available in Richard W. Lindholm, ed., *Viet-Nam: The First Five Years*, East Lansing, Michigan State University Press, 1959. A more recent collection of essays on some of the same as well as on other problems is Wesley R. Fishel, ed., *Problems of Freedom: South Vietnam Since Independence*, Glencoe, Ill., and East Lansing, The Free Press and Michigan State University Bureau of Social and Political Research, 1961.

[18] Statistics available to the author either do not extend back earlier than these years, or, when they do, do not include military energy consumption.

power structures, and, second, to develop a minimal degree of consensus in the population as to the legitimacy of the regime while beginning to meet at least its basic demands for security and development. An effective approach to either of these categories of problems could not be delayed, but some progress on the first was a prerequisite to progress on the second. Without control of the armed forces, the police, and the bureaucracy, a viable measure of reintegration of the social system as a whole would be impossible. At the same time, of course, economic collapse had to be averted.[19]

In another place I have attempted to outline the series of steps by which Ngo Dinh Diem overcame and/or gained the support of the various armed forces and police who initially opposed him.[20] Initiating and cementing personal contacts with middle and lower level field commanders, and combining the strength gained thereby with astute maneuvering at the higher (including international) levels and with the successful timing of a series of domestic political and military actions, he succeeded in bringing the military and police forces either to heel or to his support. But the bureaucracy presented a somewhat different kind of problem: whereas control of the armed forces and police could be attained by securing the support of or control over a number of key officers, such convenient control points did not exist in the civil bureaucracy. At the higher levels it was staffed by several types of officials. These included, first, a relatively small number of "Doc Phu Su," a category of southern Vietnamese administrators trained under the French, mostly for higher staff type positions. Some were capable men, but they tended to be conservative, conscious of their high status, and more expert in legal analysis than in leadership and managerial decision making. Also, the withdrawal of the French from the administration had necessitated the rapid advancement of large numbers of lower-level and less experienced Vietnamese officials as replacements. When advanced in rank, a number of these were also given the title "Doc Phu Su"—but they were referred to by many of their colleagues and subordinates as "parachutists." In addition to

[19] Survival of South Viet Nam's economy during this critical period was made possible principally by massive injections of U.S. aid, without which political reintegration could not have occurred. This chapter's focus on political and administrative development should not be understood to minimize the significance of economic aid, which cannot be dealt with here because of space limitations.

[20] John T. Dorsey, Jr., "South Viet Nam in Perspective," *Far Eastern Survey*, Vol. 27, December 1958, pp. 177-182. See also Roy Jumper, "Sects and Communism in South Viet Nam," *Orbis*, Vol. 3, Spring 1959, pp. 85-96, and Francis J. Corley, "Viet Nam since Geneva," *Thought*, Vol. 33, Winter 1958-1959, pp. 515-568.

these there were a number of comparatively experienced administrators, including refugees from the north and the center above the line of partition where, under the protectorate system, they had gained some experience in positions of management and responsibility. Mostly this experience had been at the district (sub-provincial) level, but for some it had been at higher levels. But northern and central officials could not be placed in too many positions of prominent authority; southerners were suspicious that the President, from Central Viet Nam, intended to turn the bureaucracy over to officials from the north and the center. For all of these reasons, and for still others stemming from the colonial legacy and the unstable war years, there were scattered throughout the entire upper stratum of the bureaucracy many whose capacity and experience were limited, or whose motivation was either *attentiste* or, in the final analysis, opportunistic—plus, of course, an undetermined number who were more or less competent agents of the Viet Minh.[21]

Moreover, while there was a critical shortage of managerial and technical skills, most departments and agencies were heavily overstaffed at middle and lower levels with clerical and other personnel whose work habits and attitudes were formed by a combination of the French colonial and the mandarinal administrative traditions: concern for the dignity and prerogatives of officialdom, a "business as usual" rate of activity, adherence to the letter of intricate regulations—but ability to find ways of making exceptions when particularistic or other considerations indicated the desirability of doing so—a reluctance to take initiative and responsibility, a preference for formalism and the formalities, and an ingrained deference to authority. And while overstaffing was apparent in the Saigon offices of most central government agencies, field services often existed for the most part on paper. The hazards and discomfort of rural life caused most officials at all levels to seek and cling to posts in the capital.

Fortunately for the progress of governmental work, the bureaucracy also contained in its higher levels a thin sprinkling of energetic and conscientious officials whose competence and understanding of the plight of their country was an important factor in the continued func-

[21] Discussions of Viet Nam's bureaucracy can be found in Walter R. Sharp, "Some Observations on Public Administration in Indochina," *Public Administration Review*, Vol. 14, Winter 1954, pp. 40-51 (which is, to my knowledge, the first published in English), and Roy Jumper, "Mandarin Bureaucracy and Politics in South Viet Nam," *Pacific Affairs*, Vol. 30, March 1957, pp. 47-58, and "Problems of Public Administration in South Viet Nam." *Far Eastern Survey*, Vol. 26, December 1957, pp. 183-190.

tioning of the administrative apparatus. Some of these functionaries exhibited an entrepreneurial approach to their work; others, less enterprising or with less breadth of vision, nevertheless excelled in "turning out the work." However, the very fact that the offices of such men were places of relatively high productivity resulted in the convergence upon them of disproportionately large work-flows, and bottlenecks inevitably developed.

While skill shortages and motivational factors posed serious obstacles to effective coordination and integration, other obstacles were rooted in formal structural aspects of the bureaucracy. A high degree of compartmentalization of jurisdiction, organizational structure, and work procedures inhibited horizontal coordination. The civil service system was rigidly fragmented by anchoring appointments and assignments in a multiplicity of legally defined "cadres," membership in which guaranteed status and tenure and limited the possibilities of promotion, transfer, and dismissal.

Ngo Dinh Diem's strategy for transforming his formal authority over this cumbersome, relatively unintegrated, and often ineffective structure into effective and consolidated control revealed three major facets. These were administrative centralization, the development of networks of political communication and control, and efforts throughout the bureaucracy to inculcate attitudes conducive to both political reliability and higher work productivity.

Administrative centralization was focussed on the Office of the Presidency.[22] To enable closer control of the military, Ngo Dinh Diem retained the portfolio of Minister of Defense for himself. The office of the first Minister of the Interior (controlling the police forces) was located in Independence Palace, which housed the President's offices. Province chiefs, formerly appointed by and responsible to the Minister of the Interior, were made directly responsible to the President. The powers of Regional Delegates, who had formerly supervised and coordinated the activities of Chiefs of Province in the southern and central regions, were sharply reduced; the Delegates were removed from the chain of command between the presidency and the provinces and became primarily inspectors and trouble-shooters for the President.

These measures introduced a high degree of structural centralization, but further steps were taken. A number of agencies of sub-cabinet

[22] "The Presidency" refers to the Council (of Ministers) until the deposition of Bao Dai as Chief of State in October 1955 and the proclamation of the Republic; thereafter it became the Presidency of the Republic.

status were attached directly to the presidency. These included important control agencies, such as the General Directorates of Public Service (personnel) and of the Budget. The latter, previously a relatively unimportant part of the Ministry of Finance, was combined with the Directorate of Foreign Aid and given significantly increased powers over budget planning, preparation, and execution, somewhat similarly to the U.S. Bureau of the Budget; it was placed under the authority of a particularly dynamic and capable official. But also, a number of newly created "program" or "action" agencies were attached to the presidency. These included the General Commissariat of Agricultural Development, the Special Commissariat for Civic Action, the General Directorate of Civil Guard, and others. Their attachment to the presidency was maintained until 1961, when they were transferred to various departments. To assist with the direction, coordination, and supervision of these varied and often crucial agencies, a cabinet level "Secretary of State at the Presidency"[23] was appointed—but he has never stood between the President and the attached agencies. President Ngo's energy, his intention to keep a finger on the pulse of all activities important to security and control, and his disregard of official channels (sometimes to the exasperation of some of his subordinates) resulted in a very high degree of personal as well as institutional centralization of control.

The creation of new agencies, necessitated by transition of South Viet Nam to formal independence and by the need to establish programs to cope with social and economic as well as political problems, brought about a marked increase in structural differentiation of the bureaucracy.[24] At the same time, this proliferation added to the centrifugal tendencies in the government. Such tendencies only reaffirmed the rationale of centralized control.

The formal centralization of administrative authority, however, was not enough to guarantee control of the bureaucracy. Supplemental developments moved toward the establishment of patterns of relationships which could reinforce, and if need be, supersede the network of formal authority. These relationships were established on two kinds

[23] About 1956 the titles of cabinet level department heads began to be rendered in English as "Secretary of State" rather than as "Minister."

[24] Illuminating examples of administrative behavior during the early years of independence, many of which illustrate transitional and developmental problems, are to be found in John D. Montgomery and the NIA Case Development Seminar, *Cases in Vietnamese Administration*, Saigon, National Institute of Administration and Michigan State University Vietnam Advisory Group, 1959.

of bases: familial kinship and political favor and dependency. For the first, Ngo Dinh Diem could rely primarily on his brothers. Perhaps the most important in relation to political development in Viet Nam is Ngo Dinh Nhu, an intellectual and political activist who was designated "Political Advisor to the President" and installed in Independence Palace. His contribution will be outlined separately below, but mention should be made at this point of his wife. Since the President is a bachelor, Madame Ngo Dinh Nhu became the ceremonial "First Lady" of the Republic; she also assumed responsibility for the leadership of the political activity of Vietnamese women. (As a member of the National Assembly she later sponsored a controversial "Family Bill," since enacted, which, while it guarantees feminine equality in a number of domestic relations, also prohibits divorce without the President's consent, forbids concubinage and polygamy, and denies legal rights of inheritance to any offspring other than those of a legitimate monogamous union. She presently heads the Vietnamese Women's Solidarity Movement, which she established, and is the author and most important supporter of the law that abolished the occupation of taxi dance girls and institute para-military training for school girls and women volunteers.)[25] Another of the brothers, Ngo Dinh Can, was made Political Advisor in Central Viet Nam; from his home in Hue, which he reportedly seldom leaves, he has kept a check on the political reliability and responsiveness of the bureaucracy—and on political activities in general—in his region.[26] In addition to the brothers, there were other less close family ties—for example, Madame Ngo Dinh Nhu's father was made Ambassador to the U.S.A.; the Assistant Secretary of State for Defense for the first several years after 1954, who supervises the military under the President's direction, was related to him by marriage—as was the first Secretary of State at the presidency. Other such relationships might be traced, but those mentioned are enough to illustrate how kinship has served as a criterion of dependability and loyalty in important appointments. The regime has been much criticized for carrying this practice as far as it has. However, extensive family relationships among governing groups mark no great departure from tradition in Viet Nam—and of equal importance for explaining if not justifying them in the present instance,

[25] *The Times of Viet-Nam Magazine*, III, October 22, 1961, p. 15.

[26] A third brother, Ngo Dinh Luyen, serves as ambassador to Great Britain, while the fourth, Ngo Dinh Thuc, is the Roman Catholic Archbishop of Hue (he was formerly Bishop of Vinh Long in the southern delta area) and has served as an informal advisor to the President from time to time.

the unstable political conditions of 1954 and 1955 placed a high premium on unquestionable political loyalty. Many whom Ngo Dinh Diem first approached for high positions in his government in 1954 were unwilling to commit themselves and felt it necessary to decline. But if there were reasons for such appointments in 1954 and 1955, in subsequent years they have provoked increasingly bitter criticism by many Vietnamese, including some who were at one time supporters of the regime.

The other network of political communication and control in the bureaucracy was largely organized by the above-mentioned brother, Ngo Dinh Nhu. Bearing the name "Revolutionary Personalist Labor Party" (*Can Lao Nhan-Vi Cach-Mang Dang*), it is a semi-secret organization of selectively recruited individuals, most of whom are in the bureaucracy or the armed forces—although some private businessmen are included.[27] Membership is not publicly revealed, although no attempt is made to conceal the existence of the "party" as such. But it is not a party in the usual sense; it seeks no mass following, makes no public pronouncements on issues, and offers no candidates in elections. Many of its members appear to be intellectually inclined anti-Communists, often younger men, whose governmental positions, while strategic in many instances, are not necessarily at the highest level in their agencies. Ngo Dinh Nhu has stated that the organization includes about 20,000 persons, that it "devotes much of its time to the serious study of political and social questions," that it "is organized into cells and that it provides an important source of pro-government and anti-Communist support."[28] While its effectiveness as a control device is open to conjecture, it appears to constitute a political elite, membership in which involves full commitment to Ngo Dinh Nhu and the regime's leadership. In the eyes of many in the bureaucracy, membership is a prerequisite for young officials who aspire to rapid advancement to positions of trust and responsibility.[29] That it serves also as a network for communicating downward the regime's views

[27] See P. J. H., "Progress in the Republic of Viet Nam," *Times of Viet-Nam*, March 28, 1959, p. 6, reprinted from *The World Today*, Vol. 15, No. 2, February 1959; John C. Donnell, "National Renovation Campaigns in Veitnam," *Pacific Affairs*, Vol. 32, March 1959, p. 79; and Robert G. Scigliano, "Political Parties in South Vietnam under the Republic," *ibid.*, Vol. 33, December 1960, pp. 329-330.

[28] Scigliano, *op.cit.*, p. 330.

[29] The extent to which this is true is unclear. It is true that the *Can Lao* includes a number of the more capable young men in high positions, but whether they all owe their positions to their membership more than to their abilities can hardly be ascertained by observation from the outside.

on current issues, and reporting back information on individual behavior and attitudes, goes without saying. Also, of course, the *Can Lao* has on occasion provided a channel of direct communication from within administrative agencies to the Presidency, and has thus been able to provide coordination or obtain action when formal administrative channels were clogged or otherwise ineffective. However, the secrecy of membership and the known relationship of the organization to the center of power have undoubtedly induced caution and suspicion on the part of many officials who are not members, and have thus introduced additional barriers to the flow of information and otherwise inhibited action.

Networks of political communication based on kinship and political loyalty, coupled with formal administrative centralization, however, would not suffice to ensure integrated control of the bureaucracy. In addition, the positive commitment and support of officials throughout the administration was needed. To this end the National Revolutionary Civil Servants' League (*Lien-Doan Cong-Chuc Cach-Mang Quoc-Gia*) was formed. Its objectives were to spread understanding of the regime's policies and programs through the bureaucracy, to improve administrative performance, to diffuse knowledge of Viet Minh atrocities (many officials had either suffered personally or had experienced family tragedies at the hands of the Viet Minh and were thus able to testify at the weekly "Communist denunciation" meetings held during 1957 and 1958), and to generate support for the regime. However, the semi-obligatory character of membership for large numbers of civil servants and the formalism and lack of spontaneity of many of its meetings led the employees of many government agencies to participate in the *Lien-Doan* with something less than revolutionary zeal. In some parts of the bureaucracy it has been more of a paper organization than a real one. Nevertheless, it has undoubtedly contributed to middle and lower level government employees' awareness of the regime's policies and programs, and its very presence has served to remind them of the regime's expectations concerning the propriety of their political attitudes.[30]

Also in the category of efforts to develop attitudes and motivations conducive to responsiveness and political reliability has been the re-

[30] More recently the "Republican Youth" organization, which includes many officials, has appeared as a prominent part of the regime's efforts to bolster its support and disseminate political communications.

gime's attempt to formulate an explicit and positive ideological doctrine. Aware of the waning appeal of nationalism once independence was attained, and of the sterility of mere anti-Communism, and motivated by strong religious convictions himself, Ngo Dinh Diem has presented the ideas of "Personalism" to his compatriots as an alternative to Marxism. Personalism has, in fact, become the implicitly official doctrine of the regime. Derived from the ideas of the French Catholic writer Emmanuel Mounier, Vietnamese Personalism is founded on a "spiritual conception of man in the community."[31] It rejects capitalist as well as Communist materialism, and aims at "reconciling . . . the demands of collective discipline and social justice with those of individual liberty,"[32] seeking thereby the full development of the human personality. The elaboration of the doctrine has been primarily the work of Political Advisor Ngo Dinh Nhu and Bishop Ngo Dinh Thuc, but allusions to it color many of the public utterances of other public officials. Although it is Catholic in origin, its proponents insist that it blends the best ethical values of Buddhism, Mohammedanism, Confucianism, and Christianity, and thus provides an ideological meeting ground for East and West. A school for the study and propagation of Personalism was established at Vinh Long in the Mekong delta area by Bishop Thuc. It is operated by a small number of Catholic priests, and its rotating student body consists of selected goverment officials and school teachers. However, the extent to which it is understood by the population and the seriousness with which it is regarded by officials and intellectuals are open to question.

Finally, Ngo Dinh Diem's strategy for reintegrating and consolidating his control over the bureaucracy included measures for increasing the capacity, efficiency, and effectiveness of the bureaucracy's work methods. This involved the channeling in of technical information on administration and management. A principal vehicle for this process has been the National Institute of Administration, attached to the presidency. Designed to provide a three-year pre-service training program for future members of the top administrative class, to conduct research on administrative and related problems, and to stimulate in-service training in the government, the NIA has attempted to contribute to the solution of the previously mentioned shortage of ad-

[31] Donnell, *op.cit.*, p. 82.
[32] *Ibid.*, p. 80.

ministrative skills. It was assisted from 1955 to 1962 through a technical assistance contract with Michigan State University.[33] Also through this contract, advice on reorganization and administrative methods in government agencies was provided, as was technical advice and training for Viet Nam's police forces. Other measures were instituted to contribute to the goal of improving the bureaucracy's productivity. These included efforts to induce and assist the return from Europe and America of Vietnamese who had through studies or otherwise acquired skills and knowledge needed in Viet Nam; significant numbers responded and many of them were employed in the administration. A small but steady stream of government technicians and administrators was sent abroad, chiefly to the U.S.A., for periods of study and observation ranging from a few weeks to a year or more.[34] Some reorganizations and installations of new procedures and equipment occurred, particularly in budgetary administration.[35] As noted above, new agencies were established in some instances, such as the General Commissariat for Cooperatives and Agricultural Credit and the Special Commissariat for Civic Action. At the same time stringent laws and regulations were adopted to increase the punishment for financial corruption.

While these varied activities for enlarging the instrumental capacities of the bureaucracy and tightening up its effectiveness of performance have on the whole been fairly effective, there have been inherent limitations. Institutional as well as individual training and learning are at best slow and long-range processes. Innovation in bureaucratic structures and processes is difficult, obstacle-ridden, and often does not reach the profounder springs of action; not enough is known about the cultural roots of administrative processes and behavior to permit technical advisors to advise with confidence as to outcomes. Thus this category of developments has probably not been as important as the others in increasing control over the bureaucracy.

Moreover, these changes, as well as those leading to the centraliza-

[33] See Nghiem Dang, "The National Institute of Administration," in Lindholm, ed., *op.cit.*, pp. 162-166, the following commentary by Guy H. Fox, and John T. Dorsey, Jr., "Vietnam's National Institute of Administration," *Philippine Journal of Public Administration*, Vol. 2, April 1958, pp. 115-120.

[34] Howard L. Waltman, "Cross-Cultural Training in Public Administration," *Public Administration Review*, Vol. 21, Summer 1961, pp. 141-147.

[35] Montgomery, *et al.*, *op.cit.*, pp. 20-31 ("The Decision to Introduce Mechanical Accounting in the National Budget"), and Marvin Murphy, "Overcoming Resistance to Major Change—Vietnam Budget Reform," *Public Administration Review*, Vol. 20, Summer 1960, pp. 148-151.

tion and politicization of control outlined above, produced or aggravated a number of tensions and strains throughout the system.[36] Among the consequences related to changes sketched in this paper have been such things as slowdowns in decision making and a further lessening of initiative as a result of the increased centralization, resentment of the family relationships linking some of those in top positions and of the existence of the *Can Lao*, caution and suspicion on the part of some of those not in the *Can Lao* stemming from the knowledge that they may be under unseen surveillance, orientational and age gaps that inhibit communication and cooperation as a result of the influx of young returnees from abroad and of the varied sectional origins of officials, occasional conflicts between some of the newer and more action-oriented agencies and the more conservative old-line departments, and obstructive resistance to change in some sectors affected by efforts to innovate in structure and procedure. In some instances, possibly many, these problems have led to demoralization. They underline the necessity of avoiding the oversimplified view that the bureaucracy is a unified structure of power. And they suggest the limitations of even strenuous and multi-faceted efforts to bring the bureaucracy under integrated political control.

Nevertheless, the bureaucracy has remained viable, and President Ngo Dinh Diem was able to mobilize and direct its energies to the larger task: that of restoring the minimally necessary degree of consensus in the truncated southern half of Viet Nam to legitimize his government as it sought to meet at least the basic demands for security and development.

4. The Bureaucracy and Other Political Structures and Processes

Control of the military, the police, and the bureaucracy meant control of the principal concentrations of organized human energy and communication. But survival of South Viet Nam as a social system would require not only the restoration of energy conversion and information storage and exchange to previous levels. These processes would have to be so organized and stimulated that they would steadily raise energy conversion levels, for the new country began its formal existence in a condition of political and economic dependence as well as of general disintegration. Without large inputs of political, military, and economic aid from the outside world, particularly the U.S.A.,

[36] A brief survey of these problems is essayed in the present author's chapter in Fishel, ed., *op.cit.*, pp. 139-152.

disintegrative trends would have proceeded to chaotic proportions, and the outcome would undoubtedly have been reintegration into the Communist orbit. But survival outside that orbit would require that social, economic, and political energy conversion levels rise—and keep rising—beyond dependency levels, for it could not be assumed that foreign aid would continue indefinitely. This requirement implied a differentiation and restructuring according to patterns other than those of traditional Viet Nam, for the latter entailed definite ceilings upon energy conversion levels. Also, the diffusion of new, non-traditional information during the colonial and war periods had created widespread demands which could be satisfied only by a social system based on higher levels of energy conversion. All of this pointed to the necessity of a political system which could not only re-establish control and security but which could also initiate and carry through basic and far-reaching developmental programs.

However, in Viet Nam south of the 17th parallel, the problem of security conditioned reintegration and development more than in most of the "new" nations. Before partition the Viet Minh had controlled large areas of southern Viet Nam, and upon regrouping had left behind an armed underground network. Also, the name and image of Ho Chi Minh, known in city and countryside as the leader of the resistance to the French, were semi-legendary among the population. Thus the government faced not only the chaotically mixed forces of disorganization, apathy, traditionalism, and nationalistic demands; it also had to displace a firmly ensconced and prestigious symbol of anti-colonialism and ward off the attacks of a hostile and potent subversive organization.

The attacks were not long in coming. The Viet Cong (Vietnamese Communists), as the Viet Minh agents were redesignated by the Republican government, relied primarily on propaganda and the strengthening of their organization between 1954 and 1956. But they did not neglect terrorism as a tactic, particularly against village landlords.[37] When it became apparent that the 1956 elections called for by the Geneva agreement would not be held[38] the Viet Cong underground organization began to direct its efforts more directly at the government. From 1957 to 1959 the assassination rate of village and district

[37] Roy Jumper, "The Communist Challenge to South Viet Nam," *Far Eastern Survey*, Vol. 25, November 1956, pp. 161-168.

[38] The southern government had not signed the agreement; it had opposed the partition and felt no obligation to hold the elections.

officials, police, civil guardsmen, and field agents of the central government averaged about one every two or three days; by mid-1960 the rate had risen to over three a day.[39] Terrorism and assassination were supplemented by sabotage of developmental projects and, increasingly since 1959, by military guerrilla operations against the government. Thus security considerations have underlain most government policy from the beginning, and insecure conditions in various parts of the country (particularly the southwest) have hampered developmental activities to varying degrees.

The absence in 1954 of stabilized political processes and of a working consensus among the population imposed an initial tactic on the new regime. If an integrated political system was to be created from the chaotic conditions of post-Geneva South Viet Nam, a central unifying symbol would have to be diffused throughout the country, a symbol which could elicit wide supportive activities and around which the people could rally in opposition to the charismatic image of Ho Chi Minh. The most obvious and available referent for such a symbol was Ngo Dinh Diem. A large amount of effort was therefore expended in projecting his personality (perhaps "character" would be the more appropriate word in this instance) to the population, and in identifying it with the symbols of national independence theretofore monopolized by Ho and the Viet Minh. Although many segments of the bureaucracy had to be enlisted at different phases of this effort, primary responsibility devolved upon two agencies: the Department of Information and the Special Commissariat for Civic Action. The latter is a unique type of multi-purpose agency created late in 1955 to deal with a number of village-level problems. It operates by means of a large number of mobile teams which travel in the countryside, visiting villages and hamlets. The teams provide literature, advice, and some services and equipment in support of village activities in health, education, land reform, etc.—and, at the same time, seek to stimulate support for the government. Before moving on, they try to recruit and give some training to local individuals who will carry on the work of the Civic Action team after its departure. It has provided a channel of communication for the President's statements, plans, programs, and actions. While not infrequent collisions have occurred with provincial authorities and other agencies upon whose program jurisdictions Civic Action teams infringed, and while Civic Action's younger and some-

[39] Wesley R. Fishel, "Vietnam's War of Attrition," *The New Leader*, December 7, 1959, and "Communist Terror in South Vietnam," *ibid.*, July 4-11, 1960.

times northern or urban-bred personnel may have grated upon the sensibilities of traditionally inclined villagers, the agency undoubtedly had a measure of success in informing the rural Vietnamese of the existence in Saigon of an independent national government headed by Ngo Dinh Diem.

Meanwhile, if Civic Action had some effect in its grassroots information campaign, the Department of Information was equally active with its more orthodox programs. Through the production of films, photographs, pamphlets, posters, and slogans which were distributed up and down the country by its field services, the department made a significant contribution to the popularization of President Ngo Dinh Diem's image. The department was seconded by the U.S. Information Service, which, for some time after the formation of the new government, devoted most of its efforts to publicizing the President among his own people.

In addition to these "positive" communicative activities, the government also resorted to "negative" methods of control over the information circulating publicly. Most important of these was press control, which was accomplished in several ways short of mandatory prepublication censorship of newspapers.[40] Also, foreign publications were screened before release for public sale. Such restrictions on the free circulation of information were accepted without a great deal of complaint in the early years—in fact, criticism of government agencies was permitted, and restrictions on the press were less than during the colonial period. But as they appeared gradually to tighten, the more educated elements of the population became increasingly restive and resentful of them.

These were of course not the only means employed for the ideological reintegration of the population, but they were among the most important. None of the media of communication would have been sufficient, however, were it not for a series of events at the national level which, when news of them was disseminated throughout the country, added immensely to the President's charisma. First was his outmaneuvering of the army's Chief of Staff, General Nguyen Van Hinh, and the subsequent consolidation of control over the armed forces. Then, in the spring of 1955, came the more spectacular showdown with the Binh Xuyen group which controlled the Saigon-Cholon police as well as metropolitan vice. The military defeat of the Binh

[40] J. A. C. Grant, "The Viet Nam Constitution of 1956," *American Political Science Review*, Vol. 52, June 1958, pp. 437-462, includes a discussion of methods of press control.

Xuyen in street fighting not only marked a victory over a dissident domestic force but also had symbolic overtones of the routing of colonialism, because some of the French in Viet Nam had unofficially supported the Binh Xuyen. This was followed by the national referendum in October 1955 by which Emperor Bao Dai was deposed, President Ngo Dinh Diem became Chief of State, and the State of South Viet Nam became a republic. The bureaucracy participated actively in the electoral campaign, helping to "explain the issues" and "get out the vote."[41] Subsequent auspicious events were the election of a constituent assembly, the military defeat of the remnants of the Hoa Hao (a politico-religious sect which had opposed the government in the southwest), and the adoption and promulgation of the constitution in October 1956.[42] All of these events were accompanied by considerable public ceremonial, parades, demonstrations, and nation-wide holidays and celebrations. Thus there was much for government publicists to point to in their efforts to convince the people of South Viet Nam that President Ngo Dinh Diem was the man of destiny in Viet Nam's hour of need. If the traditional "Mandate of Heaven" evidenced itself through the successes of the ruler, then Ngo Dinh Diem clearly established a claim to it during the first two or three years of his regime in Viet Nam.

An increase in stability and in the recognition of the regime's legitimacy were only the pre-conditions of effective political integration, however. New networks of organizational structure and information flow had to be woven into the coalescing fabric of the social system, to pattern and channel energy conversion, mechanical as well as human, so as to contribute to the developmental goals of the regime. Efforts were made to build up extra-bureaucratic structures for this purpose, but bureaucratic instrumentalities had to be used, *faute de mieux*, in getting them started. The bureaucracy (supported by the military and the police and controlled, on the whole, by the Ngo Dinh Diem regime) has remained the most important national structure, either overshadowing, maintaining, or directly controlling the other political, economic, or social structures which have appeared.

For example, the official party of the regime, the National Revolu-

[41] Although based mainly on a later election (1959), an article useful for understanding any election in Viet Nam is Robert G. Seigliano, "The Electoral Process in South Viet-Nam: Politics in an Underdeveloped State," *Midwest Journal of Political Science*, Vol. 4, May 1960, pp. 138-161

[42] For a discussion of the background of the constitution and its principal provisions, see Grant, *op.cit.*, and Francis J. Corley, "The President in the Constitution of the Republic of Viet Nam," *Pacific Affairs*, Vol. 34, Summer 1951, pp. 165-174.

tionary Movement (*Phong-Trao Cach-Mang Quoc-Gia*), has had important links with the bureaucracy from the beginning, and has not developed into a political force independent of it. The first two chairmen of the party were successive heads of the Information Department. Also, it has been closely coordinated with the League of Revolutionary Civil Servants, which it spawned, and in the provinces public meetings of the NRM have been presided over by province chiefs and other officials.[43] The NRM, in turn, completely dominates the "legal" party system; the other parties, all of which are minor, have either been officially absorbed by it or are hardly distinguishable from it in their programs and activities.

The National Assembly is also overshadowed by the executive bureaucracy. With an overwhelming preponderance of pro-government deputies, most of whom are members of the NRM, the Assembly depends mostly in its deliberations on information provided by the executive branch.[44] It is not effective in expressing the demands of its constituents, mainly because its members have no power base outside the regime; members are much more dependent for election upon government approval and support than upon their own political standing or upon local political structures in their constituencies. And elections are organized, conducted, and supervised by the bureaucracy.

Private associations and organizations are subject to governmental regulation and supervision. They must have the approval of the Department of the Interior to organize, and they must inform the same department of their finances, membership, and activities. The labor movement in particular operates under solicitous governmental supervision, and its leadership, if not selected by the regime (through the *Can Lao*), is at least dependent upon the regime's approval. It should be pointed out that this kind of governmental dominance of nongovernmental groups is not always due to the regime's desire to control everything in sight. Much of it derives simply from the incomprehension of many officials, particularly in Interior, of any other way of doing business. From pre-colonial as well as from French administrative practice comes the unquestioned assumption that the bureaucracy must regulate, or at least keep a close eye upon, private organizations

[43] Scigliano, "Political Parties . . . ," *op.cit.*, pp. 331-332. In the provinces of Central Viet Nam, where Ngo Dinh Can is the dominant political figure, the NRM is the only political party in evidence. At provincial and district headquarters NRM offices share premises with government offices.

[44] Robert G. Scigliano and Wayne W. Snyder, "The Budget Process in South Vietnam," *Pacific Affairs*, Vol. 33, March 1960, pp. 48-60.

of all kinds—particularly those of potential political significance. These assumptions have only been strengthened by the serious security problem in the Republic of Viet Nam.

Assumptions of the same sort, given impetus by the experience of colonial exploitation, govern the bureaucracy's relations with the economy. Precisely because of the importance to the country of the economic category of energy conversion processes, the regime and the bureaucracy have felt it necessary to maintain direction and control. But also, in some important sectors of the economy, if there were no governmental initiative and regulation there would be no development. And in other sectors, control by non-Vietnamese groups (i.e., the Chinese and the French) is deemed inimical to both national independence and development. Thus imports and exports, industrial investment, wholesale and retail trade (particularly in rice), and expansion and diversification of agricultural production have been subjected to governmental control or made dependent on governmental policy and assistance. Licenses, contracts, permits, and taxes, however, which are the essential tools of governmental regulation, also provide the main opportunities for abuses and bribery. Thus it is that in its relations with economic segments of the social system the bureaucracy has been most exposed to and most tempered by the debilitating effects of corruption. The latter, nevertheless, has not altered in any basic way the unquestioned upper hand of the bureaucracy over the economy.

While in the examples just cited bureaucratic dominance evolved over groups and organizations whose genesis and growth were mostly independent of the bureaucracy, in yet other instances the bureaucracy has initiated and sustained important organizational complexes. This has been most evident in the rural areas, and it reflects what must have been a deliberate policy decision made at an early point: to give priority in developmental efforts to projects intended to benefit the rural population. This was based on the realization that the long-run success of the regime would depend on the support of the rural peasantry, where the bulk of the population is, where the basic source of energy for the entire population is produced in foodstuffs, and where the agents of the hostile regime in North Viet Nam could be expected to be most active. Consequently a broad range of programs was undertaken, including land reform, agricultural credit, cooperative purchase of supplies and equipment and marketing of produce, distribution of seed and fertilizer, resettlement of population from overcrowded areas in abandoned or otherwise underpopulated zones, reconstruction and extension of canals and roads, and technical advice and assistance of various kinds. Refugees from the north were among the first beneficiaries of these programs; energetic action had to be taken to move them from the ports and cities and re-establish them as self-supporting communities throughout the south. While this was being done, the newly created Department of Agrarian Reform was establishing its field services. The latter set about the organization of cantonal, district, and provincial agrarian reform committees, composed partly of officials and partly of landowners and tenants. Similarly, the General Commissariat of Agricultural Credit and Cooperatives began stimulating the organization of fishing and agricultural cooperatives, lending government funds at low interest to enable the new cooperatives to get a start.[45] Somewhat later (1959) the government began the organization of a "Farmers' Association," with units in the villages and hamlets. The primary purpose was to provide assistance of various kinds to individual farmers, but, like the formation of the Republican Youth organization at about the same time, it was also prompted by political and security motivations. In the central highlands, and in some areas of the southern delta, the government began establishing entire new villages populated by volunteers from the overcrowded coastal areas in the center. Like the northern refugee villages before them, these new resettlement villages were sponsored and serviced by a central governmental agency, the General Commissariat of Agricultural Development, until they could become self-sufficient.

In short, governmental initiative, through the bureaucracy, resulted in the establishment of a number of organizations throughout the rural areas. Most of them have remained dependent on bureaucratic guidance and support for continued existence. The resettlement villages are the principal exception; most of them have attained the degree of self-sufficiency that has permitted their integration into the regular provincial administrative system. But, as will be pointed out below, the central government's bureaucracy dominates and guides village governments too.

One must conclude from the foregoing that, while the regime succeeded in reintegrating Viet Nam south of the 17th parallel as a political system, the product was a political system in which the bu-

[45] Agrarian reform is discussed by Price Gittinger, David Wurfel, Richard W. Lindholm, and "A Vietnamese Official" in Lindholm, ed., *op.cit.*, pp. 200-213, and by Wolf I. Ladejinsky in Fishel, ed., *op.cit.*, pp. 153-175. Agricultural credit and cooperatives are discussed by Tran Ngoc Lien in *ibid.*, pp. 177-189.

reaucracy (supported, of course, by the armed forces and police) was the overwhelmingly preponderant structure for the mobilization and control of energy expended in the political process. While more remains to be said about these matters and some of the problems they entail, the theoretical premises of this analysis require that we also look at other aspects of energy conversion and information processes. Unfortunately, statistics that would permit exact comparison with those given earlier in this paper are not available. However, it is possible to suggest something of what has occurred and to adduce at least some statistical data.

For example, information inputs have been increased through such means as the previously mentioned return of students from abroad, the sending of personnel abroad for training and observation, and technical assistance in a wide variety of fields. The amount of books, periodicals, and other printed material imported has been large. Quantitative data on these matters are not available, but in at least one related channel where they are available, foreign mail handled in the postal system, an increase has occurred. Pieces of such mail increased from 25.9 million in 1955 to 27.5 million in 1959.[46] Perhaps more significant for developmental implications, however, has been the sharp increase in internal circulation of information. Between 1955 and 1959, domestic airmail increased from 4.8 to 13.6 million pieces and telephone conversations from 5 million to 18.7 million. The average number of words transmitted daily by telegraph fell somewhat, from 119,000 to 102,000, probably reflecting greater use of long distance telephone. Radio sets increased from 38,000 to 87,000 over the same period.[47] Elementary school enrollment went from 330,000 in 1954-1955 to 873,000 in 1958-1959, secondary school enrollment from 21,000 to 52,000, university enrollment from 2,155 to 7,500, and technical school enrollment from 1,590 to 3,850.[48] Current figures on literacy have not come to my attention, but the government's literacy campaign over the past seven years can be presumed to have considerably improved the figures given earlier in this paper.

Figures such as these are of course only indices; they reflect only

[46] United States Operations Mission to Viet Nam, *Annual Statistical Bulletin*, No. 3, Saigon, USOM Program Office, June 1960, Table G-2, p. 111.

[47] *Ibid.* Figures have been rounded. Data on newspaper and library circulation, which would also be useful indices, are not available.

[48] Department of National Education, "Activities of the Department of National Education of the Republic of Vietnam, 1954-1959," Saigon, July 1959, mimeo. Figures have been rounded.

indirectly such changes in the rate of social communication as may have been brought about by the establishment of new organizations and the growth of old ones, or the circulation of political pamphlets, or the holding of meetings on whatever subjects. Also, they do not take into account the not inconsiderable Viet Cong propaganda activities. Even so, these figures warrant the conclusion that there is a trend toward more people being exposed to more information of all kinds, and that their attitudes and actions are being influenced as a consequence. In addition to the human energy conversion that is thereby influenced or determined, it is not implausible to suppose that there has been an increase in the circulation of information relative to the conversion of non-human energy. In any event, the available statistics show increases in agricultural production (rice paddy, for example, rose from 2.8 million metric tons in 1955 to about 4.5 million in 1959)[49] and electricity production increased from 202.8 to 267 megawatt hours in the same period while imports of petroleum products went from 335,300 to 500,300 metric tons, not including military imports.[50] While the population has also grown, if complete statistics were available on energy conversion and if they were all translated into per capita figures, it seems clear that they would show a significant net gain in energy conversion since the republic was established. Some of the gain, of course, would be accounted for merely by the resumption of war-interrupted economic activities.

The government, of course, has actively sought such increases in economic energy conversion rates. Economic development plans and projects aimed at increasing and diversifying agricultural production have been implemented through the bureaucracy, aided in many important aspects by U.S. economic and technical assistance. While their success has depended ultimately upon the work of several million nongovernmental rural people, it is certain that gains in agricultural production would have been a good bit smaller without the efforts of such agencies as the Departments of Agriculture and Land Property and Agrarian Reform, and the General Commissariat for Agricultural Credit and Cooperatives. Nor was commerce, banking, and industry overlooked. Foreign exchange controls and import-export regulations were adopted, price controls were instituted, the Bank of Indochina was nationalized and transformed into the National Bank of Viet Nam, a Commercial Bank of Viet Nam was established, and efforts were

[49] United States Operations Mission to Viet Nam, *op.cit.*, Table E-1, p. 70.
[50] *Ibid.*, Tables F-3 and F-4, pp. 99 and 100. Figures are rounded.

made to stimulate industrial development, in part through the establishment of a developmental loan fund supported by the government and foreign aid.[51] Industrial development, while modest, has nevertheless shown increases in production in some areas of light industry such as textiles and sugar refining. Progress in other areas of production has been spotty and less than hoped for. However, the question that must be asked about increases in energy conversion rates in all sectors of the economy is: has it been enough? No unequivocal answer can be given, in part because it has not been assumed that the Republic of Viet Nam will be able to survive without substantial foreign economic aid for many years to come. Unfortunately, the time available has been under constant and increasing pressure from the interrelated factors of the international situation and the domestic security problem. The importance of these factors is unhappily such that one is not entitled to exclude the possibility that no feasible rate of increase in energy conversion levels would be enough—that even if economic development had far exceeded the most optimistic hopes, Viet Nam might still be brought down by a combination of external pressure and internal subversion.

Regardless of questions such as these, however, we must look briefly at some of the important problems related to the emergence of the bureaucracy to a dominant role in the political system and to the regime's efforts to cope with the security situation.

In its activities affecting the agricultural villagers, the bureaucracy has repeatedly encountered problems and difficulties that can be classified as "articulation problems."[52] That is, the articulation of the bureaucracy with the rural population, which was seriously weakened and disrupted during the colonial period and the ensuing war, has not been effectively re-established.[53] Thus officials have found villagers reluctant to take the initiative or even to participate in the various programs and organizations sponsored by the government. Or they have encountered misunderstanding of the objectives and confusion about the procedures and methods of such programs. Cooperation and

[51] See Lindholm, ed., *op.cit.*, *passim.* For a critical view of economic development and U.S. aid in Viet Nam, see Milton C. Taylor, "South Viet-Nam: Lavish Aid, Limited Progress," *Pacific Affairs*, Vol. 34, Fall 1961, pp. 242-256.

[52] The word "articulation" is not used here in the same sense in which it is used in the Almond-Coleman schema, but rather in the sense of "connective relationship."

[53] Of course it should not be inferred that articulation was "complete" or "perfect" in the pre-colonial period—far from it. But for reasons given in the following few paragraphs, it seems clear that relationships between officials and the population in general are less close and more problem-ridden now than then.

compliance have often been purely formal, given only while the officials were physically present or able to exercise direct controls, and discontinued or avoided otherwise. Villagers, for their part, have often found government officials unsympathetic to their problems and sometimes autocratic and even abusive in their behavior. These problems have been less important in some programs than in others, of course, but they seem general enough to be considered symptomatic of an underlying weakness of articulation.

Much of the explanation of this phenomenon lies in the patterns in which information has been distributed in Viet Nam. Information leading to the acquisition of knowledge, skills, and values developed originally in the West has come into Viet Nam through its urban centers and schools. The bureaucracy is staffed by persons who have come through such schools and whose knowledge, skills, and values tend to differ from those of the bulk of the rural population. But also, insofar as this information has been diffused in both urban and rural masses, it has generated demands more rapidly than it has disseminated the knowledge and skills necessary for the satisfaction of those demands. Such technical information as is available is largely concentrated in the hands of the bureaucracy, which thus finds itself the target of demands which it cannot satisfy.

These articulation problems are sometimes aggravated by structural factors. The dominance of the central government bureaucracy over village government has already been alluded to. Thus, appointment of villagers to their village councils has been, since 1956, a responsibility of the central government's province chiefs.[54] Village budgets have had to be supported in large part by central government loans and subventions, and are subject to approval by central government officials. Moreover, the central government's power to fix village boundaries, sometimes combining several small ones into a single larger village or dividing a single large one into two or more smaller villages, has produced situations in which villagers feel little identification with the village within whose administrative jurisdiction they happen to reside. This obviously affects the degree to which a "community spirit," conducive to participation in village government and community development projects, can be generated.[55] The problem is not one that

[54] Lloyd W. Woodruff, "The Study of a Vietnamese Rural Community—Administrative Activity," I, Saigon, Michigan State University Viet-Nam Advisory Group, May 1960, mimeo., p. 53. In 1961 the President announced the government's intention to reinstitute elective councils.

[55] James B. Hendry, "The Study of a Vietnamese Rural Community—Economic Activity," Saigon, Michigan State University Viet-Nam Advisory Group, December 1959, mimeo., pp. 357-360.

can be solved simply by readjustments in village boundaries, for there is evidence that the "units of community identification" are small;[56] if used as the main criterion for drawing boundaries they would result in far too many villages for economic and administrative feasibility.

Of course, the Viet Cong have made their contribution to the exacerbation of articulation problems. Using persuasion, rumor, pamphlets, threats, sabotage, murder, and military operations, they have sought to impede government projects, discredit and intimidate officials, encourage and enforce non-cooperation with the bureaucracy, and gain active or at least passive support among the peasantry.[57] Although all of the government's difficulties in building stronger relationships with the latter cannot be ascribed to the Viet Cong, it is beyond question that the activities of this underground have seriously increased such difficulties. The Viet Cong have not only hampered the bureaucracy in many instances, but have thwarted it in some.

Thus the analysis brings us once again to the pervasive problem of subversion and insecurity. Some of its effects on the bureaucracy and on political development have been suggested, but there are others which cannot be overlooked. It has forced the regime to extend and tighten controls throughout the social system to a degree which would not have occurred in its absence. This has entailed the allocation of a large proportion of the total available governmental energy to agencies employing force (the various military and police organizations), and has required that the attention of the bureaucracy at all echelons never shift too far from security matters.

The armed forces, kept at a strength of about 150,000 since 1955 and trained and equipped through U.S. aid, are now being raised to 200,000 men, and U.S. military aid has been sharply increased since 1960. The various police forces, including the security police, the civil guard, the municipal police forces, and the village self-defense militia, have also been strengthened, armed, and trained with the help of U.S. aid. The civil guard, with a national structure but under operational control of province chiefs, was at first trained as if it were to become a rural police force somewhat comparable to state police forces in the U.S.A., but more recently it has been equipped and

[56] *Ibid.*

[57] Fishel, "Communist Terror . . . ," *loc. cit.*, Joseph J. Zasloff's "Peasant Protest in South Viet Nam" (a paper prepared for delivery at the annual meeting of the American Political Science Association, St. Louis, Missouri, September 6-9, 1961) contains a cogent analysis of Viet Cong tactics. See also Denis Warner, "The Invisible Front Lines of South Vietnam," *The Reporter*, Vol. 25, August 17, 1961, pp. 28-30.

trained as a military organization. The police forces have had to concern themselves with political as well as criminal delinquencies, and have been complemented by several "political re-education centers" or internment camps, where political prisoners are detained and efforts are made to rehabilitate them ideologically.

In provincial administration the security problem led early to the appointment of military officers as Chiefs of Province and of District in several areas. While this has not meant that social and economic programs have been neglected in such provinces (in fact, some of the younger officers in such posts have demonstrated more interest in such programs than might have been expected of some of their civilian counterparts),[58] it has reflected the necessity of giving such programs secondary priority. Even in provinces still under civilian administration, province and district chiefs are likely to think of their responsibilities basically in terms of maintaining security. Since 1960, a number of military officers have also been placed in Saigon offices of the civil administration.

Within the villages, *Lien Gia* (or "five family groups" as they are usually termed in English) have been organized for mutual observation and protection. The system, which has ancient precedents in traditional Viet Nam, is meant to maintain channels of communication through hamlet chiefs and village officials to district officials of the national government. Its effectiveness as a communication and control network depends upon the commitment of villagers to the government, for the chain can be broken at several points before it reaches national government officials.

Security considerations have also been important in the agricultural development program of resettling people from overcrowded areas in more sparsely populated parts of the Central Highlands and the Mekong delta. New villages have been located in known zones of infiltration from the north via Laos and Cambodia, on the assumption that anti-Communist villagers in such areas will constitute a barrier to Viet Cong bands. And from 1959 to 1961 in the delta area, many small scattered villages were compulsorily regrouped in larger agglomerations called "agrovilles" to provide security unavailable to smaller and more isolated hamlets. More recently a program to fortify and arm many individual "strategic hamlets" has gained momentum.

[58] Which calls to mind, of course, the argument of Prof. Guy Pauker in "Southeast Asia as a Problem Area in the Next Decade," *World Politics*, Vol. 11, April 1959, pp. 325-345.

Controls in the principal urban area, Saigon, have been manifested in such manners as indirect press censorship, the surveillance of group activities of potential political significance, political arrests and detention and official impatience with criticism. Such controls appear to have become tighter in the past two or three years; for example, a prominent oppositionist elected to the National Assembly in 1959 was disqualified on the grounds of election fraud and not allowed to take his seat. The restrictions have led to increasing resentment among Saigon intellectuals and professionals, who were already prone to criticize the regime for the family relationships among people in top positions, for the Ngo family's Catholicism, for restrictions on freedom of the press, and for the actual and alleged activities of the police and the *Can Lao*. A non-Communist opposition to the regime has existed in Saigon since 1954, mostly fragmented and ineffective, and when the government's control of the countryside began to deteriorate in 1959 and 1960, its members began to claim that the government was not only corrupt, but also that it was losing the country to the Viet Cong. Finally, in November of 1960, one group of oppositionists, with the help of a few companies of paratroopers (commanded by a nephew of one of the civilian oppositionists) attempted a *coup d'état*. The *coup* failed when the high command of the military threw its support to the President and stamped out the rebellion.[59]

The significance of the episode has not been without ambiguity. Critics of the regime could see it as a symptom of basic instability and as a protest with potentially wide support which failed only because of poor planning and mismanagement. The President and his supporters, on the other hand, could derive reassurance from the failure of such support to materialize and from the demonstration that the overwhelming preponderance of the military was still with the regime. At any rate, the regime subsequently promised far-reaching reforms, including some administrative decentralization and the popular election of village councils. To achieve the former, a majority of the many agencies attached directly to the presidency have been transferred to appropriate line departments, and the latter have been grouped under three supra-departmental coordinating secretaries of state—one for security, one for economic development, and one for cultural and social

[59] See Stanley Karnow, "Diem Defeats His Own Best Troops," *The Reporter*, Vol. 24, January 19, 1961, pp. 24-29, and Wesley R. Fishel, "Political Realities in Vietnam," *Asian Survey*, Vol. 1, April 1961, pp. 15-22. An interpretation of the psychological "atmosphere" among some Saigon students and intellectuals during this crisis can be found in Luther A. Allen, "South Vietnam: The Issue is Freedom," *The Nation*, Vol. 194, March 17, 1962, pp. 233-236.

affairs. It was announced—not, however, for the first time—that the government would take "new drastic measures against civil servants found guilty of abuse of power, brutality, or vexation toward the population; they will be mercilessly punished and immediately suspended."[60] The government proceeded to hold the scheduled election for President in 1961 (President Ngo was re-elected), but the village council elections have not yet occurred.

However, while they would help, much more than popularly elected village councils and some administrative decentralization would be required to offset Viet Cong gains and establish a more effective articulation between the bureaucracy and the population. The situation in the countryside has increasingly become one to which the only short-range solution is military. But in the longer range, even complete military elimination of the Viet Cong will accomplish nothing unless ways can be found to reintegrate the political system in Viet Nam south of the 17th parallel. Given the central role of the bureaucracy, social and economic as well as political development are all the more dependent upon such reintegration.

5. *Conclusion: Prospects for Political Development*

The preceding pages have attempted to outline the means by which a "low energy-level" society, brought to the verge of disintegration by a long war fought within its boundaries, sought to reintegrate itself, absorb new information, and accelerate the rates of its energy conversion. The principal mode of adaptation was the mobilization and concentration of information and energy control through the bureaucracy. But a crucial handicap in this adaptation has been the activity of an underground organization intent upon subverting this political system by the dissemination of hostile information and the application of destructive energy. This has contributed in a vital way to the inability of the bureaucracy to establish effective articulation with other segments of the social system—particularly the rural peasantry. At the same time, the preeminence of the bureaucracy, as the central and basic structure seeking to relate the political elite with the other components of the social system, has been such that no other structures have been able to develop to perform this function. Parties, interest groups, economic organizations, and associations of various kinds have appeared, but they are all dominated or overshadowed by the bureaucracy. Many, in fact, would be empty forms without governmental

[60] The announcement is quoted in Fishel, *ibid.*, p. 22.

support. Thus, ineffective linkages between the bureaucracy and the population as a whole constitute a weakness and vulnerability of critical proportions in the political system.

In retrospect, one could raise the question of whether President Ngo Dinh Diem and his regime chose the right pattern of adaptation for the political system. Should he have strengthened and relied so heavily upon the bureaucracy as the central mechanism for the integration of the political system in South Viet Nam? But any answer to this would only beg the prior question of whether any other adaptive process could have been chosen. Given the mandarinal administrative tradition in Viet Nam and background of the President, given his lack of a strong party to support his regime, given the absence of parliamentary experience and traditions in Viet Nam, and given the elemental need to restore governmental services and operations to at least a minimal level, was it not inevitable that the new regime would look upon the bureaucracy as its principal if not only means of effecting integration? Once consolidated control was established over the bureaucracy, what possibilities existed that other political structures to channel demands to the regime could emerge? The possibilities were limited by the struggles and violence of 1954 and 1955 through which the army, the Binh Xuyen, the Cao Dai, and the Hoa Hao were brought under control or dispersed. This eliminated alternative structures for the channeling and expression of demands, but it is extremely doubtful that they could have been peacefully integrated into a viable political system. Again, possibilities were limited by the hostility of the regime in the north and the activities of its underground apparatus in the south, which augmented the southern government's suspicion of any oppositionist activities. Finally, they were limited by the regime's efforts to organize its own mass political party, the NRM, which sought to dominate the party system and succeeded—but without becoming independent of the bureaucracy. It is possible that the odds were heavily in favor of the political system's adapting as it did—that events and other factors beyond the control of the regime structured the evolving situation in a way that precluded any significantly different outcome. On the other hand, perhaps a different leadership strategy, one aimed at more rapid liberalization of the political process, could have retained its initial hold on the popular imagination so as to compensate for weaknesses in the integration of other aspects of the political system.

These, however, are questions whose speculative nature only emphasizes the limitations of our present understanding of the processes of political development. Whether the information and energy concepts that have guided the present analysis will prove useful for deepening that understanding will depend on a good bit more research and application than has been possible in this rather rough first approximation. But on the provisional assumption that they may have some utility, what do they permit one to say about the prospects for political development in Viet Nam?

As has already been pointed out, military action, even if it is successful in eliminating or neutralizing the Viet Cong, will not be sufficient. Channels would still be needed through which the demands of the more significant groups and categories of the Vietnamese people could be effectively communicated, and through which the political leadership could mobilize the people's energies, both to resist further subversion from the north and to raise economic energy conversion rates. Whether the bureaucracy can provide such channels is doubtful, given its problems of establishing strong links with the population. The NRM might be able to do so, if it were able to divorce itself from the bureaucracy, develop more autonomous local organizations, and enforce a greater degree of responsiveness to it by the leadership rather than the reverse relationship which now prevails. But the means by which this might be brought about are far from apparent, and it is not likely that the regime would permit it. Similarly, the probability that a significant non-Communist opposition party can develop is small. Opposition leaders in Saigon have little organization, are divided among themselves, and have no following in the countryside. Thus it appears that there are few prospects of any significant structural changes in the political system in the foreseeable future (assuming that the Viet Cong are contained). Consequently, channels of the sort referred to above will probably not develop in the next few years.

The alternative means of bringing about integration would be charismatic leadership. But the popularity of President Ngo Dinh Diem has faded perceptibly in the last few years. Conceivably it could be restored by some spectacular series of events comparable to those of the period 1954-1956, or by some dramatic policy shifts which might rekindle emotions of confidence and enthusiasm throughout the country. But this is not likely, given the tenseness of the security situation, and the policy commitments and personality of the President. Otherwise, he might well be able to continue in power as long as he has the support of the military leadership. The attempted *coup* of 1960 demonstrated clearly that the army commanders can be the crucial factor in deciding who is to occupy the presidency. But whether President Ngo retains power, or is ousted in some future military take-over, the same fault in the political system will remain: ineffective integration of the bureaucracy with the population, and the absence of other sound links between the latter and the political leadership.

Over a period of years, again assuming the Viet Cong problem is overcome, economic energy levels might rise sufficiently to force changes in political structure. But present levels are so low, and they rise so slowly, that related changes in political structure are far in the future. In the meantime, it remains to be seen whether the bureaucracy can, even with the help of large injections of information and energy from external sources, provide the structures and processes of adaptation that can achieve a viable measure of integration in Viet Nam.

CHAPTER 12

Public Bureaucracy and Judiciary in Pakistan[1]

RALPH BRAIBANTI

I. Introduction

INSTITUTIONS transplanted from one milieu to another develop in unpredictable ways and may serve needs different from those satisfied in the place of origin. Ideas and structures introduced from one society are molded by those already rooted in the receiving society in a highly dynamic process of transformation which has been variously described as "culture radiation and reception," and "spiralling indigenization."[2] The forces acting upon such transformation are varied and complex; neither they nor the nature of the reciprocal actions occurring in the process are easily amenable to precise ordering.

This chapter attempts to analyze one instance in which two institutions largely of British importation—public bureaucracy and the writ jurisdiction—have been confronted by a variety of social, economic, and historical forces and have been changed thereby, serving fundamental needs of a modern state, but in a somewhat different manner than in Western countries. The contours of the two spheres of power —the bureaucratic and the judicial—are in a state of flux, with each

[1] The author wishes to record his indebtedness to several sources of support for this study. Research was carried on in Pakistan, India, and England in 1957, 1958, and 1959 under sponsorship of the Social Science Research Council and the Duke University Commonwealth Studies Center. Subsequent research was done in Pakistan in 1961 while on leave from Duke University to serve as Chief Advisor to the Civil Service Academy of Pakistan under terms of a United States Agency for International Development contract administered by the University of Southern California. The full and generous cooperation of the various agencies of the government of Pakistan, both executive and judicial, must also be mentioned with deep appreciation. This chapter was critically read by M. R. Kayani, Chief Justice of the High Court of West Pakistan; Dr. Nasim Hasan Shah, editor of the *Pakistan Supreme Court Reports;* and Agha Abdul Hamid, formerly secretary, cabinet member, and secretary to four prime ministers. The assistance of Zahid Shariff, research associate, and Abdul Rahman Bajwa, stenographer, at the Civil Service Academy, is also acknowledged. None of these organizations or persons mentioned here or in subsequent notes bears any responsibility for views expressed herein, which are solely those of the author.

[2] For further analysis, see Ralph Braibanti, "The Relevance of Political Science to the Study of Underdeveloped Areas," in Braibanti and J. J. Spengler, eds., *Tradition, Values and Socio-Economic Development,* Durham, 1961, pp. 139-181.

sphere exerting a permeative force on the other. The dynamism of the transformation is enhanced by interpretations of martial law as it affects the role of the judiciary.

Changing contours of the public bureaucratic and judicial spheres of power, as manifest through the mechanism of the writ petition, can be understood only in the context of other circumstances. The use of the writ for purposes which, in the American bureaucracy, would be regarded as matters of internal administration must be judged in terms of exigencies found within Pakistan's bureaucracy. The problems of disarticulation in the bureaucracy for the decade after partition were almost overwhelming. Neither machinery nor official disposition were adequate to deal with the urgent demands of preserving the administrative viability of the nation and at the same time rationalizing the internal structure of the bureaucracy. There were too many forces totally beyond bureaucratic control and others theoretically within its control but beyond the span of energy and attention which the bureaucracy was capable of focusing on them. One dimension of the problem—that of the shortage of executive talent at the time of partition—is dealt with in detail in Part II of this chapter. In this part there is an effort to describe with some precision the means by which values of the Indian Civil Service (ICS) were transmitted into the total bureaucracy.

Part III attempts, with less precision, to convey an impression of the climate of bureaucracy which the values of the elite ICS corps could not completely permeate and change. Part IV is a brief survey of the historic image of the judiciary as a champion of liberty and seeks to contrast such image with that of the bureaucracy. Finally, in Part V the nature of the writ jurisdiction is surveyed.

This study has obvious limitations, the first of which is the omission of any extended consideration of the influence of inadequate structure and procedure as a factor contributing to the rise of grievances within the bureaucracy. Certainly the administrative system which was well adapted to colonial administration and to relatively static conditions was technically and procedurally archaic when measured by the demands of a modern state.[3] This is not the place to analyze the mechanism of administration, for this has been done adequately by official

[3] On this point and on the need for a change in the attitude of administration, few statements are more forthright than President Ayub's address at the inauguration of the Administrative Staff College, December 24, 1960. *Speeches and Statements by Field Marshal Mohammad Ayub Khan*, Karachi, 1961, III, 72-74.

reports of the government of Pakistan.[4] This omission does not indicate in any sense that mechanism was not an important cause of factious social relations within the system. On the contrary, the relationship between system and behavior is reciprocal. Certainly antiquated procedures, especially with respect to financial matters, profoundly affected the social climate of administration and contributed to the creation of grievances for which the judiciary seemed to be the only recourse.

A second limitation is that there is no comprehensive analysis of important changes in system and disposition which have been taking place in the bureaucracy during the last three years. The bureaucratic system is in a state of flux; there is acute awareness of the problems described in Part III and there are signs of institutional change designed to remedy many of them. Analysis of these trends is precluded not only by limitations of space but by the fact that they have been dealt with by the same reports which describe the administrative system.

A third limitation is omission of technical legal aspects of the writ jurisdiction, e.g., how the writs have been applied and the standards of application which have been evolved. These issues do not directly concern service matters and must be left as the subject of another essay.

II. Administrative Disabilities of Partition

The most serious administrative problem faced by Pakistan on achieving independence in 1947 was the acute shortage of managerial talent which was experienced in the complexity of decision making at a high level of government. The disorder characterizing the partition of 1947 and the absence of accurate personnel records for the first four years of the country's existence make it difficult to ascertain reliably the situation regarding the transfer of executive talent from India. While it is well established that Muslims held few positions

[4] General analyses are found in the *First Five Year Plan 1955-60*, Karachi, 1957, pp. 91-123; *Second Five Year Plan 1960-65*, Karachi, 1960, pp. 105-125; Rowland Egger, *The Improvement of Public Administration in Pakistan*, Karachi, 1953, part of which was published as "Ministerial and Departmental Organization and Management in the Government of Pakistan," *Public Administration*, Vol. 39, 1961, pp. 149-171; Report of the *Provincial Administration Commission*, Lahore, 1960; *Report of the Administrative Reorganization Committee*, Karachi, 1961, which has not been released but is summarized in the official statement of its chairman in *Dawn*, January 27, 1961, p. 4, and in G. Ahmed, "Changes in the Administrative Organization of the Government of Pakistan since 1953," *Public Administration*, Vol. 39, 1961, pp. 353-361. See also *Report of the Economy Committee*, especially Part I, Karachi, 1957, pp. 1-10, and Part III, Karachi, 1958, pp. 17-66, 74-78; M. Parnwell, *Organization and Methods in the East Pakistan Government*, Government of East Pakistan, Dacca, 1958; Sir Archibald Rowlands, *Report of the Bengal Administration Enquiry Committee 1944-45*, Government of Bengal, Alipore, 1944.

of high rank in the upper reaches of the bureaucracy of India, the acute nature of that disproportion is not generally appreciated.[5]

It is commonly said that eighty-two members of the former Indian Civil Service and Indian Political Service joined Pakistan's new equivalent service, which in 1947 was named the Pakistan Administrative Service (PAS) and renamed in 1950 the Civil Service of Pakistan (CSP).[6] While the figure eighty-two is inaccurate by about twenty per cent, no figure has meaning unless it is further refined and related to the circumstances of the early years of Pakistan. No analysis of these figures has heretofore been made and since documents and personal corroboration of events are of diminishing accessibility, it would seem appropriate to set forth in detail the sources of administrative talent available for the task of constructing the new state of Pakistan created in August 1947.

The analysis which follows is based almost entirely on a rather narrow and arbitrary definition of demonstrated and latent administrative talent. The administrative talent dealt with here is that of the elite

[5] It would serve no useful purpose in this chapter to probe into the reasons why a greater proportion of Muslims did not attain higher positions in the government of India. Muslims were not attracted to British education and hence to government service (open only via British education) until the Aligarh movement of Sir Syed Ahmed Khan in the last decades of the nineteenth century. Background studies illuminating this problem are Ram Gopal, *Indian Muslims: A Political History, 1858-1947*, Bombay, 1959; W. W. Hunter, *The Indian Musalmans*, Calcutta, 1947; S. S. Thorburn, *Mussalmans and Moneylenders in the Punjab*, London, 1886; W. H. Moreland, *The Agrarian System of Moslem India*, Cambridge, 1929; I. H. Qureshi, "The Background of Some Trends in Islamic Political Thought," Chapter 6 in Ralph Braibanti and J. J. Spengler, eds., *Tradition, Values, and Socio-Economic Development*, Durham, 1961; Mufti Intizamullah Shikabi, "Muslim System of Education under the Later Moghuls," Chapter 8, and A. R. Malick "British Educational Policy," Chapter 9, both in Vol. II, Part I, *A History of the Freedom Movement*, Karachi, 1960; S. Moinul Haq, "The Aligarh Movement: Educational," Chapter 19, and A. Hamid, "The Aligarh Movement: Political and Social," Chapter 20, both in Vol. II, Part 2, *A History of the Freedom Movement*, Karachi, 1961. See especially the 95-page dissent by Abdur Rahim to the *Report of the Royal Commission on Public Services*, Cd. 8382, London, 1917, [Islington Report,] pp. 394-488. Statistical tables in text and appendices of the Islington Report are especially valuable sources showing the number of university degrees conferred on Muslims as against other communities. Other tables show the small number of Muslims in government service. See especially pp. 496ff. Similar data for 1876-1886 can be found in the [Aitchison] *Report of the Public Service Commission 1886-7*, C. 5327, 1888, I, 78ff. See also I. H. Qureshi, *The Muslim Community of the Indo-Pakistan Subcontinent 610-1947*, The Hague, 1962.

[6] This figure is given, for example, in the *Official Report of the Debates of the Constituent Assembly of Pakistan*, Vol. I, No. 57, January 26, 1956, p. 2,104, and is quoted by Muzaffer Ahmed Chaudhuri in "Organization and Composition of the Central Civil Service in Pakistan," *International Review of Administrative Sciences*, XXVI, 1960, pp. 278-292 and by Keith Callard in *Pakistan: A Political Study*, New York, 1957, p. 289.

corps of India—the Indian Civil Service (ICS) and its companion service, the Indian Political Service (IPS). Some positions in the Audits and Accounts Service of India and the well-known Economic (Commerce) Pool are also included; a brief analysis of the provincial services of the Punjab and Bengal is also given. But the ensuing argument supporting the notion that such talent was scarce rests almost exclusively on a study of the ICS-IPS cadres. This limitation is imposed in part by the fact that the subject matter of this chapter is exclusively that of the higher bureaucracy of Pakistan (CSP), the lineal descendent of the ICS-IPS tradition. Even without this limitation, it is doubtful if a study of the transfer of other administrative talent, such as that found in the railway service, postal services, other financial services, and the provincial services, could be made in several lifetimes, so great is the magnitude of these services, so diffuse are the records, and so fragmentary the documentation for the first few years after partition. Certainly a separate study of the Audits and Accounts Service and other superior services is warranted, but such a study must be left to subsequent research. What is sought to be traced here is the transfer of high-level, generalist, managerial talent trained for the upper policy reaches of the generalist (as opposed to the finance and specialist) bureaucracy. The ICS-IPS was the acknowledged repository of this talent and administration was organized in a manner reserving key policy posts for members of these cadres. This is not to say that comparable talent was absent in other cadres in government. On the contrary, there was such other talent chafing under the restrictions and frustrations imposed by an elitist system in which there was very little parity of esteem. But it was the accepted doctrine of pre-partition India, and of Pakistan, that the destiny of the nation was to be determined, administratively at least, by a small group of carefully chosen Guardians. The allocation of managerial talents was based on this doctrine, and it must necessarily determine the pattern of analysis which follows here.

During the first quarter of 1947, the Indian Civil Service and the Indian Political Service cadres had a strength of 1,157 officers (not including Burma). Of these, 101, or 9 per cent, were Muslims. The Muslims were unevenly distributed among the provinces of India, although about half belonged to cadres in the predominantly Muslim provinces (Bengal, Punjab, Sind), all or parts of which later became incorporated into Pakistan. This does not mean that the officers belonged ethnically or culturally to the provinces to whose cadres they were assigned. The only implications which can be drawn from provincial cadre assignment are (1) that about half the officers who came to Pakistan had been assigned to other parts of India and many of these came to Pakistan as refugees with no family connections or property in Pakistan, and (2) fully one-third of the officers available were in the Punjab government and were Punjabis by birth. Since the Punjab was a predominantly Muslim province, it was inevitable that these officers would have attained high positions before partition and that they would continue in senior positions after partition. Thus the allegation that Pakistan was dominated by Punjabi officialdom in the early years of independence in partly true, but it was the inevitable consequence of historical factors and not the deliberate machination of any particular regional clique. The distribution of ICS-IPS officers by provinces is shown in Table 1 below. A few from these cadres

TABLE 1: DISTRIBUTION OF ICS-IPS OFFICERS IN INDIA IN 1947 SHOWING MUSLIM INCUMBENTS

Province	*British*	*Hindu and Others* [a]	*Muslim* [b]	*Total*
Assam	20	17	2	39
Bengal	74	75	18	167
Bihar	53	45	4	102
Bombay	62	66	5	133
Central Provinces and Berar	38	38	3	79
Madras	63	86	12	161
Northwest Frontier Province [c]	27	0	3	30
Orissa	5	9	2	16
Punjab	93	32	27	152
Sind	19	5	5	29
United Provinces	83	67	16	166
Princely States	71	8	4	83 [d]
Total	608	448	101	1,157
Total percentage	52%	39%	9%	100%

[a] Includes unknown number of Christians and Sikhs, probably not exceeding 10.

[b] Muslims are determined by name and personal knowledge, since listing of religion is not given. List was cross-checked by several senior officers now in Pakistan and is probably accurate.

[c] IPS officers.

[d] Excluding 15 British officers serving in the Persian Gulf.

Source: Compiled from *Combined Civil List for India and Burma, No. 158, Jan.-Mar. 1947,* Lahore, 1947.

served in other provinces or in the central secretariat in Delhi. When independence came in 1947, an Indian or British officer serving in the Indian Civil Service was permitted to choose one of three alternative courses for his future. First, he might opt for service either in India or Pakistan without reduction in salary or rank and without loss of retirement privileges, which included pension benefits payable in sterling. The second alternative was to leave service with a severance allowance equal to the officer's salary from 1947 to the normal retirement date (usually at age 60). The third possibility was to leave service and then re-enter by personal contract usually for a one- or two-year term, each contract negotiated separately between the officer and the government. Of the 101 Muslim ICS-IPS officers in 1947, 95 opted for service in Pakistan; the others remained in India or retired.[7] One Christian officer, now Chief Justice of Pakistan, also opted for Pakistan. Most of the British officers who served in Pakistan resigned from service and re-entered on contract. Some 50 British officers (36 ICS, 14 IPS) entered service either by option or on contract at independence. Several left after a few months service. These officers were augmented by 11 Muslim war-service candidates who were recruited under special war-service provisions. In 1943, during the Second World War, regular competitive examinations to the ICS were held in abeyance, with the understanding that veterans of outstanding qualifications who might otherwise have been eligible for the competitive ICS examinations during the years of abeyance would later be considered for the service. In October 1946 India admitted 91 such officers into the postwar Indian Administrative Service, which became the successor to the ICS. Four of the 91 war service candidates were Muslims and 3 of them opted for Pakistan. Late in 1947, after the independence of Pakistan, 8 war service candidates were admitted to the Pakistan Administrative Service on the same basis, thus making a total of 11 who entered the CSP as war service officers.[8]

The net result was that the total strength of ICS-IPS talent in Pakistan at partition was 157 officers derived from the sources summarized in Table 2. But the figure 157 has limited significance, for

[7] Computations in this part of the essay are based on comparative analysis of *Combined Civil Lists for India and Burma, Jan.-Mar. 1947, No. 156*, Lahore, 1947; *Combined Civil List for India, Pakistan, and Burma, No. 161, Jan.-Mar. 1948*, Lahore, 1948; and *Combined Civil List for Pakistan, India and Burma, No. 168, Oct.-Dec. 1949*, Parts I, II, III, Lahore, 1949. These lists have been cross-checked with the first published gradation list of the Civil Service of Pakistan printed in the form of an appendix to Cabinet Secretariat, Establishment Branch, *Letter No. 3(1)48-SE III*, Karachi, June 6, 1951. The resulting data have been checked with senior Pakistani government officials who helped establish the government of Pakistan in 1947.

[8] I am indebted for this information to Hammad Raza, Commissioner of Lahore Division, and Qaiser Ali Khan, Registrar, High Court of West Pakistan, both of whom were war service candidates.

TABLE 2: CADRE ORIGINS OF ICS-IPS ADMINISTRATIVE TALENT IN PAKISTAN AT PARTITION, 1947

Cadre	*Number*	*Percentage*
Muslim ICS	83	53.0
Indian Christian ICS [a]	1	0.6
British ICS	36	23.0
Muslim IPS	12	7.6
British IPS	14	8.8
War Service Candidates [b]	11	7.0
Total	157 [c]	100.0

[a] One Christian opted for Pakistan; one (not included in this table) entered Pakistan service later on contract.

[b] Three officers were from the Indian Administrative Service who opted for Pakistan.

[c] Of 157 officers, 15 held judicial and 6 diplomatic assignments, thus reducing the number available for administrative posts to 136.

Source: Compiled from gradation list in Cabinet Secretariat *Letter No. 3(1)/48-SE III,* Karachi, June 6, 1951 and from personal interviews.

only 136 of these officers were available for administrative service in Pakistan. Fifteen of these officers had been posted to judicial work in India and continued in such work in Pakistan; 6 were given diplomatic assignments, mostly abroad. Some of the judicial officers made outstanding contributions to the development of administration in Pakistan,[9] but they cannot be counted for purposes of this analysis as being directly involved in the practical task of managing the bureaucracy. This task devolved largely upon a small group of officers, of whom 136 were from the ICS-IPS cadre in India. The figure 136 cannot have meaning unless refined further in terms of two dimensions of the experience of these officers: (a) length of experience in government service and (b) quality of experience as revealed by assignments held before partition. Table 3 reveals that only about 25 per cent had more than 15 years experience. But nearly half of these were British officers, most of whom left during the first two years of independence. Thus, fewer than 20 officers in service during the first two years had more than 15 years experience. Half the officers had less than a decade of service. In terms of age these data can be interpolated in this way: fewer than 20 officers were more than 40 years old; half (or 60 officers) were younger than 35 years:

[9] See below, pp. 416-418.

TABLE 3: ADMINISTRATIVE EXPERIENCE IN YEARS OF 136 ICS, IPS AND WAR SERVICE OFFICERS HOLDING ADMINISTRATIVE POSTS IN CSP IN PAKISTAN IN 1947 AFTER PARTITION[a]

Years of Experience	*ICS-IPS Officers* Muslim	British	*War Service Officers*	*Total*	*%*
25-35	0	1	0	1	0.7
20-25	6	10	0	16	11.8
15-20	10	7	0	17	12.5
10-15	27	9	0	36	26.5
5-10	24	10	1	35	25.7
1-5	17	3	6	26	19.1
0-1	1	0	4	5	3.7
Total	85	40	11	136	100.0

[a] The figure 136 excludes 15 officers (5 Muslim, 1 Christian, 9 British) holding judicial posts with experience ranging from 14 to 23 years and averaging 17 years. It also excludes 6 officers (5 Muslim, 1 British) who held diplomatic assignments with experience ranging from 9 to 22 years and averaging 16 years. These 21 exclusions, added to the 136 officers considered in this table, equal numbers 1-134 in 1951 *Gradation List,* plus 23 British officers who left service from 1947 to 1951.

Sources: Gradation Lists of CSP, 1951, 1952; interviews; corresposdence.

The quality of experience which the 136 officers brought with them is shown by Table 4. Only 8 officers held positions in the secretariat of the government of India and only 3 of these held the rank of Joint Secretary (Mian Aminuddin and M. Ikramullah in the Ministry of Commerce; Iskander Mirza in the Ministry of Defense). Although this was the third highest secretariat rank, it was a high position for a non-British officer, as is indicated by the fact that only 3 Hindu ICS officers held full secretaryships and approximately 3 Hindus were additional secretaries in India in 1947. Considering the small proportion of Muslims in the total ICS cadre, therefore, Joint Secretary was a high position. Fewer than 30 per cent had positions of policy-making responsibility in the provincial governments, and only some 10 of these were positions in the secretariats proper; the remainder were in attached operating departments. About 56 per cent of the officers had experience below that of provincial administration.

To this analysis there must be added the role of the 50 British officers who entered Pakistan service from the ICS and IPS on contract. Much has been said of the impact of the British in these formative years of Pakistan's administrative history, probably because the statistical contrast between India and Pakistan in this regard is striking. The evidence reveals clearly that at the very outset in 1947, about 28 per cent of the ICS-IPS administrative talent effectively available for administrative

TABLE 4: QUALITATIVE EXPERIENCE OF 136 ICS-IPS AND WAR SERVICE OFFICERS IN INDIA PRIOR TO JOINING CSP IN 1947[a]

Highest Position Held in India[b]	*ICS-IPS Officers* Muslim	British	*War Service Officers*	*Total*	*%*
GOVERNMENT OF INDIA					
Secretary	0	0	0	0	0
Additional Secretary	0	3	0	3	2.2
Joint Secretary	3	4	0	7	5.1
Deputy Secretary	4	0	0	4	2.9
Private Secretary	1	0	0	1	0.7
PROVINCIAL GOVERNMENT					
Chief Secretary	1	1	0	2	1.5
Secretary	6	0	0	6	4.4
Additional Secretary	6	0	0	6	4.4
Joint Secretary	5	0	0	5	3.7
Deputy Secretary	8	1	0	9	6.6
Additional Deputy Secretary	2	0	0	2	1.4
Under Secretary	3	1	0	4	2.9
Director of Department	10	3	0	13	9.6
Commissioner	11	2	0	13	9.6
Deputy Commissioner	18	6	0	24	17.7
Assistant Commissioner	12	4	0	16	11.8
MISCELLANEOUS					
Judge	0	4	0	4	2.9
Military Officer[c]	0	0	11	11	8.1
Unknown	1	5	0	6	4.4
Total	91	34	11	136	100.0

[a] The figure 136 excludes 15 officers (5 Muslim, 1 Christian, 9 British) holding judicial posts with experience ranging from 14 to 23 years and averaging 17 years. It also excludes 6 officers (5 Muslim, 1 British) who held diplomatic assignments, with experience ranging from 9 to 22 years and averaging 16 years. These 21 exclusions, added to the 136 officers considered in this table, equal numbers 1-134 in 1951 *Gradation List* plus 23 British officers who left service from 1947 to 1951.

[b] Wide variation in types of positions has been rendered into equivalent ranks listed in this table.

[c] Ranks of war service officers were 1 major, 6 captains, 1 navy lieutenant, 3 navy sub-lieutenants. All were university graduates.

Sources: Combined Civil Lists for India and Burma Jan.-Mar. 1947, No. 156 (Lahore, 1947); interviews; correspondence.

work in Pakistan was British, as Table 5 shows, but the ratio changed sharply in Pakistan because of attrition in the number of British officers after 1950 and because of increase in the CSP cadre.

It can be said with certainty that while British officials held key posts for the first few months after independence was achieved in August 1947, their influence diminished steadily after the first year and sharply after 1950. For two years after partition the governors of Bengal, the Northwest Frontier, the Punjab, and the Chief Commissioner in Baluchistan were British officers. Of the five provinces, only Sind had

TABLE 5: ROLE OF BRITISH ICS-IPS OFFICERS IN EARLY ADMINISTRATION OF PAKISTAN

Year	*Adjusted Number of Officers* [a]	*Adjusted Cadre Strength* [b]	*Per Cent*	*Year*	*Adjusted Number of Officers*	*Adjusted Cadre Strength*	*Per Cent*
1947 [c]	44	153	28.7	1955	12	220	5.4
1948	44	153	28.7	1956	12	220	5.4
1949	27	156	17.2	1957	11	240	4.5
1950	No data			1958	8	258	3.0
1951	20	149	13.4	1959	8	275	2.9
1952	19	172	11.0	1960	7	279	2.5
1953	21	180	11.6	1961	7	298	2.6
1954	13	212	6.1	1962	3	296	1.0

[a] These figures, modified to show only effective administrative strength, do not include those assigned to judicial work (averaging 5 each year for 1947, 1948, 1949 and 2 each year thereafter) or those on leave preparatory to retirement (averaging 2 each year).

[b] These figures show only effective administrative strength rather than total strength. They do not include officers assigned to judicial work, on leave preparatory to retirement, or on probationary training at the Civil Service Academy, abroad or as assistant commissioners. These exclusions average about 35 each year.

[c] Figures for 1947, 1948, 1949 are estimates based on cross-checking of several sources. Figures for 1947 and 1948 based on *The Combined Civil List for India, Pakistan and Burma, No. 161, Jan.-Mar. 1948,* Lahore, 1948. The figures for 1948 are also used for 1947, on the assumption that they were probably compiled in October or November in 1947 and are as valid or perhaps more valid for that year than for 1948. Figures for 1949 based on *The Combined Civil List for Pakistan, India, and Burma, No. 168, Oct.-Dec. 1949,* Parts I, II, III, Lahore, 1949. Neither of these civil lists has a comforting degree of reliability; cadre designations are often lacking, and the arrangement and accuracy of data reflect the administrative disarticulation consequent to partition. Although these data have been cross-checked by interviews, 5 per cent margin of error is estimated.

For 1951 on, published gradation lists have been used and the reliability of data is much greater.

Sources: Compiled from annual *Gradation Lists* of the Civil Service of Pakistan except as indicated in note c above.

a Muslim governor at the outset, and for two years his chief secretary was a British officer. Two crucial positions in the central government (Secretary of Finance and Secretary of Food and Agriculture) were held by British officers for two years, and for one year a British officer was Secretary of Evacuation and Rehabilitation. Some 10 other officers were full or deputy secretaries in provincial governments for about two years.

Quite apart from the ICS-IPS cadres here considered, British influence was otherwise important during the first year. The mint, railways, post and telegraphs, and defense forces were under the direction of British officers for a year or more. Moreover, some 50 British officers of other cadres and of middle rank remained for one or two years.

The British ICS-IPS contribution was more of a stabilizing influence, a holding action, than a long, sustained influence in government policy. There were two possible exceptions to this generalization. The first was the Establishment Division, to which British officers were assigned almost continuously from 1947 to 1961. T. Creagh-Coen and later Sir Eric Franklin served as Establishment secretaries from 1947 to 1958. British incumbency was interrupted by a brief period in 1959 when A. R. Khan was secretary, but was resumed in 1960 by the appointment of J.D. Hardy, who continued in that post until his resignation in 1961, when he was succeeded by G. Mueenud din. Even during A. R. Khan's tenure, Hardy served as his joint secretary. It was the Eastablishment Division which dealt with three important activities relating to administration: (1) administrative reorganization through an organization and methods unit, (2) service rules, composition, and training of the CSP cadre, and (3) personnel matters for the CSP, such as postings, promotions, and decorations. In all of these activities British officers were in direct charge and reported to the Establishment secretary, who was also, except in 1959, a British officer. This is the only instance in the administrative history of Pakistan that two echelons of British officers worked together in the same unit over a period of several years. From 1952 to 1958 the O and M unit was the responsibility of A. W. Redpath, a British officer of the Indian Political Service. The Civil Service Academy in Lahore, citadel of the elite corps of the orthodox bureaucracy, was headed by a British ICS officer, Geoffrey Burgess, from 1951 to 1960. Many of the early reorganization reports from 1947 to 1953 were made under the aegis of British officers. The first Reorganization Committee which dealt with secretariat requirements for the new central government and which made its report on September 15, 1947 was headed by Sir Victor Turner. Sir Jeremy Raisman prepared the report, *Financial Enquiry Regarding Allocation of Revenues Bewteen Central and Provincial Governments*, submitted December 3, 1951. K. S. Jeffries in 1952 wrote the survey *Development of Organization and Methods Work*, and Terence B. Creagh-Coen was chairman of the first Administrative Enquiry Committee which reported in June 1953.

It is true that during the first decade the pattern of administrative reform and the orientation of the civil service of Pakistan was British. The pace of change cannot be said to have been highly accelerated until the influence of the Planning Board and martial law began to be felt in 1958. The structure of the CSP remained more elitist than did its counterpart in India, the IAS.[10] The mode of entry was essentially the same as that established in the ICS tradition—namely by competitive examination taken by men between 21 and 24 years of age. There was no large-scale lateral entry until 1952 and 1960, and even then officers so recruited did not account for more than 5 per cent of the total cadre strength. Training at the Civil Service Academy followed the British pattern. The 1949 batch received training in Australia, and from 1951 to 1960 all probationers in the CSP spent one year at Oxford or Cambridge following a year at the Civil Service Academy in Lahore. Both the Australian and British foreign training were under Colombo Plan auspices. This training, combined with the fact that all the 125 (excluding 11 wartime recruits) officers who came from the ICS-IPS had been trained in England, gave a British cast to the system. In 1960, when British foreign training was ended, all but one officer of the total cadre strength of 332 had received advanced training in England or in a Commonwealth country.

British values and concepts espoused by the CSP cadre and especially in the Establishment Division were frustrating to administrative reform efforts which began, as early as 1953, to be introduced, somewhat unsuccessfully, with assistance from the United States.[11] It was commonly thought by Americans involved in the program that continued British influence was delaying effective administrative reform. This may not have been a fair assessment and probably derived from

[10] For analysis of change in the IAS, see Ralph Braibanti, "Reflections on Bureaucratic Reform in India," in Braibanti and J. J. Spengler, eds., *Administration and Economic Development in India*, Durham, 1963.

[11] The Ford Foundation engaged Professor Rowland Egger to prepare a general report on administration which was completed in November 1953. See Rowland Egger, *The Improvement of Public Administration in Pakistan*, Karachi, 1953, and a subsequently published portion of the report under the title "Ministerial and Departmental Organization and Management in the Government of Pakistan," *Public Administration*, Summer 1961, pp. 149-171. In May 1955 Bernard L. Gladieux, also under Ford Foundation auspices, submitted his report, *Reorientation of Pakistan Government for National Development* to the Planning Board. The Ford Foundation contracted with Harvard University to provide an advisory group for the Planning Board, and that activity got underway in 1955. In April 1955 the United States International Cooperation Administration contracted with the University of Pennsylvania to establish an Institute of Business and Public Administration. These efforts at administrative reform were not received with enthusiasm or even respect by the hard core of the orthodox bureaucracy; indeed in some instances there was hostility to foreign suggestions. An exception was the work of the advisory group to the Planning Board, but, even here, the proposals relating to administration of the Board's First Five Year Plan were not given much attention until the advent of martial law in 1958.

the essential incompatibility of the mechanistic, egalitarian bais of American public administration and the classical, elitist concept rooted in the ICS. Officials trained in the ICS tradition, whether British or not, knew the best days of one of the greatest administrative systems of all times—the Indian Civil Service—and their pride and confidence in that system was justifiably great. They were confronted by the brash, anti-intellectual bias of American public administration, more closely allied with the philistinism of commerce than with the ethos of platonic guardianship. The American influence showed neither understanding nor respect for the splendor of the ICS accomplishments. It was impatient with history, contemptuous of the concept of an elite corps, opposed to the pragmatic pace of change which had been the hallmark of British administration, and indissolubly wedded to doctrinaire notions of a scientific administration of spatial and temporal universal validity.

Though it is too early to judge with certainty, it is not improbable that British influence in forestalling this kind of administrative change was of some importance in this respect. But at best this is conjecture, for the Establishment Division was not the ultimate source of authority in these matters. It was part of the cabinet secretariat and later of the President's secretariat. As such it was responsible to the officer of highest position in the bureaucracy, the secretary-general, who, after 1952 was designated as secretary to the cabinet. This post was usually held by a senior Pakistani ICS officer of considerable ability and strength of views. An important factor in conditioning the status of the post of secretary-general was its incumbency from independence in 1947 until 1950 by Chauduri Mohamad Ali, a brilliant administrator who also served as cabinet secretary. When Mohamad Ali became prime minister, the senior officer of the cabinet secretariat was Agha Abdul Hamid, who served also as private secretary to the prime minister. Thus the power and prestige of the prime minister was directly felt in the cabinet secretariat. For much of this period the British Establishment's Officer was a joint secretary. These two factors circumscribed the degree of his independent discretionary power. Osman Ali, Aziz Ahmed, Agha Abdul Hamid, S. M. Yusuf, and N. A. Faruqi, all of whom held the post of cabinet secretary, were officers very highly regarded in government. Even though in some cases their position on the *Gradation List* was lower than that of other secretariat officers and in some cases their rank was that of joint secretary rather than full secretary, their influence was significant. The nature of the interaction of influence of the prime minister and cabinet secretary with the views of their British subordinates cannot be clearly established nor can the influence of the cabinet and the president. It is noteworthy that British officers were not alone in espousing the cause of an elitist cadre and conservative, gradual administrative reforms. This disposition was shared generally by Pakistani members of the ICS, who were educated at Oxford and Cambridge and who shared these values with equal and sometimes even greater conviction. Even in the case of the Civil Service Academy, which for nine years was headed by a British officer, the first two directors during the first four formative years of its development were senior Pakistani officers of considerable distinction, G. Mueenuddin and A. K. Malik. Moreover, when administrative reform was accelerated and the direction of administrative training modified in 1960 the Establishment secretary was a British ICS officer. These changes occurred under martial law and when the availability of technical assistance from the United States was greater. All of these important variables whose relative influence cannot be determined make it impossible to reach definite conclusions as to the extent of British influence on administrative matters during the first decade of Pakistan's development.

Whatever may have been the sources which continued to mold Pakistan's higher bureaucracy in a British pattern, it would be hazardous to conclude that such emphasis was detrimental to the nation. It should not appear unnatural, and may even be desirable, that in the midst of serious political instability the one stable sector, the bureaucracy, should not experiment with radical change which might unpredictably spell disaster for the nation. Adherence to values which were known and cherished might well have been the means by which the nation was able to maintain its existence rather than the reason why it did not make greater strides in political development. The British ICS officers who remained in work closely connected with service matters represented a British tradition of dedicated, responsible service to the nation. These qualities and such personal characteristics as punctuality, discipline, and integrity could not have had an adverse effect in so strategic a place as the Establishment Division, whose moral tone is felt throughout the bureaucracy.

The impact of British officers in the Ministry of Law cannot be discussed at length here since the work of that ministry was only incidentally concerned with administration. Sir Edward Snelson was joint secretary of law under Akbar Husain from 1947 until he became secretary in 1951. He remained in that position until his resignation in 1961,[12] establishing the record for the longest continuous tenure held by a British officer in Pakistan. It should be noted in passing that in one matter, however, the Law Ministry was deeply involved. It advised the government in litigation brought by civil servants through the instrument of the writ petition. The views of Sir Edward Snelson were probably of importance and his opinion that the courts were disturbing the discipline of bureaucracy may also have been the view of the central government. It is not without interest that his expression of views on the writ jurisdiction led to his ultimate sentencing for contempt of high court which was followed by his resignation in 1961.

In the judiciary itself there were always some British officers serving in the courts as judges, registrar, or legal remembrancer. The number of such judicial appointments was as high as 9 in 1947 and dropped to 2 (Sir G. B. Constantine and J. Ortcheson) in 1961. This was small representation in the total judicial body of 42 supreme and high court judges.

It is probably not inaccurate to conclude that the influence of British officers in dealing with policy over a period of several years was primarily in molding the structure and attitudes of the higher bureaucracy and in directing the pattern of administrative reform. Whatever this influence may have been, it disappeared in 1962 with the departure of all British officers except two high court judges, one contract officer with the Lahore Improvement Trust and one officer who had some years previously become a Muslim.

The role of both British and Muslim officers of the Indian Political Service[13] during the first three years in the formation of the nation also merits discussion. Two-thirds of the members of the Indian Political Service were drawn from the Indian army and one-third from the Indian Civil Service. The IPS, regarded by many as a super-elite made up of the "picked of picked men," served in the princely states and in frontier areas. The work of the IPS was less bureaucratic in an orthodox sense than that of the ICS. It combined diplomacy, intelligence work, a good deal of adventure, and, in the frontier, a rather vigorous outdoor life. Its members were, therefore, of a different temperament and outlook from the ICS. Two of the best-known members

[12] See pp. 425-427 below for analysis of the case of Sir Edward Snelson.

[13] See an account of the Indian Political Service in Philip Woodruff, *The Guardians*, New York, 1954, pp. 270-272, 293-296.

of the IPS who came to Pakistan were Lt. Col. Iskander Mirza, the first Sandhurst-trained non-British officer to pass into the Political Service and who later became president of Pakistan, and Lt. Col. A. S. B. Shah, now chairman of the Federal Public Service Commission. Of the 26, 15 held military rank. The administrative experience of the 26 officers ranged from 22 years to 3 years; 12 had more than 10 years in service. Since the work of the IPS in India involved tasks closely related to the conduct of foreign affairs, it did not appear unnatural that many of these officers were assigned to foreign relations posts. By 1951, 6 held diplomatic or foreign affairs assignments and 4 were political agents to frontier regions. The remaining officers were scattered in relatively important posts, such as defense secretary, establishments secretary, and provincial chief secretary. It can be said that the IPS officers held significant policy posts probably disproportionate to their numerical strength but that their principal influence was felt in foreign affairs. On the other hand, the influence of IPS officers as a group became rather quickly dispersed and diminished for various reasons. By 1959, only 7 of the original 1947 group remained in government service; 2 of these were in the diplomatic service, 1 was chairman of the Federal Public Service Commission. Thus only 4 remained within the CSP, occupying administrative posts. There were no special reasons for this relatively rapid diminution of IPS influence. Five of the officers were British and they departed from the service somewhat sooner than British ICS officers; Iskander Mirza became President of Pakistan; Lt. Col. A. S. B. Shah joined the Public Service Commission; the severance of the other officers from the service appears to have been uneventful. It thus appears statistically evident that the allegation that Pakistan's administration came under unusual military influence from the earliest days of independence cannot be corroborated.

To complete this analysis of the quality of experience of the 136 officers available for administrative service in Pakistan in 1947, brief comment on the 11 war service officers must be made. They were all university graduates from either Punjab, Lucknow, or Allahabad universities. Four had masters' degrees and 2 had degrees in law. Six served as army captains, 1 as a major, 3 as sub-lieutenants, and 1 as a lieutenant in the navy. At the time of partition the ages of these officers ranged from 24 to 31 years, with the average being 27 years. They did not, therefore, have civil administrative experience and had an average of only four years military experience.

No analysis of administrative talent available to Pakistan in 1947 would be either complete or fair without mention of the distinguished role played by 5 or 6 officers of the Audits and Accounts Service of India, the elite corps of finance administrators. Their contribution to administration in the crucial days of organizing the nation was far greater than their number suggests. Their distinguished work is corroboration of the observation that managerial skill was not limited to the ICS-IPS cadres alone. It is generally conceded by senior administrators who established Pakistan's administration that the leadership of Chaudury Mohamad Ali, a distinguished officer of the Audits and Accounts Service who had attained the high rank of Financial Adviser in the Military Finance Department of India, was significant in establishing the government. His role as secretary-general and cabinet secretary has already been discussed. As chairman of the Pakistan Industrial Credit and Investment Corporation he continues to play an important role in the nation's development.[14] Ghulam Mohammad, who was also a finance officer in India, served in Pakistan later as finance minister and as governor-general. Mumtaz Hasan and A. A. Burney had served as deputy secretaries in the Commerce Department of India, and played a leading role in establishing the fiscal system of Pakistan, as did S. A. Hasnie, who was joint secretary in the supply department of India. M. A. Mozaffer, of the Audits and Accounts Service, is the only government officer in Pakistan to have served on as many as five different administrative reform groups ranging from the time of partition to the end of martial law in 1962. These were the Turner Committee (1947), the first Pay Commission (1948), the Economy Committee (1958), the Provincial Reorganization Commission (1960), and the second Pay Commission which reported in June 1962. A few other officers in other services had high-level experience. G. Ahmed was deputy director of the intelligence bureau of the government of India and Qurban Ali Khan was director of anticorruption in the police service of India. The former was chairman of Pakistan's planning board for many years as well as chairman of the Commission on Administrative Reorganization. The latter played an important role in administering Pakistan's police service. The number of officers of such administrative experience outside the ICS-IPS cadre is placed for purposes of this analysis at ten. By their inclusion, the number of executives of high-level experience available to Pakistan may at this point be said to be about 146 irrespective of cadre.

[14] See p. 313 above and p. 340 below.

The same shortage of managerial talent available to Pakistan from the elite cadres of the ICS and IPS also characterized the supply of executives in the provincial civil services (PCS). In all the provinces the number of Muslims in those services was disproportionate to the Muslim component of the population. One index of Muslim representation is the composition of provincial civil service cadres. These cadres supplied some of the officers for the provincial secretariats and for local government in the districts. In the executive branch of the Punjab provincial service, for example, in 1947 there was a total cadre of 342 of whom 134, or 39 per cent, were Muslims. The approximate Muslim percentage of PCS strength in Bengal was 30 per cent; in the Sind it was 21 per cent.[15] Records are not available for determining the Muslim strength of other provincial cadres, but it is reasonable to assume that it was considerably less than in predominantly Muslim provinces. An indication of the level of experience of Muslim PCS officers in provincial secretariats is revealed by examination of the civil list postings. Table 6 shows only ranks above that of assistant secretary, since only such ranks are really important policy-making posts which provide experience in complex administration.

TABLE 6: STRENGTH OF PROVINCIAL CIVIL SERVICES IN PROVINCIAL SECRETARIATS IN INDIA IN 1947 SHOWING MUSLIM INCUMBENTS

Province	*Total Number Secretariat Posts* [a]	*Number of Muslim Incumbents* [b]
Assam	16	1
Bengal	55	6
Bihar	33	4
Bombay	30	1
Central Provinces and Berar	24	1
Madras	20	0
Northwest Frontier Province	15	2
Orissa	18	0
Punjab	40	0
Sind	12	1
United Provinces	62	6
Total	325	22 (or 7% of total)

[a] Only posts above the rank of assistant secretary are counted. Posts held by ICS or other control service cadres not included.

[b] Muslims were determined by name since there is no official listing of religion. This method is not completely accurate, but the error is probably not more than 1%.

Source: Compiled from *Combined Civil List for India and Burma, No. 158, Jan.-Mar.* 1947, Lahore, 1947.

[15] Computed (from study of names only) from *Punjab Civil List*, Lahore, 1947, Part III, pp. 15 to 26a; *Sind Civil List*, Karachi, 1947; and *Bengal Civil List No. 282*, Alipore, 1947.

There are no records accessible to show how many of the 22 Muslim secretariat officers above the rank of assistant secretary chose to serve in Pakistan. Estimates vary greatly, but a calculation that about 75 per cent or 15 officers probably joined the provincial services in Pakistan would seem not unreasonable. In the absence of precise records, there is another means of estimating the strength of provincial civil service talent available to Pakistan; i.e., the estimates of the Committee on Services and Records of the Punjab Partition Committee.[16] The committee set the needs of West Punjab for provincial officers of the executive branch at 196, but only 159 were available for service in Pakistan. The committee figures include PCS officers assigned to local government as well as to the provincial secretariat. A similar imbalance existed in the judicial branch of the provincial service; 85 was the strength, but only 58 officers were available. The evidence available seems to indicate that the provincial civil services of Sind, Bengal, Baluchistan, Punjab, and the Northwest Frontier provided few officers of high level secretariat training. PCS officers meeting this description probably did not exceed 15 in number.

If these data are integrated into generalizations which illuminate the dire shortage of administrative skill at the disposal of Pakistan in creating a completely new state and government, the following observations might be made. For the first several years of its existence Pakistan had available for administrative tasks no more than 136 officers recruited in India and destined there for high-level positions. Of these no more than 15 had experience in central secretariat work, an additional 30 had comparable experience in provincial secretariats, and about 20 more held other positions of high-level responsibility. Half of these 136 officers had less than 10 years experience and were under 35 years of age. About one quarter of the more experienced officers of 136 of ICS-IPS origin were British, most of whom left the service of Pakistan by 1958 and most of whom had substantial impact on the administrative system only during the first three or four years of Pakistan's history. Eleven of the officers were wartime recruits who had no administrative training whatever except in the military services. Five or 6 officers of the Indian Audits and Accounts Service and the police service played crucial roles in establishing the administrative system. The role of military officers does not appear to have been

[16] *Reports of Expert Committees in Connection with the Partition of the Punjab Province*, Lahore, Superintendent, Government Printing, 1947. See especially reports on skeleton cadres. These committees were made up of an equal number of Hindu and Muslim members, and the degree of reliability of the statistical data they used is very high.

crucial. The IPS officers played a greater role in diplomatic assignments than in internal administration. The shortage of talent is indicated by the fact that a large number of officers in the ICS-IPS and Audits and Accounts cadres assumed non-cadre posts as governor, minister, and even president. A hard core of posts in secretariat administration in crucial although unspectacular ministries and departments was filled by ICS officers who had similar experience in India. Experienced executive talent in the provincial services was equally scarce. Approximately 74 positions above the rank of assistant secretary had to be filled in the provincial secretariats of Pakistan, but only 22 Muslim provincial service officers had held such posts before, and it is doubtful if more than three quarters of them were actually available to Pakistan.[17] These facts speak more effectively than explanation. Most developing states have faced the trauma of independence with acute shortage of administrative skill, but at least most states had inherited a national entity which merely changed its status from colony to sovereign nation. Pakistan had to create *de novo* a state from two culturally disparate, physically separate, strife-torn areas. The odds against success were enormous. To have constructed a nation for several years with about 50 experienced government officials of reasonable maturity in policy-making positions is a singular tribute to both the British administrative heritage and Muslim perseverance.

The physical problems faced by this small group of officers were formidable. Although plans were formulated for the division of assets, records, and office equipment in a series of meetings starting in July 1947, few of these decisions were implemented. Whatever records and office equipment may have been sent from Delhi were lost in the burning and destruction of trains which accompanied independence. Thus the central government had to be organized with no records or office equipment, and had to be housed in miscellaneous buildings scattered throughout Karachi. The destruction of crucial personnel records made it necessary in many instances to rely on memory in establishing seniority. The provincial governments of West Pakistan were in somewhat better condition, for their physical properties were undisturbed. The provincial government of East Pakistan, on the other hand, had to develop a new provincial capital and secretariat in Dacca. Some of the records and secretariat library which had been in the Bengal summer capital at Darjeeling were ultimately sent to Dacca.

[17] *Agendas of the Meetings of the Punjab Partition Committee from 1st July to 11th August 1947*, Lahore, 1947, p. 68.

The vision of creating a new state based on a common religion and unquestioned devotion to the Quaid-i-Azam and the Quaid-i-Millat provided a remarkable strength and zeal which for two or three years seemed to make up for the more mundane problem of scarcity of experienced executives. But the diminution of this enthusiasm was not quickly enough supplanted by the strength of a highly rational bureaucratic organization; consequently, the corrosive effect of internal stresses was revealed. In retrospect, it is probably wise that Pakistan continued its identification with the British system of administration, for this resulted in reinvigoration of the transplanted ideas and structures of bureaucracy by contact with their source. Continued identity with such wellsprings is an important factor in maintaining the pristine vigor of externally introduced ideas. During the decade after partition, the inner ICS-oriented bureaucracy reassembled, consolidated, and enlarged its forces. It reasserted its traditional dominance in key policy-making positions at all levels of government and by so doing its permeative power as a transmitter of values throughout the total bureaucracy was thereby strengthened. It drew on the sources of its tradition. A civil service academy was organized at Lahore in 1948 and approximately 25 probationers selected by competitive examination were admitted each year for one year of training after which (until 1959) they spent a year at Oxford or Cambridge. By 1955, the CSP cadre reached a total strength of 270, of whom about 220 officers were available for administrative work.[18] Of this group, about 114 officers (in 1955) had been members of the ICS with a background of education at Oxford or Cambridge or another British university. By 1962 although the total cadre was 368, of whom about 258 were available for administrative work, the number of ICS officers was 88, or 20 per cent of the total cadre. This was a remarkably small percentage, and the CSP cadre was but a small segment of the total bureaucracy, which by 1962 approximated a third of a million persons in a population of 93 million.[19]

Yet the recruits taken into the service from 1948 onward could not strengthen the inner core to the extent suggested by statistics. The universities which they attended, reeling under the impact of parti-

[18] Figures based on gradation lists for the years shown. Probationers, officers training abroad and on judicial and diplomatic assignments are counted as unavailable for administrative work.

[19] Computation of a more precise figure is deliberately avoided at this point. With existing data, precision is almost impossible. M. Ahmed Chauduri's (see note 1 above) estimate is 286,000, but it is not known whether this includes district revenue staff.

tion and the loss of faculty, were on the verge of breakdown. Social values and bureaucratic values were in upheaval and neither the year at the Civil Service Academy nor a year of casual non-degree work in England could provide the discipline, knowledge, and sense of order which the older ICS possessed. The most important bulwark of ICS training—meticulous field training under an able deputy commissioner—collapsed under the pressure of greater urgencies.

The fact that between 100-200 key administrators of high rank and firm training formed the pivotal group which weathered the stormy transition to independence is of immense significance in understanding the relationship of bureaucracy and courts. It was this small group which was the source through which the values of the bureaucracy, regnant under the British *Raj*, were transmitted into the administrative system built by Pakistan. Breadth of view, perspective, imagination which could transcend the otherwise restrictive influences of regulations, sustained contact with high levels of government in which British influence had been dominant: these were qualities possessed by only a handful of officers. These officials had been carefully selected and had received probationary training at British universities. In intellect and training they reflected a high degree of objectivity and detachment. Trained for, and in some cases experienced in, the management of complex affairs, this small group constituted the source from which radiated the rational administrative skill of the venerable Indian Civil Service. But the task of permeating the new bureaucracy of Pakistan with such values was too great, the external pressures and demands almost overwhelming. The totality of bureaucratic behavior was separated, as it had been under the British *Raj*, into two spheres of validity in which different value systems operated concurrently. The smaller sphere was that of a disciplined, rationally disposed ICS tradition deriving its strength primarily from the cadre of about 200 men and secondarily from a larger group embracing the whole CSP cadre and others, forming a nucleus of 500-600 men. Within this sphere, the comprehension of order, intellectuality, system, law, objectivity, and rational analysis was of a high order. A second sphere consisted of Class I gazetted officers of various cadres and origins numbering some

My figure is arrived at by computing figures in *Demands for Grants (Final) Budget of the Government of Pakistan, March 31, 1959*, Karachi, 1959 and the 1960 civil lists for West Pakistan and East Pakistan, and by adding 500 persons for each district to include district revenue staff not listed elsewhere. This results in a total of 330,000.

5,000 men in 1962. Within this sphere, competence, knowledge of rules, sense of order and discipline were sometimes high, but in general these qualities had permeated less thoroughly than in the first group. This description of the first and second spheres is an artificial and somewhat misleading abstraction, for in reality some members of the second sphere possessed these qualities to a greater degree than members of the first sphere. The third and larger sphere was that of the remainder of the bureaucracy, embracing perhaps as many as a third of a million persons, among whom the values of an impersonal, rational bureaucratic system had unevenly and only marginally permeated. This large sphere drew its strength, inspiration, and values from the vernacular society of which it was an integral part but which had been disordered by partition. The larger and smaller spheres of validity were in a continuous state of interaction, the influence of each changing the contours of the other, but neither superseding its rival sphere. The permeative dynamism of the smaller sphere was great enough to preserve its identity and to affect profoundly the larger sphere. But it was in turn unable to mold attitudes and behavior sufficiently to permit internal order and satisfaction to prevail without recourse to external help.

III. Social Environment of Bureaucracy

The truism that bureaucracy, like any institution, is a reflection of the larger society of which it is a part is certainly not disproved by developments in Pakistan. In the ensuing analysis there is an effort to recreate the atmosphere in which the business of administration was conducted, and which was but a microcosmic view of national life. There is no detailed discussion of the functions of the system or changes that were made after partition. This is an attempt to systematize what probably cannot be systematized, to suggest a mood, to draw together certain amorphous qualities which, acting in concert, contributed to the rise of the role of the judiciary. To abstract such causes is to invite disagreement as to their relative importance and the pattern of their interaction. Nevertheless, some effort, however crude, must be made at this point to describe the social environment of administration if the role of the judiciary in the question of the writ petition is to be generally understood. Many of the circumstances described below are undergoing major change. Certainly, procedures and systems are being modernized rapidly; hence behavioral change may be expected to follow. Nevertheless, the description here given is not invalid, at least for West Pakistan, for the decade following partition during which the circumstances giving rise to the use of the writ petition were found.[20] The description which follows is not meant to imply that every court case seeking remedy of an employee's grievance can be traced directly to one of the situations described. On the contrary, many of these situations did not directly result in litigation. But the sum of the situations described did create an environment inimical to harmonious, non-litigious settlement of employee grievances.

(1) The fundamental determinant of social environment in the bureaucracy was a simple adverse Malthusian ratio: the supply of poorly trained, unsuitable manpower seeking employment far exceeded the work which government had been able to organize for itself. Government service was the principal employer and such service, particularly at the lower levels, afforded a semblance of marginal security. Since the wages were often below subsistence, government service at such levels served the purpose of a welfare-relief mechanism. Since alternative means of employment at all levels were almost non-existent, there was no competition between government and other activities for human services. Hence the impact of competition—which would normally compel the public bureaucracy to improve its conditions of work to retain its employees—was totally absent, and the system was deprived of the chastening and rectifying effects of vigorous competition.

(2) The second overriding determinant is the violent disturbance in the accepted patterns of security, tenure of post, assignments, and promotions. This disturbance had already been generated by the Second

[20] There is no careful description of the social environment of bureaucracy in Pakistan. This analysis is based on the writer's impressions over a five-year period, on study of several hundred writ petition cases, a few of which are mentioned in this chapter, and on extensive interviews and observation. Suggestions of the social climate can also be found in the growing body of critical literature by experienced Pakistani administrators. See, for example, papers by Masih-uz-Zaman and Raja Muhammad Afzal in a report of a government sponsored seminar, *The Expanding Role of the Public Servant in Pakistan's Democratic Structure*, Lahore, 1960; speeches of Raja Muhammad Afzal in Muhammad S. Sajid, compiler, *Images and Goals*, Peshawar, n.d.; National Assembly of Pakistan, *Parliamentary Debates, Official Report*, February 15, 1957, pp. 427ff.; address by Raja Muhammad Afzal at Academy For Village Development, Peshawar, December 30, 1961, mimeo.; "Presidential Address" by Dr. I. H. Usmani, CSP, at the inauguration of the CENTO Scientific Symposium, Lahore, January 8, 1962, mimeo.; Al Hamza, "Constitutional Success an Arduous Goal," *Pakistan Times*, Supplement of March 23, 1962, p. 1. See also Ralph Braibanti, "Reflections on Bureaucratic Corruption," *Public Administration*, Vol. 40 (Winter, 1962), pp. 357-372.

World War as early as 1943 in India when recruitment to the ICS was stopped. There was no chance to recover from the serious dislocation of personnel and postings consequent to this and to the termination of hostilities. War's end in 1945 was followed by preparations for independence, by the trauma of partition in 1947, and by a decade of turbulent politics. The results were manifold. The most important was the perceptible deterioration in morale and a sense of security after the high enthusiasm and dedication of the first two or three years vanished. This particularly affected the CSP cadre, who became the scapegoats for a bewildered public and for politicians. While members of the cadre could not be removed, their confidence and security were shaken in a variety of subtle ways which every bureaucracy has at its command as sanctional devices. First would be transfer for having offended a politician. Transfer could be to a less desirable post or it could be so frequent as to nearly ruin the personal finances of an officer. For example, three transfers in two years involving nearly a thousand miles each time would have a devastating effect. The reimbursement for movement of household effects of a mature officer with an established family never equalled the actual costs. Hidden costs such as enrollment of children in new schools which necessitated purchase of new books increased the financial burden. In later years, retirement at the request of the government was also a serious blow to morale. Normal retirement was at sixty years of age or after thirty-five years service, but government could request retirement at fifty or fifty-five years of age. The family pattern was such that most officers at that age had children in school or college, and retirement in advance with no alternative means of employment meant acute hardship during years when it could be least sustained. While not many compulsory retirements occurred, there were enough to shake the confidence and hence the crucial sense of independence of many officers. This uncertainty of tenure and post created an atmosphere in which equivocation, delay, and avoidance of courageous decision became the safest behavior.

Government officials, particularly the ICS and new CSP officers, were publicly denounced by politicians as being responsible for almost whatever complaint the public had registered and they were excoriated by the people for being too aloof and too British in their ways. They became the scapegoats for all the distresses of Pakistan. Whatever rational personnel system had been inherited from the British was now assaulted by the demands for patronage by politicians. The organization of society into factions, each with a direct channel to various combinations of politicians, brought all sorts of demands. To adhere to known canons of promotion and efficiency would bring accusations of communal or caste favoritism by employees adversely affected. This would reach the politician, who might then have the officer transferred. Under such circumstances it was nearly impossible to preserve an orderly bureaucratic mechanism.

In superior service cadres, like that of the CSP, unusually rapid promotion created problems of uncertainty and instability. In the ICS before partition, long and careful training in all aspects of administrative work was one of its most valuable characteristics. The young ICS officer was trained in the details of the work which he was later to supervise, starting with land measurement and crop analysis of the *patwari* and record keeping of the office *kanungo*. The land settlement which each officer made in his career provided rich experience in the details of revenue administration and microcosmic economic planning. This experience gave the officer that sense of confidence and expertness which can come only with the familiarity of active participation; it also conditioned his relationship with his subordinates in an intimate and crucial way, for his authority rested on knowledge and skill demonstrably equal to or greater than their's and not on the superficialities of bluff, arrogance, or exaggerated status barriers. Such training gave the officer an understanding of the work conditions and problems of his subordinates which enabled him to appreciate the causes of poor or delayed work, and to correct those causes. This appreciation of conditions did much to create a relationship of mutual respect and harmony between officer and subordinate. But this relationship was to a large extent broken if not destroyed by the trauma of partition. The slow and careful training of the new CSP officer disappeared. In pre-partition days, an officer would serve ten years as an assistant commissioner and another twenty years as deputy commissioner in charge of a district. During that period, he might have been transferred every three years, but his rank and position remained the same and his experience doing the same work in districts of varying economic, geographic, and cultural circumstances deepened his insight and sharpened his expertness. Even if transferred to the secretariat, the tenure in various assignments was long enough to permit the development of an orderly administrative system in which the duties, rights, and privileges of civil servants were widely understood. In any case, he brought to the secretariat a maturity, breadth of experience, and human touch deeply conditioned by years of contact with the masses which gave a sense of realism to his administration. After partition, rapid promotion combined with frequent transfer destroyed the orderliness of the system. The confidence of officers, which had stemmed from certainty of knowledge and skill, was destroyed, and refuge was sought in the use of artificial status barriers as a means of wielding authority. This inexperience in both rank and tenure was not helped by the fact that neither the structure of administration nor the contours of power were static. On the contrary, new responsibilities were added and old duties subtracted. Totally new functions, such as statistical units, organization and methods units, and training programs, outside the realm of experience of most officers, were added. The old order, whose hallmark had been stability and slow, cautious change, was, to some extent, shaken and the confidence of officers lessened. As a consequence, esteem and respect for officers by subordinates deteriorated and was replaced by resentment, animosity, and, in some instances, hostility. This situation was acerbated by the fact that with the disappearance of colonial rule and of most British officers, reliance on ethnic differentials and the power of empire was no longer effective as a means of wielding authority. The upsurge of freedom and consequent irresponsible behavior and demands subjected the higher bureaucracy to strains and pressures from its own compatriots which it often met with greater isolation and detachment than did the British. Finally, it cannot be overlooked that most of the new CSP officers immediately after partition came from backgrounds unaccustomed to command. In a status-conscious society of non-egalitarian values this is of immense significance. Indians recruited to the ICS usually came from families of some distinction or status derived either from wealth, learning, landholding, or hereditary tribal leadership. These families were generally known in their respective areas and the public naturally accorded such officers esteem and obedience. Since the officers themselves had been accustomed to positions of authority, they were less easily flattered by postures of obeisance and they commanded with natural ease. But the new recruitment which became much more egalitarian after 1947 produced men of different backgrounds, whose experience in command was less and whose social position played a minor or even a negative role as a source of authority.

Employees, especially in the middle ranks of the bureaucracy, were catapulted into posts from which they were ill equipped. This is a different predicament from the relatively simpler one (described in the first part of this chapter) of ICS officers coping with complex tasks in which they had little or no experience. In the case of the ICS officers, competence, education, intellect, and language facility were all present. They constituted a cadre destined for such posts; partition merely accelerated what would have normally occurred. But in the middle range of bureaucracy, government officials who ordinarily could not have hoped for positions beyond those of clerks found themselves preparing notes on major policy, without necessary education, language ability, or self-confidence. It must be remembered that there had been and still is a close correlation between level of education, social status, and position in government service. The petty functionary was thus thrust into positions beyond his remotest expectations, and his inability to muster the psychological and intellectual resources necessary to rise to the challenge was a disturbing factor in morale and bureaucratic efficiency. An attempt was made to solve this by the "section officer" scheme which allowed for the selection and promotion of capable lower ranking men to quasi-executive positions.

The circumstances described above increased misunderstandings and tensions within the bureaucracy. In short, the stabilizing influence of experience and slow evolution was not sufficient to counteract the dynamics of rapid change in personnel structure and responsibility, and the inadequate seasoning of the new CSP leadership could not provide the leavening of mature wisdom and compassionate understanding which the ICS had once provided.

(3) The intrusion of caste, communal, and familial considerations was also a fundamental factor. Even if such considerations did not, in fact, influence decisions, the suspicion that they did may have had as much or greater effect than the reality. Every action of promotion, discipline, or severance, however justly based on impersonal grounds, could be deemed capricious and based on clique animosities. There were tensions and suspicions between Punjabis and non-Punjabis, Bengalis and non-Bengalis, refugees and non-refugees,[21] among traditional lineage castes (Syeds, Sheikh, Quresh, Moghuls, Pathan),[22] among oc-

[21] For the first several years after partition, refugees from India pressed insistently for government employment. The government issued a white paper: *Statement Showing the Total Number of Persons, Employed under the Government of Pakistan Belonging to Different Provinces, States, etc., of India*, Karachi, 1950, showing 3,121 refugees employed.

[22] On caste in Pakistan, see Sir Denzil Ibbetson, *Punjab Castes*, Lahore, 1916; A. K. Nazimul Karim, *Changing Society in India and Pakistan*, Dacca, 1956; John B. Edlefsen and Jamila Akhtar, "Caste Differentials among the Muslims of West Pakistan," *The Academy Quarterly*, *I*, 1961, pp. 29-37. Perhaps the most persuasive evi-

cupational castes, and among religious sects (Sunni, Shia, Ahmediya, Christian).[23] Such cleavages are found in most societies, but they are acerbated by political insecurity, dire poverty, and occupational dislocation. In a new state which has not yet quite surmounted the problems of national integration, these regional-linguistic, sectarian cleavages, although diminishing, are significant determinants of behavior. Some of these animosities resulted from the fact that a political entity of nationhood arose before feudal tribal loyalties could be submerged in a transcendent nationalism.[24] Coupled with this was the latent fear of recrimination by someone now offended who might later be in a position of power. As a protection against individual helplessness in the face of such vindictiveness, the individual depends on his own regional or *biradri* (caste) faction and on factional alliances. He thus merged his personal fate with the collective fate of a larger group which had greater resilience as well as greater offensive capability. There was no clear conception of the separateness of personal and impersonal modes of conduct, with the consequence that government employees were incapable of construing any bureaucratic personnel decision as being devoid of selfish, factious considerations. Although there is a strong tradition of compassion and humaneness both in the Islamic tradition and in the British *Raj* from which the contemporary bureaucracy derives its values, these qualities were more latent than operative. In any society in which livelihood is precarious, the disposi-

dence of the existence of caste in Muslim society (despite the unequivocal egalitarianism proclaimed by Islam) is the plea of Muslims in India for recognition of the existence of castes in their society. See Government of India, *Report of the Backward Classes Commission*, Delhi, 1956, I, vi, 27.

[23] The height of sectarian animosity was reached in 1953, precipitated by the appointment of Zafrullah Khan, an Ahmediya, as Foreign Minister. See *Report of the Court of Inquiry Constituted under Punjab Act II of 1954 to Enquire into the Punjab Disturbances of 1953*, Lahore, 1954. The changed atmosphere in Pakistan is indicated by the fact that the appointment of Zafrullah Khan as chief of Pakistan's United Nations delegation in 1961 was not a controversial issue.

[24] Nor have these characteristics gone unnoticed by President Ayub, who said that a perusal of past events shows that "we are inclined towards provincialism, parochialism, tribalism, and selfishness" (*Pakistan Times*, November 8, 1961, p. 1). An arresting analysis of the effect of these characteristics on administration and especially on the application of British legal norms can be found in Penderel Moon, *Strangers in India*, London, 1944. Moon, a member of the Indian Civil Service, convincingly argues that British law cannot be applied effectively in India. It is of interest to note that President Ayub referred to Moon's "illuminating little book" to support his defense of extension of the Frontier Crimes Regulation. The text of Ayub's address before the High Court Bar Association in Lahore on April 27, 1962, is in *Pakistan Times*, April 28, 1962, pp. 1, 9. The novels of Philip Woodruff, *Call the Next Witness*, Oxford, 1945, and *The Wild Sweet Witch*, London, 1947, are also valuable sources of insight into the factionalism described here.

tions of aggression and self-survival, selfishness, and vindictiveness tend to be dominant. The triumphal elevation of the virtues of compassion and humaneness to a position in which they may operate as effective influences in such a situation is a task of superhuman dimensions.

(4) Another factor was the extreme compartmentalization of the bureaucracy, derived in part as a response to the assaults of factional pressures and in part from the behavior of British officers who were accessible in the districts to the masses but who held themselves aloof from their Indian subordinates within the bureaucracy. This latter behavior was well summarized by President Ayub when he described the inherited colonial administration as creating "a superior class of somewhat denationalized individuals who could maintain proper distances and rule with awe and disdain under the cover of public service."[25] Such denationalization was reflected in the physical separation of the governor, who conducted his business in Government House, removed often from the secretariat by several miles. At the lowest level, the deputy commissioner's office was in his bungalow, serenely sequestered from the milling throng waiting in attendance upon the district offices and courts. The attitude which prevailed was that of summoning a retainer to a presence, not that of informal consultation. Such attitudes were remnants of colonial rule when British governors and deputy commissioners felt it essential to keep both physical and social distance from the people. This attitude certainly was not the stated policy of British rule, for that policy urged the most humane, compassionate, and respectful attitudes possible.[26] It was, however, the inevitable result of colonial rule, and the mere fact that minutes had to be issued ordering attitudes of equality and respect was an index that such attitudes were not invariably manifest. This condition of separateness or absence of vertical communication continued even though the incumbents of superior posts were no longer British.

[25] Address to Administrative Staff College cited in note 2, above.

[26] See, for example, *Memorandum on the Subject of Social and Official Intercourse Between European Officers in the Punjab and Indians*, Lahore, 1922, an official pamphlet reproducing Sir John Malcolm's *Minute* of June 28, 1821. Both of these enjoin a high standard of idealistic behavior. This was the same John Malcolm who entered service in India as a boy of thirteen, became an eminent Persian scholar and author of several books on India and Persia. On the complex subject of British colonial attitudes see also Philip Woodruff, *The Guardians*, *op.cit.*, pp. 226ff. and Bernard Cohn, "The British in Benares," *Comparative Studies in Society and History*, IV, 1962, pp. 169-199; Robert Eric Frykenberg, "British Society in Guntur in the Early Nineteenth Century," *ibid.*, pp. 200-208; Hilton Brown, ed., *The Sahibs*, London, 1948.

Such inability to communicate very far above or below one's position in the administrative structure was further complicated by the cultural and linguistic bifurcation which characterized society. English is the language of government, but English competence diminishes as one descends in the hierarchy, and spoken English competence diminishes more sharply, ending probably with clerks and typists. Government employees in the secretariat and other large establishments in the rank of superintendent or assistant are probably the linguistic or social mediators, communicating upwards in English and downwards in a vernacular. This group is virtually the only group which has frequent face-to-face contact with their officer superiors and non-officer subordinates.[27] This is not to say that higher ranking officers are unable to speak a vernacular; on the contrary, they are universally bilingual although occasionally their skill in Urdu or a vernacular such as Pushtu, Punjabi, or Sindhi may be less than their skill in English. The point is that a social barrier was sensed and enhanced by the awareness that what went in and came out of a senior official's office was completely in written English and almost completely in spoken English.

The elaborate categorization of the government service into CSP, central superior services, provincial services, gazetted and non-gazetted officers, Class I, II, III, and IV employees was so deeply imbedded in the system and so intricately related to social status that it is nearly impossible to imagine the services without such classification.[28] That the classification is derived essentially from the Aitchison report,[29]

[27] This phenomenon of linguistic and cultural mediation is even more important in local administration than in the secretariat, precisely because the differences in society outside the secretariat are much more sharply drawn. See Ralph Braibanti, "The Civil Service of Pakistan: A Theoretical Analysis," *South Atlantic Quarterly*, LVIII, 1959, pp. 258-304. There is a positive correlation between skill in spoken English and status in the eyes of the vernacular speaking public. The same correlation exists with respect to Western dress. The same official, speaking English and dressed in Western clothes, is shown greater deference and privilege than when he dresses in Indian style clothes or speaks a vernacular. Some of the experiences of Masih-uz-Zaman in this matter are amusing though disturbing indices of the crucial problem of building a democratic society on a linguistic frame completely detached from its popular base. See Masih-uz-Zaman, "English—An Impediment to Economic Growth," *Pakistan Times*, April 30, 1962, p. 4.

[28] The Munir Commission struggling with this problem suggested regrouping the services into five groups lettered from A to E. *Report of the Pakistan Pay Commission*, Karachi, 1949, I, 18-19. Cf. India's solution to the problem, which the Das Commission sought through abolition of all such classifications within cadres. Government of India, *Commission of Enquiry on Emoluments and Conditions of Service of Central Government Employees 1957–59, Report*, Delhi, 1959, pp. 560ff.

[29] *Report of the Public Service Commission 1886-87*, Cd. 5327, 8 vols., London, 1887.

which created provincial services to meet demands for Indianization and retain power in British hands and from the Islington report[30] which modified the basis somewhat, is seldom regarded as important. The ad hoc political response of the British *Raj* now appears utterly rational and not only becomes venerated tradition, but also is supported by new reasons and vested interests.

Compartmentalization was not reduced by extreme differentials in pay among ranks and even cadres in the service.[31] This differential originated in the British *Raj* when it was thought (by the British) that British officers, because of their foreign service, required a different salary scale. The scale became associated with the post rather than with the nationality of the incumbent and was also given to those Indian incumbents who had taken the examination in London. At partition, ICS officers who opted for Pakistan were guaranteed the same pay scale. When, as a result of the recommendations of the First Pay Commission in 1950, the scale for higher ranks was sharply reduced, it did not really affect secretaries in the central government, all of whom were pre-partition ICS officers on the old ICS scale. Since there are even now about eighty such officers in the CSP cadre, it is not unlikely that they will hold such positions in the central government and key secretaryships in the provincial governments for sometime to come. On the old scale, the base salary of a full secretary was Rs. 4000 (nearly $900) a month. His stenographer's (usually a male high school graduate with special training in dictation and typing) was usually Rs. 200 (about $40). This is a ratio of 20 to 1. Based on the new scale, a secretary's monthly base pay was Rs. 2500 (about $500);[32] hence in this scale, the ratio would be 12 to 1. Either of these ratios is in marked contrast to the ratio of 4 to 1 for equivalent ranks in federal government service in the United States.[33] This differential is a vexatious problem with which the first Pay Commission valiantly strug-

[30] *Report of the Royal Commission on the Public Service in India*, Cd. 8382, London, 1917.

[31] See the excellent survey of the development of pay scales in the *Report of the Pakistan Pay Commission, op.cit.*, I. The commission also analyzed the problem of the marked Western orientation of the upper reaches of the bureaucracy and the vernacularized, tradition-oriented disposition of the masses. See especially pp. 55ff. This problem of cultural bifurcation was a favorite theme of politicians and others critical of the bureaucracy. See, for example, National Assembly of Pakistan Debates, *Official Report*, February 15, 1957, pp. 434-435.

[32] No full secretary to the central government (or chief or additional chief secretary to the provincial governments) actually was on the new scale, since all incumbents through 1961 were former ICS officers.

[33] This is a difficult and in many ways a misleading comparison to make since there are no positions of secretary and male stenographer in American bureaucracy which

gled and on which the second Pay Commission is ready to submit its report. While the differential may appear too great, from another point of view it may be too small. For it is clear that the upper reaches of the bureaucracy—most of the CSP cadre, for example, having been educated in England—have acquired the tastes and way of life of the British, a way of life much more costly to support than one geared to the economy of the rest of the nation. While the satisfaction of occupying the handsome residences set in peaceful gardens formerly used by the British *Raj* may be great, the economic reality of coping with the way of life engendered thereby may be painfully distressing. It is not here suggested that extremes in salary differential are, *qua* extremes, determinants of rigid compartmentalization. But these differences purchase two ways of life—the way of the *gymkhana* and the way of the bazaar tea stall—and hence become a fair index of the immense social distance between ranks. Certainly in terms of education, social background, way of life, language, social presence, and self-confidence, the average government employee below the elitist cadre level stands (literally) in diffidence, unease, and marked inequality in relation to his gazetted officer. This relationship is aggravated by the relative vertical and horizontal job immobility which characterized the system. The improbability that non-officers would ever become officers, that a clerk would be more than a clerk, or that a superintendent might eventually become a policy-making executive was very great. This created tensions deeply affecting social relations within the bureaucracy. Certainly there was great mobility within groups (such as engineers, CSP, Audits and Accounts Service, etc.) but little mobility from one group to another. This condition is changing rapidly, largely because of the section officer scheme, which, by recruiting a portion by internal promotion from lower ranks and a smaller portion from sources outside government, provides a means (theoretically, at least) of rising to under-secretaryship without regard to cadre or origin. But we are here analyzing the social causes for the rise of the writ petition, and the period under consideration (1947-1960) was a period during which immobility was the more pronounced characteristic of the bureaucratic scene.

It is not here suggested that this compartmentalization was altogether bad. This detachment (called "aloofness" and "snobbery" by

correspond in all essentials to these posts in Pakistan government. The United States civil service ranks of GS-16 and GS-5 are used here as the base for the rough comparison.

detractors of the CSP) is an essential posture for whomever wields power in Pakistan. A clear concept of personal loyalty and impersonal obligation to fixed bureaucratic canons has not permeated society. Loyalty to kin and caste (*biradri*) is held a greater virtue than adherence to an abstract, impersonal notion of equity. To counter this, the official must not only be physically detached but must exaggerate the drama of his detachment. To be close to the people is to place oneself in a web from which there is no escape. In a society so full of intrigue, of tribal animosity, of vengeance, and of incredible *biradri* pressures for favoritism, the mere posture of familiarity inevitably creates a reputation for partiality which leads to actual partiality. Overnight the inexorable progression of this syndrome collapses the edifice of bureaucratic equity. This situation is aggravated by the encompassing power of government. In the absence of effective voluntary organization, virtually every group action requires bureaucratic impetus and sanction. There being no escape from bureaucratic power, the total pressures of the entire social realm are brought to bear upon the single person who represents this bureaucratic power in microcosm. In the district this person is the deputy commissioner and his subordinates. In the district there can be no diffusion, no delegation, no equivocation except that which ultimately increases the forces of public pressure. Since the natural barriers of background, colonial rule, and cultural differences are gone, the Pakistani official is almost helpless against the web which threatens to strangle him. His aloofness is his instinctive response to the need for self-preservation. The insulated cellular organization which made such detachment possible functioned without serious disarticulation so long as the benevolence of paternalism undergirded a stable structure in which every member knew his place and was moderately contented with it. Such paternalistic stability was the premise on which was constructed the elaborate legal edifice of which the two central pillars were the master-servant relationship and the corollary that salary was the bounty of the state. The existence of this idyllic state of affairs is the presumption in the *Rangachari* and *Venkata Rao* cases[34] which played so important a part in subsequent Pakistan decisions relating to the services. While the trauma of partition destroyed the presumption of such attitudes, it accentuated the cellular insulation of segments of administration. Such insulation became a protection against massive assault by particularistic selfish pressures. It would be misleading to suggest that this compartmentalization

[34] See p. 424n below.

actually increased grievances within the administration. It is doubtful if the bureaucracy was ready for a radical change in the direction of egalitarian, consultative behavior after two centuries of a rigid, cellular organization based on a caste-structured society existing long before British rule. It is clear only that compartmentalization without the attitudinal prerequisites could not cope with the spectacular rise in employee grievances. Yet it is conveivable that the very same compartmentalized structure which could not resolve the problem prevented even greater deterioration not only in order but in probity as well.

(5) Administration of the district in India was another major influence shaping the social characteristics of the bureaucracy.[35] It was in the district that the ICS officer spent at least twenty of the most impressionable years of his life, and the fond nostalgia with which those days are recalled indicates how strong this impression was. "I came up to Limbo," said Catullus, in charge of a district in North India in Aubrey Menon's novel, *The Prevalence of Witches*,[36] "because I had always wanted to possess a country of my own." This sentiment perhaps better expresses the appeal of district work than any formalized, technical description. That work was essentially autocratic, involving very little consultation among equals and equally little complex staff work. A premium was placed on quick decision, independent and forceful action, both attributes akin to good military field administration. Among the best officers, such as F. L. Brayne, C. F. Strickland, James M. Douie, Malcolm Darling, and Denzil Ibbetson,

[35] The fascination of district work has captured the imagination of more than one novelist. See, for example, Philip Woodruff, *The Wild Sweet Witch*, London, 1947, and *Call the Next Witness*, London, 1945. While all of John Masters' novels on India touch on district administration, his *Lotus and the Wind*, New York, 1953, and *Far, Far the Mountain Peak*, New York, 1957, are especially illuminating. Jim Corbett's incomparably sensitive novels are valuable, especially *My India*, Oxford, 1952, and *Man Eaters of Kumaon*, Oxford, 1944. Philip Woodruff's two volumes—*The Men Who Ruled India:* Vol. I, *The Founders;* Vol. II, *The Guardians*, New York, 1954—include perhaps the most revealing quasi-biographical accounts of district life. See also H. T. Lambrick's historical biographies, *Sir Charles Napier and Sind*, Oxford, 1952, and *John Jacob of Jacobabad*, London, 1960. Other accounts are: C. W. Whish, *A District Officer in Northern India*, Calcutta, 1892; C. H. Birck, *The Assistant Commissioner's Notebook*, London, 1906; C. A. Kincaid, *Forty Years A Public Servant*, London, 1934; R. D. Macleod, *Impressions of an Indian Civil Servant*, London, 1938, Bernard Houghton, *Bureaucratic Government*, London, 1913. More recent studies of some relevance to Pakistan are S. S. Khera, *District Administration in India*, New Delhi, 1960; K. N. V. Sastri, *Principles of District Administration in India*, Delhi, 1957. See also *Report of the Provincial Administration Commission*, Lahore, 1960, pp. 181-191; *Report of the Food and Agriculture Commission*, Karachi, 1960, pp. 149-212; *First Five Year Plan, 1955-60*, Karachi, 1957, pp. 101-106.

[36] London, 1947.

there was compassionate understanding of problems of the people, but the behavior pattern was one of paternalism, in which action depended exclusively on the district officer as the source of wisdom and authority. The relative autonomy and personal character of rule in the district was not easy for either Britons or Americans to comprehend. Macaulay found need a century ago to explain to the House of Commons that "such a power as that which collectors of India have over the people in India is not found in any other part of the world possessed by any class of functionaries."[37] The net result of district experience was often a marked independence, sometimes bordering, as Philip Woodruff has described it,[38] on not unpleasant eccentricity. In any case, there was a tough-minded sense of reality, a pragmatism, and the courage to disagree with superiors and to write sharp notes of dissent to secretariat colleagues who were not always regarded with the highest esteem. These were not qualities of the British alone; they were encouraged in the young Indian collector through close association with his district superiors, a relationship described so well by Gorwala[39] and other senior ICS officers. Such attitudes and habits set the norm for the total bureaucracy. Certainly they affected the conduct of secretariat work, as Sir Richard Tottenham pointed out in 1946,[40] even though such norms may have been antithetical to those required. Masih-uz-Zaman indicates that the authoritarian values of district administration deeply affected welfare officials in Pakistan, who soon behaved like the law-and-order bureaucracy whose influence and techniques they were supposed to replace.[41] Similar permeation of district administration values via the ICS (later CSP) cadre occurred in varying degrees throughout the bureaucracy.

(6) Permeating the psychological clime of the lower reaches of the bureaucracy was a defeatist attitude which often discouraged initiative and even superior performance. The pressure towards mediocrity came, not always from superiors, who, on the contrary, often waged war against it, but from one's peers. Subtle group pressures characteristic of village life were often applied to the bureaucratic group. Parnwell was thus able to remark that in this atmosphere merit

[37] *Parliamentary Debates*, 3d series, CXXVIII, June 24, 1853, col. 745-746.

[38] *The Men Who Ruled India: The Guardians*, New York, 1940.

[39] A. D. Gorwala, *The Role of the Administrator, Past, Present and Future*, Poona, 1952.

[40] *Report in the Reorganization of the Central Government, 1945-1946*, New Delhi, 1946, Tottenham Report, p. 28.

[41] Masih-uz-Zaman, *Community Development and its Audience*, Lahore, 1960, p. 38.

could not easily make its mark,[42] and Bakar was able to say that frustration was endemic.[43] In the middle range of bureaucratic officialdom, the "babu" mentality often avoided decision, and acted by raising pettifogging issues which served to obstruct and delay. This has been characterized by one senior official as the tendency of officials to "delight in disagreeing with each other" and "to flourish their knowledge of rules only to differ and demolish."[44] Their written actions he describes as "acrimonious notings" made often for the pleasure of pointing out mistakes. This practice, which probably originated in the irresponsible attitude which inevitably characterizes those ruled by a colonial power, served as a convenient vehicle for the transmission of petty animosities and rivalries, which were thereby deepened and extended.

(7) Another factor disturbing bureaucratic harmony was the frequent inordinate delay in payment of salary. This occurred among new employees, temporary employees, and often upon transfer. It was sometimes related to the employee's refusal to accept a rank lower than that which he felt himself qualified for, or to accept a demotion, or even to recognize that he had not been promoted to a position which he thought he deserved. Contemplating the possibility of seeking a writ to redress the alleged grievance, the employee felt that acceptance of salary at the lower rate might be held as *prima facie* evidence of accepting the lower position. This situation, which was fairly common, was dramatized late in 1961 by an official's murder of his daughter and his subsequent suicide.[45] He had not accepted his pay for eight months because he refused to sign as an assistant director since he claimed he was a deputy director. This episode precipitated action by the West Pakistan government and later by the central government, which ordered that delays be reduced and their causes be eliminated. The provincial investigation revealed that new employees were rarely paid before four months and transferred employees usually waited six months for pay.[46] Most salary delay was unrelated to litigation respecting status and was due simply to tortuous procedures. It was endemic at all levels and in all branches of government. Yet this

[42] M. L. Parnwell, *Organization and Methods in the East Pakistan Government*, Dacca, 1958, p. 13.

[43] S. N. Bakar, *Report of the Secretariat Reorganization Committee, March-April, 1954*, Dacca, 1954.

[44] Mian Anwar Ali, "The Role of the Senior Administrator, II," *Pakistan Times*, June 7, 1961, p. 4.

[45] *Pakistan Times*, November 11, 1961, p. 1.

[46] *Ibid.*, November 13, 1961, p. 1; December 8, 1961, p. 10.

is not to say that delayed payment occurred chronically for all groups. Once technical difficulties were resolved, and salary began to arrive, most employees continued to be paid on time. At any given moment there was, however, a large number of new recruits, temporary employees, and "unusual" cases whose pay was delayed. Major portions of the salaries of teachers in Montgomery, for example, had not been paid in five years because of "technical complications."[47]

(8) A further cause of distress was the frustration felt by technical administrators who were usually prevented from occupying generalist positions as heads of departments, even when those departments had technical functions. Whether justified or not, the feeling was acute, and it became more so with the appointment of a CSP officer as education secretary in West Pakistan replacing a professional educator. The outcry against this caused the governor to issue an explanation of this action, which was due, he said, to the need for making more rapid progress in educational reform.[48]

(9) There was resentment on the part of provincial service officers of long seniority who found themselves blocked from advancement to posts reserved for the CSP. The latter, on the other hand, regarded the provincial service officers as inferior in training and experience, and feared that the integration of the two cadres would jeopardize the effectiveness of the CSP as an elite corps.[49]

(10) Although relative immobility between cadres and major classes of ranks has been suggested in paragraph 4 above as a source of factiousness and discontent within the bureaucracy, the opposite—i.e., extreme mobility of CSP officers—must also be cited as a determinant, not necessarily of factiousness, but of a climate of uncertainty and perhaps some instability. In the upper reaches of the bureaucracy, both in the CSP cadre and among technical officers such as in the Audits and Accounts Service, length of assignment has been remarkably short. This has probably been unavoidable because of the rapid increase in government responsibilities, organizational changes, and the small number of qualified executives who must be used as trouble-shooters or as agents for organizing a new activity. Change of assignment in the CSP cadre occurred with such frequency that it is virtually impossible to ascertain from the annual gradation lists. Other assignments

[47] *Ibid.*, December 3, 1961, p. 5.

[48] *Ibid.*, December 21, 1961, p. 1.

[49] For both points of view, see exchange of letters in *Pakistan Times,* August 1, 1959, p. 4; August 2, 1959, p. 4; September 26, 1961, p. 4; October 1, 1961, p. 6; December 27, 1961, p. 4.

occur between publication dates so that the lists reflect only the assignment at the moment. A precise, statistical computation of frequency of assignment needs yet to be made, and at this point only impressionistic generalizations can be advanced. Few CSP assignments were held for more than two years, and a large number of officers, perhaps nearly half of the total cadre, changed assignments oftener than each year. While the situation in the abstract might have stabilized in recent years, any increased stability has probably been offset by the rise in the number of officers attending in-service training. Such courses require the officers' replacement and usually result in their reassignment to a post for which the training has presumably prepared them. A graphic instance of the change in length of incumbency is provided by study of the plaques invariably in display in the office of the deputy commissioner of any district in Pakistan.[50] In Peshawar, for example, where the plaque bears such well-known names as Sir Olaf Caroe and Iskander Mirza, who served as deputy commissioners, the length of incumbency before partition was at least two years, and often three and four years. After 1947, the incumbency was an average of six months. While the Peshawar experience may not be typical, it is more common than uncommon. In the secretariats, such frequency of change was perhaps straining too far the notion of a universal science of administration applicable without regard to substantive context. Mastery of the content to be administered is improbable in so short a time. Personnel problems became even more difficult as the effective, operative power of resolving them devolved by default upon a subordinate functionary whose familiarity was probably based on long tenure of post. Since such an official is invariably more vernacular than English-oriented and will rarely be detached from the network of factionalism —indeed he may be a manipulator of such forces in the system—personnel problems may be aggravated rather than reduced. When this occurs, the argument that a quasi-itinerant administrator at the top level brings detachment and objectivity to the solution of personnel issues is invalidated. Such objectivity is achieved inter alia by independence (in tenure, promotion etc.) from the consequences of factionalism. This independence may be helped by the knowledge that a posting is not of lifetime permanence, but not necessarily by too frequent transfer, which shifts internal power to an undetached official.

[50] Another means of ascertaining the rate of turnover is by examination of the list of deputy commissioners in every district gazetteer. These lists usually appear as Table 33 in the statistical volume of the gazetteer.

In any event, even without the statistical verification by which a final judgment can be made, most CSP officers agree that changes in assignment have been far more frequent than before 1947 and that this was an important factor in engendering psychological uncertainty and a kind of instability in internal administration.

(11) While the pattern of social relations within the bureaucracy made redress of grievances difficult to achieve, a series of large-scale readjustments of personnel increased the incidence of situations conducive to grievance. The first readjustment and perhaps the most serious was the partition of 1947,[51] in which there was a deeply felt moral obligation to continue in government service those employees who left India for Pakistan. While, as has already been described, there was a serious shortage of senior executives, there was an excess of lower-ranking government employees. Such employees had to be integrated in posts often inappropriate to their talents and their respective seniorities established without necessary records. The grievances created thereby did not begin to reach the courts until 1956, after the Constitution was in effect, and many of the decisions are only now beginning to appear.[52] Occurring at about the same time was the vexing problem of fixing seniority of new employees who had been in military service during the war. The Punjab government, for example, gave preference in both appointment and seniority to war service candidates. The war had also resulted in a large number of temporary appointments and it was difficult to rationalize the seniority of these temporary incumbents with eligibility of the returning veterans.[53]

The second large personnel shift was occasioned by the integration of the Punjab, Sind, Northwest Frontier Province, and Baluchistan into the single province of West Pakistan in 1955.[54] This involved not

[51] There is, unfortunately, no adequate description of the trauma created by this disarticulation and its legacy in the administration. A suggestion can be found in a speech by Mushtaq Ahmad Gurmani in Constituent Assembly (Legislature) *Debates*, October 1, 1953, pp. 731-734. See also *Report of the Economy Committee Appointed to Review the Expediture of Central Government and Suggest Economies*, Karachi, 1958, Part I, pp. 2-10.

[52] Perhaps the best-known writ cases resulting from the dislocation of partition are *Pakistan v. Naseem Ahmad*, P.L.D. 1961, S.C. 445, involving the status of 17 police officers of Karachi, and *Pakistan v. Sheikh Abdul Hamid*, P.L.D. 1961, S.C. 105, in which a clerk's seniority was changed because of transfers.

[53] See *Manzur Ahmad v. Province of West Pakistan* (1961) 1 P.S.C.R. 151; *Muhammad Athar v. Pakistan* P.L.D., 1962, S.C. 367.

[54] A relevant statute is the Establishment of West Pakistan Act 1955, discussion of which can be found in 29 successive daily reports of National Assembly of Pakistan, Parliamentary Debates, *Official Report*, Vol. 1, No. 9, August 23, 1955, to No. 38,

only amalgamation of governments but also of the provincial public service commissions handling records and personnel matters. As at partition, the rights of all employees were respected and, despite great disparity in training, competence, and pay-scales, an effort was made to integrate the various cadres. But this integration caused acute seniority and pay problems largely because the commitment that terms of service would not be impaired by integration was interpreted to mean that even prospects of promotion would not be less favorable after integration than before.[55] This made integration exceedingly difficult, if not impossible. It was only in 1960 that this situation was alleviated by a Supreme Court ruling that the adverse effect on promotion prospects does not involve a vested legal right and that while government may consider such effect *ex gratia*, it is not legally bound to do so.[56] The disarticulation of the 1955 integration of services was still not resolved by the end of 1961, when the cabinet of the central government, announcing a series of provincial administration changes, ordered that the discrepancies created in 1955 be adjusted.[57]

Both major readjustments in 1947 and in 1955 were made during years of political instability, in an atmosphere of irresponsible charges by politicians against bureaucracy and by bureaucracy's retreat behind a wall of secrecy. The first readjustment was accompanied by the immense distress of millions of refugees, thousands of whom were government officials and all of whom had to start life anew, with no assets, and often with the anguish of family members killed in the massacres accompanying partition.

(12) There were other changes in structure which created new causes for possible grievance. The introduction of the section officers' scheme in the central secretariat in 1959 provided for both direct recruitment and promotion to the new posts.[58] Since it was the first

September 30, 1955. The complexity of the problem of integrating the various services and governments can be appreciated by study of the *Report of the West Pakistan Integration of Services Cadres Committee*, Lahore, 1955.

[55] In *Attaur Rehman Khan v. Province of West Pakistan and others* P.L.D., 1958, 2, Lahore, 180, it was held that government must assign the employee so as to afford the same prospects of promotion he formerly had. See also *Fida Muhammad Khan v. Government of West Pakistan* P.L.R., 1957, I.W.P., 1954.

[56] The judgment in *Fida Muhammad's* case (note 55) was overturned by *Government of West Pakistan v. Fida Muhammad Khan*, 1959, 2 P.S.C.R. 187. Cf. *Pakistan v. Hasan Ali Jafari and another*, 1960, 1 P.S.C.R 26; *Government of West Pakistan v. Fateh Ullah Khan*, 1959, 2 P.S.C.R. 192; *Province of West Pakistan v. Mohammad Akhtar*, P.L.D., 1962, S.C. 428.

[57] President's Secretariat, *Press Communique*, December 27, 1961.

[58] See *Abdul Latif Sethi and others v. Pakistan and another*, P.L.D., 1961, Karachi, 457 for description of this scheme.

opportunity for major advancement to an important post for lower-ranking employees, the scheme attracted wide attention. It was a significant, beneficial, and far-reaching reform, but inevitably its implementation put increased emphasis on seniority and eligibility and on criteria by which selection was to be made. A further change was the merger of Karachi, which had been a federal territory, with West Pakistan in 1961; this required integrating the service cadres as well.[59]

Another important cause of grievance resulting in seeking a writ was the problem of promotion of civil servants temporarily officiating at posts. In many instances employees held such temporary posts for several years and then were reverted to their former posts. This was often construed as a reduction in rank and hence a punishment. Writs were then sought on the ground that this was punishment without adhering to the Civil Service (Classification Control and Appeal) Rules. In such cases the Supreme Court defined reduction in rank,[60] and held that reversion did not necessarily amount to reduction in rank and that only the executive could determine if reversion were in the best interests of the state.[61] A related problem was that of relative seniority of officers recruited from out of government and those promoted from within the department and the similar problem of integration of "emergency cadres" into regular cadres with officers who were regularly appointed.[62] The same question of determining seniority was encountered in cases of police personnel promoted to officer rank from enlisted rank and those holding corresponding posts who were already members of the Indian Police Service by virtue of entry as cadets. In the leading case on this issue,[63] it was held that the High Court was correct in laying down five "propositions" to guide the executive in determining police seniority. This was not construed as judicial interference in the executive's immediate control over its officers. On the contrary, the High Court action was regarded by the

[59] See *Report on the Merger of Karachi with West Pakistan*, Karachi, 1961.

[60] *Pakistan v. Moazzam Hussain Khan*, 1958, 2 P.S.C.R. 272.

[61] *Pakistan v. Hikmat Hussain*, 1958, 2 P.S.C.R. 257; *West Pakistan Province v. Bashir Ahmad Qureshi and others*, 1959, 1 P.S.C.R. 59. See also *Province of East Pakistan v. Muhammad Abdu Miah*, 1959, 1 P.S.C.R. 259. *Muhammad Akram Khan v. Additional Inspector-General of Police*, 1958, 1 P.S.C.R. 268. *Muhammad Hassan Abidi v. Pakistan*, 1959, 2 P.S.C.R. 170.

[62] See an excellent description of this problem by Chief Justice Cornelius in *Province of West Pakistan v. Akram Wasti*, P.L.D., 1960, S.C. 93. See also the unpublished case, *Civil Appeal Nos. 96/1960 and 1,2,3 of 1961, Pakistan v. A. P. Hassumani and A. R. Malik*, Supreme Court, April 19, 1962. On emergency cadres see *Pakistan v. A. P. Hassumani*, P.L.D., 1962, S.C. 409.

[63] *Bashir Ahmad Khan v. Mahmud Ali Khan Chodhary*, 1958, 2 P.S.C.R. 242.

Supreme Court as "calculated to assist government in exercising such control peacefully and harmoniously." In the *Bashir Ahmad Khan* case the fact that the government decided the seniority of the same three police officers on five occasions during a six-year period, each time rendering a decision different from the previous ones, illustrates the state of affairs within the bureaucracy which the judiciary deplored.

(13) Much of the litigation on service matters focuses on whether there was any restriction on the power of government to dismiss its employees at pleasure. Section 240 of the Government of India Act stated that members of the civil service held office at His Majesty's pleasure and the essence of this provision became incorporated in Article 181 of the Constitution of Pakistan. In the leading judgment, *I. M. Lall's* case,[64] the Privy Council held that the Crown's pleasure was limited by the mandatory provisions that no authority lower than the appointing authority could order reduction or dismissal and that adequate show cause notice had to be given. The reasoning in I. M. Lall's case was sustained by a long line of Pakistan decisions.[65] The application of this doctrine to instances of employees without permanent status whose services have been terminated has been the subject of several cases. In the *Isaacs* case[66] the court, distinguishing between temporary and permanent employees, held that if the former were released upon expiration of the temporary period by means of notice, this was not removal or dismissal. But for permanent employees, the show cause and other provisions of section 240 must be met. In the subsequent *Fayyaz Ahmed* case,[67] a majority opinion written by Chief Justice S. A. Rahman challenged the soundness of the *Isaacs* doctrine by holding that if termination of services of a temporary employee is made in accordance with terms of a contract it need not constitute removal or dismissal and the provisions of Section 240 are inapplicable. Chief Justice Kayani, supported by Justice Shabir Ahmed, dissented in the *Fayyaz Ahmed* case. He argued that termination of service or discharge, whichever the term used, amounts to removal and is governed by Section 240. Kayani's dissent was subsequently supported

[64] *High Commissioner for India and High Commissioner for Pakistan v. I. M. Lall*, 75 I.A. 225, 1948.

[65] *Muhammad Ayub v. Government of West Pakistan*, P.L.D., 1957, Lahore, 487; *Raja Muhammad Afzal Khan v. Federation of Pakistan*, P.L.D., 1957, Lahore, 17; *Federation of Pakistan v. Fayyaz Ahmad*, P.L.D., 1958, Lahore, 500. *Punjab Province v. Athar Ali*, P.L.D., 1956, Lahore, 886.

[66] *Mrs. A. V. Isaacs v. Federation of Pakistan*, P.L.D., 1954, Lahore, 800; *Federation of Pakistan v. Mrs. A. V. Isaacs*, 1956, P.S.C.Rs. 224.

[67] See citation in note 65 above.

by the Supreme Court in an appeal made by Ghulam Sarwar (one of the respondents in the *Fayyaz Ahmed* case) decided on March 19, 1962.[68] The significance of this case, which would affect thousands of contract employees, is indicated by the fact that a special bench of seven judges, including three co-opted from the High Court, made the judgment, which was one of the longest (100 pages) in the court's history. It was also the first time that a bench of more than five judges was used by the Supreme Court. In seven separate concurring opinions, the court unanimously held that when services of a government servant are terminated in accordance with conditions of his contract, such termination amounts to dismissal. Hence the power to terminate services in this manner is subject to Section 240, which includes the requirement of a reasonable opportunity to the employee to show cause against his discharge.

A closely related issue is the power of the judiciary to compel the government to pay arrears in salary if the employee is found, as a result of a court decision, not to have been legally dismissed from service. In this matter the regnant doctrine was that of the *I. M. Lall* case: while the courts may declare a dismissal void and inoperative by a writ, payment of salary is the bounty of the Crown and cannot be judicially ordered.[69] Such payment could be sought through political or administrative means and the court would hope that the government would, *ex gratia*, pay due arrears. This legal inability of the courts to order payment of salary was a very vexing problem for civil servants. The concept of the bounty of the Crown had been reinterpreted even in England by distinguishing between a servant of the Crown and a government official. It was resolved in India by the Supreme Court's interpretation of Section 240 of the 1935 Government of India Act, thus making it possible for the courts to *mandamus* arrears.[70] The Pakistan Constitution Commission, headed by retired Supreme Court Justice M. Shahabuddin, noted with approval the Indian interpretation and suggested that something similar be done in Pakistan.[71] Chief Justice Kayani in a decision in 1962 held that the Supreme Court had departed from the position that the courts could

[68] *Khwaja Ghulam Sarwar v. Pakistan*, P.L.D., 1962, S.C. 142. The facts of this case are an especially good example of the way in which intrigue, recrimination, and victimization distort justice within the bureaucracy, thus creating a situation which can be rectified only by the courts.

[69] *State of Pakistan v. Mehrajuddin*, 1959, 1 P.S.C.R. 34; *Government of West Pakistan v. Fazal-e-Haq Mussarratt*, 1960, 1 P.S.C.R. 125.

[70] *The State of Bihar v. Abdul Majid*, 1954, 41 A.I.R. S.C. 245.

[71] *Report of the Constitution Commission, Pakistan, 1961*, Karachi, 1961, p. 113.

not *mandamus* payment of arrears[72] and that this departure was suggested in *Hayat's* case, in which it was ruled that a *mandamus* could be issued to compel government to pay an employee's salary at a certain rate.[73] Kayani held that it is only logical to say further that *mandamus* can issue to require government to pay his salary to a government servant or to pay arrears of salary. Kayani noted further that *Hayat's* case made no reference to the *Mehrajuddin* case, which had upheld the *I. M. Lall* ruling. Thus the legal position relating to use of judicial power to compel payment of arrears appears to have been reversed by the Kayani judgment. It remains to be seen if this judgment will be appealed to the Supreme Court and, if appealed, whether it will be sustained or rejected.

Interpretations of the Civil Service (Classification Control and Appeal) Rules—CS (CCA)—in a manner construed by the courts as being denial of fundamental rights is a common source of the writ petition. The discharge of an employee without serving a show cause notice by purporting to abolish his post which, in fact, was not abolished is one circumstance illustrative of this problem.[74] Another issue is disagreement as to the authority competent to impose a penalty. The CS (CCA) rules require this to be the appointing authority merely to review and approve a penalty.[75] The penalty must be initiated by the appointing authority. Another issue is that of determining the finality of employment. In one case an official was appointed pending receipt of character affidavits. Upon his severance from service he filed for a writ which the Supreme Court denied him on the ground that his appointment was not final.[76] In another instance, an employee who entered the service under certain promotion rules alleged that the rules had changed and that he should be subject only to the rules in force when he entered service. But the Supreme Court, overturning the High Court, ruled that since his post was upgraded to Class II, government had the right to raise the efficiency of the services and that this action, because he could compete for the post, did not infringe his rights.[77]

Another employee sought a writ to have adverse remarks made on

[72] *Muhammad Anwar v. Government of Pakistan*, P.L.D., 1962, Lahore, 443. Kayani's view of the bounty of the crown doctrine was publicly expressed as early as December 7, 1959 in an address before the Student's Union of Panjab University.

[73] *Pakistan v. Muhammad Hayat*, P.L.D., 1962, S.C. 28.

[74] *Muhammad Din v. Corporation of the City of Lahore*, P.L.D., 1960, Lahore, 242.

[75] *Inayat Shah Hashmi v. Military Accountant General*, P.L.D., 1960, Lahore, 1001.

[76] *Federation of Pakistan v. Muhammad Afzal Khan*, 1958, 1 P.S.C.R. 196.

[77] *Central Board of Revenue v. Asad Ahmad Khan*, 1959, 2 P.S.C.R. 215.

his character roll expunged, alleging that they were made for personal reasons and that they affected his promotion. The Supreme Court sustained the High Court's denial of the writ, stating that government was the sole judge of promotion unless *mala fides* could be proved and that remarks on the character roll could not be expunged by the courts.[78]

There was disagreement in the bureaucracy as to application of retirement rules. A civil servant contended that the government could not require his retirement until he reached the age of 60. The Supreme Court upheld the unfettered discretion of government to require retirement after 55.[79]

(14) Paradoxically, while use of the writ petition by civil servants was partly the consequence of deficiencies within the bureaucracy and served as a remedy for personal injustices incurred, the institutional deficiencies were not corrected by reliance on the writ. It is conceded by members of the excutive and judiciary alike that while personal justice was achieved by the writs there were some unsettling institutional consequences. The courts were aware of this problem, as the judgment in the *Bashir Ahmed Khan* case shows. In that case the High Court set forth positive propositions for guiding the administration in determining seniority, and the Supreme Court concurred, stating that "so far from being an inconvenient interference with the day to day control of that service by the Government, is indeed an action calculated to assist the Government in exercising such control peacefully and harmoniously." Nevertheless, the use of the writ did produce some deleterious effects, one of which was change in the relationship between superiors and their subordinates resulting from the knowledge that the latter could have certain decisions of the former invalidated through court action. Government officers view this as a deterioration of discipline, but it might just as well be construed as deterrence of further injustice. Secondly, a substantial portion of the time of establishments and law departments of the central and provincial governments had to be spent preparing government's defense in writ cases. It is sometimes argued that such time and energy might have been devoted to construction of an effective personnel system. The third and probably the most serious result was the uncertainty and confusion caused by the lapse of time between filing a writ and

[78] *Mohammad Aboo Abdullah v. Province of East Pakistan and another*, 1960, 1 P.S.C.R. 53.

[79] *Pakistan v. Liaqat Ali Khan*, 1958, 2 P.S.C.R. 234.

the ultimate final decision. During this period a whole sequence of assignments, transfers, promotions, and other personnel decisions might be held in abeyance pending a decision. Chief Justice Cornelius in the *Md. Abdu Miah* case,[80] called attention to the period (in this instance, two years) during which "the general efficiency of the staff is adversely affected by . . . a state of uncertainty and by retention of certain persons in posts to which their claims are doubtful." Thus the courts were faced with the dilemma of not only being unable to correct the institutional arrangements which gave rise to injustice, but also of aggravating these arrangements somewhat. Former Justice Akhlaque Husain suggested that the writ jurisdiction is not really a source of conflict between the judiciary and executive; rather it is "an inherent and eternal conflict between the interests of the individual and the administration. . . . The possibility of occasional hitches in the efficient running of the government is perhaps not too great a price to pay for the protection of the people's interests against the errors of the government."[81]

Yet, the judiciary chose wisely on the side of personal justice, for it is likely that without the use of the writs, personal injustice would have been far greater and institutional efficiency might have suffered much more from lowered morale than it did from whatever uncertainty the use of the writs may have produced.

In conclusion, the social environment of the bureaucratic system inherited from the British *Raj* was one of unstable equilibrium. The bureaucracy was strong enough and resilient enough to withstand the immense external pressures without disintegrating. This in itself is a remarkable accomplishment. But it was not equipped to deal with the internal pressures generated by the instability of society generally. The system was premised on assumptions of polite, respectful subservience to British superiors and on the notion that government employment was a rare privilege and distinction. Moreover, it was based on a more or less static society, not yet awakened fully to the freedom and its abuses which sovereignty brings in its wake. Responsibility for service matters was diffused throughout government, shared by the Establishment Division, Finance Ministry and other ministries, and by general administration departments in the provinces. There was no central personnel agency formulating and administering uniform per-

[80] *Province of East Pakistan v. Md. Abdu Miah*, 1959, 1 P.S.C.R. 259.

[81] Unpublished case *Muhammad Yahya Ali Khan v. Government of West Pakistan, Writ Petition No. 584 of 1958*, High Court of West Pakistan, August 5, 1958.

sonnel policies. Any employee could, of course, seek redress of grievance by consultation with superiors, but the foregoing analysis has been an effort to demonstrate that this was more a legal right than a socially convenient solution in which much faith was reposed. There were elaborate rules which had been carefully framed and from which a sophisticated body of case law had developed. For the central government services, these were known as the Civil Services (Classification, Control and Appeal) Rules which had been enacted under the Government of India Act in 1930 and were in force in Pakistan until superceded in some provisions by emergency screening rules in 1959. The provincial governments had adopted similar rules.[82] The CS (CCA) rules provided for elaborate hearing procedures designed to insure due process of law and to protect the government servants' rights. But they were designed to be administered by officials who were either British or who were carefully trained by the British and who were conversant with values implicit in due process of law. During the years after partition, these rules were applied, but the disarticulation of the system was too great; confidence in the rules and in those who applied them was lacking—and the next step was the judiciary. There was no mechanism such as Whitley Councils or other institutions either inherited or evolved. There were employees' unions such as the provincial civil service and CSP associations, and from time to time they functioned as important interest groups, but they were not fully institutionalized nor were they equipped to handle individual grievances in a systematic manner. The federal and two provincial public service commissions struggled to maintain what power they possessed and could not reorient their dispositions or mobilize their forces to deal effectively and positively with personnel matters even when such were within their jurisdictions. The commissions deplored their own weaknesses and tried to rise to the powerful position of a governing personnel authority, but they were victims of the trauma of the times and the shortage of skilled talent for their own staffs.[83]

[82] The most significant case in this regard is *Noorul Hassan v. Federation of Pakistan*, 1956, P.S.C.R. 128. The briefer judgment of the High Court in the same case includes a good analysis of the provincial civil service rules of Sind. *Noorul Hassan v. Federation of Pakistan*, P.L.D., 1955, Sind, 200.

[83] A candid statement of the inadequate powers of the public service commission (in this instance, provincial) can be found in the *Annual Report of the Working of the West Pakistan Public Service Commission for the Period 14 October 1955 to 31 December 1956* and in the following annual report for 1957. See criticism of the role of commissions in *The First Five Year Plan 1955-60*, Karachi, 1957, pp. 115-117. See also Chief Justice Kayani's stern criticism of government's disregard of the role of the public service commission which he regarded of fundamental importance: *S. I.*

It is admittedly unrealistic to limit this analysis of bureaucratic social environment to administrative matters. Transcending all of these determinants was the problem of political instability, changes in ministries, declarations of martial law prior to 1958, and other factors which profoundly affected and perhaps even caused the circumstances here described. The political conditions cannot possibly be discussed here; they have been extensively and competently dealt with elsewhere.[84]

Moreover, conditions within the bureaucracy were but a reflection of the disarticulation of society, displacement of millions of people, massacre of perhaps half a million, upheaval of social values—all of which could not have been avoided. The bureaucracy stood when other segments of society faltered and collapsed. It conducted the business of government. It helped forge a new state. It could not deal effectively with the burdens of internal strains and stresses; indeed no bureaucracy faced with a similar set of problems would have been able to meet the needs adequately. It was in this context of acute human distress that the judiciary felt that its duty was to act to extend justice and compassion which the bureaucracy could not generate from within.

IV. Historic Image of the Judiciary

Reliance on the courts through the mechanism of the writ to attain justice within the bureaucracy is related to the image of the judiciary as a symbol of compassionate justice and independence. The significance of this symbol extends beyond the bureaucracy itself to all grievances involving citizen and government. For example, students alleging injustice in grading and in types of examinations sought writs against professors and professors sought writs against vice-chancellors and the government. As in the bureaucracy, this is probably partly due to conditions of trauma and disarticulation in the universities caused by

Mahbub v. Province of West Pakistan and Islamic Republic of Pakistan, 1959, P.L.R. 2, WP. 1275. See the case of *Abdul Latif* (cited note 57 above) for account of the Federal Commission's effort to play an effective role in selection of section officers and the court's support of this role. One of the most distinguished and vigorous chairmen of the Federal Public Service Commission, Mian Afzal Husain, has written critically of the weakness of the commission in "They Way to a Clean Administration," *Pakistan Times Supplement*, October 27, 1960, p. 17.

[84] See Mushtaq Ahmad, *Government and Politics in Pakistan*, Karachi, 1959; G. W. Choudhury, *Constitutional Development in Pakistan*, Lahore, 1959; Nasim Zakaria, *Parliamentary Government in Pakistan*, Lahore, 1958; Khalid Bin Sayeed, Pakistan: *The Formative Phase*, Karachi, 1960. See especially *Report of the Constitution Commission, Pakistan* (Shahabuddin Commission), Karachi, 1961, pp. 5-14; Leonard Mosley, *The Last Days of the British Raj*, New York, 1961; Penderel Moon, *Divide and Quit*, London, 1961.

(1) the departure of teaching faculties most of whom were Hindu and British, (2) restlessness of students, and (3) discontent of professors because of the low estate of scholarship as a profession.[85] Three examples of the use of writs by students will illustrate the problem of judicial participation in the quest for justice in educational matters. Students entered a university in 1958 when the requirement was that the final examination count for 40 per cent of the total grade.[86] Two years later the requirement was changed to 45 per cent. The students' qualification for graduation was based on the new requirements and they failed to qualify. They sought a writ of *mandamus* to compel the university to use the 1958 requirement as a basis for qualification. The High Court dismissed the writ and the Supreme Court upheld the dismissal.

The university's retrospective application of the changed requirement is illustrative of conditions of administrative disarticulation within the university and imperfect understanding of the paramountcy of fundamental concepts of justice. These conditions create the necessity of the court's extension of the writ jurisdiction into what might otherwise be regarded as internal matters. A second example shows the type of agitation which leads to seeking the writ. A number of employees of the West Pakistan University of Engineering and Technology were displeased with the appointment of a new vice-chancellor. Several subordinate employees made public statements urging his removal. The vice-chancellor, regarding a group of professors as being particularly antagonistic, allegedly ordered four of them to go to Karachi, Dacca, and Lahore and prepare lists of books and journals.[87] The High Court considered the application but refused to grant the

[85] An impressionistic account of the circumstances in Indian universities which is, in almost all respects, applicable as well to universities in Pakistan is Edward Shils, "Indian Students," *Encounter*, September, 1961, pp. 12-20. See also Alex Page, "Asyntasia; or Learning Attitudes in Pakistan," *The Educational Record* Vol. 43 (1962), pp. 269-271; Robert J. Kibbee, "Higher Education in Pakistan," *Journal of Higher Education*, Vol. 33 (1962), pp. 179-189. The university problem has been dealt with extensively in various government reports. See especially *Proceedings of the Educational Conference Held at Karachi 4-5 December, 1951*, Karachi, 1956; Ghulam Jilani and B. M. Omar, *An Enquiry into the Factors Influencing the Academic Atmosphere of the Dacca University*, Dacca, 1956; *Report of the Educational Reforms Commission—East Pakistan, 1957*, Dacca, 1957, 2 vols.; *Report of the Commission of National Education January-August, 1959*, Karachi, 1960; *Report of the Scientific Commission of Pakistan*, Karachi, 1960; M. Bashir, "The Scholar and Society in Pakistan," *The Scholar and Society, Bulletin 13 of the Committee on Science and Freedom*, Manchester, England, 1959, pp. 59-64.

[86] *Sultana Khokar v. University of the Punjab*, P.L.D., 1962, S.C. 35.

[87] For various accounts see *Civil and Military Gazette*, December 27, 1961, p. 4.

writ.[88] In another university case, a student was "rusticated" or suspended for one year by the College Council for allegedly copying in an examination.[89] Since the College Council did not call for an explanation from the student, the High Court granted a writ ordering the Council to hold a meeting to decide afresh as to the student's guilt. The court maintained that justice requires that no person be condemned without being heard and that all persons and institutions with power to condemn must observe this principle of justice. This case would probably startle an American observer, for such matters would rest exclusively and privately with the professor, who might, conceivably, not observe such conditions and yet could not be challenged. Indeed the contrast between this case and American practice points to the reason for the use of the writ in such matters in Pakistan. There is highly uneven absorption of standards of Anglo-Saxon justice and high expectation that these standards are not understood or, if understood, not observed. This places the burden of enforcement on the judiciary, which becomes thereby the chief means by which Anglo-Saxon notions of justice gradually permeate the totality of social custom. Whatever the reasons, the universities, like the bureaucracy, appeared to have no satisfactory mechanism for the adjustment of these disorders, and the void was filled by turning to the judiciary.

Since the use of the writ goes beyond the bureaucracy itself, the historic image of the courts as the hope of the people must also be considered. The high courts of the subcontinent are venerable institutions, the first ones having been established in Bombay, Madras, and Calcutta in 1862. The High Court of West Pakistan was established as the High Court of Lahore in 1919, after existing as Chief Court of the Punjab since 1865. The symbol of hope which the courts represent in Pakistan is not unrelated to the historic conception of the courts as being essentially Indian and providing an open, public means of achieving personal freedom and to the converse impression of the bureaucracy as essentially foreign, secretive, and exclusivist in its attitudes. These stereotypes seem to be reflected in the two institutions by many characteristics. It is, for example, far easier to gain access to court sessions than it is to the civil secretariats. District and sessions

[88] *Mumtaz Husain Qureshi and three others v. Vice-Chancellor of West Pakistan University of Engineering and Technology, Writ No. 832*, High Court of West Pakistan, December 27, 1961.

[89] *Muhammad Munir Shah v. The Principal, Government College, Sargodha*, P.L.D., 1958, Lahore, 466.

courts, particularly, usually teem with humanity and present a picture of humane justice administered close to the people. The secretariats, on the other hand, are removed from the maelstrom of life not only physically but in the attitude conveyed to the citizenry. A larger proportion of texts of judgments of the Supreme and High Courts are published in the English language press than is the case in most Western countries and the decisions are read avidly and discussed with fervor in the coffee houses and other gathering places. Legal terms and references to provisions of the criminal and civil codes are commonly used in the press on the correct assumption that the reading public understands the references without further explanation. In 1925 Darling noted the "almost passionate love of litigation in the Punjab," and supported his observation by the Civil Justice Committee Report of 1925 and various settlement reports.[90] He notes from the 1907 settlement report for Mianwali, for example, that "to people who are not only delighted to take advantage of the smallest chance of joining in an affray or trying their strength, but are also desperately fond of civil litigation, years of plenty offer an irresistible temptation to spend money in connection with cases which in the long run prove utterly ruinous to many of them."[91] Noting that what was true of the Punjab was generally true for India, the Simon Report in 1930 observed that in Bengal, judicial stamps were a source of public revenue to the provincial government second only to land.[92] There was almost universal confidence in the capacity, efficiency, and integrity of the judiciary, and this reputation was well earned and deserved.[93] The closeness of the courts to the masses of people was in part accounted for by the more rapid pace of Indianization. The Simon Report shows that in 1929 in the Punjab nearly half, and in Madras 57 per cent, of the judges in the High Court, district courts, sessions courts, and magistrates courts were Indian. The chief justice of the Punjab High Court was Indian and 6 justices were European and 6 Indian. A more detailed analysis for 1932 reveals the same pattern. In that year, 37

[90] Sir Malcolm Darling, *The Punjab Peasant in Prosperity and Debt*, Oxford, 1925, p. 68.

[91] *Idem.*

[92] *Report of the Indian Statutory Commission, 1930*, Cmd. 3568, I, 295-296.

[93] This reputation may have deeper roots than those suggested here. Derrett suggests that the attractiveness of British courts, evident as early as the eighteenth century, lay in the immediacy of the remedy and in high prizes if the case was won. J. Duncan M. Derrett, "The Administration of Hindu Law by the British," *Comparative Studies in Society and History*, IV, 1961, p. 18.

(44 per cent) of the 84 judges of the high courts and chief courts of India were Indian.[94] Three of these were chief justices of the high courts of the Punjab, United Provinces, and Bengal, the latter being regarded as the senior high court in India. In contrast, the civil lists for the executive branch reveal that of 54 posts of secretary to the government of India or to provincial governments, only 3 (5.5 per cent) were held by Indians. These posts were actually below that of high court judge, but come nearest to them for rough comparison.[95] Another way of determining the difference in degree of Indianization of the executive and judicial departments is by total composition of the two cadres. In 1932 the ICS had a total strength of 1,099 officers (excluding Burma), of whom 306 (27.9 per cent) were Indian. In the same year, in addition to the 84 high court judges already mentioned, there were 97 district and sessions court judges, of whom 32 (32.9 per cent) were Indian. In the magistrates' and small cause courts all 86 judges were Indian. Thus, of the total cadre of 183 judges assigned to courts below the high courts, 64.4 per cent were Indian.

This high degree of Indianization contributed much to the emotional feeling which the public has had for the courts, a feeling certainly deeper and friendlier than its attitude toward the executive bureaucracy. To the already shining symbol of the courts as a champion of individual liberty, the writ jurisdiction was added and quickly acquired deep meaning both in jurisprudence and as a public symbol. This feeling was summarized by retired Justice Syed Akhlaque Husain of the West Pakistan High Court when he said,

"It would be no exaggeration to say that for the first time after the country was freed from the crippling yoke of foreign rule, that Article (Art. 170 of the 1956 Constitution) has brought to us a sense of real liberty. The average citizen feels it. Even the majority of the officials in the hierarchy of the officialdom feel it. The amazing speed with which the word 'writ' has become a part of our language, even of the undeveloped regional language, is eloquently significant. Article 170, and Part II, which lays down the fundamental rights of the citizen,

[94] Compiled from names in *Combined Civil List for India No. 100, April-June 1932*, Lahore, 1932.

[95] According to the Warrant of Precedence in India in effect in 1932, following are the relative ranks of the posts here compared: chief justice of the Bengal High Court, 7; chief justices of other high courts, 12; judges of high courts, 20; secretaries to government of India, 24; secretaries to provincial governments, 35.

have truly made our Constitution a matter for joy and pride. They have brought the Rule of Justice within our grasp. We have only to take it and keep it with fond reverence."[96]

It is of interest to note that while the high courts and Supreme Court are independent of the executive, there exists in the frame of government left by the British *Raj* a mutual interest between bureaucracy and judiciary. This mutual interest is expressed in two institutional forms. First, at certain levels of government there was a partial convergence of judicial and executive functions, a convergence which was the subject of several reports by various committees both on justice and civil service in pre-partition India. The well-known dissent by Abdur Rahim in the Islington Commission Report is a particularly cogent analysis of the problem.[97] At the local level of government, executive officers who may be members of the civil service of Pakistan or of the provincial services serve as magistrates along with their other duties as deputy commissioners and collectors of revenue. This does not mean that they are permanently assigned to the judiciary but only that it is an important aspect of their district work, for they do not do judicial work when they leave the district for the secretariats. These officers, even in their judicial work, come under the control of the executive branch rather than the courts. The effect of this system is that, of the four levels of courts (Supreme Court, High Court, District and Sessions Courts, and the district magistrate's courts) the lowest level remains outside the control of the regular court system. The Law Commission was unanimous in its recommendation for changing this aspect of the executive-judicial convergence by separating the two functions.[98] It proposed that all judicial magistrates at all levels be placed under the direct control of the High Court for judicial and administrative matters. The commission's answer to the familiar argument that the district officer needs judicial powers to enhance his prestige and enforce his decisions was that local administration had to change its sanctional base from one of fear to one of persuasion and leadership. The commission suggested, however, that powers under the preventive and security sections of the Criminal Procedure Code remain with the district officer, who, in the exercise of this respon-

[96] Syed Akhlaque Husain, "Writ Jurisdiction of Superior Courts in Pakistan," P.L.D., 1958, *Journal*, p. 10. See also his decision in the unpublished case, *Muhammad Yahya Ali Khan v. Government of West Pakistan*, cited in note 79 above.

[97] *Report of the Royal Commission on Public Services, 1915*, Cd. 8382, 20 vols. 1917, Vol. I.

[98] *Report of the Law Reform Commission 1958-59*, Karachi, 1959, pp. 25ff.

sibility, would be known as an "executive magistrate." The proposal to separate executive and judicial functions "as soon as practicable" was included in the 1956 Constitution as a directive principle of state policy (Part III, article 30). Even after martial law the central government announced that such separation would be accomplished when the new 1962 Constitution was made effective in June 1962.[99] Many eminent jurists and government officers who doubt that this separation will actually take place support their view by the fact that the concept of separation is nowhere mentioned in the new 1962 Constitution.

The second dimension of this problem is the assignment of officers of the CSP more or less permanently to judicial work at high levels, including the benches of the high courts. The practice in India had been to assign some ICS officers to what was known as the judicial branch of the ICS, in which work they would advance to higher judgeships, some eventually being appointed to reserved posts on the High Court and (though without special reserved posts) to the Supreme Court. The Civil Justice Committee 1924-1925 deplored this situation and other commissions were concerned about it. After partition the government of Pakistan decided against creating a judicial branch of the CSP, but in 1954 the policy was changed somewhat when it was decided to permit former ICS and CSP officers to serve on the judicial side, and in 1962, 2 of the judges on the Supreme Court and 5 of the 26 judges of the West Pakistan High Court were former ICS officers, and 9 CSP officers were posted as district or sessions judges or in other judicial assignments. At this level of the judiciary, the courts are entirely independent of the executive and the judges are full-time career judges. The Law Commission concurred with the government policy to transfer selected CSP officers to the judiciary. It suggested further that such selection be made before the fifth year of service (29 years of age) and that those selected be given two years of intensive civil law training. The judicial branch was to be made as attractive in terms of salary and amenities as the executive branch and certain posts such as Solicitor to Government and Law Secretary were to be opened to members of the judicial branch. Three members of the commission vigorously dissented from this view. Mahmud Ali suggested instead the establishment of a separate judicial service equal in status to the CSP.[100] He also favored not appointing CSP officers to the High Court

[99] *Pakistan Times,* Sept. 11, 1961, p. 9.
[100] *Ibid.,* p. 133.

unless they had extensive judicial experience. Enayetur Rahman was more emphatic in his opposition to using CSP officers in the judiciary.[101] Citing the *Sixth Report of the Pakistan Public Service Commission*, which deplored the low standard of education of those who passed the CSP examination, he felt that such ill-prepared officers, who had no legal training and no experience, could not strengthen the judiciary. Rahman urged a separate judicial service made up of those with law degrees who had successfully passed an examination. M. A. Majid similarly argued that those assigned to judicial work should have law degrees, though he did not comment on establishing a separate judicial service.[102]

These two aspects of relationship between judiciary and bureaucracy have not appeared in any way detrimental to the impartiality and independence of the courts or the judges. As in the *Conseil d'Etat* of France, the fact that some judges belong to the same ICS cadre as administrators has not resulted in impartiality for or against administration. Nor has it conduced to any absence of humility with respect to the intricacies of administrative problems, as is indicated by Justice Cornelius' statement: "The strength of the executive in the discretionary field lies in this, namely, that it knows the necessities of the administration and is seized of the large question of the overall public interest . . . [a purely judicial court] lacks the necessary minimum knowledge to follow the ramifications of administrative action. . . ."[103]

Despite this disclaimer, judges in Pakistan have, in fact, played an important role in analysis of administrative problems, which has unquestionably deepened their insight and understanding of bureaucracy. Former Supreme Court Chief Justice Muhammad Munir was chairman of the first pay commission which prepared a comprehensive study of conditions of service and pay scales in 1949.[104] In 1953, Chief Justice Munir and the present chief justice of the High Court of West Pakistan, M. R. Kayani, were members of the commission which investigated the Punjab disturbances of 1953. A major part of that report was an analysis of the causes of weaknesses in civil administration which allowed the trouble to develop.[105] The chairman

[101] *Ibid.*, p. 136.

[102] *Ibid.*, p. 141.

[103] Address before All-Pakistan Lawyers Convention, October 1, 1960, *Pakistan Times*, October 4, 1960, p. 6.

[104] Cited in note 28, above.

[105] Cited in note 23, above.

of the Constitution Committee which presented its report in 1962 and which necessarily dealt *inter alia* with service matters was former Supreme Court Chief Justice M. Shahabuddin, ICS, Retired Chief Justice Munir, Chief Justice Shahabuddin, and the present chief justices of the Supreme and High Courts are eminently respected in intellectual circles and by the public generally. The position of the High Court is reinforced by the rather special role of its chief justice in Pakistan life. Since the executive government must take an official stand against each writ petition when it is sought, it might be expected that government officers would be against the use of the writ jurisdiction in service matters. Most government officers are not opposed to the writ and certainly there is no feeling in the bureaucracy against one of the staunchest defenders of the writ, Chief Justice M. R. Kayani. In 1962 he was serving his seventh consecutive term as president of the CSP Association and that same year was elected president of the Association of Alumni of British Universities for a third term. Both of these are influential interest groups of officials and private citizens educated in England. From his installation as Chief Justice of the High Court of West Pakistan in April 1958 to May 1, 1962, Kayani has made no fewer than twenty public addresses, which, however, have become far more important commentaries on Pakistan's affairs than ordinary speeches. This rather special position of Kayani's speeches is indicated by the fact that most of the Urdu and English papers print the full text, sometimes in two or even three installments. This verbatim reporting of speeches is very rarely done. That it is done in M. R. Kayani's case is symptomatic of the high regard in which he is held both by the English-reading and vernacular-reading public. His use of allegory and parable based both on Qur'anic and Western literature is a very effective means of commenting on moral and mundane affairs in a manner easily grasped by both Urdu and English-reading audiences. His sharp wit and deceptively rambling but brilliantly satirical style and the forthrightness of his views have contributed to this position which, in turn, has enhanced the esteem of the High Court. The speeches which he has written in English have been compiled in a volume entitled *Not the Whole Truth.*[106] It is noteworthy that President Ayub has written a foreword in which he states that, while the usual role of the witness is to tell the truth, the whole

[106] The speeches have been compiled by Iftikhar Ahmad Khan, an officer of the Civil Service of Pakistan, and were scheduled to be published in Lahore by the Pakistan Writers Cooperative Society in 1963.

truth, and nothing but the truth, and the judge's duty is to ascertain the truth, Justice Kayani has assumed the role of the witness in Pakistan's public life and his doing so under martial law is an index of the measure of freedom which prevails. From this statement by the President, Justice Kayani had selected the title of the collection of speeches.

The senior puisne judge of the High Court, Shabir Ahmed, has tried some of the most spectacular cases in which government officials were defendants. His vigorous assertions of the independence of the judiciary and his refusal to be influenced by the power of the executive branch have won him high prestige which has also redounded to the credit of the court.

Chief Justice A. R. Cornelius of the Supreme Court is also universally respected and is very much in the public eye as chairman of the second Pay Commission, which submitted its report in the middle of 1962 on structure and pay of the public bureaucracy. Chief Justice Cornelius has given several public addresses of a serious, scholarly nature, probing deeply into problems of law and bureaucracy.

Indeed, the detachment of the judges from the minutiae of bureaucratic problems, their insight into the nature of bureaucracy, and their deep sense of compassion for employee grievances, place their utterances among the most constructive made in Pakistan.

V. The Writ Jurisdiction

The writ jurisdiction involves exercise of the well-known instruments of English jurisprudence whereby the courts may compel the executive to act or may restrain the executive from acting injuriously to rights deemed to be of superior concern. These instruments, *mandamus, certiorari,* prohibition, *quo warranto,* and *habeas corpus,* have been regarded as extraordinary remedies, or as a "short-handed means of rectifying wrongs" deriving from excess or failure of jurisdiction by judicial, quasi-judicial, and administrative authorities.[107] The writs also came to be known as "prerogative writs" because in the development of English common law they were originally issued by the crown and later by the Curiae Regis. With gradual separation of executive and judicial functions, the writs came to be addressed by the courts

[107] A cogent summary of the development of writs (especially of mandamus) is found in Chief Justice Cornelius' judgment in *The State of Pakistan v. Mehrajuddin,* 1959, 1 P.S.C.R. 34. See also A. K. R. Kiralfy, *Potter's Outline of English Legal History,* London, 1958; G. W. Keeton, *Elementary Principles of Jurisprudence,* London, 1949; A. T. Carter, *History of English Courts,* London, 1944.

against other agents of the crown performing executive functions. Under British rule in undivided India, the principle embodied in the writ of *mandamus* was included in the Specific Relief Act of 1877 and was first vested in the Calcutta High Court only. The principle of *habeas corpus* was included in the Criminal Procedure Code in 1898 and the principle embodied in the writ of *certiorari* was granted in 1908.

The writ jurisdiction entered the legal system of Pakistan even before the 1956 Constitution, when, in July 1954, the Constituent Assembly approved a proposal of the Law Ministry amending the Government of India Act of 1935.[108] The resulting section 223-A of the Government of India Act of 1935 gave to all the high courts the power to issue "writs including writs in the nature of" the five writs of English law to any person, authority, or government in Pakistan.[109] At least one High Court judge viewed the words "in the nature of" as conferring on the courts the positive right to redress wrongs unhampered by the "limitations and technicalities which have in the course of time grown around the prerogative writs in England on account of historical causes peculiar to the past and present conditions in that country."[110] In any event, there was no chance for judicial construction of the wording of the Government of India Act of 1935, for the language of Article 170, of the new Constitution of Pakistan enacted in 1956, permitted an even more expansive interpretation of the writ jurisdiction than might have been construed from the words "in the nature of." This was made possible by reading the writ provisions with the provisions on fundamental rights (Article 5-22 of Part II). Article 22 of the 1956 Constitution guaranteed the right to move the Supreme Court for enforcement of fundamental rights conferred by the Constitution and gave the Supreme Court the power to issue directions, orders, or writs for enforcing fundamental rights. Article 163 further empowered the Supreme Court to issue directions, orders, decrees, or writs as necessary

[108] Constituent Assembly (Legislature) of Pakistan Debates, *Official Record*, July 6, 1954, p. 189.

[109] A major constitutional crisis in Pakistan in 1954 hinged on interpretation of the validity of section 223-A. The President of the Assembly had petitioned the court under section 223-A to issue a mandamus preventing the governor-general from dissolving the Assembly. The Federal Court overturned the High Court and ruled that section 223-A, not having received the assent of the governor-general, was not part of the law of Pakistan. See *Tamizuddin Khan v. Federation of Pakistan*, 1955, I F.C.R. 155. For extended discussion of this issue, see Sir Ivor Jennings, *Constitutional Problems in Pakistan*, Cambridge, 1957.

[110] See Syed Akhlaque Husain's view in his "Writ Jurisdiction of Superior Courts in Pakistan," P.L.D., 1958, x, Journal, 3. See also his unpublished judgment cited in note 80 above.

to do complete justice in any matter pending before it. But the widest jurisdiction was given to the high courts, which were empowered by Article 170 to issue directions, orders, or writs not only for the enforcement of fundamental rights but for any other purpose. The limitation imposed by Article 163 on the Supreme Court that the order relate to a cause or matter before it was not placed on the High Court jurisdiction. It is because of this rather special position of the High Court that the writ jurisdiction is more commonly associated with the high courts than with the Supreme Court. The possibility of issuing directions or orders going beyond the confines of the power given in issuing writs seems to have been reduced by the Supreme Court judgment in the *Mehrajuddin* case.[111]

In general the view of the Supreme Court has been that the law of writs in Pakistan follows the practice of English courts "in all essential respects."[112] Interpretations of the Privy Council are followed although they are not legally binding since that body has had no jurisdiction over Pakistan decisions since 1950, when the Constituent Assembly passed the Privy Council (Abolition of Jurisdiction) Act, 1950. The High Court of West Pakistan has inclined somewhat more to the view forcefully and cogently expressed by former Justice Akhlaque Hussain in *Yahya Ali Khan's* case. This view holds that the political, social, and administrative conditions of Pakistan are vastly different from those of England and that it was recognition of these differences which led the framers of the 1956 Constitution to confer special jurisdiction on the high courts. Such power might then be used, as Akhlaque Hussain wrote, "by . . . successive generations of . . . judges according to their wisdom and sagacity and in accordance with the circumstances of their times."

The earliest important judgment in the writ jurisdiction after the 1956 Constitution was in effect was made by M. R. Kayani, then a puisne judge of the High Court of West Pakistan in the *Salamat Ali Jafri* case.[113] The issue was whether Article 170 of the new Constitution which conferred the writ power on the high courts could be used as a

[111] *State of Pakistan v. Mehrajuddin,* 1959, 1 P.S.C.R. 34. In this judgment Chief Justice Cornelius stated that the inclusion of the terms "directions" and "orders" in Article 170 related to the amendment of English law in 1938 abolishing certain writs but authorizing the issuance of orders of the same kind. From this he reasoned that the authority to issue directions and orders cannot exceed the authority to issue the five standard writs.

[112] *Lahore Central Co-operative Bank, Limited v. Saif Ullah Shah,* 1959, 1 P.S.C.R. 34.

[113] *Salamat Ali Jafri v. Province of West Pakistan,* P.L.D., 1956, Lahore, 548.

remedy for a grievance which occurred before the Constitution was in effect. Kayani declared that when a statute creates a new right, it operates prospectively, but when it provides a new remedy for an existing right, it has retrospective effect. By this reasoning it became possible to embrace within the protection of Article 170 grievances which had been suffered prior to its enactment.

After the 1956 Constitution went into effect, the number of writs sought in the courts increased markedly. As Table 7 shows, the total

TABLE 7: INCIDENCE OF WRIT PETITIONS FILED IN HIGH COURTS AND SUPREME COURT OF PAKISTAN (THROUGH JULY 31, 1962)

Year	*Supreme Court*		*High Court of West Pakistan*	*High Court of East Pakistan*	*Total*
	Original	Appellate			
1955	0	5	54	19	78
1956	6	83	734	374	1,197
1957	15	58	1,576	190	1,839
1958	13	74	1,863	203	2,153
1959	12	85	1,285	108	1,490
1960	12	132	1,666	111	1,921
1961	16	88	2,275	260	2,639
1962 (July 31)	5	50	2,276	210	2,541
Total	79	575 [a]	11,729	1,475	13,858

[a] Duplication in these totals resulting from the fact that some of the appellate cases originated in one of the high courts cannot be precisely determined. An official estimate is 150 cases; in any event, duplication cannot exceed 575 cases.

Percentage of writs sought by civil servants seeking redress of service grievances is 36% for the Supreme Court. Records are not available for the statistical determination of this percentage for the high courts. An official estimate for the High Court of West Pakistan is 30% and for the High Court of East Pakistan 8%.

Sources: Chief Justices of the Supreme Court of Pakistan and of the high courts of West Pakistan and East Pakistan.

number sought through July 31, 1962 approximates 14,000. Of these, approximately 3,000 (or about 500 a year after 1956) were writs sought by government employees seeking redress of grievance relating to employment matters. This does not mean that these actions resulted in granting of writs or even of admitting them for consideration. The number of writs sought is symptomatic of its wide use as a means of redress. This is an unusually high incidence of cases in which the courts seek to render justice in matters which, under other circumstances, would be rectified by some means within the bureaucracy. Grievances for which redress is most commonly sought by a writ involve determination of seniority for promotion, payment of back salary, and severance of service, involving alleged failure to adhere to rules and also infringement of the fundamental rights of government servants. Most of the writs are sought in other matters characteristic of problems of administrative law in other countries, namely, application by a citizen to compel government to act or restrain it from acting. Discussion of writs in this paper is limited to service matters, bulking less than a third of the writ petitions sought.[114]

Chief Justice M. R. Kayani of the West Pakistan High Court perhaps best summarized the arguments in an address to the High Court and the Karachi Bar Association on December 16, 1958 in which he justified use of the writ jurisdiction by public servants seeking redress:

"Important persons have told me that they have heard that the writ jurisdiction is sometimes abused, and I have told them that hearing is not like seeing. What have we done except to help the government in resolving for it entangled questions relating to seniority and salaries—the railway particularly, and for what we have done for the railway underdog, I think we are entitled to a railway saloon. As for the other civil departments, the officers who protest most are senior civil servants of the status of Secretaries and Commissioners and high police officers, but you will be surprised to know that they also come running to us when a small misfortune affects their private seniority. At this moment we have pending with us petitions of this nature affecting about ten such officers and we have already settled the seniority of police officers in respect of whom the Government took three or four decisions, each time reversing the previous decision, according as the Government in power was democratic or republican. Consequently you need have no fear that the writ jurisdiction has been curtailed. Mandamus and certiorari are flowers of paradise, and the whole length and breadth of Pakistan is not wide enough to confine their perfume. If in England the Judges could stretch certiorari even to the rate inspector's assessment by the necessity of a situation, we who are less conservative in interpretation and are often faced with situations more liberal in political vicissitudes, will compel ourselves to go much farther. Certiorari varies with the imaginative consciousness of the judicial mind, and there is plenty of it in the High Court.

"There may have been occasional lapses. After all, we are learning: we are all learning. After all this is a new jurisdiction. And there is a

[114] The leading case setting forth principles for the application of the writ jurisdiction generally (not solely in service matters) is *Tariq Transport Co. Lahore v. Sargodha—Bhera Bus Service and others*, 1958, P.S.C.R. 71.

Supreme Court to rectify our mistakes. Sometimes we deliberately commit mistakes, in order that the Supreme Court may correct them. And out of the hundreds of cases that we have disposed of, the number of lapses can be counted only on our fingers."[115]

The installation of M. R. Kayani as chief justice of the High Court of West Pakistan in 1958 proved to be an occasion for a forceful defense of the writ jurisdiction by the bar and by the new Chief Justice. Mahmud Ali Qasuri, a distinguished barrister who was then president of the High Court Bar Association, referred to the view of many ministers and administrators that the high courts "have a tendency to interfere in writ jurisdiction in cases in which the framers of the constitution never expected there would be interference."[116] Asserting that the Constitution clearly provided for equal protection of the laws, he found no case in which the courts interfered with executive discretion "except in the vindication of rights and justice." He confirmed the deep attachment which the people have for the judiciary and warned that curtailment of the powers of the high courts' writ jurisdiction would cause widespread dissatisfaction and might be "an invitation to the people to take extra-legal means for the redress of their grievances." In a reference to the internal conditions of bureaucracy, he upheld the right of a man who has failed to secure justice from the executive, to whom freedom has been denied, for whom "social justice is a mere mirage," to appeal to the High Court for redress. But it was the new Chief Justice in his installation address who elevated the function of the judiciary to the celestial realm. Referring to 1955, when the Governor-General's use of the ordinance power laid the writ jurisdiction "low in the dust," he was reminded that the High Court decided several original suits challenging government. Even though the writ jurisdiction was curtailed, it made no difference to the High Court, "for we thought," concluded Kayani, "that God fulfils Himself in many ways and that we are the humble instruments of His fulfilment."[117]

The judiciary in the exercise of the writ jurisdiction manifests awareness that it is the abnormal circumstances prevailing in the services which have, to some extent, compelled the courts to use the writ. Even when the Supreme Court has not supported such extension in law, it has shown a quality of compassion for the difficulties of civil servants.

[115] Address by Chief Justice M. R. Kayani, as published in *Pakistan Bar Journal*, 4, 1959, pp. 4-15.

[116] See full text of Mahmud Ali's address in *Pakistan Times*, April 3, 1958, p. 6.

[117] Full text of address in *idem*.

In the *Mehrajuddin* case, Chief Justice Cornelius, while overruling the high courts' use of a *mandamus* and contempt action to get certain railway employees paid, could not refrain from observing that the government did not show proper regard for the needs of their employees.[118] Again, the Supreme Court, overruling the High Court, deplored the failure of government to honor a court decree and to pay an employee salary arrears. Justice S. A. Rahman found it "impossible to withold our sympathy from the unfortunate subjects whose desperate condition very probably inspired the initiative taken by the High Court."[119] The Supreme Court has frequently quoted with approval the Privy Council decisions in *Rangachari's* case[120] and the *Venkata Rao* case,[121] in which the view was affirmed that redress is the "responsibility . . . and their Lordships can only trust, will be the pleasure, of the executive Government." But this may be a vain hope, for according to Chief Justice Cornelius, whatever may have been the conditions in government in 1936 "when the Privy Council used the inspiring words which adorn the judgment in the case of *Venkata Rao*, we have to observe with regret that any expectation based on a similar belief today would be illusory, at any rate in a comparative sense."[122]

A strong sense of compassion is one of the most characteristic distinctions of the high and supreme courts. In a significant statement expounding a philosophy of democratic administration, Chief Justice Cornelius called for equality of opportunity for the creative development of individual talents within the bureaucracy.[123] While compassion is not explicitly mentioned by the Chief Justice, his plea for the creative development of each individual is based explicitly on belief in the sacredness of human personality, which is the wellspring from which compassion flows. Chief Justice Kayani pointedly expressed this view: "I ask you to allow compassion and humaneness to inspire your governmental conduct. The quality of mercy is not strained, and it is mightiest in the mightiest. If this is pointed out to you occasionally by the High Court, do not say that the High Court is causing headache to you over the public servant or over any other section of society for that matter. The High Court is yours and the public servant is yours. The High Court maintains balance for you and maintains your bal-

118 *State of Pakistan v. Mehrajuddin*, 1959, 1 P.S.C.R. 34.

119 *Government of West Pakistan v. Fazal-e-Haq Mussarrat*, 1960, 1 P.S.C.R. 124.

120 *R. T. Rangachari v. Secretary of State*, A.I.R., 1937, Privy Council 27.

121 *R. Venkata Rao v. Secretary of State*, A.I.R., 1937, Privy Council 31.

122 *Pakistan v. Abdul Hamid*, 1961, 1 P.S.C.R. 1.

123 Address before Lahore Rotary Club on September 1, 1961, *Pakistan Times*, September 2, 1961, p. 7.

ance, and the public servant runs the country for you."[124] Again, in an address to the Village Development Academy, Kayani stated that the administrators do not possess "compassion and humaneness in the application of their knowledge to the needs of people. These qualities I was commending the other day to public servants in general and now to the Government. I am now commending them particularly to those who deal with villagers. But in my present context compassion and humaneness assume a different aspect. Here I am commending to them the quality of mercy."[125]

The issue of writ jurisdiction, both in its emotional dimension as a popular symbol of liberty and in its legal dimension as an assertion of judicial independence and popular rights, reached climatic heights with the trial of Sir Edward Snelson, Secretary of the Law Ministry, for contempt of the High Court in 1961.[126] The case arose because of comments regarding the high courts and the writs. In the mind of the literate citizenry who followed the case with deep interest, the issue between what they regarded as an arrogant bureaucracy dominated by martial law and a sympathetic judiciary, defender of liberty, was joined. It was the more dramatic because the defendant was one of two remaining British members of the ICS in the service of the central government and hence had become a symbol in the popular mind of the colonial bureaucracy of the British *Raj*. The status of the judiciary was enhanced by the High Court of West Pakistan, which, unanimously finding the Law Secretary guilty of contempt, asserted in unequivocal terms its independence and its sense of duty to prevent derogation of its dignity and prestige. Public approbation of the decision was immediate and was reflected in an editorial in the *Pakistan Times* which declared that the "power of the law has thus manifested itself in all its majesty, and the position of the Judiciary has been fully vindicated. . . . Fresh lustre has been imparted to the record of the Judiciary as an independent and fearless dispenser of justice. The people's confidence in its capacity to protect their legal rights and liberties has been heightened. And the country's prestige in the world outside has been enhanced."[127]

Sir Edward Snelson had given, upon invitation, a talk to a group of civil servants on the "Transitional Constitution of 1958." The talk was

[124] *Pakistan Times*, December 12, 1961, p. 6.

[125] *Pakistan Times*, January 1, 1962, p. 10. See also *ibid.*, April 18, 1962, p. 7.

[126] *The State v. Sir Edward Snelson*, P.L.D., 1961, Lahore, 78; *Sir Edward Snelson v. Judges of High Court of West Pakistan*, P.L.D., 1961, S.C. 237.

[127] *Pakistan Times*, May 7, 1961, p. 6.

subsequently printed by the central government and distributed to government offices. In the course of his remarks he commented on the High Court's writ jurisdiction, asserting, *inter alia*, that the high courts had claimed a "jurisdiction to interfere with the Government itself without reference to the strictly defined frontiers of the prerogative writs." He suggested that failure to adhere to known limits would lead to "chaos, duplication, fraction, usurpation of function, uncertainty, and public confusion." One of the strongest assertions of judicial independence arose indirectly from a comment of the Attorney-General. In the course of the government's defense of the Law Secretary, the Attorney-General referred to the court's publication of portions of the Snelson talk, which had appeared in a pamphlet classified for official use only. Mr. Justice Shabir Ahmad construed this as being "nothing but a hint that the sword of Damocles in the shape of appropriate action for contravention of the Official Secrets Act, 1923, hung over the heads of the Judges" of the High Court. In countering this "hint," Justice Shabir Ahmad reaffirmed the settled doctrine that when "the Central Government of Pakistan is a party in a proceeding before a Court of law however humble the Court may be, it has no better rights than any other party to the proceedings before that Court." In dealing with the remarks of Snelson, all three judges in separate but concurring opinions unqualifiedly found his comments on the courts' writ jurisdiction contemptuous. In the Supreme Court judgment, Chief Justice Cornelius characterized the case as appearing to be "unique in the annals of even so well documented a branch of law as that dealing with contempt of Courts." He regarded it "as a matter of acute regret" that so much attention was given by the High Court to the Attorney-General's statement, which had been construed as a threat and, indeed, did not agree with the High Court in its interpretation of this statement. But he upheld the judgment of the High Court and agreed with its view "that the words of which they complained do constitute libel upon the court, such as is calculated to interfere with the proper administration of justice by the High Courts." The significance of the case is indicated by the fact that the four other justices of the Supreme Court wrote separate concurring judgments, thus making the eighty-three-page judgment one of the longest in recent Pakistan law. It should be noted, however, that the four concurring judgments did not agree with Chief Justice Cornelius' view of Shabir Ahmed's distaste for the Attorney-General's "threat." That the Snelson case emerged because of disagreement between the Law Secretary and the judiciary as to the latter's interpretation of the use of writs suggests the existence of differing views held by the judiciary and the executive government. That the Law Secretary was found guilty of contempt illustrates again the high degree of courage and independence of the judiciary and the remarkably high regard in which the writ as an instrument of justice is held.

The judiciary has not been unmindful of the problems raised by reliance on the writ jurisdiction as a means of redressing grievances of civil servants. In some 12 judgments out of 24 major decisions on service matters, the Supreme Court has not been in agreement with the High Court. Its dilemma has been to strike a balance between "the interest of the public service and of the public in general" and the claims of individual public servants. The court attempted to lay down a guiding principle in this respect when Chief Justice Cornelius said that there is a "presumption that official acts are regularly performed, that a finding of excess or irregularity is not to be lightly reached, and that the approach must be from the point of view of the larger public interest, of which such private right forms only a small part."[128] Three alternative remedies have been advanced. Chief Justice Cornelius of the Supreme Court first suggested at the 1959 convocation of Law College, Lahore,[129] the introduction of administrative tribunals similar to the French system. Praising the French system, he showed awareness of the problems raised by interference in the internal operations of bureaucracy. Interference by elected ministers might have deleterious consequences, but government might also "be embarrassed and the efficiency of its process . . . gravely prejudiced by action at the hands of the courts, when they are induced to interfere in matters concerning promotions, appointments, and the general conditions of service of civil servants." In support of this Cornelius cited instances when "judicial decisions have been given that a particular officer and not another should be the Inspector-General of a particular province." True, these decisions have been given in forms of law and have been supported by plausible reasons, and yet it is impossible to deny that thereby interference has been effected in the very structure of the executive government. . . ." To avoid this he urged consideration of some system of administrative law as practiced in France.

Cornelius pursued this proposal further as a means of preserving the probity of the public services. In an address to the Lahore Rotary

[128] *Province of East Pakistan v. Md. Abdu Miah*, 1959, 1 P.S.C.R. 259.
[129] See text in *Pakistan Bar Journal*, IV, 1959, pp. 9-10.

Club on August 12, 1960, he stated that the introduction of administrative tribunals with necessary powers "would provide a strong agency for suppression of corruption among public servants, at the instance of members of the public who have suffered injury at the hands of such public servants."[130] He expanded this view in an address to the All-Pakistan Lawyers Association on October 1, 1960, in which he urged consideration of a system similar to that of the French *droit administratif*.[131] The regular courts cannot have, he said, the expertness necessary to interfere in the exercise of discretionary power by the executive, yet the exercise of discretion may result in deprivation of a valuable right. In the English tradition of the writ jurisdiction, there is judicial deference to the executive in such discretionary matters, but in the French system preservation of rights in the face of exercise of administrative discretion can be quickly and easily achieved. An administrative tribunal, Cornelius continued, offered the best chance of controlling corruption in administration. The Chief Justice reiterated his advocacy of administrative tribunals in an *obiter dictum* given in a judgment relating to the writ jurisdiction handed down May 31, 1961. His brief, cogent defense of the French institution merits quotation:

"Here, I may diverge a little from the main discussion to express regret that in our country there is no procedure similar to that of French Administrative Law which with variations appears to be in operation over the whole of Europe with the exception of the United Kingdom, or to a system of Administrative Courts which prevails in the United States. Under each of these systems there is a quasi-judicial Tribunal provided to which a person injured by any action of a public servant performed in the exercise of public powers may have instant recourse, and these Tribunals are invested with powers to bring all the underlying processes into the light of day, and apply necessary correction to the executive action by issuing appropriate directions to the executive authorities. In our law, apart from departmental appeals on the executive side, the judicial remedy lies only in the prerogative writs, which the superior Courts are empowered to issue. The pro-

[130] Full text in *Pakistan Times,* August 16, 1960, p. 4.

[131] Full text in *Pakistan Times,* October 4, 1960, p. 6. Cornelius' proposal for consideration of the French system stimulated controversial discussion as to its feasibility. The Constitution Commission dealt with the problem (see page 71 below) and a few commentaries by lawyers have been published. See, Hafizullah Khan, "Administrative Law for Pakistan," *Law Journal,* XLI, 1961, pp. 24-62; Mushtaq Ahmad Khan, "Administrative Tribunals and their Desirability in the Legal System of Pakistan," *ibid.,* pp. 116-125; Nasim Hasan Shah, "The Concept of Administrative Law," *Pakistan Times,* January 18, 1961, p. 4; *ibid.,* January 19, 1961, p. 4.

cedure, as these cases illustrate, is cumbersome and lengthy. Four years of waiting have been imposed upon the injured party in this case, to gain redress in regard to a trading license which was its main source of revenue."[132]

A second approach to a solution was suggested by Justice S. A. Rahman of the Supreme Court. Deploring the failure of government to honor a declaratory decree, Justice Rahman thus identified one of the principal legal reasons for reliance on the writ, namely, that it is judicially enforceable, whereas in declaratory decrees the court must depend on the sense of duty of the executive. Ordinarily it would be supposed that such sense of duty would be as effective as the threat of judicial sanction, for the "state . . . stands in no higher footing than an ordinary litigant and its duty to honor the Court's decree in the letter and the spirit would be too obvious to require any emphasis in this court."[133] Justice Rahman continued that the state had an even higher responsibility in maintaining the authority of the courts. Searching for a means whereby civil servants could effectively move the state with respect to salary arrears, he praised the position in Great Britain with the passage of the Crown Proceedings Act of 1947 and suggested that it was time for the government of Pakistan to pass legislation enabling civil servants to obtain relief with respect to salary claims against the state. He proposed modification of the Civil Procedure Code which would make this possible or, alternatively, a law similar to the Crown Proceedings Act which might be "found to be more in consonance with the spirit of the times."

The Law Commission recognized the problems inherent in the writ jurisdiction of the high courts but rejected the idea of creating separate administrative tribunals and did not refer to Justice Rahman's proposal for an adaptation of the British Crown Proceedings Act. The commission's proposal, more conservative than either of these suggestions, sought to preserve the writ jurisdiction as it is with some minor modifications to render speedier and more efficient justice. Acknowledging that the large number of writs sought by civil servants led to congestion of work, especially in the West Pakistan High Court, the commission proposed that district judges be allowed to issue writs on matters relating to non-gazetted civil servants. It suggested that students not be allowed to seek writs but that a special university

[132] *Faridsons Ltd. and Friederike, Ltd. v. Government of Pakistan*, P.L.D., 1961, S.C. 537.

[133] *Government of West Pakistan v. Fazal-e-Haq Mussarratt*, 1960, 1 P.S.C.R. 124.

tribunal be established for their grievances and that single judges rather than division benches be allowed to dispose of writ petitions. The commission suggested further that the High Court in East Pakistan should be allowed to issue writs to the central government even though that government is outside the court's geographical area.

Some impetus was added to the Cornelius' proposal for consideration of the French system of administrative law by the widely publicized comments of the distinguished former prime minister, Chaudhry Mohamad Ali.[134] The comments were given in Mohamad Ali's written answer to a questionnaire sent by the Constitution Commission to thousands of citizens. The full text of Mohamad Ali's answers which appeared subsequently in the press[135] merits special attention because of the high esteem in which Mohamad Ali is generally held in Pakistan, because of his distinguished service in establishing the bureaucracy in the first months after partition as Secretary-General and later as Prime Minister. In response to Question 27 of the Constitution questionnaire in which the commission asked if the respondent felt that the introduction of the administrative law concept would be an advantage to Pakistan, Mohamad Ali answered: "The introduction of an administrative law modified to suit conditions in Pakistan would probably be of advantage. With the introduction of such a law the power of writ exercised by the High Court and the Supreme Court in respect of the civil administration should be withdrawn. The procedure under the administrative law should be as simple as possible so that complaints whether by civil servants against unjust orders of the government or by the public against corruption, nepotism and high-handed behaviour of civil servants are promptly dealt with. In the past the civil services have been demoralised by the feeling that they were at the mercy of Ministers. On the other hand, the ordinary procedure for action against civil servants for dishonesty and maladministration is so dilatory and complicated that corrupt officials are seldom brought to book and still more rarely punished. If the administrative law remedies these defects it could be of great benefit to the country."

The proclamation of martial law on October 7, 1958 marked the beginning of a significant phase in the development of the writ jurisdiction. Initially it was thought that martial law would result in an effective curtailment of the use of writs. But, in fact, a series of interpretations by the courts has restored almost all the pristine vigor of

[134] See p. 377 above.

[135] *Pakistan Times*, June 13, 1960, p. 8.

the writs. The legal reasoning by which this has been accomplished is a remarkable episode in the evolution of Pakistani jurisprudence. In this essay, however, only the broadest outline of this development is possible.

The first order issued by the President after the October 7, 1958 Proclamation was President's Order (Post-Proclamation) No. 1 of 1958 Laws (Continuance in Force) Order. Under this instrument the courts were allowed to function, although their writ jurisdiction was somewhat modified. Art 2 (4) of the Continuance Order specifically gave the supreme and high courts the power to issue the five named writs, but it did not refer to the power to issue orders and directions which had been mentioned in Article 170 of the 1956 Constitution. The Continuance Order also omitted the words "in appropriate cases, to any government" which were also part of Article 170. The 1961 Constitution Commission commented that these omissions were probably "due to the fact that it was thought that the courts might unduly interfere in administration."[136] The commission thought that this caution was not necessary since the Supreme Court in the *Tariq Transport* case had ruled that the words "direction and orders" did not confer on the high courts any authority to issue orders except with respect to those portions of executive acts which are clearly judicial in nature.[137] Nevertheless, the government may have felt that the *Tariq Transport* doctrine might be overturned by subsequent construction. Whatever the reasons, these words were omitted in the martial law definition of the scope of the writ jurisdiction. This omission has not, however, been the source of judicial interpretation of martial law intent.

That interpretation has derived from Art. 2 (5) of the Continuance Order, which states that "No writ shall be issued against the Chief Administrator of Martial Law, or the Deputy Chief Administrator of Martial Law, or any person exercising powers or jurisdiction under the authority of either." The Supreme Court has interpreted paragraphs 2 and 5 of Article 2 when read together to mean that "the intention was to leave the writ jurisdiction intact, and not to add to or take away from it."[138] The jurisdiction of the courts has further been asserted by its construction of the titles given in Article 2 (5). It is quite clear that the Chief Martial Law Administrator is Field Marshal

[136] *Report of the Constitution Commission, Pakistan, op.cit.*, p. 95.

[137] *Tariq Transport Company v. Sargodha Bhera Bus Service*, 1958, 2 P.S.C.R. 71. Subsequently in the *Mehrajuddin* case, the Supreme Court defined the permissible scope of "directions and orders" even more explicitly. See note 110 above.

[138] *Pakistan v. Muhammad A. Hayat*, P.L.D., 1962, S.C. 28, at 34.

Muhammad Ayub Khan since he was so designated in the original Proclamation of October 7, 1958. But it is not clear who the Deputy Chief Martial Law Administrator (DCMLA) is, for after Aziz Ahmed held that title until October 28, 1958, it is uncertain that there was a "Deputy." The three commanders of the armed forces had been appointed deputies and later three generals were appointed "administrators of martial law" in three zones, A, B, and C, into which Pakistan was divided. In the well-reasoned *Gulab Din* judgment[139] Justice Shabir Ahmed concluded that immunity from writs could not extend to zone administrators or to entities appointed by them. Immunity can extend only to the chief and the deputy martial law administrators. Since it is not clear that there are deputies, this suggests that unless Ayub Khan himself issues the martial law order, the court's jurisdiction has not been ousted. It is clear in judgments of both the supreme and high courts that orders issued by the Chief Martial Law Administrator or his Deputy are exempt from judicial scrutiny.[140] The courts also asserted their jurisdiction by interpretation of three categories of instruments, ordinances, orders, and regulations.[141] In the *Khuhro* case it was held that a martial law *Order* could not be questioned by the courts, but an *order* issued under a martial law *Order* could be questioned.

When a legal instrument issued under Article 2 (5) by anyone except the Chief or Deputy Martial Law Administrator specifies that the courts cannot call such an action into question, the courts have not regarded their jurisdiction as being ousted. Only when five conditions were met would they acknowledge that their ouster was complete. These conditions were specified as (1) the authority should have been constituted as required by the statute, (2) the person proceeded against should be subject to the jurisdiction of the authority, (3) the ground on which action is taken should be within the grounds stated by the statute, (4) the order made should be such as could have been made under the statute, and (5) the proceedings should not be in *mala fides* and the statute not be used as a cloak to cover an act which in fact is not taken though it purports to have been taken under the statute. This reasoning has been supported in several cases[142] which make clear

[139] *Gulab Din v. A. T. Shaukat*, 1961, P.L.D., Lahore, 952.

[140] *Hayats'* case cited in note 138 above and *Muhammad Ibrahim v. Government of Pakistan*, P.L.D., 1960, Lahore, 1073.

[141] *Khuhro v. Pakistan*, P.L.D., 1960, S.C. 237, *Iftikhar-ud-Din v. Muhammad Sarfraz*, P.L.D., 1961, S.C. 585.

[142] *Zafar-ul-Ahsan v. Republic of Pakistan*, P.L.D., 1959, Lahore, 879; *Zafrul*

that both the Supreme and High Courts do not accept the ousting of their writ jurisdiction except under judicially defined circumstances and (as the Supreme Court said in *Zafrul Ahsan's* case) "in accordance with a long line of decisions in England."

While the courts have thus defined their jurisdiction in issues relating to martial law matters, there remains the question of the status of the writ when sought in matters not related to specific martial law legislation. In such matters the jurisdiction of the courts seems to turn on the issue of whether or not fundamental rights were invalidated when the 1956 Constitution was abrogated by martial law. The reasoning in three major cases—*Dosso's*, *Wakf*, and *Iftikhar-ud-Din*,[143]—deals with this remarkably complicated question. In *Dosso's* case, the first major court decision after martial law was proclaimed, Chief Justice Munir reasoned that fundamental rights were part of the Constitution which had been abrogated by martial law; hence the courts could not issue a writ on the ground of violation of these fundamental rights. This doctrine was upheld in the *Wakf* case, though Chief Justice Cornelius in this case reasoned that fundamental rights had not lost their validity and that they derive their force from martial law because Article 2 (1) of the Continuance Order, subsumed into martial law, asserts that Pakistan shall be governed in accordance with the late Constitution. In this judgment, Cornelius implies, but does not specifically assert, the natural law origin of rights.

In summary: with respect to writs based on fundamental rights, the present position is that they have been abrogated, but there is a strong leaning by Cornelius in the direction of their existence. In the more recent *Iftikhar-ud-Din* case, the issue of their existence was averted. When writs are sought in matters activated by martial law instruments, the ousting of judicial scrutiny is contingent upon such factors as the nature of the instrument and who issued the order. Even when the instrument ousts jurisdiction in specific categories, the courts will determine if the ouster is valid only if five conditions are met.

The future of the writ jurisdiction was carefully considered in the

Ahsan v. Republic of Pakistan, 1960, 1, P.S.C.R. 41; *Muhammad Zaman Khan v. M. B. Nishat and others*, P.L.D., 1962, S.C. 22; *Muhammad Ali v. Commissioner, Lahore Division*, P.L.D., 1960, Lahore, 64; *Pahlomal—Motiram v. Chief Land Commissioner*, P.L.D., 1961, Karachi, 384; *Syed Anwar Ali Shah v. Fiayaz Ali Khan*, P.L.D., 1962, Lahore, 483.

[143] *The State v. Dosso and another*, 1958, 2 P.S.C.R. 180; *Province of East Pakistan v. Md. Mehdi Ali Khan*, 1959, 2 P.S.C.R. 1 (commonly called the *Wakf* case); *Iftikhar-ud-Din v. Muhammad Sarfraz*, P.L.D., 1961, S.C. 585.

new constitutional framework for Pakistan created in 1962. The Constitution Commission did not propose any radical change in the status of the writ jurisdiction as it had existed under the 1956 Constitution before the proclamation of martial law. The only major change it suggested was that the High Court of East Pakistan be given the power to issue writs against the central government if the case arises from the central government employee posted in East Pakistan. This can be rightly construed as increasing rather than diminishing the effective power of the writ jurisdiction. The commission rejected the suggestion of administrative courts and concluded that "there is no reason to apprehend that writs filed by government servants, against any orders passed against them, would lead to dislocation of administrative work."

The Constitution eventually promulgated by the President under martial law on March 1, 1962, departed in major substantive respects from the Constitution Commission's recommendations. The status of the writ jurisdiction under the new Constitution is not yet clear, since there is room for judicial construction of the provisions. It would appear, however, that the writ jurisdiction has not been greatly altered. The Constitution does not mention the term *writ,* nor does it use the well-known Latin terms for the five writs. Article 98 (2) clearly authorizes the High Courts to issue *orders* in five categories of actions. These categories are definitions of the five writs, even though the terms are not used. Orders cannot, however, be issued in service matters involving members of the defense services. Nor can orders be made in relation to other government employees in respect to terms and conditions of service, except a term or condition of service specified in the Constitution. Since terms and conditions of service are more carefully detailed in Part VII of the Constitution than they were in the 1956 Constitution, the use of the writ in service matters is likely to continue. For example, dismissal only after a show cause notice is given is a specified condition. Fixed retirement age and remuneration may not be changed to the employee's disadvantage. It is conceivable that such issues as determination of seniority, which is not specifically mentioned as a condition of service in the Constitution, may be excluded as a matter in which a writ may be sought. But this exclusion does not seem probable, for the implications of *remuneration,* which is specifically listed as a condition of service, can properly be construed to include seniority, upon which promotion and hence remuneration ultimately depend.

VI. Summary

Pakistan's bureaucracy developed under greater handicaps than is generally supposed. The strongest single factor in reassembling a bureaucratic system was the influence and experience of a small group of Muslim officers, mostly but not exclusively from the ICS cadre who had distinguished careers in India. For the first two years the role of British officers as a transitional, stabilizing force was also important. This small group of officers whose system of order and administrative values was derived from the British was buffeted by a larger sphere of administrative values more intimately connected with vernacular, non-British values of Pakistani society. The resilience and staying power of the small group were considerably enhanced by maintaining contact with the radiating source of its values, namely British education. This was accomplished by continuing a British pattern in training recruits to the civil service of Pakistan and by sending them to England for further training. But the quality of such training was inferior to that of pre-partition training, largely because the time spent in England was too short and was not subject to the disciplined study of a degree course. Limiting the size of the CSP cadre to about four hundred men and admitting only young recruits (except for twelve PCS officers) in small numbers each year did much to prevent ICS values from being overwhelmed by the vernacular, non-British values of the total bureaucracy.

Order, rationality, and depersonalized bureaucratic norms emanating from the small sphere of ICS-oriented officialdom could not sufficiently permeate the total bureaucracy. The circumstance of a bifurcated culture had a dual contradictory effect. On the one hand, the higher bureaucracy, because it was partially detached from society in its values, was able to maintain its strength and preserve its identity in the face of political upheaval and social trauma. On the other hand, such detachment provoked hostility in the society at large and generated within the bureaucracy a loss of confidence in its capacity to resolve conflict.

The judiciary, particularly the High Court, a century-old symbol of independence, was juxtaposed with the bureaucracy, which had been a symbol of alien rule. The writ petition, which had been accorded a remarkably high legal status, filled a void in the bureaucracy's internal requirements of orderly conflict resolution. The High Court interpreted its writ jurisdiction to achieve a measure of natural justice for government employees, who constituted the largest group of institutionally employed persons in the nation. The judiciary was motivated by a strong sense of compassion and humaneness and did not appear to be extending its authority into the bureaucracy for the sake of power alone. The judiciary was also motivated by a keen awareness of its own historical role as an instrument of preserving liberty and a just society. The judiciary was better able than the bureaucracy to withstand the influence of non-British norms of law and order for several reasons: (1) it was secure in tenure and protected from political onslaught, (2) its leadership was of an uncommonly high order in courage and independence, (3) its relative detachment from the urgencies and pressures of administration had an insulating effect, (4) its attachment to and immersion in the source of radiation of its legal norms was more continuous and more profoundly intellectual. Of these four factors, probably the last is the most important. The judiciary was keenly aware that the roots of its norms were not in its own culture. It was compelled by the mere process of rendering judgments which entered the realm of Western legal scholarship to fit indigenous practices to Western norms. The application of the doctrine of *stare decisis*, the almost exclusive reliance on British precedent, a sense of identification of the judges with a body of jurisprudence transcending national cultural limits—all of these helped the judiciary maintain a pristine vigor. The result was that the judiciary became a source for the continued permeation of Western norms in the bureaucracy, not in administrative technique or organization, but in values of order in employee relations and due process in conflict resolution. In spite of the inadequacy of the internal order of the bureaucracy, it was the judiciary which made constructive, positive proposals for reform, proposals based on understanding of social environment, on knowledge of comparative jurisprudence, and on a sense of its own limitations.

With the promulgation of martial law in 1958, the judiciary felt compelled to accommodate the fact of the ultimate sovereignty of martial law with a philosophically and historically derived sense of judicial responsibility. The paramountcy of martial law was acknowledged, but the judiciary continued to assert that government had no special privilege before the courts. Acquiescing in martial law's curtailment of the writ jurisdiction when specified by certain categories of martial law instruments when issued by certain martial law officials, the judiciary reasserted the legal doctrine that it alone would determine when its jurisdiction had been ousted and that it would acknowledge such ousting only when certain conditions had been met.

No major, responsible, organized, adverse criticism has been able effectively to weaken the power of the writ jurisdiction. That power received support from the Law Commission and the Constitution Commission, and ultimately reappeared in slightly different though untarnished form in the 1962 Constitution. An important instrument of justice since 1956, it has survived the uncertainties of martial law for four years and the vagaries of constitution making in 1961 and 1962. Such vigor, power, and adaptability are qualities not easily lost in the subsequent evolution of bureaucracy and courts. Chief Justice Kayani said in 1959 that the writ jurisdiction would survive so long as there was an "imaginative consciousness of the judicial mind." There was "plenty" of it then, he said.

But it is by no means clear that the High Court of West Pakistan will continue to assert so vigorously what it has long regarded as its positive—indeed, sacred—responsibility for rectifying the wrongs within the bureaucratic apparatus. Several influences are even now changing the role of the High Court in Pakistan's political life. First, there have been twelve significant Supreme Court decisions which have overruled the High Court's interpretation of the writ jurisdiction.[144] This fact is obscured by the Supreme Court's concurrence in the High Court's sentencing of Sir Edward Snelson for contemptuous remarks of its interpretation of the writ jurisdiction. In these remarks, Snelson stated that "some very severe observations by the Supreme Court on the other (hand) have at least had the effect of indicating that after all there are limits and that the limits must be observed." While Snelson did not support this observation by case citation, an affidavit was presented listing some appeals presented to the Supreme Court in 1960 in which that Court ruled that such writs could not be issued. These cases are not listed in the judgments,[145] which do not deal with whether it was true that the Supreme Court had viewed the

[144] *Abdul Karim v. West Pakistan Province* (1956) 1 PSCR 116; *Pakistan v. Liaqat Ali Khan* (1958) 2 PSCR 234; *Pakistan v. Hikmat Hussain* (1958) 2 PSCR 257; *Pakistan v. Hasan Ali Jafari and another* (1959) 1 PSCR 26; *Lahore Central Cooperative Bank Ltd. v. Saif Ullah Shah* (1959) 1 PSCR 164; *Province of East Pakistan v. Md. Abdu Miah* (1959) 1 PSCR 259; *Pakistan v. Ali Afyal* (1959) 2 PSCR 160; *Government of West Pakistan v. Fida Muhammad Khan* (1959) 2 PSCR 187; *Government of West Pakistan v. Fateh Ullah Khan* (1959) 2 PSCR *Central Board of Revenue v. Asad Ahmad Khan* (1959) 2 PSCR 215; *Province of West Pakistan v. Akram Wasti* (1959) 2 PSCR 285; *Government of West Pakistan v. Fazal-e-Haq Mussarratt* (1960) 1 PSCR 124.

[145] See citations in n. 126 above.

writ jurisdiction differently from the High Court. The judgments focused on the contemptuous manner in which the remarks were made by Snelson, on the effect of those remarks and on certain clearly erroneous statements he made. Neither the Supreme Court nor the High Court judgment admitted or denied the implication of over-ruled writ judgments in the Snelson talk. Despite such judicial silence, the fact remains that the Supreme Court has progressively constructed channels within which the discretionary power of the High Courts to issue writs must flow. While such continuing definition and refinement of the scope of the High Courts' discretion does not deny the power to issue writs, in the long run it will necessarily reduce the sphere of exercisable power of writ issuance. This clearly discernible disposition of the Supreme Court is given additional significance by the intense personal interest which at least two Supreme Court justices—A. R. Cornelius and S. A. Rahman—have in finding alternative remedies for the redress of bureaucratic grievances. Secondly, the retirement from the High Court of Chief Justice M. R. Kayani in October, 1962 at the mandatory retirement age of sixty deprived that Court of its most articulate, formidable, and effective champion of the writ jurisdiction. Kayani's subsequent death in Chittagong on November 15, 1962 removed him from private political life where he was a powerful influence. With the retirement of his equally courageous colleague, Shabir Ahmed, scheduled for late 1963, the High Court will have lost its two most powerful judges. Thirdly, the appointment of Manzur Qadir as Chief Justice of the High Court in October 1962 may also change the Court's attitude toward writs. A distinguished barrister, Manzur Qadir served as Foreign Minister in the martial law cabinet of President Ayub and is generally regarded as the author of the 1962 constitution. It was Manzur Qadir who toured the country explaining and defending the 1962 constitution to bar associations, civil servants, and other educated groups. Since the constitution does not provide for judicial review of legislative action, Manzur Qadir's reputed authorship and support of it was regarded by many as a betrayal of his legal training. Because of his closeness to the President, he is thought also to have shared the latter's reputed disdain for judicial power. Manzur Qadir became the target of vicious attacks when the 1962 constitution went into effect and again when it was rumored that he was to be appointed Chief Justice of the West Pakistan Hight Court. On June 10, 1962 at the second session of the new National Assembly convened under the 1962 constitution, Mohammad Ali Bogra, successor to Manzur Qadir as foreign minister, referred to his predecessor as a "Rasputin-like architect of the Constitution." In August, district bar associations of Chittagong, Khulna, Gujrat Peshawar, and Lahore and the Karachi Bar Association passed resolutions opposing the appointment of Manzur Qadir as Chief Justice.[146] The tempo of vicious allegations against Qadir prompted his issuance of a formal statement of denial and explanation.[147] Probably Qadir was used as a scapegoat for widespread dissatisfaction with the new Constitution. Whatever the reasons, the campaign of slander indicates the extent of public feeling that he was closely associated with Ayub's views concerning the judiciary. Whether or not this is true is not known; certainly this public feeling cannot be taken at its face value. Only a series of subsequent judgments by the new Chief Justice on the writ jurisdiction will reveal his attitude. Certainly Manzur Qadir is an erudite student of law, as a study of his carefully prepared briefs in Supreme Court cases immediately reveals. His knowledge of Western case law is prodigious and his legal reasoning is rationally based and relatively devoid of extraneous, temperamental considerations—a quality rarely found in legal reasoning on the subcontinent. How these commendable emotional and intellectual characteristics will ultimately affect the writ jurisdiction cannot be conjectured. Lastly, a series of ordinances issued on July 7, 1962,[148] the last day of martial law, may have consequences on the writ jurisdiction. Although the ordinances took effect on June 7, 1962, it was reliably reported that the High Court of West Pakistan did not receive the notification promulgating the ordinances until June 16, 1962.[149] Such delay is a common occurrence in government affairs and is due usually to a lag in printing and distribution of the official *Gazette*. While little significance can be attached to this delay as such, it is important to note that the High Court was not formally notified or consulted in

[146] *Pakistan Times*, August 4, 1962, p. 1; August 7, 1962, p. 7; August 9, 1962, p. 5.

[147] *Ibid.*, August 9, 1962, p. 1.

[148] *Ordinance XLIII Limitation (Amendment) Ordinance 1962; Ordinance XLIV of 1962; Code of Civil Procedure (Amendment) Ordinance, 1962; Ordinance XLV, Registration (Amendment) Ordinance, 1962; Ordinance XLVII, Sale of Goods (Amendment) Ordinance, 1962; Ordinance XLIX, Negotiable Instruments (Amendment) Ordinance, 1962; Ordinance L of 1962, Appellate Jurisdiction (High Courts and Supreme Court) Ordinance, 1962; Ordinance LI of 1962, Provincial Small Causes Courts (Amendment) Ordinance, 1962; Ordinance LII of 1962, Court Fees (Amendment) Ordinance, 1962.* These ordinances all appeared in the *Gazette of Pakistan, Extraordinary*, June 7, 1962.

[149] Maqbul Shariff, "Civil Laws and Amendments," *Pakistan Times*, June 24, 1962.

advance concerning these ordinances. The most significant provision of the July 7 judicial ordinance is curtailment of the High Court's appellate jurisdiction. The power of the High Court to hear appeals from decisions of single benches, originally granted to the Court in 1919, has been abolished and the power transferred to the Supreme Court. The net consequence of these ordinances is an increase in jurisdiction of the lower district and sessions courts and the higher Supreme Court. This is in consonance with the report of the Law Commission, although the detailed implementation varies somewhat from the Commission's recommendations. The ultimate effect of this curtailment of jurisdiction is difficult to assess or to predict. Coupled as it is with the other factors here discussed, it may lower the prestige of the High Court and ultimately its effectiveness in adjudicating service cases. Further, the new review rules are likely to reduce the time lag between High Court judgment and Supreme Court review and thus may render the High Court more immediately responsive to the Supreme Court's views. On the other hand, consequent lessening of the High Court's burden in appellate civil cases may enlarge the attention it gives to writ cases which usually originate in the High Court.

Clearly, 1962 marks a new era in the development of Pakistan's judiciary. The preeminence of the writ jurisdiction as a powerful instrument to rectify bureaucracy seems somewhat less assured than at any time since 1946.

CHAPTER 13

INTERNATIONAL BUREAUCRACIES AND POLITICAL DEVELOPMENT

WALTER R. SHARP

THE role of bureaucracy in the political evolution of the developing countries may be viewed from at least two distinct angles. First, and foremost, there is the direct impact of the native administrative corps on the forces of political change within a country. Various facets of this impact have been the subject of preceding chapters in this book. Second, but much less obviously, it is possible to detect influences emanating from the international staff groups now operating in almost all of the less-developed nations of the non-Communist world.

Except for a few small missions in Latin America, under the auspices of the Organization of American States, these international *field* bureaucracies, so to speak, form part of the operational structure of the United Nations family of agencies.[1] It is with the political impacts of such groups that this chapter purports to deal.

The analysis rests on two main assumptions: first, that even though the rationale of United Nations technical assistance is that it "shall not be a means of foreign economic and *political* interference in the internal affairs of the country concerned,"[2] it is inherent in the nature of assistance programs that national political institutions and processes, broadly construed, cannot help being affected by the activities of foreign administrative and technical missions assigned to a country by organs of the international community; economic and social development, in other words, is inseparable from political evolution, particularly in transitional societies. In the second place, it is assumed that, difficult though the task may be, one can discover specific types of impacts. Whether, without more systematic research than has as yet been undertaken, it is possible to evaluate the depth of such impacts is highly doubtful; this being so, the concluding section of this chapter

[1] The Colombo Plan, which sends field missions to Southeast Asian countries, is really a scheme for coordinating economic and technical assistance on a *bilateral* rather than a multi-lateral basis.

[2] This quotation, with italics added, is from ECOSOC Resolution 222 (IX), dated 10 August 1949, authorizing the UN Expanded Program of Technical Assistance (EPTA).

ventures to suggest kinds of research that might usefully be designed with this end in view.

Proliferation of UN Assistance Programs

The constitutional basis for United Nations sponsored programs of economic and technical assistance is to be found in Chapter IX of the UN Charter. This chapter pledges member states to take "joint and separate action in cooperation with the Organization" for the promotion of "higher standards of living, full employment, and conditions of economic and social progress and development"; as well as "for solutions of international economic, social, health, and related problems," including "international cultural and educational cooperation." The Economic and Social Council (ECOSOC) is given responsibility for initiating studies, making reports, formulating recommendations for action, and coordinating the activities of the UN and its specialized agencies in this broad domain. Several of the major specialized agencies, notably the Food and Agriculture Organization (FAO), the World Health Organization (WHO), the International Labor Organization (ILO), and the United Nations Educational, Scientific and Cultural Organization (Unesco), are authorized by their respective constitutional instruments to provide technical aid to member governments and peoples, each within its particular province.

Under these constitutional provisions, modest programs of technical assistance were inaugurated by the UN itself and by certain of the above-mentioned agencies even before the inception of the Expanded Program in 1950. These early programs, so far as the UN itself was concerned, were designed to aid in the establishment of advisory social welfare services, in furthering economic development, and in strengthening public administration. Later came authorization to set up advisory services relating to "human rights," perhaps the most clearly political of the enormous variety of assistance activities undertaken by the United Nations.

Among the specialized agencies, WHO from the outset allocated a larger portion of its regular budget to field programs than did any other. WHO's program embraced assistance for the improvement of national health administrations, campaigns for the control and eradication of communicable diseases, and arrangements for training health administrators, sanitary engineers, nurses, and laboratory technicians.[3]

[3] In addition to funds allocated from WHO's own budget, the Pan American Health Organization, its regional affiliate, provides substantial support for similar work in Latin America.

Next in size came the diverse educational and related kinds of aid financed by Unesco out of its regular budget. Unesco's program included the dispatch of educational missions to selected countries, the conduct of country surveys, the sponsorship of national and regional training centers, aid in teaching the natural and social sciences, and the provision of advisory services to educational and scientific institutions. In 1956 Unesco inaugurated a number of ten year "major" projects, among which, notably, was one to promote the extension of primary education in Latin America.

Although FAO, during its earlier years, did not institute any continuing program of direct technical aid to national governments, it sent agricultural survey missions to a number of countries on request and established regional commissions to study the technical aspects of rice production, forestry, fisheries, and the control of foot-and-mouth disease.

On a restricted scale shortly after World War II, the International Labor Organization decided to inaugurate operational programs in workers' education and vocational training. Certain activities of a field character, moreover, were inherent in the objectives of the International Civil Aviation Organization (ICAO), to wit: the "monitoring" by field staffs of the application by national governments of regional plans for the provision of air navigation facilities and services to international civil aviation.

Mention should also be made of the role of the United Nations Children's Fund (UNICEF) in the evolving picture of international aid. Set up by the UN General Assembly originally on a temporary (emergency) basis, UNICEF was in 1953 accorded permanent status as a semi-autonomous, subsidiary arm of the UN for the support of welfare and health aids to needy children, nursing mothers, and pregnant women, at first in war-torn Europe and later in non-Western countries. UNICEF's resources, however, stem mainly from voluntary contributions by states outside their regular budgetary assessments. UNICEF, relying chiefly on WHO and FAO for technical advice, handles the distribution of milk, clothing, and drugs, as well as the provision of transport and equipment for the mass immunization of millions of children against tuberculosis.

While the importance of international technical assistance was, as outlined above, given recognition as early as the 1940's, it was the establishment in 1950 of the Expanded Program (EPTA), under the impetus of President Truman's Point Four proposal, that provided the great stimulus for "the spread of operational activities around the globe. . . . Indeed, it is not too much to say that the impact of EPTA converted certain of the specialized agencies from essentially reporting and debating societies into 'service' institutions and, in effect, vitalized their work."[4] This new program, for which from $20 million to $30 million has been made available annually through voluntary contributions since 1950, is a multi-agency operation involving the UN and most of its specialized institutions (including currently the International Atomic Energy Agency). The purpose of EPTA, as stated officially, "is to help under-developed countries to strengthen their national economy through the development of their industries and agriculture with a view to promoting their economic and political independence in the spirit of the Charter, and to ensure the attainment of higher levels of economic and social welfare for their entire populations."[5] Without describing in detail the administration of EPTA, it is in order to note that since 1956 each recipient government has been required to present its requests for assistance in the form of a "balanced" country program drawn up until recently on an annual basis and now biennially. These country-programming operations are typically carried out in consultation with Resident Representatives of the Technical Assistance Board (RTARs), who are stationed permanently in some forty countries collectively accounting for around ninety per cent of the program. The RTAR acts as the overall coordinator in the process of adjusting rival claims for project aid among national ministries and other institutional units, while field representatives of the project-executing bodies (the UN and the specialized agencies) advise on the "technical soundness" of project requests.

In 1958, an additional technical assistance program was established by the United Nations in the form of the so-called Special Fund. This move, representing a compromise between advocates and opponents of a UN capital-granting fund for economic development (SUNFED), was designed to promote longer-term and larger-scale field projects than had been possible under EPTA auspices, with a view to creating conditions that would attract capital investment. Like EPTA, the Special Fund's resources are derived from voluntary contributions—roughly in the same amount for the two related programs. To date projects approved by the Special Fund authorities have taken the form mainly of surveys of natural resources and of aid in establish-

[4] Quoted from the author's study of *Field Administration in the United Nations System*, New York, Frederick J. Praeger, 1961, p. 29. Much of the factual data on which the present chapter is based was derived from this larger study.

[5] Appendix I, Annex I, of ECOSOC Resolution 222 (IX), *op.cit.*

ing permanent training and research centers in such fields as public administration, statistics, technology, industry, and agriculture. Of 326 project requests received from governments by the spring of 1961, 157 had been authorized, involving an aggregate expenditure of approximately $130 million.[6] Projects are from two to six years' duration. Among the criteria governing selection of applications for approval, the relative urgency of the needs of requesting countries and the prospect of early and tangible results are given high priority. As will be noted later, the Special Fund utilizes for liaison and investigational purposes the field machinery of the Technical Assistance Board (TAB) although the fund operates under the control of a separate governing council appointed by ECOSCO and is administered by its own managing director (Mr. Paul Hoffman). The execution of fund projects, including the recruitment of mission experts, is normally handled by the UN itself or by an appropriate specialized agency. The managing director, however, has authority to contract directly for the services of other agencies, private firms, universities, or research institutes, but this authority had not been invoked up to the time these lines were written.

The field programs briefly described above have one thing in common: they all involve the dispatch of persons, whether on project assignments or as members of field office staffs, to developing countries around the globe. Over one hundred countries and dependent territories are served by EPTA alone, while a growing number are now becoming beneficiaries of Special Fund projects. This brief sketch of multi-lateral assistance under UN system auspices, however, would not be complete without reference to the somewhat different type of field operations carried on by the International Bank for Reconstruction and Development (IBRD) and the International Monetary Fund (IMF).

In the main, the field operations of the IBRD are related to the process of negotiating and supervising agreements for loans, under government guarantee, for developmental purposes. In this connection the Bank's headquarters frequently sends out staff groups for first-hand reports on loan applications and later, during the life of the loan, "end-use" missions for an assessment of the progress of the undertakings being financed in whole or in part. Apart from the lending process, the Bank performs various advisory functions on request, e.g., general economic surveys in a score of countries; limited survey mis-

[6] UN Doc. SF/L.50, May 29, 1961.

sions in a smaller number of places (often in conjunction with FAO on the agricultural side); aid in the setting up or strengthening of national development banks; and the assignment of resident representatives to gather information, maintain liaison with governmental authorities, or, in a few instances, to act as advisers on economic development and financial policy. In general the Bank does not maintain any continuing field organization such as do the UN and the major specialized agencies. As we shall observe later, this does not mean that the Bank's impact on national development is without significance.

The field activities of the International Monetary Fund are confined largely to the provision of advice to governments on an informal basis concerning such matters as central banking policy, exchange controls, statistical procedures, and monetary stabilization. This advisory function is performed in part by short-term field missions and in part, more recently, by appointing country advisers for periods of a year or two. For these purposes the Monetary Fund uses only members of its headquarters staff: it does not recruit outside specialists, as do the Bank to some extent and other UN agencies on a much wider basis.

Geographic Dispersion of Personnel

As suggested above, the implementation of UN system field activities has involved the assignment of personnel to developing countries in two principal ways: (1) for the staffing of permanent field offices and (2) for the conduct of operational and advisory projects. Taken together, these two groups of personnel constitute the international bureaucracies with which this chapter is concerned.

For the entire UN system, the number of field offices now approximate 250.[7] Roughly 80 of these offices are located in the more advanced member nations, chiefly European and North American. A few others are maintained in developing areas by the United Nations Commissioner for Refugees (UNHCR) and the United Nations Relief and Works Agency for Palestinian Refugees (UNRWA). This leaves some 150 offices of relevance to the subject of this chapter.

It is estimated that in 1960 slightly more than 1,200 established posts were filled by international recruitment for this group of offices. In addition, a substantial number of persons recruited locally performed routine services at such offices. The range in size of their pro-

[7] Statistics regarding field offices cited here are drawn mainly from Sharp, *op.cit.*, chap. 4; see also UN Doc. A/C.5/786, October 6, 1959.

fessional and administrative staffs was from around 200 down to only one or two individuals, depending on the importance of the country (or region) served by an office and the functions delegated to it by central headquarters. By far the largest international staffs are to be found at the secretariats of the UN Regional Economic Commissions (Santiago de Chile, Bangkok, and Addis Ababa) and at the regional offices of WHO (Alexandria, Brazzaville, New Delhi, and Manila). Much smaller regional offices are operated by FAO, ILO, Unesco, and ICAO. The jurisdiction of the vast majority of field offices, however, extends to a single country and in two cases (e.g., the U.A.R. and Pakistan) to distinct geographic sections of the same country. Aside from these two instances, all field offices except the WHO regional office at Alexandria and two ILO offices at Istanbul and Bangalore, respectively, are located in national capitals, primarily in order that there may be easy and direct contact with national administrations. Clusters of UN agency offices are to be found at some 12 to 15 major centers, notably Mexico City, Santiago, Lima, Cairo, Beirut, New Delhi, Bangkok, and Manila. During recent years efforts have been made, but with only moderate success, to consolidate the premises of offices at such centers. At Manila a new WHO building now houses all the UN system offices located in that city. Plans are under way at Santiago for the construction of a UN building that can accommodate the entire group of offices there. In a few other places (e.g., Cairo and New Delhi) negotiations to this effect have been undertaken with the host government. Progress has thus far been inconclusive.

The kinds of personnel assigned to field offices depends in large part on the terms of reference of an office. Field machinery may be, and has been, set up for various purposes. A field office may, for example, be intended merely to serve as an outpost of headquarters and to provide it with a listening post vis-à-vis national governments. Broadly, this has been the function of the United Nations Information Centers now maintained in some thirty places. These centers, incidentally, help to publicize locally the work of the UN system in the economic, social, and cultural domain. For the most part the small professional staffs of the centers are specialists in mass communication, either recruited directly for such assignments or detailed from the UN Office of Public Information in New York.

Over and beyond this kind of activity, there has been a distinct trend toward the devolution to major field offices of authority to make either administrative or substantive decisions, or both, affecting operational programs in the country or region concerned. WHO affords the most advanced example of this sort of decentralization. Under its constitution, "regional organizations" could be, and have been, established, each consisting of a sizable regional office and a regional committee representing the national health administrations of the region. Each regional director submits annually to the committee a draft program of work under the regular budget after consultation with national health authorities. This program, as approved by the committee, is then forwarded to the central organs of WHO as a recommendation which is normally adopted without appreciable change. In this kind of context, it has proved advisable to assign to the regional offices a substantial number of professional specialists, e.g., on communicable diseases, maternity and child health, vital statistics, the training of health administrators, and the like. The regional offices are typically headed by an ex-minister of health or some senior officer of a national health service. The organizational unit of each office dealing with budgetary, personnel, and procurement matters is staffed accordingly—largely by detail from WHO headquarters.

A somewhat similar type of regional decentralization is to be found in the UN regional economic commissions: (1) for Latin America (ECLA) at Santiago, (2) for Asia and the Far East (ECAFE) at Bangkok, and (3) for Africa (ECA) at Addis Ababa. These bodies (including one for Europe as well) were established by ECOSOC on the assumption that differential regional needs called for regional representative organs to facilitate economic reconstruction (after World War II) and then the long-term development of each major region. In 1960, ECOSOC broadened the terms of reference of these commissions to include "social" as well as "economic" development problems. Each commission is serviced by a secretariat of 50 to nearly 100 professional officers, largely economists, statisticians, and industrial and agricultural technicians, together with an appropriate complement of administrative and financial personnel. The secretariat carries on research and makes reports to the commission; it also arranges for and follows up on special conferences and training seminars held in the region. Since the inauguration of EPTA, moreover, the regional commission staffs have increasingly undertaken on their own initiative to stimulate requests for technical assistance from governments and have performed technical backstopping functions for aid projects in the economic and social field.

In 1960 ECOSOC adopted a resolution requesting the secretary-general to draw as fully as possible on the services of the regional commissions, "especially in the planning and execution of programs for advancing regional development."[8] The General Assembly, at its ensuing session, stressed even more strongly the advantages of decentralizing operations regionally and of using the staff facilities of the commissions.[9] Plans for implementing these resolutions, as announced in June 1961, will involve a steadily wider role for the regional commission secretariats and will require their members to move about their regions frequently with a view to maintaining contact with national ministries of finance, economics, trade, and agriculture, as well as economic planning bodies.

As already indicated, the country field offices of TAB have, since 1956, played a significant part in the formulation of country programs under EPTA. Most of the Resident Representatives managing these offices are individuals with extensive previous international experience, whether with the League of Nations or UN agencies, with the foreign services of national governments, or with voluntary organizations.[10] While they represent a wide variety of occupational backgrounds, with few exceptions they may be characterized as mature diplomatic and operational "generalists." The RTAR, in the less important countries, is seldom assisted by more than one subordinate professional officer—sometimes only by locally recruited clerical staff. In the major countries, such as India and Mexico, he will usually have one or more younger assistants with backgrounds roughly similar to his own. Most RTARs have jurisdiction over a single country, but for reasons of economy "regional" RTARs are used in Central America, Southeast Asia, and parts of Africa covering groups of the newly independent states.

For the field office establishments of the other specialized agencies—FAO, ILO, Unesco, ICAO—suffice it to say that their staffs consist of varying combinations of generalists and specialists.[11] None of these agencies has decentralized substantive control over program making under their own budgets to anything like the extent of WHO although there are signs that FAO may be slowly moving in this di-

[8] Resolution 793 (xxx).
[9] In Resolution 1518 (xv).
[10] For career profiles of a substantial sample of RTARs, see Sharp, *op.cit.*, pp. 173-177.
[11] The following agencies have not set up field offices: Universal Postal Union (UPU), International Telecommunications Union (ITU), World Meteorological Organization (WMO), and International Atomic Energy Agency (IAEA).

rection. These offices serve variously as liaison units and to handle procedural aspects of program operations, including briefing and backstopping services for field experts. FAO follows the practice of "outposting" to its regional and "zonal" offices a considerable number of technical specialists from the Rome headquarters staff for periods of two years or more. These men help the directors of such offices to supervise and inspect FAO projects, and they are expected to circulate through the region often enough to keep in effective touch with governmental reactions to FAO's program.

Let us now turn our attention from the field office bureaucracies to the much larger corps of UN system employees on field *project* assignments. According to available estimates, this group, for 1960, had reached the following dimensions:[12]

This group was scattered through more than 100 countries and dependent territories on assignments ranging from a few weeks to three or four years. For the most part, the group is specially recruited for technical assistance work, although an appreciable proportion consists of agency headquarters staff detailed for temporary duty in developing areas, with the expectation of returning to headquarters at the termination of such assignments. Except in the case of Special Fund projects, almost none of these "shirt-sleeve diplomats" are initially appointed for periods longer than two years.[13] In practice, however, a good many appointments are extended for an additional year or more, with the result that, for a recent typical year, some fourteen per cent of EPTA experts then in the field had served over three years.[14] Also, there has been a tendency to retain field experts for longer periods by transfer to similar projects in other countries. On the question of duration of assignments, there is a growing feeling in UN circles that periods of only a few weeks or months are too short for incoming

[12] As indicated in the Report of TAB for 1960, Annex IX, UN Doc. E/3471, and the Report by the Managing Director of the Special Fund, UN Doc. SF/L.49, May 12, 1961.

Categories	*Number*
Regular budget	1,046
EPTA-financed	2,258
Special Fund	123
Total	3,427

[13] Only WHO, among UN agencies, offers initial contracts for two years as a matter of policy.

[14] Report of TAB for 1957, UN Doc. E/3080, p. 80.

experts to gain the sort of intimate acquaintance with local conditions essential to effective technical assistance operations.

Table 1 shows how UN system personnel were distributed among the ten countries which had the largest contingents in 1960.

TABLE 1: UN SYSTEM FIELD STAFFS IN TEN UNDERDEVELOPED COUNTRIES 1960

Country	*Office Staffs* (excluding locally recruited)	*Project Personnel*		*Total Personnel*
		EPTA	Regular Budget	
India	218	145	61	424
U.A.R.	235 (Cairo, Alexandria, Damascus)	106	24	365
Thailand	162	48	21	231
Chile	106	50	10	166
Indonesia	9	71	29	109
Iran	4	73	31	108
Mexico	52	21	19	92
Pakistan	4	66	29	89
Afghanistan	6	61	22	89
Brazil	16	48	22	86

Sources: Annual Report of TAB for 1960 (UN Doc. E/3471), and *Information Annex III to Budget Estimates for the Financial Year 1960* (UN. Doc. A/C.5/786). The totals given in this table do not include experts attached to Special Fund projects, less than 50 in all.

The countries listed in Table 1 are the major beneficiaries of technical assistance programs in terms of dollar expenditure, which also includes a substantial item for travelling fellowships and an inconsequential amount for equipment and supplies. The number of UN-sponsored experts decreases steadily as the population and area of receiving countries decline. By major regions, EPTA project costs were distributed percentage-wise as follows for 1960:[15]

Africa	15.4 (not including the special Congo program)
Asia-Far East	33.3
Europe (chiefly Greece-Yugoslavia)	6.0
Latin America	25.9
Middle East	17.9
Inter-regional projects	1.5

As might be expected, the allocation for Africa is now increasing rapidly.

In contrast to field office staffs, project experts are not concentrated

[15] Report of TAB for 1960, *op.cit.*, Chart v.

in the national capitals in the larger countries. Probably half of such experts spend most of their time at project sites located at various points over the country in rural villages and provincial towns, at dam and factory sites, in mountain valleys (for geological survey work), and so on. During 1958, for example, UN technical assistance personnel were assigned to as many as twenty different locations in India. Despite this dispersion, most experts are able to make contact with their associates in the national capital at least once or twice a year. The office of the TAB Resident Representative, as well as agency field offices to a lesser extent, serves as a central point of reference for this purpose. As the years have gone on, the Resident Representatives have increasingly encouraged group meetings for the exchange of experience by experts working on different but related undertakings. The esprit de corps of UN project personnel at national capitals has also been aided by social gatherings sponsored by Resident Representatives at fairly frequent intervals. By and large, however, these international field bureaucracies do not "colonize" among themselves as much as do comparable staff groups under the United States Point Four program. "On the other hand, there seems to be considerably more social intercourse, in many countries, between UN groups and local people than is true of the United States colony."[16]

The professional identifications of the 3,000 to 4,000 UN project experts on duty during a given year range over an impressive variety of specialities: industrial management and engineering, agriculture, forestry, postal and radio communications, health, general and vocational education, social welfare, rural sociology, public administration (generalists and technicians), statistics—to mention only the broader categories. By principal forms of action, their assignments may be classified as follows: (1) demonstration and pilot undertakings, e.g., on the use of seeds and fertilizers, or on the treatment of a particular disease; (2) survey missions preliminary to program planning or capital investment; (3) advisory missions (and individual advisory experts), e.g., on the use of some new technique or method in an industry, railroad system, or government department; (4) the establishment or improvement of local training facilities, e.g., centers, institutes, laboratories, libraries, workshops, etc.; and (5) quasi-operational projects. During recent years there has been a noticeable trend away from short-term demonstration projects and toward the longer-range provision of advisory services, particularly toward aid in establishing permanent

[16] Sharp, *op.cit.*, p. 464.

training and research institutions of various kinds. Projects involving advice to governmental and educational units on their organization and methods often shade over into "operational" activities, since the dividing line between advice and operations is not easy to maintain. Many of the UN civilian experts sent to the Congo in 1960-1961, although advisers in the technical sense, have had, *faute de mieux*, to act as *de facto* administrators of major public services, for the UN personnel confronted during the early months of the Congo crisis a virtual administrative vacuum that had somehow to be filled.

In this general connection, reference is appropriate here to a relatively new UN program, known in bureaucratic terminology as OPEX, which was inaugurated by the 1958 General Assembly at the suggestion of Secretary-General Hammarskjold.[17] The object of this program is to provide personnel to governments for the performance of high-level "executive, operational, or administrative" services. It differs, however, from "orthodox" technical assistance in that the foreign personnel recruited by the UN are integrated into governmental employment with paid civil service status, the UN providing such supplementary emoluments and allowances as may be necessary to bring the personnel in question up to the compensation level to which they would be entiled as UN field experts. It is assumed in the working agreement made by the UN with receiving governments that such OPEX personnel will not only be given operational responsibilities but will undertake concurrently to train their successors from among their local associates.

Branded by Soviet bloc opponents in the original Assembly debates on this program as a "new multi-lateral form of colonialism," it had nevertheless been sought by early 1961 by 48 different governments, for which 56 posts were then either filled or at various stages of recruitment. These posts called for appointment contracts of from one to two years, with the expectation that in some cases there would have to be renewals for an additional year or two. Although the UN part of the OPEX program is financed directly from the organization's regular budget ($800,000 for 1961), its subject-matter coverage embraces the specialized agencies as well. Recruitment is through the UN Office of Personnel after consultation with the appropriate agencies. During the first year of operation, OPEX appointments included an economist, a statistician, an industrial manager, a legal officer, a finance officer, a fisheries specialist, a milk production manager, and a high-

[17] By Resolution 1256 (XIII).

way building engineer. There have since been appointments in natural resources development, power, transport and communications, civil aviation, agriculture, and meteorology. It would appear that most governments have preferred to seek OPEX personnel for politically non-sensitive positions. There have as yet been few requests for public administration generalists. Even so, this program, if it develops well, clearly has interesting potentialities for influencing the context of political development in a number of countries.

Nationality and Language Factors in Field Assignments

United Nations technical assistance work involves criss-crossing networks of trans-cultural operations. The attempted transfer of technology, by teaching and example, while essentially from advanced Western to less advanced non-Western countries, embraces a wide range of national economic development stages—from areas just emerging from tribalism through those approaching the industrial "take-off" stage and on to those probably capable of sustained economic growth. No one country or even any small cluster of countries, however generally advanced in the economic sense, is able to provide for foreign employment appropriately qualified experts in all occupational fields. The distribution of skills and experience is affected by geography, climate, and technological factors. Experts in tropical agriculture, for instance, do not abound in the United States; nor is it the most important source of fisheries and forestry specialists or of experts in rice production. The industrial experience of the Western European and North American regions may not be the most valuable for countries of the Middle East or of Southeast Asia. In the field of public administration, sheer organizational size, together with the lavish provision of staff services, may not make the large nations like the USA or the USSR the most suitable places from which to obtain advice on management and personnel problems for countries with relatively simple administrative systems and agrarian economies.

The foregoing observations are intended to remind the reader that UN field bureaucracies have a multi-national composition. Increasingly, since the inception of EPTA over a decade ago, its managers have endeavored to widen the national sources of project experts. For 1960, such experts were drawn from 57 different countries, well over half of which were themselves recipients of UN technical assistance. India, for instance, received 145 UN experts and supplied 99 of its own nationals for UN assignments abroad, largely in closely related cultural regions of South Asia and the Middle East. For the U.A.R., incoming experts totalled 106 and the outgoing contingent 48, chiefly to other Arab countries. The Philippines accepted 30 foreign specialists and provided 15; Brazil got 48 and supplied 21. In all, some 27 per cent of the corps of UN agency experts on technical assistance assignments that year came from areas other than Europe and North America, to wit: 12 per cent from Asia, 9 per cent from Latin America, 5 per cent from the Middle East, and 1 per cent from Africa. Over half of the countries receiving experts' services provided one or more of their own nationals to serve other countries.[18]

The annual reports of TAB contain interesting examples of individual cross-cultural assignments within this global context. Thus, during 1960, an agricultural extension specialist from Greece worked in Iraq, an Indian geologist in Brazil, a Brazilian agricultural statistician in Venezuela, a Venezuelan aviation adviser in Ethiopia. Similar examples could be cited.[19] It should of course be recognized that a considerable proportion of the technicians emanating from non-Western countries have had Western training either directly or indirectly. Even so, their cultural and linguistic identification remains non-Western.

It is fairly typical for project teams to include both Western and non-Western personnel within their membership. Such arrangements, although occasionally giving rise to internal stress and strain, appear usually to produce the adjustments essential for integrated group action. Opportunity to promote the cause of world community through the United Nations often acts as a strong stimulus to this end, helping thus to minimize personality and nationality differences.

Communication within project teams, and even more across to host country officials, is sometimes complicated by linguistic pluralism. On the whole, however, language barriers present a less serious problem for the UN field bureaucracies than for foreign advisers emanating from a single nation such as the U.S.A. For one thing, language skills are more widely spread among UN field experts, while a somewhat larger proportion have had previous cross-cultural experience than has thus far been the case with their American counterparts. When the cultural gap is a relatively narrow one between UN teams and their local administrative associates, as is not infrequently the case, semantic misunderstandings are less likely to occur than with groups exclusively recruited from a single highly developed Western nation.

[18] Report of TAB for 1960, *op.cit.*
[19] *Ibid.*, para. 18.

With regard to the composition of field office staffs, UN agencies have in principle favored the assignment of non-nationals of the host country as office directors, with a view to minimizing the possibility of unduly favorable treatment of its requests for UN assistance. There have, however, been exceptions to this rule, each of which could be justified on special grounds. Three of WHO's regional offices were for many years headed by host country nationals. Similarly, FAO's Cairo office has been directed successively by officials of Egyptian nationality. In these cases the argument was advanced that it was important during the formative years of the organization to have as field office heads persons with wide acquaintance and close contacts with the host country administrations, especially when the host country happened to be the dominant nation in the region. It is TAB's policy never to assign a resident representative to his own country, while in the case of the UN Information Centers the practice has been not to use host country nationals as office directors but generally to appoint such nationals as deputy heads.

Since the assignment of UN field project personnel to member countries must have the consent of their governments, objection has in some instances been raised to candidates of certain nationalities or religions. No Arab government, for example, will accept Jewish experts, and there is reluctance to taking persons who, though themselves not Jewish, have previously served in Israel. "The Government of Brazil has shown some unwillingness to approve experts hailing from other Latin American countries; while Thailand was for a time not inclined to welcome Japanese."[20] The assignment of Soviet bloc experts, totalling in 1960 about 80 in all, has for political reasons been limited to such "neutralist" countries as India, the U.A.R., Burma, and Afghanistan, along with Yugoslavia. Contrary to popular impression, comparatively few UN-sponsored Soviet experts have been able to communicate in the indigenous languages of the host countries. Soviet field teams are not infrequently accompanied by an official Russian translator.

Channels of Contact and Influence

By way of generalization, it may be said that the official contacts of UN field bureaucracies are primarily with the largely Western-educated ruling elites in the host countries. Although these elites may include agrarian, industrial, educational, labor, or scientific groups,

[20] Sharp, *op.cit.*, p. 141.

they are principally governmental and administrative in composition. UN assistance programs are designed to aid *governments*, directly or indirectly, and all agreements covering aid arrangements are normally routed through the Ministry of Foreign Affairs, of Finance, or of Economics of the recipient country. Even in areas where oppositional political groups exist, UN project missions are not likely to have much to do with them, although this is not to say that the long-range impact of successful UN aid projects may leave unaffected the status of such groups in the political system.

During the conduct of preliminary negotiations for project agreements, the field representatives of UN agencies, including the TAB Resident Representative, develop fairly close informal contacts with senior officials of the subject-matter ministries and institutions involved. This is particularly true of the technicians attached for considerable periods to agency field office staffs who often form lasting personal friendships with such host country officials. The closeness of these contacts is influenced both by the attitudes of the receiving bureaucrat toward foreign aid and by the degree of cultural sympathy displayed by the international staff man.

More specifically, it is important to note the extent to which the advent of international assistance programs has stimulated the establishment or strengthening of national machinery for coordinating country aid requests. At the outset of EPTA, few of the then independent developing countries had any coordinating machinery worthy of the name; now nearly all, except, to be sure, some of the *newly* independent nations, have administrative arrangements of this sort. In many cases, the TAB Resident Representative has been influential in persuading the recipient government leadership to set up coordinating machinery, sometimes by suggesting helpful forms of UN aid on the personnel, organizational, or procedural aspects of the problem. Advisory groups were, on request, set up by ECLA in 1959 to help certain Latin American governments organize national economic programming machinery.

National coordinating arrangements exhibit three distinct patterns. Most of the earlier arrangements—and some even now—were centered in a bureau of the Foreign Office, typically that dealing with international organizations and conferences. Where this situation obtains, the results have tended not to be very satisfactory in terms of promoting a thorough consideration of the relative merits of aid proposals from competing subject-matter ministries and institutions. The staff of such a bureau is likely to be so swamped with political and diplomatic business that "it will have little time—or competence—to focus effectively on technical assistance problems."[21]

The second type of coordinating machinery, sometimes combined with the first, consists of an inter-ministerial committee or board which may or may not be serviced by an adequate staff unit. Here the tendency has often been for the members of such committees to bargain with one another for slices of the technical assistance pie. As a consequence of this log-rolling process "a multiplicity of small projects without regard to relative needs or priorities" is frequently recommended to the top-level political decision maker—president or prime minister. Where the inter-departmental board representing claimant ministries is endowed with a permanent professional staff of high hierarchical status, the latter can mitigate the proneness to "vote-trade" in the committee. This is the situation in a few of the better-organized national bureaucracies.

Probably the most effective arrangement, the writer would conclude on the basis of direct observations in fourteen countries, lodges the power of decision on project proposals with a single high-level official independent of the Foreign Office, or with a small executive group on which the subject-matter ministries are not themselves represented. This type of arrangement obviously requires a strong technical staff attached to one of the major economic agencies of the government—Ministry of Finance, Budget, or Economics, the Prime Minister's office, or the national economic planning machinery if any. The more closely the technical aid staff unit is geared to the over-all economic programming organization, the more likely its screening of ministerial requests will take into account long-range development goals; also, the more probably will its own analytical thinking take place in a cumulative planning context. In one South American country there is a Central Office of Coordination and Planning which acts as the secretariat for the Economic Committee of the Cabinet. Other minor deviations from the patterns outlined above exist in various countries.

Most of these coordinating arrangements have one common weakness—the lack of a thoroughly trained and experienced professional staff with courage to withstand powerful political pressures within and on the government. It should not be surprising that in some of the looser regimes the planning and coordinating process is still largely a paper creation. Incidentally, it is not uncommon for the developing

[21] *Ibid.*, p. 395.

countries to utilize development banks and/or semi-autonomous public corporations as instruments in their economic program implementation, thus expanding the public sector of their economies.

In one way or another, the TAB Resident Representative must maintain continuing contact with the host government's aid coordinating unit. This contact is as much necessary during the conduct of the country technical assistance program (or of a Special Fund project) as during the formulating stage. For one of the responsibilities of the aid-coordinating staff is usually to follow up on the execution of projects by the operational units involved. In some countries, moreover, the coordinating staff group is expected to evaluate the results of completed aid undertakings, although appropriate criteria for such evaluations have seldom been developed.

The relationships of the Resident Representative with the top political leadership of host nations vary widely. In some countries he may be consulted by cabinet ministers, or even the prime minister, for advice relative not only to technical assistance programs but to public policy in a broader sense. The late Secretary-General Hammarskjold referred to this type of relationship in defending EPTA against charges in the UN General Assembly of involvement by technical assistance missions in the "political" affairs of recipient countries. Some missions, he said, had a "kind of political impact" or "significance" but "in a way entirely under the control of the government." Was it to be considered "illegal if the resident representative in a regular technical assistance mission was frequently called in by cabinet ministers for discussions and even had direct access to the Chief of State"?[22] This sort of relationship must of course be a confidential one: any serious indiscretion on the UN side would put an end to such high level intercourse. Indeed, the contacts of UN Resident Representatives with top policy elites, in many countries, tend to remain formal, limited, and largely by correspondence. Personality factors may be decisive in determining how close—or distant—such contacts are; likewise, the political stability or instability of national elites, whether a regime is civilian- or military-dominated, and so on.

During the operation of UN assistance projects, the most continuous form of contact between project personnel and the receiving bureaucracy is by way of so-called "counterpart" arrangements. Counterparts are usually national (or local) officials assigned to assist international advisers in their work. The counterpart and the UN project adviser

[22] UN Doc. A/C.5/769, October 20, 1960.

ordinarily occupy the same or adjoining offices in the ministry or institution where the project is based. Not only is the counterpart supposed to facilitate the international adviser's operations administratively, but the latter is often expected to provide on-the-job training for his counterpart. Where advanced study abroad seems desirable, the international adviser may suggest to the counterpart's superior that he be nominated by the government for an appropriate UN agency fellowship. According to recent TAB surveys, a substantial proportion of individuals designated as counterparts have not proved satisfactory because of inadequate professional training or experience. There have also been a few cases where the local counterpart, resenting the intrusion of a foreign technician into his working milieu, has placed procedural obstacles in the path of the latter, thus provoking an annoying sense of frustration. Even so, it is through the counterpart that the international adviser can most readily infiltrate new ideas as to organization, method, or technique; and most counterparts, being at the middle management level, are in a good position to disseminate such proposals through their respective units or agencies.

A somewhat similar situation obtains in training and "institution-building" projects as between UN instructional staffs and their professional associates of host country nationality. Opportunities abound in daily conversation and in staff meetings to suggest administrative or policy proposals on a purely informal or unofficial basis. While many such proposals fall on fallow ground, some make their way up the hierarchy to action levels.

Finally, it would be inaccurate not to recognize the existence of contacts with semi- and non-governmental groups of various kind. Important among these is the newspaper and radio press, which, whether governmentally controlled or free, is cultivated by the UN field bureaucracies with a view to building up as favorable a climate as possible for support of their project activities. Student and teacher groups constitute another channel of varying importance for the influencing of opinion, especially in connection with educational missions. Active contacts with business, labor, and agrarian organizations are more scattered in view of the ill-defined organizational character of such groups in the majority of developing areas. The ILO productivity missions appear to have enjoyed the closest relationships with industrial and labor groups, while some of FAO's project teams concerned with land reform and agricultural credit arrangements have developed contacts with farmers' associations where they exist. Civic groups of a voluntary character are not a significant feature of the community life of many of the less-developed areas, but mention should be made of the "associations for the United Nations" which function as propaganda and informational groups in various countries. These, also, have here and there been useful as channels of influence by UN field personnel. In this general context, the celebration of "United Nations Day," each October, is highlighted much more in non-Western than in advanced Western countries. In one Southeast Asian country, a few years ago, the national army produced for this occasion thousands of facsimiles of the UN flag to be pasted by the Boy Scouts on buses and taxis all over the capital. In such an environment the United Nations serves as a symbol of material help rather more than one of a peace-regulating institution.

Impacts on Institutions, Personnel, Methods, and Techniques

The substantive impacts of the activities of the UN field bureaucracies on host countries tend to fall into two major categories. On the one hand there are the influences affecting institutional structures and the staffs, methods, and techniques which they employ. On the other are the effects of UN assistance on the general stream of public policy and in particular on the allocation of budgetary resources for national programs. This second category of impacts is on the whole much less specific or immediate than the first: the policy- and budget-influencing impacts of international assistance programs radiate out from the operational core of projects to government offices and counsels concerned with major policy decisions, somewhat like the ripples caused by a stone thrown into a body of water. The effect usually tends to diminish as the bureaucratic distance from the immediate project base increases; sometimes, to be sure, there is no effect whatever. It is these latter types of effect, however, that probably impinge more on basic *political* change than do the former, in terms of stimulating the development of community services; through education, by promoting social mobility; and, in some areas, by increasing citizen participation in politics.

Let us now briefly illustrate some of the kinds of impact that may take place under the first of the two broad headings suggested above. For this it is proper to begin with the administrative framework of the developing country. As the years have progressed, UN agencies have found it wise to devote increasing attention to efforts of the public services at reform. Without honest, reasonably efficient, and imaginative administration, coordinated economic and social development faces an insurmountable roadblock. Yet, to quote from a recent statement issued by UN headquarters, "each country has to evolve its own institutions and patterns appropriate to its own culture and traditions." Experience has shown that for this purpose "a concerted advance on all fronts, i.e., governmental organization and procedures, personnel management and training, budgeting and financial controls, fiscal policy and administration, etc., is more fruitful than a piece-meal approach on individual sectors."[23]

How to achieve any such concerted advance, however, has proved to be exceedingly difficult to work out in practice. During 1960 the services of UN experts were provided to help plan administrative reform in over thirty countries, from such relatively advanced areas as Argentina and Venezuela to newly independent African states like Ghana and Togo. For the most part these efforts consisted of small separate projects limited to personnel improvement, organization and methods (O and M), fiscal administration, tax assessment, cost accounting, and auditing. A series of workshops on budget forms and methods was held over the period from 1953 to 1961 for the regions of Latin America, Asia, and Africa. In 1960 an Asian workshop "centered on program and performance budgeting." Various projects for improved tax administration have been undertaken on a long-range basis. Special attention has been given to the training of statistical experts for the conduct of national censuses. At New Delhi, in December 1960, an Asian regional seminar was organized under UN and Unesco auspices on the "Public Administration Problems of New and Rapidly Growing Towns"—now a world-wide sociological phenomenon!

One of the most intractable problems faced by UN technical assistance groups has been—indeed still is—that of over-centralization in administration. This is traditional in most of the developing countries and, unless modified, the breach between the national capital and the countryside may widen as development proceeds. Excessive centralization of authority in top executives is also a chronic phenomenon within the national administration itself, resulting in part from the insecure status of ministries and government departments. Commenting on the situation in Latin America, a senior UN official has recently observed that it "induces an unwillingness and incapability

[23] UN Doc. E/3474, May 8, 1961.

of assuming responsibility and of taking initiative. Under these circumstances the subordinate official is always more apt to be penalized for innovation than for routine or even neglect."[24]

The UN Division for Public Administration at New York has during the last few years given special attention to ways in which overcentralization, whether laterally or vertically, may impede the effective implementation of development programs. In this connection the division recently sponsored an extensive comparative study of the role of local government and field administration in decentralizing governmental functions and in increasing popular participation in public affairs.[25] A Working Group on the Administrative Aspects of Decentralization met at Geneva in October 1961 for the purpose of discussing this whole problem and projecting future lines of attack by the UN on it. Thus far, at the field level, it has proved difficult to make any very concrete impact on the situation. The initial attack, it is believed, "should be concentrated upon the reform of administrative institutions and on personnel administration."[26]

A companion problem has to do with training for administrative, professional, and technical personnel. Within the UN assistance framework, personnel training has been promoted in two ways. One has been through a series of travelling fellowship programs financed partly out of agency regular budgets and partly from EPTA funds. During the decade 1950-1960 over 20,000 men and women from more than 100 countries and territories have had the opportunity to study abroad (chiefly in Western countries) on UN fellowships for periods of a few months to two or three years. Although fellowship candidates must in all instances be formally nominated by their governments, favoritism in this matter has been checked substantially by the frequent intervention of UN project experts who, as indicated earlier in this chapter, propose as candidates persons with whom they have been closely associated on work assignments and with whose qualifications they are familiar. The selection process, however, is still marked by the lingering influence of nepotism and the occasional choice of protégés of ministers and senior officials.

[24] Herbert Emmerich, "Administrative Roadblocks to Co-ordinated Development," UN Doc. ST/TAO/CONF.6/L.C-4/ Rev. 1, April 28, 1961.

[25] This study, arranged under contract by the UN with the International Political Science Association, was conducted by Professor Henry Maddick of the University of Birmingham.

[26] Cf. Emmerich, *op.cit.*

In nominating fellowship candidates, governments assume the obligation of providing suitable employment for returned fellows over a specified period (usually two or three years). During recent years TAB and certain of the specialized agencies have undertaken systematic surveys of what actually happens to ex-fellows. These studies indicate that around 90 per cent had returned home and accepted employment in their respective fields of study. Roughly half of this number had won promotions or held positions calling for greater responsibilities than they had before the fellowship experience. A substantial proportion were engaged in training local personnel, including the introduction of new operating methods. The TAB survey for 1958 cited "numerous examples of former fellows who are now holding responsible positions in the national or local civil services of their governments—at the rank of director-general, director, deputy-director, or inspector of important administrative departments. Others were making significant contributions to national development programs as officers of planning boards or managers of development corporations. A considerable number occupied educational posts as deans or professors of university faculties or research institutes."[27] In a growing number of countries an inventory of all returned fellows is now being maintained by the national aid coordinating machinery.

The second pattern of personnel training is that of establishing regional and national institutes within the developing areas themselves. This pattern has been utilized increasingly since the middle 1950's partly for reasons of economy and partly because of the belief that more realistic training arrangements can be devised on home soil than through overseas study. The two systems in fact are regarded as complementary.

According to the results of a survey conducted during 1960 by the TAB Secretariat, 119 long-term institutes (lasting over a year) and 22 short-term institutes had benefitted from UN aid since the inception of EPTA. Of the long-term institutes 95 were national and 24 regional in scope. For every dollar contributed by UN agencies two were made available by the participating governments, the aggregate expenditures on all types of institutes totalling slightly more than $65 million. For 85 institutes on which reliable information was avail-

[27] Sharp, *op.cit.*, p. 491. There are in addition certain special training programs of limited dimensions, such as the UN program for African economists carried on at UN headquarters, a similar program for Latin-American economists under ECLA's auspices, and the Economic Development Institute operated on a permanent basis by the International Bank in Washington.

able, approximately 30,000 trainees had completed their training by the end of 1960.[28]

By subject-matter fields, the long-term *national* training institutes and centers were distributed as follows:

Public administration	7
Statistics	2
Communication	2
Civil aviation	12
Industrial development and productivity	6
Agricultural development	3
Technical education	16
Vocational training	17
Medical and allied education	13
Fundamental education, including teacher training for rural areas	17

For the greater part the training made available through the institute pattern is of an in-service character, although there are examples where basic preparatory education has been provided. Some institutes have an independent status; others are a part of, or closely affiliated with, existing schools or universities. A typical feature has been an effort to ensure "multiplier effect" by training teachers to train others. This has been especially true of the centers for vocational training and for fundamental education, and to some extent of the public administration institutes. Gradually, as an institute acquires a solid foundation, the UN's contribution to its staffing is diminished and eventually the host government takes over full responsibility for its management and financing. In a good many cases, however, UN agencies have been requested—and have agreed—to continue to supply a limited number of specialized personnel for periods up to six or eight years and even longer in certain instances.

It is too soon to estimate the contribution of these UN-aided undertakings to the trained manpower pool of the recipient nations. Most of the graduates have not yet been at work long enough to produce much of an impact on the economy or the polity. Nor, to the writer's knowledge, has there been any detailed objective study of institute recruitment, planning, or operation. It would be interesting to know from what social classes the institutes are drawing their student clientele; to what extent there are potentialities for increasing social mobility through the opportunities offered; and so on. From his limited observation it is the writer's impression that the curricula of most

[28] The data on training institutes cited here are drawn from the Report of TAB for 1960, *op.cit.*

of the institutes provide what is essentially *technical* training which, however valuable in itself, does not stress the inculcation, for example, of democratic values into authoritarian systems of education or public administration. This may in some instances represent a byproduct but probably not a very important one.

Over and beyond the kinds of UN-assisted projects thus far outlined in the present section of this chapter, one notes a multitude of short-term projects of a pilot or demonstrational character. Space will permit the citation of only a few examples of this category of action by the international field bureaucracies, much of which is designed to improve either agricultural or industrial production. On the agricultural side, such projects include demonstrations of the use of new seeds and fertilizers and of the application of better fisheries and forestry methods. Rice production in several Asian countries has been increased through the introduction of more suitable techniques, as has salt production in the Philippines. In the industrial domain, apart from vocational training, the main emphasis has been on the provision of technical advice to small-scale enterprises and on the development of handicrafts. The ILO has been active in persuading a number of governments to set up productivity and labor-management relations centers with the cooperation of ministries of industry and labor and of organized labor groups where they exist. Only in the fairly well-developed countries have such undertakings appeared to yield substantial results: there must be some industrial base to start with. In the domain of transport and communication, technical aid has here and there been supplied for the improved operation of railways, on how to expand port facilities, and concerning the setting up of telephone and radio systems and weather services. So also for the construction of dams and power plants.

Not least are to be noted the advisory and operational activities of UN field staffs in health, education, and welfare. In addition to the specialized training centers described above, these activities take myriad forms. Most notable, in the health field, are the campaigns sponsored by WHO for the control or eradication of widespread diseases like malaria, yaws, and trachoma. Such campaigns bring WHO specialists into direct contact not only with local health authorities but with village communities. The anti-malaria campaign has attained world-wide dimensions and attracted special support from various donor governments, including the U.S.A. WHO has in addition given assistance to national health administrations for the establishment of rural health centers. Unesco's forays in the domain of educational and scientific aid cover a variety of operations affecting elementary and secondary school curricula, library management, equipment for research laboratories, the teaching of the natural and social sciences in universities, and the production of special teaching materials for illiterate adults. The UN itself, WHO, ILO, FAO, and Unesco have cooperated in a number of community development programs intended to stimulate villagers to apply the "self-help" principle to the improvement of various facets of life in the rural communities of Asian and Middle Eastern countries. WHO and FAO have provided nutritionists to advise on diet improvement. ILO has for many years been sending out to Latin America, and more recently to other regions, field missions competent to advise on the establishment or improvement of social security systems. Further examples could be given if space allowed.

Finally, we come to a unique type of assistance that lies squarely in the political-legal domain. This consists of advisory services designed to aid countries in the implementation of "human rights" as defined by the United Nations. On the initiative of the United States, a few years ago, it was agreed by ECOSOC and the General Assembly that the "educational" approach to the problem of human rights might prove more productive than the seemingly interminable effort to achieve an international convention to which most states would adhere. Consequently, *inter alia*, a small appropriation (now $100,000 annually) was made to the UN budget for the organization of regional seminars on the national instrumentalities of human rights protection. A few such seminars have since been held dealing with the role of substantive criminal law in such protection, with the administration of criminal justice, with the political and legal status of women, with the freedom of information, and with judicial and other remedies against the abuse of administrative authority. Among countries offering to act as the host for seminars have been Mexico, Costa Rica, India, and Ethiopia, along with a number of more advanced nations such as Japan, Sweden, New Zealand, and Austria. The UN Division of Human Rights in New York prepares the agenda and working papers for each seminar in consultation with outside experts as necessary. Participants, for the most part officials of ministries of justice, practicing attorneys, and professors of public law, are invited by the UN from each country in a designated region. The experience of nations with a strong tradition of judicial independence is examined comparatively in the discussions with the object of discovering helpful guideposts for countries in course of building up their legal structures and processes. Except in one or two instances this type of assistance has not involved the stationing of field experts for extended periods in the countries being aided. The seminars themselves last only a few weeks. As to what their consequences have been "back home," there is little or no direct evidence as yet. At best, they represent tiny, rather isolated efforts to induce governments to emulate the examples of other countries in strengthening the political and juridical foundations of human rights.

Impacts on Basic Policy and the Allocation of Resources

The cluster of impacts described in the preceding section overlap with a second major category having to do with long-term trends in public policy and in the allocation of national resources for public purposes—often in the direction of modernization. The sources of this second type of impact are much less easy to identify than for the first category. Shifts in policy and budgetary priorities may result from a multitude of domestic and outside influences, among which these emanating from UN action are only peripheral. For most countries the aggregate expenditure of UN aid funds annually (apart from World Bank loans) constitute only a very minor fraction of the total outlays for national development. As already suggested, the UN impact derives almost entirely from people (technicians, administrators, eduactors, etc.) rather than from capital investments. Even so, it is possible to discover a number of instances where governments have altered their spending patterns as a consequence of a UN or World Bank survey team's recommendation. In UN circles there is growing recognition that "the ultimate objective of economic development is a social objective: higher levels of living and the well-being of the community and the individuals who compose it. There are still wide divergences of views as to which economic programs are best designed to further social progress and which social programs can best contribute to economic growth. . . . No ready answers have been found, but the search is on."[29] The theme of "balanced economic and social development" is being given more than lip service in countries with strong national planning arrangements. What this typically means is increased appropriations for educational, health, and welfare programs in comparison with those aimed directly at the expansion of agricultural and/or industrial output. Broadly speaking, the trend has been to

[29] UN Doc. E/3347, May 5, 1960.

emphasize the strengthening of infra-structure rather than the direct increase of production. WHO has frequently helped with the problem of how to plan for national health administrations adequate to the needs of agrarian societies. Unesco, for its part, during 1960 conducted planning missions in 23 countries and territories in sub-Saharan Africa to determine the contours of the special technical assistance educational program for Africa about to be launched by that organization.

The completion of UN field projects of an advisory nature is often accompanied by specific recommendations for continued legislative support of the undertakings after the departure of the international experts. Such recommendations, while not carried out by any means in all cases, have caused a considerable number of governments to adopt a policy line involving positive budgetary action. The new UN Special Fund, in negotiating its project agreements, has insisted on firm commitments of "local" financial support during the life of each project (often four or five years). It is the fund's policy to require receiving governments to more than match its own monetary contribution. Here again lies an opportunity to start governments on a fixed policy of supporting new or enlarged research or training institutions and/or of seeking domestic or foreign capital investments to help finance, for example, river basin or mineral resources development.

While UN and World Bank experts have assisted at times with advice on the technical aspects of new tax schemes, there is little indication that the impetus for basic tax reform has come from such field groups. The UN's role has rather been to help in the implementation of reform proposals already adopted by the government.[30] Nor do the international staff groups appear to have had much impact on the *substantive* features of agrarian reform, although advice has been given on how to carry out a land reform program through, for instance, appropriate credit and cooperative arrangements. This is perhaps another way of saying that the United Nations agencies are seldom in a position to influence directly national policy changes that may run counter to powerful interest groups, e.g., the landlord class. At most, the UN's role is that of a catalytic agent.

Resistances to UN Recommendations

The "modernizing" implications of the activities of international field staffs for the new national communities to which they render technical and administrative assistance are by no means immediately

[30] As, for example, in Nepal during 1960.

evident. UN project recommendations confront various kinds of resistances from political leaders and administrators. Certain of these obstacles relate to the motivations behind aid requests in the first place. Sometimes applications for UN aid are submitted by a governing group with a view to enhancing its own prestige in a power struggle with other groups. Contrarywise, international experts have in some situations been sought "to cover up the failures of national program-planning, the responsible politicians thus trying to shift the blame to foreign advisers."[31] In either case the psychological climate for effective implementation of field project proposals may not be particularly favorable.

A more common aspect of "still-born" aid recommendations is the sheer administrative inertia in which they get bogged down. As a senior UN official recently has expressed it, such a state of affairs is often the result of a "system of hit and miss selection and frequent turn-over of personnel . . . [and] when the process of implementation or installation begins there is a great wall not only of opposition at the lower echelons but more often one of complete inertia, misunderstanding, and silent sabotage."[32] Anything that may jeopardize their job security is not likely to be viewed with favor by the local bureaucrats.

The impact of foreign economic and social assistance on the balance of political forces in a developing area may be potentially upsetting in proportion to the substantive dimensions of the aid rendered. Accordingly, some increase in political instability may frequently be anticipated, the status of the ruling elite being weakened by the rising position of a rival group, civilian or military, either more or less democratic in outlook. Although the long-range "modernizing" effects of such changes in the body politic may be important, their short-term impact may be to block the official adoption of UN-sponsored policy recommendations. When there occurs a change of regime, whether by revolution or *coup d'état,* between the formal approval of an aid program and its implementation, the newly installed regime has been known to refuse the necessary executive or legislative authorization for the UN field projects concerned. On occasion UN agency personnel have arrived in a host country only to discover that "the government has forgotten all about its original request for their services. Or a new group of senior officials, unsympathetic to the requests made

[31] Sharp, *op.cit.,* p. 450.
[32] Emmerich, *op.cit.*

by their predecessors, may place roadblocks in the path of the UN project advisers attached to their ministry."[33]

In only one instance, however, has a government requested the withdrawal of all UN field groups before the completion of their assignments. Such a move was taken by Guinea in February 1961, allegedly because of its doubt as to the "neutrality" of UN technical assistance in terms of world political cleavages. Presumably this action had a significant relation to the then decided orientation of the government of Guinea toward the Soviet bloc. This situation, even though thus far unique, illustrates the exposure of UN technical aid teams to national political currents which, if they become strong enough, may undermine the UN's usefulness. The field bureaucracies of the international community, in other words, must always be on guard not to offend the political sensitivities of "sovereign" governments by word or deed. The former can function effectively only in an atmosphere of freely granted consent and confidence: to exert undue pressure on the host country officialdom may be to risk the disintegration of the entire technical assistance enterprise. This is the dilemma facing the practitioners of international aid for economic and social development. They have to recognize that the bogey of "colonialism" may plague even the most unselfish efforts of internationalists if exceptional care is not taken to convince the beneficiaries of aid that their role is consistently one of non-interference in domestic political problems.

Research Problems

It will have by now become apparent to the reader that no discussion dealing with "International Bureaucracies and Political Development" can, at the present stage, do more than indicate in descriptive terms the kinds of operations performed by these bureaucracies and the more obvious types of impact resulting. For several reasons, no attempt could be made to estimate the political ramifications of such impacts. In the first place, the time period spanned by UN-sponsored field programs is still too short to provide an adequate perspective. Second, UN agency teams, far from operating alone, often participate in joint projects involving American Point Four and/or Colombo Plan groups as well, the precise UN role being difficult to assess. Thirdly, as mentioned earlier, the dimensions of UN aid programs normally represent only a minor fraction of the develop-

[33] Sharp, *op.cit.*, p. 451.

ment activities within a country, and "to attempt to isolate the contribution made by (EPTA and other programs) and to subject it to quantitative measurement would be an illusory operation."[34] Finally, in view of the officially *non*-political orientation of UN aid operations, many of their actual effects on national *political* development are necessarily covert rather than overt, indirect rather than direct, diffuse rather than specific, and thus not easy to identify clearly.

It should further be recognized that any attempt to carry on intensive field research designed to reveal the extent, character, and depth of these international impacts on national political development would require extraordinary tact and subtlety on the part of the investigators. In view of the delicacy of the subject, it would probably be essential to disguise in some way or other the actual objectives of the research. Otherwise, a research team, no matter under whose auspices, would be unlikely to gain access to the necessary sources of information whether from UN field personnel or host country people. Few UN agency missions would be willing to provide clues as to the political repercussions of their operations while still on assignment in a country even though anonymity were assured by the interviewers: the possibility of "leaks" would be apt to put potential informants on guard. On the other hand, they would perhaps be more willing to talk freely, although still on a confidential basis, after the termination of their term of overseas duty. Among important sources of data would be the progress and terminal reports submitted by technical assistance experts to UN agency headquarters, as well as the reports of Resident Representatives to TAB headquarters, provided consent could be obtained to use them under conditions acceptable to the United Nations.

On the assumption that the foregoing difficulties could be overcome, how should the research be designed with a view to yielding illuminating insights on the role of international bureaucracies in the political "modernization" of developing areas? Presumably, such studies would have two principal objectives: (1) to classify different kinds of impacts in terms of the structure and functions of the political system concerned, and (2) to assess the relative importance of various factors conditioning such impacts—on the one hand, the indigenous factors (e.g., the stage of economic development, the length of time the country has been politically independent, the position of the native bureaucracy in the power constellation of the society, and the degree

[34] Report of TAB for 1958, ECOSOC, O.R.,: 28th Sess., 1959, Suppl. No. 5, p. 57.

of internal "competitiveness" in the political system); and on the other hand, the United Nations factors (e.g., the size and duration of country program projects, the cultural composition of project teams in relation to the host country's culture, etc.). Under the first objective it would be necessary to devise ways of translating what superficially appear to be economic or technical impacts into relevant categories for purposes of political comparison, with special reference to the diffusion (or concentration) of political power. This would not be an easy operation, but it could perhaps be done in enough instances to become meaningful.

In large part, such research would need to be conducted, it is believed, by means of a series of case studies in pairs or clusters of countries so selected as to facilitate the comparative assessment of significant variables in the relationships under examination. Thus, for example, one might take one or two countries which have escaped colonial control (e.g., Ethiopia, Liberia, Thailand) and compare the situation there with one or two fairly recently independent areas as nearly similar as possible in other respects to the non-colonial countries. Other sets of areas might be selected so as to highlight the effect of the stage of economic development on the sensitivity of recipient areas to proposals susceptible of affecting political change. A particularly interesting target of inquiry would be the discovery of conditions most (as well as least) favorable to introducing into the native bureaucracy itself rational in contrast to traditional value patterns.

If the writer of this chapter has conveyed to the reader the impression that he attributes a *decisive* importance to the role of the United Nations field bureaucracies in the political evolution of developing areas, it was not his intention. By the very act of describing in some detail the character and range of the various UN field programs, with which the writer himself happens to have had contact, their impact in the context of this symposium may have seemed to be exaggerated. If the writer were himself undertaking intensive research of the kind outlined above, he would anticipate, as a working hypothesis, that much of the work of technical assistance groups has had no ascertainable effect on political institutions or processes, that a considerable portion of the recommendations made by such groups have been ill-adapted to the host country's environment, that some were too grandiose and others were confusingly formulated. This would appear to be part of the "lost motion" inherent in any international aid program. A second tentative assumption would be that programs designed to strengthen basic institutions and to train personnel, with all their shortcomings, will make a deeper penetration on the political future of a country than projects intended to demonstrate methods of increasing economic output. Ironically enough, however, it is the former kind of penetration that least lends itself to quantitative evaluation. A decline in the incidence of disease is relatively easy to measure; not so the cumulative role of trained personnel with leadership potential, or the impact of a scheme of administrative decentralization.

With this caveat the conclusion of this chapter is in order. What it has tried to do is to view the role of international staff groups in political development with an appropriate perspective. In short, this role appears to be appreciable and growing but thus far quite subsidiary to other forces, sporadic and uneven, and primarily indirect. These limitations could be tested by attitude surveys which would almost certainly reveal how little actual knowledge of local UN operations has reached elite groups, let alone the masses. The United Nations is plowing new ground with woefully meagre resources in relation to the vast need for help. What it is doing is undoubtedly useful, but it would seem to affect political modernization chiefly as a concealed byproduct of its economic, social, and technical activities.

CONTRIBUTORS

CARL BECK, born in Pittsburgh in 1930, is Associate Professor of Political Science and Senior Research Associate in the Administrative Science Center of the University of Pittsburgh. As holder of a Social Science Research Council Fellowship, he traveled and conducted research in Europe in 1958-1959. He has also held the James B. Duke Fellowship at Duke University and was a Fulbright Grantee. His field of teaching and research concentration is comparative government. He has written *Contempt of Congress* and has published articles in several political science journals.

RALPH BRAIBANTI, born in Danbury, Connecticut, in 1920, is Professor of Political Science and Chairman of the Program in Comparative Studies on Southern Asia at Duke University. In the past, he has held a Ford Foundation Fellowship and has been a consultant to the Governmental Affairs Institute and the National War College. In recent years, he served as the Chief Advisor to the Civil Service Academy of Pakistan. He has conducted extensive research in Southern Asia, and his major area of interest is comparative government and administration of Asia. In addition to being author of articles published in several professional journals, he is co-editor and co-author of *Tradition, Values, and Socio-Economic Development* and *Administration and Economic Development in India.*

JOHN T. DORSEY, born in Atlanta, Georgia, in 1924, is Associate Professor of Political Science at Vanderbilt University. He has held a Fulbright Award, under which he conducted research in France. He has traveled extensively in Europe and Asia and has been involved in technical assistance in the field of public administration to the government of South Viet Nam. His primary field of teaching and research interest is comparative administration. He has published in several of the professional journals and is a contributor to *Problems of Freedom* and *Papers in Comparative Administration.*

S. N. EISENSTADT, born in Warsaw in 1923, is Professor of Sociology and Chairman of the Department of Sociology at the Hebrew University, Jerusalem. His travels include every major area of the world. In 1955-1956, he was a Fellow at the Center for Advanced Study in the Behavioral Sciences. He has held visiting professorships at the University of Oslo, University of Chicago, University of Buenos Aires, and the Massachusetts Institute of Technology. His major fields of research interest are political sociology and comparative institutions and modernization. He has published on these subjects in most of the social science journals. His major works include *Absorption of Immigrants, From Generation to Generation, Bureaucracy and Bureaucratization, Essays on Sociological Aspects of Political and Economic Development*, and *Political Systems of Empires.*

MERLE FAINSOD, born in McKees Rocks, Pennsylvania, in 1907, is Professor of Government at Harvard University, where he also held the position of Chairman of the Department of Government from 1946 to 1949. He is currently the Director of the Russian Research Center of Harvard University. He has traveled widely in Europe and Asia. His many publications have appeared in all of the major journals in political science, and his major works include *American People and Their Government*, *International Socialism and the World War*, *Government and the American Economy*, *How Russia Is Ruled* and *Smolensk Under Soviet Rule*.

BERT F. HOSELITZ, born in Vienna in 1913, is an economist and a member of the Research Center in Economic Development and Cultural Change at the University of Chicago. His work in the past has involved him as a consultant to the government of India, to Unesco, and to other agencies of the United Nations Organization. In 1955-1956 he was a Fellow at the Center for Advanced Study in the Behavioral Sciences. His primary research and teaching interests include the fields of economic growth and history and the history of economic thought. He is editor of *The Progress of Underdeveloped Areas* and *Economic Development and Cultural Change*, and author of *Sociological Aspects of Economic Development*.

J. DONALD KINGSLEY, born in Cambridge, New York, in 1908, is the Resident Representative of the Ford Foundation to West Africa. In the past, he has taught at Antioch College. In addition, he has accumulated over the years a vast experience with federal and international administrative agencies. His primary field of interest is foreign policy and international administration. He is co-author of *Public Personnel Administration* and author of *Representative Bureaucracy*.

JOSEPH LAPALOMBARA, born in Chicago in 1925, is Professor of Political Science at Michigan State University, and he was Chairman of the Department of Political Science there from 1958 to 1963. He has lived and conducted research in Western Europe and has traveled widely in Asia. In 1962-1963 he was a Fellow at the Center for Advanced Study in the Behavioral Sciences. His main field of research is comparative political development, with particular reference to the role of the bureaucracy in that process. He is co-editor of *Elezioni e Comportamento Politico in Italia*, and author of *Guide to Michigan Politics*, *The Italian Labor Movement: Problems and Prospects*, and other works.

FRITZ MORSTEIN MARX, born in Hamburg, Germany, in 1900, is Professor of Political Science and Dean of Administration at Hunter College. In addition to frequent teaching and research visits to Western Europe, he has held the position of Visiting Professor at such institutions as New York University, Columbia University, Yale University, Harvard University, the University of Southern California, and the University of Puerto Rico. In addition, he has had important administrative experience with the U.S. federal government, including periods of assignment to the Bureau of the Budget and the Executive Office of the President. He is a specialist in comparative governments and in political theory. His major publications include *Elements of Public Administration*, *Foreign Governments*, and *The Administrative State.*

FRED W. RIGGS, born in Kuling, China, in 1917, is Professor of Comparative Administration at Indiana University. He has held fellowships from the Social Science Research Council and from the East-West Center of the University of Hawaii. He has been very active as a member of the Comparative Administration Committee of the American Society for Public Administration, and he is the director of a graduate program in comparative and development administration at the Indiana University which is financed by a grant from the Carnegie Corporation. His primary field of research and teaching interest is comparative administration and governments, and in its furtherance he has traveled extensively in various parts of the world. His major published work includes *Pressures on Congress*, *Formosa Under Chinese Nationalist Rule*, and *Ecology of Public Administration.*

WALTER R. SHARP, born in Greenwood, Indiana, in 1896, is Professor of Political Science and Director of Graduate Studies in International Relations at Yale University. He has held fellowships from the Social Science Research Council, the American Field Service, and the John Simon Guggenheim Foundation. In the past, he has held administrative positions with the U.S. Department of State and with agencies of the United Nations Organization, including the position of co-director of the U.N. Egyptian Institute of Public Administration. His primary fields of interest are international relations, comparative governments, and organization and management. Since 1922, he has published many works in political science, among the most significant of which are *Government of the French Republic*, *Field Administration in the United Nations System*, and *Contemporary International Politics*, of which he is co-author.

JOSEPH J. SPENGLER, born in Piqua, Ohio, in 1902, is James B. Duke Professor of Economics and Director of Graduate Studies in Economics at Duke University. He has traveled extensively in Africa, Asia, Europe, and Canada. During his distinguished career, he has held fellowships from the Ford Foundation, The Brookings Institution, and the John Simon Guggenheim Foundation. His teaching, research, and writing interests are concentrated in the fields of population problems, history of economic ideas, and economic development. He has published extensively in the professional journals, and his major works include *Natural Resources and Economic Growth*, *Tradition, Values, and Socio-Economic Development*, and *Administration and Economic Development in India*, of which he is co-author and co-editor, and *Essays on Economic Thought: Aristotle to Marshall.*

A Selected Bibliography

PREPARED BY

GARRY D. BREWER

Introduction

Selecting this bibliography from the extensive literature extant in the diverse, yet relevant, fields of political development, public administration, social theory, behavioralism, value theory, economic development, and political-military affairs has been both demanding and somewhat frustrating. It has been demanding in that so much good material had to be consulted in so many varied areas; and it has been frustrating in the sense that many excellent and pertinent sources had to be culled from this final listing in the interests of concision.

This bibliography is intended to be representative of the literature that in the last decade has become germane to an understanding of bureaucracy and political development. Certainly the seminal works of Weber and Parsons are much in evidence both as direct citations and as citations of those scholars who in varying degrees are in their intellectual debt. Nevertheless, one will find that the behavioral and normative views have not been ignored.

Much has happened since 1963, when *Bureaucracy and Political Development* was originally published; and, in the interim the functional approach to political development has increasingly turned one's attention to a polity's "output" or "capabilities." Certainly the identification and conceptualization of the various crises of political development have done much to delineate and to suggest the vital role a bureaucracy may play in these greater processes. Thus, the literature of the functional approach is represented in the bibliography.

Hopefully this listing will serve as a solid source for the beginning scholar, as a handy guide for the practitioner, and as a useful reminder to the serious student of the range and richness of the literature that comprises the promising study of administration and political development.

BIBLIOGRAPHY

I. ORIGINS OF BUREAUCRATIC ORGANIZATION

Bureaucracies in historical context.
Theoretical treatment of the bureaucracy.
Theoretical treatment of political development.
Methodological studies; analytical frameworks.
Generalized literature on bureaucracy.

1. Almond, Gabriel A. "A Developmental Approach to Political Systems," *World Politics*, Vol. 17 (January 1965), pp. 183-214.
2. Almond, Gabriel A. "Political Systems and Political Change," *The American Behavioral Scientist*, Vol. 6 (June 1963), pp. 3-10.
3. Almond, Gabriel A., and James S. Coleman (eds.). *The Politics of the Developing Areas.* Princeton: Princeton University Press, 1960.
4. Apter, David E., and Carl Rosberg. "Some Models of Political Change in Contemporary Africa," in D. P. Ray (ed.). *The Political Economy of Contemporary Africa.* Washington, D.C.: National Institute of Social and Behavioral Sciences, 1960.
5. Berger, Morroe. "Bureaucratic Theory and Comparative Administration," *Administrative Science Quarterly*, Vol. 1 (March 1957), pp. 518-529.
6. Beyer, William C. "The Civil Service of the Ancient World," *Public Administration Review*, Vol. 19 (Autumn 1959), pp. 243-249.
7. Braibanti, Ralph. "Administrative Reform in the Context of Political Growth," in Fordyce Luikart (ed.). *Symposium on the Research Needs Regarding the Development of Administrative Capabilities in Emerging Countries.* Washington, D.C.: The Brookings Institution, 1966.
8. ———. *Research on the Bureaucracy of Pakistan.* Durham, N.C.: Duke University Press, 1966 (published for Duke University, Commonwealth Studies Center).
9. Brecht, Arnold. "How Bureaucracies Develop and Function," *The Annals of the American Academy of Political and Social Science*, Vol. 292 (March 1954), pp. 1-10.
10. Carter, Gwendolyn, and W. O. Brown (eds.). *Transition in Africa: Studies in Political Adaptation.* Boston: Boston University Press, 1958.
11. Coleman, James C. (ed.). *Education and Political Development.* Princeton: Princeton University Press, 1965.
12. Crozier, Michel. *The Bureaucratic Phenomenon.* Chicago: University of Chicago Press, 1964.
13. Cutright, Philips. "National Political Development: Measurement and Analysis," *American Sociological Review*, Vol. 28 (April 1963), pp. 253-264.
14. Deutsch, Karl W. "Towards an Inventory of Basic Trends and Patterns in Comparative International Politics," *American Political Science Review*, Vol. 54 (March 1960), pp. 34-57.
15. Diamant, Alfred. "Bureaucracy in Development Movement Regimes: A Bureaucratic Model for Developing Countries," *CAG Occasional Papers.* Bloomington, Indiana: CAG/American Society for Public Administration, 1964.
16. ———. "The Relevance of Comparative Politics to the Study of Comparative Administration," *Administrative Science Quarterly*, Vol. 5 (June 1960), pp. 87-112.
17. Dorsey, John T., Jr. "A Communication Model for Administration," *Administrative Science Quarterly*, Vol. 2 (December 1957), pp. 307-324.
18. Dorwart, Reinhold A. *The Administrative Reforms of Frederick William I of Prussia.* Cambridge: Harvard University Press, 1953.
19. Eisenstadt, S. N. "Bureaucracy, Bureaucratization, and Debureaucratization," *Administrative Science Quarterly*, Vol. 4 (December 1959), pp. 302-320.
20. ———. "Political Struggle in Bureaucratic Societies," *World Politics*, Vol. 9 (October 1956), pp. 15-36.

21. ———. "Primitive Political Systems: A Preliminary Comparative Analysis," *American Anthropologist*, Vol. 61 (April 1959), pp. 200-220.
22. ———. *The Political Systems of Empires: The Rise and Fall of the Historical Bureaucratic Societies.* New York: The Free Press, 1963.
23. Esman, Milton J. "The Politics of Developmental Administration," *CAG Occasional Papers.* Bloomington, Indiana: CAG/American Society for Public Administration, 1963.
24. Ghosal, Akshoy Kumar. *Civil Service in India Under the East India Company: A Study in Administrative Development.* Calcutta: University of Calcutta, 1944.
25. Hall, R. H. "Concept of Bureaucracy: An Empirical Assessment," *American Journal of Sociology*, Vol. 69 (July 1963), pp. 32-40.
26. Heady, Ferrel. "Bureaucratic Theory and Comparative Administration," *Administrative Science Quarterly*, Vol. 3 (March 1959), pp. 509-525.
27. ———. *Public Administration: A Comparative Perspective.* Englewood Cliffs, New Jersey: Prentice-Hall, 1966.
28. Hsieh, P. C. *The Government of China, 1644-1911.* Baltimore: Johns Hopkins University Press, 1925.
29. Huntington, Samuel P. "Political Development and Political Decay," *World Politics*, Vol. 17 (April 1965), pp. 386-430.
30. Kahin, G. McT., Guy J. Pauker, and Lucian Pye. "Comparative Politics of Non-Western Countries," *American Political Science Review*, Vol. 49 (December 1955), pp. 1022-1041.
31. Lantzeff, George V. "The Russian Colonial Administration: Its Origins and Development to the End of the 17th Century, With Special Reference to Siberia." Unpublished Ph.D. dissertation, University of California, Berkeley, 1938.
32. LaPalombara, Joseph. "Alternative Strategies for Developing Administrative Capabilities in Emerging Nations," in Fordyce Luikart (ed.). *Symposium on the Research Needs Regarding the Development of Administrative Capabilities in Emerging Countries.* Washington: The Brookings Institution, 1966. Published as *CAG Occasional Paper*, Bloomington, Indiana, 1966.
33. ———. "Public Administration and Political Development: A Theoretical Overview," in Charles Press and Alan Arian (eds.). *Empathy and Ideology: Aspects of Administrative Behavior.* Chicago: Rand McNally, 1967.
34. Litwak, Eugene. "Models of Bureaucracy Which Permit Conflict," *American Journal of Sociology*, Vol. 67 (September 1961), pp. 177-184.
35. Lybyer, Albert Howe. *The Government of the Ottoman Empire in the Time of Suleiman the Magnificent.* Cambridge: Harvard University Press, 1913.
36. Maine, Henry. *Lectures on the Early History of Institutions.* London: J. Murray, 1893.
37. Michael, Franz. *The Origin of Manchu Rule in China: Frontier and Bureaucracy as Interacting Forces in the Chinese Empire.* Baltimore: Johns Hopkins Press, 1942.
38. Montgomery, John D., and William J. Siffin (eds.). *Approaches to Development: Politics, Administration and Change.* New York: McGraw-Hill, 1966.
39. Morstein-Marx, Fritz (ed.). *Elements of Public Administration*, 2nd ed. Englewood Cliffs, New Jersey: Prentice-Hall, 1963.
40. ———. *The Administrative State.* Chicago: University of Chicago Press, 1957.
41. Nigro, Felix A. "Ancient Greece and 'Modern' Administration," *Personnel Administration*, Vol. 23 (March-April 1960), pp. 11-19.
42. Pfiffner, John M., and Frank P. Sherwood. *Administrative Organization.* Englewood Cliffs, New Jersey: Prentice-Hall, 1960.
43. Prasad, Beni. *Theory of Government in Ancient India.* Allahabad: Indian Press, 1928.
44. Pye, Lucian W. (ed.). *Communications and Political Development.* Princeton: Princeton University Press, 1963.
45. ———. "The Non-Western Political Process," *Journal of Politics*, Vol. 20 (August 1958), pp. 468-486.

46. Riggs, Fred W. *Administration in Developing Countries: The Theory of Prismatic Society*. Boston: Houghton Mifflin, 1964.
47. ———. *The Ecology of Public Administration*. New York: Asia Publishing House, 1961.
48. Siffin, William J. (ed.). *Toward the Comparative Study of Public Administration*. Bloomington, Indiana: Department of Government, Indiana University, 1957.
49. Singer, Milton B. (ed.). *Traditional India: Structure and Change*. Philadelphia: American Folklore Society, 1959.
50. Slesinger, Jonathan A. "A Model for the Comparative Study of Public Bureaucracies," *Papers in Public Administration*, No. 23. Ann Arbor: Institute of Public Administration, University of Michigan, 1957.
51. Thompson, James D., *et al. Comparative Studies in Administration*. Pittsburgh: University of Pittsburgh Press, 1959.
52. Tout, Thomas F. *Chapters in the Administrative History of Medieval England*. Manchester: The University Press, 1920.
53. Von Mises, Ludwig. *Bureaucracy*. New Haven: Yale University Press, 1962.
54. Ward, Robert E., and Dankwart A. Rustow (eds.). *Political Modernization in Japan and Turkey*. Princeton: Princeton University Press, 1964.
55. Wittfogel, Karl A. *Oriental Despotism—A Comparative Study of Total Power*. New Haven: Yale University Press, 1957.
56. Yih, Dachin. "The Formation of the Chinese Bureaucracy." Unpublished Ph.D. dissertation, Harvard University, 1947.

See also: II-8, II-11, III-30, III-39, III-55, III-68, VI-5, VI-26, VI-31, VII-52, VII-61, VIII-6, X-28.*

* Roman numerals refer to sections of the bibliography in which additional citations may be found.

II. ADMINISTRATIVE ORGANIZATION AND AUTHORITY SYSTEMS

Literature based on Weberian criteria relevant to development.
Traditional authority systems.
Transitional-charismatic authority systems.
Legal-rational authority systems.

1. Appleby, Paul H. *Public Administration in India, Report of a Survey.* New Delhi: Government of India Press, 1957.
2. Apter, David E. *The Gold Coast in Transition.* Princeton: Princeton University Press, 1955.
3. Barghoorn, Frederick C. *Politics in the USSR: A Country Study.* Boston: Little, Brown, 1966, esp. Chapters 5, 7, 8, and 10.
4. Berger, Morroe. *Bureaucracy and Society in Modern Egypt.* Princeton: Princeton University Press, 1957.
5. Binder, Leonard. *Iran: Political Development in a Changing Society.* Berkeley: University of California Press, 1962.
6. Black, Max. *The Social Theories of Talcott Parsons.* Englewood Cliffs, N.J.: Prentice-Hall, 1962.
7. Blau, Peter M. "Critical Remarks on Weber's Theory of Authority," *American Political Science Review*, Vol. 57 (June 1963), pp. 305-316.
8. Bloch, Marc. *Feudal Society.* L. A. Manyon (tr.). Chicago: University of Chicago Press, 1961.
9. Braibanti, Ralph, *et al. Asian Bureaucratic Systems Emergent from the British Imperial Tradition.* Durham, N.C.: Duke University Press, 1966 (published for Duke University, Commonwealth Studies Center).
10. Constas, Helen. "Max Weber's Two Conceptions of Bureaucracy," *American Journal of Sociology*, Vol. 63 (January 1958), pp. 400-409.
11. Corson, John J., and Joseph P. Harris (eds.). *Public Administration in Modern Society.* New York: McGraw-Hill, 1963.
12. Crozier, Michel. "Power Relationships in Modern Bureaucracies," *Indian Journal of Public Administration*, Vol. 7 (March 1961), pp. 32-38.
13. Davison, Roderic H. *Reform in the Ottoman Empire, 1856-1876.* Princeton: Princeton University Press, 1963.
14. Delany, William. "The Development and Decline of Patrimonial and Bureaucratic Administration," *Administrative Science Quarterly*, Vol. 7 (March 1963), pp. 458-501.
15. Diamant, Alfred. "The Bureaucratic Model: Max Weber Rejected, Rediscovered, Resurrected," in Ferrel Heady and Sybil L. Stokes (eds.). *Papers in Comparative Administration.* Ann Arbor: Institute of Public Administration, University of Michigan, 1962, pp. 59-96.
16. Donnison, F. S. V. *Public Administration in Burma.* London: Royal Institute of International Affairs, 1953.
17. Drake, St. Clair. "Traditional Authority and Social Action in Former British West Africa," *Human Organization*, Vol. 19 (Fall 1960), pp. 150-158.
18. Dube, S. C. "Bureaucracy and Nation Building in Transitional Societies," *International Social Science Journal*, Vol. 16 (June 1964), pp. 229-236.
19. Ecker, Frank A. "Transition in Asia: Uzbekistan Under the Soviets." Unpublished Ph.D. dissertation, University of Michigan, 1953.
20. Fainsod, Merle. *Smolensk Under Soviet Rule.* Cambridge: Harvard University Press, 1958.
21. ———. "The Control of the Bureaucracy-Public Administration in the Soviet Union," in *How Russia is Ruled*, rev. ed. Cambridge: Harvard University Press, 1963.
22. Fortes, M., and E. E. Evans-Pritchard (eds.). *African Political Systems.* London: Oxford University Press, 1940.
23. Friedrich, Carl J. "Political Leadership and the Problem of the Charismatic Power," *Journal of Politics*, Vol. 23 (February 1961), pp. 3-24.

24. Gable, Richard. *Government and Administration in Iran.* Los Angeles: University of Southern California Press, 1959.

25. Gerth, H. H., and C. Wright Mills. *From Max Weber: Essays in Sociology.* New York: Oxford University Press, 1946.

26. Gluckman, Max. *Custom and Conflict in Africa.* New York: The Free Press, 1955.

27. Goodnow, Henry Frank. *The Civil Service of Pakistan: Bureaucracy in a New Nation.* New Haven: Yale University Press, 1964.

28. Hopkins, Terence K. "Bureaucratic Authority: The Convergence of Weber and Barnard," in Amitai Etzioni (ed.). *Complex Organizations.* New York: Holt, Rinehart & Winston, 1961.

29. Hoselitz, Bert F. (ed.). "Agrarian Societies in Transition," *The Annals of the American Academy of Political and Social Science*, Vol. 305 (May 1956).

30. Jumper, Roy. "Problems of Public Administration in South Viet Nam," *Far Eastern Survey*, Vol. 26 (December 1957), pp. 183-190.

31. Kearney, Robert N., and Richard L. Harris. "Bureaucracy and Environment in Ceylon," *Journal of Commonwealth Political Studies*, Vol. 2 (November 1964), pp. 253-266.

32. Merton, Robert K. *Social Theory and Social Structure.* rev. ed. New York: The Free Press, 1957.

33. Meyer, Poul. *Administrative Organization: A Comparative Study of the Organization of Public Administration.* London: Stevens and Sons, 1957.

34. Needler, Martin C. "The Political Development of Mexico," *American Political Science Review*, Vol. 55 (June 1961), pp. 308-312.

35. Norman, E. Herbert. *Japan's Emergence as a Modern State.* New York: Institute of Pacific Relations, 1940.

36. Oh, Chung Hwan. "The Civil Service of the Republic of Korea." Unpublished Ph.D. dissertation, New York University, 1962.

37. Parsons, Talcott. "Authority, Legitimation, and Political Action," in Carl J. Friedrich (ed.). *Authority, Nomos I.* Cambridge: Harvard University Press, 1958, pp. 197-221.

38. ———. "Some Principal Characteristics of Industrial Societies," in Cyril E. Black (ed.). *The Transformation of Russian Society.* Cambridge: Harvard University Press, 1960, pp. 13-42.

39. ———. *Structure and Process in Modern Societies.* New York: The Free Press, 1960.

40. ———, and Edward A. Shils. *Toward a General Theory of Action.* Cambridge: Harvard University Press, 1959.

41. Pike, Douglas. *Viet Cong: The Organization and Techniques of the National Liberation Front of South Vietnam.* Cambridge: The M.I.T. Press, 1966.

42. Pye, Lucian W. "The Spirit of Burmese Politics: A Preliminary Survey of a Politics of Fear and Charisma." Cambridge: Center for International Studies, M.I.T., #C/59-11, April 1959.

43. Radcliffe-Brown, A. R. *Structure and Function in Primitive Society.* New York: The Free Press, 1952.

44. Richards, Allan R. *Administration—Bolivia and the United States.* Albuquerque: University of New Mexico Press, 1961.

45. Riggs, Fred W. *Thailand: The Modernization of a Bureaucratic Polity.* Honolulu: East-West Center Press, 1967.

46. ———. "The Ambivalence of Feudalism and Bureaucracy in Traditional Societies," paper delivered at the annual meeting of the American Political Science Association, Chicago, September 1964.

47. Schapera, I. *Government and Politics in Tribal Societies.* London: C. A. Watts, 1956.

48. Scott, Robert E. *Mexican Government in Transition.* Urbana: University of Illinois Press, 1959.

49. Sharp, Walter. *The French Civil Service: Bureaucracy in Transition.* New York: Macmillan, 1931.

50. Shaw, Stanford J. *The Financial and Administrative Organization and Development of Ottoman Egypt, 1517-1798.* Princeton: Princeton University Press, 1962.
51. Shils, Edward A. "The Concentration and Dispersion of Charisma: Their Bearing on Economic Policy in Underdeveloped Countries," *World Politics*, Vol. 11 (October 1958), pp. 1-19.
52. Smith, Thomas C. *The Agrarian Origins of Modern Japan.* Stanford: Stanford University Press, 1959.
53. Thomas, S. B. *Government and Administration in Communist China.* 2nd rev. ed. New York: Institute of Pacific Relations, 1955.
54. Toennies, Ferdinand. *Gemeinschaft und Gesellschaft* (1887). Charles P. Loomis (tr.). *Fundamental Concepts of Sociology.* New York: American Book, 1940.
55. Vernon, Raymond. *The Dilemma of Mexico's Development.* Cambridge: Harvard University Press, 1963.
56. Ward, Robert E., and Roy C. Macridis (eds.). *Modern Political Systems: Asia.* Englewood Cliffs, N.J.: Prentice-Hall, 1963.

See also: I-28, I-46, I-55, III-20, III-65, IV-11, IV-12, IV-24, IV-28, IV-34, V-14, VI-2, VI-14, VI-21, VI-31, VI-43, VII-53, IX-28.*

* Roman numerals refer to sections of the bibliography in which additional citations may be found.

III. ADMINISTRATIVE ORGANIZATION AND BEHAVIOR

Theoretical behavioral literature.
Cross-cultural examples; behavioral variations.
Leadership; elites.
Decision making.
Human relations.

1. Albert, Ethel M. "Socio-Political Organization and Receptivity to Change: Some Differences Between Ruanda and Urundi," *Southwestern Journal of Anthropology*, Vol. 16 (Spring 1960), pp. 46-74.
2. Apter, David E. *The Political Kingdom of Uganda: A Study in Bureaucratic Nationalism.* Princeton: Princeton University Press, 1961.
3. Argyris, Chris. *Understanding Organizational Behavior.* Homewood, Illinois: Dorsey Press, 1960.
4. Armstrong, John. *The Soviet Bureaucratic Elite: A Case Study of the Ukrainian Apparatus.* New York: Frederick A. Praeger, 1959.
5. Benda, Harry J. "Non-Western Intelligentsias as Political Elites," *Australian Journal of Politics and History*, Vol. 6 (November 1960), pp. 205-218.
6. Berliner, Joseph S. *Factory and Manager in the USSR.* Cambridge: Harvard University Press, 1957.
7. Blau, Peter M. *The Dynamics of Bureaucracy: A Study of Interpersonal Relations in Two Government Agencies.* Chicago: University of Chicago Press, 1955.
8. ———, and W. Richard Scott, *Formal Organizations: A Comparative Approach.* San Francisco: Chandler Publications, 1962.
9. Braibanti, Ralph. "Reflections on Bureaucratic Corruption," *Public Administration*, Vol. 40 (Winter 1962), pp. 357-372.
10. Bundy, William P. "The Intellectual and the Bureaucrat." (Decennial Conference on Ideas and Action, Dedham, Mass., May 18-21, 1961.) Cambridge: Center for International Studies, M.I.T., #C/61-17, 1961.
11. Cartwright, Dorwin, and Alvin Zander (eds.). *Group Dynamics, Research and Theory.* New York: Harper & Row, 1960.
12. Chapman, Brian. *The Prefects and Provincial France.* London: Allen and Unwin, 1955.
13. Doob, Leonard W. *Becoming More Civilized: A Psychological Explanation.* New Haven: Yale University Press, 1960.
14. Dubin, Robert (ed.). *Human Relations in Administration: The Sociology of Organization.* 2nd ed. Englewood Cliffs, New Jersey: Prentice-Hall, 1961.
15. Edinger, L. J. "Continuity and Change in the Background of German Decision-Makers," *Western Political Quarterly*, Vol. 16 (March 1961), pp. 17-36.
16. Eisenstadt, S. N. "Internal Contradictions in Bureaucratic Polities," *Comparative Studies in Society and History*, Vol. 6 (October 1958), pp. 58-75.
17. Etzioni, Amitai. *A Comparative Analysis of Complex Organizations.* New York: The Free Press, 1961.
18. ——— (ed.). *Complex Organizations: A Sociological Reader.* New York: Holt, Rinehart & Winston, 1961.
19. Fagg, Donald R. "Authority and Social Stratification: A Study of Javanese Bureaucracy." Unpublished Ph.D. dissertation, Harvard University, 1958.
20. Fried, Robert C. *The Italian Prefects: A Study in Administrative Politics.* New Haven: Yale University Press, 1963.
21. Getzels, Jacob W. "Administration as a Social Process," in Warren G. Bennis, *et al. The Planning of Change: Readings in the Applied Behavioral Sciences.* New York: Holt, Rinehart & Winston, 1961, pp. 376-384.
22. Glover, J. D., and R. M. Hower. *The Administrator: Cases on Human Relations in Business*, 4th ed. Homewood, Illinois: Richard D. Irwin, 1963.
23. Gourlay, Walter E. *The Chinese Communist Cadre: Key to Political Control.* Cambridge: Russian Research Center, Harvard University, 1952.
24. Hagen, Everett E. *On the Theory of Social Change.* Homewood, Illinois: Dorsey Press, 1962.

25. Haire, Mason (ed.). *Modern Organization Theory.* New York: John Wiley & Sons, 1959.

26. Inkeles, Alex. "Social Stratification and Mobility in the Soviet Union, 1940-1950," *American Sociological Review*, Vol. 15 (August 1950), pp. 465-479.

27. Kaplan, Abraham. *The Conduct of Inquiry: Methodology for Behavioral Science.* San Francisco: Chandler Publications, 1964.

28. Kasar, Michael. "The Reorganization of Soviet Industry and its Effect on Decision Making," in Gregory Grossman (ed.). *Value and Plan.* Berkeley: University of California Press, 1960, pp. 213-234.

29. Kingsbury, Joseph B., and Tahin Aktan. *The Public Service in Turkey: Organization, Recruitment and Training.* Brussels: International Institute of Administrative Sciences, 1955.

30. Klyuchevsky, Vasily. *Peter the Great.* Archibald Translation. London: Macmillan, 1958.

31. Lansberger, Henry. *Hawthorne Revisited.* Ithaca: Cornell University Press, 1958.

32. Lauterbach, Albert. "Perceptions of Management: Case Materials from Western and Northern Europe," *Administrative Science Quarterly*, Vol. 2 (June 1957), pp. 97-109.

33. Leff, Nathaniel. "Economic Development through Bureaucratic Corruption," *American Behavioral Scientist*, Vol. 8 (November 1964), pp. 8-15.

34. Mannoni, O. *Prospero and Caliban: A Study of the Psychology of Colonization.* Pamela Powesland (tr.). 2nd ed. New York: Frederick A. Praeger, 1964.

35. Matthews, A. T. J. *Emergent Turkish Administrators.* Ankara: Institute of Administrative Sciences, University of Ankara, 1955.

36. Merton, Robert K. (ed.). *Reader in Bureaucracy.* New York: The Free Press, 1952.

37. Metcalf, Henry C., and Lyndall Urwick. *Dynamic Administration: The Collected Papers of Mary Parker Follett.* New York: Harper, 1942.

38. Montgomery, John D. *Forced to be Free: The Artificial Revolution in Germany and Japan.* Chicago: University of Chicago Press, 1957.

39. ———. "The Role of Induced Elite Change in Political Development," in Montgomery and Arthur Smithies (eds.). *Public Policy, XIII.* Cambridge: Graduate School of Public Administration, Harvard University, 1964.

40. ———, and the National Institute of Administration Case Development Seminar. *Cases in Vietnamese Administration.* Saigon, Vietnam: NIA and Michigan State University Vietnam Advisory Group, 1959.

41. Pages, G. "La vénalité des offices dans l'ancienne France," *Revue historique*, Vol. 169 (1932), pp. 477-482.

42. Plamenatz, John. *On Alien Rule and Self-Government.* London: Longmans, Green, 1960.

43. Presthus, Robert V. "Authority in Organizations," *Public Administration Review*, Vol. 20 (Spring 1960), pp. 86-91.

44. ———. "Behavior and Bureaucracy in Many Cultures," *Public Administration Review*, Vol. 19 (Winter 1959), pp. 25-35.

45. ———. "Decline of the Generalist Myth," *Public Administration Review*, Vol. 24 (December 1964), pp. 211-216.

46. ———. *The Organizational Society.* New York: Alfred A. Knopf, 1962.

47. ———. "Toward a Theory of Organizational Behavior," *Administrative Science Quarterly*, Vol. 3 (June 1958), pp. 48-72.

48. Pye, Lucian W. "Administrators, Agitators, and Brokers: Roles Relating to Modern and Traditional Patterns of Politics," *The Public Opinion Quarterly*, Vol. 22 (Fall 1958), pp. 342-348.

49. ———. "Personal Identity and Political Ideology," in Dwaine Marvick (ed.). *Political Decision Makers.* New York: The Free Press, 1960.

50. Raeff, Marc. "The Russian Autocracy and Its Officials," in H. McLean, *et al.* *Russian Thought and Politics.* Harvard Slavic Studies, Vol. 4 (1957).

51. Richards, Audrey (ed.). *East African Chiefs.* London: Faber and Faber, 1960.
52. Rivkin, Arnold. "Incentives in African Life," *Journal of African Administration*, Vol. 12 (October 1960), pp. 224-227.
53. Rokeach, Milton. "Authority, Authoritarianism and Conformity," in Irwin A. Berg and Bernard M. Bass (eds.). *Conformity and Deviation.* New York: Harper & Bros., 1961, pp. 230-257.
54. Rubinstein, Albert H., and Chadwick H. Haberstroh (eds.). *Some Theories of Organization.* Homewood, Illinois: Dorsey and Irwin, 1960.
55. Selznick, Philip. *Leadership in Administration.* Evanston, Illinois: Row Peterson, 1957.
56. ———. *T.V.A. and the Grass Roots.* Berkeley: University of California Press, 1949.
57. Seton-Watson, Hugh. "Intelligentsia and Revolution," *Soviet Survey*, No. 29 (July-September 1959), pp. 90-96.
58. Shils, Edward A. "The Intellectual in the Political Development of the New States," *World Politics*, Vol. 12 (April 1960), pp. 329-368.
59. Simon, Herbert A. *Administrative Behavior: A Study in Decision Making Processes in Administrative Organizations.* New York: Macmillan, 1957.
60. ———. *The New Science of Management Decision.* New York: Harper & Bros., 1960.
61. ———, Donald W. Smithburg, and Victor A. Thompson. *Public Administration.* New York: Alfred A. Knopf, 1950.
62. ———, and James March. *Organizations.* New York: John Wiley & Sons, 1958.
63. Singer, Marshall R. "Leadership in Ceylon: A Comparative Study of Elites." Unpublished Ph.D. dissertation, Massachusetts Institute of Technology, 1962.
64. "Special Number on Administrative Reforms since Independence," *Indian Journal of Public Administration*, Vol. 9 (July–September 1963).
65. Swart, K. W. *Sale of Offices in the Seventeenth Century.* The Hague: Nijhoff, 1949.
66. "The '50-50 Agreement.'" in Raul P. de Guzman, ed. *Patterns in Decision-Making, Case Studies in Philippine Public Administration.* Manila: University of the Philippines, 1963, pp. 91-120.
67. Thompson, Victor A. *Modern Organization.* New York: Alfred A. Knopf, 1961.
68. Woodruff, Philip. *The Men Who Ruled India.* New York: St. Martin's Press, 1954.
69. Wraith, Ronald, and Edgar Simpkins. *Corruption in Developing Countries.* London: Allen & Unwin, 1963.

See also: I-14, I-30, I-47, II-24, II-41, III-20, V-5, V-11, V-12, VI-3, VI-14, VI-36, VI-39, VII-16, VII-75, VIII-9, IX-16, X-6, X-7, X-9, X-14, X-35.*

* Roman numerals refer to sections of the bibliography in which additional citations may be found.

IV. NORMATIVE VIEWS OF BUREAUCRACY

PODSCORB literature.
Responsibility, ethics, and other Western values.
Non-Western and cultural views of administration.
Ideologies.

1. Appleby, Paul H. *Morality and Administration in Democratic Government.* Baton Rouge: Louisiana State University Press, 1952.
2. Banfield, Edward. *The Moral Basis of a Backward Society.* New York: The Free Press, 1958.
3. Bin Sayeed, Khalid. "Religion and Nation Building in Pakistan," *Middle East Journal*, Vol. 28 (Summer 1963), pp. 279-291.
4. Brown, Bernard E. *New Directions in Comparative Politics.* New York: Asia Publishing House, 1962.
5. Cleveland, Harlan. "A Philosophy for the Public Executive," in Edmund N. Fulker (ed.). *The Influences of Social Scientific and Economic Trends on Government Administration.* Washington, D.C.: U.S. Dept. of Agriculture, 1960.
6. Cropsey, Joseph. "The Right of Foreign Aid," in Robert A. Goodwin (ed.). *Why Foreign Aid?* Chicago: Rand McNally, 1962.
7. Emmerich, Herbert. *Essays on Federal Reorganization.* University, Alabama: University of Alabama Press, 1950.
8. Finer, Herman. "Administrative Responsibility in a Democratic Government," *Public Administration Review*, Vol. 1 (Summer 1941), pp. 335-350.
9. Friedrich, Carl J. "Public Policy and the Nature of Administrative Responsibility," in Carl J. Friedrich and Edward S. Mason (eds.). *Public Policy, I.* Cambridge: Harvard University Press, 1940.
10. ———. "The Dilemma of Administrative Responsibility," in Carl J. Friedrich (ed.). *Responsibility, Nomos III.* New York: Atherton Press, 1960, pp. 189-202.
11. ———, and Taylor Cole. *Responsible Bureaucracy: A Study of the Swiss Civil Service.* Cambridge: Harvard University Press, 1932.
12. Gable, Richard. "Culture and Administration in Iran," *Middle East Journal*, Vol. 13 (Autumn 1959), pp. 407-421.
13. Gulick, Luther, and Lyndall Urwick. *Papers on the Science of Administration.* New York: Harper & Bros., 1937.
14. Gusfield, Joseph R. "Equalitarianism and Bureaucratic Recruitment," *Administrative Science Quarterly*, Vol. 2 (March 1958), pp. 521-541.
15. Hauser, Philip M. "Cultural and Personal Obstacles to Economic Development in the Less Developed Areas," *Human Organization*, Vol. 18 (Summer 1959), pp. 78-84.
16. Hyneman, Charles S. *Bureaucracy in a Democracy.* New York: Harper & Row, 1950.
17. Karve, D. G. *Public Administration in Democracy.* Poona, India: Gokhale Institute of Politics and Economics, 1950.
18. Kluckhohn, Clyde. "Toward a Comparison of Value Emphases in Different Cultures," in Leonard White (ed.). *The State of the Social Sciences.* Chicago: University of Chicago Press, 1956, pp. 116-132.
19. Lepawsky, Albert. *Administration: The Art and Science of Organization and Management.* New York: Alfred A. Knopf, 1949.
20. Malenbaum, Wilfred. *East and West in India's Development.* Washington, D.C.: National Planning Association, 1959.
21. Montgomery, John D. "Public Interest in the Ideologies of National Development," in Carl J. Friedrich (ed.). *The Public Interest, Logos V.* New York: Atherton Press, 1962.
22. Leys, Wayne A. R., and Charner Perry. *Philosophy and the Public Interest.* Chicago: Committee to Advance Original Work in Philosophy, 1959.

23. Pfiffner, John M. "Administrative Rationality," *Public Administration Review*, Vol. 20 (Summer 1960), pp. 125-132.
24. Presthus, Robert V. "Weberian vs. Welfare Bureaucracy in Traditional Society," *Administrative Science Quarterly*, Vol. 6 (June 1961), pp. 1-24.
25. Sayre, Wallace C. "Trends of a Decade in Administrative Values," *Public Administration Review*, Vol. 2 (Winter 1951), pp. 1-10.
26. Schubert, Glendon. *The Public Interest.* New York: The Free Press, 1961.
27. Sigmund, Paul E., Jr. (ed.). *The Ideologies of the Developing Nations.* New York: Frederick A. Praeger, 1963.
28. Singer, Floyd L. "*Pao Chia*: Social Control in China and Vietnam," *U.S. Naval Institute Proceedings*, Vol. 91 (November 1965), pp. 36-45.
29. Sjoberg, Gideon. "Political Structure, Ideology, and Economic Development." The Carnegie Faculty Seminar on Political and Administrative Development. Bloomington, Indiana: Indiana University, 1963 (mimeographed).
30. United Nations. *A Handbook of Public Administration: Current Concepts and Practice with Special Reference to Developing Countries.* New York: U.N. Department of Economic and Social Affairs, 1961.
31. United Nations, Special Committee on Public Administration Problems. *Standards and Techniques of Public Administration.* New York: Technical Assistance Administration, 1951.
32. Waldo, Dwight. *The Administrative State: A Study of the Political Theory of American Public Administration.* New York: Ronald Press, 1948.
33. Wallace, Schuyler. *Federal Departmentalization: A Critique of Theories of Organization.* New York: Macmillan, 1944.
34. White, Leonard D. *The Civil Service in the Modern State.* Chicago: University of Chicago Press, 1930.
35. Wickwar, W. Hardy. *The Modernization of Administration in the Near East.* Beirut, Lebanon: Khayats, 1963.
36. Willbern, York. "Professionalization in the Public Service: Too Little or Too Much?" *Public Administration Review*, Vol. 14 (Winter 1954), pp. 13-21.
37. Young, Tien-cheng. *International Civil Service: Principles and Problems.* Brussels: International Institute of Administrative Services, 1958.

See also: II-31, II-33, II-42, II-51, III-1, III-9, III-37, III-64, VII-19, VII-59, VII-83, VIII-14, VIII-15, VIII-16, IX-9, IX-18.*

* Roman numerals refer to sections of the bibliography in which additional citations may be found.

V. BUREAUCRACY AND OTHER POLITICAL INSTITUTIONS

Generalized relationships of the bureaucracy to other institutions.
Parties.
Interest groups.
Students.
Labor groups.

1. Apter, David E. "Some Reflections on the Role of a Political Opposition in New Nations," *Comparative Studies in Society and History*, Vol. 4 (January 1962), pp. 154-168.
2. Beck, Carl. "Party Control and Bureaucratization in Czechoslovakia," *Journal of Politics*, Vol. 23 (May 1961), pp. 279-294.
3. Galenson, Walter (ed.). *Labor in Developing Countries*. Berkeley: University of California Press, 1962.
4. Grassmuck, George L. "Polity, Bureaucracy, and Interest Groups in the Near East and North Africa," *CAG Occasional Papers*. Bloomington, Indiana: CAG/American Society for Public Administration, 1965.
5. Houghes, Jerry F. "The Technical Elite vs. the Party: A First-hand Report," *Problems of Communism*, Vol. 8 (September–October 1959), pp. 56-59.
6. International Labor Office. *Reports of the ILO on a Manpower Survey in Pakistan*. Karachi, Pakistan: United Nations Publications Office, 1959.
7. Jumper, Roy. "Mandarin Bureaucracy and Politics in South Vietnam," *Pacific Affairs*, Vol. 30 (March 1957), pp. 47-58.
8. Jurczenko, A. "Administrative Reorganization and the Building of Communism," *Bulletin of the Institute for the Study of the USSR*, Vol. 7 (January 1960), pp. 14-23.
9. LaPalombara, Joseph. *Interest Groups in Italian Politics*. Princeton: Princeton University Press, 1964.
10. Liebman, C. S. "Electorates, Interest Groups, and Local Government Policy," *American Behavioral Scientist*, Vol. 4 (January 1961), pp. 9-11.
11. Lorwin, Val R. *The Politicization of the Bureaucracy in Belgium*. Stanford: Center for Advanced Study in the Behavioral Sciences, 1962.
12. Park, Richard L., and Irene Tinker (eds.). *Leadership and Political Institutions in India*. Princeton: Princeton University Press, 1959.
13. Revai, Jozsef. "The Character of a 'People's Democracy,'" *Foreign Affairs*, Vol. 28 (October 1949), pp. 143-152.
14. Rustow, Dankwart A. *The Politics of Compromise: A Study of Parties and Cabinet Government in Sweden*. Princeton: Princeton University Press, 1955.
15. Scalapino, Robert. *Democracy and Parties in Pre-War Japan*. Berkeley: University of California Press, 1953.
16. Schachter, Ruth. "Single Party Systems in West Africa," *American Political Science Review*, Vol. 55 (June 1961), pp. 294-307.
17. Silverstein, Josef, and Julian Wohl. "University Students and Politics in Burma," *Pacific Affairs*, Vol. 37 (Spring 1964), pp. 50-65.
18. Sutton, Joseph L. (ed.). *Problems of Politics and Administration in Thailand*. Bloomington, Indiana: Institute of Training for Public Service, Indiana University, 1962.
19. Tinker, Hugh. *Ballot Box and Bayonet: People and Government in Emergent Asian Countries*. New York: Oxford University Press, 1964.
20. Tsuji, Kiyoaki. "The Cabinet, Administrative Organization, and the Bureaucracy," *The Annals of the American Academy of Political and Social Science*, Vol. 38 (November 1956), pp. 10-17.
21. Tucker, Robert C. "On Revolutionary Mass-Movement Regimes," in *The Soviet Political Mind: Studies in Stalinism and Post-Stalin Change*. New York: Frederick A. Praeger, 1963, pp. 3-19.
22. Weiner, Myron. *Party Politics in India: The Development of a Multi-Party System*. Princeton: Princeton University Press, 1957.

23. Weiner, Myron (ed.). *State Politics in India.* Princeton: Princeton University Press, 1967.

See also: I-10, I-15, I-20, I-55, II-20, II-34, II-55, III-23, III-51, VI-20, VI-22, VI-38, VI-39, VI-44, VII-41, VII-47, VII-61, VII-83, VIII-3, X-20.*

* Roman numerals refer to sections of the bibliography in which additional citations may be found.

VI. BUREAUCRACY AND THE HISTORICAL CRISES OF POLITICAL DEVELOPMENT

Identity.
Legitimacy.
Participation.
Integration.
Penetration.
Distribution.
Sequencing; timing.

1. Abueva, José. "Bridging the Gap between the Elite and the People in the Philippines," *Philippine Journal of Public Administration*, Vol. 8 (October 1964), pp. 325-347.
2. Ashford, Douglas E. *Political Change in Morocco.* Princeton: Princeton University Press, 1961.
3. Binder, Leonard. "Political Recruitment and Participation in Egypt," in Joseph LaPalombara and Myron Weiner (eds.). *Political Parties and Political Development.* Princeton: Princeton University Press, 1966, pp. 217-240.
4. ———. "Prolegomena to the Comparative Study of Middle East Governments," *American Political Science Review*, Vol. 51 (September 1957), pp. 651-668.
5. Black, C. E. *The Dynamics of Modernization.* New York: Harper & Row, 1966.
6. Bondurant, Joan V. *Regionalism vs. Provincialism: A Study in Problems of Indian National Unity.* Berkeley: University of California Press, 1958.
7. Buchman, Jean. *L'Afrique noire indépendante.* Paris: Librairie Générale de Droit et de Jurisprudence, 1962.
8. Coleman, James S., and Carl Rosberg (eds.). *Political Change and Integration in Tropical Africa.* Berkeley: University of California Press, 1964.
9. Crowley, Daniel J. "Politics and Tribalism in the Katanga," *Western Political Quarterly*, Vol. 16 (March 1963), pp. 68-78.
10. Deutsch, Karl W. "Social Mobilization and Political Development," *American Political Science Review*, Vol. 55 (September 1961), pp. 493-514.
11. Deutsch, Karl W., and William J. Foltz (eds.). *Nation-Building.* New York: Atherton Press, 1963.
12. Eisenstadt, S. N. *Modernization: Protest and Change.* Englewood Cliffs, New Jersey: Prentice-Hall, 1967.
13. Evers, Hans-Dieter. "The Formation of Social Class Structure: Urbanization, Bureaucratization, Social Mobility in Thailand," *American Sociological Review*, Vol. 31 (August 1966), pp. 480-488.
14. Fallers, L. A. *Bantu Bureaucracy: A Study of Integration and Conflict in the Political Institutions of an East African People.* Cambridge, England: Heffer and Sons, 1956.
15. Hamilton, William B. (ed.). *The Transfer of Institutions.* Durham, N.C.: Duke University Press, 1964 (published for Duke University, Commonwealth Studies Center).
16. Hermann, Charles F. "Some Consequences of Crises Which Limit the Viability of Organizations," *Administrative Science Quarterly*, Vol. 8 (June 1963), pp. 61-82.
17. Johnson, Chalmers. "Civilian Logistics and Guerrilla Conflict," *World Politics*, Vol. 14 (July 1962), pp. 646-661.
18. Johnson, J. J. *Political Change in Latin America: Emergence of the Middle Sectors.* Stanford: Stanford University Press, 1958.
19. LaPalombara, Joseph. "Distribution and Development," in M. Weiner (ed.). *Modernization: The Dynamics of Growth.* New York: Basic Books, 1966, pp. 218-229.
20. Lewis, John. *Quiet Crisis in India.* Washington D.C.: The Brookings Institution, 1962.

21. Lipset, Seymour M. *The First New Nation: The United States in Historical and Comparative Perspective.* New York: Basic Books, 1963.
22. Lunev, A. E. *Forms of Participation of Masses in Activity of State Organs of Chinese People's Republic.* Washington, D.C.: Joint Publications Research Service, November 18, 1958 (JPRS 374).
23. Milbrath, Lester W. *Political Participation.* Chicago: Rand McNally, 1965.
24. Pye, Lucian W. *Aspects of Political Development.* Boston: Little, Brown, 1966.
25. ———. *Politics, Personality, and Nation Building: Burma's Search for Identity.* New Haven: Yale University Press, 1962.
26. ———. "The Concept of Political Development," *The Annals of the American Academy of Political and Social Science*, Vol. 358 (March 1965), pp. 1-13.
27. ———. "The New Politics of National Building," *AID Digest* (August 1962), pp. 12-16.
28. ———. "The Roots of Insurgency and the Commencement of Rebellions," in Harry Eckstein (ed.). *Internal War.* New York: The Free Press, 1964, pp. 157-179.
29. Rokkan, Stein (ed.). *Approaches to the Study of Political Participation.* Bergen: Christian Michelsen Institute, 1962.
30. Rustow, Dankwart A. "The Vanishing Dream of Stability," *AID Digest* (August 1962), pp. 8-11.
31. Shils, Edward A. *Political Development in the New States.* The Hague: Mouton, 1962.
32. Shinoda, Minoru, *et al.* "Some Problems in Public Administration in Developing Countries," *Occasional Papers on Research Translations.* Honolulu: East-West Center Press, Institute of Advanced Projects, 1966.
33. Soemardjian, S. "Bureaucratic Organization in a Time of Revolution," *Administrative Science Quarterly*, Vol. 2 (September 1957), pp. 182-199.
34. Spengler, Joseph J. "Economic Development: Political Preconditions and Political Consequences," *Journal of Politics*, Vol. 22 (August 1960), pp. 387-416.
35. Tambiah, S. J. "Ethnic Representation in Ceylon's Higher Administrative Services, 1870-1946," *University of Ceylon Review*, Vol. 13 (April–July 1955), pp. 113-134.
36. Tilman, Robert O. *Bureaucratic Transition in Malaya.* Durham, N.C.: Duke University Press, 1964 (published for Duke University, Commonwealth Studies Center).
37. Tinker, Hugh. "People and Government in Southern Asia," *Transactions of the Royal Historical Society*, 5th Series, Vol. 9 (1959), pp. 141-167.
38. Von der Mehden, Fred R. *Politics of the Developing Nations.* Englewood Cliffs, New Jersey: Prentice-Hall, 1964.
39. Weiner, Myron. "Congress Party Elites," *The Carnegie Seminar on Political and Administrative Development.* Bloomington, Indiana: Department of Government, Indiana University, 1966.
40. ——— (ed.). *Modernization: The Dynamics of Growth.* New York: Basic Books, 1966.
41. ———. "Political Integration and Political Development," *The Annals of the American Academy of Political and Social Science*, Vol. 358 (March 1965), pp. 52-64.
42. Wriggins, Howard. *Ceylon: Dilemma of a New Nation.* Princeton: Princeton University Press, 1960.
43. Younger, Kenneth. *The Public Service in New States.* London: Oxford University Press, 1960.
44. Zolberg, Astride. "Mass Parties and National Integration: The Case of the Ivory Coast," *Journal of Politics*, Vol. 25 (February 1963), pp. 36-48.

See also: I-1, I-29, II-5, II-45, IV-27, V-3, V-16, VIII-11, IX-5, X-6, X-25.*

* Roman numerals refer to sections of the bibliography in which additional citations may be found.

VII. BUREAUCRACY AND SOCIO-ECONOMIC CHANGE

Theory; theoretical literature.
National examples of the bureaucracy in socio-economic change.
Technical assistance; foreign aid.
Developmental administration; reforms.
Planning.
Public enterprise.

1. Adams, Walter, and John Garraty. *Is the World Our Campus?* East Lansing, Michigan: Michigan State University Press, 1960.
2. Alexandrides, Costas G. "The United Nations Economic Assistance to the Republic of Korea: A Case Study of Economic Reconstruction and Development." Unpublished Ph.D. dissertation, New York University, 1961.
3. Baker, Burton A. (ed.). *Public Administration, a Key to Development.* Washington, D.C.: Graduate School, U.S. Department of Agriculture, 1964.
4. Bauer, P. T., and Basil S. Yamey. *The Economics of Under-Developed Countries.* Chicago: University of Chicago Press, 1957.
5. Belassa, Bela. *The Hungarian Experience in Economic Planning.* New Haven: Yale University Press, 1959.
6. Berger, Morroe. "The Public Bureaucracy and Economic Growth," in *Problems of Administration.* Cairo: Congress for Cultural Freedom, 1959, pp. 52-58.
7. Bock, Edwin A. *Fifty Years of Technical Assistance.* Chicago: Public Administration Clearing House, 1954.
8. Boh, Lim Tay. "The Role of the Civil Service in the Economy of Independent Malaya," *Malayan Economic Review*, Vol. 4 (April 1959), pp. 1-9.
9. Braibanti, Ralph. "Transnational Inducement of Administrative Reform," *CAG Occasional Papers.* Bloomington, Indiana: CAG/American Society for Public Administration, 1964.
10. ———, and Joseph J. Spengler (eds.). *Administration and Economic Development in India.* Durham, N.C.: Duke University Press, 1963 (published for Duke University, Commonwealth Studies Center).
11. ———. *Tradition, Values, and Socio-economic Development.* Durham, N.C.: Duke University Press, 1961 (published for Duke University, Commonwealth Studies Center).
12. Brown, David S. "Concepts and Strategies of Public Administration: Technical Assistance," *CAG Occasional Papers.* Bloomington, Indiana: CAG/American Society for Public Administration, 1964.
13. ———. "Key to Self-Help: Improving the Administrative Capabilities of the Aid Receiving Countries," *Public Administration Review*, Vol. 24 (June 1964), pp. 67-77.
14. Burov, Boris. "The Reorganization and Administration of the Bulgarian National Economy," *Pravna Misal*, Vol. 4 (July–August 1960), pp. 3-13.
15. Caldwell, Lynton K. "Technical Assistance and Administrative Reform in Colombia," *American Political Science Review*, Vol. 47 (June 1953), pp. 494-510.
16. Carlson, Sune. *Development Economics and Administration.* Stockholm: Svenska Bokförlaget, 1964.
17. Ditz, Gerhard W. "Industrial Administration in Communist East Europe," *Administrative Science Quarterly*, Vol. 4 (June 1959), pp. 82-96.
18. *Education for Social Change: Establishing Institutes of Public and Business Administration Abroad.* Washington, D.C.: The Brookings Institution, 1961.
19. Emmerich, Herbert. *Administrative Roadblocks to Coordinated Development.* United Nations Document ST/TAO/Conf., 6/LC-4/Rev. I, April 1961.
20. Fox, G. H., and John T. Dorsey, Jr. "Vietnam's National Institute of Administration," *Philippine Journal of Public Administration*, Vol. 2 (April 1958), pp. 115-120.

21. Friedman, John. "The Social Context of National Planning Decisions: A Comparative Approach," *CAG Occasional Papers*. Bloomington, Indiana: CAG/American Society for Public Administration, 1963.
22. Gable, Richard (ed.). "Partnership for Progress: International Technical Cooperation," *The Annals of the American Academy of Political and Social Science*, Vol. 323 (May 1959).
23. Hackett, John, and Anne-Marie Hackett. *Economic Planning in France*. Cambridge: Harvard University Press, 1963.
24. Hagen, Everett E. *Planning Economic Development*. Homewood, Illinois: Richard D. Irwin, 1963.
25. Hanson, A. H. *Public Enterprise and Economic Development*. London: Routledge and Kegan Paul, 1959.
26. Heady, Ferrel. "Bureaucracies in Developing Countries: Internal Roles and External Assistance," Conference of Comparative Administration Group, Baltimore, Maryland, April 1966 (mimeographed).
27. Higgins, Benjamin. *UN and US Foreign Economic Policy*. Homewood, Illinois: Richard D. Irwin, 1962.
28. Hirschman, Albert O. *Journeys Toward Progress*, New York: Twentieth Century Fund, 1963.
29. ———. *The Strategy of Economic Development*. New Haven: Yale University Press, 1958.
30. ———, and Charles E. Lindblom. "Economic Development, Research and Development Policy Making: Some Converging Views," *Behavioral Science*, Vol. 6 (April 1962), pp. 211-222.
31. Hoover, Calvin B. (ed.). *Economic Systems of the Commonwealth*. Durham, N.C.: Duke University Press, 1962 (published for Duke University, Commonwealth Studies Center).
32. Hoselitz, Bert F. *Sociological Aspects of Economic Growth*. New York: The Free Press, 1960.
33. Hsia, Ronald. *Economic Planning in Communist China*. New York: Institute of Pacific Relations, 1955.
34. Hsueh, S. S. "Technical Cooperation in Development Administration in South and Southeast Asia," *CAG Occasional Papers*. Bloomington, Indiana: CAG/American Society for Public Administration, 1966.
35. Ilchman, Warren F. "New Time in Old Clocks: Productivity, Development, and Comparative Public Administration," *CAG Occasional Papers*. Bloomington, Indiana: CAG/American Society for Public Administration, 1967.
36. ———. "Rising Expectations and the Revolution in Development Administration," *Public Administration Review*, Vol. 25 (December 1965), pp. 314-328.
37. Jackson, Sir Robert. *The Case for an International Development Authority*. Syracuse: Syracuse University Press, 1959.
38. Kraus, Hertha (ed.). "International Cooperation for Social Welfare—A New Reality," *The Annals of the American Academy of Political and Social Science*, Vol. 329 (May 1960).
39. Kuznets, Simon, Wilbert E. Moore, and Joseph J. Spengler (eds.). *Economic Growth: Brazil, India, Japan*. Durham, N.C.: Duke University Press, 1955.
40. LaPalombara, Joseph. "Theory and Practice in Development Administration: Observations of the Role of the Civilian Bureaucracy," *CAG Occasional Papers*. Bloomington, Indiana: CAG/American Society for Public Administration, 1967.
41. ———. *The Politics of Economic Planning in Italy*. Syracuse: Syracuse University Press, 1966.
42. Lepawsky, Albert. "Technical Assistance: A Challenge to Public Administration," *Public Administration Review*, Vol. 16 (Winter 1956), pp. 22-32.
43. Lewins, Leon. "The Polish Economy, The Problems and Prospects," *Problems of Communism*, Vol. 7 (May–June 1958), pp. 14-23.

44. Li, Choh-ming. *Economic Development of Communist China: An Appraisal of the First Five Years of Industrialization.* Berkeley: University of California Press, 1959.
45. Lockwood, William. *The Economic Development of Japan.* Princeton: Princeton University Press, 1954.
46. Malenbaum, Wilfred. "The Role of Government in India's Third Five Year Plan," *Economic Development and Cultural Change*, Vol. 8 (April 1960), pp. 225-236.
47. Mason, Edward S. *Economic Planning in Underdeveloped Areas: Government and Business.* New York: Fordham University Press, 1958.
48. Milne, R. S. "The New Administration and the New Economic Program in the Philippines," *Asian Survey*, Vol. 2 (September 1962), pp. 36-42.
49. Montgomery, John D. *The Politics of Foreign Aid: American Experience in Southeast Asia.* New York: Frederick A. Praeger, 1962.
50. ———, and Milton J. Esman. *Development Administration in Malaysia, Report to the Government of Malaysia.* Kuala Lumpur: Government of Malaysia, 1966.
51. Mosher, Frederick C. *The Administrative Science Program at Bologna.* Berkeley: Bureau of Public Administration, University of California, 1959.
52. Myrdal, Gunnar. *The Political Element in the Development of Economic Theory.* Cambridge: Harvard University Press, 1954.
53. Natu, W. R. *Public Administration and Economic Development.* Poona, India: Gorkhale Institute of Politics and Economics, 1954.
54. Nelson, Joan M. "Central Planning for National Development and the Role of Foreign Advisors: the Case of Burma." Unpublished Ph.D. dissertation, Radcliffe, 1960.
55. Paauw, Douglas S. "Economic Progress in Southeast Asia," *Journal of Asian Studies*, Vol. 23 (November 1963), pp. 69-92.
56. Papanek, Gustav F. "Framing a Development Program," *International Conciliation*, No. 527 (March 1960), pp. 307-372.
57. Peacock, A. T. "The Public Sector and the Theory of Economic Growth," *Scottish Journal of Political Economy*, Vol. 6 (February 1959), pp. 1-12.
58. Pye, Lucian W. "Soviet and American Styles in Foreign Aid," *Orbis*, Vol. 4 (Summer 1960), pp. 159-173.
59. ———. "The Political Impulses and Fantasies Behind Foreign Aid," *The Annals of the American Academy of Political and Social Science*, Vol. 339 (January 1962), pp. 8-27.
60. Riggs, Fred W. "Public Administration: A Neglected Factor in Economic Development," *The Annals of the American Academy of Political and Social Science*, Vol. 305 (May 1956), pp. 70-80.
61. ———. "Relearning an Old Lesson: The Political Context of Development Administration," *Public Administration Review*, Vol. 25 (March 1965), pp. 70-79.
62. Rivkin, Arnold. "The Role of External Assistance in African Development," *International Journal*, Vol. 14 (Summer 1959), pp. 157-167.
63. Rosenstein-Rodan, Paul N. "International Aid for Underdeveloped Countries," *Review of Economics and Statistics*, Vol. 43 (May 1961), pp. 107-138.
64. Roxas, Sixto K. *Organizing the Government for Economic Development Administration.* Manila: National Economic Development Commission, 1964.
65. Schenk, Frank. *Magie der Planwirtschaft.* Cologne: Kiepenheuer und Witsch, 1960.
66. Schultz, Theodore W. *Transforming Traditional Agriculture.* New Haven: Yale University Press, 1964.
67. Sharp, Walter. *International Technical Assistance.* Chicago: Public Administration Service, 1952.
68. Shaw, Leander J., Jr. "A Documentary and Descriptive Analysis of the Admin-

istration of Educational Programs under Point Four in Brazil, Iran, and Thailand." Unpublished Ph.D. dissertation, Pennsylvania State University, 1955.

69. Smith, Thomas C. *Political Change and Industrial Development in Japan: Government Enterprise, 1868-1880.* Stanford: Stanford University Press, 1955.

70. Spulber, Nicolas. *The Economics of Communist Eastern Europe.* New York: John Wiley & Sons, 1957.

71. State of California, "The Chile-California Program: A Report to the Governor." Sacramento, California, June 18, 1964 (mimeographed).

72. Storm, Bruce, and Richard W. Gable. "Technical Assistance in Higher Education: An Iranian Illustration," *The Educational Record* (April 1960), pp. 175-182.

73. Swerdlow, I. (ed.). *Developmental Administration: Concepts and Problems.* Syracuse: Syracuse University Press, 1963.

74. Tanham, George K. *War Without Guns: American Civilians in Rural Vietnam.* New York: Frederick A. Praeger, 1966.

75. Thompson, Victor A. "Administrative Objectives for Developmental Administration," *Administrative Science Quarterly*, Vol. 9 (June 1964), pp. 91-108.

76. Ul-Haq, Mahub. "Planned Capital Formation in an Underdeveloped Economy: The Case of Pakistan." Unpublished Ph.D. dissertation, Yale University, 1958.

77. U.S. Agency for International Development. *Improving the Public Service through Training.* Washington, D.C.: U.S.A.I.D., 1962.

78. Vrancken, Fernand. *Technical Assistance in Public Administration: Lessons of Experience and Possible Improvements.* Brussels: International Institute of Administrative Sciences, 1965.

79. Waltman, Howard L. "Cross-Cultural Training in Public Administration," *Public Administration Review*, Vol. 21 (Summer 1961), pp. 141-147.

80. Weidner, Edward W. *Technical Assistance in Public Administration Overseas: The Case for Developmental Administration.* Chicago: Public Administration Service, 1964.

81. ———. "The American Education of Foreign Administrators: Lessons from American Training Programs in Foreign Countries," *Technical Assistance in Training Administrators.* Bloomington, Indiana: Institute of Training for Public Service, Indiana University, 1962.

82. Wolf, Charles, Jr. "National Priorities and Development Strategies in Southeast Asia," *Philippine Economic Journal*, Vol. 4 (Second Semester 1965), pp. 156-172.

83. Wurfel, David. "The Bell Report and After: A Study of the Political Problems of Social Reform Stimulated by Foreign Aid." Unpublished Ph.D. dissertation, Cornell University, 1960.

84. Yanov, Yanko. "A Transfer of the Function of State Organs to Public Organizations," *Pravna Misal* (Bulgaria), Vol. 4 (August 15, 1960).

See also: I-23, I-32, I-46, II-1, II-13, III-6, III-24, III-40, III-64, IV-6, IV-15, IV-20, IV-29, IV-30, VI-34, VII-46, VIII-2, VIII-4, VIII-7, VIII-10, VIII-17, VIII-18, IX-11, IX-15, IX-27, IX-29, IX-41, X-24, X-32, X-36, X-39.*

* Roman numerals refer to sections of the bibliography in which additional citations may be found.

VIII. BUREAUCRACY AND PUBLIC POLICY

Bureaucracy as a policy making body.
Recommendations of policy either from bureaucracy or for the bureaucracy.

1. Appleby, Paul H. *Policy and Administration.* University, Alabama: University of Alabama Press, 1949.
2. Balogh, T. "Economic Policy and the Price System," *Economic Bulletin for Latin America,* Vol. 6 (March 1961), pp. 41-53.
3. Bator, Francis M. *The Question of Government Spending: Public Needs and Private Wants.* New York: Harper & Bros., 1960.
4. Bauer, P. T. *Indian Economic Policy and Development.* New York: Frederick A. Praeger, 1961.
5. Center for International Studies, Massachusetts Institute of Technology. *The Objectives of United States Economic Assistance Programs.* Study prepared for the Committee on Foreign Relations, United States Senate. Washington, D.C.: Government Printing Office, 1956.
6. Gaus, John M. *Reflections on Public Administration.* University, Alabama: University of Alabama Press, 1947.
7. Golay, Frank. *The Philippines: Public Policy and National Economic Development.* Ithaca, New York: Cornell University Press, 1961.
8. Hoselitz, Bert F. "Economic Policy and Economic Development," in Hugh G. J. Aitken (ed.). *The State and Economic Growth.* New York: Social Science Research Council, 1959.
9. Janowitz, Morris, and William Delany. "The Bureaucrat and the Public: A Study of Informational Perspectives," *Administrative Science Quarterly,* Vol. 2 (September 1957), pp. 141-162.
10. Khera, S. S. *Government in Business.* Bombay: Asia Publishing House, 1963.
11. Millikan, Max F., and Donald L. M. Blackmer. *The Emerging Nations: Their Growth and United States Policy.* Boston: Little, Brown, 1961.
12. Musgrave, Richard A. *The Theory of Public Finance.* New York: McGraw-Hill, 1959.
13. Myrdal, Gunnar. *Beyond the Welfare State: Economic Planning and Its International Implications.* New Haven: Yale University Press, 1960.
14. Spengler, Joseph J. "Social Value Theory, Economic Analyses, and Economic Policy," *American Economic Review,* Vol. 42 (May 1953), pp. 340-345.
15. Stein, Harold. *American Civil-Military Decisions.* University, Alabama: University of Alabama Press, 1963.
16. Stein, Harold (ed.). *Public Administration and Policy Development: A Casebook.* New York: Harcourt, Brace and World, 1952.
17. Tinbergen, Jan. *The Design of Development.* Baltimore: Johns Hopkins University Press, 1958.
18. Tobin, J. "Economic Growth as an Objective of Government Policy," *American Economic Review,* Vol. 54 (May 1964), pp. 1-27.

See also: I-39, IV-32, V-10, VII-27, VII-30, VII-37, VII-57.*

* Roman numerals refer to sections of the bibliography in which additional citations may be found.

IX. BUREAUCRACY AND TERRITORY

Federalism.
Provincialism; state level.
Local.
Community or rural development examples.
Field administration.

1. Abueva, José V. *Focus on the Barrio.* Manila: University of the Philippines, Institute of Public Administration, 1959.
2. Baun, Bernard H. *Decentralization of Authority in a Bureaucracy.* Englewood Cliffs, New Jersey: Prentice-Hall, 1961.
3. Brady, Alexander. *Democracy in the Dominions,* 3rd ed. Toronto: University of Toronto Press, 1958.
4. Brett, Cecil C. "The Government of Okayama Prefecture: A Case Study of Local Autonomy in Japan." Unpublished Ph.D. dissertation, Michigan, 1957.
5. Dow, Maynard W. *Nation Building in Southeast Asia.* Boulder, Colorado: Pruett Press, 1966.
6. Ensminger, Douglas. "Community Development and its Contribution to National Development," *Community Development Review,* Vol. 6 (1961), pp. 10-16.
7. Fesler, James W. *Area and Administration.* University, Alabama: University of Alabama Press, 1949.
8. Ghosh, D., Christopher Sower, and C. F. Ware. *Report of a Rural Development Evaluation Mission in Ceylon.* New York: United Nations Technical Assistance Administration, October, 1962.
9. Goodrick, M. George. "Integration vs. Decentralization within the Federal Field Service," *Public Administration Review,* Vol. 9 (Autumn 1949), pp. 272-281.
10. Hickey, Gerald C. *Village in Vietnam.* New Haven: Yale University Press, 1964.
11. Hicks, Ursula, *et al. Federalism and Economic Growth.* New York: Oxford University Press, 1961.
12. Horrigan, Frederick J. "Local Government and Administration in Thailand: A Study of Institutions in their Cultural Setting." Unpublished Ph.D. dissertation, Indiana University, 1960.
13. Hoven, W., and A. van den Elshout. *Local Government in Selected Countries: Ceylon, Israel, Japan.* New York: United Nations Technical Assistance Administration, 1963.
14. Jacob, Herbert. *German Administration Since Bismarck: Central Authority vs. Local Autonomy.* New Haven: Yale University Press, 1963.
15. Jayme, V. R. "The Mindanao Development Authority: A New Concept in Philippine Economic Development," *Philippine Journal of Public Administration,* Vol. 5 (October 1961), pp. 321-329.
16. Kaufman, Herbert. *The Forest Ranger: A Study in Administrative Behavior.* Baltimore: Johns Hopkins University Press, 1960.
17. Lower, A. R. M., F. R. Scott, *et al. Evolving Canadian Federalism.* Durham, N.C.: Duke University Press, 1958 (published for Duke University, Commonwealth Studies Center).
18. Lutz, Edward A. *The Role of Local Government in Philippine Democracy.* Quezon City: University of the Philippines, College of Agriculture, 1958.
19. Luykx, Nicolaas G. M. "Some Comparative Aspects of Rural Public Institutions in Thailand, the Philippines, and Vietnam." Unpublished Ph.D. dissertation, Cornell University, 1962.
20. Macmahon, Arthur W. (ed.). *Federalism Mature and Emergent.* Garden City, New York: Doubleday, 1955.
21. Maddick, Henry. *Decentralization for National and Local Development.* New York: United Nations, Division for Public Administration, 1962.

22. Maryanov, Gerald S. "The Establishment of Regional Government in the Republic of Indonesia." Unpublished Ph.D. dissertation, Indiana University, 1960.
23. Montgomery, John D., Rufus B. Hughes, and Raymond H. Davis. "Rural Improvement and Political Development: The JCRR Model." Washington, D.C.: U.S.A.I.D., 1964 (mimeographed).
24. Ness, Gayle D. "Central Government and Local Initiative in the Industrialization of India and Japan." Unpublished Ph.D. dissertation, University of California, Berkeley, 1961.
25. Nyce, Roy. "The New Villages of Malaya: A Community Study." Unpublished Ph.D. dissertation, Hartford Seminary, 1962.
26. Opler, Morris E. "Political Organization and Economic Growth: The Case of Village India," *International Review of Community Development*, Vol. 5 (1960), pp. 187-197.
27. Riggs, Fred W. "Economic Development and Local Administration: A Study in Circular Causation," *Philippine Journal of Public Administration*, Vol. 3 (January 1959), pp. 56-147.
28. Robinson, Geroid T. *Rural Russia under the Red Regime*, (*A History of the Landlord-Peasant World, and a Prologue to the Peasant Revolution of 1917*). New York: Macmillan, 1957.
29. Sady, Emil. *Public Administration Aspects of Community Development Programs*. New York: United Nations, Office of Public Administration, 1959.
30. Sanders, Irwin T. *Summary of Conference on Community Development and National Change*. Washington, D.C.: International Cooperation Administration, March 1958.
31. Sanjian, A. K. *The Armenian Communities in Syria under Ottoman Dominion*. Cambridge: Harvard University Middle Eastern Studies, 1965.
32. Sharp, Walter. *Field Administration in the United Nations System*. New York: Frederick A. Praeger, 1961.
33. Steiner, Kurt. "Local Government in Japan." Unpublished Ph.D. dissertation, Stanford University, 1955.
34. Tinker, Hugh. "Authority and Community in Village India," *Journal of African Administration*, Vol. 12 (October 1960), pp. 193-210.
35. ———. *The Foundations of Local Self-Government in India, Pakistan and Burma*. London: University of London, 1954.
36. Tripathy, Sridhar. "Village Governments in India." Unpublished Ph.D. dissertation, Columbia University, 1957.
37. United Nations. *Public Administration Aspects of Community Development*. New York: St/TAO/,/ 14, 1959.
38. Vucinach, A. "The State and the Local Community," in C. E. Black (ed.). *The Transformation of Russian Society*. Cambridge: Harvard University Press, 1960.
39. Ward, Robert E. (ed.). *Far Eastern Quarterly*, Vol. 15 (February 1956), pp. 157-238. Special issue on local and village government.
40. ———. "The Socio-Political Role of the Buraku (hamlet) in Japan," *American Political Science Review*, Vol. 45 (December 1951), pp. 1,025-1,040.
41. Wiles, P. J. D. "Rationality, the Market, Decentralization, and the Territorial Principle," in Gregory Grossman (ed.). *Value and Plan*. Berkeley: University of California Press, 1960, pp. 184-203.
42. Yang, C. K. *A Chinese Village in Early Communist Transition*. Cambridge: Harvard University Press, 1959.

See also: I-31, I-37, II-19, II-20, III-56, IV-7, V-10, VI-1, VI-6.*

* Roman numerals refer to sections of the bibliography in which additional citations may be found.

X. MILITARY AS AN ELEMENT OF THE BUREAUCRACY

Role; general literature; organization and authority structure.
Politically stabilizing: military, government, peace keeping, counter insurgency.
Politically destabilizing: revolutions, coups d'état.
Economic development force.
Military assistance programs.

1. Berger, Morroe. *Military Elite and Social Change: Egypt Since Napoleon.* Princeton: Center of International Studies, Princeton University, (Research Monograph #6), 1960.
2. Bobrow, Davis B. "Political and Economic Role of the Military in the Chinese Communist Movement, 1927-1959." Unpublished Ph.D. dissertation, Massachusetts Institute of Technology, 1962.
3. Braibanti, Ralph. "The Occupation of Japan: A Study in Organization and Administration." Unpublished Ph.D. dissertation, Syracuse University, 1949.
4. Chiu, Sin-ming. "The Chinese Communist Army in Transition," *Far Eastern Survey*, Vol. 27 (November 1958), pp. 168-175.
5. Daalder, Hans. *The Role of the Military in the Emerging Countries.* The Hague: Institute of Social Studies, 1962.
6. Dupuy, Trevor N. "Burma and Its Army: A Contrast in Motivations and Characteristics," *Antioch Review*, Vol. 20 (1960-1961), pp. 428-440.
7. Finer, S. E. *The Man on Horseback: The Role of the Military in Politics.* New York: Frederick A. Praeger, 1962.
8. Franck, Thomas M. "UN Law in Africa: The Congo Operation as a Case Study," *Law and Contemporary Problems*, Vol. 27 (Autumn 1962), pp. 632-652.
9. Frey, Frederick W. *The Turkish Political Elite.* Cambridge: The M.I.T. Press, 1965.
10. Friedrich, Carl J., *et al. American Experiences in Military Government in World War II.* New York: Rinehart, 1948.
11. Greene, Fred. "Political Factors: Modernization and Related Problems in Developing Nations," Symposium Proceedings, U.S. Army, Limited War Mission and Social Science Research, Washington, D.C.: Special Operations Research Office, 1962.
12. James, Alan. "Law and Order Forces," *World Today*, No. 12 (December 1962), pp. 503-513.
13. Janowitz, Morris. *The Military in the Political Development of New Nations.* Chicago: University of Chicago Press, 1964.
14. ———. *The Professional Soldier: A Social and Political Portrait.* New York: The Free Press, 1960.
15. Johnson, John J. (ed.). *The Role of the Military in Underdeveloped Countries.* Princeton: Princeton University Press, 1962.
16. Jones, Richard A. "The Nationbuilder, Soldier of the Sixties," *Military Review*, Vol. 45 (January 1965), pp. 63-67.
17. Khadduri, Majid. "The Role of the Military in Middle East Politics," *American Political Science Review*, Vol. 47 (June 1953), pp. 511-524.
18. Lansdale, Edward G. "Civic Action Helps Counter the Guerrilla Threat," *Army Information Digest*, Vol. 17 (June 1962), pp. 50-53.
19. Lerner, Daniel, and Richard D. Robinson. "Swords and Ploughshares: The Turkish Army as a Modernizing Force," *World Politics*, Vol. 13 (October 1960), pp. 19-44.
20. Lev, Daniel S. "The Political Role of the Army in Indonesia," *Pacific Affairs*, Vol. 36 (Winter 1963-1964), pp. 349-364.
21. Lieuwin, E. "The Military: A Revolutionary Force," *The Annals of the American Academy of Political and Social Science*, Vol. 334 (March 1961), pp. 30-40.

22. Liu, Frederick F. "The Nationalist Army of China." Unpublished Ph.D. dissertation, Princeton University, 1951.
23. Morris, I. I. "The Significance of the Military in Post-War Japan," *Pacific Affairs*, Vol. 31 (March 1958), pp. 3-21.
24. President's Committee to Study the United States Military Assistance Program. *Composite Report* ("Draper Report"). Washington, D.C.: Government Printing Office, 1959.
25. Pye, Lucian W. "Armies in the Process of Political Modernization," *European Journal of Sociology*, Vol. 2 (1961), pp. 82-92.
26. ———. *Military Development in the New Countries*. Cambridge: M.I.T. Center for International Studies, #C/62-1, December 1961.
27. ———. "Military Training and Political and Economic Development," in D. C. Piper and Taylor Cole (eds.). *Post-Primary Education and Political and Economic Development*. Durham, N.C.: Duke University Press, 1964, pp. 75-94 (published for Duke University, Commonwealth Studies Center).
28. Rapoport, David. "A Comparative Theory of Military and Political Types," in S. P. Huntington (ed.). *Changing Patterns of Military Politics*. New York: The Free Press, 1962, pp. 71-100.
29. Riggs, Fred W. *Formosa under Chinese Nationalist Rule*. New York: Macmillan, 1952.
30. Rustow, Dankwart A. "The Army and the Founding of the Turkish Republic," *World Politics*, Vol. 11 (July 1959), pp. 513-552.
31. ———. "The Military in Middle Eastern Society and Politics," in Fisher (ed.). *The Military in the Middle East*. Columbus: Ohio State University Press, 1963, pp. 3-20.
32. Sadli, Mohammad. "The Influence of the Military on Economic Development: An Analysis Drawn Mainly from Indonesian Experience." Cambridge: Center for International Affairs, Harvard University, 1964 (mimeographed).
33. Shahan, James B. "American Colonial Administration in the Western Pacific: A Study in Civil-Military Relations." Unpublished Ph.D. dissertation, Ohio University, 1951.
34. Stambuck, George. *American Military Forces Abroad: Their Impact on the Western State System*. Columbus, Ohio: Ohio State University Press, 1963.
35. Stouffer, Samuel, *et al. The American Soldier*. 2 vols. Princeton: Princeton University Press, 1949.
36. Unger, Jess P. "The Military Role in Nation Building and Economic Development," *CAG Occasional Papers*. Bloomington, Indiana: CAG/American Society for Public Administration, 1963.
37. Vatikiotis, P. J. *The Egyptian Army in Politics: Pattern for New Nations?* Bloomington, Indiana: Indiana University Press, 1961.
38. Von der Mehden, Fred R., and Charles W. Anderson. "Political Action by the Military in the Developing Areas," *Social Research*, Vol. 28 (Winter 1961), pp. 459-479.
39. Walinsky, Louis J. "The Role of the Military in Development Planning: Burma," *The Philippine Economic Journal*, Vol. 4 (Second Semester 1965), pp. 310-326.
40. Walterhouse, Harry F. "Civic Action: A Counter and Cure for Insurgency," *Military Review*, Vol. 42 (August 1962), pp. 47-54.

See also: V-15, VI-28, VIII-15.*

* Roman numerals refer to sections of the bibliography in which additional citations may be found.

INDEX

achievement orientation, in political systems, 44-46
action patterns of bureaucracy, 75-86
adaptation, in social systems, 172-173
Adebo, Chief Simeon, 307
Adelman, I., 211n
administration, centralization of, 355-356, 462-463; centralization of in Viet Nam, 334-335; compartmentalization in, 390-395; in differing political systems, 177-178; dual bureaucracy variety, 181-183; localization of, 308-310; need for specialization, 178-179; reform of, 339-341; reform of in Pakistan, 372n; reorganization in, 283-285; of technical assistance, 457-461
administrative elite, in Pakistan, 372-374
administrative independence, 69
administrative reorganization, in Eastern Europe, 283-285
administrative system, in Eastern Europe, 278-282
administrators, as policy advisors, 312-313; shortage of in Pakistan, 362-382
Adu, A. L., 222n
Afzal, Raja M., 384n
agrovilles, 354
Ahmad, M., 409n
Ahmed, G., 362n
Aitken, Hugh G. J., 188n, 215n
Alhaique, Claudio, 231n
Ali, C. Mohamad, 373ff
Ali, Mian A., 397n
Allen, L. A., 355n
Almond, Gabriel, 96n, 111n, 168, 176-177, 179, 271n, 322n
apparatchiki, 294-296
Appleby, Paul, 71
Apter, David E., 188n
ascriptive commitment, diminution of, 99
associations, *see* interest groups
autonomy, administrative, 288-289, 291
Avery, R. W., 268n

Bajaki, V., 290n
Bakar, S. N., 397n
Bales, Robert F., 168n
Balogh, T., 211n
Banfield, E., 201n
Barber, C. L., 219n
Bares, G., 274n
Bashir, M., 410n
Bass, R. H., 275n
Bauer, P. T., 213n
Bauer, R. A., 300n
Beck, Carl, 282n, 298n
beggars' democracy, 132n
Bendix, R., 297n
Berger, Morroe, 13
Berliner, J. S., 285n
Birck, C. H., 395n
Bismark, O. von, 79-80, 85
Black, Cyril E., 270n, 247n
Black, E. R., 220
Bloch, Marc, 178n, 190n
Bobrowski, C., 285n
Bolivia, 149-150
Bolsheviks, and administrative reform, 249
Boorstein, D. J., 299n
boyar, 240
Braibanti, Ralph, 54n, 106n, 148n, 360n, 363n, 372n, 384n, 391n
Britain, impact on Pakistani bureaucracy, 374-375
Brown, B. E., 269n, 270n
Brown, H., 390n
Brzezinski, Z., 272n, 274n, 275n, 277n
Bulgaria, 268ff
bureaucracies, classified as to functions, 237; dual nature of, 12-14; of the developing areas, and corruption, 24-25; types of, 234-239
bureaucracy, action patterns of, 75-86; administrative generalists in, 54; Africanization of, 308-311; allocation of resources, 15; and Anglo-American norms, 51-53; characteristics of, 49-50; classic theory of, 269-270, 297-300; commitment to management activities, 75-77; and constitutional government, 64-65; as control in political struggle, 110; and the courts, 153-158; definition of, 6-8; definition of goals, 15; and democratic development, 22-27; disappearing colonialism, 16; and displacement of service goals, 115-116, 118; dual variety, 181-183; and economic development, 199-232; and economic modernity, 12; and the electorate, 131-139; and the execu-

bureaucracy, action patterns of, (*cont.*) tive, 158-164, 334-341; functional specialization, 20-21
in historical empires, 113-114, 115; impact of functional specialists on, 71-73; importance of weakness in, 126; in India, 56; as instrument of political regulation, 112; as instrumental agency, 51-53; instrumental nature of, 66, 340; and interest groups, 139-142; as interest group, 116-117; inter-bureaucratic conflict, 16; and the judiciary in Pakistan, 360-440; and legislature, 145-147; and levels of economic performance, 168-198; limiting powers of, 59; limits on power of, 25-26; managerial roles, 7; military type and development, 31-33; and modernization, 105-110; international, multi-national character of, 454-456; mutual interest between bureaucracy and judiciary, 414-416; and national integration, 316-317; neutrality of, 93-95, 332; in non-colonial new state, 108-109; and other political institutions, 55-61, 341-356; obstruction to development, 116-117; organizational characteristics, 109-110; as overwhelming power, 348-349
political control of in Viet Nam, 331-341; political neutrality of, 14-17; political orientations, 113-119; and political parties, 127-131; political role, 121-122; and political socialization, 110-113; and post-colonial society, 111-113; and the public interest, 16; reform supporter, 90-93; relationship to political development, 54-61; and response to demands, 27-30; responsible neutrality of, 16-17; self-interest of, 66; with service orientations, 115; and its social environment, 383-408; as a social system, 173-183; under Stalin, 256-257; and voluntary associations, 52; Weberian conception of, 10; Weberian formulation, 49-50; Western norms concerning, 51-53
bureaucratic administrations, in post-colonial empires, 106-108
bureaucratic attitudes, in new states, 107
bureaucratic centralization, 131-133
bureaucratic disharmony, causes of in Pakistan, 384-409
bureaucratic evasion, 260-261
bureaucratic leadership, localization of in Nigeria, 308-310
bureaucratic power, limitation of, 26
bureaucratic systems, models of, 8-9
bureaucratic talent, American exportation of, 19; importation of, 18-19; improvement of, 18-21; scarcity of, 17-22
bureaucratization, 113; development of autonomy in, 282-291; impact on political institutions, 268ff; selection of leaders in, 291-297
bureaucrats, antagonism toward, 385-386; British officers in Pakistan, 368-371; causes of grievances among, 400-406; in charismatic systems, 161-162; compensation of in Pakistan, 392-393; and courts, 157; defenders of status quo, 87; dismissal of in Pakistan, 403-406; divisionist tendencies in, 88-90; elitist values in, 372-374; as functional specialists, 20-21; involvement in politics, 121-122; recruitment of, 86, 127-130, 216-218; recruitment of in Eastern Europe, 291-296; recruitment of in Nigeria, 304-308; role in policy council, 77-80; role in program formulation, 80-83; role in public management, 83-86; sale of office to, 193-195; training of, 463-465; unseasoned variety, 313-314
international: on direct project assignments, 450-454; geographic dispersion of, 446-454; in field and regional offices, 447-450; nature of assignments, 452-453
Burov, B., 287n
Buttinger, J., 328n
Bystrina, I., 291n

Callard, K., 363n
capital, foreign, 227-229; importance to economic growth, 207-208; shortage in developing countries, 219-220
Carroll, H. N., 268n
Carter, A. T., 418n
centralization, 352, 355-356; too much of, 462-463; in the U.S.S.R., 256ff; in Viet Nam, 334-335
Chang, Chung-li, 130n
change, impact of international bureaucrats on, 456-469; relative importance of political over economic, 473-474; resistances to, 469-471
political: dimensions of, 39-48
charisma, 161, 343, 358
charismatic regime, 162-163
Chatelain, Jean, 217n
Chatterjee, B. R., 224n
Chaudhuri, M. A., 217n, 363n
China, 127; impact on Viet Nam, 327
Chipman, J. S., 212n

Choudhury, G. W., 409n
Chulalongkorn, 160
Civic Action in Viet Nam, 343-344
civil service, defined, 63-64; higher civil service, 62-95
Civil Service Academy of Pakistan, 374ff
Civil Service of Pakistan, 362ff
Clarkson, Jesse D., 240n
classic theory, limitations of, 298; of bureaucracy, 269-270
Cohn, Bernard S., 131n, 155n, 156n, 390n
Cole, R. T., 222n, 310, 312n, 316n
Coleman, J., 96n, 111n, 168n, 322n
Colombo Plan, 441n
colonial administration, 125; bureaucracy, 106-108
colonialism, administrative characteristics of, 301-303, 312
Colonial Service, characteristics of, 312; Nigerians in, 307
Communist doctrine and development, 278
Communist Party of the Soviet Union, as instrument of bureaucratic control, 258-260
compartmentalization, of administrative units, 390-393; necessity of, 394-395
compensation, delays of in Pakistan, 397
comradely courts, 290
conflict, of caste-family in commune in Pakistan, 388-390
Corbett, Jim, 395n
Corley, F. J., 332n
Cottrell, F., 321n
Council of Ministers, powers of, 279
Csergo, Janos, 293n
Czechoslovakia, 268ff

Dahl, R. A., 196, 197n
Daimant, Alfred, 157n
Dang, Nghiem, 340n
Darling, Sir M., 412n
Dean, A. L., 222n
decentralization, in Eastern Europe, 279-281; industrial, 285-289; under Khrushchev, 259-260; need for, 356
decision strategies, 272n
demands, articulation of, 100-102; on bureaucracy, 27-30; management of, 358; on Pakistan bureaucracy, 386; and political systems, 96-98; rapid generation of, 352
democratic centralism, 284
democratic development, in the United States, 60
democratic political development, as a goal, 27
democracy, and representative bureaucracy, 235
Derrett, J. D. M., 412n
Deutsch, K. W., 324n
Deutscher, I., 262n
developing countries, changes induced by international bureaucracies, 456-469; lack of interest group autonomy in, 141-142; price systems of, 210-211; relations of political elites to technical assistance personnel, 456-460; role of bureaucracy in, 121-122; scarcity of capital in, 219-220; scarcity of educated personnel in, 220-222
developing nations, and economic liberalism, 30; function of bureaucrats in, 92-93; need for political institutions, 167; and political liberalism, 30
development, defined, 122; negative type, 116
Devillers, P., 329n
devolution, administrative, 289-291
Dickens, C., 299n
Diem, Ngo Dinh, 330ff
differential compensation, 392
differentiation of structures, in development, 122-123
dismissal in Pakistan, causes for, 402-406; powers of judiciary concerning, 404-406
district administration, importance of in shaping bureaucracy, 395-396
Ditz, G. W., 285n
Djilas, M., 292
Donnell, J. C., 337n
Dorsey, J. T., 320n, 321n, 332n, 340n
dual bureaucracies, 181-183
dual economy, 328-329
dualism, in transitional societies, 123
Duchacek, I., 275n

ECOSOC, 442ff
EPTA, 443ff; purpose of, 444
Eastern Europe, political development in, 268-300; changes in political elite, 291-296
Easton, David, 96n
Eckstein, Otto, 215n
economic assistance, inevitable political impact of, 441
economic development, definition of, 199-201; determinants of, 204-212; evidence of in Viet Nam, 350-351; goal setting in, 202ff; impact on administrative structures, 183; importance of private sector in, 58-60; input transformation in, 203ff; need to deemphasize, 57; as paramount goal, 23-25;

economic development, (*continued*) political-legal requisites of, 205-206; political requisites of, 191; processes of, 202-204; role of bureaucracy in, 223-232, 347-348; role of entrepreneur in, 142-143
economic growth, *see* economic development
economic liberalism, 30
economy, inter-sectional relations, 212-215
education, of bureaucrats, 293; and economic growth, 209; as instrument of change, 255-256; of Nigerian bureaucrats, 311-312; and political change, 59; and political development, 166
Egger, R., 362n, 372n
Eisenstadt, S. N., 97n, 98n, 106n, 111n, 113n, 117n
Emmerich, H., 462n, 470n
energy, in societies, 319-325
energy conversion, and political development, 320
English language, as status symbol in Pakistan, 391n
enterprise, and economic growth, 208-209
entrepreneur, 142-144; in developing countries, 157; importance to economic growth, 223-224
Erlich, A., 252n
Establishment Division, of Pakistan, 371ff
Evans-Pritchard, E. E., 185, 189
executive, in traditional systems, 158-159; relationship to bureaucracy, 158-164
executive branch, defined, 204n
expatriate bureaucrats, 308-310

FAO, 442-443
Farberov, N. P., 274n
feudalism, 190, 192-193
field training, importance in Pakistan, 386-387
Fishel, W. R., 331n, 343n, 353n, 355n, 356n
Fixnan, W. F., 222n
foreign aid, 148-149, 227-228
formalism, 151-153
Fortes, M., 185, 189
Fox, Guy H., 340n
France, historical pattern of bureaucratic recruitment in, 195-196; National School of Administration, 79
French institutions, impact on Viet Nam, 328-331
Friedrich, Carl J., 121, 271n
Frolov, K., 279n
Frykenberg, R. E., 390n
functional expertise, 70-74; impact on bureaucracy, 71-73, 94

Ganshof, F. L., 190n
generalists, tension with specialists, 398
gentry, 130
Gerth, H. H., 180n, 269n
Gheorghiu-Dej, 275n
Ginsburg, N., 319n
Gittinger, P., 348n
Gladieux, B. L., 372n
Gluckman, Max, 184n
goal gratification, in social systems, 171ff
goals, systemic, 171
Gomulka, W., 277n
Goodall, M. R., 223n
Gopal, Ram, 363n
Gorwala, A. D., 396n
government programs, role of bureaucracies in, 80-82
Griffith, W. E., 277n
Grossman, G., 285n
Gurmani, M. A., 400n

Halperin, E., 292n
Hamid, Agha A., 360n
Hamid, A., 363n
Hammarskjold, Dag, 453, 459
Hammer, E. J., 329n
Hammond, P. B., 272n
Hamza, Al, 384n
Hanson, A. H., 223n, 229n, 230n, 231n
Hawkes, R. W., 272n
Heady, F., 320n
Hegel, F., 85
Hendry, J. B., 352n
Hershlag, Z. Y., 224n, 225n
higher civil service, as action group, 66-67; composition in India before partition, 365-368; education of in Pakistan, 382-383; length of assignments in Pakistan, 398-400; motivational factors, 94-95; prevailing attitudes, 65; responsibility in, 72-73; role in development, 89-93; unattractive to Muslims, 363n
historical empires, function of bureaucracy in, 113-114, 115
Hochfeld, J., 288n
Holzman, F. D., 211n
Hoover, C. B., 289n
Hoselitz, Bert F., 172n, 187n, 188n, 215, 215n, 221n
Hough, J. F., 288n
Houghton, B., 395n
Hsiao-tung Fei, 137n
Hsieh, P. C., 194n

Hunter, H. H., 363n
Husain, Mian A., 409n
Husain, S. A., 414n, 419n
Hyneman, Chas. S., 121n

ILO, 442ff
India, 25, 56, 221n
Indian Civil Service, 362ff
Indian Political Service, 364ff
industrialization, attractiveness of Soviet model, 264-265; misunderstandings concerning, 265-266; relation of mass education to, 266-267; in Russia, 246, 261-262; by totalitarian means, 251ff
information, in societies, 319-325
Inkeles, A., 293n, 294n, 296n
input transformation, 203-204
institution, meaning of, 179ff
integration, in bureaucracies, 174; difficulties of in Pakistan, 380-383; ineffective, 359; methods of, 341-356; relation of bureaucracy to, 316-317; role of bureaucracy in, 341-356; in social systems, 170ff
intellectuals, and development, 221n; in Communist parties, 293-294
interest groups, 116, 119, 139-142; and bureaucracy, 52; as bureaucratic instruments, 140-141; consequences of absence of, 394; control of in Viet Nam, 346-347; reasons for lack of autonomy, 141-142
International Bank for Reconstruction, and Development, 445-446
international bureaucracies, field and regional offices, 447-450; geographic dispersion of personnel, 446-454; and political development, 441-474
International Monetary Fund, 445-446
Italy, national development in, 55; structural differentiation in, 42
Iu, A., 247n

Japan, 160-161
Jelenski, K. A., 277n
Jennings, Sir I., 419n
Johansen, Leif, 212n
Johnson, Lyndon B., 65n
Johnson, J. J., 224n
Johnson, W. L., 199n
Johnston, B. F., 224n
judiciary, exploitation by bureaucrats, 157; role in developing countries, 154-158; in Pakistan, as democratic force, 436-437; in Pakistan, historic image of, 411-414; in Pakistan, reaction to martial law, 432-433
Jumper, Roy, 327n, 332n, 333n, 342n

Junker, B. H., 272n
Jurczenko A., 285n

Kahan, Arcadius, 260n
Kahin, George McT., 122n
Kahn, M. A., 361ff
Kaplan, Abraham, 124n
Karnow, S., 355n
Kasar, M., 285n
Kayani, M. R., 360n, 416ff
Keeton, G. W., 418n
Kemmerer Mission, 150
Kersten, H., 277n
Khan, H., 428n
Khan, I. A., 417n
Khan, M. A., 428n
Khera, S. S., 395n
Khrushchev, N., 257ff
Kibbee, R., 410n
Kincaid, C. A., 395n
Kingsley, J. D., 311n
Kiralfy, A. K. R., 418n
Klyuchevsky, Vasily, 241n
Knapp, J., 285n
Koo, A. Y. C., 219n
Kornai, J., 285n
Kuznets, S., 213n, 214n, 224n

Laberge, E. P., 222n
Ladejinsky, W. I., 348n
Lamb, H. B., 224n
Lambrick, H. T., 395n
land owners, contribution to economic growth, 224n
Lasswell, Harold, 124n
Lebkicher, Roy, 227n
legal rationalism, and bureaucracy, 269-278
legislatures, role in development, 145-147
legitimacy, 299-300; of bureaucracies, 75-77
Lenin, V. I., 249ff, 249n, 289n
Le Thanh Khoi, 328n
Lewins, L., 277n
Lewis, A. B., 134n
Lewis, Oscar, 201n
Lieuwin, E., 224n
Lim Tay Boh, 223n
Lindblom, C. E., 196, 197n
Lindholm, R. W., 331n, 348n, 351n
Lipset, S. M., 271n, 299n
literacy, relationship to political development, 263
local autonomy, in Soviet Union, 260
local self-government, 132-135
long ballot, 136
Lowenthal, R., 292n

Macleod, R. D., 395n
Macridis, Roy C., 269n, 270n, 299n
magnitude, in political systems, 42-44
Maine, Henry, 131n
Malara, Jean, 276n
Malick, A. R., 363n
management, public, 82-86
managerial personnel, scarcity of, 220n, 221n
managerial skill, lack of in Viet Nam, 332-334; shortage of in Africa, 314
managerial talent, shortage of in Pakistan, 362-382
Manolov, P., 287n
manpower, shortage of, 220-221
March, J. G., 231
Marx, F. Morstein, 67n
Masih-uz-Zaman, 384n, 391n, 396n
Masters, J., 395n
Mattei, Enrico, 55
Mears, L., 211n
Meiji Japan, 25
Mellor, J. W., 224n
Merton, R. K., 271n
middle class, absence of in Nigeria, 316; role in development, 223ff
Migon, W., 287n
Miladinov, D., 287n
military, as developmental force, 31-33; as dominant bureaucracy, 236; coup d'état, 163, 355; bureaucracy, 57
Mills, C. W., 180n, 269n
Minh, Ho Chi, 342ff
models, 168-169; economic, 285n; information-energy type, 319-325
modern, *see* modernity
modern government, merit bureaucracy essential to, 74
modernity, as a concept, 9; confusion regarding meaning of, 35-36, 38; and corruption, 11; definition of, 9; deterministic views concerning, 38-39; and economic change, 10; as normative concept, 36-37
modernization, bureaucracies in, 238-239, 247-248; characteristics of, 99; defined, 233-234; examples of, 98; historical role of bureaucracies in, 105-110; impact on administrative structures, 184; impact on bureaucracy, 270; patterns of, 188n; process of, 191
money economy, 180-181
Montesquieu, de Charles S., 194n
Montgomery, John D., 148n, 335n, 340n
Moon, P., 389n
Moore, W. E., 224n
Moore, Wilbert F., 187n
Moreland, W. H., 363n
Mosca, Gaetano, 62n, 70
Mosley, L., 409n
movement-regimes, 145n
Murphy, M. E., 220n, 222n, 223n
Murphy, Marvin, 340n
Musgrave, R. A., 213n, 214n

Nagy, Imre, 276n
National Front, 278
national policy, impact of technical assistance on, 468-469
nationality, as factor in technical assistance assignments, 455-456
nepotism, in Viet Nam, 336
neutrality, 93-95; of bureaucracy, 322; responsible, 16
new classes, 291-297
Nhu, Ngo Dinh, 336-337
Nigeria, 301-307
nobility, in bureaucracy, 244-245
Norman, E. Herbert, 124n

OPEX, 453-454
opposition parties, 130-131
Oroszi, I., 287n

Page, A., 410n
Pagès, G., 193n
Pakistan, 56; administrative law in, 429-430; 1962 constitution, 438-439; introduction of administrative tribunals, 427-428; martial law in, 430-433; personnel of higher civil service, 362-382; political conditions of, 409n; shortage of administrative talent in, 362-368; sources of bureaucratic insecurity, 384-388; use of British administrative officers, 368-371
Palmer, Norman, 121n
para-judicial bodies, 290
Paranjape, H. K., 231n
para-police organizations, 289-290
pariah entrepreneurship, 142-145
parliamentary systems, requisites of, 146-147
Parnwell, M., 362n, 397n
Parsons, Malcolm B., 126n
Parsons, Talcott, 168, 210n, 215n, 270n
pattern of maintenance, in social systems, 169ff
Pauker, Guy, 354n
Peacock, A. T., 214n, 215n, 227n
people's committees, 279-281, 283-284, 286-287, 290
Pepeliasis, A., 211n
Personalism, in Viet Nam, 339
Peska, P., 274n

Peter the Great, 241-244
petwari, 386ff
Poland, 268ff
policy, pseudo rule making, 152
political articulation, problems of, 351-353
political change, achievement orientation in, 44-46; and bureaucracy, 271-272; dimensions of, 39-48; magnitude in, 42-44; secularization in, 46-48; structural differentiation in, 39-42
political communication, networks of, 337-338
political control, of bureaucracy in Viet Nam, 331-341
political controls, 355
political culture, and bureaucracy, 271
political demands, 58
political development, definition of, 96, 139-140, 318, 322; difficulties of conducting field research on, 472; factors impeding, 357; impact of education on, 166; impact of international bureaucracy on, 461-469; military in, 31-33; phases of, 272n, 272-278; resistances to, 469-471; role of bureaucracy in, 54-61; role of international bureaucracies, 441-474
political elites, 117, 118; and economic change, 202, 203; importance to development, 117-119; recent changes in Eastern Europe, 291-296; in developing countries, relations with international bureaucrats, 456-460; in developing countries, resistances to change, 469-471
political institutions, impact of bureaucracy on, 341-356
political integration, *see* integration
political liberalism, 30
political orientations, of bureaucracy, 113-119
political parties, and administrative control, 281-282; and control of bureaucracies, 258-260; as integrative structures, 101-102; relation to bureaucracy in Viet Nam, 345-346; in Viet Nam, 337-338
political recruitment, 45-46, 175-176
political regulation, 112
political socialization, 110-113, 174-175, 297n; phases of, 175
political stability, role of bureaucracy in, 86-90
political structures, 177; survival powers, 42
political system, changes in, 39-48; characteristics of, 37-38; reaction to change, 103-104; role of demands in, 96-98; types of, 185-187
poly-functionalism, 130
population explosion, 165-166
Prasad, Parmanand, 227n
Presthus, Robert V., 173n, 298n
price system, shortcomings in developing countries, 211n
private sector, in economic development, 212ff
program formulation, 80-83
promotion, negative consequences of rapidity of, 387
Przblya, J., 277n
public administration, by bureaucracy, 49-50; functional specialists in, 40-41; and political change, 48-55; in transitional systems, 49; in the USSR, 50-51
public corporations, 226, 229-232; shortcomings as developmental agents, 230-231
public finance, in developing countries, 147-149
public management, 83-86
public sector, in economic development, 212ff, 347-348; factors affecting importance, 213-215
Pye, L. W., 224n, 297n

Qureshi, I. H., 363n

Raeff, Marc, 244n
Rahim, Abdur, 363n
Ramanadhan, V. V., 229n
rationality, 78, 237-238
Rattinger, B., 274n, 279n
recruitment, bureaucratic, 193-195; of bureaucrats, 293-297; of bureaucrats in Nigeria, 304-308; faulty discrimination in, 216-217n; in public and private sectors, 216-218
reform, administrative, 339-341; of bureaucracy in Nigeria, 315; recommendations concerning Pakistan, 372n; role of bureaucrats, 90-93
reorganization, administrative, 283-285; territorial, 285-288
research, difficulties of conducting in the field, 472; important subjects concerning political development, 472-473
retirement, as a weapon against bureaucrats, 385
Revai, J., 273n
revisionism, 276-278
Revolutionary Personalist Labor Party, 337-338

Riggs, Fred W., 39n, 116n, 124n, 126n, 129n, 138n, 318n, 324n
Ritvo, H., 279n, 289n
Rosberg, Carl, 188n
Rosenstein-Rodan, P. N., 219n
Rowlands, Sir A., 362n
Rucker, Sir A., 311n
Rumania, 268ff
Russia, historical role of bureaucracy in, 240-248
Russian bureaucracy, development under Peter the Great, 241-243

SUNFED, 444-445
Sajid, M. S., 384n
Salter, Lord, 231n
Sandor, J., 294n
Sarte, Jean-Paul, 277n
Sastri, K. N. V., 395n
Sayeed, K. B., 409n
Schenk, Fritz, 282n
Schwartz, Harry, 211n
Scigliano, R. G., 337n, 346n
Scott, R. E., 109n
secularization, in political systems, 46-48; rationality in, 46-47
security, impact on development, 353-355; impact on political development, 342-343
Sedlak, J., 284n
Seewald, H., 277n
seniority, determination of in Pakistan, 402-403
service goals, displacement of, 115-116, 118
service orientation, 118; in historical empires, 115
Seton, F., 285n
Seton-Watson, H., 275n, 292n
Shah, N. H., 360n, 428n
Shariff, M., 439n
Sharp, W. R., 333n, 444n, 446n, 452n, 456n, 464n, 470n, 471n
Shavrov, Y. M., 273n
Shikabi, Mufti I., 363n
Shils, E. A., 111n, 168n, 220n, 221n, 222n, 266, 410n
short ballot, 136-138
Siffin, W. J., 106n, 157n, 223n
Simon, H. A., 231
Siroky, W., 276n
Smelser, Neil J., 169n, 187n, 215
Snelson, Sir E., 374ff, 425-426
Snyder, W. W., 346n
social action, adaptive variety, 172; characteristics of, 169-173
social system, bureaucracy as example, 173-183
Socialism, in Eastern Europe, 274ff
societal development, phases of, 188-189
Soemardjan, S., 271n
solidarity structure, 189-190
Solo, R., 224n
Soviet Union, administrative reform in, 249-260; Five Year Plans, 254; New Course doctrine, 275-276
Spengler, J. J., 106n, 111n, 148n, 224n, 360n, 363n, 372n
spoils, in bureaucracy, 306
spoils system, importance to development, 128-130
Stalin, J., 253ff, 254n, 289n
Stalinism, 274
state bureaucracy, 235-236
status officialdom, 67-70; dimensions of, 67-68; main tendencies, 70-74; as source of bureaucratic strength, 69-70
Steanu, P. B., 274n
Stepan, L., 285n
Stepanek, 228n
Stillman, E. O., 275n
Stokes, S., 320n
strategic hamlets, 354
structural differentiation, 184-186; patterns of, 197-198
structure functionalism, model of, 169
Sumner, B. H., 243n
Sun Yat-Sen, 131
Supple, B. E., 221n
Swart, K. W., 193n
Swearer, H., 260n
Szalai, Sandor, 288n

tahsīldār, 155
Tamasi, A., 288n
taxation, *see* public finance
taxes, and economic growth, 227n
Taylor, M. C., 351n
Taylorism, 252
technical assistance, difficulty of assessing impact, 471; impact on change, 461-474; main beneficiaries of UN assistance, 451; patterns of, 125-126; short-run projects, 466-468; type of assignments, 452-453; type of coordinating machinery, 457-461; types of impact, 461-469
  personnel: channels of influence for, 456-469; duration of UNO assignments, 450-451; geographic dispersion of, 446-454; nationality and language in field assignments, 455-456; relations to host country counter-parts, 459-460
technical intelligentsia, 294-295
technology, and economic growth, 208

Tei-chert, Pedro, 224n
Thompson, J. D., 268n, 272n
Thorburn, S. S., 363n
Toeplitz, J. L., 287n
Toma, P. A., 294n
Toynbee, Arnold J., 124n
traditional society, 269
Trainin, I. P., 272n
transitional society, 135
transitional societies, 120, 121-122, 123; classified as to executive authority, 159-162
tsar, 240ff
Tucker, Robert C., 145n
Tuden, Arthur, 272n

UNICEF, 443
Ulam, A. B., 288n
Unesco, 442ff
United Nations Organization, 441ff; employees on field project assignments, 447-450; geographic assignment of technical assistance personnel, 446-454; nature of field offices, 447-450; proliferation of assistance programs, 442-446; specialized technical assistance agencies, 442-446; type of technical assistance rendered, 452-453
United States, and democratic development, 60
university men, 79

value systems, relation to economic change, 202-203, 210
Vella, Walter, 124n
venality of office, 193-195; relation to corruption, 194
Viet Cong, 342ff
Viet Minh, 329-330
Viet Nam, 318-359; communications pattern in, 325-326; impact of Chinese institutions on, 327; impact of French institutions on, 328-331; increases of information in, 349-350; methods of political control in, 343-345
village values, impact on administration, 396-397
voluntary association, *see* interest groups
Vornesensky, N. A., 289n
Vucinach, A., 247n

WHO, 442-443
Wagner, Güntner, 186
Waltman, H. L., 340n
Ward, Robert E., 137n, 138n
Warner, D., 353n
Weber, Max, 10ff, 77, 100, 161, 180, 183, 189, 192, 269ff; model of bureaucracy, 49-50
Whish, C. W., 395n
White, L. A., 321n
Wiles, P. J. D., 285n
Williams, A. A., 222n
Wiseman, Jack, 214n, 215n
Wittfogel, Karl A., 132n
writs in Pakistan, defense of, 428-429; factors leading to use of by bureaucrats, 400-406; incidence of petitions, 421; jurisdiction of, 419-427; and martial law, 430-434; negative effects of, 406-407; relationship to justice, 407; types of, 418
Woodruff, P., 352n, 375n, 389, 390n, 395n, 396
Wurfel, D., 348n

Yang, Martin, 132
Yanov, Y., 291n
Yoichi Itagaki, 182n
Younger, K., 308n, 310
Yutin, I., 274n

Zakaria, N., 409n
Zasloff, J. J., 353n
Zemstvo reforms, 246-247